Advancing the Miami Process:
Civil Society and the Summit of the Americas

Advancing the Miami Process:
Civil Society and the Summit of the Americas

Robin Rosenberg and Steve Stein, editors

North·South Center Press
UNIVERSITY OF MIAMI

The mission of the North-South Center is to promote better relations and serve as a catalyst for change among the United States, Canada, and the nations of Latin America and the Caribbean by advancing knowledge and understanding of the major political, social, economic, and cultural issues affecting the nations and peoples of the Western Hemisphere.

To order or to return books, contact Lynne Rienner Publishers, Inc. at 1800 30th Street, Suite 314, Boulder, CO 80301-1026, 303-444-6684, fax 303-444-0824

Permission to use the logo of the Summit of the Americas on the cover of this book has been granted by the Host Committee and cannot be reproduced by any other parties or for any other event or matter.

Permissions to reprint the documents in this volume have been granted to the University of Miami North-South Center by each of the sponsoring agencies. Requests to reproduce, in whole or in part, any of the documents herein must be directed to the individual sponsoring agency.

Cover photograph © The Miami Herald

*HC
94
A558
1995*

Cataloging-in-Publication Data
Advancing the Miami process: civil society and the Summit of the Americas
        / Robin Rosenberg, Steve Stein, editors.
            p. cm.
        Includes index.
        ISBN 0-935501-99-1 (pbk. : alk. paper)
            1. Summit of the Americas (1994: Miami, Fla.) 2. Western
Hemisphere—Economic conditions—Congresses. 3. Western Hemisphere —
– Economic integration—Congresses. I. Rosenberg, Robin L.
II. Stein, Steven J.
HC94.A558 1995   95-25293
337'.09181'2—dc20   CIP

Printed in the United States of America
00 99 98 97 96 95 6 5 4 3 2 1

Advancing the Miami Process: Civil Society and the Summit of the Americas

PROPOSALS FROM NON-GOVERNMENTAL SECTORS

I. Preserving and Strengthening the Community of Democracies of the Americas

II. Promoting Prosperity Through Economic Integration and Free Trade

Contents

CONTENTS

Foreword

Robin Rosenberg and Steve Stein, editors

The extraordinary growth in the number and the power of non-governmental actors and organizations over the past few decades has led to increased pressure on government to "democratize" foreign policy initiatives, by providing channels for input and establishing a formal role for civil society in international diplomacy. Public diplomacy has long been a feature of U.S. foreign policy, but its transformation into "participatory diplomacy" is a much more recent development. The Summit of the Americas, held in Miami in December 1994, represents the most significant instance to date of the implementation by the United States of this process of participatory diplomacy. While public diplomacy, as exemplified by the many informational, cultural, and educational exchange programs funded by the government, has long been oriented toward building support and understanding of U.S. positions and policy objectives overseas, participatory diplomacy represents the direct involvement of civil society in various aspects of the policy-making process and in the implementation and monitoring of the provisions of international agreements. The Summit experience has demonstrated that new forms of participatory diplomacy, in which responsibility for policy initiatives is shared with representatives from civil society, often is a cumbersome arrangement which must overcome significant barriers on both the governmental and non-governmental side. But the experience of civil society involvement in the Summit of the Americas, as well as the exhausting political fight in Congress over implementing legislation for the North American Free Trade Agreement (NAFTA) — wherein many non-governmental actors were in opposition — demonstrates that having influential non-governmental actors as stakeholders in major foreign policy initiatives can be of enormous benefit.

In recent years, certain non-governmental actors or "NGAs" (business and labor associations, academic and research institutions, advocacy and community groups) have increasingly participated in international policy formulation. This trend was clearly evident in the various United Nations summit initiatives, as exemplified by the 1992 Earth Summit in Rio de Janeiro, where government and NGAs worked either jointly or in parallel during planning sessions and the official gatherings. Nevertheless, the kind of "partnership" in the planning, consultation, negotiation, and implementation of policy initiatives leading up to the Summit of the Americas is unprecedented in the inter-American context. This is the case not only for the United States, where recent political changes reflect a reexamination of the relationship between citizens and their government, but also for Latin American and Caribbean countries, where the strengthening of civil society and its role in democratic governance is a policy objective in itself. For this reason, the very deliberate, if not always balanced or successful, efforts to involve the civil society and the non-governmental community in the Summit of the Americas and the ongoing

"Miami Process" are of tremendous significance in the history of inter-American relations and of U.S. foreign policy in particular. In his address to the non-governmental policy community in September 1994 (included in this volume), Richard Feinberg, Special Assistant to the President and Senior Director for Inter-American Affairs at the National Security Council, speaks of the "potential for a much broader policy constituency for American foreign policy than ever before." The involvement of civil society reflects not only the realization that government has neither all the answers to complex problems nor the appropriate resources to implement solutions, but also, that in democracies a robust and vibrant civil society with access to a responsive public sector is the ultimate guarantor of the success of major economic, political, and social initiatives.

The December 1994 Miami Summit of the Americas marked the beginning of a new era in inter-American relations in a number of significant areas. In dramatic contrast to previous hemispheric summits, the Miami meeting took place in a post-Cold War context of shared values regarding democratic governance, the primacy of free markets, and the importance of hemispheric integration. And contrary to U.N. summit initiatives, in the "Miami Process" the traditional North/South debate has been replaced by a broader hemispheric dialogue in which major U.S. policy concerns are largely the same as those advanced by Canada and the Latin American and Caribbean countries. Unlike the last full hemispheric Summit in 1967 in Punta del Este, Uruguay, which was held under the auspices of the Organization of American States (OAS), the Summit of the Americas was convened by the invitation of U.S. President Bill Clinton. In accord with the emphasis on democracy that has characterized inter-American relations in recent years, the invitation to the Summit was issued only to the other thirty-three "freely elected" heads of government and state of the Americas. With his invitation, the U.S. president established a new hemispheric summit process outside the formal diplomatic context of the OAS, and he communicated a strong political message. The Summit would be the largest gathering of hemispheric leaders, embracing all of the independent countries of the Western Hemisphere, with the notable exception of Cuba. It would be a meeting of democracies (the justification for excluding Cuba). The extension throughout Latin America of democratic forms of government and the strong U.S.

commitment to democratic politics in the region, as emphasized by former President George Bush in his June 1990 speech announcing the Enterprise for the Americas Initiative (EAI), have clear implications for hemispheric relations. In a region which appears to have a much greater capacity to carry through on shared regional policy initiatives, democratic credentials, which, significantly, were not necessary for the Punta Del Este meeting, hold out the promise that governments that signed on to the Summit of the Americas' *Declaration of Principles* and *Plan of Action* would be able to work in partnership with their people and institutions in meeting the detailed objectives and timetables agreed to in Miami. Pre- and post-Summit processes will be key to the realization of this promise.

Nevertheless, the efforts to democratize the pre-Summit planning process have not always been seen in an incontrovertibly positive light. Indeed, the participatory diplomacy leading up to the event may have contributed to the widely shared perception among observers from both inside and outside the U.S. government that the planning and consultation process for the Summit got a very late start, leaving the impression of a somewhat chaotic and uncoordinated initiative. After Vice President Al Gore made the announcement of Clinton's invitation in Mexico City in December 1993, there were few signs of visible progress in setting the agenda. There was an initial round of consultations by U.S. officials in the spring of 1994, but through the spring and into the summer, planning proceeded largely at the staff level and did not appear to receive high-level support. Then, late in the summer, an interagency working group issued a "Fourteen-Point Summary of Summit Initiatives" that would serve as a basis for discussion in consultations around the hemisphere. While the document presented an impressive array of issues, from trade integration and democratic governance to sustainable development, there was concern among many non-governmental actors influential in the policy community that the Summit lacked a "centerpiece" that would provide a catalyst to guarantee the Summit's diplomatic and political success.

For its part, the national media gave very little coverage to the Summit process. This apparent lack of interest may have been the result of the absence of a strongly formulated central Summit theme until only a very short time before the Miami gathering. While the relative neglect of Latin American and Caribbean issues in the national media is by no means a new phenomenon, the lack of coverage was reinforced by an increasingly inward-looking political system that focused more on President Clinton's domestic political problems than on the historical significance of the Summit of the Americas. In any case, the relative anonymity of the Summit process in this country contrasted sharply with the excitement displayed by the rest of the hemisphere's media leading up to and during the Summit.

The Summit picture began to change significantly when parts of the NGA community, along with the inter-American multilateral institutions (Inter-American Development Bank (IDB), the United Nations Economic Commission on Latin America and the Caribbean (ECLAC), and the Organization of American States) became increasingly vocal about the primacy of trade integration in the Summit agenda. From July through September 1994, a variety of reports, press releases, and white papers had appeared from important members of the NGA community, including the Institute of International Economics; the Council of the Americas, the Association of American Chambers of Commerce in Latin America, and the U.S. Chamber of Commerce; the OAS, IDB and ECLAC; the Inter-American Dialogue; and the North-South Center. Their shared concern regarding the issue of trade integration echoed a firm consensus among Latin American and Caribbean governments that President Clinton's invitation to Miami in December must contain the promise of concrete progress on economic issues, most especially on the trade integration front. Subregional integration was already advancing rapidly, particularly in southern South America with the Mercado Común del Sur (MERCOSUR); for Latin American and Caribbean nations, the question of U.S. market access had become the primary item on the Summit agenda. Even many of the environmental, labor, and other NGAs whose issues were addressed in varying degrees on the original fourteen-point summary acknowledged — some reluctantly, some as a matter of pragmatism — that the trade issue had indeed gained primacy for the Summit.

It is difficult to determine to what degree the NGA expressions ultimately influenced the Clinton administration in its decision to take the bold steps necessary to pursue agreement in Miami to complete negotiations on a Free Trade Area of the Americas (FTAA) by 2005. Senior officials were certainly listening and reading, but they were also busily consulting with their Latin American and Caribbean partners who were equally unambiguous about their priorities for the Miami *cita*. The real complications on the trade policy front were, in fact, with the U.S. Congress, where the administration was under intense pressure to obtain approval for implementing legislation for the long-delayed Uruguay Round of the General Agreement on Tariffs and Trade (GATT). In order to strengthen its position for the GATT vote, in September the administration pulled the "fast-track" provision out of the GATT implementing legislation. Fast-track, which grants the administration authority to pursue free trade agreements and submit them to Congress without the possibility of amendments, had been bogged down by bitter disputes over the inclusion of environmental and labor negotiating objectives (an unresolved set of issues that will inevitably complicate the Miami Summit objectives). Many observers interpreted the Clinton administration's reticence to push for agreement on trade integration at the Summit of the Americas as a simple waiting game for fast-track authority from a 103rd Congress that was taking entirely too long to pass the GATT implementing legislation. Whatever the reason, without fast-track, it seemed, the administration would be in a very difficult position to offer any concrete proposals on trade integration at the Summit of the Americas.

The NGA input on the trade issue came at a strategic juncture in the Summit planning process. The administration was clearly wary of free trade initiatives after the bruising NAFTA debate in Congress and showed itself willing to sacrifice fast-track negotiating authority for at least another year in the interest of gaining approval for the long-delayed GATT global trade pact. In the context of the host-country's weak position on the Western Hemisphere trade front in September, the NGA community — particularly the private business sector — makes a convincing case for having prodded the U.S. administration to announce in Miami in early October that trade would indeed be the centerpiece of the Summit of the Americas.

But trade integration was certainly not the only aspect of the Summit agenda strongly influenced by NGA involvement. By September there was evidence of significant civil society involvement in setting other key aspects of the evolving Miami agenda. The August "Fourteen-Point Summary of Summit Initiatives" had been divided into three major issue areas, or "baskets," which eventually became the following four broad initiatives in the Summit *Declaration of Principles* and *Plan of Action*: "Promoting Prosperity Through Economic Integration and Free Trade," "Preserving and Strengthening the Community of Democracies in the Americas," "Eradicating Poverty and Discrimination in our Hemisphere," and "Guaranteeing Sustainable Development and Conserving Our Natural Environment for Future Generations."

During the summer, administration officials had been quietly sounding out the non-governmental community in Washington regarding the democracy and sustainable development issue areas. The administration went so far as to set up a special Associate Directorship for NGA liaison in the Inter-American Affairs Directorate at the National Security Council (NSC) to facilitate and channel NGA input. At the same time, the White House Office on Environmental Policy was actively engaged in developing a detailed sustainable development agenda with an NGO working group led by the major Washington- and New York-based environmental NGOs that had supported the Clinton administration in the struggle for NAFTA implementing legislation. Similar working groups were established by the State Department for the issues of democratic governance, poverty, and discrimination. The introduction to this volume, written by Cathryn L. Thorup, former Associate Director at the NSC, outlines the clear and deliberate policy priority at senior levels of the administration to take on the bureaucratic, domestic, and hemispheric political challenges that NGA access would inevitably bring. In the view of both Cathryn Thorup and Richard Feinberg, the policy was well worth the trouble and the risks: it played a major role in producing the richness of the documents that eventually emerged from the Summit.

Despite the strong evidence of civil society's varied impact on the Summit agenda, as some of the postscripts to the NGA documents in this volume testify, satisfaction about the process was not shared by all of the non-governmental groups that attempted to channel input into the Summit consultations. The variety and magnitude of the obstacles to NGA input are given ample treatment in Thorup's introduction. From the NGA perspective, especially that of the activist groups, civil society's concerns were not adequately reflected in the Summit agenda, and those concerns that did receive consideration were not expressed in sufficiently strong language. Overall, those groups who weighed in with succinct recommendations seemed to have made the biggest imprint

on the Summit agenda and final documents. Also, inputs that reflected some kind of hemispheric NGA "consensus," such as the North-South Center's three hemispheric working group *Policy Proposals*, appear to have received substantial attention. While direct access to Summit planners in working groups or consultations at the White House or Department of State left a strong imprint on the Summit agenda and official documents, some among the environmental community, for example, spoke of being initially "smothered by access" to senior U.S. officials only to be disappointed later by the final documents that emerged from the official consultations with Latin American and Caribbean governments.

In terms of the concrete impact of NGA initiatives, it is important to note that the very question of civil society input and public participation was on the line from the very beginning of the consultations for the Summit of the Americas. As Cathryn Thorup recounts, the receptiveness of Latin American and Caribbean governments to NGA involvement in the consultations varied widely, from the deliberate [albeit selective] initiatives in countries such as Argentina and Chile, to clear displeasure in Brazil and Mexico. It is not clear if Latin American and Caribbean governments were reacting to the well-known fact that U.S. NGAs were already deeply involved in helping the host government draft Summit documents for consultation, thus adding a nationalistic dimension to their existing sensitivity to intervention by non-official players. The peremptory treatment of some environmental NGO leaders who accompanied senior U.S. representatives at official consultations in Brazil and Mexico may have represented a reaction to a perceived North American assault on national sovereignty. No doubt contributing to this perception was the transparent agenda of those NGO leaders — ultimately unsuccessful — to link trade to environmental protection through possible sanctions, a position considered to be at the vanguard of "green protectionism."

However, the sovereignty issue goes beyond the intervention of persistent U.S.-based NGOs who challenged Latin American and Caribbean governments on particularly controversial issues. It directly addresses the very source of sovereignty in a democracy: the principle that the people, that is, civil society, and not only the government that represents civil society, is sovereign, constituting the ultimate legitimizing force. Historically, much of the hemisphere has been weak on this principle; yet the "new moment" in hemispheric relations brought on by the end of the Cold War and the long, hard-fought process of democratization over the past fifteen years has facilitated civil society's new-found vibrancy and relevance throughout the hemisphere.

Ironically, the de facto involvement of NGAs in the consultation process helped bring to the fore the question of civil society's very role in the process of hemispheric integration, leading to disagreements over language in the official Summit documents originally designed to commit governments to a partnership with civil society. The successive drafts of the official Summit *Declaration of Principles* and *Plan of Action*, leaked during the final few weeks of consultations before the Miami *encuentro*, reveal the difficulties faced in forging a consensus on what language, if any, would be used to open the door to civil society and make it a stakeholder in the "Miami Process."

Though these final consultations in late November and early December 1994 at Airlie House were not public, detailed markings on the successive drafts seem to indicate that, in general terms, the United States, Canada, and the Caribbean Common Market and Community (CARICOM) countries were at odds with some Latin American governments who were uncomfortable with the original language, apparently proffered by some Caribbean countries, which did not carefully qualify the public sector's commitment to accessibility and responsiveness. The final document ultimately represents a compromise in this area: the thirty-four nations promised to "assure public engagement and commitment" with NGAs in "both our national and regional efforts" but only "in accordance with national legislation." This last restriction asserts the sovereignty of national governments, and its inclusion reflects the still uneasy relationship between hemispheric governments and their civil societies. The "national legislation" limitation protects not only against the imposition of non-governmental initiatives from abroad (especially those from the North), but also against internal critics who would intrude on government's traditional monopoly on power.

Many of the NGAs who had worked tirelessly to have their concerns included in the Summit drafts were dismayed to find that strong statements on everything from human rights and collective action in defense of democracy to the link between trade and the environment were either watered down or eliminated during the final few weeks of official consulta-

tions. In the case of collective action, for example, decisive language that would have committed the thirty-four nations to a collective military response to threats to democracy — and that would have gone further in tone and substance than the historic 1991 *Santiago Declaration* of the OAS — was weakened substantially in the final *Declaration of Principles.*

One of the most striking cases of civil society's frustration with the final Summit product was that of the environmental activists who had worked very closely with the White House on producing a comprehensive and strongly worded draft Summit agreement on the environment. This group was extremely disappointed that in the final action plan, original language that had advocated specific "national" and "international" initiatives across a wide range of sustainable development issues was both watered down and substantially shortened. What is worse, the ardent attempts by environmentalists, led by the U.S. NGO community, to obtain strong language establishing the reciprocal linkage between trade and the environment seems to have had quite the opposite effect. The *Declaration of Principles* ended up expressing the philosophical converse to their position: that environmental benefits would trickle down from the process of trade integration. This perspective, in effect, establishes a philosophical and contractual basis for ignoring concrete mechanisms to address environmental protection in the negotiations for the FTAA, a position clearly borne out in the *Declaration of Ministers* from the post-Summit Denver Trade Ministerial in June 1995, the first major post-Summit gathering in the Miami Process.

Various NGAs were quick to blame the Clinton administration for either ignoring their concerns altogether or for being seemingly eager to negotiate their positions away for the image of a harmonious Summit of the Americas. Here is where, perhaps, the late start in the consultation process mattered the most. The pressure to prepare long and complex documents in time for the Summit undoubtedly contributed to the strengthening of opposition, particularly from some governments in Latin America, to NGA positions and ultimately did not brighten the prospects for full civil society participation in the post-Summit Miami process. Nevertheless, in the final analysis, if the draft documents that emerged during the final days of official consultations at Airlie House in the Washington area did not represent a "hemispheric consensus" among the governments, neither were they the Clinton administration's draft documents to defend. After the initial outrage, a sobering realization seems to have descended over the NGA community, confirming something that they probably had suspected from early on: that outside Canada and the United States and with some exceptions in the Caribbean, much work still needs to be done to secure the access to and responsiveness of the public sector to NGA involvement and input.

Efforts by the NGA community to secure balanced public participation in the Denver Trade Ministerial in June 1995, the first major event in the post-Summit of the Americas era, revealed just how much work needs to be done. At the "Hemispheric Forum," a conference hosted by the U.S. Department of Commerce immediately after the Denver ministerial, NGA representation on the national delegations was disturbingly unbalanced. The conference, which had originally been planned for the Miami Summit, brought together over one thousand private business sector participants from throughout the hemisphere to discuss the various structural, technical, and political issues related to trade integration in the hemisphere. Few non-business representatives were invited to participate on the Latin American and Caribbean delegations; in some cases credentials were denied to those who requested them from their national delegation. The conference, moreover, was held *after* the ministers had met and issued their declaration. It is important to note that the Ministers' declaration failed to address the need for more formal mechanisms for public participation in constructing the FTAA. Under a section entitled "Other Matters," the document makes only a vague commitment to "transparency in the FTAA process" by welcoming "the contribution of the private sector and appropriate processes to address the protection of the environment and the further observance and promotion of worker rights, through our respective governments." There was no agreement on what role the private sector might play in working groups or in future negotiations, and there was an overall suggestion that the involvement of other non-business NGAs from important sectors related to trade was not entirely welcome. Again, the battle over public participation appeared to pit the United States against certain Latin American countries, most notably Brazil, which reluctantly accepted the weak language on civil society's participation in the trade integration process in exchange for concessions elsewhere in the Denver agenda. The United States

had already dropped its proposal for a working group on trade and the environment in the face of the opposition of some Latin American countries. As the Miami Summit documents suggested, the work on the FTAA would proceed without the integration of environment and labor issues into the technical work programs. Although there are plans to make the Hemispheric Forum a permanent fixture of the FTAA process, if Denver and the official working group activities on the FTAA are any indication, there is an urgent need to address the major gap regarding the establishment of a more formalized role for NGAs in the Miami Process.

Despite these setbacks for civil society, overall there is certainly cause for substantial satisfaction with the Summit process. The final Summit *Declaration of Principles* and *Plan of Action* remain documents rich in fundamental agreement around the great challenges facing the hemisphere, and, notwithstanding their shortcomings in terms of civil society expectations, they bear the imprint of an unprecedented participation by non-governmental actors. As senior administration officials attest, a number of initiatives draw word for word from some of the documents submitted to official "summiteers" and reprinted in this volume. Public participation was integrated into a truly hemispheric process, and governments will be held accountable to the promises made in Miami in December 1994.

These promises of the Summit are not just vague principles to which governments can pay lip service. The *Plan of Action* has specific targets and deadlines that invite a public monitoring process beyond the tripartite institutional framework set up with the OAS, IDB, and ECLAC. For the NGA community, there is a new and exciting challenge: to utilize organizational capacity and resources to monitor the progress of the Summit accords and continue to propose policy alternatives, thereby strengthening its role as a powerful participant in the movement toward hemispheric integration.

In publishing these contributions of civil society to the Miami Process, the North-South Center is mindful of the fact that this volume is more than an historical record of the raw material that was fashioned into a finished product in Miami by the thirty-four freely elected heads of government and state of the Western Hemisphere. For the "Miami Process" is by no means finished. Those who have spoken through these documents, or through other means, will continue to shoulder a major responsibility for a process that has as a fundamental principle the partnership between government and civil society. For their part, governments will have to be even more forthcoming in the future regarding the establishment of concrete mechanisms for non-governmental involvement in the post-Summit "Miami Process." We trust that *Advancing the Miami Process: Civil Society and the Summit of the Americas* will serve as reminder to both governmental and non-governmental actors and groups of the opportunities that lie ahead, as well as the shared responsibilities that have been acquired in pursuing the Summit's lofty goals.

Acknowledgments

In many ways, compiling such a comprehensive set of documents is a much more complicated and daunting task than editing a work of original scholarship. The editors would like to express a great debt of gratitude to the many people at the North-South Center, in government, and in non-governmental organizations whose support and collaboration made this volume possible.

Thanks must first be given to the North-South Center Summit of the Americas team: Carlos Monge (of CEPES, Peru); Genie Becerra; and North-South Scholars Leda Pérez, José Luis Huiza, and Joe Domask. This team was responsible not only for the Center's intellectual input into the Summit agenda, but also for establishing the networks with non-governmental actors necessary to generate interest and support for this volume. We would also like to express our deep appreciation to Lou Falino, USIA Diplomat in Residence, for his invaluable support as liaison with government agencies.

Our thanks to Sherry Tross, Program Associate, for her work at the outset of the project to secure support from many of the collaborating governmental and non-governmental organizations. For the arduous work in securing documents and managing correspondence with dozens of organizations, we deeply appreciate the support of Omaida Hennessey, Staff Associate to the Deputy Director. Her persistence and patience resulted in a richer, more representative volume. Many thanks also to María Padilla, Nancy Colón, and Norma Laird of the North-South Center, and North-South Center Scholars Laura Hernández and Tim Withee, who worked long hours to generate the original index list, making it a valuable tool for scholars and practitioners.

To our colleagues at the North-South Center Press, suffice it to say that because of your professionalism — and patience — the Center's publications are timely, relevant, and academically sound. First, our thanks to Richard Downes, Director of Communications, for his support in getting the book published in such a short time frame. We would like to thank Kathleen Hamman, Editorial Director, for overseeing each stage of the editing/proofreading process; Jayne Weisblatt, Editor, for painstakingly correcting the scanned documents and for proofreading all the documents at various stages; Cynthia Jenney, Editor, for translating a lengthy document and proofreading; and Diane Duys, Editorial Assistant, for her support. On the production team, our deep appreciation goes to Mary Mapes, Publications Director, for the brilliant cover design and formatting the text; to Susan Holler, Associate Director of Publications, for formatting the text and for her support in bringing the work to completion; and to Stephanie True Moss, Publication Design Consultant, for meticulously creating the index.

To Edwards Brothers Inc., of Lillington, North Carolina, we extend our thanks for printing the book on such a tight deadline.

A special note of thanks must go to Richard E. Feinberg, Special Assistant to the President and Senior Director for Inter-American Affairs at the National Security Council, whose commitment to public participation in the Summit process is evident throughout this volume and without whose ideas and support this work would not have been published.

Robin Rosenberg and Steve Stein, editors

Advancing the Miami Process: Civil Society and the Summit of the Americas

President William Jefferson Clinton

In December 1994, the leaders of our hemisphere came together in Miami to seize an historic opportunity to build a community of nations committed to the values of liberty and the promise of prosperity. At the Summit of the Americas, we worked to strengthen the remarkable movement towards democracy that has taken hold of our nations. We agreed on principles to help open new markets and to create a free trade area throughout our hemisphere. We dedicated ourselves to improving the quality of life for all our people by improving their education, their health and their environment.

The Summit of the Americas launched a partnership that will lead to expanding freedoms, increased opportunities and rising prosperity for our children and for generations to come.

But this partnership goes beyond governments. Forgetting national borders and narrow interests, an extraordinary group of individuals united to help define a 21st century agenda for the Americas. Indigenous leaders, academics, businessmen and labor organizers took up the challenge to help chart our hemisphere's future. Women's activists, human rights advocates and environmentalists brought their expertise to the table. Community organizers joined with economists to make sure all voices were heard.

Their ideas, their service and their cooperation energized the "Spirit of Miami" that reigned during the days of the Summit. This volume captures that spirit of trust and possibility. It portrays the excitement of exploring new ideas, of building a common vision, of creating a plan to make that vision a reality. It demonstrates the diversity of suggestions and strategies that the Summit organizers sought and captured. And it reproduces the final Summit documents — the *Declaration of Principles* and the *Plan of Action* — which record the hopes we share for our hemispheric community and our commitment to make them real.

The agenda we embraced at the Summit of the Americas is broad and ambitious. It imagines a hemisphere where disputes among and within nations are peacefully resolved, where cultures and nations are universally respected, where no person's rights are denied nor labor abused and where work is rewarded and families and communities are strong. It reflects the belief that we will only succeed if all of us — in villages, classrooms, factories, offices and government corridors — come together to make freedom, opportunity and prosperity the common property of the people of the Americas. This is the vision of the Summit of the Americas and the challenge that lies before us as a new century dawns.

Building Community Through Participation: The Role of Non-Governmental Actors in the Summit of the Americas

Cathryn L. Thorup

Cathryn L. Thorup worked at the National Security Council, Directorate for Inter-American Affairs, as Associate Director and Senior Summit Liaison for Non-Governmental Actors from June-December 1994. She is currently Director of the Office of Development Partners and Deputy Coordinator of the New Partnerships Initiative at the U.S. Agency for International Development (USAID). The views expressed here are the author's alone and do not necessarily represent the policy or views of the U.S. government as a whole nor of the specific agencies with which she is now or has been associated.

The 1994 Summit of the Americas was a critical catalyst for action and collaboration in the Western Hemisphere, directly contributing to a strengthening of civil society in that region. Both the process by which the Summit initiatives were developed and the content of the initiatives themselves were key to a process of active engagement of the public and private spheres unparalleled in scope and depth for a gathering of heads of state.

In preparing for the 1967 Punta del Este Summit, the U.S. government consulted with only a handful of business and non-governmental leaders (primarily academics). Preparations for the 1994 Summit of the Americas were markedly different. The Clinton administration quite consciously paired traditional diplomacy with a new participatory diplomacy in order to expand the range of actors involved in the consultative process and to deepen their degree of participation.

This approach reflected the realignment already underway within the Western Hemisphere in the relative division of labor between government and civil society. During the 1980s, the relative roles of the business community and the public sector were redefined; the 1990s are witness to a similar phenomenon in terms of the role of non-governmental organizations (NGOs). Ultimately, it was not simply thirty-four governments that convened in Miami, Florida, in December 1994, but rather an evolving community of thirty-four nations. The results of the consultative process engendered by this event demonstrated the value of partnership among government, business, and the non-governmental community on the full range of social and public policy issues.

This volume is itself both part of and testimony to this broad-based effort to engage a wide range of non-governmental actors (NGAs) in the official preparations for the Summit of the Americas. It captures one particularly important aspect of the multiple ways in which non-governmental actors (business and labor organizations, grassroots development and community organizations, and advocacy and research organizations) participated in the Summit process, serving as an official repository of the written contributions made by many of these actors to the *Declaration of Principles* and accompanying *Plan of Action* endorsed by the heads of state in Miami.

While this chapter addresses a number of concerns and experiences common to public and private sector actors throughout the hemisphere,

The author gratefully acknowledges the comments and contributions of Richard E. Feinberg, Ramón Daubón, Constance R. Dunham, Mark Rentschler, and Linda A. Robertson. A special debt of gratitude is owed to Cheryl Morden for her thoughtful insights.

it does so through a U.S. lens and from the vantage point of the public sector. It is left to the many public and private sector participants located elsewhere to report directly and in detail the ways in which their own experiences evolved.

Benefits of Partnership: Strategic Objectives

Early during the U.S. lead-up to the Summit of the Americas, the role to be played by non-governmental actors was discussed by key policymakers in the White House and the Department of State. Gradually, a consensus emerged around the potential benefits attached to their active involvement in the Summit process:

1. It would assist policymakers in identifying those issues in the hemisphere where the urgency was greatest and where concerted, collective action was most likely to produce sustainable, tangible benefits;

2. Engaging a broad cross-section of the non-governmental community from throughout the hemisphere in an exchange of views and a sharing of "best practices" would help build bridges between and within nations and promote economies of scale;

3. It would foster the development of new skills and the professionalization of the non-governmental community (in terms of greater accountability, transparency, and efficiency) in ways that would make it possible for ever broader segments of that community to respond even more effectively, rapidly, and proactively to future such initiatives;

4. It would build political constituencies for the Summit initiatives and foster public support for broader U.S. foreign policy goals in the region;

5. Drawing upon the full range of creativity and energy of the widest array possible of social actors would highlight the priority needs of previously marginalized sectors and provide impetus for more far-reaching reforms;

6. It would guarantee non-governmental actors a legitimate role in the implementation process, a stake in its success, and a clear sense of shared responsibility for the results;

7. It would build upon the notion of a new partnership between government and civil society to provide the outlines of a new social compact, underscoring *shared* rights, risks, and responsibilities.

Building a Partnership: The Process

Public discussion of the Summit initiatives began from the moment the Summit was first announced. Consultations took place throughout 1994, with the greatest concentration of activity occurring during the final three to six months prior to the Summit. Many of the joint public/private sector discussions were initiated in the United States, either by the U.S. government or by U.S. non-governmental actors. A significant number of consultations were the product of other hemispheric actors — particularly non-governmental actors — in Canada, Latin America, and the Caribbean. In each country context, the style of involvement was different. Similarly, public participation varied somewhat depending on the type of issue under discussion — with the sustainable development issues being the most highly participatory and some of the economic issues being less so.

In the United States

The Clinton administration utilized a variety of different mechanisms to engage U.S. non-governmental actors in preparations for the Summit of the Americas and, by extension, to encourage other governments in the hemisphere to enrich their planning processes through similar means. Special attention was paid to ensuring that this participation was as balanced as possible in terms of the types of groups engaged and the subjects under discussion. In some cases, this led to proactive efforts to address certain topics or to engage specific non-governmental actors — particularly those that were relatively less experienced, less responsive, and, therefore, less visible. These mechanisms included the following:

• participation by non-governmental actors in official inter-agency working group meetings to design the initial U.S. initiatives proposed for the Summit;

• inclusion of non-governmental actors on certain U.S. official delegations to consult on the Summit initiatives with other governments in the hemisphere;

• cross-sectoral consultative discussions and briefings with a broad array of non-governmental groups at once;

• targeted consultative sessions with individual sectors such as human rights, environmental, and indigenous rights groups; Latino leadership; labor; academics and non-governmental policy influentials, and others;

• numerous public speeches to non-governmental groups, including the Business Roundtable, the Inter-American Dialogue's network of NGOs, and the Meeting of Western Hemisphere Women Leaders;

• preparation by the business community of a "white paper" on Summit-related economic issues;

• selected press interviews and journal articles on the Summit for non-governmental audiences;

• designation of special contact persons at the National Security Council, USAID, the Office of Environmental Policy, and the U.S. Department of Treasury for non-governmental actors;

• access to Summit briefings, press conferences with government officials, and official Summit documents for NGAs whose publication activities allowed them to obtain press accreditation;

• participation of invited non-governmental actors in the Summit itself, including a special reception offered by President Clinton and Vice President Gore to recognize the contributions of these actors; two cabinet-level briefings for non-governmental actors; and attendance at the final Plenary Session;

• development of a Summit initiative designed to foster an enabling environment for civil society throughout the hemisphere and specific tie-ins with non-governmental actors in numerous other Summit initiatives;

• delineation of specific roles for non-governmental actors in implementing the full range of Summit initiatives.

The way in which the Summit *Declaration of Principles* and *Plan of Action* were developed also enhanced the prospects for non-governmental actors to work hand-in-glove with governments throughout the hemisphere. For those more accustomed to UN-type summits — where issues are negotiated during the course of the gathering itself, with governments and non-governmental actors working either jointly or in parallel sessions — it is useful to view the Summit of the Americas not as a three-day leaders-only gathering but, rather, as the formalization of a process of consultation and negotiation that covered a period of more than six months.[1] During that entire time, a broad cross-section of non-governmental actors played a key role in the design of the Summit initiatives. These dynamic, working partnerships with government will be sustained and expanded upon during the implementation phase of the Miami Process.[2]

Elsewhere in the Hemisphere

Throughout the hemisphere, the Summit of the Americas provided an opportunity for public/private sector partnership in both its design and implementation phases. Government responses, however, varied greatly. In a number of countries, preparations for the Summit of the Americas opened new channels of access and communication and afforded the possibility of significant cooperation between national policymakers and certain sectors of the non-governmental community. In other nations, it served to further strengthen previously existing collaborative relationships. In still others, there was little or no involvement of non-governmental actors.

The degree of NGA involvement in the Summit preparations varied from issue to issue and between one type of non-governmental actor and another. Some governments were reluctant to allow environmental groups to take part in the planning process, for example, while in other countries environmental groups were welcome but human rights groups were not. In some countries, business actors were welcomed into the process, but other non-governmental actors were excluded. In some instances, government reaction varied depending upon whether it was a home-based non-governmental actor or a "foreign" one.

The manner in which non-governmental actors were incorporated into the formal preparations by their governments (as opposed to their participation through non-governmental channels) also varied greatly. The Canadian government, for example, organized a highly structured, extremely participatory process. Some governments (Ecuador and Trinidad and Tobago, for example) hosted regional conferences for the discussion of Summit initiatives that involved both governmental and non-governmental players. Other governments limited their activities to briefings of non-governmental actors, while others were not at all proactive.

Regardless of the predisposition of particular governments, the strength of non-governmental actors overall was enhanced by the process of the Summit preparations, as networks were built and/or strengthened across borders and across sectors.

The Summit Documents

The two official documents[3] produced at the Summit of the Americas are replete with specific references to the role to be played by non-governmental actors as doers, facilitators, and as beneficiaries. The Summit's *Declaration of Principles*, for example, states: "To assure public engagement and commitment, we invite the cooperation and participation of the private sector, labor, political parties, academic institutions and other non-governmental actors and organizations in both our national and regional efforts, thus strengthening the partnership between government and society."

Similarly, commitments made by the heads of state in the Summit's *Plan of Action* set the stage for concerted efforts to strengthen civil society. Under the initiative entitled "Invigorating Society/Community Participation," each signatory pledged to work toward a strong and diverse civil society through legal and regulatory reform, the encouragement of local private philanthropy, technical and financial support, increased civic participation (particularly on the part of groups traditionally marginalized from policymaking), and the professionalization of the non-governmental community in terms of accountability and transparency. The *Plan of Action* also contains community-based initiatives in health and education and other initiatives specifically designed to promote dynamic public/private sector partnerships in microenterprise and small business development and in the areas of energy use, biodiversity, and pollution prevention.

While the Summit's *Plan of Action* provides a fairly detailed framework (including performance indicators, timetables, and a delegation of responsibility) to ensure steady, measurable progress toward these objectives, the active engagement of civil society actors in Summit follow-up will contribute additional specificity and momentum where necessary. All segments of civil society are explicitly invited to participate in implementing each of the twenty-three Summit initiatives agreed to by the heads of state.[4]

Participatory Diplomacy: Transcending Barriers to Entry

The Summit of the Americas established a benchmark for public consultation and provided a number of lessons for future exercises in participatory diplomacy. At the same time, collaboration between the public and private spheres in this instance progressed in fits and starts due to certain "barriers to entry."

While some branches of the U.S. government were, from the outset, extremely receptive to and proactive regarding the participation of non-govern-

mental groups in the elaboration of the proposed U.S. initiatives for the Summit, others were more reluctant, given their own lack of experience in working with such groups, time constraints, the perceived sensitivity of a particular issue, or the anticipation of a negative reaction on the part of other governments in the hemisphere. Similarly, there were marked differences in the way in which different sectors within the non-governmental community responded to the opportunity to work closely with the U.S. government. Some of these barriers to entry were resistant to bridge-building efforts; others were more easily overcome.

One set of such barriers resided in the *prevailing institutional cultures* of the various public and private sector actors. Alongside the process of political opening in Latin America that has been evolving since the 1980s, many non-governmental actors have moved from political opposition to a search for greater "concertación" with their governments. While this approach has emphasized peaceful dialogue, negotiation, and accommodation, there is still today a need for confidence building between government and the non-governmental sector as both move toward constructive engagement.[5] This is particularly challenging where perspectives differ.

Collaborative efforts require time, trust, and tenacity and are more difficult where there is a legacy of friction (for example, with human rights groups in the aftermath of the conflicts in Central America in the 1980s or vis-à-vis labor organizations in the post-NAFTA era). Where there are clear mutual interests and economies of scale (such as business groups or environmental organizations), the process is more fluid.

In the case of the Summit of the Americas, there was a marked diversity of opinion in the first weeks and months among those U.S. officials — at times even within the same agency — who proactively sought to encourage non-governmental participation, those who thought it "couldn't hurt," and those who viewed it as problematic. Into the latter category fell those concerned that a participatory process might delay and complicate the planning process, alienate other governments in the hemisphere, raise unrealistically high expectations on the part of NGAs, and/or politicize the event itself to the detriment of the Clinton administration or the other participating governments. Some officials felt (as did some in the non-governmental community as well) that the notion of having "government" promote the participation of the non-governmental sector was itself an inappropriate blurring of the lines separating the public and private spheres. Overall, the range of opinion was directly related to variations in personal and organizational experience and differences in agency mandates, priorities, and constituent bases.

A number of steps were taken by particular Clinton administration officials to facilitate and foster the more general adoption of a participatory approach: non-governmental actors were defined as broadly as possible in order to incorporate a wide ideological and professional spectrum (the inclusion of business actors was important in this regard); strong working relationships were built among receptive individuals within each U.S. agency involved in Summit planning;[6] NGAs were reminded that consultation did not guarantee the automatic incorporation of their suggestions into the Summit agenda; references to the potentially positive contribution to be made by non-governmental actors were incorporated into as many public presentations as possible;[7] key U.S. government officials galvanized other U.S. actors with their deep-seated belief in the need for an inclusionary process;[8] and an extremely active relationship was developed with those non-governmental entities prepared to devote considerable time and energy to the Summit process. Additional momentum was afforded by institutions such as the Inter-American Development Bank, whose president sparked significant rethinking among other senior bank officials from throughout the hemisphere regarding the role of non-governmental actors.[9]

Among non-governmental groups as well, there was considerable variation in their degree of openness to cooperation with government officials. For virtually all of these groups, work on the Summit would require an unexpected shift in resource allocation, and some were skeptical regarding the seriousness of the U.S. government's invitation to them to participate. Again, reactions varied largely as a result of past personal and organizational histories.

A second set of obstacles resided in the *organizational capacity of the non-governmental actors*. During the early stages of Summit planning, environmental NGOs and business groups were the most proactive. These organizations had the requisite resources (both human and financial) to devote to the process and the political savvy to determine where best to focus their efforts. They knew exactly how to weigh-in to press their concerns in the most efficient and effective manner and were fluent in the language of bureaucratic politics.

Other groups — drawn from more traditional development and anti-poverty organizations, religious groups, think-tanks, and human rights, indigenous rights, and women's rights organizations — found participation required the development of new organizational skills or a refocusing of pre-existing skills. Some non-governmental actors simply did not have experience in working with the U.S. government and were unsure how, whether, and where to weigh-in. In some cases, non-governmental groups were more comfortable maintaining a low profile. Other groups, while quite experienced in working with the U.S. government regarding their particular areas of interest (knowing exactly whom to contact, for example), had to develop new knowledge and skills in order to address these issues within the broader context of a hemispheric summit. In some cases, the process of collaborative work itself contributed to institutional strengthening, as more experienced non-governmental actors shared experiences with those who were less so.

Some non-governmental actors were accustomed to a more adversarial relationship with government and found that a process requiring a combination of both collaboration and advocacy posed new challenges. Others were accustomed to working in the international arena and found that working on national policy proposals for the regional context required some reorientation. Finally, some organizations were challenged by the need to address not only their particular sectoral concerns, but a broad array of cross-cutting issues as well.

This issue of organizational capacity benefits from additional nuancing regarding the way in which non-governmental groups view their advocacy role and the question of representativity. While it may slow or otherwise complicate their ability to work with government, some would consider U.S. non-governmental groups that work closely with counterparts in other areas of the hemisphere as having greater organizational capacity than those groups that do not prioritize advocacy grounded in cross-border partnerships. In the case of the Summit of the Americas, these relationships both enriched and constrained the advocacy capacity of organizations that were committed to introducing the perspectives of their southern counterparts into the policy-making process.[10]

A third barrier to participatory diplomacy had to do with the *nature of the work agenda* and the identification of the areas within which the public and private spheres would interact (i.e., which players would be welcome where). U.S. officials were particularly interested in the participation of non-governmental actors on issues relating to the strengthening of civil society. Some groups, however, were disinclined to circumscribe their activities to any one area, preferring instead to address a range of issues including, for example, macroeconomic concerns. Meanwhile, government players charged with developing initiatives in the economic arena — particularly at the outset — were reluctant to open this area much beyond business actors.

Ultimately, participatory diplomacy advanced more quickly in the areas of democracy and governance, and sustainable development (including both the environmental and social agendas) with regard to NGOs. Other non-governmental actors — such as business — found that their participation was also welcome within the economic arena by, for example, the Department of Commerce. Thus, the level of participation varied according to the issue area and the degree of coincidence of interests among the players.

A fourth barrier to entry related to the *start-up time* involved in engaging non-governmental actors. For their part, U.S. government officials devoted considerable energy to a careful assessment of the relative risks and rewards of a participatory approach. Consultation takes time and slows the preparatory process. It also fosters the empowerment of non-governmental actors, which in turn increases the pressure upon government officials to "do" certain things. This led some officials to suggest that it would be better to handle Summit preparations in a very low-profile manner, staving off outside pressure as long as possible. Others argued against such an approach, stating that when that pressure did emerge, it would be all the more intense and potentially disruptive as it would be born out of the anger of exclusion, rather than a constructive force emanating from authentic involvement. Further, they stated that while it was true that increased societal participation would reduce the ability of state actors to "direct" the process, it was also the case that the long-term results would be more sustainable.

During planning for the Summit of the Americas, U.S. officials stressed to NGAs the need to participate early and often rather than waiting until the end of the process.[11] For many U.S. non-governmental actors, however — particularly those groups without extensive experience in working with government — there

was a significant lag time between the decision to participate in the Summit planning process and their ability to notify their counterparts in the region, encourage them to participate, work through concerns of northern NGO dominance, process their input, consult with one another, and present their joint views to government policymakers.

Non-governmental actors wanted to be certain that they were in fact to be authentic partners to government and not window dressing for the Summit. In this context, they raised a number of concerns prior to the Summit: whether they would be allowed to be physically present and/or take part in the Miami event; the level of their participation in all aspects of the Summit planning processes (including trade-related issues, for example); the role of labor in the consultation; parity among NGOs and business; participation on official consultation teams; the level of attention afforded to issues of particular concern (women's rights, indigenous rights, the nexus between trade expansion and environmental issues, poverty, immigration, policy toward Cuba, and human rights); the level of consultation with other governments in the hemisphere and with non-governmental groups; competing priorities (the International Conference on Population and Development in Cairo, the World Summit for Social Development in Copenhagen, and the Fourth World Conference on Women in Beijing); the degree of attention accorded to disparities between North and South (rather than an exclusive focus upon the Western Hemisphere as a cohesive whole); and the level of support to be provided for NGA on-site activities (press conferences, xeroxing, and so on).

Another concern was related to the way in which some U.S. NGOs viewed the process of "partnered advocacy" with their southern counterparts. Some were reluctant — based on the burden of responsibility they felt as a result of their relatively greater access to information and decisionmakers in the United States — to be too hasty in advocating a major investment of resources by their southern partners before having a clear sense of the Summit process and confidence regarding its potential impact.

Ultimately, the participation of non-governmental actors in the process was determined by a number of factors: a belief that the solicitation of their views was sincere; that their interaction was part of a credible process and that there was a clear mechanism for this process of engagement; that there would be resources available to support their efforts; that they would have access to policymakers and the potential for influence; and that there would be a lasting value to their participation. For Latin American and Caribbean non-governmental actors in particular, there was a desire to open political space and secure recognition of the potential contributions to be made by NGAs.

Although some non-governmental groups initially believed that their physical presence at the Summit itself would be more significant than any up-front contributions, a consensus emerged that early involvement was the only "real" involvement since the Summit documents would be negotiated among the governments well in advance of the formal signing in Miami. Nevertheless, written input and requests for appointments grew steadily as the date of the Summit approached, and it became increasingly difficult for policymakers to incorporate this input into the ever-more tightly scheduled and highly structured process of government-to-government consultations.

As non-governmental participation in these sorts of events becomes more routine, the problems associated with a slow start-up time can be significantly reduced. For this to be the case, however, governments will need to modify their processes to further facilitate the participation of non-governmental actors, and NGAs will need to develop more flexible and agile ways to respond to collaborative opportunities. A jointly developed framework for partnership — that builds upon the Miami experience and is mutually agreed upon early in the planning process — would enhance significantly future cooperative endeavors.

A fifth barrier to entry was related to the issue of *national sovereignty*. U.S. non-governmental actors were hampered in their ability to achieve economies of scale by working cross-nationally with NGAs in other parts of the hemisphere where access to decision-making spheres in some cases was either extremely limited or nonexistent. At the same time, there was a fairly general consensus within the U.S. government that it would be "inappropriate" or imprudent for the U.S. government directly to encourage non-governmental actors outside the United States to take part in Summit planning, as this might be viewed by the other leaders in the hemisphere as an unwarranted intrusion into their domestic spheres of influence.

To a large extent, then, it fell to the non-governmental actors themselves to serve as a bridging

mechanism to bring forward the views of NGAs with less access to their own governments or to regional fora. For example, U.S. human rights and indigenous rights organizations transmitted the views of non-U.S. NGAs in these sectors to U.S. policymakers — forwarding their materials directly or raising concerns in their name.

Thus, the Indian Law Resource Center transmitted a letter to U.S. government officials from the Indigenous Parliament of America. Human Rights Watch endeavored to provide information and access for non-U.S. NGOs. Frequently, U.S. and non-U.S.-based NGAs would join forces to press a point. For example, the proposal by the Ad Hoc U.S. NGO Working Group on the Summit on ways in which NGOs could participate at the Summit itself was endorsed by a group of regional organizations of agricultural producers, small and medium-sized businesses, NGOs, trade unions and grassroots organizations throughout the hemisphere.

A second way in which non-U.S., non-governmental actors participated was through the development of proposals in concert with U.S. NGAs. For example, non-governmental actors from the entire region participated, in early October, in the development of the *Communiqué of the Women's Hemispheric Roundtable to the Summit of the Americas*. A similar phenomenon took place with the preparations by U.S. and Latin American NGAs of a proposed Summit declaration on human rights.

Interestingly, when initial efforts to influence the Summit agenda on women directly proved unsuccessful, the non-governmental actors involved approached both U.S. congresswomen (who subsequently lobbied the executive branch on their behalf) and the Nicaraguan government. The latter then raised the issue successfully at the final official negotiation among the governments of the hemisphere held at Airlie House. Similarly, some non-governmental actors in Latin America and the Caribbean kept U.S. officials advised of their efforts to contribute to the Summit process in case their own governments were less responsive. Thus, interesting temporary alliances can develop between the non-governmental actors of one country and the government of another in order to influence other actors.[12]

Academic institutions and think-tanks like the North-South Center of the University of Miami, the Inter-American Dialogue, and the International Center for Research on Women convened conferences involving a broad range of non-governmental actors throughout the hemisphere to develop policy recommendations. The North-South Center, for example, established three hemispheric policy working groups that cut across borders and sectors to involve academic experts, government officials, business and labor, and NGOs throughout the hemisphere in the elaboration of proposals related to every area of the Summit agenda. Organizations like Church World Service/Lutheran World Relief spent significant time in discussions with counterparts throughout the region in the development of policy proposals.

Another way in which U.S. non-governmental actors involved numerous non-governmental actors from elsewhere in the hemisphere in the Summit was through the establishment of three electronic networks by Florida International University, the National Audubon Society, and Church World Service/Lutheran World Relief. These networks for the exchange of information and perspectives also served to disseminate official Summit-related documents to a broader audience than would otherwise have been the case.

One particularly ambitious Latin American non-governmental effort was that of the Fundación Futuro Latinoamericano. Based in Ecuador, the organizers built upon national non-governmental consultations in fourteen countries (the results of which were to be transmitted to the respective heads of state) to develop a consensus document during a regional consultation in Bogotá.

The self-ascribed goal of the exercise was to ensure that the interests of Latin NGOs not be established by actors from outside the region — either governmental or non-governmental.

In their efforts to expand the points of access for non-governmental actors, U.S. officials encouraged other governments in the hemisphere to open their Summit planning process to non-governmental actors. To this end, a cable[13] was sent to U.S. embassies throughout the hemisphere instructing them to express U.S. support for non-governmental involvement to their host governments and — in consultation with those governments — to be responsive if approached by local non-governmental actors. The objective was to secure active, pre-Summit involvement by a broad cross-section of non-governmental

actors and to contribute to the establishment of innovative public/private sector partnerships.

One effective — and relatively unobtrusive way — to foster such dialogue was by example, and U.S. officials in meetings with their counterparts described the ways in which non-governmental actors were participating within the United States and discussed the advantages to be derived from a rethinking of the traditional division of labor between the public and private spheres.

A final and more direct approach to the encouragement of non-governmental involvement in the Summit planning involved the inclusion of a number of environmental NGOs on the official U.S. delegations to some of the bilateral and multilateral consultations on the Summit agenda. The U.S. teams traveled with a small number of environmental NGOs — usually two or three — to bilateral consultations in Argentina, Brazil, Chile, Colombia, Mexico, and Nicaragua. Though constrained in the range of their activities by the ground rules set out in advance, the signal sent to other governments in the hemisphere was dramatic nonetheless. In some countries, for example, the host government reciprocated by inviting their own local NGOs to join the discussions. In the case of Argentina, highly respected civic-action NGOs took part in the discussions. In Brazil and Mexico, on the other hand, the host governments responded quite differently, barring the U.S. NGOs from the discussions altogether.

Similarly, U.S. NGOs and NGOs from other countries of the hemisphere took part in multilateral consultations on the environment (in Quito, Ecuador) and on the microenterprise and small business initiative (in Trinidad and Tobago).

The case of the microenterprise meeting in Trinidad and Tobago in early November is a particularly good example of the benefits to be accrued from a more highly participatory negotiation.[14] A list of the top NGOs that assist microenterprises throughout the region was developed jointly by the Ford Foundation, Inter-American Foundation, Inter-American Development Bank, and USAID. These groups — and a number of the key multilateral organizations — were then invited to take part in the official consultation on ways in which key barriers to microenterprise and small business finance and development could be eliminated. The NGOs and multilaterals played a key role in this two-day event, providing technical expertise to government participants from seventeen countries. The non-governmental actors selected six of their own to present formal remarks at the meeting. Following an intensive and highly participatory debate and extensive negotiation, the attendees produced a consensus action plan that became part of the Summit *Plan of Action.*

These examples underscore some of the ways in which non-governmental actors contributed to the Summit planning process. The special role of U.S. environmental NGOs is noteworthy here, underscoring once again how far cooperation between the public and private spheres in this sector has advanced. In the future, one objective of U.S. officials and non-governmental actors alike almost certainly would be to incorporate an even more diverse array of players, building upon the relationships established and knowledge gained in the Summit of the Americas exercise.

Measurable Results

Non-governmental actors were involved to an unprecedented degree in all phases leading up to (and including) the Summit of the Americas and are actively engaged in the implementation of the *Plan of Action.* The active involvement of a wide array of non-governmental actors left an unmistakable imprint upon both the tone and content of the Summit of the Americas *Declaration of Principles* and the accompanying *Plan of Action.* It was reflected in the richness and range of the Summit initiatives — particularly those focused upon women, human rights, indigenous rights, civic participation, microenterprise and small business development, and the environment. The input of the business community was particularly visible in the initiatives relating to economic prosperity. The presence of a range of non-governmental actors at the final official signing ceremony (the Plenary Session) highlighted emerging cross-border and cross-sectoral linkages in the hemisphere.

According to both official and non-governmental participants, the Summit of the Americas served to remove significant barriers to partnership in a number of different countries in the hemisphere. Not only did it promote active working partnerships between governments and non-governmental actors, but it also underscored the benefits of cross-sectoral networks (encompassing, for example, the environment, human rights, women's rights, business, labor, and

academics) and among non-governmental groups from different countries, cross-border networks of NGAs. It signaled the involvement of a broad community of actors engaged in a new partnership cutting across both sectors and borders to involve the citizens of the hemisphere in a joint effort with government to address priority needs in a way that will produce sustainable, tangible results.

Similarly, the specific success of this collaborative process in the United States was recognized by key actors in both the public and private spheres. President Clinton offered a special reception in Miami recognizing the contributions of the business and NGO communities to the U.S. preparations for the Summit. Similarly, Vice President Gore received a letter in February 1995 from twelve leading U.S. NGOs stating, "The role played by NGOs in the preparations for the Summit was unprecedented for this type of presidential level meeting, and conveyed a powerful message about the importance of citizen participation to government officials throughout the Americas."[15]

The Summit of the Americas established a new benchmark for public/private sector cooperation in the Western Hemisphere. The decision of many non-governmental actors to take part early in the process rather than to mount an alternative Summit or to choose not to participate derived from their genuine involvement.[16] The level of engagement reached was reflected by the breadth of the Summit initiatives and the level of detail regarding implementation; the number of sectoral and regional non-governmental meetings that took place; the quantity of high-quality proposals for the Summit agenda (as evidenced in this volume); and the many requests for additional information. Non-governmental actors throughout the hemisphere also provided constant feedback and suggestions on an informal basis; direct input into U.S. initiatives and those in other countries; and technical expertise.

Participatory diplomacy produced other results during the lead-up to the Summit: reducing the natural parochialism of government agencies and non-governmental actors accustomed to focusing on one particular issue or sub-set of issues; contributing to an emerging notion of collective action within the hemisphere rather than a traditional North/South divide; pushing actors beyond an outdated notion of foreign assistance and/or entitlement to a collective sense of responsibility for the future of the hemisphere; raising the comfort level around public/private sector partnership; providing government officials with conceptual grounding and technical expertise; enhancing the enabling environment for NGAs by opening political space for service providers, research, and advocacy organizations and by mobilizing government, foundation, and private resources for the work of non-governmental actors; and fostering tie-ins with the International Conference on Population and Development (Cairo), the World Summit for Social Development (Copenhagen), and the Fourth World Conference on Women (Beijing).

As noted above, the Summit also served to spark a great deal of ancillary activity — with a strengthening of cross-sectoral and cross-border integration throughout the hemisphere. As a result, activities are under way, people are talking with one another, organizations are working together, and agenda items have moved from the back burner to the front burner in ways that would not otherwise have occurred — particularly in such a concentrated period of time or in such a focused manner.

The Summit of the Americas provided an unusual opening to engage U.S. domestic audiences on issues related to U.S. foreign policy, particularly with regard to Latin America. It was an occasion to highlight the direct relevance of foreign policy to the everyday concerns of U.S. citizens across the country, underscoring the anachronism of the traditional divide between foreign policy and domestic concerns. Simultaneously, it provided the U.S. public an opportunity to reflect upon U.S. interests within the context of the Western Hemisphere as a whole and to explore a range of issues specific to U.S. relations with Latin America and the Caribbean within an environment of potential collaboration.

Still, there is significant room for further advancement in the area of participatory diplomacy. This would include expanding the range of players, for example. While quite involved in other areas of the hemisphere, labor was a less active participant than other non-governmental actors in the United States due to a confluence of factors. Economic issues were generally less permeable to the involvement of non-governmental actors; labor was relatively uninterested in working on political or social issues; and there remained a legacy of unease in the aftermath of the previous years' battles over NAFTA. Had the moment been different, it might have been possible

to engage labor in a more fruitful discussion of social safety nets and adjustment assistance.

Similarly, respect for the sovereignty of the various participating governments meant that U.S. official actors were restricted in their ability to work directly with the non-governmental actors of non-U.S. participants. In retrospect, this could have been pushed further in the case of the Summit of the Americas and public sector roadblocks born out of inexperience, excessive sensitivity, and/or legitimate concern that might have been overcome.

At the same time, non-governmental actors might have directed greater energy toward encouraging other governments in the hemisphere to be more participatory in their preparations for the Summit rather than expecting that push to come primarily from the U.S. government. Non-governmental groups — both U.S. and non-U.S. — tended to direct their lobbying efforts toward U.S. policymakers in order to influence the Summit agenda or to encourage the U.S. government to use its influence to weigh-in with other governments on specific issues. Similarly, there was a tendency to work through the U.S. government to encourage other governments to open political space to non-governmental actors rather than to lobby those governments directly.

At similar future events, some governments in the hemisphere will now be more likely to include a broad range of non-governmental actors as part of their delegations. A number of governments brought business leaders to the Miami event, for example, and this practice might be expanded to include other non-governmental actors, such as women's, environmental, or human rights groups (as the United States did in this case). At the Miami event, there was concern on the part of some U.S. officials that providing numerous special on-site NGA events might distract from the meeting of the leaders themselves; encourage large numbers of NGAs to forego early involvement in the planning process in favor of simply showing up at the Summit itself (thereby provoking frustration when it became apparent that it was too late for meaningful input); and isolate the non-governmental groups.

As an alternative, as indicated above, a significant number (well over one hundred) of the U.S. NGAs most heavily involved in the pre-Summit planning and/or representative of a broad range of constituencies were invited to a few select Summit events. This worked well but could have been expanded to include additional activities. NGAs might have been invited not simply to attend the final Plenary Session, but to also speak there, publicly endorsing the Summit initiatives and pledging their participation in the Summit follow-up.

Finally, events such as the Summit of the Americas serve to build a domestic constituency for U.S. foreign policy. Even more could have been done in this regard. Public outreach in the United States tended to be heavily Washington-based. Although many, if not most, non-governmental groups have representatives in Washington,[17] there is much to be gained from targeted consultations with non-governmental actors around the country.[18] Such activity is extraordinarily time-intensive if it is to be truly participatory and inclusive, and would need to be undertaken very early in the planning process.

Lessons Learned

Overall, the results of adopting a participatory approach to the planning for the Summit of the Americas were extremely significant and formed a strong base for future endeavors.

The experience of the Summit of the Americas demonstrates that certain agencies and departments of the U.S. government are considerably more comfortable than others in working with the non-governmental sector. Based on greater experience, overlapping agendas, and/or the political will to experiment, some agencies will move more quickly than others to consolidate public/private partnerships and will find themselves at an immediate advantage vis-à-vis those parts of the government that confine themselves to business as usual. The establishment of active working partnerships with the non-governmental community will provide agencies with strong advocates outside the formal halls of power; more effective programming (based upon a more accurate assessment of the dimensions of the problem and upon solutions that enjoy broad-based support among those that will participate); reinforcement of government openness, accountability, and transparency; and greater cost-effectiveness. These working partnerships also will enhance the prospects for the long-term sustainability of results. Similarly, within the U.S. government itself, important alliances can be built among agencies on the basis of a shared interest in working with non-governmental actors.

For their part, non-governmental actors may want to explore new ways to work collaboratively across sectors, based upon their experience with the Summit of the Americas. Early in the U.S. planning process, at a joint meeting of U.S. officials and NGAs to discuss ways to increase citizen partnership in the environmental arena, it was decided to invite a broad cross-section of non-governmental actors to the next meeting in order to contribute to the building of networks and the strengthening of cross-sectoral ties. The initial response from one invited women's rights organization was, "We don't do the environment." While the desire to concentrate resources is understandable in times of budget stringencies, greater cost effectiveness may, in fact, be derived in the medium term through the building of cross-sectoral ties and the sharing of lessons learned.

A second lesson for the non-governmental community is related to the ways in which they intersected with the planning process. Last minute input in the form of long documents was difficult for policymakers to assimilate. Succinct, policy-oriented, consensus documents did command attention — particularly when they were the products of processes that were cross-cutting in geographic and sectoral terms.[19] Well-known non-governmental actors, in some case relying on long-standing personal relationships with government officials, were effective advocates. Ultimately, the lesson for non-governmental actors seeking to influence the policy process successfully was to be loud, be specific, and be reasonable. Groups that are highly representative, timely,[20] concise, pragmatic, and persistent are most likely to be successful in influencing policy.

One objection that some government actors raise to explain their reticence to work with and through NGAs is that they are not elected and therefore do not "represent" anyone. Clearly, not all NGAs are equally "representative," which is why there are systems (often quite elaborate to the point of being cumbersome) for their registration.[21] In order to be registered, NGAs must satisfy a series of criteria regarding organizational structure, financial systems, etc. While in some cases, some government actors may use the argument regarding representation as an excuse to avoid working with NGAs, it is equally true that non-governmental actors bear a responsibility to move their organizations toward the same accountability, transparency, and participatory structures that they demand of their government counterparts. True partnership is a two-way street.

One of the challenges in such a partnership is achieving the right mix of collaboration and independence between the public and private spheres. A healthy degree of separation between the two is vital to the integrity of each, but cooperation is also critical to the vitality of both. Non-governmental actors must decide for themselves the appropriate degree of autonomy they require from government. For their part, public sector actors tend to expect that greater accessibility will translate into support, believing that at the end of the day — after pushing hard to influence the official process and working hard to improve it — non-governmental actors will help to make the event a success and will support it publicly. Such support is not automatic, however, but rather the result of true collaboration.

Much has been learned from this exercise, and preparations for a future Summit can build on the learning that took place in this instance in both the public and private spheres. Non-governmental actors will start with more developed organizational skills and stronger networks. Government players will have much greater experience in working with external partners and even more enthusiasm for doing so. Concern over national sovereignty will be tempered by the knowledge of the benefits to be accrued from spirited collaboration.

Public and private actors are in the process of reassessing the costs and benefits of joint action. There is an emerging consensus that government cannot do it all and that non-governmental groups can themselves accomplish more if — at times — they work in concert with government. For U.S. government officials involved in this process, it no longer seems out of the ordinary to consult with non-governmental actors in the development of policy initiatives — to have them present at inter-agency meetings or to take part in official consultations with other governments. Similarly, from the perspective of non-governmental actors, there is a growing willingness to explore new ways in which to influence policy. From a relationship that was often routinely adversarial, there is today movement on both sides toward dialogue and cooperation. While this does not imply automatic agreement, the pooling of skills is deeply beneficial to both. Preparations for the Summit of the Americas were constructed upon this evolving relationship and served to spur it further.

Next Steps

The Miami process did not end on December 11, 1994, with the signing of the Summit *Declaration of Principles* and the *Plan of Action*. As mentioned above, the other significant way in which the Summit of the Americas differed from Punta del Este is that it produced an actionable set of agenda items with clear implementation mechanisms, performance indicators, and delineation of responsibilities. As is clearly underscored in the *Declaration of Principles* and the *Plan of Action*, the active participation of the full range of non-governmental actors is essential to the realization of that agenda. Across the hemisphere, non-governmental actors have both the right and the responsibility to involve themselves in the full range of Summit initiatives.

The Summit of the Americas set a new benchmark in the exercise of participatory democracy, opening significant political space for non-governmental actors. The Miami process offers them an opportunity to go further. With the Summit *Plan of Action* in hand, non-governmental actors throughout the hemisphere can approach their governments and suggest ways in which they can serve as full partners in the implementation process. It also affords non-governmental actors the opportunity to perform a watchdog function, serving to monitor the compliance of governments with the agreed-upon implementation plan and timetable for results. Part of the Summit follow-up might usefully include efforts to expand the participation beyond those non-governmental actors that took part in the Summit to include others who were not previously involved.

. Official actors have a similar responsibility. The participation of non-governmental actors in the Summit is but the first step in a long process. Over time, partnership may become second nature for the majority of government officials (for many, it already is). In the meantime, public actors must consistently push themselves toward greater participation and partnership, ensuring that accessibility and collaboration did not end in Miami, but rather that a deeper and richer involvement began there. Ultimately, partnership between non-governmental actors and governments is likely to transcend the specific arena of the Summit of the Americas. Public and private sphere actors can be expected to build upon the bridges established during the course of the Summit preparations to initiate collaborative activities in other areas as well.

In sum, both in the United States and in a significant number of countries throughout the rest of the hemisphere, non-governmental actors played an unprecedented role in planning for the Summit. This reflected a recognition on the part of governments that non-governmental actors are a necessary, valuable, and legitimate partner to government both in terms of service delivery and in order to promote a healthy civil society. It was, as well, testimony to the enormous energy, creativity, and dedication of the non-governmental community.

To advance both national and hemispheric agendas, government and civil society must work in close collaboration. Democracy occurs within a multi-interest arena and — to be effective over the long term — must build upon the reality of that diversity. Partnership — both between and within societies — on the full range of social and public policy issues is the best guarantor of equity, good governance, and democratic pluralism.

This is not business as usual. The Summit of the Americas helped to establish the initial outlines of a new relationship between the public and private spheres. In this sense, it is both a cause of celebration and a spur to actors in both arenas to secure and build upon these advances.

NOTES

1. The author is grateful to Ramón Daubón, Deputy Assistant Administrator of the Bureau for Latin America and the Caribbean, USAID, for this point.

2. The "Miami Process" refers to the post-Summit implementation phase of the Summit of the Americas. The emphasis is upon an ongoing process, rather than a one-shot event.

3. *Summit of the Americas Declaration of Principles — Partnership for Development and Prosperity: Democracy, Free Trade and Sustainable Development in the Americas* and *Summit of the Americas Plan of Action.*

4. In fact, the Appendix to the *Plan of Action*, which details the division of labor for implementation, begins by stating, "The primary responsibility for implementing this Plan of Action falls to governments, individually and collectively, **with participation of all elements of our civil societies** [highlighting by the author]."

To further facilitate this process, a document was prepared subsequent to the Miami event that lists the appropriate contact person in the U.S. government for each initiative. See *Summit of the Americas — Implementation of the Summit Plan of Action: Contact Points for the Private Sector and Non-Governmental Organizations.*

5. The author is grateful to Cheryl Morden, Associate Director for Development Policy at Church World Service/Lutheran World Relief, for this point.

6. This process had the added benefit of fostering collaboration between U.S. officials devoted primarily to foreign policy issues and those focused upon U.S. domestic policy.

7. "Address Given by César Gaviria Trujillo upon Assuming Office as Secretary General of the Organization of American States," Washington, D.C., September 15, 1994; "Remarks Prepared for Delivery by Vice President Al Gore to the Inter-American Development Bank," September 16, 1994; "The Summit of the Americas: An Architecture for Inter-American Relations," remarks by Richard E. Feinberg, Special Assistant to the President and Senior Director for Latin America, National Security Council before the Inter-American Dialogue, Washington, D.C., September 20, 1994; "Remarks by Alexander F. Watson, Assistant Secretary of State, to the Inter-American Dialogue and International Center for Research on Women — Meeting on Investing in Women," Washington, D.C., October 6, 1994; "Remarks by U.S. Secretary of Commerce Ronald H. Brown at the Summit of the Americas Business Leaders Dinner, Miami, Florida, October 28, 1994; "Remarks by Secretary of State Warren Christopher at Cabinet Breakfast with Business and Non-Governmental Organization Representatives," Intercontinental Hotel, Miami, Florida, December 10, 1994.

8. "In concert with a number of countries and institutions, including the Inter-American Development Bank, we are exploring ways to help create vibrant civil societies in which non-governmental actors and civic associations can flourish. These efforts are designed to promote public participation and encourage local private philanthropy with a view toward creating a new partnership between government and society." Vice President Al Gore in a speech to the Inter-American Development Bank, Washington, D.C., September 16, 1994.

9. "Remarks by President Enrique V. Iglesias at the IDB Conference on Strengthening Civil Society," Washington, D.C., September 12, 1994.

10. The work of the Ad Hoc U.S. NGO Working Group on the Summit of the Americas exemplifies this point.

11. Although U.S. officials began to encourage such involvement more than eight months prior to the Summit, the full dimensions of that opportunity developed somewhat gradually in the absence of a tried and true blueprint for partnership and the need to work through differing opinions within the United States bureaucracy.

12. For an analysis of the potential impact of cross-border and cross-sectoral alliances such as these upon government to government negotiations, see Thorup, Cathryn L., "Redefining Governance in North America: The Impact of Cross-Border Networks and Coalitions on Mexican Immigration into the United States," DRU-219-FF, RAND: Santa Monica, California, April 1993.

13. This was an unclassified action cable (283748) sent from the Department of State to U.S. embassies throughout the Western Hemisphere in October 1994.

14. For a more detailed analysis of this event by one of the protagonists, see Constance R. Dunham, "After the Summit: Microenterprises Command More Attention," in *SuperVisions*, Volume 10, No. 2, February 1995, Washington, D.C.: Comptroller of the Currency, Administrator of National Banks.

15. Letter to Vice President Gore from the following NGOs: National Audubon Society, Partners of the Americas, Environmental Law Institute, The Humane Society of the United States, Indian Law Resource Center, Center for International Environmental Law, Healing Forest Conservancy, International Institute for Energy Conservation, National Wildlife Federation, World Wildlife Fund, Sierra Club, and the Natural Resources Defense Council, February 21, 1995, p. 3.

16. In other cases, a decision not to participate reflected insufficient resources, lack of clarity regarding the event itself and the role to be played by NGAs, and/or a decision that scarce resources could be more productively allocated elsewhere.

17. Despite advances in electronic networking, geographic proximity to policy circles remains highly advantageous.

18. Plans for a Summit of the Americas outreach tour were dropped due to logistical difficulties and resource constraints. The tour would have involved town meetings in five U.S. cities with a wide array of community groups to solicit input into the Summit planning process.

19. The Environmental and Energy Study Institute, for example, submitted a consensus document from seventy citizens' groups from throughout the hemisphere on principles of public participation.

20. Of course, as was signaled earlier, there may be an inherent tension in the non-governmental sector between representativity and rapid response.

21. Registration requirements are insufficient to ensure representativity, however. New mechanisms that encourage and facilitate strong linkages between NGAs and their grassroots are needed.

OFFICIAL SUMMIT DOCUMENTS

Fourteen Summit Agenda Initiatives Presented by the United States to Governments of the Hemisphere

The United States believes the Summit of the Americas will accelerate the development of a hemispheric community based on democratic rule, increased economic integration, and shared values and interests. It represents an unprecedented opportunity for the leaders of this hemisphere to affirm a joint vision of the future and to lay a foundation for hemispheric cooperation into the next century. Taken together, initiatives developed in preparation for the Summit will unite the governments and people of the hemisphere in an historic partnership. The following proposed initiatives are being discussed throughout the hemisphere.

THEME ONE — MAKING DEMOCRACY WORK: REINVENTING GOVERNMENT

Initiative 1

No to Corruption: A hemispheric call on governments and international businesses to recognize the need for transparency and accountability, to refrain from offering or seeking bribes, and to take specific actions necessary for compliance. Discussions might include 1) how to participate in implementation of the May 1994 recommendation of the Council of the OECD on bribery in international business transactions; 2) development of national action plans to strengthen formal and operational mechanisms for combatting corruption, e.g., review of law and practice relating to management of public funds, procurement, conflict of interest of public officials, donations to political parties, and auditing structures; 3) adoption of strong criminal, civil, and administrative prohibitions against bribery of foreign officials in international business transactions; and 4) greater cooperation to improve public procurement, civil service, and business regulation.

Initiative 2

Battle Plan against the Cartels: A hemisphere-wide commitment to law enforcement measures against the major drug traffickers and to demand/production targets.

The initiative would focus on moving our long-established efforts on the continent to a new plateau of cooperation and sophistication. The theme would be a call for a modernized, forward-looking drug agenda grounded on the understanding that the narcotics trade is a fundamental threat to democracy and sustainable development throughout the hemisphere.

We will pursue discussions, commitments, and initiatives focused on two separate but reinforcing objectives. The first will be an enforcement challenge to the cartels that calls for regional and institution-building programs that deprive traffickers and their operations the opportunity to elude law enforcement. This will be broad enough to encompass the particular interests of each participating government: chemical controls for some; money laundering, interdiction, and kingpin investigations for others. Several Latin American governments have expressed particular interest in strengthening regional efforts against money laundering.

The second objective will be a call to reject the legalization of drugs and commit to a substantial reduction in drug cultivation and consumption by the year 2000. The goal will be to eliminate opium poppy production and significantly reduce illicit coca cultivation by the year 2000 and to resume, at a faster rate, the downward trend in drug abuse in the United States. For its part, the United States will be willing to step up technical, operational, and financial support for eradication and to lead an international effort to raise billions of dollars in sustainable development assistance over the remainder of the decade to create economic alternatives for drug producers.

Initiative 3

Regulatory Reform: Financial market integrity and investor protection are necessary to maximize capital inflows. Leaders could endorse the activities of existing regional regulatory bodies such as the Council of Security Regulators of the Americas (COSRA) and the Center for Monetary Studies of Latin America (CEMLA), lending them greater legitimacy. In addition, the U.S. is prepared to expand IRS and customs programs that provide training to national authorities in the collection of taxes and tariffs.

Initiative 4

Making Civil Society Work: An integrated program would include a model legal/tax framework for the operation of NGOs, start-up financing through an IDB civil society fund, better support through organized hemispheric networking, and an OAS prize to recognize outstanding individual contributions. The Summit would react to existing analyses and proposals for improving the climate for creation and operation of civic-minded NGOs and private voluntary associations. It would endorse the creation of a fund within the IDB which would stimulate private philanthropy by providing matching funds for the endowment of "Mentor Foundations" in the civic development area. The mentors would advocate needed tax and regulatory policy reform in individual countries and help other organizations get started. The Summit would also endorse networking among NGOs to share experience.

Initiative 5

Enhance OAS Capacity to Strengthen Democracy: Commitment for OAS 1) to assist member states to strengthen their legislative branches though technical assistance and increased interaction with their democratic counterparts and 2) to enhance the capacity of the organization to preempt or manage situations in member states that threaten the democratic order. A proposed mediation and reconciliation service would be able to call on outside notables to facilitate peaceful constitutional solutions before the democratic order is broken. Creation of a crisis management center would enable the OAS to respond more effectively when and if a breakdown occurs.

THEME TWO — MAKING DEMOCRACY PROSPEROUS: HEMISPHERIC ECONOMIC INTEGRATION

Advancing Trade and Investment
Strengthening Financial Linkages

Initiative 6

Hemispheric Free Trade: The Summit offers the opportunity to affirm the vision of free trade in the Western Hemisphere based on the principles of "open regionalism." Senior U.S. government trade officials will consult with governments of the hemisphere on ways and means to make this powerful vision a reality.

Initiative 7

Hemispheric Capital Movements Liberalization:
Barriers to the free movement of capital hamper investment and economic growth. Leaders could commit to progressive liberalization of capital flows. Those leaders prepared to move ahead now could give momentum to this process by agreeing to launch negotiations for a Hemispheric Capital Movements Code that would provide for a standstill and the progressive liberalization of capital restrictions. This code would facilitate the free flow of capital, promote comparable financial standards, bolster transparency, and reduce opportunities for corruption. Development and advancement of the code may require establishment of a committee on hemispheric capital markets comprised of senior financial officials meeting periodically to examine issues related to cross-border capital flows in the region.

In addition, the leaders might consider other agreements that could provide private investors assurances about the future openness of their investment regimes.

Initiative 8

Hemispheric Infrastructure:

Part A — Hemispheric Infrastructural Protocol:
The goal of this initiative is to reduce the cost of financing the tremendous infrastructure requirements of the hemisphere, including those in the telecommunications, transportation, energy, and public utility grids. Leaders could agree to develop a protocol to facilitate international financing for private infrastructure projects that could 1) enunciate the policies and principles that governments should follow to support private financing of infrastructure; 2) establish procedures for consultations before enacting policy changes affecting an infrastructure project; and 3) agree to compensate investors in private sector infrastructure projects for damages caused by government failure to respect the commercial integrity of such projects.

In addition, this initiative would benefit from harmonization of inconsistent standards and regulations across borders. It would complement initiatives in the environmental domain to ensure that infrastructure development is consistent with sound environmental policies.

Part B — Information for the Americas: Sharing information is essential to making markets work and to promoting democratic institutions and sustainable development. Today, the primary means of sharing information is electronic. The leaders could endorse private investment, competition, open access to networks, universal service, and flexible regulatory frameworks as the basic principles of a hemispheric information infrastructure linked to the global information infrastructure. These could be achieved through an energized Inter-American Telecommunications Commission (CITEL) that would serve as the regional forum and focal point for telecommunications development activities. Working individually and through CITEL, countries could set a goal to put the Americas online by ensuring hemisphere-wide access points connecting major hospitals, universities, libraries, and research institutions to the Internet within one year.

THEME THREE — MAKING DEMOCRACY ENDURE: SUSTAINABLE DEVELOPMENT

Major challenges are investing in people, the hemisphere's most valuable resource, and creating an alliance with nature to ensure that our natural resources are available to sustain future generations.

A. Investing in People

The Summit offers the opportunity to call for policies that would allow all members of the hemisphere's societies to partake of the benefits of development. The proposed initiatives in this area focus on population segments — the poor, women, and indigenous populations — likely to remain excluded from full benefits of development unless specific policy measures are taken.

Initiative 9

Universal Access to Quality Primary Education:
Obtain a commitment from the hemisphere's governments to refocus existing resources more effectively toward quality primary education. A hemispheric partnership proposes to achieve 100 percent primary school completion rates and 75 percent secondary school enrollment by the year 2000. Aim at education sector reforms in financing, decentralization, and a reordering of budget priorities, so that an increased proportion of government budgets would be invested in primary education. The hemisphere initiative would approve the design of a plan of action involving all

nations. The action plan would be monitored by a region-wide consultative partnership involving governments, NGOs, the business community, and international organizations. Achievement of the goal would enable all citizens to participate productively and democratically in a maturing economic and political environment.

Initiative 10

Equitable Access to Basic Health Care: Summit leaders would call for each country's commitment to ensure equitable, universal access to basic health services so as to reduce child mortality rates in the region by one-third and maternal mortality rates by one-half by the year 2000. Health reform commissions would be designated in each country and include public and private participants and donors to help plan, monitor, and mobilize resources for reforming the health sector and ensuring equitable access to services. Under the country plans, reforms will include decentralizing services, reorienting budgetary allocations to favor essential services for the poor, developing new financial mechanisms, and encouraging privatization of some services and greater use of NGOs. As a result, countries should be able to ensure access to a basic, cost-effective WHO and World Bank-endorsed package of clinical and public health services. The Pan American Health Organization (PAHO) and other existing regional mechanisms will monitor implementation of the country plans, consistent with the Nariño Accord, and provide a forum for sharing information and expertise.

Initiative 11

Nurturing Microenterprises: The IDB group could take the lead in crafting a pilot project to integrate the poor into the formal economy through reducing legal obstacles to enterprise growth and through development of financial services targeted specifically at small businesses and microenterprises. Specifically, it could 1) provide assistance to improve the marketing, management, and financial capabilities of NGOs that sponsor successful savings associations and financial companies for microenterprises so that they can operate on market terms and conditions; 2) provide financial and technical assistance to commercial banks and saving institutions to help lower transaction costs associated with originating and monitoring small loans to entrepreneurs; 3) develop and provide seed

capital and technical support for a network of locally owned business advisory services affiliates; and 4) assist in efforts to reduce legal obstacles to microenterprises, e.g., simplification of business registration and tax codes and improved land titling.

B. Alliance with Nature

The alliance with nature's overall objectives are 1) to ensure that resource use today does not reduce the quality of life of future generations, 2) to halt and reverse resource waste and environmental degradation in the hemisphere, and 3) to strengthen natural resource stewardship by facilitating increased participation of indigenous people, local communities, and non-governmental organizations.

The initiatives described below build on the agreements reached at UNCED 1992, including the Climate Change and Biodiversity Conventions and Agenda 21. Follow-up would be focused on at a ministerial-level meeting on sustainable development, proposed to be held in Bolivia in 1995.

Initiative 12

Energy: Summit leaders would agree to begin implementation by 1998 of programs to promote sustainable energy use based on the principles of integrated resource planning and consideration of the full range of energy and capacity resources. Leaders would call for the identification and financing of non-conventional renewable energy and energy efficiency, especially by the multilateral development banks, which would be asked to increase financing for sustainable energy projects. As a first step, energy ministers will develop national work programs to promote energy efficiency, renewable energy, and natural gas use for discussion at the November 1995 meeting of the Latin American Energy Organization (OLADE). Technical cooperation could be coordinated by OLADE and Renewable Energy in the Americas (REIA).

Initiative 13

Hemispheric Partnership for Nature: The leaders would reaffirm their commitment, utilizing existing international agreements and the newly replenished Global Environmental Fund (GEF) to build cooperative action on the management and conservation of living resources. The partnership would focus on enhancing scientific and management capacity in forest management, management of coral reef and marine resources, and parks, reserves, and migratory species. Special emphasis would be placed on support for natural resource management efforts of indigenous communities. The leaders would call on the OAS to establish a Western Hemisphere convention office to report on progress of the initiative.

Initiative 14

Environmental Protection and Compliance Regimes: Leaders would agree to pursue an agreement to develop and strengthen compatible environmental laws, standards, and enforcement regimes to reduce environmental problems and negative impacts, promote a level playing field for industries operating in the hemisphere, increase demand for environmental technologies and services, and offer opportunities for public participation in the environmental policy-making process. This "upward" harmonization of environmental standards in the Americas would strengthen legal frameworks, enhance environmental compliance and enforcement capacity, and build institutions through technical cooperation, training, and education. A first step would be to focus on a sector or sectors of critical importance to human health, such as pesticides, lead, mercury, or industrial pollution, as well as on developing mechanisms to promote public involvement in the decision-making process. Leaders should also call on appropriate regional institutions to provide technical coordination linking government agencies, NGOs, the private sector, and professional groups. Leaders could announce an initial set of principles and commitments, e.g., pollution prevention, cost internalization, ecosystem protection, and the right of nations to adopt levels of protection more stringent than international levels.

Declaration of Principles

Partnership for Development and Prosperity: Democracy, Free Trade and Sustainable Development in the Americas

The elected Heads of State and Government of the Americas are committed to advance the prosperity, democratic values and institutions, and security of our Hemisphere. For the first time in history, the Americas are a community of democratic societies. Although faced with differing development challenges, the Americas are united in pursuing prosperity through open markets, hemispheric integration, and sustainable development. We are determined to consolidate and advance closer bonds of cooperation and to transform our aspirations into concrete realities.

We reiterate our firm adherence to the principles of international law and the purposes and principles enshrined in the United Nations Charter and in the Charter of the Organization of American States (OAS), including the principles of the sovereign equality of states, non-intervention, self-determination, and the peaceful resolution of disputes. We recognize the heterogeneity and diversity of our resources and cultures, just as we are convinced that we can advance our shared interests and values by building strong partnerships.

To Preserve and Strengthen the Community of Democracies of the Americas

The Charter of the OAS establishes that representative democracy is indispensable for the stability, peace and development of the region. It is the sole political system which guarantees respect for human rights and the rule of law; it safeguards cultural diversity, pluralism, respect for the rights of minorities, and peace within and among nations. Democracy is based, among other fundamentals, on free and transparent elections and includes the right of all citizens to participate in government. Democracy and development reinforce one another.

We reaffirm our commitment to preserve and strengthen our democratic systems for the benefit of all people of the Hemisphere. We will work through the appropriate bodies of the OAS to strengthen democratic institutions and promote and defend constitutional democratic rule, in accordance with the OAS Charter. We endorse OAS efforts to enhance peace and the democratic, social, and economic stability of the region.

We recognize that our people earnestly seek greater responsiveness and efficiency from our respective governments. Democracy is strengthened by the modernization of the state, including reforms that streamline operations, reduce and simplify government rules and procedures, and make democratic institutions more transparent and accountable. Deeming it essential that justice should be accessible in an efficient and expeditious way to all sectors of society, we affirm that an independent judiciary is a critical element of an effective legal system and lasting democracy. Our ultimate goal is to better meet the needs of the population, especially the needs of women and the most vulnerable groups, including indigenous people, the disabled, children, the aged, and minorities.

Effective democracy requires a comprehensive attack on corruption as a factor of social disintegration and distortion of the economic system that undermines the legitimacy of political institutions.

Recognizing the pernicious effects of organized crime and illegal narcotics on our economies, ethical values, public health, and the social fabric, we will join the battle against the consumption, production, trafficking and distribution of illegal drugs, as well as against money laundering and the illicit trafficking in arms and chemical precursors. We will also cooperate to create viable alternative development strategies in those countries in which illicit crops are grown. Cooperation should be extended to international and national programs aimed at curbing the production, use and trafficking of illicit drugs and the rehabilitation of addicts.

We condemn terrorism in all its forms, and we will, using all legal means, combat terrorist acts anywhere in the Americas with unity and vigor.

Recognizing the important contribution of individuals and associations in effective democratic government and in the enhancement of cooperation among the people of the Hemisphere, we will facilitate fuller participation of our people in political, economic and social activity, in accordance with national legislation.

To Promote Prosperity Through Economic Integration and Free Trade

Our continued economic progress depends on sound economic policies, sustainable development, and dynamic private sectors. A key to prosperity is trade without barriers, without subsidies, without unfair practices, and with an increasing stream of productive investments. Eliminating impediments to market access for goods and services among our countries will foster our economic growth. A growing world economy will also enhance our domestic prosperity. Free trade and increased economic integration are key factors for raising standards of living, improving the working conditions of people in the Americas and better protecting the environment.

We, therefore, resolve to begin immediately to construct the "Free Trade Area of the Americas" (FTAA), in which barriers to trade and investment will be progressively eliminated. We further resolve to conclude the negotiation of the "Free Trade Area of the Americas" no later than 2005, and agree that concrete progress toward the attainment of this objective will be made by the end of this century. We recognize the progress that already has been realized through the unilateral undertakings of each of our nations and the subregional trade arrangements in our Hemisphere. We will build on existing subregional and bilateral arrangements in order to broaden and deepen hemispheric economic integration and to bring the agreements together.

Aware that investment is the main engine for growth in the Hemisphere, we will encourage such investment by cooperating to build more open, transparent and integrated markets. In this regard, we are committed to create strengthened mechanisms that promote and protect the flow of productive investment in the Hemisphere, and to promote the development and progressive integration of capital markets.

To advance economic integration and free trade, we will work, with cooperation and financing from the private sector and international financial institutions, to create a hemispheric infrastructure. This process requires a cooperative effort in fields such as telecommunications, energy and transportation, which will permit the efficient movement of the goods, services, capital, information and technology that are the foundations of prosperity.

We recognize that despite the substantial progress in dealing with debt problems in the Hemisphere, high foreign debt burdens still hinder the development of some of our countries.

We recognize that economic integration and the creation of a free trade area will be complex endeavors, particularly in view of the wide differences in the levels of development and size of economies existing in our Hemisphere. We will remain cognizant of these differences as we work toward economic integration in the Hemisphere. We look to our own resources, ingenuity, and individual capacities as well as to the international community to help us achieve our goals.

To Eradicate Poverty and Discrimination in Our Hemisphere

It is politically intolerable and morally unacceptable that some segments of our populations are marginalized and do not share fully in the benefits of growth. With an aim of attaining greater social justice for all our people, we pledge to work individually and collectively to improve access to quality education and primary health care and to eradicate extreme poverty and illiteracy. The fruits of democratic stability and economic growth must be accessible to all, without discrimination by race, gender, national origin or religious affiliation.

In observance of the International Decade of the World's Indigenous People, we will focus our energies on improving the exercise of democratic rights and the access to social services by indigenous people and their communities.

Aware that widely shared prosperity contributes to hemispheric stability, lasting peace and democracy, we acknowledge our common interest in creating employment opportunities that improve the incomes, wages and working conditions of all our people. We will invest in people so that individuals throughout the Hemisphere have the opportunity to realize their full potential.

Strengthening the role of women in all aspects of political, social and economic life in our countries is essential to reduce poverty and social inequalities and to enhance democracy and sustainable development.

To Guarantee Sustainable Development and Conserve Our Natural Environment for Future Generations

Social progress and economic prosperity can be sustained only if our people live in a healthy environment and our ecosystems and natural resources are managed carefully and responsibly. To advance and implement the commitments made at the 1992 United Nations Conference on Environment and Development, held in Rio de Janeiro, and the 1994 Global Conference on the Sustainable Development of Small Island Developing States, held in Barbados, we will create cooperative partnerships to strengthen our capacity to prevent and control pollution, to protect ecosystems and use our biological resources on a sustainable basis, and to encourage clean, efficient and sustainable energy production and use. To benefit future generations through environmental conservation, including the rational use of our ecosystems, natural resources and biological heritage, we will continue to pursue technological, financial and other forms of cooperation.

We will advance our social well-being and economic prosperity in ways that are fully cognizant of our impact on the environment. We agree to support the Central American Alliance for Sustainable Development, which seeks to strengthen those democracies by promoting regional economic and social prosperity and sound environmental management. In this context, we support the convening of other regional meetings on sustainable development.

* * * * *

Our Declaration constitutes a comprehensive and mutually reinforcing set of commitments for concrete results. In accord with the appended Plan of Action, and recognizing our different national capabilities and our different legal systems, we pledge to implement them without delay.

We call upon the OAS and the Inter-American Development Bank to assist countries in implementing our pledges, drawing significantly upon the Pan American Health Organization and the United Nations Economic Commission for Latin America and the Caribbean as well as sub-regional organizations for integration.

To give continuity to efforts fostering national political involvement, we will convene specific high-level meetings to address, among others, topics such as trade and commerce, capital markets, labor, energy, education, transportation, telecommunications, counternarcotics and other anti-crime initiatives, sustainable development, health, and science and technology.

To assure public engagement and commitment, we invite the cooperation and participation of the private sector, labor, political parties, academic institutions and other non-governmental actors and organizations in both our national and regional efforts, thus strengthening the partnership between governments and society.

* * * * *

Our thirty-four nations share a fervent commitment to democratic practices, economic integration, and social justice. Our people are better able than ever to express their aspirations and to learn from one another. The conditions for hemispheric cooperation are propitious. Therefore, on behalf of all our people, in whose name we affix our signatures to this Declaration, we seize this historic opportunity to create a Partnership for Development and Prosperity in the Americas.

Plan of Action

Table of Contents

Summit of the Americas Plan of Action

The heads of state and government participating in the 1994 Summit of the Americas in Miami, Florida, desirous of furthering the broad objectives set forth in their Declaration of Principles and mindful of the need for practical progress on the vital tasks of enhancing democracy, promoting development, achieving economic integration and free trade, improving the lives of their people, and protecting the natural environment for future generations affirm their commitment to this Plan of Action.

I. PRESERVING AND STRENGTHENING THE COMMUNITY OF DEMOCRACIES OF THE AMERICAS

1. Strengthening Democracy

The strengthening, effective exercise and consolidation of democracy constitute the central political priority of the Americas. The Organization of American States (OAS) is the principal hemispheric body for the defense of democratic values and institutions; among its essential purposes is to promote and consolidate representative democracy, with due respect to the principle of non-intervention. The OAS has adopted multilateral procedures to address the problems created when democratic order has been interrupted unconstitutionally. In order to prevent such crises, the OAS needs to direct more effort toward the promotion of democratic values and practices and to the social and economic strengthening of already-established democratic regimes.

Governments will:

- Give expeditious consideration to ratifying the Cartagena de Indias, Washington and Managua Protocols to the OAS Charter, if they have not already done so.

- Strengthen the dialogue among social groups and foster grass roots participation in problem solving at the local level.

- Support efforts by the OAS to promote democracy by:

- Encouraging exchanges of election-related technologies and assisting national electoral organizations, at the request of the interested state.

- Strengthening the Unit for the Promotion of Democracy so that it can provide assistance at the request of the interested state on such matters as legislative and judicial processes, government reforms (including administration of justice, technical modernization of national legislative bodies, simplification of government regulations and promotion of participation by community organizations in local democracy), and other institutional changes.

- Encouraging opportunities for exchange of experiences among member states' democratic institutions, particularly legislature-to-legislature and judiciary-to-judiciary.

- Fostering understanding, dialogue and political reconciliation, at the request of the affected state and bearing in mind that national reconciliation comes from within.

- Requesting the OAS to promote and follow up on these commitments.

2. Promoting and Protecting Human Rights

Great progress has been made in the Hemisphere in the development of human rights concepts and norms, but serious gaps in implementation remain. While courts ultimately have the responsibility for enforcing legal rights and obligations, reforms in other institutions are needed to contribute to the further development of a climate of respect for human rights. There must also be universal access to justice and effective means to enforce basic rights. A democracy is judged by the rights enjoyed by its least influential members.

Governments will:

- Give serious consideration to adherence to international human rights instruments to which they are not already party.

- Cooperate fully with all United Nations and inter-American human rights bodies.

- Develop programs for the promotion and observance of human rights, including educational programs to inform people of their legal rights and their responsibility to respect the rights of others.

• Promote policies to ensure that women enjoy full and equal legal rights within their families and societies, and to ensure the removal of constraints to women's full participation as voters, candidates and elected and appointed officials.

• Review and strengthen laws for the protection of the rights of minority groups and indigenous people and communities to ensure freedom from discrimination, to guarantee full and equal protection under the law, and to facilitate active civic participation. Support a process to review and enhance the protection of indigenous rights in OAS member states and to develop promptly an effective United Nations declaration on indigenous rights.

• Review national legislation affecting people with disabilities, as well as benefits and services for them, and make any changes needed to facilitate the enjoyment by these individuals of the same rights and freedoms as other members of society.

• Undertake all measures necessary to guarantee the rights of children, and, where they have not already done so, give serious consideration to ratifying the United Nations Convention on the Rights of the Child.

• Guarantee the protection of the human rights of all migrant workers and their families.

• Take the necessary steps to remedy inhumane conditions in prisons and to minimize the number of pretrial detainees.

• Review training curricula for law enforcement agents to ensure that they adequately cover proper treatment of suspects and detainees as well as relations with the community.

• Exchange experiences on protection of human rights at the national level and, where possible, cooperate in the development of law enforcement and security force training or other programs to reduce the potential for human rights violations.

• Call on the OAS and the Inter-American Development Bank (IDB) to establish or to reinforce programs, as appropriate, to support national projects for the promotion and observance of human rights in the Western Hemisphere.

• Further strengthen the Inter-American Commission on Human Rights and the Inter-American Court of Human Rights.

3. Invigorating Society/Community Participation

A strong and diverse civil society, organized in various ways and sectors, including individuals, the private sector, labor, political parties, academics, and other non-governmental actors and organizations, gives depth and durability to democracy. Similarly, a vigorous democracy requires broad participation in public issues. Such activities should be carried out with complete transparency and accountability, and to this end a proper legal and regulatory framework should be established to include the possibility of obtaining technical and financial support, including from private sources.

Governments will:

• Review the regulatory framework for non-governmental actors with a view to facilitating their operations and promoting their ability to receive funds. This review will emphasize the management and oversight of resources as well as transparency and the accountability to society of said actors.

• Take steps to improve the participation in social activities and initiatives of groups traditionally marginalized, including women, youth, indigenous people and the extremely poor.

• Exchange progress reports on activities in the civil society area at the 1996 Summit Conference on Sustainable Development in Bolivia.

• Consider the development by the IDB of a new Civil Society Program to encourage responsible and accountable philanthropy and civic engagement in public policy issues.

4. Promoting Cultural Values

Cultural development is a fundamental and integral component of development in the Americas and has an inherent capability to enrich our societies and to generate greater understanding among our countries.

In order to promote cultural values, governments will:

• Encourage more dynamic relations among public and private institutions and organizations, including universities, museums, and centers of art and literature, as well as among individual cultural actors. Such exchanges emphasize our cultural diversity, recognize the value of our local cultures and contribute to improving hemispheric understanding.

• Request that the OAS and IDB reinforce their plans and programs to facilitate these cultural exchanges and the flow of cultural and historical information within and among our nations.

5. Combating Corruption

The problem of corruption is now an issue of serious interest not only in this Hemisphere, but in all regions of the world. Corruption in both the public and private sectors weakens democracy and undermines the legitimacy of governments and institutions. The modernization of the state, including deregulation, privatization and the simplification of government procedures, reduces the opportunities for corruption. All aspects of public administration in a democracy must be transparent and open to public scrutiny.

Governments will:

• Promote open discussion of the most significant problems facing government and develop priorities for reforms needed to make government operations transparent and accountable.

• Ensure proper oversight of government functions by strengthening internal mechanisms, including investigative and enforcement capacity with respect to acts of corruption, and facilitating public access to information necessary for meaningful outside review.

• Establish conflict of interest standards for public employees and effective measures against illicit enrichment, including stiff penalties for those who utilize their public position to benefit private interests.

• Call on the governments of the world to adopt and enforce measures against bribery in all financial or commercial transactions with the Hemisphere; toward this end, invite the OAS to establish liaison with the OECD Working Group on Bribery in International Business Transactions.

• Develop mechanisms of cooperation in the judicial and banking areas to make possible rapid and effective response in the international investigation of corruption cases.

• Give priority to strengthening government regulations and procurement, tax collection, the administration of justice and the electoral and legislative processes, utilizing the support of the IDB and other international financial institutions where appropriate.

• Develop within the OAS, with due regard to applicable treaties and national legislation, a hemispheric approach to acts of corruption in both the public and private sectors that would include extradition and prosecution of individuals so charged, through negotiation of a new hemispheric agreement or new arrangements within existing frameworks for international cooperation.

6. Combating the Problem of Illegal Drugs and Related Crimes

The problems of illegal drug and related criminal activities pose grave threats to the societies, free market economies, and democratic institutions of the Hemisphere. Drug use imposes enormous social costs; drug money and income are net drains on economic growth; and drug lords and criminal organizations endanger the security of our people through corruption, intimidation, and violence. While drug trafficking continues to be a significant source of illegal funds, the money laundering industry increasingly deals with the proceeds of all types of criminal activity. An integrated and balanced approach that includes respect for national sovereignty is essential to confront all aspects of these problems. For these reasons, a broad coordinated hemispheric strategy to reduce drug use and production, including new enforcement methods that can disrupt drug trafficking and money laundering networks and prosecute those engaged in such activities, is required. In this context, governments note the work of the 1992 San Antonio Summit, endorse the efforts of the Inter-American Commission on Drug Abuse Control, and agree to work together to formulate a counter-narcotics strategy for the 21st Century.

Governments will:

• Ratify the 1988 United Nations Convention Against the Illicit Traffic of Narcotics and Psychotropic Substances and make it a criminal offense to launder the proceeds of all serious crimes.

• Enact legislation to permit the freezing and forfeiture of the proceeds of money laundering and consider the sharing of forfeited assets among governments.

• As agreed by ministers and representatives of Caribbean and Latin American governments in the Kingston Declaration, November 5-6, 1992, implement the recommendations of the Caribbean Financial Action Task Force on Money Laundering and work to adopt the Model Regulations of the Inter-American Commission on Drug Abuse Control (CICAD).

• Encourage financial institutions to report large and suspicious transactions to appropriate authorities and develop effective procedures that would allow the collection of relevant information from financial institutions.

• Work individually and collectively to identify the region's narcotics trafficking and money laundering networks, prosecute their leaders, and seize assets derived from these criminal activities.

• Adopt programs to prevent and reduce the demand for and the consumption of illicit drugs.

• Adopt effective and environmentally sound national strategies to prevent or reduce substantially the cultivation and processing of crops used for the illegal drug trade, paying particular attention to national and international support for development programs that create viable economic alternatives to drug production.

• Pay particular attention to the control of precursor chemicals and support comprehensive drug interdiction strategies.

• Strengthen efforts to control firearms, ammunition, and explosives to avoid their diversion to drug traffickers and criminal organizations.

• Hold a working-level conference, to be followed by a ministerial conference, to study and agree on a coordinated hemispheric response, including consideration of an inter-American convention, to combat money laundering.

• Convene a hemispheric-wide conference of donors, including multilateral development banks and UN agencies, to seek resources for alternative development programs aimed at curbing the production, trafficking, and use of illicit drugs, and the rehabilitation of addicts.

• Support the discussion the OAS has initiated with the European Union on measures to control precursor chemicals.

• Support the convening of a global counter-narcotics conference.

7. Eliminating the Threat of National and International Terrorism

National and international terrorism constitute a systematic and deliberate violation of the rights of individuals and an assault on democracy itself. Recent attacks that some of our countries have suffered have demonstrated the serious threat that terrorism poses to security in the Americas. Actions by governments to combat and eliminate this threat are essential elements in guaranteeing law and order and maintaining confidence in government, both nationally and internationally. Within this context, those who sponsor terrorist acts or assist in their planning or execution through the abuse of diplomatic privileges and immunities or other means will be held responsible by the international community.

Governments will:

• Promote bilateral and subregional agreements with the aim of prosecuting terrorists and penalizing terrorist activities within the context of the protection of human rights and fundamental freedoms.

• Convene a special conference of the OAS on the prevention of terrorism.

• Reaffirm the importance of the extradition treaties ratified by the states of the Hemisphere, and note that these treaties will be strictly complied with as an expression of the political will of governments, in accordance with international law and domestic legislation.

8. Building Mutual Confidence

The expansion and consolidation of democracy in the Americas provide an opportunity to build upon the peaceful traditions and the cooperative relationships that have prevailed among the countries of the Western Hemisphere. Our aim is to strengthen the mutual confidence that contributes to the economic and social integration of our peoples.

Governments will:

• Support actions to encourage a regional dialogue to promote the strengthening of mutual confidence, preparing the way for a regional conference on confidence-building measures in 1995, which Chile has offered to host.

II. PROMOTING PROSPERITY THROUGH ECONOMIC INTEGRATION AND FREE TRADE

9. Free Trade in the Americas

1) While pursuing economic integration and free trade in the Hemisphere, we reinforce our strong commitment to multilateral rules and disciplines. We

endorse full and rapid implementation of the Uruguay Round, active multilateral negotiations in the World Trade Organization, bilateral and subregional trade agreements, and other trade arrangements that are consistent with the provisions of the GATT/WTO and that do not raise barriers to other nations.

2) Extraordinary achievements have been made by countries of the Hemisphere in trade liberalization and subregional integration. Free trade and increased economic integration are key factors for sustainable development. This will be furthered as we strive to make our trade liberalization and environmental policies mutually supportive, taking into account efforts undertaken by the GATT/WTO and other international organizations. As economic integration in the Hemisphere proceeds, we will further secure the observance and promotion of worker rights, as defined by appropriate international conventions. We will avoid disguised restrictions on trade, in accordance with the GATT/WTO and other international obligations.

3) We will strive to maximize market openness through high levels of discipline as we build upon existing agreements in the Hemisphere. We also will strive for balanced and comprehensive agreements, including among others: tariffs and non-tariff barriers affecting trade in goods and services; agriculture; subsidies; investment; intellectual property rights; government procurement; technical barriers to trade; safeguards; rules of origin; antidumping and countervailing duties; sanitary and phytosanitary standards and procedures; dispute resolution; and competition policy.

4) We recognize that decisions on trade agreements remain a sovereign right of each nation. In addition, recognizing the importance of effective enforcement of international commitments, each nation will take the necessary action, in accordance with its own legislation and procedures, to implement the agreements in the areas covered by this Plan of Action.

5) As we work to achieve the "Free Trade Area of the Americas," opportunities such as technical assistance will be provided to facilitate the integration of the smaller economies and increase their level of development.

Immediate Action Agenda

We direct our ministers responsible for trade to take the following concrete initial steps to achieve the "Free Trade Area of the Americas."

6) With the objective of ensuring full and complete discussion among the parties to the various trade agreements in the Hemisphere, we direct that meetings be held under existing trade and investment fora. Members of these fora will determine areas of commonality and divergence in the particular agreements under review and should consider the means of improving disciplines among them and bringing them together. We further direct that members of these fora inform ministers of the status of their discussions and make recommendations for achieving the "Free Trade Area of the Americas."

7) Transparency in, and a clear understanding of, the subregional and bilateral agreements achieved to date among the nations in the Hemisphere are critical for advancing trade and investment integration in the Americas. We will direct the OAS Special Committee on Trade, with the support of the IDB, ECLAC, and other specialized regional and subregional organizations, to assist in the systematization of data in the region and to continue its work on studying economic integration arrangements in the Hemisphere, including brief comparative descriptions of the obligations in each of the Hemisphere's existing trade agreements. We will further direct the Special Committee on Trade to prepare a report of its work by June 1995 for the meeting of ministers.

8) We direct our ministers responsible for trade to: (a) review the progress of work undertaken in the fora noted in paragraphs 6 and 7; (b) provide guidance with respect to further work; and (c) consider areas for immediate attention—such as customs facilitation and product testing and certification with a view to mutual recognition agreements—that could be taken up in the appropriate fora.

9) Therefore, today we launch the "Free Trade Area of the Americas" by initiating the following process. We will direct the OAS to assist the host country in arranging the ministerial meetings.

January 1995 • Initiation of work programs and establishment of schedules in the fora in paragraph 6 and in the Special Committee on Trade.

June 1995 • Meeting of Ministers responsible for trade.

— preliminary report on status of work in the fora described in paragraph 6.

— preliminary Special Committee on Trade report.

— areas for immediate consideration.

March 1996 • Meeting of Ministers responsible for trade.

— final report to ministers by the Special Committee on Trade.

— final reports to ministers from the fora described in paragraph 6.

— timetable for further work.

10. Capital Markets Development and Liberalization

The availability of capital at competitive rates is essential to finance private sector investment—a vital ingredient in economic development. Developing, liberalizing and integrating financial markets domestically and internationally, increasing transparency, and establishing sound, comparable supervision and regulation of banking and securities markets will help to reduce the cost of capital by enhancing investor and depositor confidence.

Governments will:

• Form a Committee on Hemispheric Financial Issues to examine steps to promote the liberalization of capital movements and the progressive integration of capital markets, including, if deemed appropriate, the negotiation of common guidelines on capital movements that would provide for their progressive liberalization.

• Prepare, in cooperation with the Inter-American Development Bank, a comprehensive list of national capital regulations in order to promote transparency and support the discussions in the Committee on Hemispheric Financial Issues.

• Support the cooperative endeavors of the Association of Latin American and Caribbean Bank Supervisors and the Council of Securities Regulators of the Americas to provide sound supervision and regulation that support the development and progressive integration of markets.

The Committee on Hemispheric Financial Issues should also review problems of debt in the Hemisphere, taking account of ongoing work and drawing, as appropriate, on a broad range of expertise.

11. Hemispheric Infrastructure

Development in this Hemisphere depends on urgent infrastructure measures, including the priority allocation of financial resources, in accordance with national legislation and with the participation of both the public and private sectors. Strengthening the flow of private productive capital to economically and environmentally sound projects has become increasingly vital to countries throughout the Hemisphere as the growth of official sources of capital has failed to keep pace with the area's needs.

Governments will:

• Charge multilateral development banks to work with governments and, as appropriate, private concerns, to develop mechanisms to deal with lending and investment issues.

• Draw on other regional and sub-regional experiences within the Hemisphere to support infrastructure development.

• Governments that so wish will develop suitable mechanisms, including multilateral and bilateral commitments on regulatory and legal rules and practices, to encourage private investment, both domestic and foreign, in national and transboundary infrastructure projects.

12. Energy Cooperation*

The nations of the Hemisphere have begun a new era of economic growth. This new era is based on greater economic cooperation, freer trade, and open markets. Sustainable economic development requires hemispheric cooperation in the field of energy.

Governments will:

• Convene a follow-up hemispheric officials' meeting in the first semester of 1995 to encourage cooperation to study ways to develop the energy industry within the Hemisphere, consistent with the least cost national energy strategies and the activities described in the "Partnership for Sustainable Energy Use" in the following areas:

• Consideration of ways to use the energy sector to promote sustainable economic growth.

• Cooperation to study ways to optimize and facilitate the financing mechanisms of international financial institutions to support the development of projects in the energy sector, especially including those pertaining to the enhancement of efficiency in the use of energy and to non-conventional renewable energy.

• Cooperation to promote capital investment and to foster the use of innovative financial mechanisms to increase investment in the energy sector and the enhancement of efficiency in the use of energy and non-conventional renewable energy, in accordance with each country's legislation and developmental needs.

• Promotion of the use of efficient and non-polluting energy technologies, both conventional and renewable, leading to a higher degree of knowledge and technical expertise in this area.

• Consideration of the enhancement of ongoing efforts to establish electric and other energy facilities in accordance with domestic regulatory frameworks and, where appropriate, under sub-regional agreements.

* This initiative is integrally linked with the Partnership for Sustainable Energy Use item.

13. Telecommunications and Information Infrastructure

A country's information infrastructure — telecommunications, information technology, and broadcasting — is an essential component of political, economic, social and cultural development. The information infrastructure development needs in the Americas are immense. The governments of the Americas intend to meet these needs by engaging in multiple actions, where consistent with their respective governing laws, such as: encouraging private sector investment to increase participation in the telecommunications and information infrastructure sectors; promoting competition; implementing flexible regulatory regimes; stimulating diversity of content, including cultural and linguistic diversity; providing access to information networks for service and information

providers; and ensuring universal service, so that the benefits of the information infrastructure will be available to all members of our societies.

Governments will:

• Engage in ongoing discussions at the international level of the actions referred to above and endeavor to take those actions in their own countries, taking account of domestic conditions and circumstances.

• Undertake efforts to make government information more publicly available via electronic means.

• Review the availability and interoperability of connections to international networks that facilitate trade, improve education and improve access to health care.

• Encourage major universities, libraries, hospitals and government agencies to have access to these networks, building on the work of the OAS Hemisphere-Wide Inter-University Scientific and Technological Information Network.

• Via the OAS Inter-American Telecommunications Commission (CITEL), and in coordination with the sub-regional telecommunications organizations, develop and carry out a work program to:

• Evaluate regulatory, technical and legal means to promote liberalization, common standards, interoperability of networks and compatible use of the radio spectrum.

• Examine ways to promote greater consistency of the certification processes for telecommunications equipment among member countries.

• Develop regional guidelines for the provision of international value-added network services.

• Support a meeting by 1996, coordinated by CITEL, of senior telecommunications officials to conduct further discussions of the above actions.

14. Cooperation in Science and Technology

There is a need to re-assess the ongoing interaction among the region's science and technology (S&T) infrastructure and cooperative mechanisms; to provide impetus for improved cooperation; to reduce barriers to collaboration; to augment the demand for technology; and to disseminate information about technological opportunities using new advances in information technology; and generally to improve communications among the key S&T organizations, researchers in the region, and growing technology-based small and medium-sized enterprises.

The commitment of the countries of the Americas to non-proliferation has gained new momentum with the acceptance of the international safeguard regime by some of our countries. The outstanding progress achieved in this field is to be commended and should contribute to enhanced opportunities for cooperation in the area of advanced goods and technologies.

Governments will:

• Convene a meeting of ministers responsible for science and technology in the Hemisphere within the next year to assess progress and to promote the Bolívar Programme and the OAS Common Market of Scientific and Technological Knowledge (MERCOCYT) program, to provide the necessary support to improve scientific partnerships and technological ventures in the region, and to explore the possibility of establishing a council on science and technology.

• Use existing multilateral mechanisms in the region to address a wide number of common S&T interests, including enhanced professional technical training, development and implementation of national policies and regional programs, dissemination and standardization of science and technology (including metrology and other technical norms), environmental technology development, and more effective partnerships to promote learning and competitiveness.

• Stimulate greater S&T interaction in the Hemisphere and support efforts already undertaken in other fora, including the Inter-American Institute for Global Change Research, and the International Research Institute for Climate Prediction. Governments will serve to advance and communicate new initiatives such as the Global Learning and Observations to Benefit the Environment (GLOBE) program.

• Confirm their interest in participating in new initiatives driven by a demand from private sector and non-government interests in technological opportunities.

• Confirm their national commitments to share S&T information with others in the Hemisphere, in accord with their respective laws, and to expand cooperation in scientific and environmental research.

15. Tourism

Tourism is important to our economies and valuable in promoting understanding among the people of the Americas.

Governments will:

• Undertake initiatives to stimulate tourism in the Hemisphere.

III. ERADICATING POVERTY AND DISCRIMINATION IN OUR HEMISPHERE

Large segments of society in our Hemisphere, particularly women, minorities, the disabled, indigenous groups, refugees and displaced persons, have not been equipped to participate fully in economic life. Nearly one-half of the Hemisphere's population still lives in poverty. Expanded participation of the poor in the region's economies, access to productive resources, appropriate support for social safety nets and increased human capital investments are important mechanisms to help eradicate poverty. In pursuit of these objectives, we reaffirm our support for the strategies contained within the "Commitment on a Partnership for Development and Struggle to Overcome Extreme Poverty" adopted by the OAS General Assembly.

The World Summit for Social Development to be held in Copenhagen in March 1995, as well as the United Nations World Conference on Women in Beijing in September 1995, will provide unique opportunities to define strategies to promote social integration, productive employment and the eradication of poverty.

16. Universal Access to Education

Universal literacy and access to education at all levels, without distinction by race, national origin or gender, are an indispensable basis for sustainable social and cultural development, economic growth and democratic stability.

Governments will:

• Guarantee universal access to quality primary education, working with public and private sectors and non-governmental actors, and with the support of multinational institutions. In particular, governments will seek to attain by the year 2010 a primary completion rate of 100 percent and a secondary enrollment rate of at least 75 percent, and to prepare programs to eradicate illiteracy, prevent truancy and improve human resources training.

• Promote, with the support of international financial institutions and the private sector, worker professional training as well as adult education, incorporating efforts to make such education more relevant to the needs of the market and employers.

• Improve human resources training, and technical, professional and teacher training, which are vital for the enhancement of quality and equity of education within the Hemisphere.

• Increase access to and strengthen the quality of higher education and promote cooperation among such institutions in producing the scientific and technological knowledge that is necessary for sustainable development.

• Support strategies to overcome nutritional deficiencies of primary school children in order to enhance their learning ability.

• Support decentralization including assurance of adequate financing and broad participation by parents, educators, community leaders and government officials in education decision-making.

• Review existing regional and hemispheric training programs and make them more responsive to current needs.

• Create a hemispheric partnership, working through existing organizations, to provide a consultative forum for governments, non-governmental actors, the business community, donors, and international organizations to reform educational policies and focus resources more efficiently.

• Urge the March 1995 World Summit for Social Development and the September 1995 Fourth World Conference on Women to address the issue of universal access to education.

17. Equitable Access to Basic Health Services

Despite impressive gains in the Hemisphere, limitations on health services access and quality have resulted in persistently high child and maternal mortality, particularly among the rural poor and indigenous groups.

Governments will:

• Endorse the maternal and child health objectives of the 1990 World Summit for Children, the 1994

Nariño Accord and the 1994 International Conference on Population and Development, and reaffirm their commitment to reduce child mortality by one-third and maternal mortality by one-half from 1990 levels by the year 2000.

• Endorse a basic package of clinical, preventive and public health services consistent with World Health Organization, Pan American Health Organization (PAHO) and World Bank recommendations and with the Program of Action agreed to at the 1994 International Conference on Population and Development. The package will address child, maternal and reproductive health interventions, including prenatal, delivery and postnatal care, family planning information and services, and HIV/AIDS prevention, as well as immunizations and programs combating the other major causes of infant mortality. The plans and programs will be developed according to a mechanism to be decided upon by each country.

• Develop or update country action plans or programs for reforms to achieve child, maternal and reproductive health goals and ensure universal, non-discriminatory access to basic services, including health education and preventive health care programs. The plans and programs will be developed according to a mechanism to be decided upon by each country. Reforms would encompass essential community-based services for the poor, the disabled, and indigenous groups; stronger public health infrastructure; alternative means of financing, managing and providing services; quality assurance; and greater use of non-governmental actors and organizations.

• Strengthen the existing Inter-American Network on Health Economics and Financing, which serves as an international forum for sharing technical expertise, information and experience, to focus on health reform efforts. The network gathers government officials, representatives of the private sector, non-governmental institutions and actors, donors and scholars for policy discussions, analysis, training and other activities to advance reform; strengthens national capabilities in this critical area; and fosters Hemisphere-wide cooperation.

• Convene a special meeting of hemispheric governments with interested donors and international technical agencies to be hosted by the IDB, the World Bank and PAHO to establish the framework for health reform mechanisms, to define PAHO's role in monitoring the regional implementation of country plans and programs, and to plan strengthening of the network, including the co-sponsors' contributions to it.

• Take the opportunity of the annual PAHO Directing Council Meeting of Western Hemisphere Ministers of Health, with participation of the IDB and donors, to develop a program to combat endemic and communicable diseases as well as a program to prevent the spread of HIV/AIDS, and to identify sources of funding.

• Urge the March 1995 World Summit for Social Development and the September 1995 Fourth World Conference on Women to address the issue of access to health services.

18. Strengthening the Role of Women in Society

The strengthening of the role of women in society is of fundamental importance not only for their own complete fulfillment within a framework of equality and fairness, but to achieve true sustainable development. It is essential to strengthen policies and programs that improve and broaden the participation of women in all spheres of political, social, and economic life and that improve their access to the basic resources needed for the full exercise of their fundamental rights. Attending to the needs of women means, to a great extent, contributing to the reduction of poverty and social inequalities.

Governments will:

• Recognize and give full respect for all rights of women as an essential condition for their development as individuals and for the creation of a more just, united and peaceful society. For that purpose, policies to ensure that women enjoy full legal and civil rights protection will be promoted.

• Include a gender focus in development planning and cooperation projects and promote the fulfillment of women's potential, enhancing their productivity through education, training, skill development and employment.

• Promote the participation of women in the decision-making process in all spheres of political, social and economic life.

• Undertake appropriate measures to address and reduce violence against women.

• Adopt appropriate measures to improve women's ability to earn income beyond traditional occupations, achieve economic self-reliance, and

ensure women's equal access to the labor market at all employment levels, the social security systems, the credit system, and the acquisition of goods and land.

• Cooperate fully with the recently appointed Special Rapporteur on Violence Against Women, its Causes and Consequences, of the United Nations Commission on Human Rights.

• Support and actively work to secure the success of the United Nations World Conference on Women that will take place in Beijing in September 1995.

• Encourage, as appropriate, ratification and compliance with the International Convention on the Elimination of all Forms of Discrimination Against Women and the Inter-American Convention on the Prevention, Punishment and Eradication of Violence Against Women.

• Further strengthen the Inter-American Commission on Women.

• Call upon regional and international financial and technical organizations to intensify their programs in favor of women. Encourage the adoption of follow-up procedures on the national and international measures included in this Plan of Action.

19. Encouraging Microenterprises and Small Businesses

Microenterprises and small businesses account for a large percentage of the employment of the poor, particularly women, and contribute a considerable percentage of the gross domestic product of our countries. Strengthened support for microenterprises and small businesses is a key component of sustainable and equitable development.

Governments will:

• Further pursue or initiate programs of deregulation and administrative simplification.

• Increase efforts to enable enterprises to obtain information on appropriate technologies (especially those that are environmentally sound), markets, processes, raw materials and management systems that will permit them to be more competitive in the global economy.

• Develop programs of financial deregulation to reduce costs in credit transactions and strengthen the institutional capacity of the financial sector servicing microenterprises and small businesses, and encourage the active participation by multilateral and bilateral agencies, development banks, commercial banks and other intermediary credit organizations, consistent with strict performance standards.

• Strengthen the institutions and programs that supply services and facilitate access to training and technical assistance to make possible this sector's participation in the global economy through export of its products and services.

• Encourage cooperation among businesses in this sector to enable them to benefit from the advantages of economies of scale without losing their distinctive characteristics.

• Promote the strengthening of relations among the public, private and mixed (public/private) institutions that support the microenterprise and small business sector through programs of information, training, technical assistance, financing and association-building, enabling this sector to thrive over the long term.

• Recommend to the multilateral development organizations, especially the World Bank and the IDB, the establishment or fortification of funds and other mechanisms to support microenterprises and small businesses.

20. White Helmets — Emergency and Development Corps

The "White Helmets Initiative" is based on the conviction that a concerted international effort of developing and developed countries can facilitate the eradication of poverty and strengthen the humanitarian rapid response capability of the international community to emergency humanitarian, social and developmental needs.

The countries of the Americas could pioneer this initiative through the creation of national corps of volunteers that could respond to calls from other countries in the region. These national corps could eventually be put at the disposal of the United Nations.

Governments will on a voluntary basis:

• Establish, organize and finance a corps of volunteers to work at the national level and, at the same time, be at the disposal of other countries of the Hemisphere and, eventually, the United Nations system, on a stand-by basis, for prevention, relief, rehabilitation, technical, social and development cooperation, with the aim to reduce the effects of natural disasters, social and developmental needs and emergencies.

• Through the creation of a national corps of volunteers, be responsible for the following:

• Selection and training of its national volunteer corps;

• Financing of its national corps of volunteers, encouraging the involvement of the private sector;

• Preparedness to send specialized volunteers, on short notice and at the request of the United Nations, to cope with situations generated by or to prevent the effects of natural disasters and humanitarian emergencies.

• Contribute to the formation of this corps and invite private enterprises, foundations and regional financial institutions to do so.

• Contribute to the development of an international roster of volunteers to be maintained in a master plan in the United Nations to be drawn upon to complement the activities of existing UN mechanisms. The IDB, OAS, and PAHO should be invited to participate and assist in developing this corps.

IV. GUARANTEEING SUSTAINABLE DEVELOPMENT AND CONSERVING OUR NATURAL ENVIRONMENT FOR FUTURE GENERATIONS

21. Partnership for Sustainable Energy Use*

Consistent with Agenda 21 and the Framework Convention on Climate Change, sustainable energy development and use promote economic development and address environmental concerns. Governments and the private sector should promote increased access to reliable, clean, and least cost energy services through activities and projects that meet economic, social, and environmental requirements within the context of national sustainable development goals and national legal frameworks.

Governments will:

• Pursue, in accordance with national legislation, least cost national energy strategies that consider all options, including energy efficiency, non-conventional renewable energy (i.e., solar, wind, geothermal, small hydro, and biomass), and conventional energy resources.

- Emphasize market-oriented pricing, which discourages wasteful energy use.

- Identify for priority financing and development at least one economically viable project in each of the following areas: non-conventional renewable energy, energy efficiency, and clean conventional energy.

- Promote, in cooperation with the private sector and rural and isolated communities, rural electrification programs which take into account where appropriate the utilization of renewable energy sources, in accordance with the domestic regulatory framework.

- Seek to ratify and begin implementation of the provisions of the Framework Convention on Climate Change which entered into force on March 21, 1994.

- Encourage the World Bank and IDB to increase promptly and substantially, as a portion of energy lending, financing of projects in energy efficiency and renewable energy and financing to improve the environmental sustainability of conventional energy sources, in accordance with economic rationality.

- Call on the multilateral financial institutions and other public and private financial institutions to finance regional and national programs in support of this Action Plan, such as training and exchange programs as well as technology cooperation, in accordance with the needs and conditions of receiving countries.

- Assist with coordination and technical cooperation between countries, using existing regional organizations, including project identification and implementation, training programs, and personnel and information exchanges to increase capacity.

- Promote the identification and implementation of private sector projects that reduce greenhouse gas emissions.

- Convene a Sustainable Energy Symposium in the first half of 1995 to discuss follow-up activities relative to this initiative. In the spirit of cooperation countries will share their experiences and discuss progress on implementing this Action Plan.

*This initiative is integrally linked with the Energy Cooperation item.

22. Partnership for Biodiversity

Our Hemisphere contains over half the world's biodiversity. To sustain the Hemisphere's social and economic development, we must intensify efforts to understand, assess, and sustainably use this living resource base. We must act now to increase the technical and management capacity and public awareness of national and international efforts in this area. Agenda 21, the Convention on Biological Diversity, and other related international instruments recognize these needs and call for the conservation and sustainable use of biodiversity resources.

Governments will:

- Seek to ensure that strategies for the conservation and sustainable use of biodiversity are integrated into relevant economic development activities including forestry, agriculture, and coastal zone management, taking into account the social dimension and impact of these activities.

- Develop and implement the policies, techniques, and programs to assess, conserve, and sustainably use terrestrial, marine, and coastal biodiversity resources.

- Seek to ratify the Convention on Biological Diversity and pursue opportunities for collaboration under it, and, as appropriate, other international and regional environmental instruments.

- Support democratic governmental mechanisms to engage public participation, particularly including members of indigenous communities and other affected groups, in the development of policy involving conservation and sustainable use of natural environments. The forms of this participation should be defined by each individual country.

- Develop national plans and programs to establish and strengthen the management of parks and reserves, seeking links to economic, social, and ecological benefits for local people.

- Build capacity for the conservation and sustainable use of biodiversity, through programs on management of parks and protected areas, forests and wetlands management, the Small Islands Developing States Action Plan, the Coral Reef Initiative, CITES support projects, and the Caribbean Regional Marine Pollution Action Plan, among others.

- Launch a "Decade of Discovery" to promote hemispheric technical and scientific cooperation and to facilitate the exchange of information relevant to the conservation and sustainable use of biological diversity.

• Increase support of training and education initiatives addressing sustainable use of biodiversity resources and foster activities by universities, non-governmental actors and organizations and the private sector to assist in the training of managers and to empower local communities.

• Call on multilateral financial institutions, including the IDB and the Global Environment Facility, to support eligible regional and national projects.

• Discuss progress on implementation of national and international activities described above at the 1996 Summit Conference on Sustainable Development in Bolivia, and at subsequent annual sustainable development ministerials.

23. Partnership for Pollution Prevention

As recognized in Agenda 21, sound environmental management is an essential element of sustainable development. Cooperative efforts are needed to develop or improve, in accordance with national legislation and relevant international instruments: (1) frameworks for environment protection and (2) mechanisms for implementing and enforcing environmental regulations. To achieve this goal, a new partnership will promote cooperative activities for developing environmental policies, laws, and institutions; increasing technical capacity; promoting public awareness and public participation; continuing to pursue technological, financial and other forms of cooperation; and facilitating information exchange, including on environmentally sound technologies. The activities of the partnership will build on and advance the implementation of international agreements and principles including those agreed to at the 1992 United Nations Conference on Environment and Development and the 1994 Global Conference on the Sustainable Development of Small Island Developing States, in areas identified as priorities by countries of the Hemisphere.

Governments will:

• Strengthen and build technical and institutional capacity to address environmental priorities such as pesticides, lead contamination, pollution prevention, risk reduction, waste and sanitation issues, improved water and air quality, access to safe drinking water, urban environmental problems, and to promote public participation and awareness.

• Develop and implement national action plans to phase out lead in gasoline.

• Strengthen national environmental protection frameworks and mechanisms for implementation and enforcement, and include sustainability criteria and objectives in national and other development strategies.

• Undertake national consultations to identify priorities for possible international collaboration.

• Support democratic governmental mechanisms to engage public participation, particularly from members of indigenous and other affected communities, in the consideration of policies regarding the environmental impact of development projects and the design and enforcement of environmental laws.

• Convene a meeting of technical experts, designated by each interested country, to develop a framework for cooperative partnership, building on existing institutions and networks to identify priority projects. These projects will initially focus on (1) the health and environmental problems associated with the misuse of pesticides, and (2) the impacts of lead contamination from gasoline and other sources. Subsequent activities could address waste, air, water quality, marine pollution from ships and other sources, and problems associated with urbanization.

• Promote the participation of organizations, such as the IDB, MIF, the World Bank, PAHO, the OAS, and non-governmental actors and organizations, as appropriate, to finance, develop and implement priority projects.

• Develop environmental policies and laws with the goal of ensuring that economic integration of the region occurs in an environmentally sustainable manner.

• Establish mechanisms for cooperation among government agencies, including in the legal and enforcement areas, to facilitate environmental information exchange, technology cooperation and capacity-building.

• Develop compatible environmental laws and regulations, at high levels of environmental protection, and promote the implementation of international environmental agreements.

• Discuss progress on implementation of international and national activities described above at the 1996 Summit Conference on Sustainable Development in Bolivia and at subsequent annual sustainable development ministerials.

Appendix

The primary responsibility for implementing this Plan of Action falls to governments, individually and collectively, with participation of all elements of our civil societies.

Existing organizations or institutions are called upon to implement the package of initiatives that has emerged from this Summit of the Americas. In many instances we have proposed that specific issues be examined by meetings of ministers, senior officials or experts. We are also proposing that some of these initiatives be carried out in partnerships between the public and private sector. Wanting to benefit from existing hemispheric mechanisms, and considering the various proposals included in this Plan of Action, we offer the following recommendations, which shall not impede any government from approaching other institutions not cited herein, as appropriate.

I. Principal Initiatives in Which International Organizations and Institutions Will Be Involved

A) The OAS will have a paramount role in following up on the various decisions of this Summit meeting. Regarding the Plan of Action, the OAS has a particularly important supporting role in connection with the following:

- Strengthening Democracy
- Promoting and Protecting Human Rights
- Combating Corruption
- Eliminating the Threat of National and International Terrorism
- Building Mutual Confidence
- Free Trade in the Americas
- Telecommunications and Information Infrastructure

The Action Plan also envisages roles for the OAS in the following areas:

- Promoting Cultural Values
- Combating the Problem of Illegal Drugs and Related Crimes
- Cooperation in Science and Technology
- Strengthening the Role of Women in Society

- Partnership for Pollution Prevention

B) We call on the Inter-American Development Bank to support the activities specified in this Plan of Action. The policies agreed in the recently completed augmentation of its capital and replenishment of the Fund for Special Operations already move in the directions identified and should receive special emphasis. The IDB has a particularly important role in connection with the following:

- Universal Access to Education
- Equitable Access to Basic Health Services
- Encouraging Microenterprises and Small Businesses
- Partnership for Sustainable Energy Use
- Partnership for Biodiversity
- Partnership for Pollution Prevention

In addition, the Action Plan envisages roles for the IDB and its affiliates in the following areas:

- Promoting and Protecting Human Rights
- Invigorating Society/Community Participation
- Promoting Cultural Values
- Combating Corruption
- Combating the Problem of Illegal Drugs and Related Crimes
- Free Trade in the Americas
- Capital Markets Development and Liberalization
- Hemispheric Infrastructure
- Cooperation in Science and Technology
- White Helmets—Emergency and Development Corps

C) Other international organizations, notably ECLAC and PAHO in the Hemisphere, as well as the World Bank and all agencies of the UN system active in the Hemisphere, are called upon to assist in the implementation of the action items where appropriate.

II. High-Level Meetings

The following high level meetings and conferences are called for to carry out the mandates emanating from the Summit:

- Summit Conference on Sustainable Development (Bolivia, 1996) with follow-on Annual Ministerials

- Ministerial Conference on Combating Money Laundering (preceded by working level meeting)

- Conference of Donors for Alternative Development Programs to Curb Narcotics Trafficking

- Global Counter-Narcotics Conference

- Special OAS Conference on Combating Terrorism

- Regional Conference on Confidence-Building Measures (Chile, 1995)

- Meetings of Ministers Responsible for Trade (June 1995, March 1996)

- Meeting of Committee on Hemispheric Financial Issues

- Hemispheric Meeting on Development of Energy Industries (first semester 1995)

- Meeting of Ministers Responsible for Science and Technology (1995)

- Meeting Between Governments and Donors/Technical Agencies to Establish Health Reform Mechanisms

- Sustainable Energy Symposium (first half of 1995)

III. Initiatives in Which Public and Private Sector Partnerships Play an Important Role

- Strengthening Democracy
- Promoting and Protecting Human Rights
- Invigorating Society/Community Participation
- Promoting Cultural Values
- Combating Corruption
- Hemispheric Infrastructure
- Cooperation in Science and Technology
- Universal Access to Education
- Equitable Access to Basic Health Services

- Encouraging Microenterprises and Small Businesses

- White Helmets — Emergency and Development Corps

- Partnership for Sustainable Energy Use
- Partnership for Biodiversity
- Partnership for Pollution Prevention

Postscript:
Implementation of the Summit *Plan of Action*: Contact Points for the Private Sector and Non-Governmental Organizations

The *Plan of Action* proposed for adoption at the Summit of the Americas contains twenty-three initiatives grouped in four broad categories: strengthening democracy, promoting prosperity through economic integration and free trade, eradicating poverty and discrimination, and guaranteeing sustainable development and the conservation of our natural environment. The Summit leaders call for "the participation of all elements of our civil society" in implementing the *Plan of Action.* Below are brief summaries of each initiative, including a sketch of the U.S. implementation strategy. The public at large is encouraged to participate in the "Miami Process." For more information on individual action items, please contact the persons listed below.

I. PRESERVING AND STRENGTHENING THE COMMUNITY OF DEMOCRACIES OF THE AMERICAS

The Summit of the Americas 1994 is an opportunity to celebrate and consolidate the remarkable democratic transformation of the Western Hemisphere since the last summit of 1967. Sharing the recognition that participatory democracy is required for — and supported by — economic prosperity and sustainable development, the leaders endorse the following actions to be taken by governments and multilateral organizations.

1. Strengthening Democracy: The leaders agree to support an expansion of efforts by the Organization of American States (OAS) to promote and consolidate democracy in the hemisphere. OAS actions will include providing technical assistance in electoral, legislative, and judicial matters; encouraging the exchange of experiences among member states' democratic institutions; and fostering political dialogue and reconciliation at the request of the affected state.

The U.S. will strongly support Secretary Gaviria's initiatives to strengthen democracy, including bolstering the OAS Unit for Democracy. The OAS effort will concentrate on strengthening democratic institutions and on promoting democratic values and practices.

Contact: William Millan
Permanent Mission of the U.S. to the Organization of American States
Department of State, Rm. 6494
2201 C Street N.W.
Washington, D.C. 20520
(202) 647-9376, FAX (202) 647-0911

2. Promoting and Protecting Human Rights: The governments agree to promote policies that guarantee and protect human rights and universal access to justice. They will give serious consideration to adherence to international human rights instruments to which they are not already party. They agree to specific actions in support of the rights of women, minority groups, indigenous people, people with disabilities, children, prisoners, and migrant workers and their families.

The U.S. will review its own performance on human rights and will support OAS and IDB efforts to establish or to reinforce programs to support national projects for the promotion and observance of human rights in the Western Hemisphere. The U.S. will cooperate with other Summit governments in the development of law enforcement and security force training and other programs to reduce the potential for human rights violations. The U.S. will sign the UN Convention on the Rights of the Child.

Contact: Fay Armstrong
Office of Policy Planning, Coordination and Press
Bureau of Inter-American Affairs
Department of State
2201 C Street N.W.
Washington, D.C. 20520
(202) 647-5333
FAX (202) 736-7450

Contact: Marshall Carter
Bureau of Democracy, Human Rights, and Labor
Department of State
2201 C Street N.W.
Washington, D.C. 20520
(202) 647-2551
FAX (202) 647-9519

3. Invigorating Society — Community Participation: The governments agree to review national regulations in order to facilitate the operations of non-governmental organizations (NGOs) and promote their ability to raise private funds, while emphasizing their accountability. Governments will also encourage participation in society by marginalized groups and consider the creation of a Civil Society Program at the Inter-American Development Bank (IDB).

The U.S. will initiate a national review of the rules governing NGOs. Consulting with NGOs both at home and abroad, the U.S. will seek to strengthen the ability of NGOs to participate effectively and effi-ciently in their societies. USAID will initiate a project to strengthen NGO networks throughout the hemisphere.

Contact: Sharon Epstein
Bureau for Latin America and the Caribbean
Office of Regional Sustainable Development
U.S. Agency for International Development,
Rm. 2242
Washington, D.C. 20523
(202) 647-8093
FAX (202) 647-8098

4. Promoting Cultural Values: The leaders agree to encourage dynamic relations among public and private cultural institutions and to facilitate cultural exchanges through the OAS and the IDB.

The U.S., through the U.S. Information Agency, will fund and facilitate numerous exchanges of artists, writers, and other professionals in the arts and humanities. USIA will develop and broadcast media products on cultural themes. The U.S. will cooperate with hemispheric governments to enhance appreciation of indigenous cultures and cultural artifacts.

Contact: Jerome J. Oetgen
U.S. Information Agency, Rm. 750
301 4th St. S.W.
Washington, D.C. 20547
(202) 619-6873
FAX (202) 619-5172

5. Combating Corruption: The *Plan of Action* commits governments to establish transparency and accountability in government by ensuring proper oversight of government functions and by establishing conflict-of-interest standards for public employees. The Plan calls on the governments of the world to adopt and enforce measures against bribery in all financial and commercial transactions with the hemisphere. Summit governments will also develop cooperative mechanisms in the judicial and banking areas and within the OAS to assist in investigation and restitution in corruption cases.

The U.S. is supporting OAS efforts to develop a hemispheric approach to acts of corruption and to work with the OECD on the corruption problem. A hemispheric anti-corruption convention proposed by Venezuela is currently being considered. The U.S. is also supporting IDB efforts to address corruption, e.g., through the modernization and streamlining of fiscal administration.

Contact: Fay Armstrong
Office of Policy Planning, Coordination and Press
Bureau of Inter-American Affairs
Department of State
2201 C Street N.W.
Washington, D.C. 20520
(202) 647-5333
FAX (202) 736-7450

6. Combating the Problem of Illegal Drugs and Related Crimes: The leaders agree to formulate a broad coordinated hemispheric strategy to reduce drug production, trafficking, and consumption. Governments that have not done so will ratify the Vienna Convention Against the Illicit Traffic in Narcotics and Psychotropic Substances, and they will make it a criminal offense to launder the proceeds of all serious crimes. Governments will enact legislation to permit the freezing and forfeiture of the proceeds of money laundering, and they will implement existing anti-money laundering regulations and recommendations. The Summit participants will hold a ministerial conference to consider a coordinated hemispheric response to the money laundering problem. They will convene a hemispheric-wide conference of donors to seek resources for alternative development programs.

The U.S. and Mexico are producing a draft Counter-narcotics Strategy for the 21st Century, which the U.S. hopes will be signed by all 34 Summit governments by mid-1995. The U.S. will support anti-drug and anti-money laundering efforts through a wide range of cooperative projects in the Hemisphere.

Contact (anti-drug element): James Dandridge
Bureau of International Narcotics and Law
 Enforcement Affairs
Department of State, Rm. 7811
2201 C Street N.W.
Washington, D.C. 20520
(202) 647-8984
FAX (202) 646-4291

Contact: (anti-money laundering element):
Pete Balanon
Financial Crimes Enforcement Network
Department of the Treasury
2070 Chain Bridge Road, Ste. 200
Vienna, VA 22182
(202) 622-3500
FAX (202) 622-7154

Contact: (anti-money laundering element):
Lester M. Joseph
Department of Justice, Rm. 8403
1400 New York Ave. N.W.
Washington, D.C. 20005
(202) 514-1758
FAX (202) 616-1344

7. Eliminating the Threat of National and International Terrorism: The governments reaffirm their determination to combat and eliminate terrorism, which they describe as not only a violation of the rights of individuals but an assault on democracy itself. They will convene a Special Conference of the OAS to address the terrorism problem.

The U.S. will work closely with other Summit governments on the problem of terrorism, and will support an OAS conference on the prevention of terrorism to be held in Washington in the fall.

Contact: Joseph Reap
Office of the Coordinator for Counterterrorism
Department of State, Rm. 2507
2201 C Street N.W.
Washington, D.C. 20520
(202) 647-8682
FAX (202) 647-0221

8. Building Mutual Confidence: Governments agree to encourage a regional dialogue on building mutual confidence in security matters. They will hold a conference on confidence and security building measures (CSBMs) in Chile in 1995.

The U.S. will support activities within the Organization of American States to foster security confidence. In preparation for the CSBM conference in Chile, the U.S. will consult with hemispheric governments and non-governmental organizations.

Contact: Giovanni Snidle
Bureau of Non-Proliferation and Regional Arms
 Control
U.S. Arms Control and Disarmament Agency
320 - 21st St. N.W.
Washington, D.C. 20451
(202) 647-3799
FAX (202) 736-4833

II. PROMOTING PROSPERITY THROUGH ECONOMIC INTEGRATION AND FREE TRADE

Recognizing that economic progress depends on sound economic policies, sustainable development, and dynamic private sectors and that the key to prosperity is trade without barriers and an increasing flow of productive investments, the leaders resolve to construct the Free Trade Area of the Americas, in which barriers to trade and investment will be progressively eliminated. They further agree to encourage investment by cooperating to build more open and transparent markets.

9. Free Trade in the Americas: The leaders agree to set in motion immediately a process to construct "The Free Trade Area of the Americas" and to maximize market openness through agreements that reduce tariff and non-tariff barriers. They resolve to conclude the negotiation of the FTAA no later than 2005. They agree to have ministers responsible for trade meet to decide in June 1995 on next steps and again in March 1996 to determine further work, vowing to make concrete progress toward the free trade area by the end of this century.

Intensive consultations are being held to prepare for the meeting of Trade Ministers in Denver in June. Immediately following the trade ministerial, the U.S. will host a Hemispheric Trade and Commerce Forum involving the public and private sectors.

Contact: Michaelle Burstin
Office of the United States Trade Representative
600 17th St. N.W., Rm. 100
Washington, D.C. 20506
(202) 395-6120
FAX (202) 395-3692

10. Capital Markets Development and Liberalization: The leaders agree to form a Committee on Hemispheric Financial Issues to promote the liberalization and progressive integration of capital markets, possibly negotiating common guidelines on capital movements. Opportunities for increased cooperation to advance regulatory reform will be explored. The Committee will also review debt problems in the hemisphere.

The U.S. will be a member of the Committee and will also support the work of the regional associations of banking and securities regulators.

Contact: Bruce Juba
Office of Latin American and Caribbean Nations
Department of Treasury
1500 Pennsylvania Ave. N.W., Rm. 5413
Washington, D.C. 20220
(202) 622-1282
FAX (202) 622-1273

11. Hemispheric Infrastructure: The leaders request multilateral development banks to develop mechanisms to deal with lending and investment issues. Governments may voluntarily commit to regulatory practices to encourage private investment in national and transborder infrastructure projects.

The U.S. will be working with interested governments, private financial interests, the international financial institutions, and national export credit agencies to develop new mechanisms to foster private investment in areas that have traditionally been the province of the public sector.

Contact: Glen Rase
Office of International Energy Policy
Department of State
2201 C Street N.W.
Washington, D.C. 20520
(202) 647-2875
FAX (202) 647-4037

12. Energy Cooperation: The leaders agree to convene a follow-up hemispheric officials' meeting in 1995 to encourage cooperation to develop an energy industry consistent with least-cost strategies, efficiency, and the use of renewable energy sources.

The U.S. is consulting with the government of Venezuela on planning for this meeting.

Contact: Aimee Christensen
Office of International Energy Policy
U.S. Department of Energy, P.O. — 73
1000 Independence Ave. S.W.
Washington, D.C. 20585
(202) 586-4576
FAX (202) 586-6148

13. Telecommunications and Information Infrastructure: The leaders agree to undertake efforts to improve access to international networks that facilitate trade and improve education and access to health care. They also task the Inter-American Telecommunications Commission (CITEL) of the OAS to take actions to upgrade telecommunications in the hemisphere.

The U.S. participates actively in CITEL, which will prepare a report in June on its work. The U.S. is also organizing a ten-nation public/private conference on telecommunications.

Contact: Ed Malloy
Office of International Communication and
Information Policy
Department of State, Rm. 2533A

2201 C Street N.W.
Washington, D.C. 20520
(202) 647-6842
FAX (202) 647-0158

14. Cooperation in Science and Technology:
The leaders agree to convene a Science and Technology ministerial in 1995 to improve scientific partnerships and technological ventures and explore the possibility of establishing a council on science and technology.

Preparations for the meeting of science officials are under way.

Contact: Cathy Campbell
Executive Office of the President
Office of Science & Technology Policy
Old Executive Office Building, Rm. 435
Washington, D.C. 20500
(202) 456-6058
FAX (202) 456-6028

15. Tourism: The leaders agree to explore ways of expanding tourism development in the hemisphere.

The U.S., in consultation with the other nations of the hemisphere, will prepare for a Meeting of Ministers in Argentina in 1995.

Contact: Wanda Barquin
U.S. Travel and Tourism Administration
Department of Commerce
14th and Constitution Ave. N.W.
Washington, D.C. 20230
(202) 501-8105
FAX (202) 482-2887

III. ERADICATING POVERTY AND DISCRIMINATION IN OUR HEMISPHERE

Recognizing that strong democracies depend on the health and well-being of their people, the leaders affirm support for strategies to provide health services and to curtail the devastating effects of poverty. Noting that governments and economies flourish when all segments of the population participate fully in society, leaders agree to invest in education and small business.

16. Universal Access to Education: The leaders commit to refocus existing resources more effectively toward universal quality education, literacy programs, and employment training through reforms in financing and decentralization. The goal is to achieve 100% primary school completion rates and 75% secondary school enrollment by the year 2010, paying particular attention to the unmet needs of women, indigenous peoples, and other disadvantaged groups.

The U.S. government's centerpiece for education reform will be USAID's Partnership for Education Reform in the Americas (PERA) project. It is planned to be launched by the First Lady, Hillary Rodham Clinton, in October, prior to the opening in Paraguay of the next Meeting of the Wives of Heads of States and Governments of the Americas.

Contact: Sharon Epstein
Bureau for Latin America and the Caribbean
Office of Regional Sustainable Development
U.S. Agency for International Development,
Rm. 2242
Washington, D.C. 20523
(202) 647-8093
FAX (202) 647-8098

17. Equitable Access to Basic Health Services: Governments decide to expand access to basic health services, with minimum goals for the year 2000 of reducing the region's child mortality rate by one-third and maternal mortality rate by one-half from 1990 levels. Leaders endorse the provision of basic health services recommended by international organizations and the development of national plans encompassing accessible essential services for poor and indigenous groups, stronger public health infrastructure, and advancing alternative means of financing and providing services, involving community resources and greater use of non-governmental organizations.

The U.S. will continue its support for health care services through the Pan-American Health Organization, funding agencies, and the Inter-American Network on Health Economics and Financing. A national action plan will be developed as described above, and will include the First Lady, Hillary Rodham Clinton, launching in April the campaign for Measles Elimination in the Americas.

Contact: Sharon Epstein
Bureau for Latin America and the Caribbean
Office of Regional Sustainable Development
U.S. Agency for International Development,
Rm. 2242
Washington, D.C. 20523
(202) 647-8093
FAX (202) 647-8098

18. Strengthening the Role of Women in Society: The leaders commit their governments to promote policies to ensure that women enjoy full legal and civil rights protection and participate in decision-making at all levels. Leaders also agree to support the work of multilateral fora on women's issues.

The U.S. will support progressive positions at the World Conference on Women and will seek to secure ratification of the Convention on the Elimination of All Forms of Discrimination Against Women.

Contact: Sharon Epstein
Bureau for Latin America and the Caribbean
Office of Regional Sustainable Development
U.S. Agency for International Development,
Rm. 2242
Washington, D.C. 20523
(202) 647-8093
FAX (202) 647-8098

19. Encouraging Microenterprises and Small Businesses: The leaders decide to support and strengthen microenterprises and small businesses by means of improved legal and regulatory environments and simplified administration, strengthened financial-sector support from national and international sources, enhanced access to training and technical assistance, increased public-private cooperation, and involvement by non-governmental organizations.

Domestically, the U.S. will focus on making operational the Administration's various initiatives designed to aid microenterprises and creating a new broad consultative mechanism. The backbone of international action will consist of implementation of USAID's existing programs in the area and encouragement of World Bank and IDB activities in the microenterprise sector.

Contact: Constance Dunham (Domestic)
Economic and Policy Analysis, Room 6-6
Comptroller of the Currency
Washington, D.C. 20219
(202) 874-4793
FAX (202) 874-5394
E-mail: 76532.1017@compuserv.com

Contact: Sharon Epstein
Bureau for Latin America and the Caribbean
Office of Regional Sustainable Development
U.S. Agency for International Development,
Rm. 2242
Washington, D.C. 20523

(202) 647-8093
FAX (202) 647-8098

20. White Helmets — Emergency and Development Corps: Countries will establish, on a voluntary basis, a national corps of volunteers dedicated to reducing the effects of natural disasters and to meeting social and developmental needs and emergencies. They would respond to calls from the region, and would eventually be at the disposal of the United Nations. Each government will be responsible for their training and financing.

The U.S. will continue to support Argentina, author of the initiative, in developing this project under the auspices of the United Nations framework. It also is examining ways in which the U.S. can contribute its own expertise.

Contact: Dr. Johanna Mendolson
Bureau for Humanitarian Response
Office of Transition Initiatives
U.S. Agency for International Development
Washington, D.C. 20523
(202) 647-3390
FAX (202) 647-0218

IV. GUARANTEEING SUSTAINABLE DEVELOPMENT AND CONSERVING OUR NATURAL ENVIRONMENT FOR FUTURE GENERATIONS

Seeing the need for wise management of the hemisphere's environmental resources to ensure their use by future generations, the leaders agree to promote partnerships in the fields of energy, pollution prevention, and the sustainable use of biological resources.

21. Partnership for Sustainable Energy Use: The participating countries commit to increase access to reliable, clean, and less costly energy services.

The U.S. is developing a National Energy Policy Plan, pursuing least-cost energy strategies and promoting market-oriented pricing. The U.S. Department of Energy is organizing a symposium of hemispheric partners to advance implementation of the Partnership. The U.S. is working with the multilateral development banks to increase their financing for sustainable energy use projects within their energy-related lending.

Contact: Aimee Christensen
Office of International Energy Policy
U.S. Department of Energy, P.O. — 73
1000 Independence Ave. S.W.

Washington, D.C. 20585
(202) 586-4576
FAX (202) 586-6148

22. Partnership for Biodiversity: The participating countries commit themselves to build capacity (indigenous, local, and national) for the protection and sustainable use of biodiversity resources, within the policy framework of existing international agreements, and the resources of the Inter-American Development Bank and the newly replenished Global Environmental Facility.

The U.S. is building strategies to conserve and sustainably use biodiversity in economic development, strengthen park and reserve management, and promote hemispheric technical and scientific cooperation through a "Decade of Discovery."

Contact: Suzanne Fleeck
Office of Policy Analysis
U.S. Department of the Interior
1849 C St. N.W., Mail Stop 4429
Washington, D.C. 20520
(202) 208-5978
FAX (202) 208-4867

23. Partnership for Pollution Prevention: The participants agree to strengthen technical and institutional capacity to address environmental priorities such as control of pesticides, reducing lead contamination, improved water and air quality, and urban environmental problems. They will use existing institutions such as the OAS and the resources of the multilateral development banks to develop legal frameworks, environmental compliance and enforcement capacity, and public participation.

The U.S. will host an "International Workshop on Phasing Lead out of Gasoline" (Washington, March 14-15), and it is planning to present short, professional training courses on environmental management, beginning with a course on risk management to be held in Venezuela (July 1995) that will be sponsored by the Pan-American Health Organization. The U.S. is working with Central American representatives to develop a legal network and technical assistance projects to implement CONCAUSA, the U.S.-Central American agreement on sustainable development.

Contact: Cam Hill-Macon
Office of International Activities
Environmental Protection Agency
401 M St. S.W. (2621)
Washington, D.C. 20460

(202) 260-6009
FAX (202) 260-4470

Note: Copies of the complete Summit documents — *Declaration of Principles* and *Plan of Action* — may be obtained from:

Summit Coordinating Office
Department of State, Rm. 3250
2201 C Street N.W.
Washington, D.C. 20520
(202) 736-7533/FAX (202) 736-7618

Speech to the North Texas Commission Dallas/Fort Worth, Texas August 18, 1994

Ambassador Charles A. Gillespie, Jr. served as the U.S. State Department's senior coordinator for the Summit of the Americas. He has served as senior director for Latin America and the Caribbean at the National Security Council and as U.S. ambassador to Chile and to Colombia.

U.S.-Latin American Relations in the Nineties: New Opportunities and Challenges

Ambassador Charles A. Gillespie, Jr.

From Consensus to Partnership

This is a defining moment in our relationship with the world. Emerging out of the old divisions of the Cold War and the old confrontations between North and South is a broad new consensus in favor of democratic government and market economies. It is a striking trend in many parts of the world.

- In Asia, the dramatic economic successes of the Asian Tigers are evolving into open political systems. By developing their economies and particularly by developing their human resources through education, these countries set up the conditions wherein citizens demanded a stake in the political process and full accountability from their governments.

- In East Europe, countries have thrown off the old yoke of authoritarian government and state-directed economies and are struggling with enormous difficulties to build open societies and open economies.

- In South Africa, we have just witnessed the birth, after a strenuous effort, of a society which will offer equal political and economic opportunities to all.

In Latin America, the progress toward democracy and market economics has been dramatic, even though it has tended to be overshadowed by the speed and surprise of events in East Europe or South Africa.

- The Americas are now overwhelmingly governed by elected leaders. There is a strong sense throughout the hemisphere that elections must be fair and credible and that governments must have full legitimacy at home and internationally in order to serve their country properly.

- Governments in the hemisphere are increasingly committed to market economics. Most are well into the process of implementing monetary and fiscal discipline, reforming taxes, privatizing state enterprises, opening to international trade, and freeing internal markets.

- The benefits of these reforms are beginning to be felt. Latin America is experiencing its third year of solid growth, inflation is receding and is at single-digit levels in countries which not so long ago were struggling with three-digit rates, and capital inflows are triple the levels of the 1980s.

- Most important is the synergy among these reforms. Democratic reforms are a powerful impetus to greater social equity and to more effective and responsive government. These in turn build the broad-based citizen support and political stability which reassure investors and maximize the flows of capital, technology, and trade. That adds up to greater growth. Completing the cycle, broad-based growth sustains citizen support for the changes which are under way.

The Economic Stakes

These transformations are important to the interests of citizens of all the nations of the hemisphere. The Americas constitute a big market, and it is growing. In the next five years — by the turn of the century — our hemisphere's population will approach 820 million. Gross product is expected to exceed $12 trillion. Along with our neighbors, the United States has an economic and political stake in the prosperity and stability of the region. And it is this enduring U.S. interest which underlies our policies supporting democratic and market reforms.

Today, 37 percent of U.S. exports go to Western Hemisphere nations, with a quarter of those to non-NAFTA markets. We sell as much to Brazil as to China and more to Venezuela than to Russia. We export more to Ecuador than to Hungary and Poland combined. We already sell more to our hemispheric market than we do to either Western Europe or Asia, including Japan. This trade reflects tremendous new opportunities for American business and has generated hundreds of thousands of new jobs for American workers. As trade barriers in the region continue to fall, more American jobs will be created.

Looking at the hemisphere from pole to pole, as early as 1995 this region will probably account for close to $200 billion in U.S. exports. That's considerably more than what we sell to all Europe (West and East) plus Russia and more than to East and South Asia combined.

Looking just at Latin America, our exports are growing at three times the global rate. If current trends continue, by the end of the century U.S. exports to Latin America will exceed those to the European Union. Well over one million U.S. jobs are directly supported by exports to Latin America and the Caribbean.

This region is, of course, particularly important to Texas. Forty-four percent of the state's exports go to Latin America. Last year, Texas sent $13 billion of merchandise exports to Mexico alone and another $3 billion to the rest of Latin America and the Caribbean.

A trend which is particularly worth watching is the impact of regional integration. Early next year, the five countries of the Andean Pact are expected to become a single market, with free internal trade and a common external tariff no greater than 20 percent. At that point, they will become one of our top 12 markets, accounting for more than $10 billion in U.S. exports. We sell more to the Pact's 95 million people than to China's 1.2 billion, and while the Andean Pact buys more than a third of its total imports from us, China buys less than a tenth.

By any standard, Latin America will become an increasingly important force in the world economy. With a population approaching half a billion, a growing and sophisticated entrepreneurial class oriented toward international markets, and relatively high standards of living by developing country standards, Latin America is capturing the imagination of investors seeking new "tigers" — or should we say "jaguars?"

The agenda of reforms is creating extraordinary new opportunities for entrepreneurs and for the citizens of the entire hemisphere.

New and Common Challenges

The story, obviously, is not over. There are a great many challenges ahead. Let me touch on some of the challenges which the region faces in what has been called the second generation of reforms.

The first generation aims at taking government out of the things that it doesn't do well and probably shouldn't do at all and empowering markets to be the main decisionmakers for the economy. The second generation of reforms aims at giving government the capacity to do well what only governments can do and what markets cannot do or do only imperfectly. The idea here is to make growth inclusive, to give a stake to all elements of society in the market-based democracies now being built.

In a broad sense, we face similarly daunting new challenges throughout the Americas and, indeed, throughout the world:

- We are all seized with the need to restructure our economies so that we can compete effectively in a world economy which technology is constantly remaking.

- We are all looking for ways of reviving our various domestic communities so that growth and job opportunities reach all parts of our societies.

- We all need to re-examine and reform our social systems so that health, education, and essential social services are delivered efficiently at a reasonable cost, free of abuses and responsive to the needs of all our people.

- We are all faced with the challenge of making sure that the incentives are there to protect our countries' resources for sustainable, environmentally sound use.

- We all face the need to constantly re-invent and strengthen our political institutions so as to make democratic government more effective and more responsive to citizens' needs and to sustain citizen support.

Effective Government and Effective Democracy

I'd like to discuss some of these issues in more detail — first, about deepening democracy. Democracy is, of course, about more than elections. The everyday functioning of government — its efficiency and honesty — is critical to making democracy a reality in the lives of ordinary citizens. Corruption is a particularly pernicious threat.

Popular insistence on government accountability is mounting throughout the hemisphere. In country after country, people are insisting that the politicians they elect and the bureaucrats whose salaries they pay — even diplomats — be more responsive and more efficient. Decentralization is another potential trend. Efforts to give local institutions greater authority in allocating funds and administering programs are a dramatic and healthy departure from the past.

The Clinton administration is re-inventing government at home and, recognizing the same trends elsewhere, we support complementary efforts by other governments and international institutions to make public administration more effective, efficient, and relevant. The Organization of American States

(OAS) has formally recognized the need to improve legal, regulatory and administrative structures so as to prevent corruption and improve government performance. The Inter-American Development Bank (IDB), at its recent replenishment meeting in Guadalajara, adopted "modernization of the state" as one of its guiding principles.

Free Markets, Growth and Poverty

An equal challenge before us is how to make free markets work so as to bring growth to all parts of society. We have all heard talk of "reform fatigue" in the hemisphere, but, in President Clinton's words, we must "compete, not retreat." Indeed, we simply cannot afford to retreat from the reforms which are under way. History shows that a critical mass of reforms and restructuring must be sustained for the process to succeed and to yield greater growth throughout society. Countries which went only halfway in the reform process have ended up with disastrous results, paying the high costs of transition while achieving very few of the expected gains. Expectations in Latin America have been raised by the initiation of the reform process. If these are not met, then a despairing populace will turn to other political and economic models — such as populist economics or authoritarianism — which cannot produce the broad-based and self-sustaining growth or the participatory politics, which citizens increasingly demand.

The issue then is to show that markets work. For Latin America, showing that markets work to help *all* elements of society is particularly important because of the pervasiveness of poverty. By various estimates, between one-third and one-half of Latin America's people live in poverty. Regrettably, income inequality is greater in Latin America than in any other region of the world. Moreover, the disparities between wealth and poverty are increasingly apparent — and politically volatile — with increasing urbanization and improved communication. If free markets and democracy fail to deliver, the ideological victory will be lost.

The challenge before reformist governments is thus to convey to their electorates tangible evidence that their programs will benefit all parts of society and that the lives of ordinary citizens will improve in the foreseeable future. Without this elementary perception of fairness, neither democracy nor free markets can survive. As Milton Friedman has said, "History suggests that capitalism is a necessary condition for political freedom. Clearly, it is not a sufficient condition."

Fortunately, there is a growing awareness that economic reform must include more than deregulation, trade liberalization and privatization. We've seen innovative programs (like Mexico's Solidarity, Bolivia's Social Fund, and Peru's FONCODES, the National Social Compensation and Development Fund) which offer a helping hand to those at the margins of the economy and those disadvantaged in the short run by reforms.

The recent, historic capital replenishment of the Inter-American Development Bank — which increased the IDB's capital from $60 to $100 billion and added almost another billion to its Fund for Special Operations — also marked agreement on reorienting the Bank's lending to investment in health and education, to protection of the environment, and to harnessing the energy of the private sector.

There is also increasing hard-headedness about the operation of social programs. Facing severe budget restraints, many countries are beginning to refocus their spending away from programs that benefit elites or all groups in society, and instead focus on those in urgent need. Governments which seek to be fiscally responsible and which accept the fact that they cannot do it all have begun to identify priorities and make tough decisions.

In that context, it is clear that there is a great benefit to society as a whole, as well as to individuals, in investments in basic education and primary health care. That is one of the clearest lessons that we all can learn from the so-called "East Asian miracle;" these countries were able to combine long-lasting high growth with decreased income inequality by emphasizing investments in human capital. They have shown that policies of *shared* growth can also be policies of *high* growth. And it goes without saying that educated, healthy people can more actively and effectively participate in democratic society.

New Priorities at the Summit of the Americas

These new priorities — consolidating today's democratic and market reforms and moving forward toward growth shared throughout society — are reflected in the themes which we anticipate will occupy the leaders of this hemisphere when they gather for the Summit of the Americas, to be held this December in Miami.

The Summit will present an unparalleled opportunity to transform the broad, although far-from-perfect consensus within the hemisphere into a new partnership for action to address our common problems and approach our common goals. Thirty-four democratic leaders from the hemisphere will be able to converse about the whole range of challenges which our societies face, each bringing individual insights and experience, with the aim of identifying those priority concerns ripe for cooperative endeavors. The leaders face common challenges: making democracy work, making democracy prosperous, and making democracy endure.

We envision that the Summit will produce a declaration of principles to guide relationships among our nations and the policies they will pursue and an action plan of specific initiatives. We have found support and enthusiasm for a Summit built around the themes of democracy and effective government, shared prosperity, and sustainable development.

We have concluded a first round of comprehensive formal consultations as well as numerous informal discussions. We plan additional consultations to fully engage our partners in the Summit process. We also look forward to receiving input on the Summit from a variety of private sector and non-governmental groups.

While our thinking is still evolving, two examples may help illustrate our aims:

- We believe the Summit can give impetus and direction to the consolidation and defense of democracy; government accountability, efficiency and transparency; empowering civil society; and the rule of law, including steps to combat the dangerous narcotics cartels.

- We see a renewal of the region's commitment to all its peoples as a key focus of the Summit. We may explore innovative approaches to developing regional health, labor, environmental and educational standards.

Trade Expansion in the Hemisphere

The expansion of trade in the hemisphere will clearly be a major focus of the Summit. The interest in the region in this issue is intense. And because of North Texas' strategic position in North American trade, I expect your interest is strong as well. Let me expand just a little on this subject.

First, let me note that, under President Clinton's leadership, the U.S. has experienced the most important year in trade in our history. Highlights include the passage of NAFTA, the Asia Pacific Summit, and the conclusion (after seven years of gridlock) of the Uruguay Round, which will create hundreds of thousands of U.S. jobs and increase global growth.

But we look at these achievements as the beginning, not the end of the road. The President sees the transition occurring in this hemisphere as an historic opportunity and sees trade cooperation as a means of supporting this transition.

The President has made clear his personal commitment to the goal of closer trade ties in the hemisphere. Last November, immediately after the passage of the NAFTA, he noted that he saw NAFTA as "just the first step in our effort to expand trade." The President stated his desire: "to reach out to the other market-oriented democracies of Latin America to ask them to join in this great American pact that I believe offers so much hope to our future."

The Clinton administration is currently developing a strategy for achieving this goal. In the context of the Uruguay Round implementing legislation, it is the Administration's intention to propose a renewal of authority to negotiate trade agreements and so-called fast-track procedures to ensure rapid Congressional passage of such agreements. We are seeking a full range of options, including global agreements and negotiations with individual countries.

During the visit of Chilean President Eduardo Frei Ruiz-Tagle to Washington in June, President Clinton reaffirmed his firm commitment to negotiate a free trade agreement next with Chile. The two presidents asked U.S. Trade Representative Mickey Kantor and Chilean Minister of Finance Eduardo Aninat to provide them a joint recommendation on the best avenue for a free trade agreement — whether bilateral or NAFTA accession.

In May, Vice President Al Gore announced the Interim Trade Program for the Caribbean Basin to respond to the concerns about the impact of NAFTA on CBI countries. The program would provide treatment substantially equivalent to NAFTA for textile and apparel products. In return, beneficiaries would be asked to join the World Trade Organization, improve treatment of investment and intellectual property rights, and provide commitments on labor and the environment — all measures which would enhance the CBI nations' ability to attract investment and to compete on the world market.

Incidentally, the use of the word "interim" is deliberate because we want to convey the idea that this new program is a transition to some later date when we have worked out a fully reciprocal trade arrangement with interested CBI countries.

Of course, expanding the NAFTA to the countries of Latin America and the Caribbean will take time. We fully acknowledge the accomplishments of many countries in the hemisphere in adopting market-oriented policies and liberalizing their trade regimes. However, countries need to continue to move forward. They need to understand better NAFTA's high standards, to be prepared to accept reciprocal market access requirements, and to continue to reform their economies so as to stimulate the private sector to ready itself for the benefits and obligations of trade expansion. We also believe it is in our mutual interest to work on improving the environment and raising labor standards.

I want to emphasize that, from the perspective of the Clinton administration, trade expansion involves much more than the simple exchange of goods and services. We see it in a broader context, as providing the basis for stronger linkages among our societies as a whole. As such, closer trade cooperation can be a powerful tool for supporting democracy and economic restructuring in the hemisphere and for helping develop patterns of international cooperation on a whole range of transnational issues (such as control of narcotics, curbing illegal immigration, and control of the proliferation of weapons) that go far beyond trade.

Conclusion

The sweeping reforms of the past several years have led to an extraordinary convergence of interests among the nations of the Americas, from Canada in the north to Chile in the south, and from our own westernmost points to Barbados and Brazil in the east. Renewed and deeper commitments to democracy and market economics mean that these core values are now shared throughout the hemisphere and form the basis for developing a true community of nations — one committed to democracy and human rights, bound together by open markets and rising standards of living, and dedicated to the peaceful resolution of disputes.

Such a community implies a new kind of relationship between the United States and its neighbors, one which is more mature and modern, based on mutual respect and cooperation to achieve common objectives. Let me finish with a quote from Colombia President César Gaviria, soon to be Secretary General of the OAS: "We will see born a new hemisphere that calls for solidarity and cooperation to develop economic and trade relations based on parity and dignity."

*Speech to
the Inter-American
Dialogue*

*September 20, 1994
Washington, D.C.*

*Richard E. Feinberg is
special assistant
to the President
of the United States
and senior director for
Inter-American Affairs
of the National
Security Council.*

The Summit of the Americas: An Architecture for Inter-American Relations

Richard E. Feinberg

It's a pleasure to be with so many friends today. I appreciate this opportunity to exchange thoughts with you as we approach the Summit of the Americas, now less than three months away. The Miami meeting could be the most important and successful Summit in the history of hemispheric relations. It could set the spirit and agenda for the rest of this decade and beyond.

Vice President Gore announced the Summit last December in Mexico City. That sparked an intensive process of preparation within the U.S. government, between government agencies and our civil society, and among governments of the region. The Summit has unleashed a torrent of energy and surfaced an enormous backlog of thoughtful proposals. Haiti and Cuba capture the daily headlines, but I can assure you that Summit preparations are proceeding apace at an accelerating rate.

This spring, senior U.S. officials undertook a first round of consultations throughout the region to determine the Summit's broad themes. Vice President Gore led two of these visits to Central America and Canada. We are now in the midst of a second round of consultations on the more detailed agenda for action. Tomorrow, we will host representatives from the Rio Group to continue these increasingly in-depth discussions on specific initiatives.

We are also drawing on the expertise of the two most prominent regional institutions. President Clinton will meet this afternoon with OAS Secretary General César Gaviria, and Ambassador Harriet Babbitt is chairing a working group within the OAS on the Summit agenda. Vice President Gore spoke last Friday at an Inter-American Development Bank conference on democracy and the modernization of the state. The IDB, through its president, Enrique Iglesias, is helping to craft many of the Summit's initiatives and will have a role in implementing them.

The consultation process is not limited to officialdom. We have welcomed the suggestions from a wide range of civil society — that whole spectrum of private sector associations and non-governmental organizations interested in hemispheric affairs. This morning, Ambassador Tony Gillespie appeared before the Washington, D.C., Liaison Committee on Latin America. Last week, we exchanged views with the Council of the Americas. We have benefited from the input of a large number of non-profit advocacy groups and think tanks, and many more exchanges will occur. During October, Summit of the Americas citizen consultations will be held with the private sector and NGO leaders around the country. We have also read with great interest the proposals advanced by a group of distinguished experts assembled by the UN Development Programme and the IDB.

By example and persuasion, we have sought to stimulate other governments to also involve their own civil society in Summit preparations. In Argentina, representatives of *Conciencia* and of *Poder Ciudadano* participated in our bilateral consultations. In Central America, experts from both U.S. and local environmental groups are deeply involved in designing the Alliance for Sustainable Development. We have heard from our business leaders that private sector groups in Mexico, Argentina, Brazil, and Chile are working closely with their own governments.

In this way, when the Summit leaders call for a deepening of democracy and for more cooperative interchange between government and civil society, their words will ring true. There will be a consistency between the form and the substance of the Summit process. The Summit preparations are advancing those very values and institutions that the Summit declarations will proclaim.

We want to involve the private sector and NGOs in Summit preparations for another reason: so that they can assist in the implementation of its recommendations. In the promotion of democracy, in encouraging trade and investment flows, in educational reform and the design of environmental projects, partnerships between governments and civil society can be essential elements of change and part of the standard machinery of hemispheric governance.

This expanding array of consultations with civil society serves yet another purpose for U.S. foreign policy. With the end of the cold war, fears arise that Americans could turn their backs on the rest of the world. We must build a new coalition for an affirmative foreign policy. Its constituency lies among U.S. firms and workers whose livelihood depends on trade. It includes environmentalists and other public policy groups that see the links between the actions of foreign governments and their own objectives. It also includes religious and ethnic groups legitimately concerned about the welfare of their brethren and families overseas. Among these and other groups, there is a potential for a much broader constituency for American foreign policy than ever before. By involving many of these groups, the Summit process can help strengthen the foundations of hemispheric relations.

The Summit in Historical Perspective

A Summit is a bold undertaking. There have only been two hemispheric Summits in the post-war period, in Panama in 1956 and in Punta del Este, Uruguay in 1967. It is already clear that this Summit will be distinct and historic in a number of respects.

First, the extent of consultations with civil society. Accounts of the 1967 Summit make reference to meetings with a few well-known business and labor leaders and intellectuals. That was before the broad spectrum of American civil society became so deeply involved in hemispheric affairs. Certainly, the inclusion of Latin American civil society in Summit preparation is unprecedented. Still more needs to be done to make hemispheric diplomacy more accessible and transparent, but the Summit has already advanced this democratizing process.

Second, previous Summits were attended by many leaders whose power derived from bullets not ballots. This is the first Summit of solely democratically elected leaders. The Miami Summit will be a celebration of the consolidation of democracy. Our democracies are far from perfect, but we should not lose sight of the dramatic process made since the days when authoritarianism was at its apogee.

Third, this is the first hemispheric Summit hosted by the United States and the first held in this country. In earlier years, the hemisphere was split along a north-south divide and the confrontational stances spawned by the cold war. These tensions would have made it difficult for any U.S. president successfully to convene such a meeting. The previous two hemispheric Summits were hosted in Latin America under OAS auspices to compensate for the asymmetries of power and purpose that separated the United States from the rest of the hemisphere. Today, Latin America welcomes the United States' commitment to hemispheric solidarity that the Summit signals. In the 1990s, there is a shared desire to work closely with one another to address our common agenda.

Fourth, we are in an era of substantive symmetry — a shared agenda based on synchronic domestic concerns that can best be addressed cooperatively. We face similar agendas rooted in our common participation in the one-world economy. A traveler encounters common conversations in Santiago, São Paulo, and San Francisco. We are all concerned with overcoming citizen alienation and with bringing government closer to the people. We are all dedicated to increasing job security and raising productivity. We all seek broad access to health care and quality education. Preoccupation with foreign aid has given way to intense interest in free trade zones that create mutual prosperity. Fears of unilateral American interventionism have been superseded by interest in strengthening the capacity of the UN and the OAS to enable the hemisphere to defend democracy collectively.

The president's decision to host the Summit in the regional center of Miami follows this theme in the administration's foreign policy: In a world of integrated markets, domestic interests and foreign policy are tightly intertwined. The daily lives of U.S. citizens are deeply affected by our relations with Latin America, the Caribbean, and Canada. Job creation through trade and investment, population and immigration, drug trafficking, and money laundering, these regional phenomena — some good, some bad — link the welfare of all the inhabitants of this hemisphere. Miami is a hub of the hemisphere, a crossroads of cultures and commerce. Miami's diversity richly displays the interconnectedness of the Americas.

Recent events in the Caribbean Basin underscore the stake that Miami has in the region. Just as prosperity abroad generates jobs in the United States, so do the after-shocks of instability cast a long shadow across our shores. The Summit location and agenda recognize that our fates are inextricably linked to the fates of our hemispheric neighbors. Today, all politics, like economics, is global.

Fifth and finally, this Summit will create an architecture for hemispheric relations to assure that its plan of action is implemented and the results are measurable. As Secretary General Gaviria warned in his inaugural address last week, "The confidence and hope of the American nations cannot survive another round of empty rhetoric and unfulfilled promises." At this Summit, the leaders will mandate a network of implementing mechanisms including functional partnerships around specific objective, periodic ministerials, strengthened regional institutions, and public-private sector interactions. Many of the initiatives under discussion will be mandated to the OAS and the IDB. Make no mistake; the Summit will enhance the authority of both of these multilateral agencies. Other Summit initiatives will be implemented by senior officials from the responsible national ministries and regulatory bodies. In numerous areas, the expertise and perspectives of private business and NGOs will join with governmental authori-

ties. Together, these mechanisms will amount to a genuine inter-American system capable of sustained action.

We are working to help craft a Summit agenda which lays forth an inspiring vision of the future — one which is concrete and relevant to the daily lives of the average citizen of the hemisphere. When leaders return home after Miami, each should be able to report to their constituents exactly how the Summit initiatives will improve their lives and those of their children. Better government, new jobs, easier access to quality education, healthier air to breathe, these, we hope, will be the living legacy of the Miami Summit.

Inclusive participation of civil society, legitimacy accorded only to democratic authority, a new maturity of relations between North and South America, substantive symmetry and follow-on architecture, these are five of the innovative hallmarks of the process that is the Summit of the Americas 1994.

Conceptual Convergence

This is an era of overlapping agendas in hemispheric relations. The common problems we face have increasingly impelled us to share common approaches to resolving these problems. There is, indeed, a notable conceptual convergence throughout the hemisphere around certain basic ideas. With these shared interests and values, it becomes much more feasible to arrive at common solutions to our hemispheric agenda.

Hemispheric leaders have reached agreement on the three broad themes for the Summit: democratic governance, shared prosperity, and sustainable development.

Government reform is at the top of the political agenda throughout the region. Leaders are seeking to identify themselves with cleaner, more effective public administration. If the challenge of the 1970s was the protection of human rights and if the triumph of the '80s was the rejection of authoritarianism, as Vice President Gore said last week at the IDB, "The challenge of the '90s is the creation of an effective, efficient, and transparent state." The Summit is an opportunity to share ideas on how to institutionalize representative, accountable, and effective government capable of confronting threats to democracy, including corruption and narcotics trafficking. In our consultations, we are also discussing how to deepen democracy by encouraging a vibrant civil society. The IDB is exploring the creation of a civil society fund designed to promote public participation and encourage local private philanthropy. The Summit will also strengthen the capacity of the OAS to assist members in fortifying democratic institutions and discouraging threats to democracy.

The region's leaders also understand that greater economic integration will promote the dynamic growth that comes from expanding markets. The Summit setting lets them take a long-range view on measures to reduce trade barriers. The Summit will foster economic integration, including financial market reform, and promote greater financial and infrastructure linkages in sectors such as telecommunications, transportation, and energy.

Sustainable development encompasses the goals of improving the well-being of the people of the Americas. It recognizes the importance of protecting environmental resources for future generations. Summit measures to expand access and improve the quality of educational and health services, stabilize population growth, prevent pollution, preserve biodiversity, and more wisely husband our natural resources will strengthen the region's democratic institutions.

Together, the three themes of reinventing government, economic integration, and sustainable development amount to a comprehensive and coherent paradigm for national development. The Summit holds the promise of ratifying and building upon the emerging consensus on the fundamental ideas which will guide inter-American relations into the next century.

Haiti

The Haitian military dictatorship has been the antithesis of the values that the Summit will seek to consolidate. Government for the *de factos* has existed not to educate and nurture but to extort and exploit. The Haitian kleptocracy has left most of the population illiterate and without potable water. The Haitian countryside has been stripped of its natural resources, transforming it into an ecological wasteland.

Haiti could be a test case for the aspirations of the Summit. Having defended democracy collectively, the hemisphere and the international community will join with Haitians in the task of constructing a government of and for the people. Having lifted the embargo, the international community will share its financial resources and expertise to build infrastructure, attract investment, and create jobs. We must invest in the Haitian people by helping to provide primary education and health care. We will also help to repair the land, to reforest the hills, and purify the waters.

The Summit and the Interests of Americans

One measure of the Summit's success will be its relevance for all the hemisphere, from the poorest country, which is Haiti, to the richest which is the United States. For us, the Summit will succeed if it improves the hemispheric neighborhood we inhabit. It will also succeed for Americans if it spurs us forward to continue to reinvent our own government, to improve our global competitiveness, to nurture our piece of the earth.

Ultimately, the Summit should be an exercise not only in international relations but also in domestic renewal. It should speak to Americans as partners to the hemisphere at the same time as it addresses our own daily agenda. It should address our foreign and domestic interests. That will make it significant and historic. It will be a Summit for our times and for the twenty-first century.

INTERGOVERNMENTAL PUBLICATIONS

*The Presidents of the
Central American
governments have adopted
this regional, integral
strategy for sustainable
development*

Central American Alliance for Sustainable Development

INTRODUCTION

The Presidents of the Republics of Costa Rica, El Salvador, Guatemala, Honduras, Panama, and the representative for the Prime Minister of Belize, meeting together at the Central American Ecological Summit for Sustainable Development, have agreed that the circumstances prevailing in the region compel us to pursue a new course. Thus, we have decided to adopt an integral strategy for sustainable development in the region.

As manifested in the Declaration of Guácimo, we have embodied this option in a national and regional strategy called the Alliance for Sustainable Development, a Central American initiative concerning politics, ethics, economics, social welfare, and ecology. We propose this strategy in the form of a concrete plan which we hope will serve as a model for other regions.

The Alliance for Sustainable Development is a policy initiative comprising short-, medium-, and long-term programs that delineate a change in development scheme as well as in our individual and collective attitudes, in local, regional, and national policies and measures promoting political, economic, cultural, and environmental sustainability in our societies.

The Alliance is a strategy of regional cooperation and a consensus on interests, development initiatives, and the harmonization of rights. The implementation of the Alliance is founded upon institutionality and in no way replaces existing mechanisms and instruments of regional integration but rather complements, supports, and strengthens them, intra-regionally and extra-regionally, particularly in the process of promoting sustainable development as the central strategy and policy of the countries of the region. The Alliance reaffirms and broadens the agreements that have already been made by our countries for the new process of sustainable development in the Isthmus.

With this initiative and commitment to the sustainable development of the Central American community, we assume responsibility for the better use and more efficient management of the resources in the region.

In this regard, we consider that the international community can and should contribute to sustainable development in Central America by means of a change in its attitudes, policies, and demeanor toward the region, a change which would wholly redefine the relations between the international community and the countries of the Isthmus in a mutually beneficial manner.

The Central American Committee for Sustainable Development, at the urging of the Alliance and with the full agreement and support from those institutions which are directly responsible at the regional and national levels, will negotiate and promote the signing of agreements in

*Translated by Cynthia L. Jenney
for the University of Miami
North-South Center.*

countries and between groups of countries and regions as well as regional and international agencies for cooperation.

Central America will define the rights and responsibilities framed in Agenda 21 of Rio de Janeiro with the object of aspiring to become a model of sustainable development for all those countries in which peace; respect for life in all of its manifestations; the continual betterment of the quality of life; respect for the richness and diversity of our land and the multiculturalism and ethnic diversity of our peoples; participative democracy; the respect, promotion, and protection of human rights; the economic integration of the region with the rest of the world; and the intergenerational commitment to sustainable development will be the principles which will guide us toward the future.

The Concept of Sustainable Development

Due to the particular characteristics and idiosyncracies of the region, we have adopted the following concept of sustainable development:

> Sustainable development is a process of progressive improvement in the quality of life for all human beings, who are the focus and prime beneficiaries of development through economic growth with social equity and a change in production methods and consumption patterns. This process has as its foundation the ecological balance and the support of all forms of life in the region. It implies respect for local, regional, and national cultural and ethnic diversity as well as the strengthening and broadening of citizen participation within a framework of peaceful coexistence and harmony with nature, guaranteeing the quality of life for future generations.

Principles of the Alliance for Sustainable Development

Below, we enumerate the seven fundamental principles that we agree to adopt to achieve sustainable development. These principles will prevail in all policies, programs, and activities promoted by the Central American nations, individually or jointly, as well as by civil society, for whose benefit these objectives and shared commitments are made.

1. Respect for Life in All Its Manifestations

The basis of life is a code of ethics and moral values based on respect, personal responsibility, and consideration for other living things and the earth itself. Sustainable development will not be achieved at the expense of other groups or future generations, nor will it threaten the survival of other species.

2. The Betterment of the Quality of Human Life

The goal of sustainable development is to improve and guarantee the quality of human life. This will permit all people to develop their potentials and lead a decent, fulfilling life. To achieve this end, it is imperative to establish security and well-being by means of human development, the promotion of popular participation in the democratic process, respect for cultural pluralism and ethnic diversity, access to education, and the fostering of technical and professional development, which will lead to equitable economic growth.

3. Respect for and the Use of the Vitality and Diversity of the Earth in a Sustainable Manner

Local, national, and regional development shall be based upon the sustainable use and management of natural resources and the protection of the structure, functions, and diversity of the ecosystems upon which human beings and other species depend. To this end, the necessary actions will be taken to:

• Conserve those ecosystems which support life and the ecological processes which affect atmospheric conditions and the quality of the air and the water, regulate the water supply, recycle essential elements, create soils, and permit the ecosystems to regenerate themselves.

• Protect and conserve the biodiversity of plant and animal life and other organisms, of the genetic pools within each species, and the variety of ecosystems.

• Ensure the sustainable exploitation of natural resources — particularly the soil, all wild and domesticated species, forests, cultivated land, and fresh- and salt-water ecosystems.

4. The Promotion of Peace and Democracy as Basic Forms of Human Co-existence

Political freedom; respect for and the promotion of human rights; combatting violence, corruption, and impunity; and respect for duly celebrated international treaties are essential for the promotion of peace and democracy as basic forms of human co-existence.

Peace and democracy are strengthened by means of the full participation of the citizenry. Similarly, democratic institutions and mechanisms which promote both participation and constitutional governance must be strengthened in order to promote sustainable development.

5. Respect for the Multiculturalism and Ethnic Diversity of the Region

To a greater or lesser extent, the countries of Central America are societies characterized by an ethnic and cultural diversity which must be preserved, creating conditions that are conducive to all forms of cultural expression, particularly that of indigenous groups, which, in spite of being native to the region, have been subjugated since the Conquest and the colonization of the Americas. The right to a cultural identity is a fundamental human right and the basis for co-existence and national unity.

Areas of great biological diversity are generally inhabited by indigenous groups, which in some cases have life styles that advocate and support the conservation of the environment. The world view held by these groups is favorable to this objective in that they perceive nature as being inseparable from human beings.

For this reason, respect for ethnic diversity and the development of indigenous cultures, which is an objective in itself, coincides with respect for the environment. Nonetheless, in order for this respect to translate into coherent policies, there must be options for sustainable development which are accessible to the people.

Respect for ethnic diversity can become a reality only within the context of peace and democracy and by facilitating access to the opportunities offered by sustainable development.

6. Greater Economic Integration on the Regional and International Levels

Within the framework of globalization, it is indispensable that the benefits of free trade be accessible to the entire region, particularly by means of the more developed countries' promoting and implementing policies that would lead to the creation of a large free trade zone characterized by economic integration. All of the countries of Central America must have access to this free trade zone under adequate conditions and safeguarding their respective levels of development.

7. An Intergenerational Commitment to Sustainable Development

The strategies, policies, and programs implemented by the countries of Central America shall promote sustainable development and the well-being of the present and future generations, which will make it possible to improve the human condition in different areas — political, economic, social, cultural, and environmental.

The Bases of the Alliance for Sustainable Development

Sustainable development entails a holistic approach to development which requires the simultaneous implementation of initiatives in the Alliance's four fundamental issue areas.

Democracy, characterized by popular participation in the decision-making processes that affect society, requires that public policy and the people's means of making a living and interrelating be broad and participative. Likewise, in order to succeed in the alleviation of poverty, it is necessary for there to be economic growth. Economic growth depends, in turn, on the development of human resources and on social policies that increase economic opportunities for the most disenfranchised sectors of the population.

Democracy and economic and social development are not sustainable unless the environment and our natural resources are conserved. This implies that the contribution made by this perspective on sustainable development is precisely its emphasis on the need to work simultaneously to achieve democracy, equitable economic growth, social development, the sustainable management of natural resources, and an improvement in environmental conditions.

1. Democracy

Democracy, a basic form of human co-existence, and sustainable development are intimately linked. Only in a democratic, participative society governed by constitutional rule will justice and well-being be reached in Central America.

Support for the consolidation of democracy and the defense and guarantee of human rights are expressions of respect for human dignity. Therefore, democracy is one of the principal goals of sustainable development.

Attempts to decentralize the political, economic, and administrative activities carried out by the state contribute to the viability of the process as do the strengthening and consolidation of democratic institutions and municipal governments. The strengthening of non-governmental and community organizations is also of great importance.

The solid and lasting peace that is derived from this type of human co-existence permits the achievement of sustainable development — a goal which requires harmonious relations among human beings, who must in turn live in harmony with the environment.

2. Sociocultural Development

The fundamental priority in the social sphere is to eradicate extreme poverty in the region. In the countries of Central America, poverty is proof of the grave state of backwardness and the inequality which constitute obstacles to harmonious conciliation and national integration as well as a latent threat to the democratic way of life and a solid and lasting peace.

As a component of sustainable development in Central America, social development is based on mutual aid, solidarity, cooperation, initiative, and attention to the basic needs of the people as well as on the participation and empowerment of communities.

The principal parties responsible for social development shall be the communities and community organizations, intermediary institutions, and local governments. The success of sustainable development in the region depends on the creation and strengthening of the municipal agents responsible for community organization and broad popular participation as well as on social services implemented according to the principle of decentralization and with the full participation of beneficiaries.

Initiatives in this area shall address the following:

a. Investment in human resources. Priority will be given to basic education, preventive medicine, training and development programs, and environmental sanitation;

b. Implementation of programs in support of the family and populations that are at risk in order to ensure the full development of minors, adolescents, the elderly, and women;

c. Widening the access of lower income groups to social services and social and economic infrastructure;

d. Increasing employment opportunities, which includes creating the conditions necessary to generate productive activities by means of strengthening credit to micro and small businesses, providing technical assistance, and implementing any other measures that would improve the economic opportunities available to the neediest sectors of society.

A fundamental component is increasing public awareness of the importance of sustainable development.

The respect for life in all of its manifestations and its natural support system, the environment, necessitates a value system that is favorable to the development of a national identity within a framework of cultural pluralism and ethnic diversity. In the same manner, sustainable development establishes a set of attitudes, values, habits, and life styles that strengthen solidarity and identity. The region's cultural and historical heritage as well as its abundant natural resources shall be properly respected and utilized for the promotion of sustainable economic and social activities. In addition, creativity in the areas of the arts, science, and technology shall be fostered throughout the region.

3. Sustainable Economic Development

The sustainable economic development of the Isthmus is based on freedom, dignity, justice, social equality, and economic efficacy.

The rational, efficient management of macroeconomic and sectoral policies, together with the implementation of clear, congruent, consistent norms, is an indispensable requisite for the achievement and subsequent consolidation of economic and social stability. Our future socioeconomic order will call into play all the elements that are essential for peaceful co-existence and the establishment of a humanistic economy, which incorporates a cost-benefit approach to those matters relating to the deterioration of the environment and the exploitation of natural resources.

In order to increase the productivity of the economies in the region and to foster economic growth in general, it is also necessary to improve the existing infrastructure, especially in the areas of electrification, telecommunications, and transportation.

The vulnerability of our economies, which to a great extent depend on the exportation of a limited number of raw materials, has been reflected in the persistence of a significant external balance of trade gap. In consequence, it is imperative that we achieve greater access to the industrialized economies for our products.

The burden of the external debt and its servicing have greatly restricted our countries' ability to accelerate growth and eradicate poverty. Thus, to achieve these ends, it is necessary to find a lasting solution to the external debt problem as soon as possible.

The financial strategies that are needed to ensure sufficient resources to fuel sustainable development will be forthcoming from both domestic and international sources. The mechanisms of forgiveness, debt conversion, and refinancing could be considered for bilateral and multilateral debts, in accordance with the particular circumstances that exist in each country. The establishment of rotating funds and trust funds as well as the restructuring of national budgets could also be considered, giving priority to the objectives of sustainable development and adjusting expenditures on security and defense to reflect our countries' realities and the climate of peace that is making advances in the region.

The region's model for sustainable development promotes the increasing participation of the private sector and the full development of its creative capacities. The model focuses on the promotion of direct investment for the provision of services to the neediest sectors of society, among other programs, as this is a means of increasing productivity and business competence as well as alleviating poverty.

In addition, initiatives promoting savings, trade, investment in sustainable productive ventures, the rational utilization of renewable sources of energy, and the downsizing and decentralization of public administration shall be developed. This model also advocates support for research and the development of environmentally friendly technologies through the establishment of research centers that would advance the development of environmental standards for the region. These research and development centers would serve as quality control agents in the certification of the quality of our export products. They would also contribute to the process of industrial modernization that is currently underway in the region as well as to industry's implementation of sustainable production processes, which incorporate preventive measures such as the permanent monitoring of the impact on the environment.

Human resource development is not only a necessary condition to improve productivity but also an important vehicle to achieve greater social equity. For this reason, special emphasis should be given to investment in the area of education and health, especially for the most marginal sectors, as a means of boosting productivity, increasing competitiveness, and fighting poverty in the region.

Due to the conditions of the tourist industry in the region, it is necessary to guarantee a dynamic equilibrium between the preservation of the environment and the development of the tourist trade, maintaining respect for our natural and cultural heritage.

The strengthening and consolidation of the Central American commitment to integration are fundamental elements for improving the quality of life of our peoples, increasing inter-regional trade, opening new markets, and inserting Central America into the global economy.

Insertion into the global economy requires that all countries implement existing treaties that put an end to protectionism and widen access to markets, especially those that are of interest to developing countries. It is urgent to improve access to these markets for our principal products, particularly through the gradual elimination of trade barriers which restrict the importation of raw materials and processed goods from the countries in Central America and through a significant, though gradual, reduction of the types of support (e.g., subsidies for production and exportation) that lead to non-competitive ventures.

4. The Sustainable Management of Natural Resources and Improvement of Environmental Conditions

The deterioration and exhaustion of our natural resources pose a problem for future development in

Central America. Air, water, and ground pollution have increased dramatically in the region and will probably continue if the current development programs and industrial processes are not reoriented. The principal threats are deforestation and a reduction in the supply and quality of water. The lack of a clean water supply is one of the primary causes of illness and death, especially in the marginal sectors of our societies.

The ecological processes and genetic diversity which are essential for the support of life in our region can be protected through the sustainable management of natural resources and the improvement of environmental conditions. In the same way, these initiatives contribute to the ongoing effort to preserve biological diversity and protected lands; to prevent the contamination of the water, land, and air; and to permit the sustainable utilization of the ecosystems as well as the recuperation of those that have deteriorated.

In order to guarantee that the environment be used as an instrument to promote sustainable development, we have committed ourselves to the elaboration of policies with a domestic and international framework for the areas of land planning, energy, transportation, community planning, forests and biological diversity, and pollution control and prevention for our water, land, and air, among other resources.

Given the serious situation that confronts Central America, it is imperative that we formulate a master plan regarding the production, sale, and consumption of energy, promoting the use of renewable and alternative forms of energy, efficiency programs, and a Central American electricity network.

Objectives of the Alliance for Sustainable Development

1. To achieve peace, freedom, democracy, and development in Central America by means of promoting a change in attitudes on the personal and social levels, ensuring the building of a model for sustainable development in the political, economic, social, cultural, and environmental domains according to the framework established by Agenda 21.

2. To manage the environment in a wholly sustainable manner to guarantee the preservation and conservation of the biodiversity in the region for our benefit and that of the global community.

3. To inform the international community of the advances made by the Alliance as well as of the importance and the common advantages that derive from supporting this model for sustainable development in Central America.

4. To create conditions that permanently strengthen civil society's level of competency and participation in order to improve the quality of life in the present as well as in the future.

These objectives will be elaborated in further detail in the Annex, which forms an integral and inseparable component of this Alliance for Sustainable Development.

Instruments of the Alliance for Sustainable Development

1. The National Council for Sustainable Development

Our governments have agreed to form National Councils for Sustainable Development composed of representatives from both the public sector and civil society.

The respective National Councils for Sustainable Development shall be responsible for harmonizing national policies, programs, and projects with the strategies for sustainable development.

2. The Central American Council for Sustainable Development

Our governments have agreed to create the Central American Council for Sustainable Development, whose members shall be the presidents of the Central American states and the Prime Minister of Belize or their representatives.

The Council will adopt and execute its decisions, commitments, and other agreements with the assistance of Central American entities and institutions. The Council of the Central American Ministers of Foreign Relations, in conjunction with the Chancellor of Belize, will serve as the entity that coordinates decisions made at the presidential level and will receive the support of the General Secretariat of the System of Central American Integration (SC-SICA), which will work in close association with the Technical Secretariats of the regional subsystems and entities.

The Central American Council for Sustainable Development will adopt mechanisms to ensure the participation of civil society in the entire process of sustainable development, particularly the Consulting Committee to which the Protocol of Tegucigalpa refers.

José María Figueres Olsen
President
Republic of Costa Rica

Armando Calderón Sol
President
Republic of El Salvador

Ramiro de León Carpio
President
Republic of Guatemala

Carlos Roberto Reina Idiaquez
President
Republic of Honduras

Violeta Barrios de Chamorro
President
Republic of Nicaragua

Ernesto Pérez Balladares
President
Republic of Panama

Henry Young
Representative for the Prime Minister of Belize

Annex

Specific Objectives of the Alliance for Sustainable Development

Political Objectives

1. Support the processes of peacemaking and reconciliation that are initiated by the countries in the region.

2. Promote the full protection and enforcement of human rights.

3. Strengthen constitutional democracy and democratic institutions.

4. Combat corruption and impunity.

5. Strengthen the administrative and municipal capacity to address local problems directly.

6. Perfect the mechanisms which promote political and electoral participation.

7. Support all types of community organizations which preserve the national identity within a framework of cultural pluralism and ethnic diversity.

8. Combat the causes which give rise to violence and crime, including drug trafficking.

9. Modernize government institutions to enable them to carry out their functions more efficiently.

Economic Objectives

1. Promote a strategy of sustainable development and internal and global integration based on the growth of the internal market and the promotion of national and foreign investment.

2. Promote policies that reduce the intra-regional disequilibria which affect the sustainable development of the region.

3. Increase economic growth rates, which would lead to the eradication of poverty and thereby guarantee the social and political sustainability of democratization and the opening of markets in the region.

4. Seek joint solutions for managing the external debt.

5. Harmonize macroeconomic and sectoral policies at the regional level.

6. Foster investment and sustainable productive processes.

7. Promote research and debate regarding the economic and institutional reforms that the countries of Central America should foster to enable the negotiation of a free trade treaty and investment at the hemispheric level.

8. Promote the creation and sharing of environmentally friendly technologies to increase productivity and the development of technical environmental standards and to stimulate production without degrading the environment.

9. Promote and develop an ecologically sustainable tourist industry.

10. Formulate policies that justify and encourage agricultural activities which foment rural development, boost the intra-regional trade of agricultural products, guarantee the quality of foodstuffs, and increase and diversify exports, strengthening productive, commercial, and service networks.

11. Strengthen the incorporation of science and technology in the productive processes by upgrading the technical training and professional development of the region's workers, creating and strengthening research centers, and promoting entrepreneurship and the development of technologies.

12. Foment the overhaul, rehabilitation, and modernization of infrastructure at the regional level, especially in regard to transportation, telecommunications, and energy, in order to increase the efficiency and competitiveness of the productive sectors at the national, regional, and international levels.

Social Objectives

1. Eliminate legal and de facto discrimination against women to enable them to better their social standing and improve their standard of living.

2. Reduce the rate of extreme poverty, especially by means of the creation of opportunities for employment.

3. Reintegrate, in a Central America characterized by safety and stability, those individuals who have been exiled, displaced, and dispossessed so that they can fully exercise their citizenship rights and improve their quality of life in the context of equality of opportunity.

4. Integrate the criteria of subsidization, solidarity, community, social responsibility, and self-help in policies designed to redress poverty through development, community participation, and the economic and administrative decentralization of the state.

5. Prioritize investment in human beings in order to promote their self-realization.

Cultural Objectives

1. Promote a system of ethics that advances and fortifies sustainable development.

2. Strengthen national identity within a framework of cultural and ethnic diversity.

3. Promote, protect, and benefit from our cultural and natural heritage in an appropriate manner.

4. Encourage all forms of cultural expression that are conducive to a more adequate relationship with the environment.

5. Promote awareness about the preservation and sustainable use of our natural resources.

6. Foster the restitution and return of those cultural assets that have been exported illicitly.

Environmental Objectives

1. Harmonize and modernize environmental standards and legislation as well as the national agencies responsible for the protection of the environment.

2. Reduce air and water pollution as well as the contamination and erosion of the soil, all of which affect the quality of life.

3. Preserve, acknowledge, and utilize the biodiversity of the region, promoting the development of wildlife preserves, protected lands, and botanical gardens, among others.

4. Strengthen the regulatory and oversight capacities and the implementation of environmental norms as well as the identification and classification of crimes against the environment.

5. Promote the increasing awareness and participation of the citizenry by incorporating environmental education in the curricula of formal and informal educational institutions.

6. Decrease the rate of deforestation while simultaneously promoting reforestation and productive forestry ventures at the regional level.

7. Manage the watershed in an adequate manner so as to guarantee the diverse application of an abundant, high quality water supply.

8. Promote discussion at the regional level of joint policies regarding environmentally compatible products, green labeling, and environmental research.

9. Foment sustainable development projects in border zones.

Managua, Nicaragua
October 12, 1994

A Pre-Summit Initiative by the Inter-American Development Bank

The Inter-American Development Bank, the oldest and largest regional multilateral development institution, was established in December of 1959 to help accelerate economic and social development in Latin America and the Caribbean. The Bank was created in response to a longstanding desire on the part of the Latin American nations for a development institution that would focus on the pressing problems of the region. A resolution calling for the creation of such a bank was adopted at the First International American Conference, held in Washington, D.C., in 1890. In 1958, President Juscelino Kubitschek of Brazil proposed that the countries of the Western Hemisphere embark upon a bold cooperative effort to promote the economic and social development of the region. His proposal received support from throughout the hemisphere, and shortly thereafter a special committee of the Organization of American States drafted the Articles of Agreement Establishing the Inter-American Development Bank. The Bank's Charter states that its principal functions are to utilize its own capital, funds raised by it in financial markets, and other available resources for financing the development of the borrowing member countries; to supplement private investment when private capital is not available on reasonable terms and conditions; and to provide technical assistance for the preparation, financing, and implementation of development plans and projects.

Summary Report of the Conference on Strengthening Civil Society

A. INTRODUCTION

1. Organized by the Inter-American Development Bank (IDB), the Conference on Strengthening Civil Society was held at the Bank's headquarters between 12 and 14 September 1994. It was attended by representatives of member governments of the Bank, legislative bodies from several countries of Latin America and the Caribbean, international organizations, bilateral cooperation agencies, civil society organizations from the Bank's developed member countries, and numerous civil society organizations from countries in the region.

2. The Bank's purpose was to provide governments, international agencies, and civil society organizations (CSOs) with an opportunity to reflect together and to hold a constructive and respectful dialogue on the subject of strengthening civil society. Starting from the mandate created by the governors of the Bank at the time of the Eighth General Increase in the Bank's Resources, approved at Guadalajara in April 1994, the specific aims of the Conference were (a) to publicize the Bank's interest in supporting member countries in strengthening civil society, as an essential part of a comprehensive, sustainable and equitable process, and in consolidating democratic societies; (b) to analyze the program and operating guidelines required for an effective Bank effort in terms of rethinking the relations between the State and civil society, strengthening the latter and seeking appropriate financing mechanisms; (c) to exchange specific experiences of governments, international agencies and civil society organizations, and to promote an ongoing dialogue on the issue; and (d) to stimulate the mobilization of domestic and international resources, including philanthropy and other forms of financing, as part of the commitment by the countries and the international community to dynamic, participatory, equitable and sustainable development.

3. The Conference provided an opportunity to hear the views of several international organizations and bilateral cooperation agencies. Also presented were a number of cases of concrete experiments carried out in member countries of the Bank, which were discussed in working groups, each of which focused on one of the four main issues around which discussions on the strengthening of civil society had been organized: (a) civic participation, (b) socioeconomic participation, (c) financing, and (d) regulatory and institutional framework. The reports by each of these working groups were presented to and commented on at plenary meetings. The agenda and structure of the Conference allowed full participation by those attending and an intensive and constructive exchange of opinions and experiences. Participants repeatedly commented favorably on the Bank's initiative and encouraged it to continue

its efforts in the area of strengthening civil society. Those attending supported, in particular, the Bank's efforts in response to the mandate from the Eighth General Increase in Resources to build economic reform, social reform, and reform of the State into a single comprehensive development agenda, within the framework of strengthening civil society.

4. Speakers at the inaugural ceremony were Mr. Fernando Zumbado, Regional Director for Latin America and the Caribbean of the United Nations Development Programme (UNDP); Mr. Mark Schneider, Administrator for Latin America and the Caribbean of the U.S. Agency for International Development (U.S.AID); Ambassador Christopher Thomas, Acting Secretary-General of the Organization of American States (OAS); and Mr. Enrique V. Iglesias, President of the Inter-American Development Bank (IDB). The closing ceremony was addressed by Mr. Juan Antonio March Pujol, Director General of the Institute of Ibero-American Cooperation (ICI); Mr. Carlyle Guerra de Macedo, Director-General of the Pan American Health Organization (PAHO), and Mr. Enrique V. Iglesias. These representatives of international organizations and bilateral cooperation agencies congratulated the IDB on its initiative in organizing the Conference and in broadening the scope of its programs in support of member countries and reiterated their willingness to coordinate efforts with a view to supporting the strengthening of civil society. The President of the IDB thanked those representing governments, parliaments, international organizations, bilateral cooperation agencies, and civil society organizations (CSOs) for participating in the Conference and for the suggestions they had made to help the Bank fine-tune its policies and programs to accommodate the strengthening of civil society.

B. SUMMARY

1. Before summarizing the comments and discussions which took place in each working group, it should be pointed out that participants were unanimous in stressing the inseparable links between civic participation, socioeconomic participation, financial support, and the regulatory and institutional framework, which were the topics around which, for operating purposes and to facilitate broader participation, the working groups had been organized. In this connection, during the plenary meetings at which the working group reports were commented on and which provided an opportunity to bring a more

comprehensive and integrating perspective to bear, the following main points of broad consensus were highlighted as desirable ingredients for a program structure aimed at strengthening civil society:

(a) Strengthening civil society is a complex task that needs to be approached from several closely interrelated perspectives: political, social, economic and juridical.

(b) Strengthening civil society is primarily a domestic process which cannot be imposed from outside. At the same time, it is a process in which all the agents in each society should be involved: governments, businesses trade unions, political parties, churches, NGOs, foundations, intermediary and grassroots organizations, and individual citizens. Although the strengthening of civil society is a fundamentally domestic process set against widely differing and specific circumstances, it needs to be supported by the international community. In this connection, it was recognized, on the one hand, that a process of democratic consolidation and economic and social reform is under way in the region that is conducive to the strengthening of civil society, and, on the other, that the international environment is favorable for the mobilization of resources and the pooling of efforts among countries and international agencies and organizations to support the strengthening of civil society. The IDB was especially urged to continue the efforts which it has begun in this direction, by exploring options for establishing appropriate financing mechanisms with this goal in mind.

(c) Strengthening the citizenry lies at the heart of the process of strengthening civil society, which can thrive only where there are basic democratic freedoms and meaningful economic opportunities for all citizens. From this standpoint, reforms aimed at consolidating macroeconomic stability, broadening the entrepreneurial base, boosting employment, restoring growth, and putting our economies back on the global scene on a stronger competitive footing must be combined with social reform and reform of the State into a unified development strategy conducive to growth and socioeconomic equity in a context of increasingly stronger democratic systems. It was recognized that the fight against poverty, which engulfs vast segments of Latin America's population who lack dignified participation in the economy, must be central to the process of strengthening civil society. In the final analysis, it was felt that this process is both a prerequisite for and the outcome of dynamic, equitable and sustainable development.

(d) There is a close relationship between modernization and reform of the State and the strengthening of civil society. It was acknowledged that the quality of government rests ultimately on the quality of the citizens themselves in terms of their opportunity and capacity to help shape public policies and monitor their implementation. The rule of law and democratic institutions and the promotion of sound government and governance can be strengthened *only if civil society is also strengthened*. In this respect, it was recognized that redefining the role of the State and resizing it mean, on the one hand, strengthening its capacity to promote competition, which is the essence of market efficiency, and to promote equity, which is the essence both of its legitimacy and that of the democratic system; on the other, they mean strengthening the capacity of citizens, individually or in partnerships, through profitmaking activities or otherwise, to assume responsibilities — some of them economic — that the State has been shedding and to monitor and supervise the act of governing.

C. THE WORK OF
THE WORKING GROUPS

Civic Participation

1. To some working groups, civic participation meant individual or collective participation by the citizenry in policy, government, and social affairs of public interest. This can take place at both the national and the local level, but the latter is more common. However, if society is to benefit, these local inputs must be part of a national vision and must seek the common good.

2. The concept of civil society was found to have evolved over time and had come to mean different things in different countries. In fact, whereas some regard civil society as being composed primarily of NGOs and philanthropic organizations, in the poor countries it also includes the weakest links in the socioeconomic chain. Cases in point are micro-, small, and medium-sized companies, workers in the informal sector, poor municipalities, grassroots social and local organizations, vulnerable groups, and a large proportion of women and young people. Although it would be presumptuous to aim at a hard-and-fast definition of civil society organizations, it should be stressed that the term has a singular capacity to pull together all the individual and collec-

tive elements that come into play to influence — through participation — the decisions which are taken by the organs of the State with respect to political and social development and to economic growth and income redistribution.

3. The most novel and essential elements of contemporary civil society are the exercise of citizenship, representation, and participation. Here, education, information, and public debate play a crucial role. The greater the separation between public and private discussion, the greater the erosion of civic participation and responsibility among the various partnership groups.

4. The different experiences that were shared brought to light a very interesting assortment of successful initiatives that have been implemented to strengthen civil society. Some of them are described below:

- Organization of forums to discuss national issues at the local level. The purpose of these gatherings is to make it easier to identify and define the issues that are most relevant to the community, to promote thoughtful discussion of them, and to suggest options from among complex alternatives by first mapping out a framework of common ground. Most issues selected have a bearing on the major trends in the world today — the strengthening of democracy and of civil society — and are based on or aimed at eliciting specific actions.

- Similarly, efforts have been encouraged to smooth the transition to democracy or to strengthen it in many corners of the continent. The methods used have ranged from campaigns to promote voter registration and training aimed at informed voting, to citizen control of the plebiscite and later the electoral process, all in the context of promoting a climate of peace that removes the latent threat of intervention in those processes.

- As one way to continue this process beyond the electoral context, there has been a need perceived to train citizens not only in the civic alternatives available in the country and their inescapable responsibility in this regard, but more especially in the avenues open to them to use their power as citizens in daily life. In this connection, numerous projects have been carried out in the field of political representation, education, justice, the control of corruption, and citizen safety. The same mandate was also felt to include firm support for processes of political and administrative decentralization, the creation of intermediary organizations, and the training of leaders, particularly among young people, women, indigenous peoples, the poorest, and among local or municipal officials.

5. Also highlighted was the increased awareness of the dramatic changes taking place in the State, in civil society, and in the relationship between the two. A number of institutions have made efforts to support this process by helping with study and training, but more particularly by facilitating meetings and relations in general among the different actors. There is a consensus today regarding the indissoluble relationship between the State and civil society. Accordingly, reform of the State must be built around the strengthening of civil society, with the latter's active participation as its linchpin.

6. In summary, there was consensus on the following basic points:

- The role of civil society consists of building channels of participation and empowering citizens to take full advantage of them.

- This calls for changes not only in the State but also in the way policy is made and in the structure of the parties and legislative bodies.

- One common denominator of our governments is the explosion of sector interests and demands in search of new institutional outlets.

- Although citizen participation is normally more effective when the sectors of civil society organize themselves, civic participation can take both individual and collective forms.

- The importance of education, especially at university level, should extend beyond its scientific and professional function and train agents with civic awareness, responsibility, and spirit.

7. Similarly, there was consensus that civil society acts as a repository for the following demands on the State and the political class:

- The restructuring and opening up of political parties to community and individual demands from the citizenry.

- A smaller State, but one that is more responsive, capable, sensitive, and amenable to social participation.

- Resizing of the constraints and challenges which the State faces in shaping new public policies that give preference to the values of the people, greater degrees of collaboration and decentralization, and increased institutionalization of the principles of transparency and accountability as a more reliable guarantee of effectiveness, respect for the autonomy of civil society, and effective curbs on corruption.

Socioeconomic Participation and Financing

1. As far as financing is concerned, building up the citizenry, which is the heart of the process of strengthening civil society, is predicated on political freedoms and on opportunities for meaningful entry into the economy. In the private enterprise sector, there are growing signs of a marked trend toward channeling resources to well-structured socioeconomic development projects and programs, provided that they are carried out by recognized civil society organizations, which, in order to achieve their goals, use well-designed management and financial practices. The institutions and the international community can support the process but cannot be a substitute for the domestic effort.

2. Latin America and the Caribbean have accumulated a wealth of important and successful experience in strengthening civil society. Some agencies have had a singular impact on civil society, starting with a clear vision of how to improve the quality of life of the least protected groups and to stimulate private sector participation in social issues. Many experiments have grown into modern entrepreneurial organizations in a cohesive private sector and have become leaders of a network of civil society organizations collaborating with a corporate conglomerate created to serve civil society. Examples include diversification of the activities of foundations at the national level, providing technical assistance, advice, training, institutional strengthening, contributions and grants, and delivering a broad range of financial services and products.

3. Without being exhaustive, the following common threads run through these successful experiences:

- A clear mission and objectives.

- Identification of solutions consistent with the actual conditions in which each institution operates.

- Response to an identified and quantified market.

- Having a stable and open macroeconomic situation that facilitates operations and provides confidence and predictability.

- Properly evaluating the risks pertinent to the country and the operating institution.

- Establishing an appropriate scale of operations, a sound administration, and a modern, efficient, and effective organization.

- Building a track record.

- Having a suitable legal and tax framework, for continuity, transparency, and accountability in the use of resources is key to maintaining confidence for both raising and using funds.

- Availability of technical assistance and training from qualified personnel paid at market rates and responsible beneficiaries.

4. There are lessons to be learned from the failures of organizations and funds in Latin America and the Caribbean that were wiped out by decapitalization due to major macroeconomic adjustments (inflation, devaluation), poor administrative management, and the granting of unnecessary subsidies, which undermined their ability to remain financially self-sustaining and curtailed their chances of becoming involved in the economy and thereby strengthening civil society. The group looking into IDB activity in the area of strengthening civil society appeared to have a range of views, but consensus centered around a vision of the IDB as an energizing force with the capacity to assemble the parties involved, provide both cohesion and financing, and play a key catalytic role through its ability to innovate.

5. Another of the topics discussed was the creation of a fund to finance civil society initiatives or some alternative system of special financing. Other suggestions: to extend the decentralization of the Bank so that the country offices have the capacity to address the civil society issue; to step up funding for

the small projects programs; and to foster changes in the country structure to facilitate the strengthening of civil society, etc. And, although there is not at present sufficient systematized information to support the immediate drafting of an action plan to devise new ways for governments, the private sector, and civil society proper to pool their efforts, there is a broad consensus on the expanded role that civil society needs to play in alleviating poverty and in socioeconomic development, especially in all areas affecting the lowest income groups in society.

6. It is interesting to point out that some of the successful experiments received financial support from the Bank, which helped to consolidate the institutions involved, whether through a combination of technical cooperation operations for small projects, microenterprise programs, or venture capital from the Corporation. For this reason, it makes sense to promote activities that make it easier to replicate the handful of cases which have mounted successful financing schemes and have demonstrated their purposefulness and commitment to diversifying into activities that have a practical impact on citizen-building.

7. In order for governments, private enterprise and civil society to forge effective partnerships in socioeconomic development activities, especially for purposes of carrying out poverty reduction programs and projects — there is a need to design effective mechanisms for channeling sizable volumes of resources in the form of loans and grants. Such instruments should provide a way to reach civil society organizations at both national and grassroots levels.

Regulatory and Institutional Framework

1. The process of accommodating civil society vis-à-vis the State is predicated on the existence of new and heterogeneous social sectors that are claiming operating room previously denied to them by an interventionist model which turned a blind eye to or — in the worst of cases — tried to sidetrack citizen participation of this kind. Forces now at work are bringing the two sectors together, and only those blind to the extent to which these two intrinsically compatible pillars of contemporary democracy are growing together can still argue that they are at odds with each other.

2. Setting the rules of the game within a constitutional, legal, and regulatory context was seen as an overarching issue because of its potential for either

facilitating or hindering progress in these outward manifestations of civil society. In the same vein, attention was drawn to the dominant role which the implementation and administration of normative mandates play in a scenario that is not confined to legislative reform alone. The potential of the law to generate immediate changes in society will ultimately depend both on the human element and how well people are trained and on how well what is prescribed in the laws is complied with and effectively implemented.

3. The search for transparency and uniformity when defining the rules of the game was identified as a prerequisite for stimulating the creation of citizen initiatives within civil society. If there is one thing that characterizes the regulatory field to date, it is its opaqueness with respect to the dissimilar requirements and conditions which each of the states imposes before organizations can become institutions. Many, if not most, of them, far from encouraging the formation of such organizations, stand as roadblocks. In spite of this, some states have begun to move toward constitutional recognition of the state's duty to contribute to the organization, promotion and empowerment of such institutional manifestations of civil society.

4. Notwithstanding the foregoing, a review of constitutional regulations reveals that in most cases there is no body of provisions that can accommodate the different activities of public and community interest that civil society puts forward. The paradigm of a state virtually immune to the efforts of these organizations has even prevented the need to compile a typology of them from being mooted, owing to the maintenance of constructs of private law that date back to Roman times but have now been overtaken by the imperatives of the altered circumstances.

5. Modern legal statutes capable of accommodating both new and old expressions of civil society are a prerequisite for moving ahead with the process of institutionalization. The growing involvement of these entities in processes of public and collective interest require not only that they be covered by the rules of law but also that they be classified in terms of such variables as their assets, radius of action, type of social goals pursued, etc. Naturally, this classification should be mainly for purposes of encouragement and promotion, although it should be borne in mind in some cases that certain checks and balances need to be introduced, not to hamper but to make it easier to respond effectively to the social objectives to which they are committed.

6. These same arrangements for the internal regulation of civil society organizations need to be reviewed so as to compile a record of comparative experience that will help to identify the major gaps and deficiencies that currently stand in the way of realistic prospects for funding. While still recognizing the plurality, heterogeneity, and diversity which are the hallmarks of these organizations, it is clear that assimilating experience from other countries can prove instrumental in pinpointing internal operating rules that will be conducive to their institutionalization and sound operation. The highly specific nature of many of these organizations cannot prevent the exchange of positive and negative experiences from opening the way and pointing to new avenues of action.

7. It is therefore essential to engage in a broad regional dialogue, initiated at this Conference by the IDB, as a basis for establishing the current situation in each country of the region with respect to the rules and regulations that currently govern civil society activities, while taking advantage of the experience and progress already made by some organizations in the comparative analysis of pertinent legislation. The improvement, rationalization, and modernization of this regulatory framework should flow from the public debate that must be encouraged from this point on. Although the chapter on tax incentives will be paramount in promoting and financing civil society organizations, it is also clear that the review of rules and regulations must also be expanded in scope to take in civil, administrative, and economic law, in order to explore how such regulations affect the creation, operation, and professional performance of those entities.

8. Careful analysis of the different legislative developments affecting civil society organizations will provide both the IDB and the organizations participating in this Conference with clear inputs for launching a wide-ranging diagnosis that will enable initiatives to be proposed for constitutional, legislative, and regulatory reform, taking into account the specific conditions in each state and the degree of development of the organizations. The fact, for example, that there is no study on "patronage laws," nor, for that matter, on tax rules designed to encourage the operation of institutions of community interest is one of the main constraints at this time on such a diagnosis.

9. In similar fashion, initiatives aimed at internal regulation and favored by organizations themselves cannot help but be germane to their own way of operating. Proposals for self-regulation mechanisms

made by the sectors involved will very often hold the potential to inhibit stifling intervention by the state if they are capable of demonstrating their effectiveness. Topics like the introduction of codes of internal conduct within organizations, specific rules on fund raising, provisions for incompetence, and incompatibility, etc. ought to be included right now on the list of concerns of anyone who wishes to take a forward-looking approach to potential conflicts to come.

10. Building a genuine concept of citizenship that is linked to the exercise of public duties and responsibilities going beyond philanthropy, in the narrowest sense of the term, must mean endowing the dull-sounding freedom of association with a new content that addresses the need for conceptual enrichment, reassurance, and practicality. Overcoming individualism as a solution to the problem of the paradigm of the modern state has thrust new protagonists onto the stage who are calling for fresh leadership. The emergence of collective rights within the context of "third generation rights" provides a very tangible framework of action for carrying on civil society activities. And the panoply of constitutional guarantees includes the one that is exercised when the time comes to verify whether the state, through the powers that be, is or is not truly serving the rights of its citizens.

11. Promoting the culture of social responsibility should be the product of institutionalizing civil society organizations. It is therefore hard to conceive of scenarios of democratic governance in which the rights of the citizens are not seen as inextricably linked to their duties and responsibilities to society. The sense of social and political responsibility has been whetted by the unstoppable force of a civil society which no longer has to seek permission from the state to tread the institutional stages of contemporary democracy.

12. The strategy of decentralization adopted by most countries in the region should be accompanied by the creation of meaningful operating room for civil society. Decentralization does not of itself provide any real guarantee for the strengthening of civil society organizations unless it occurs in tandem with reforms to the regulatory framework at the local level that not only permit but promote the creation of grassroots organizations and other communities of interests, within a context of strengthening local democracy. Checks and balances on this process from the grassroots level are also an irreplaceable complement.

13. The awakening of civil society to realities hitherto beyond its grasp is bound to have immediate practical results. Integrating new sectors into the new scenarios of democracy therefore means that new playing rules are needed. The growing presence of the so-called informal sectors in the region's economies means that appropriate spaces must be created to accommodate the equally new tools peculiar to citizen participation in a context of direct democracy. Legal ordinances cannot remain impervious to phenomena of social life which are ready to break away from the moorings of outmoded regulatory systems if these systems are not equal to the challenge of opening their doors to the new demands of democracy.

14. Democracy in the region has witnessed an "outbreak" by groups of citizens who had never before been able to exercise the right to participate but who are doing so today, not as passive recipients of the system's largesse but as active and demanding protagonists in a process that is being called upon to meet their demands. These demands spring from the grass roots of democracy in a context of local governance and the solution of local problems, but they cast their shadow beyond the territorial boundaries of the state to become intertwined today, and rightly so, with other supranational and regional phenomena, which already constitute real networks for the internationalization of local actors. In this as in other fields, the regional and subregional regulatory frameworks must also be counted among the integration processes that pervade the continent.

15. Similarly, a great deal of thought was given to the relationship between corruption and civil society, with attention focusing on the two-way relationship between the two. First, civil society bears the costs of corruption directly, whether those costs are economic (diversion of development resources), political (popular disaffection and weakening of the democratic regime), or social (spread of illegalities and cronyism). Second, where principles of accountability and transparency thrive, both in the state and in the civil society associations themselves, the result is a healthy climate conducive to development. By the same token, where these principles are lived up to, they guarantee the autonomy of those associations. It was emphasized that one of the ways to increase public transparency and responsibility is for the civil society associations to provide certain services that used traditionally to be state monopolies. This reportedly helps to enhance the competence, efficiency, and responsibility of those who provide such services.

16. Finally, looking to the future and to the close follow-up that needs to be given to the outcome of this Conference, it is worth mentioning a few possible lines of action. For example: the creation of data bases and information and communications systems, intended for use by the network of civil society organizations generated by this event, should be replicated at the regional, subregional, and state levels; the role of the universities and educational centers in promoting culture, civic education, and the dissemination of information in these areas; the inclusion of these new issues in the IDB's sector programs as the result of direct dialogue with interlocutors who come from those organizations and from civil society in general, etc. From the financial standpoint, the possibility should be explored of devising legal asset-management constructs, such as special funds and trusts, that will generate substantial flexibility when it comes to forming organizations to assist the most marginalized segments of society. Finally, to the extent that we are involved in an agglutinative rather than a fragmentary process, civil society issues need to be made a permanent part not only of the new themes of democracy but also of the operating processes and mechanisms that are created to bring about the changes which the continent is anxiously awaiting.

On the threshold of the twenty-first century, the commitment by the states and by the bilateral and multilateral agencies cannot be other than to usher in, through the wide portals of democracy, the paramount issue on the political agenda for the future.

Organization of American States

Inter-American Development Bank

United Nations Economic Commission for Latin America and the Caribbean

The Fight Against Poverty in the Hemispheric Agenda

November 30, 1994

The Organization of American States (OAS) is the world's oldest regional organization, dating back to the First International Conference of American States, held in Washington, D.C., from October 1889 to April 1890. The basic purposes of the OAS are as follow: to strengthen the peace and security of the continent; to promote and consolidate representative democracy, with due respect for the principle of nonintervention; to prevent possible causes of difficulties and to ensure the pacific settlement of disputes that may arise among the Member States; to provide for common action on the part of those States in the event of aggression; to seek the solution of political, juridical and economic problems that may arise among them; to promote, by cooperative action, their economic, social and cultural development; and to achieve an effective limitation of conventional weapons that will make it possible to devote the largest amount of resources to the economic and social development of the Member States.

The Inter-American Development Bank (IDB), the oldest and largest regional multilateral development institution, was established in December of 1959 to help accelerate economic and social development in Latin America and the Caribbean. The Bank was created in response to a longstanding desire on the part of the Latin American nations for a development institution that would focus on the pressing problems of the region. A resolution calling for the creation of such a bank was adopted at the First International American Conference, held in Washington, D.C. in 1890. In 1958, President Juscelino Kubitschek of Brazil proposed that the countries of the Hemisphere embark upon a bold cooperative effort to promote the economic and social development of the region. His proposal received support from throughout the Hemisphere, and shortly thereafter a special committee of the Organization of American States drafted the Articles of Agreement Establishing the Inter-American Development Bank. The Bank's Charter states that its principal functions are to utilize its own capital, funds raised by it in financial markets, and other available resources for financing the development of the borrowing member countries; to supplement private investment when private capital is not available on reasonable terms and conditions; and to provide technical assistance for the preparation, financing, and implementation of development plans and projects.

*The United Nations Economic Commission for Latin America was founded in 1948 to coordinate policies for the promotion of economic development in the region. In 1984, the title **Economic Commission for Latin America and the Caribbean (ECLAC)** was adopted. ECLAC* *normally meets every two years and has permanent bodies with various subcommittees. Its activities are undertaken in cooperation with regional governments and often with other UN agencies to analyze economic problems and formulate development plans. ECLAC has become involved in the issues of economic growth promotion by suggesting production pattern changes, educational reforms, and the reduction of poverty and social inequality.*

Table of Contents

EXECUTIVE SUMMARY

This document has been prepared in light of the upcoming Presidential Summit with the view of contributing to the formulation of an hemispheric agenda. Thus, its analysis and recommendations stress those aspects of poverty alleviation that can be addressed within an hemispheric context.

Poverty is the greatest challenge for the economies of Latin America and the Caribbean. Between 1980 and 1990 it worsened as a result of the crisis and the adjustment policies, wiping out most of the progress in poverty reduction achieved during the 1960s and 1970s. Recent estimates place the number of poor at the beginning of this decade, depending on the definition of poverty, somewhere between 130 and 196 million. While the incidence and severity of poverty remains greater in the rural areas, poverty is increasingly becoming an urban problem. By 1990 more than half of the poor lived in urban areas.

Closely linked to poverty is inequality. Recession and adjustment in the 1980s also increased income inequality in most of the region. In the countries with the most highly concentrated income distribution, the richest 10% of households receive 40% of total income.

While there are no set formulas that can be applied to any country to eliminate poverty, there are three key elements that need to be part of any policy framework to successfully address the problem. These are growth, investment in people, and reforms.

Economic growth is a necessary condition to sustain poverty reduction. It should be central to any effort to reduce poverty. Without growth it will be very difficult to achieve greater equity. Past experience of growth with inequality has taught the region that growth and greater equity should be addressed simultaneously, by selecting policies that strengthen their complementarity and reduce trade-offs between both of these major objectives.

Faster growth will require higher levels of savings and investment, better allocation of resources and increased levels of productivity. A stable macroeconomic environment and increasing access to international markets will also be required for more dynamic growth. According to the World Bank, the region must grow at an annual rate of about 6.5% for the rest of the decade in order to achieve significant poverty reduction.

Investments in people are a second key element in fighting poverty. They are crucial for poverty alleviation and the achievement of greater equity and eventually contribute to sustain growth. Investments in education and training are essential to expand social opportunities, speed technological change, and train for jobs necessary to compete in the international economy. Parallel efforts also need to be made to ensure that there is equitable access to more and better health care and improved nutrition for the poor.

Since women spend more of their income on their families, investment to increase their productivity and income will contribute significantly to sustained poverty alleviation. Such investments will also be an effective way of blocking the intergenerational transmission of poverty.

Reforms required to ensure that the needs of the poor are given priority constitute the third key element for poverty reduction. The fiscal systems need to be made more equitable, without losing sight of the goals of efficiency, simplicity and revenue sufficiency. Reforms should also be introduced to remove obstacles that impede the poor from acquiring and accumulating capital. Among such efforts should be reforms in financial and capital markets that introduce innovative ways to overcome the problem of inadequate loan guarantees and promote savings, as well as reforms in land markets that will regularize titles, tax land on the basis of its production value, and introduce systems that facilitate land purchases by the poor.

The Summit participants could agree to formulate national agendas that, while being country-specific, could include the following three specific benchmark targets:

1) To reduce poverty by one-third during the next ten years. For this purpose economic growth has to accelerate so that employment growth is proportionately greater than that of the labor force.

2) To increase the share of public outlays devoted to investment in people, through enhanced basic education, health and nutrition for the poor, particularly children, women, and indigenous people.

3) To carry out reforms in the rest of the decade that improve and modernize fiscal policies, tax systems, and labor, land and capital markets.

Finally, the Summit should summon hemispheric and international organizations to support the Latin American and Caribbean countries in their efforts to reduce poverty and meet the stated targets.

I. INTRODUCTION

1. The economies of Latin America and the Caribbean have regained moderate growth in the past few years. As a result of the adjustment policies and reforms implemented, the countries of the region have been gradually changing the bases on which their economies function. Most of the economies are expanding moderately, with relative price stability, in the context of progress toward pluralist and participative societies.

2. Today, the countries of the region are in a much better position than they were at the beginning of the decade to launch a frontal attack on the main blemish that darkens this progress. Poverty is the greatest challenge found in the region's path leading to development for all.

3. There are no general formulas to fight poverty that can be applied to any country. Each will have to choose a specific combination of policies and areas of priority. But in a broad sense—as this paper highlights—there are common elements and actions in any useful approach to fight poverty and inequality. To succeed, such an approach will demand a strong commitment by individuals and social groups, by governments, and by the international community.

II. POVERTY IN THE WESTERN HEMISPHERE

4. In the early 1980s, after three and a half decades of sustained economic and social change, the living conditions of vast sectors of Latin American and Caribbean societies had improved. Still, a large share of the population—perhaps as many as 40%—were living in poverty, although their education, health, and income were better than 30 years before. Subsequently, economic and social setbacks contributed to an increase in poverty and to a marked deterioration of income distribution.

5. The most recent estimates indicate that at the end of the 1980s somewhere between 130 million and 196 million people in Latin America, or between 31% and 46% of the population, were poor, depending on the definition of poverty. But regardless of how it is

defined, poverty increased greatly between 1980 and 1990, wiping out most of the progress in poverty reduction achieved during the 1960s and 1970s.

6. Even though the incidence and severity of poverty remains greater in rural areas, the major part of the increase in poverty over the 1980s was urban. By 1990 more than half of the poor were urban—in sharp contrast to the situation in 1980—making poverty in Latin America an increasingly urban problem.

7. Latin America has one of the most inequitable distributions of income in the world. Recession and adjustment in the 1980s made the situation even worse. The gap between the incomes of the poorest 40% of households and the richest 10% widened during the 1980s. The top decile receives over 40% of the total income in the countries with the most highly concentrated income distribution patterns and slightly less than 30% in only two cases. Also, a sharp decline in both real wages and employment opportunities in most countries had a particularly strong impact on the unskilled and those at the bottom of the income pyramid. The overall result was a significant increase in income inequality in most countries in the region.

8. Poverty and inequality are major concerns not only in Latin America and the Caribbean but also in Canada and the United States.

III. KEY ELEMENTS FOR POVERTY REDUCTION

9. Growth, investment in people, and reforms are three key elements of a successful approach to poverty reduction. These elements are compatible, they are interdependent, and they can be mutually supportive. Growth and poverty alleviation can be pursued simultaneously through policies that strengthen their complementarity and mitigate trade-offs. This demands investing in people to increase their human capital and implementing reforms to ensure that the benefits of growth are widely shared.

Growth

10. Economic growth is a necessary condition to sustain poverty reduction. In effect, it is at the core of any effective strategy to this end. Without growth it is extremely difficult to achieve greater equity. Without growth it will not be possible to generate the jobs essential for poverty reduction or the fiscal revenues to pay for basic social services that benefit the poor.

The World Bank estimates that, in order to make a dent in poverty levels, the region must double its economic growth rate to about 6.5% a year for the rest of the decade. In fact, the region must grow by at least 3.4% a year just to keep poverty from increasing.[1]

11. As is suggested by the experience of Latin America and the Caribbean during the postwar period, which was characterized by a combination of dynamic growth and inequality, the type of growth is crucially important. Growth and equity can be promoted simultaneously through policies that emphasize complementarity and reduce trade-offs.

12. The poverty impact of economic growth can vary greatly depending on its sectoral composition and changes in inputs within sectors—especially the share of lower skilled labor. There is no greater engine for reducing poverty over the medium term in most of the countries than the expansion of jobs and eventually the productivity and wages for lower skilled labor who are typically the poor.

13. Raising savings and investment, improving resource allocation and increasing productivity are major levers for speeding growth. These are in turn related to other important objectives, such as increasing exports with high value-added content, which requires increased access to international markets.

14. Faster growth with greater social equity in Latin America and the Caribbean will require a stable macroeconomic environment and a sustained expansion of exports. Both are crucial to prevent the regressive distributive effects of inflation and promote the creation of employment opportunities, especially for the poor.

15. Higher investment and saving ratios are also necessary. In 1993, for instance, investment in Latin America was on average 18.5% of gross domestic product (GDP), relatively low when compared to the investment rates of the 1970s and early 1980s.

16. Increasing the rate of investment to support faster progress in the long term involves a substantial expansion of savings. For example, the Economic Commission for Latin America and the Caribbean (ECLAC) has estimated that increasing the investment rate from 16% to 22% of GDP requires resources of over $70 billion per year for the region as a whole.[2] In this regard, the net external capital flowing into the region in recent years — which amounted to $55 billion in 1993 — has been an essential factor in the recovery of the region and will have to continue.

---

[1] World Bank, "Latin America's Development: Achievements, Challenges and Opportunities," September 27, 1994.

[2] ECLAC, Changing Production Patterns with Social Equity, LC/G.1601(SES.23/4), Santiago, Chile, 1990, p.49.

17. Regardless of the extent of availability of external financing, the bulk of additional growth will require higher domestic savings to raise overall investment.

Investment in People

18. Investment in education and training is of prime importance to promote social equity as well as growth based on technical progress, since this requires a population capable of absorbing and adapting to technological change.[3] The changes at the global level require that the Latin American and Caribbean educational systems train students for jobs required by an internationally competitive economy, foster technological change, expand social opportunities, and prepare people for a democratic citizenship.

19. Nowhere in Latin America and the Caribbean are all these educational demands being fully met. While more children than ever before attend school, the quality and value of the education they receive is inadequate in most countries. Only half the students who begin primary school complete it. The educational system is incapable of meeting the needs of development and leads to inequity and differentiation. The quality of education (and training) varies enormously, ranging from world class schools and universities, attended mainly by students from higher income families, to ill-equipped, inadequately staffed, and otherwise miserable public schools for the children of the poor. The administration of public education tends to be overly centralized and bureaucratic, hampering efficiency and responsiveness to local needs. Administrative and institutional reforms, possibly radical in many instances, are warranted, emphasizing greater participation, autonomy, and responsibility at the provincial and municipal levels.

20. New strategies are needed to improve the quality, efficiency, and relevance of education and training. The goal should be to transform educational and training systems to ensure that everyone has access to modern education, giving priority to poor children and aligning education with the skills required to compete in the world economy. Individuals deprived of good basic education in their youth are condemned to a life of low productivity work outside the sphere of modern production and thus low income or outright poverty. This is a major gear driving intergenerational poverty. As the performance of education systems, or parts of them, approaches acceptable norms, many countries would enhance their development prospects by increasing the share of national income devoted to education.

21. As a consequence of demographic and epidemiological transitions in a context of significant income inequality, health conditions and demands for services are characterized by the emergence of a health profile similar to that of developed societies in the urban middle and upper socioeconomic categories and the maintenance of a traditional underdeveloped health profile among the poor. As a result, increased spending and investment in health do not necessarily represent an improvement in equity of access to health care. On the other hand, these actions are often regressive because they result from economic pressure brought to bear by the population covered by health insurance (private or public) for modern health services (medical specialties, clinical services, etc.).

22. Health care reforms are needed to achieve more equitable access to publicly funded health services and greater efficiency in resource use, including more effective health interventions. Governments need to do more to deliver services to the poor through a package of basic and progressively extended health care. Together with far more emphasis on preventive health interventions, such strategies would improve the well-being of the poor, raise their productivity and thereby their income, and thus reduce poverty.[4]

23. Investments that support individual decisions on reproductive patterns are crucial to poverty alleviation and overcoming inequity, since one element of the intergenerational transmission of poverty is the predominance of high fertility rates. In addition to expanding educational and work opportunities for young women and increasing health services, the promotion of greater and more equitable access to family planning, and the enhancement of nutritional program coverage for children will contribute to improving the chances of poor families to escape the vicious circle of poverty and, in particular, the chances that poor children will not have to replicate their parents' social and living patterns.[5]

---

3 ECLAC and UNESCO, *Education and Knowledge: Basic Pillars of Changing Production Patterns with Social Equity*, LC/G.1702/Rev.1-P, Santiago, Chile, 1992.

4 ECLAC and PAHO, *Health. Social Equity and Changing Production Patterns in Latin America and the Caribbean*, LC/G.1813(SES.25/18), Santiago, Chile, 1994.

5 ECLAC, *Population... Social Equity and Changing Production Patterns*, LC/DEM/G.131, Santiago, Chile, 1993.

24. In reducing poverty, women play a fundamental role. Investments in women are vital to growth and poverty alleviation as they pay off in terms of greater economic benefits and better prospects for the children. Investing in women leads to improvements in children's health and education, thus also contributing to the avoidance of the intergenerational transmission of poverty.

25. Providing access to continuing education and training to women in the labor market (including both the "informal" and the "formal" sectors, wage earners and the self-employed) deserves special attention in most countries. Compared to men, women spend more of their income on outlays that enhance their family's human capital. It is therefore crucial for sustained poverty reduction to increase women's education and income. In addition to providing more education and training opportunities, and incentives for exercising them, the goal of raising women's income would be furthered by improving the overall economic, social, and legal environment bearing on women's access to resources. Such improvements are essential for addressing women's needs and, since Latin American and Caribbean women are disproportionately poor, reducing overall poverty.

26. The indigenous peoples of Latin America account for almost 10% of the region's population and in some countries their share exceeds 50%. Poverty among them is pervasive and severe.[6] Most indigenous people live in conditions of extreme poverty, they have less education than non-indigenous people, and they suffer from severe health problems. Thus, policies focused on strengthening their human capital and reducing the educational gaps between indigenous and non-indigenous people tend to reduce earnings differentials and poverty.

27. To alleviate the social costs of the crisis of the 1980s and the adjustment policies, and as a means of decentralizing and expediting governmental action, a series of innovative mechanisms were created in many of the countries of Latin America and the Caribbean. The Social Investment, Compensation and Emergency Funds and other mechanisms were designed to offset or lessen conditions of extreme poverty and meet demands originating from groups of potential beneficiaries. Their experience in channeling resources for the execution of projects addressed to the very poor, building basic social infrastructure, supporting grassroots organizations, community participation, employment creation, and increasing household incomes has been systematized in a Social Network of Funds and other Programs that merit consideration and support.

Reforms

28. For poverty reduction to be sustainable, it has to be supported by reforms ensuring that the needs of the poor are not displaced by the interests of those with greater decision-making power. First, fiscal systems require a more equitable orientation, without losing sight of the goals of efficiency, simplicity and revenue sufficiency. Public sector finances need to be consolidated on the basis of a reasonable level of revenue, rather than through mere reductions of expenditure regardless of the circumstances. There is room for improving the vertical and horizontal equity of the tax systems of many countries without adversely affecting incentives by raising the effective tax burden and by securing greater effective progressivity of the corresponding tax structure.

29. This requires a broadening of the tax base coupled with a serious and permanent decision, taken at the highest national and subnational political levels, to reduce tax evasion and institutionalize a culture of compliance with the tax code. Tax administrations should be given all necessary means to enforce the statutory tax burden and the legislated progressivity. To that end, it would be advisable to make them independent of political cycles and influences.

30. Reforms on the revenue side should be complemented by a restructuring of public expenditures. This calls for reallocating outlays towards basic social services, especially those that directly contribute to developing the human capital of the poor, cutting unproductive expenditures, and improving the efficacy of the rest. To be sustainable, such changes in public spending patterns, both across and within sectors, require shifting social and political priorities towards activities that promote equity as well as growth. Increasing the efficacy of public expenditures on social projects and programs will require, among other things, that benefits be better targeted to the neediest groups.

31. The allocation of public expenditures can be improved in yet other ways. For instance, in many countries military spending remains excessive relative to social outlays benefiting the poor. There is also

---

[6] George Psacharopoulos and Harry Anthony Patrinos, editors, *Indigenous People and Poverty in Latin America*, World Bank, 1994.

great potential for supporting the neediest groups through intersectoral reallocations. For example, the poor can benefit from a greater emphasis on improved primary health care financed by shifting resources from expensive curative health care to preventive medicine, which increases efficacy in health delivery. In the education sector, financial resources can be shifted from subsidizing university education regardless of need or academic merit to primary and secondary education, where the rates of return are greater and benefits will more directly accrue to children from lower-income families.

32. Another important way to strengthen public finances while increasing the efficiency and equity of the system is by improving social security and transfer programs. Not only are many of them grossly inefficient and inequitable, particularly those that entail the delivery of health services, but most social security institutions are also insolvent. A promising approach to social security reform entails a mixed system that fosters equity and financial solvency. A version of this approach features a universal component of basic benefits financed from general resources and predicated on social solidarity. Another component apportions benefits according to the amounts contributed by each individual. Reforms should address these crippling problems while seeking to expand coverage to the neediest sectors who receive very few benefits.

33. A sustained reduction in poverty and greater equity also require actions that improve and complement markets with the objective of enabling the poor to accumulate capital. In particular, improving the operation of labor markets involves the modernization of labor relations, including the exploring of innovative ways of paying for work.

34. Reforms in financial and capital markets demand that mechanisms be devised to remove obstacles that prevent access to resources, especially access to credit by small enterprises. This is essential to promote savings as well as establishing new rules for institutional saving, including the improvement of pension systems.

35. Another area to be looked at for promoting growth with poverty reduction and greater equity is the functioning of the land market. Land tenure in Latin America is much more concentrated than in most other regions in the world.[7] Key elements to improve the land market are regularizing land titles where this is a problem and, as appropriate, taxing land on the basis of its production value, and improving capital markets to finance land acquisition.

36. Finally, most of the reforms discussed in this document that would improve the lot of the poor in Latin America and the Caribbean are unlikely to be implemented or sustained where the poor continue to be systematically excluded from economic, social, and political decisions affecting them. Designing and implementing on a sustained basis policies and reforms to address the problems of the poor are impossible without their effective participation in the political process. Broad participation also enhances the ability of governments to respond to social concerns. In democratic processes, reforms to ensure more equitable sharing of the fruits of growth will call for consensus-building and the collaboration of powerful groups of society.

IV. TOWARD POVERTY REDUCTION

37. The Summit of the Americas provides an opportunity for the Heads of State to jointly reaffirm the pre-eminence of the goal of significantly accelerating poverty reduction in the Western Hemisphere. The intent is to point out the elements of a policy framework to deal with the challenge through the agreement on certain benchmark targets.

Elements of a Policy Framework

38. 1) Sustained poverty reduction is impossible without faster and more equitably shared economic growth, greatly enhanced investment in people, and institutional reform.

2) While significant amounts of foreign capital are needed to achieve the more ambitious growth targets, domestic savings must increase substantially. To foster higher savings and investment, and to increase equity, the fiscal systems in most countries need substantial reform and more importantly, major improvements in enforcing the law.

3) To propel faster growth, enhanced investment in people should focus on improving the health and nutrition and the education and training of the young. In practice, this implies greatly improving the performance of the public agencies responsible for ensuring social services to the lower-income groups.

4) To block the intergenerational transmission of poverty among the most deprived families,

---

7 ECLAC, *Social Equity and Changing Production Patterns: An Integrated Approach,* LC/G.1701 (SES.24/3), Santiago, Chile, 1992, p. 179.

in addition to alleviating their poverty in the short run, attention should largely focus on mother-child health and nutrition among the poorest households and on the access to and subsequent quality of education of these children.

5) Because they are disproportionately poor, single parent households headed by women as well as indigenous people deserve special attention in the poverty reduction strategy.

6) At a time when the public sector is being downsized, the collective commitment to fight poverty demands efficient and effective public actions. Besides fostering human capital accumulation among the poor, it is also important to remove labor market imperfections and obstacles to the fair access to credit and accumulation of assets. This can be accomplished through reform of the institutions bearing on the capital and land markets.

7) Unless there is a national consensus among key social, political, and economic groups in support of a coherent strategy for poverty reduction, it is unlikely that the effort will be sustained for very long. Also, unless the poor participate in its design and implementation, the strategy is unlikely to be effective. Empowerment of the poor to solve their own problems forms part of any poverty-reducing strategy.

Progress Targets

39. Summit participants could agree to actively promote the national consensus and participatory work towards the formulation of an operational national agenda to accelerate poverty reduction. These national agendas, while being country-specific, could include time-bound and quantifiable commitments in the form of the following specific benchmark targets.

1) To reduce poverty by one-third during the next ten years. For this purpose, economic growth has to accelerate so that employment growth is proportionately greater than that of the labor force.

2) To increase the share of public outlays devoted to investment in people, through enhanced basic education, health and nutri-

tion for the poor, particularly children, women, and indigenous people.

3) To carry out reforms in the rest of the decade that improve and modernize fiscal policies, tax systems, and labor, land and capital markets.

Institutional Support

40. The Summit should summon hemispheric and international organizations to support national efforts to strive towards the poverty-reduction goal and meet the stated targets. Summit leaders could:

1) Reaffirm the Inter-American Development Bank's (IDB) mandate to increase the share of lending to improve social conditions and reduce inequities in Latin America and the Caribbean and to provide special support to social programs in such areas as health, education and microenterprise development.

2) Request a continuation of ECLAC's efforts in the understanding and measurement of poverty in the region as well as in incorporating the social dimension into the formulation of development policies.

3) Ask the Organization of American States (OAS) to further its support in the operation of the Latin American and Caribbean Social Network as a mechanism of horizontal cooperation between countries and in the areas of poverty, youth skills training, and promotion of small and micro enterprises.

4) Request the continued assistance of the Pan American Health Organization (PAHO) in the area of health, including disease control, food and nutrition surveillance, water supply and sanitation.

41. Finally, Summit leaders could pledge that regular meetings be held in order to monitor the progress achieved and examine the needs for external support. A forum for such meetings could be the OAS, with technical support provided by the IDB, ECLAC, and PAHO.

Sponsored jointly by the Inter-American Development Bank and the United Nations Development Programme

The Inter-American Development Bank (IDB), the oldest and largest regional multilateral development institution, was established in December of 1959 to help accelerate economic and social development in Latin America and the Caribbean.

The United Nations Development Programme (UNDP), the world's largest multilateral source of grant funding for development cooperation, was established in 1965 by the United Nations General Assembly to help developing countries foster their economic growth.

Our Common Agenda for the Americas: A Report of the Latin American and Caribbean Commission on Development and Environment

In recognition that the Summit of the Americas presents a momentous opportunity to usher in a new era in hemispheric relations, it is with great satisfaction that we present this report of the Latin American and Caribbean Commission on Development and Environment. The Commission was established in 1988 as an independent advisory group under the auspices of the United Nations Development Programme and the Inter-American Development Bank. The work of the Commission is based on the conviction that humanity must renew its pledge of global solidarity to ensure a balance between developing countries' priorities — to combat poverty and foster economic development — and environmental priorities which are of worldwide concern. As a contribution to the 1992 Earth Summit, the Commission published "Our Own Agenda," which appealed for dramatic changes in the development patterns of all countries of the Americas. A second Commission report, "Amazonia Without Myths," represents the vast consensus and will to improve the conditions among the people of Amazonia while protecting this magnificent ecosystem. "Our Common Agenda for the Americas" is the culmination of an eight-month-long process that engaged Commission members, governments, experts, grass roots, national, and international NGOs throughout the hemisphere. The process began with a February 1994 meeting which brought together leading political and intellectual figures from the Americas to discuss an agenda for substantive decisions at the Summit. A working draft of "Our Common Agenda for the Americas" was then presented as the centerpiece of discussions at broad-based national and subregional meetings. This process culminated in an August 1994 Commission meeting during which the members supported this document as a substantial contribution to the Summit and to the follow-up activities which will extend into the next millennium.

Enrique V. Iglesias
President,
Inter-American Development Bank

Fernando Zumbado
Regional Director,
Latin American and the
Caribbean, United Nations
Development Programme

THE LATIN AMERICAN AND CARIBBEAN COMMISSION ON DEVELOPMENT AND ENVIRONMENT

Members

Mr. Oscar Arias, former President of Costa Rica

Mr. Manuel Arango Arias, Chairman of the Mexican Foundation for Environmental Education

Mr. Arnoldo Gabaldón, former Senator of Venezuela

Mr. José Goldemberg, former Minister of Science and Technology, Brazil

Mr. Oswaldo Hurtado, former President of Ecuador

Mr. Jaime Lerner, former Mayor of Curitiba, Brazil

Mr. Miguel de la Madrid, former President of Mexico

Ms. Margarita Marino de Botero, Director of the Green College, Colombia

Ms. Rigoberta Menchu, Nobel Peace Prize Winner, Guatemala

Mr. Misael Pastrana, former President of Colombia

Mr. Javier Pérez de Cuéllar, former Secretary General of the United Nations, Peru

Mr. Augusto Ramírez Ocampo, former Regional Director for Latin America and the Caribbean, UNDP

Mr. Shridath Ramphal, former Secretary General of the Commonwealth; former Foreign Minister of Guyana

Mr. Domingo Santa María, President of the Development Bank of Chile

Mr. José Sarney, former President of Brazil

Mr. Jorge Terena, Director for the IFAD/CAF Programme in Support of Indigenous People in the Amazon

Mr. Patterson A. Thompson, Executive Director, Caribbean Association of Industry and Commerce, Barbados

Editorial Contributors

Deborah Bleviss, President, International Institute for Energy Conservation

Antonio Brack, Ph.D., Project Coordinator, GEF Amazonia Project

Alvaro Camacho, PAHO

René Cortázar, Ph.D., CIEPLAN, Santiago, Chile

Leandro Despouy, Ph.D., Human Rights Specialist

Rodrigo Gamez Ph.D., Executive Director, INBio

José Goldemberg, Ph.D., Professor, São Paulo University

Francisco J. Gutiérrez Ph.D., Executive Secretary, OLADE

Raúl Hinojosa, Ph.D., Visiting Scholar, IDB

Thomas Lovejoy, Ph.D., Deputy Director, Smithsonian Institution

Guillermo O'Donnell, Ph.D., International Affairs Academic Director, University of Notre Dame

Maria Tereza Jorge Padua, Ph.D., FUNATURA/Conservation International

Theodore Panayotou, Ph.D., Harvard University

Walter Reid, Ph.D., Vice President for Programs, WRI

Ronald Sprout, Ph.D., Trinity College, Washington, D.C.

Carlos Suárez, Director, Bariloche Foundation

Coordination and Editing

Emma Torres, Chief, Division for the Regional Program, Regional Bureau for Latin America and the Caribbean, UNDP, (212) 906-5408

James C. McGowan, UNDP Consultant on Environment and Development

We are grateful to the many individuals who have contributed important ideas to this document. We wish to thank especially the following people who assisted our efforts in focusing on crucial hemispheric issues at the beginning of the document development process:

Walter Arensberg, Executive Director, CIDE, WRI

John Biehl del Río, Chilean Ambassador to the United States

Deborah Bleviss, President, International Institute for Energy Conservation

Janet Welsh Brown, Senior Fellow, WRI

Jorge Castenada, Professor of Political Science, UNAM

Marc Dourojeamii, Chief, ENV/PRA, IDB

Arnoldo Gabaldón, fomer Senator, Director, Presidential Commission for State Reform, Venezuela

José Goldemberg, former Minister of Science and Technology, Brazil

Michael Gucovsky, Interim Coordinator, GEF/UNDP

Israel Klabin, President, Brazilian Foundation for Sustainable Development

Anton Kruiderink, Deputy Director, RBLAC/UNDP

Felipe Larrain, Professor, Economics Institute, Pontificia Universidad Católica, Chile

James Lemoyne, UNDP/RBLAC Special Advisor on Central America

Russell Mittermeier, President, Conservation International

Fernando Naranjo, Foreign Minister, Costa Rica

Hugo Navajas-Mogro, former Regional Director, UNDP/RBLAC

David Runnals, Senior Policy Advisor, IDRC, Canada

Jeffrey Sachs, Economist and Professor, Harvard University

Oscar Serrate, Advisor, Project for Sustainable Development, Bolivia

Patricio Silva, former Chilean Ambassador to the United States

James G. Speth, Administrator, UNDP

Emma Torres, Chief, Division for the Regional Programme, RBLAC/UNDP

Sarah Timpson, Deputy Administrator, BPPE/UNDP

Alvaro Umana, former Minister of Natural Resources, Costa Rica

Fernando Zumbado, Regional Director, UNDP/RBLAC

Table of Contents

The views and opinions expressed herein do not necessarily represent the official positions of the Inter-American Development Bank or the United Nations Development Programme.

I. EXECUTIVE SUMMARY

The Summit of the Americas will be the first congress of Western Hemisphere countries since 1967. It presents a historic opportunity to initiate a new spirit of cooperation among the countries of Latin America, North America, and the Caribbean. As an independent advisory group dedicated to advancing sustainable human development throughout the region, the Latin American and Caribbean Commission on Development and Environment offers this document as a contribution to the success of the Summit and to hemispheric solidarity for the pursuit of sustainable development.

The Americas: A New Reality

People of the Americas are full of hope as the dawn of the new post-Cold War era brightens the horizon. After a long period of authoritarian governments, democracy has returned to almost all of our countries. After long years in which the Latin American economies suffered from economic stagnation and runaway inflation, most countries have brought their inflation rates under control, and today the region has the second fastest growing economy in the world.

The re-establishment of democracy was possible through great personal sacrifices on the part of millions of citizens and leaders who made coexistence, cooperation, and consensus building the first priorities. The economic gains of today are the fruit of sweeping, and often painful, economic adjustments and reforms that reduced deficits, liberalized international trade and investment, and produced many other changes that are examples of the technical and political effectiveness of the new Latin American democracies.

The Shared Goal of Sustainable Human Development in the Americas

These important advances allow us to face the future challenges of the Americas with confidence. To embrace the 21st century with a new spirit of hemispheric cooperation and solidarity, many detrimental aspects that remain part of our present realities need to be addressed through new initiatives. Consumption patterns in the North continue to affect the environmental and social conditions in the South. All countries must work to perfect their democratic systems of government and raise the quality of governmental services. All countries must confront poverty and social inequality with commitments that are backed by political resolve. We can no longer afford the current rate of environmental degradation, and we must affirm the need to manage the environment in ways that will assure a better quality of life for both the present generation and for those generations to come. The transcontinental dimensions of immigration and population pressures require greater attention to the regional impacts on the global challenges of today. The concept of sustainable human development integrates the many dimensions of development needed for attaining a better quality of life. It is human-centered development because it promotes economic growth with equity, nondiscrimination, and broad access to basic services and governmental decisionmaking. It is environmentally sustainable because it seeks a balance in the utilization of natural resources that will preserve the resource base as a heritage for future generations. It is development that will stabilize growth patterns over the long term and soften cyclical effects such as stagnation that produce frustration and hopelessness. Growth that benefits just a few will ultimately be rejected and reversed by the larger population. Only equitable and participatory development can foster the social legitimacy that will allow policy reforms to be politically and economically self-sustaining.

Therefore, we believe that the concept of sustainable human development could be the guiding criteria for discussions at the Summit and provide the operating principle for any proposals that result from the Summit.

Our Common Agenda for the Americas

The following initiatives are priorities for sustainable human development in the Americas:

1. The Promotion of Economic and Social Equity, Trade, and Investment in the Region

To confront decisively the conditions that trap millions of people in a cycle of malnourishment, disease, illiteracy, and destitution, a ten-year plan to reduce poverty must be formulated that includes a specific focus on assistance to women and raising children out of poverty. Educational systems need to be reformed to open opportunities for the marginalized and to meet the competitive challenges of the global marketplace.

Participants in the Summit of the Americas must send forth the clear message that sustainable development requires the consolidation of a new and mutually beneficial trading and investment relationship between our countries. International trade and investment could be powerful instruments for sustainable human development if certain preconditions are met, including the incorporation of environmental costs into the prices of commodities and products, the elimination of subsidies and tariffs, and the improvement of standards throughout the hemisphere. For sustained growth, it is vital to provide a viable financial and technological platform for small businesses which generate most new jobs and employ a large segment of the work force.

2. The Consolidation of Democracy and the Reconstruction of Government

A basic consensus must be cultivated among the main social and political components to develop strong support for sustainable human development strategies. One important development internal to countries of the region in recent years has been the awakening of an active citizenry. Further efforts must be made to foster this movement and to decentralize government to the local level so that it becomes more responsive to the needs of citizens.

Modernization of the state apparatus is needed through increasing the technical support for parliaments, strengthening of the judicial systems and social service agencies, reforming government institutions, and enhancing coordination among the different branches of government, particularly between the branches that develop social, economic, and environmental policies. The renewal of effective governmental functioning is a prerequisite for confronting many urgent problems such as inequity, corruption, arms trafficking, the drug trade, and human rights infringements — especially those involving indigenous people. As the basis for a "Culture of Peace" in the Americas, Summit participants must make a firm commitment to curtail strictly the sales of conventional arms throughout the region.

3. The Sustainable Management of Natural Resources and the Environment

Many new policies need to be instituted and existing ones reformed for the sustainable management of nonrenewable resources and the fight against pollution. One major step forward would be for the private sector to assume the costs associated with the contamination it generates and the nonrenewable resources it consumes. Also, incentives should be provided for the adoption of environmentally friendly technologies.

All countries need to develop their capacity to study, sustainably utilize, and appreciate their heritage of biodiversity. Local communities should be empowered with rights and economic rewards adequate to protect the biodiversity under their guardianship, and codes of conduct and policies need to be developed regarding the use of genetic resources. As the storehouse of these resources, and the supplier of goods and services such as clean water and carbon dioxide (CO_2) fixation, greater attention must be paid to the proper management of the hemisphere's extensive network of protected areas.

4. Energy Efficiency and Clean Energy Development

Energy efficiency and clean energy development activate economic growth while reducing impacts to the local and global environments. New energy investments must focus on demand-side management, energy-efficient transportation, urban planning, and renewable energy technologies. Another priority is the elimination of discriminatory trade practices that are now permitting the export of energy-inefficient vehicles and appliances that do not meet their own national standards.

5. Financing Sustainable Human Development in the Americas

Multilateral funds need to be redeployed and reinforced and the energies of the private sector catalyzed to finance integration and sustainable human development in the Americas. A number of strategies could be pursued simultaneously at the national level including the reform of fiscal policies to change incentive structures, the elimination of wasteful subsidies, reductions in armaments spending, enforcement of the "polluter pays" principle, and the further decentralization of taxation and government. At the international level, resources must be mobilized to improve coordination, communication, and exchange among countries and societies of the Americas. Over the long term, hemispheric integration may require special financing mechanisms designed to assist sectors of the population that are particularly affected by economic changes.

Sustainable Human Development: Mechanisms for Cooperation and Interchange

The definition of common goals shared by all countries of the Americas will promote interchange and cooperation among our countries. In order for the Summit's joint statement to be effective, it should include not only the definition of common criteria and shared priorities but also the definition of a program that provides an effective mechanism for future exchange and cooperation. We believe that such a program should have two types of activities:

1. A permanent mechanism for coordination among governments. Countries' foreign offices and international organizations (UNDP, OAS, IDB, and others) could build upon their vast experience in our region and contribute to this mechanism. The principal matters addressed would include the security and commercial relationships among countries and activities that produce environmental impacts beyond national borders.

2. A mechanism for exchange and cooperation among countries and societies. The challenge of sustainable human development for the countries of the region extends beyond governmental responsibilities to include our societies at large. The private sector, educational systems, groups working to prevent violence, corruption, and drug abuse, and environmental NGOs are a few of the many social actors that would benefit greatly from enhanced cooperation and exchange. However, no effective mechanisms currently exist to facilitate such activity at the regional level.

A Program for Exchange and Cooperation Among the Americas

The fact that the Western Hemisphere is a heterogeneous region (which is normally a problem for international treaties) offers great possibilities provided that each country shares its specific strengths with the others through exchange and cooperation. The *Sustainable Development Program for the Americas* would make possible:

1. Visits by delegations of social and political leaders to a country that has been successful in a specific area. For example, a delegation of union and business leaders or a group of parliament members could visit a country that has reformed its social security system, created successful regulatory frameworks, transferred environmental technologies, or decentralized governmental decisionmaking.

2. Workshops, conferences, and seminars could be formulated at the local level, with emphasis on the participation of the different sectors of society that are affected by particular issues.

3. Exchange programs, joint research, and other similar partnerships and activities would be promoted in the fields of judicial systems, municipal government, trade and investment, environmental affairs, indigenous community issues, regulatory institutions, health care, education, urban planning, and the many other founding principles necessary for a successful society.

This proposal recognizes that areas where change is needed vary from country to country and that different countries will proceed at different paces and along different paths toward sustainable human development. The intention is not to create a new institution but rather a small administrative team responsible for the coordination of preexisting organizations like UNDP, IDB, CEPAL, governmental agencies, and NGOs. The cost would be very modest in comparison with the potential benefits, such as helping to build a basic consensus in countries where change is needed, stimulating reciprocal apprenticeships, and promoting greater understanding throughout the region as a whole.

Three Principal Results Required to Make the Summit a Success

If these three steps are achieved, the Summit will not be merely an isolated event of symbolic value but the inauguration of a new and productive era of cooperative relations among the countries and peoples of the Americas.

1. A Commitment to Pursuing Sustainable Human Development in the Americas

A joint statement identifying a series of shared priorities and common challenges for the interrelated areas of trade, investment, and sustainable human development in the Americas.

2. The Establishment of Plans and Mechanisms for Action

The establishment of action plans and efficient mechanisms for pursuing the shared priorities identified in the joint statement. Two such mechanisms are recommended: a permanent intergovernmental mechanism for cooperation and a program for exchange and cooperation among societies of the Americas — the *Sustainable Development Program for the Americas*.

3. Implementation Schedules

Schedules for periodic future meetings among governments and for the establishment of the cooperation and exchange mechanisms among societies of the Americas. It must be recognized that the Summit can represent only the beginning of a new and permanent process of dialogue among our peoples, institutions, and governments.

II. INTRODUCTION

The most important day has not arrived. We have expelled our oppressors, but we must still lay the foundation of the social pact that will make this new world into a Nation of Republics.

Simón Bolívar

The period following World War II saw the development of many unprecedented initiatives for international cooperation, and the end of the Cold War signals another such opportunity. Freed from the distorting patterns of East-West confrontation, countries can now cultivate international relationships that are based wholly on peace, justice, and sustainable prosperity for all. Advancing toward this horizon is the foremost challenge of the new millennium, and nowhere on Earth is this challenge more vividly evident than in the joined Northern and Southern continents of the Western Hemisphere.

The Summit of the Americas presents a historic opportunity to meet this challenge. To make the Summit a success, country representatives must agree to establish a timetable for periodic meetings in the future, to empower an institutional framework for systematically addressing hemispheric issues, and to initiate a flexible plan of action that will catalyze the changes necessary in the development patterns of both North and South. The pledge to pursue authentic hemispheric solidarity and the improvement of all standards among countries of the Americas is now crucial as increasing trade and investment bring these already linked zones even closer together, ultimately intertwining their fates.

This report does not focus on what the countries of the North owe those of the South or what the countries of Latin America and the Caribbean should do to improve their functioning. Instead, it focuses on the steps that all countries must take to strengthen democracy, enhance collective prosperity, and preserve the rich and diverse hemispheric ecosystem. As integration proceeds, accelerated progress in any one country is linked to the simultaneous advancement of the human condition throughout the entire region. Since all countries share the common aspiration of improving the quality of life for their citizens in a sustainable and equitable manner, sustainable human development could be the unifying principle for the Summit. The concept of sustainable human development recognizes vital interdependencies, and it is the common thread that runs throughout this document.

Without a human resource base that is educated, healthy, and prepared for the challenges of the future, there can be no progress on any of the vital issues now facing the region. The special challenges facing women and the need to raise children out of poverty are two priorities that must be addressed. This first section, A Sustainable Human Development Strategy for the Americas, directly confronts this crucial component, and the following specialized sections each point out the necessity of developing human capacities and resources for meeting the challenges of hemispheric integration. Trade, investment, and human development are not isolated from each other; all three areas are interdependent and mutually supporting. Successful trade and investment processes require an educated, vital, and productive population. To be complementary, the instruments of trade and investment must actively support the development of the requisite human and institutional capacities that are the foundation for a lasting prosperity.

The Latin American and Caribbean (LAC) countries are steadily integrating and stabilizing their economies while simultaneously building closer ties with the United States and Canada. Now, the gradual opening of a free Western Hemisphere trade zone based on principles appropriate to the realities of the Americas could contribute significantly to economic growth. From Alaska to Tierra del Fuego, the Americas are graced with stunning cultural and ecological diversity. Unfortunately, the ecological quality of life is declining while social inequality is increasing throughout the region. In Latin America, poverty and environmental degradation were aggravated as a consequence of the debt crisis and the ensuing economic adjustments. A vigorous North-South partnership is now required to address the constellation of economic, environmental, and governmental issues that will accompany integration. Strengthened multilateral efforts should be combined with domestic measures to ensure that social and environmental progress follows the accelerated pace of economic reforms. The expansion of trade, investment, and physical infrastructure needs to be complemented by a strengthened social and governance infrastructure that broadens opportunities, enhances democratic participation, provides essential services, and safeguards the environmental resource base. Success in any one of these areas demands equal attention to all the others.

We have prepared this document in the hope that it will help Summit participants take full advantage of the opportunity now at hand to begin a new era marked by pragmatic collaboration among the Americas. This document acts as a bridge between conceptual frameworks and practical realities that could lead to specific and substantial measures for the Summit agenda and follow-up. The outline format is designed to present the issues in summary, with the understanding that each major recommendation put forward will require detailed and comprehensive elaboration in the coming months. The most important point and the central requirement overriding all these policies is that adequate resources be mobilized for implementing any hemispheric initiatives catalyzed by the Summit. Redefining priorities and mobilizing additional financial resources through innovative mechanisms at the local, national, and hemispheric levels will be required if sustainable development for the Americas is not to remain on paper as one more list of wishful but financially infeasible changes.

The true substance of the Summit will be measured by the effectiveness of the follow-up mechanisms that are put in place. A partnership among governments and multilateral organizations including the United Nations Development Programme (UNDP), the Inter-American Development Bank (IDB), and the Organization of American States (OAS) could form part of the backbone of an institutional framework mandated by the Summit to assist in carrying the Summit compact forward into the next millennium.

III. A SUSTAINABLE HUMAN DEVELOPMENT STRATEGY FOR THE AMERICAS

A. Overview

Sustainable human development is the principal challenge facing all the countries participating in the Summit of the Americas. The Western Hemisphere is richly endowed with natural resources which, if properly managed, can serve as the foundation for sustainable development. However, of all its resources, the region's most valuable asset is its people, both as the ultimate source and objective of economic growth. There are no underdeveloped countries; there are only underdeveloped people. Sustainable human development promotes growth with equitable opportunity, social integration, sound governance, and protection of the environment. The Summit should be conceived as crucial for unleashing the energies — domestic and international — needed to begin imaginative strategies reinforced by firm commitments to meet this challenge.

Throughout Latin America, enormous progress has been made in recent years in many crucial areas. Countries that were authoritarian are now democratically governed. Where there was conflict and tension, there is now peace and international security. Economic reform and privatization have fostered stability and growth in many countries, and the liberalization of trade is allowing international commerce to expand rapidly. These positive changes allow us to proceed to the next stage of development that focuses on social inequalities, persistent poverty, loss of biodiversity and forests, and rising water and air pollution. Unless certain fundamental changes take place to advance sustainable human development and not just overall growth, economic growth and trade liberalization threaten to add new pressures to the regional and global environment.

The developmental approach of wealth maximization measured by GNP does not come to terms with environmental degradation and individual predicaments of extreme deprivation. Growth patterns showing a close correlation between GNP and indicators of quality of life pivot on the use of extra income in the specific fields of public education, health, and the reduction of absolute poverty. Since such investments correlate into a big expansion of basic human capabilities, policies should specifically target equity and quality of life. Economic growth and quality of life are not only directly connected, but they are also contingent on how far the additional resources resulting from economic growth are used to support services to the public.

Our intergenerational responsibility demands that we do not plunder or contaminate the common stock of natural resources, leaving future generations unable to enjoy the opportunities that we take for granted. However, in our efforts to protect future generations, we cannot ignore the deprived people of today. Preservation of the resource base does not imply that all exhaustible resources must be preserved intact. It does require that we replace non-renewable resources with reproducible capital formation, whether human or physical. This policy incorporates a moral obligation to protect and enhance the well-being of people who are presently poor and deprived while allowing future generations the capability to sustain the income of the present generation.

Alleviating poverty is a prerequisite for environmental conservation. The poor are the victims and often the agents of environmental damage. Initiatives to conserve the environment should relate concretely to people's ability to generate for themselves more income and other means of good living. Recent works on human capital formation and economic growth have demonstrated the far-reaching role of education, health, and other human qualities in generating economic growth. The importance of human capital indicates that the pivotal role of education, health, training, etc. are important not just in raising productivity but also in devising ways and means of dealing with the challenges of environmental protection and the transfer and integration of new technologies. While taking full note of the instrumental importance of human quality in expanding the material basis of human life, we must not lose sight of the central importance of the quality of human life as an end in itself.

B. Increase Social Equity and Participation

1. Although the means may vary according to the different national realities, the widest possible participation of our citizens must be secured in the political, economic, and social decisionmaking that affects their lives. Decentralized and participatory government, respect for minority rights, and a process of social integration based on equal opportunities for education, employment, and repre-

sentation are the primary means to securing broad public participation and consensus.

2. If economic reforms do not benefit main social groups, they will lack the support that will guarantee their sustainability. The sustained (at least in the medium run) development of countries that have succeeded highlights some of the ingredients required for successful sustainable human development strategies in the LAC region:

   a. investment in people (education and training);

   b. a high degree of social and political consensus;

   c. macroeconomic growth and price stability;

   d. high savings and investment;

   e. modernization of state operations;

   f. high social equity and a significant reduction of poverty;

   g. allocation of resources for the capacity to adapt to change.

3. The issue of women's affairs illustrates the problems of increasing participation and the obstacles to the expansion of democracy to all levels of society. Social and educational policies must address the specific obstacles faced by women and girls, particularly those who are impoverished.

4. Social policies must be as important as economic policies, and they should be part of an integrated development strategy. Efforts should be made to gather and analyze the social policies, particularly policies at the local level, that have been attempted by democratic governments. This information could inform the many other LAC countries currently in similar situations.

C. Build the Social Infrastructure and Human Capital

1. In the Americas, natural resources are abundant and wealth is generated, but under conditions of unacceptable inequality. Two hundred seventy million Latin Americans exist in poverty, and half of these people are unable to maintain a basic level of nutrition. Economic growth with the capacity to distrib-

ute it and a return to the human and social dimensions of development are preconditions not only to a reduction in poverty but also to the liberation of the region's productive energies.

2. Countries should develop a ten-year hemispheric plan for poverty reduction. They should reaffirm the commitments they made under the Nariño Accord, which was adopted by participants to the "Second Meeting on Children and Social Policy in the Americas, Agenda 2000: Children Now," including:

   a. a long-term commitment to raise children out of poverty;

   b. adequate resources for health care and immunization programs.

3. Educational reform is vital to the region's future success in economic development, social advancement, and democracy. Open economies and increased competition bring new demands on citizen and state alike. Unfortunately, per capita spending on public education in the LAC region represents just one-tenth that of industrialized countries. Only half of the students in the region complete primary school. Therefore, educational reform is crucial and it should be designed to:

   a. expand social opportunities for the poorest segment of the population;

   b. prepare citizens for democratic participation and social integration;

   c. train students for jobs in an internationally competitive economy.

4. Currently, only 7 percent of government-to-government assistance is directed toward human priority areas such as basic education, primary health care, nutrition, water supply, and family planning.

5. The multitude of technical cooperation initiatives that are now in operation throughout the region need to be coordinated.

D. Policies and Reforms for Sustainable Human Development

1. Policies that are detrimental to both the economy and the environment should be reformed. For example, energy subsidies and deforestation incentives should be phased out gradually by all countries of the region.

Such major reforms will require actions to protect against short-term loss of competitiveness and to counterbalance against domestic vested interests.

2. Declare adherence and joint commitment to move gradually toward:

   a. the "polluter pays" principle;

   b. full-cost pricing of natural resources and commodities (internalization of resource depletion and environmental costs in the prices of goods and services);

   c. a least-cost approach to environmental protection to preserve competitiveness in world markets;

   d. changing incentive structures by progressively lowering income taxes and concomitantly raising taxes on consumption to increase efficiency and control pollution.

3. Promote the establishment of well-defined and secure property rights (whether private, communal, or state) to ensure long-term and sustainable management of forests, land, biodiversity, and water. Regional cooperation is needed to share experiences on alternative approaches toward establishing ownership security or responsible stewardship over natural resources.

4. Increased trade and investment opens new opportunities for cooperation on the improvement of standards and the use of better technologies. Governments and institutions should be prepared to identify and develop these opportunities.

5. Joint commitments should be pursued for increased reliance on economic instruments (taxes, charges, permits, bonds, etc.) as supplements to environmental regulations for the internalization of environmental externalities. This is a means of achieving environmental protection without constraining economic growth. Exchange experiences in this regard are a low-cost regional activity that promises large dividends.

E. Trade and Investment in a Western Hemisphere Free Trade Area (WHFTA)

1. Participants in the Summit of the Americas must send forth the clear message that ad-

equate resources will be committed toward resolving the challenges posed by the consolidation of a WHFTA that benefits all the people and the environment of the Americas. The pursuit of sustainable human development in the hemisphere must also include a strategy to integrate the countries of the region into the world economy. There are three complementary and mutually reinforcing routes by which this integration should proceed: unilateral trade liberalization, regional accords, and global trade liberalization.

2. Unprecedented opportunities exist for hemispheric cohesion and prosperity stemming from (a) widespread domestic reforms among the LAC countries, (b) the resurgence of regionalism focusing this time on trade creation rather than diversion, and (c) the mutual recognition that genuine North-South hemispheric interests prevail. While the stage is set for a WHFTA capable of producing significant benefits for the Americas, many risks and uncertainties also lie ahead since this is a road that has not been traveled before, here or elsewhere. Furthermore, the window to this opportunity might be open only temporarily. Tangible progress toward a WHFTA over the coming years could go far toward leveraging recent gains from the hemispheric reform process and securing a more sustainable path for continued progress.

3. Regional trade accords — which effectively become important investment policy tools as well — should be viewed as opportunities to manage an ongoing process of growing interdependency and as mechanisms to pursue sustainable human development cooperatively.

4. Principles Toward a "Benevolent WHFTA":

   a. Preservation of subregional schemes. Widening or extending trade pacts should be crafted to minimize damage to existing subregional schemes and should not occur to the exclusion of integration deepening.

   b. GATT-plus accords. At a minimum, barriers to nonmembers should not be raised, and exceptions (by sectors or products) to barrier reductions among members should be minimized. It is better to slow the liberalization process to allow sensitive sectors to adjust than to liberalize unevenly across sectors. Explicit rules for accession should be put forth. Transparency, particularly as regards rules of origin, is vital.

   c. Compatibility among trade accords. If the integration agreements are ever to converge, rules between accords must be made compatible over time.

   d. Multilateral over bilateral accords. Bilateralism can increase the likelihood of developing incompatible accords. It can result in greater trade diversion and a dampening of investment incentives and ultimately set in motion forces which block the process of an inclusive and benevolent WHFTA. While multilateralism may be more cumbersome initially and may slow the integration process for select countries currently "ready," it is more likely to simplify the process over the long term and facilitate the desired outcome, including preserving subregional groups.

   e. Inclusiveness. The striking heterogeneity among countries in terms of level of development and progress toward reforms must be accommodated in a way that all countries of the Americas can be brought into the WHFTA process.

   f. Minimize transition and adjustment costs. While freer trade and investment are in the interest of every country, how a nation gets there factors significantly into the cost-benefit equation. Further, market forces may tend to exacerbate inequalities between and within countries, at least initially, during a WHFTA transition. Efforts (such as adjustment assistance) will be necessary to counter these market tendencies.

   g. Appropriate institutions. Existing institutions should be tapped and the path to WHFTA well defined before new, permanent institutions are created. Ancillary support can and should be developed in stages, in part to remain synchronous with the political process.

   h. Environmentally sustainable. As enunciated elsewhere in this document, the trade and investment liberalization process must be made more compatible with environmental sustainability. The link between trade and the environment should be examined comprehensively in the broader context of sustainable development, with equity as a central operating principle.

i. Social justice. Problems such as child exploitation, forced labor, and the denial of workers' rights to free speech and free association must be addressed in all trade pacts.

5. Paths and Mechanisms to a WHFTA:

a. Domestic preparation. There is much that can be done domestically — and needs to be done — to influence the cost-benefit equation of an FTA membership for LAC. Such concerns include a focus on macroeconomic stability and market reforms including further unilateral trade liberalization, addressing inequalities and poverty, and shifting toward more dynamic (and environmentally and socially sustainable) comparative advantages. The latter is largely achieved over time through human resource development, with a primary emphasis on education.

b. The regional process. Hemispheric heterogeneity can be accommodated to achieve an inclusive process in one of two ways: equal trade accord memberships with variable transitions or different types of memberships with different levels of benefits and obligations roughly consistent with the progress of each country's economic reforms and/or its desired level of commitments (an arrangement of so-called "concentric circles").

c. Whichever inclusive process is taken, there may be two viable ways that convergence to a WHFTA could happen. Both would need to include major players of the hemisphere — the countries of NAFTA and Brazil, in particular — preferably sooner than later. Both need not be mutually exclusive.

(1) FTAs among subregions. This may be the most ideal in theory if not in practice because it could serve to strengthen existing subregions and deepen integration among them and allow for a more equal and inclusive negotiation process within the hemisphere. A WHFTA would go far toward being realized if priority were given to bridging NAFTA with either MERCOSUR or the emerging South American Free Trade Area (SAFTA).

(2) Building on NAFTA. This is popular among many observers because (a) it is relatively straightforward and (b) a coherent core agreement already exists which establishes relatively "open regionalism" and includes some important environmental and labor considerations. A main disadvantage from the perspective of nonmembers is that future negotiations would be over the terms of accession to NAFTA rather than an FTA itself. A certain asymmetry in power and privilege between NAFTA members and nonmembers would likely prevail. Further, few LAC countries are able to comply in the foreseeable future with the stringent NAFTA membership conditions (on such issues as labor, environment, intellectual property rights, and investment), and it is not clear that complying with some of these conditions is in the interest of some LAC countries. For this path to be realized, some form of "fast track" authorization must be given to the U.S. executive branch from Congress, and the accession process would need to be better defined.

F. Trade, Investment, and the Environment

1. Trade liberalization can improve or damage the environment depending on the conditions and constraints under which it takes place. If natural resources such as forests, land, water, and fisheries are open access or without well-defined and secure property rights, trade liberalization may lead to expansion of exports of natural resource-based commodities and agricultural and livestock products at the expense of the resource base and long-term sustainability. Similarly, if energy is subsidized and no regulating mechanisms and economic instruments are in place

for internalization of environmental costs, the increased exports of manufacturers following trade liberalization are likely to lead to increased air and water pollution.

2. If, on the other hand, property rights over resources are well defined and secure and if instruments for the internalization of environmental costs are in place and enforced, free trade can be a potent instrument for environmental protection: it minimizes the waste of resources, improves economic efficiencies, eliminates inefficient and often highly polluting import-substituting industries, helps diversify the economy away from dependence on natural resource-based exports, and it enhances the overall range of options.

3. Environmental policies, laws, and regulations, particularly with respect to natural resource degradation, are relatively weak in Latin America and the Caribbean, as are monitoring and enforcement. Hence, the costs of natural resource degradation are not reflected in the export prices of the LAC region's primary commodities. The high incidence of primary commodities in the region's exports demands that environmental costs resulting from the exploitation of natural resources be incorporated into the export price of primary commodities. However, multilateral negotiations for strengthening environmental regulations and reducing subsidies must also preserve the region's competitive strength in the world market.

4. Taking the Basel Convention as a possible model, there should be studies and negotiations to prevent the export of hazardous substances, products, and technologies, particularly those that have been banned or restricted in some countries. This process could be initiated with pesticides and other toxic chemicals, asbestos, pharmaceutical drugs, and activities related to genetic engineering.

5. Trade distortions through export subsidies and trade restrictions are often major sources of environmental degradation and nonsustainable development. In most cases, trade liberalization of agriculture results in higher world market pricing for agricultural products from developing countries, justify-

ing improved land management (provided agri-chemicals and water are priced at full environmental costs). To the extent that the demand for natural resource-based exports is price inelastic, the consumers in industrialized countries would be paying a larger share of the environmental costs associated with their consumption patterns.

6. Good environmental policies can help to improve gains from trade and avert trade conflicts. Trade liberalization can lead to better environmental quality if conducted with adequate safeguards.

7. The relative lack of environmental controls in Latin America may tend to encourage foreign (and domestic) investment in heavily polluting industries, although the magnitude of this effect is unclear at the moment.

8. Imbalances in trade policies discriminate without providing incentives for environmental protection. For example, Latin American exports to OECD countries must meet very strict environmental requirements, while exports from OECD countries to Latin America are subject to minimal environmental restrictions.

9. The existence of tariff and non-tariff barriers to products with value-added intensifies natural resource exploitation. In many cases, such tariffs have led to the over-exploitation of these resources because such activities become the only viable option for earning foreign exchange.

10. The U.S. Ex-Im Bank and international lending institutions such as the International Finance Corporation should practice non-discrimination among country standards. Products exported from the North should comply with the standards of the country of origin. Export standards should be consistent with domestic standards.

11. The contribution of freer trade to sustainable development critically depends upon whether trade liberalization is accompanied by the internalization of environmental costs through economic and regulatory instruments. Economic instruments such as pollution charges and taxes are the preferable instruments because they do not act as barriers to trade as long as they are levied at the same level on

domestically produced and imported products. They do, however, affect competitiveness for products with price-elastic demand, a factor that discourages individual countries from fully internalizing environmental costs. This problem can be solved through hemispheric or global cooperation. In light of the prospects for hemispheric economic integration, common environmental standards for the hemisphere can be agreed upon with differing compliance schedules depending on the country's level of economic development. To speed up compliance to common standards, the Americas might agree to a special fund for environmental and social spending to strengthen weaker partners entering into free trade agreements with stronger neighbors.

12. Trade Policy Changes that Produce Environmental Benefits:

a. Reduce agricultural protectionism and domestic agricultural policy distortions. Agricultural protectionism leads to more uneconomical, chemical-intensive farming that exacerbates soil loss, chemical run-off, loss of biodiversity, and the conversion of natural ecosystems to cropland.

b. Slowly reduce trade barriers to exports of labor-intensive manufactures from the LAC region. Trade liberalization of manufacturing is likely to improve the environment by attracting unemployed and underemployed labor from natural resource encroachment and degradation into labor-intensive manufacturing for exports. However, the results are contingent on the absence of subsidies for capital, energy, and materials and the existence of environmental standards or pollution charges that fully internalize the environmental cost of manufacturing activities. Otherwise, the wrong type of industries (polluting and energy and material intensive) are likely to develop.

c. Create the capability to institute and enforce environmental regulations in the region. This would ensure that international transactions are based on actual production costs.

d. Promote partnerships and joint ventures to produce sustainable energy and environmental technologies for the regional, hemispheric, and world markets.

13. Environmental Policy Changes that Benefit International Trade:

a. Regulate unpriced environmental externalities in countries where such regulations do not exist. By obscuring true production costs, such export subsidies distort trade patterns. The OECD governments agreed to the "polluter pays" principle twenty years ago to avoid trade distortions resulting from government subsidizing industry's cost of compliance with environmental regulations.

b. Eliminate underpricing of natural resources. Water for agriculture and timber production in national forests are heavily subsidized in the United States, and other countries do the same. These subsidies distort international trade and encourage the overuse of natural resources.

G. The Role of Science and Technology

1. Science and technology are indispensable tools for sustainable development. Although private sector competitiveness is a driving factor in technological progress, the state has an essential role in creating the solid social foundation necessary for the successful transfer and adoption of new technologies. The development of human resources through proper education and health care and investment in research and development are vital public sector responsibilities that establish the underlying conditions necessary for innovation in science, the transfer of technology, and the effective integration of this new technology into the development process.

2. The goal of the hemispheric community should be to widen the multilateral dialogue toward agreeing on comprehensive and balanced non-proliferation objectives as an integral means to enhancing high technology for peaceful uses. Such a commitment by the states should be complemented by a commitment to ensure access to these technologies for peaceful purposes. These measures would greatly improve existing structures for the

international transfer of goods, services, and know-how in high technology.

3. The multilateral and multi-sector nature of technology transfer would be best served through an enhanced mechanism within the United Nations for an integrated approach to science and technology issues as they relate to sustainable human development.

4. The adoption of environmentally sound technologies by poorer countries would be greatly facilitated through the provision of enabling incentives. These incentives could take the form of an "environmental benefit fee" or financing of the "incremental cost of technology switching" where this has regional or global benefits and such incentives are critical to the adoption of new technology. Resources from bilateral and multilateral institutions will be needed to enable local governments to invest in environmental technologies. Other essential factors include:

   a. Cost. There are some low cost or even net benefit options to technologies; however, environmentally sound technologies frequently impose additional costs, and a part of this cost may be a license fee or royalty.

   b. Information. The diversity of possible technologies and the different needs and actors involved makes choices difficult without adequate information about what is available. Local capacity for making the right choices combined with international assistance in making information available will be crucial. Successful adaptation of new technologies will also require local education, infrastructure, and support.

   c. Market Needs. The existence of local demand is the best driver for adoption of new technologies. This demand is influenced by price signals and the regulatory environment.

5. The transfer of technology for the purpose of minimizing environmental degradation depends upon:

   a. Joint ventures in the private sector that are good business deals for both the Northern and Southern partners,

   b. Existence of legislation in developing countries that guarantees fair remuneration for patent rights as well as the needed local infrastructure to permit the transfer and adoption of the technologies,

   c. Firm government decisions to implement policies that might require a shift of expenditures in order to reduce environmental degradation.

6. Small businesses generate new jobs at greater rates than large corporations. Enhancing access to technology among small- and medium-sized enterprises would be an enormous stimulus to productivity and job growth. The recognized need for environmentally sound technology transfer is but one example of how essential it is for developed and developing economies to achieve a real partnership. Entrepreneurship should be fostered and systems of assistance designed to meet the special challenges faced by small businesses, including small farming operations that do not degrade the environment.

H. Reform National Accounts to Reflect Sustainable Human Development

1. National accounting standards (GNP, GDP) do not include information on social indicators (health, life expectancy, literacy, inequality) or on environmental indicators (resource depletion and recovery and environmental degradation or improvement). Reformed indicators would record the depletion or accumulation of natural, human, and man-made resources. Sustainability should be defined as non-declining productive capacity (aggregate resource stocks) and non-declining amenity and ecological capital without close substitutes. The development of such new indicators is an ideal subject for hemispheric cooperation, especially in light of prospects for economic integration. This project can be undertaken by a joint working committee from the statistical offices of all countries in the Americas assisted by academics and the participation of representatives from UNDP, ECLAC, UNSO, IDB, and the OAS.

I. Build the Physical Infrastructure

1. Projects that will deliver safe drinking water are a priority. Currently, safe drinking water is available to only 56 percent of rural Latin Americans. Even low-income developing countries have access rates 5 percent higher. Many areas must also install electrification and other infrastructure services. Overall, major investments are needed in all areas of physical infrastructure.

2. Engage the private sector in infrastructure development. Develop new mechanisms that permit full-cost pricing for the use of physical infrastructure and contribute such revenues to the financing of new projects.

3. Wherever possible, the focus should be on investing in the rehabilitation of existing infrastructure. All investments should utilize state-of-the-art environmental knowledge and technologies.

J. Establish the Sustainable Development Program for the Americas

1. Current organizations only link governments, not societies. A few of the many groups that would greatly benefit from an exchange and coordination program for sustainable development include NGOs, public agencies, universities, and labor unions of the Americas. Areas where change is necessary depend on the initial conditions and the specific economic, social, and political characteristics of the various countries of the hemisphere. A very practical way to promote learning of the most effective ways to advance sustainable human development would be through a Sustainable Development Program for the Americas (SDPA). The projects and programs sponsored by such a coordinated group of people would also contribute to consensus building among the different societies on sustainable human development and further hemispheric cooperation, integration, and the development of a common regional identity. The fact that we are a heterogeneous region is not a liability as long as different countries share their strengths.

2. The Sustainable Development Program for the Americas would promote cooperation and exchange of knowledge, skills, and technology among civil society and governmental leaders in environmental protection, judicial systems, trade unions, municipal government, protected-area management and biodiversity conservation, indigenous affairs, civilian police, professional journalism, fair electoral practices, and the many other founding principles needed for a successful society. In the initial stage, the Sustainable Development Program for the Americas could target scientific, technological, and administrative cooperation for the hemispheric implementation of the Climate Change and Biodiversity Conventions. The overall goal is to improve standards throughout the hemisphere.

3. The SDPA would assist the process of bringing about a Western Hemisphere Free Trade Area. The SDPA would help coordinate the integration process by enhancing the exchange of information between countries and institutions in an effort to make the various subregional accords more consistent and open.

4. The task of creating or rehabilitating indispensable public sector institutions lags far behind the requirements of the new economic reforms. Sluggishness in creating new public agencies (regulatory, antitrust, antidumping, consumer protection, social safety-net, and environmental agencies) which are critical for the functioning of an open, market-based economy is the biggest threat to regional economic stability. Market reforms will be impossible to consolidate if the performance of public institutions does not improve dramatically. The Sustainable Development Program for the Americas would focus on developing the human resources needed to meet these challenges.

5. Since the support of key actors from government and civil society is crucial for the pursuit of sustainable human development, representatives of these different social sectors from different countries will need to interact. Some of the Sustainable Development Program for the Americas initiatives would include:

   a. Visits by small delegations of leaders from one country to those in another that has had success in a specific area. These people would learn from each other and, as a result of this process, develop a common basis for mutual understanding.

b. Organize regional training workshops, conferences, and seminars on all of the above-mentioned issues.

c. Sponsor exchange programs among universities of the hemisphere.

d. Conduct joint research and publish independent reports.

e. Develop public environmental awareness campaigns.

f. Facilitate joint partnerships among governments, multilateral organizations, NGOs, and universities throughout the hemisphere.

K. Strengthen the Capabilities of Existing Trade Organizations to Focus on Issues of Trade and Investment in the Americas

1. Utilize the instrument of trade as a vehicle for sustainable human development throughout the hemisphere. Provide an organized system for intergovernmental dialogue on trade and investment.

2. Ensure that the United States, Canada, and Brazil give first priority to the Americas before embarking on extra-hemispheric free trade agreements that will discriminate against countries of the Americas.

3. In a hemispheric context, trade and the environment should be seen as mutually supporting rather than conflicting. Both trade liberalization and environmental regulation have as their principal goal the more efficient use of available resources.

IV. CONSOLIDATING DEMOCRACY AND RECONSTRUCTING THE STATE

A. Overview

The emergence of democratic systems providing the citizenry with political representation has been one of the most important developments in the recent history of Latin America. In the 1970s, the armed forces controlled political power in many Latin American countries. During the 1980s, a return to democracy was achieved by Brazil, Argentina, Chile, Uruguay, Paraguay, Bolivia, Guatemala, El Salvador, Honduras, Nicaragua, Panama, and Haiti. Since there are no democratic traditions in many of these countries, the road to full democracy continues to be a long one. Steps must be taken to reinforce and consolidate democratic governance — particularly in areas where extreme poverty, inequality, and arbitrary rule still prevail. Most of these reforms and activities are the internal affairs of domestic governments, but there is a clear role for international assistance in the exchange of information and expertise. Democratic governments must now enable their national economies to prosper in an equitable manner, since for many people of the LAC region, "democracy speaks to the soul but has yet to fill the belly." Under these circumstances, democracy itself might not be sustainable.

Equity and social and political participation are preconditions for the creation of a national consensus and cooperation. Consensus and cooperation are in turn crucial for growth, development, and social peace. Investment naturally flows to those economies which are characterized as having low "country risks" — where uncertainty has been substantially reduced through adherence to a sound development path. This can only take place, in an open polity, if there is a generally accepted common view among the main social and political actors with respect to the basic orientations of the development process. The main social and political actors will not be part of the consensus if they do not benefit (equity) and are not part (participation) of the important economic and political decisions. As part of a balanced and integrated development strategy, social policies should be analyzed together with economic policies, with the goals of social justice given the same hierarchy and urgency as economic growth.

Therefore, the primary task for countries of the LAC region is to create a strong political and social majority that respects democratic procedures and legitimacy of the rule of law. The countries must also develop and implement governmental policies that promote growth with equity and environmental sustainability. An effective, unbiased judicial system that provides equal access for people from all socioeconomic levels is an essential component of democratic government. A regeneration of ethics in the public and private sectors will provide the moral authority necessary for the full functioning of democracy in today's complex world. Political ethics require transparency and accountability to the citizenship.

The reconstruction of the state begins with a citizenry that is unified in purpose and that is freely able to participate in governmental decisionmaking both directly and through effective political parties. Citizenship is the tie that binds together democracy and sustainable human development. Building a strong citizenship is the horizon toward which democratic governance and sustainable human development should jointly aim. Free and fair elections, legal guarantees for individual autonomy, and fair judicial processes are basic to the development of a strong and active citizenship.

Most of the recent advances toward democratic governance in the LAC region come from domestic actions and decisions. However, international institutions can reinforce the domestic sectors involved with this process by aiding their efforts with monetary and knowledge resources. The Sustainable Development Program for the Americas would make it possible for key actors from governments and civil societies to interact, learn from each other, and improve their domestic decisions and actions. The time is ripe to bring together liberty and participation, efficiency and equity, democracy and solidarity, ethics and politics.

B. Governance for Sustainable Human Development

1. It is not possible to achieve democratic development or social stability unless the alarming level of poverty in many countries is overcome. Therefore, the agenda items for poverty reduction listed in the above section, "A Sustainable Human Development Strategy for the Americas," must be addressed by all the countries participating in the Summit.

2. The only means to overcome stagnation and breach poverty is through the joint action of the market as the resource allocator and through the state as the political catalyst dedicated to widespread investment in human capital. Following almost two centuries of decolonization, many countries are burdened with the legacies left by dictators such as a lack of democratic roots, violence, impoverishment, corruption, and disorder in public affairs. Modernizing these countries means fully developing their human capa-

bilities, improving the systems of citizen participation and oversight, and fostering transparency in governmental operations. Democracy is secured through a long-term commitment to education and the fostering of a democratic culture. Strong domestic support is required to promote this process, including the mobilization of universities, the press, grassroots organization, churches, and intellectuals.

3. An outstanding recent development in Latin America is the awakening of a dynamic citizenry that is organizing for participation in a democratic society. From Mexico's campaign for election oversight to Argentina's anti-corruption organizations to the Campaign for Hunger and Poverty in Brazil, a conscious and self-reliant citizenry pressing for changes has proven to be vital for the expansion of democracy. Support for an active citizenry increases political participation, social justice, and the consensus required for policy reforms.

C. Reinforce Democratic Governance

1. Overseeing elections — the Summit should make a clear statement regarding the whole electoral process as a single unit which must be observed:

    a. Registration procedures before the elections, voting procedures during the elections, and ballot counting after the elections;

    b. Electoral procedures and systems must not fragment civil society.

2. Ensure equal access to the media for opposition parties.

3. Reinforce laws on campaign financing to increase transparency and decrease private funding.

4. Strengthen the technical capacity of national parliaments.

5. To strengthen the party system, enforce democratic policies within parties. Establish vote thresholds below which parties cannot elect congresspeople.

6. Enforce a separation of powers among branches of government.

7. Establish the office of a truly independent controller general or ombudsman. The development of this position must be closely linked to the task of modernizing the state apparatus so that controls do not obstruct creativity and risk-taking among civil servants. The position must have clear authority and be free of corruption.

D. Strengthen the Judiciary

1. The very survival of democracy in many Latin American countries depends upon whether they can empower their judicial branches with the capability to uphold the rule of law. Special attention should be paid to combating corruption and strengthening local courts. Those courts are more directly connected with the daily concerns of marginalized people and their exercise of basic human rights including the right to a healthy environment. All citizens should be able to bring a case to their local court and have it attended to within ten days.

   a. Guarantee the independence and budgetary autonomy of the judicial branch through, among other measures, adequate systems for the appointment of judges.

   b. Facilitate access to local courts and improve legal assistance for the marginalized. Many environmental crimes occur in the regions where these people live, so such strengthening will increase environmental quality. Improve local court functioning by promoting service in those courts as an integral part of a judicial career

   c. Make educational and training opportunities available for judges and magistrates. Establish minimum standards for candidates for the posts of judge and magistrate. Appoint more young and highly motivated judges, prosecutors, and public defenders.

   d. Create a "Judicial Clearing House" formed by retired judges available for consultation by those young magistrates (also electronically).

   e. Increase services to these courts including electronic access to legislation, jurisprudence, and doctrine.

E. Reconstruct State Institutions and Functioning

1. Fragile democracies do not command enough resources to support a strong civil society, and this further weakens those democracies. The receipts of Latin American tax agencies are dismal. Industrialized countries achieve an average tax collection of 24 percent of GDP, but Latin American collections hover at 14 percent, which is 1.0 percent below the average for all developing countries. These poor results can largely be blamed on administrative incapacity, and this incapacity is reflected in a rapid decline in revenues from easily administered taxes on trade. The state's ability to cope with regional economic transformation will be in serious doubt as long as national tax bases remain small and revenues poorly collected. Adequate governmental resources are crucial because the success of a market-driven strategy rests on the ability of the state to ensure the smooth delivery of infrastructure and other public goods from myriad sources.

2. Increase wages for public employees. Of all formal sectors, public employees suffered the deepest cuts in real wages during the 1980s. Real salaries dropped 30 percent over the decade. Wage increases, training, and proper organization are needed throughout the entire public sector, particularly among the police and officials of the judicial system. In those countries in which it does not already exist, the creation of an authentic civil service career designed to attract high quality professionals is vital.

3. The more solid democracies are those in which local power has been strengthened and where there is a full recognition of the importance of community. Decentralizing power to the local level is a means to return politics to a more human dimension by bringing it closer to the people. Autonomy of local power requires the development of competent local authorities and ensuring that adequate resources are available to the community. Municipalities could assume many functions now in the hands of the central government.

4. Governmental decisionmaking needs to be supported by adequate information and interdepartmental coordination, particularly between the economic and political ministries. Coordination also needs to be extended between government officials and members of parliament and between government officials and social leaders.

5. Banking supervision is lacking in many countries, which has led to periodic bank failures. Bank examiners are under-skilled and underpaid. Consumers and businesses must now pay for these inefficiencies through tighter credit.

F. Guarantee Freedom of the Press

The press has been playing an immensely important role in creating an environment for consensus and democratic culture. It has been also been unveiling cases of human rights violations, corruption, denial of justice, and environmental abuse. This role must be encouraged and reinforced. Through the Sustainable Development Program for the Americas, initiate exchange fellowships for investigative reporters, editors, and news managers.

G. Protect the Rights of Indigenous Peoples

1. The concerns of indigenous people need to be addressed by all organizations and governments in North, Central, and South America. The lack of political representation for indigenous populations causes frustration and desperation in communities where Indian people feel they have no voice in the nation's economic development decisions and no stake in the new economic model. Biodiversity capital and carbon sinks are largely located in areas inhabited by indigenous people, and their rights as the stakeholder and beneficiaries of these resources must be recognized and enforced. Several countries have made major strides toward securing indigenous land titles and other rights. However, national policies must not cause dislocations among indigenous cultures and economies. More efforts could also be made to reduce the level of conflict between indigenous people and military/police units.

2. The incorporation of the diverse identities held by indigenous peoples into the social conscience, the political agenda, and the formal structures of the Latin American nations today is a precondition for future peace, stability, and progress.

   a. States could redraw municipal boundaries to create majority indigenous electoral and administrative districts. This would ensure greater representation in seats elected by district, and greater community control over local issues.

   b. Incorporate local people who understand the local indigenous culture and language into the operations of police and armed forces. Train national armed forces to be sensitive to indigenous cultures and issues.

3. Develop intercultural, bilingual educational systems to guarantee respect for language, world vision, and customs as well as the implementation of social policies aimed at improving conditions among indigenous people. Access to bilingual education could also spur the development of indigenous leaders and political organizations. At a minimum, indigenous people must not be punished for using their language or other cultural expressions in Spanish-only or English-only schools.

4. Most indigenous political mobilizations have involved the struggle for possession, legal recognition, demarcation, protection, and enforcement of indigenous land titles. Environmental destruction associated with resource exploitation has led to numerous health problems for Indians in adjacent territories.

   a. Demarcate and protect indigenous territories.

   b. Establish independent national oversight for the fair and peaceful resolution of conflicts over indigenous territories.

5. Increase the capacity of courts to provide indigenous cases with a fair hearing. The Inter-American Court of Human Rights should also be bolstered for the capacity to hear more indigenous cases.

6. Multilateral Organizations:

a. Engage the participation and consultation of indigenous representatives during project planning;

b. Provide direct support for projects developed and managed by indigenous groups;

c. Expand existing indigenous forums at multilateral organizations such as UNDP, IDB, PAHO, and OAS.

H. Protect All Human Rights

1. The protection of human rights is a minimal condition for democracy. The basic principles include Life, which is the foundation for all the other rights; Liberty, which guarantees the freedom of the individual against arbitrary power; Equality, which guarantees a minimum sustenance and fair access to goods; and Solidarity, which guarantees rights to the collective world including a healthy environment, peace, and democracy.

2. The dictatorships of the Latin American Southern Cone and the violence in Central America have been largely overcome. The agenda for change now demands increased vigilance in denouncing isolated or systemic human rights violations wherever they may be found, in purging security organizations of their authoritarian tendencies, in mobilizing people in support of their social and economic rights, and in initiating human rights education programs that combat all forms of despotism.

3. Strengthen the Inter-American Court on Human Rights by expanding the Court's purview to cover a broader definition of human rights, including political rights and the right to a clean environment. Bolster the Court from eight to a minimum of 50 lawyers handling cases from the 34 countries.

I. Reduce Violence and Combat Drug Consumption, Production, and Trafficking

1. Statistics indicate that in half of the countries homicide constitutes the second leading cause of death among young people and that with very few exceptions homicide rates are on the rise in countries throughout the region. This violence strikes most at the dispossessed sectors of society and bears witness to the fragility of democracy. The cost of violence in human and financial resources undermines the social fabric and the foundations for a harmonious existence. Therefore, an unavoidable task of all who value democracy is to devote greater efforts at eradicating all forms of violence. Such efforts should be logically linked to the operation of a democratic government and a community cognizant of its rights.

2. Illegal drug production and trafficking and drug money laundering are fueling corruption and distorting local and national economies. They also have a profound impact on public morality and trust in government. Drug producing plants cultivated in tropical rain forests are degrading ecological and water qualities. The "narco-economy" of the hemisphere, which is estimated at $200 billion per year, has left its mark on the economy, the environment, the judiciary, the security apparatus, and the politics of the region. To be addressed effectively, the drug problem must be viewed in its entirety, with the recognition that drug consumption in the North plays a central role in creating the huge demand that drives this vicious cycle.

3. The multicausal and multifaceted nature of violence demands an interdisciplinary and multisectoral approach that fosters the interaction among various social players. Since violence poses a direct and immediate threat to health, the Pan American Health Organization (PAHO) has been promoting mechanisms such as Safe Communities, Healthy Cities, and Local Health Systems. These programs move beyond the treatment of disease to address its root causes, including the prevention and control of violence.

4. The PAHO Directing Council has adopted a resolution urging governments to develop national policies and mobilize resources for the prevention and control of violence. The resolution also calls for the formulation of a Regional Plan of Action on Violence and Health designed to develop comprehensive activities for the prevention of violence.

5. To provide the occasion for ratifying the determination to confront violence and seek its eradication in the societies of the region,

PAHO has organized a conference with the goal of producing a declaration addressed to the Hemispheric Summit. This declaration will call upon the countries of the Americas to take up these concerns and demonstrate their solidarity with the peoples, the countries, and the international cooperation agencies working to achieve more democratic and less violent societies. Decisive support for this declaration and the PAHO Regional Plan of Action will be a giant step toward the prevention of violence and the reaffirmation of the value of democracy.

J. Foster a "Culture of Peace" in the Americas

1. Regulations must be instituted on conventional arms sales throughout the hemisphere. Consideration should be given to the creation of a hemispheric commission dedicated to stopping the proliferation of conventional arms. Serious action needs to be taken against illegal arms trafficking. On a daily basis, illegal weapons are used with deadly force by narco-traffickers, terrorists, criminals, and guerrillas.

2. Strengthen civil control over the military. The strengthening and stabilization of democracy requires a redefinition of the functions of the armed forces. Effective and concerted strategies should be proposed that will significantly reduce the drain on national budgets caused by military budgets. The military can be engaged in new tasks such as monitoring weapons proliferation, infrastructure improvement, the fight against drug trafficking, and protection of human rights.

K. Build a Basic Consensus

1. A new political culture — one that favors consensus — is needed to consolidate the rule of law. The creation of a strong political and social majority is necessary to support the state and the required policies for sustainable development. As a precondition to strengthening governance, there needs to be a more or less common view among the citizenship and the political actors with respect to the basic orientations of the development process.

2. Ethics must be recuperated since they are of supreme value for social harmony. To foster a consensus and govern effectively, a political culture based upon ethics must permeate the state at all levels. Ethics can and should take the place of ideologies. Politicians and public employees are required to be responsible, and they are obligated to be accountable to the citizenry. Respect for human rights, including collective environmental rights and the capacity to attack corruption, are two basic goals that depend upon the revitalization of ethics in both the public and private sectors.

V. BIODIVERSITY PRESERVATION

A. Overview

On average, the Latin American region holds a much greater diversity of plant species richness per unit than any other part of the world. The fate of these biological resources are closely tied to the fate of forests, which contain some of the richest biodiversity yet face some of the most serious threats. Forests also serve a multitude of vital atmospheric and ecosystemic purposes, such as ensuring stable supplies of clean water and serving as global carbon sinks. Over half of the world's tropical forests exist in Latin America, and this region also leads the world in total tropical forest area lost each year. Timber and forest products feature prominently in many national economies, yet forest people typically wield little legal or political power, which means that they rarely receive any benefits and often pay high costs from the exploitation of forest resources.

In terms of direct human consumption, just a few of the hundreds of important food crops domesticated by pre-Columbian cultures include maize, beans, potatoes, squash, tomatoes, peppers, and cassava. They were chosen by indigenous people several millennia ago for their nutritional, agronomic, technical, and socioeconomic needs. These species represent only a fraction of the thousands of species still available in neotropical wildlands, and many of these wild plant varieties are undoubtedly capable of providing useful products. They are potential sources of pharmaceuticals, natural chemical products, and germplasm for the improvement of existing crops. Protecting the rights of indigenous people and other local stakeholders as the primary guardians of these resources is the first step toward the preservation of both. Other vital measures include managing protected lands, gathering basic information on the traits of the organisms, developing gene and species banks, expanding the basic knowledge of tropical biology, and securing the financial resources necessary to support these activities.

Countries throughout the region have taken considerable measures to conserve forest biodiversity, including an extraordinary effort to establish protected areas and adopt international environmental conventions. Until the economic crisis of the mid-1980s, most of the protected areas were relatively well managed. However, the current situation is perilous. In Brazil, for example, there are only 700 officers to manage more than 36 million hectares of protected land. Most of this land is privately owned, and although only $2 billion is needed to purchase it, at the current rate, acquisition would take 400 years. In total, the protected-area network in Latin America is significant, though not yet sufficient to ensure the survival of many ecosystems with unique biodiversity. These ecosystems are either not yet protected, or the protected areas are too small to ensure the survival of the genetic resources they contain. This situation is by no means limited to the South. In the North, old growth forests of the United States and Canada are rapidly being fragmented and destroyed, and marine ecosystems are under intense pressure from over-exploitation and pollution.

The most urgent goal of North-South cooperation and coordination is to finance the national systems of protected areas in the South. Funds mobilized at the country level should be complemented by multilateral funding for biodiversity conservation. A lack of qualified personnel and modern equipment for monitoring has opened the way for colonization and illegal exploitation activities which are subjecting protected areas to slow destruction. This process can only be reversed through joint programs for biodiversity conservation that build upon a strengthened local capability to protect and manage the biological wealth of the hemisphere. It is impossible to manage these areas with current funding, and the time to apply sound management is becoming dramatically short. The management of shared biodiversity resources demands especially intensive international coordination for the preservation of species and ecosystems that overlap national boundaries.

B. Biodiversity Is a Major Economic Asset, Not a Cost

1. Biodiversity contributes vastly more to economic activity and human well-being than is currently recognized. Its potential is enormous and central to any aspiration for sustainable development.

2. Just at the time when awareness of the economic value of biodiversity is growing, international treaties have been developed based on the assumption that conservation is a "cost." Biodiversity has a fundamental historical function as well as an ongoing role in the progress of society as a whole. Multilateral institutions have been slow to incorporate the essential importance of biological resources to human society. The Summit of the Americas should acknowledge the fundamental economic, ecological, and ethical importance of biodiversity.

3. Forested and protected areas should be perceived as providers of local services (recreation, scientific research, education, eco-tourism) and materials (genetic materials, natural products). These services are equally important to the services provided by agroscape. Viewing protected areas as providers of different local, national, and global goods and services should help countries address the issue of how to cover the cost of management.

4. The cost of land acquisition for protected areas is an investment. Managing this investment calls for the development of national technical capabilities and collaborative international networks that would help countries find sustainable uses of their biodiversity in the modern global economy. Support for scientific research would improve policies and continue the process of uncovering the economically important aspects of biodiversity resources.

C. Trade, Investment and Biodiversity Impacts to Be Reversed

1. Oil exploration being undertaken or proposed in protected areas is causing intense and in some cases critical pressure on biodiversity. The Amazon rain forest has

been subjected to rapid exploitation of oil resources by foreign companies that do not comply with the regulations in force in their own countries.

2. As other readily accessible timber supplies are depleted, many South-East Asian timber importers have turned their attention to Latin America.

3. The irrational overexploitation of timber is often a result of the desperation of poor local populations who have no alternative means of support. Northern barriers to value-added products from the South exacerbate their plight.

4. Gold and precious stone mining is degrading forests, waters, and protected areas.

5. Illegal trade in threatened wildlife and plants continues despite the international conventions prohibiting such activities.

6. An expanding hydroelectric infrastructure has flooded vast areas of forest.

7. The transportation infrastructure is increasing through areas with irreplaceable biological diversity.

8. The drug trade and the cultivation of poppy plants and coca are serious contributors to deforestation.

D. Initiatives for the Summit of the Americas

1. Build the capacity to study, save, and sustainably use biodiversity.

   a. The rights of local stakeholder need to be strengthened. Local and indigenous communities must not only be consulted, they must be empowered with the right to protect and sustainably manage the biological resources within their domains.

   b. There is a serious need for crash training programs in protected area and natural resource management, systematics, and ecology. The human resource shortage can be addressed in part by paramedic equivalents, such as INBio's parataxonomists. Researchers need ready access to hemispheric collections, which are largely in North America.

c. Every country needs to conduct the kind of ecological/economic zoning exercise that Brazil is conducting in its Amazon region. This includes a review of current protected area systems for the purpose of strategically defining management programs that respond to the prevailing social contexts.

d. Provide support for extractive reserve processes to widen the range of resource utilization, including non-timber forestry, fisheries, and wildlife management. Local communities that are sustainably managing extractive reserves should be appropriately compensated for the regional and global services they provide, such as CO_2 fixation, clean water, biodiversity preservation, etc. Greater efforts are needed from international financial institutions to support sustainable extractive activities in tropical regions as alternatives to destructive activities. These projects should seek to improve the marketing and distribution possibilities for extractive products and build capacity for processing such products within the region.

2. Ratify the Convention on Biological Diversity (CBD) [also known as the Convention on Biodiversity]. All countries at the Summit should pledge to sign and ratify the CBD. Western Hemisphere countries should also negotiate a regional accord for implementation of the Convention.

   a. Create a hemispheric fund for the management of protected areas. Although developing countries have created an extensive network of protected areas, funds for management are insufficient, and so the areas are being destroyed by colonization and illegal extractive activities. The fund would therefore support the management of protected areas, indigenous lands, and the development of productive activities based on biodiversity that would benefit local people.

   b. The services provided by forested and protected areas (use of genetic resources, CO_2 fixation, fresh water production, tourism, etc.) should be calculated and charged, nationally or internationally, and the funds allocated for sustainable management of those areas.

c. Examination of intergovernmental debt could provide important opportunities for debt/nature and debt/biodiversity swaps.

3. Safeguard Biodiversity under Liberalized Trade

a. As precursors to regulations with enforcement mechanisms, international codes of conduct could influence oil and mining activities. These activities represent serious threats to biodiversity throughout the Americas. Problems are exacerbated in countries with weak environmental protection standards. Countries may wish to establish different standards, but the Summit should call for a code of conduct. In the absence of norms, companies should be held to regulations of their "home" country. However, nothing will replace the development and enforcement of national norms and regulations, strengthened by international conventions and financial support programs.

b. Develop a code of conduct for companies that exploit biodiversity's genetic material. A portion of their profits should foster the preservation of the resources and compensate local communities that protect the biodiversity and provide information about its use.

c. Leaders should reaffirm their commitment to achieving sustainable forest management with specific criteria for evaluation, including equitable and sustainable human uses of forest products, integrated local and regional management, informed participation by all stakeholders, ecological integrity, and respect for the rights of indigenous and other forest-dependent peoples.

d. Many biodiversity issues, particularly those involving migratory species and species resources which straddle borders, can only be dealt with through international cooperation. International institutions should enable collaborative research and development and create a strategy for supporting the interests of informal networks of small-scale farmers and sustainable users of biodiversity according to bioregion.

e. Improve the monitoring of forest cover and status. Data on forest status and trends are poor, which presents a serious obstacle to planning forest conservation and use. Remote sensing would provide a strategic monitoring and enforcement tool. Such information must also be distributed effectively.

4. The 1940 Convention on Nature Protection and Wildlife Preservation in the Western Hemisphere also known as the Western Hemisphere Convention, provides an existing ready-made framework for conservation action and implementation. In view of the rates of destruction, it is important and useful to move forward within the context it already provides rather than delay until it is revised and improved or some other instrument becomes available.

5. The Central American Convention for the Conservation of Biodiversity and the Protection of Priority Wildlands, signed by all Central American presidents in June 1992 and already ratified by several countries, could be a model for the hemisphere. In summary, it provides a basis for assessing needs and priorities for policy changes and training needs. A similar Western Hemisphere Agreement on Forests could couple national commitments with international agreements on assistance, training, and collaboration.

E. Guidelines for Regulating Access to Genetic Resources

1. Regulations should require that consent be obtained from local communities or indigenous groups when prospecting, gathering usage information, or making land claims.

2. A code of conduct should ensure that contracts share benefits from commercialization. A portion of the profits should be returned for conservation and the local community.

3. All countries should develop a policy framework for regulating access to genetic re-

sources. This framework includes both policy and legislation.

a. Ensure fair payment for the supply of chemical extracts with valued-added information. Provide legal guarantees of fair participation in royalties derived from the commercialization of genetic materials.

b. Share economic benefits with conservation areas.

c. Develop local scientific-technological capacity by strengthening basic local infrastructure and technology transfer processes.

4. It is essential to recognize that arrangements of this nature require development of the human capacities needed to conduct national and international commercial negotiations. Without all these capacities, countries will never be in a position to mobilize their biotic wealth or recognize the value of traditional knowledge for solving modern problems. The issue of capacity building is also fundamental to the implementation of the Convention on Biodiversity and to any other agreements that might be proposed at the Summit. Such capacity building demands extensive hemispheric collaboration, both North-South and South-South. The Sustainable Development Program for the Americas could be a catalyst for information sharing on knowing, using, and saving biodiversity.

F. Overall Strategies for Biodiversity Conservation

1. All countries need to conduct national biological surveys as required by the Biodiversity Convention. National, regional, and hemispheric biodiversity information networks need to be created for facilitating access to this biological information. The availability of information on the biodiversity contained by protected areas allows for the promotion of myriad types of non-destructive uses of wild biodiversity.

2. Countries should clearly define the portions of their territory they want to preserve as representative samples of their biodiversity and manage them accordingly.

3. Public education is vital. Most people are devoid of understanding biodiversity and its

fundamental importance to society. The ability to implement a sensible agenda is largely dependent upon an improved public understanding. This can be advanced in at least three ways.

a. Inclusion in basic curricula for schools and universities.

b. General efforts at public education via the media.

c. Exciting new opportunities through electronic media, such as GLOBE.

4. Future development relies on the participation of local populations and benefits from their knowledge, their ancestral and traditional cultures and practices, and their needs. NGOs and international institutions should focus greater support for grass roots organizations and work to ensure that local communities play a principal role in managing and administering protected areas. Costa Rica is making substantial progress along these lines with the creation of the National System of Conservation Areas.

VI. ENERGY

A. Overview

Energy is one of the essential ingredients of development. A crucial short-term problem is that the societies most affected by energy shortages are those that can least afford to be without the energy needed for their climb out of mass poverty. The striking differences in the level of affluence and access to basic services between North American (NA) and Latin American and Caribbean (LAC) countries is due in good part to the lack of energy services in the countries of LAC. This is clearly reflected by the fact that the consumption per capita in Latin American and Caribbean countries is approximately eight times smaller than in North America (see Table 1). Our urgent and collaborative task is to promote policies and devise instruments for the efficient use and sustainable development of energy resources.

If one wishes to reduce infant mortality, increase life spans, and reduce illiteracy, more useful energy will have to be made available to the population of LAC countries. The priority is to increase the energy services available for the people and socioeconomic activities of the hemisphere and not necessarily spur an overall growth in primary energy consumption. Optimization of energy use would slow the increase in primary energy consumption, but consumption per capita is so low in some of the LAC countries that it is bound to increase appreciably in rural areas.

Energy efficiency and clean energy activate economic growth and make good business sense, but they also reduce greenhouse gas emissions and reduce the environmental degradation associated with the development of conventional energy supplies. The Americas need a coherent and comprehensive energy strategy that incorporates environmental impacts and development requirements. The changes occurring in international relations and the world oil market have not done away with the strategic nature of energy; they have only attenuated it. Over the long term, interactions of market forces may once again shift because energy security continues to depend on supplies coming from a group of countries located in the Middle East and Northern Africa which are characterized by a complex political, ethnic, and religious situation. A forward-looking integration policy for the Americas would include an energy strategy that targets hemispheric energy independence.

Table I. Commercial Primary Energy Consumption in the Americas (1992)

	Energy (million toe*)	Population (million)	Per capita Consumption (toe/inhabitant)
LAC	445.4	445.0	1.0
NA	2270.4	282.0	8.0
Total	2715.8	727.0	3.7

*toe = tons of oil equivalent

The expected growth in energy consumption in Latin American and Caribbean countries will impose a serious financial strain on their economies. They must either import fossil fuels and/or invest heavily in hydroelectric or thermal power generating plants. In Latin America, approximately 20 percent (and growing rapidly) of all new investments are in the energy area, which represents an extraordinary drain on the resources available to a number of countries in the area.

The sources of primary energy in the North and South are very different. In LAC countries, oil and natural gas represent 68 percent of consumption and coal only 4.3 percent. In NA countries, coal, a larger producer of greenhouse gas (GHG) emissions, represents 23 percent, while hydrocarbons represent an additional 63 percent. On the other hand, hydroelectricity is abundant in Latin America; it provides 7.2 percent of present-day consumption and can continue to grow without increasing the CO_2 content of the atmosphere. In NA countries, hydroelectricity covers only 2.2 percent, while nuclear energy, with all its associated risks, represents 8.3 percent of total output.

Table II. Commercial Primary Energy Consumption 1992 (millions of toe)

	NA	%	LAC	%
Oil	864.1	36.1	249.0	45.3
Natural Gas	586.4	24.5	79.4	14.4
Coal	520.5	21.7	20.6	3.7
Hydro	153.9	6.4	103.8	18.8
Biomass*	80.5	3.4	95.1	17.2
Nuclear	188.5	7.9	3.2	0.6
Total	2393.9	100	552.0	100

Source: British Petroleum Statistical Review of World Energy (June 1994). * 1994 OLADE estimate.

In addition to commercial primary energy (oil, natural gas, coal, nuclear, and hydroelectricity), non-commercial energy sources (biomass, fuel wood, sugarcane, and agricultural residues) are still important in LAC countries, representing 19 percent on average, and in the rural areas of the least developed countries, up to 80 percent of all energy consumed. Although deforestation in LAC is mainly the result of clearing land for agriculture and cattle grazing, virgin forests are being depleted due to fuel wood consumption.

LAC countries are minor contributors to global greenhouse gas (GHGs) emissions since their overall energy consumption is only 16 percent of the total in the Americas, and they also have a bigger share (23.4 percent versus 15 percent) of energy sources that do not emit GHGs. However, if energy consumption grows 4 percent to 5 percent per year in Latin America, which is the goal of most planners, the situation will change dramatically in 25 years as the LAC countries' share of the total energy consumption in the Americas skyrockets.

The growth in energy consumption in Latin America also represents a serious threat to the environment in a number of high population density areas such as Mexico City, Santiago, and Cubatão in the Brazilian state of São Paulo. Some of these problems arise from the use of buses and automobiles and have characteristics which are not dissimilar to the problems of Los Angeles. Others have to do with polluting industries which benefit from weak environmental regulations.

Statistics show that the region is consuming energy less efficiently due to under-utilization, technological obsolescence, poor levels of maintenance, and a major reduction in investment. The incorporation of concrete policies for the rational use of energy would lead to important energy savings with a low level of investment. By applying measures that require little investment, the region could reduce its energy imports by 40 percent. It is in the interest of all the countries in the Americas to try to steer sustainable development in ways that will prevent the LAC region from becoming a large contributor to local and global pollution. Some of the ways that this can be achieved without curtailing development include the following.

B. Promote Energy-Efficient Technologies, Processes, and Management in Latin America and the Caribbean

1. After the first oil crisis in 1973, crucial progress was achieved in NA countries through the "decoupling" of economic growth from energy consumption. Structural changes in the economy, an expansion of the service sector, and the introduction of energy-efficient devices for motive power, lighting, refrigeration, etc. all played important roles in this decoupling. In LAC countries, the structural change went toward energy-intensive industrial development, with a slower introduction of energy-efficient devices and processes. Now, new mechanisms are needed for the provision of technical assistance and financing to facilitate the adoption of appropriate equipment, technologies, processes, and energy management expertise. Organizations like the UNDP, IDB, OLADE, the International Energy Agency, and the Export-Import Bank of the United States should be engaged in this effort.

   a. Make loans for energy conservation and/or renewables as easily available as loans for new, conventional energy supplies. Financial institutions should give due consideration to the environmental impacts of additional conventional energy supplies when evaluating energy project financing.

   b. A significant shortfall of investment resources exists for energy management service, conservation, and sustainable energy-production enterprises in the small and medium size. Multilateral funding could move in to help close this gap by supporting such enterprises.

   c. Invest in energy-efficient infrastructure. Consider the downstream costs of a project's energy requirements in the future.

   d. Cogeneration of heat and electricity proved to be an excellent investment in the United States and should be stimulated in Latin America and the Caribbean countries.

   e. Substitute construction and other materials that are produced using high levels of energy-intensity with those requiring low energy-intensity.

   f. Recycle materials and use urban wastes to produce heat and electricity.

   g. Institute labeling and heavy import duties on inefficient equipment.

   h. Set up energy-efficiency testing facilities.

   i. Develop regional energy-efficiency standards.

C. Promote Integrated Energy Planning and Demand-Side Management

Strategic energy planning will reduce the pressure to increase primary energy consumption. Emphasis should be placed on meeting energy services needs rather than simply expanding energy resource use or building more infrastructure. Promote all measures for better demand-side management and to supply development that takes into account all environmental costs, particularly those related to the Climate Convention.

D. North/South Cooperative Initiatives

1. Countries currently export products that do not meet their own national minimum standards. Inefficient vehicles, energy-wasting consumer appliances, and other products are being shipped to the South. Such discriminatory trade practices should be eliminated.

2. Promote technical cooperation for human resource development and technology transfer. Develop joint partnerships for technology transfer, demand-side management, and extending the competitiveness of hemispheric energy resources.

3. Taking into account the vast diversity of experiences in the energy field throughout the Americas, it is very important to develop programs for technical cooperation and training in the field of integrated energy planning and sustainable energy development. Organizations such as UNDP, OLADE, IDB, and the OAS could contribute to this task and also improve the flow of information and technologies. The Sustainable Development Program for the Americas could also play a major role in promoting the cooperation needed.

   a. Interactions and partnerships between utility professionals should be promoted to implement energy-efficiency measures. Promote government-to-government and public utility commission interactions to aid the development of regulations and regulatory frameworks. Utility regulations which encourage investments in conservation and renewable energy sources are particularly important.

   b. Create networks for exchanging information on regulation, energy conservation, and renewable sources.

   c. Develop self-sustaining structures for international public and private partnerships.

   d. Support vertical and horizontal cooperation and institution building among NGOs.

E. Reduce the Environmental Impacts Caused by Energy Systems

1. Require foreign energy exploration, extraction, transport, and processing firms to abide by the environmental regulations of their "home" country or the country in which activities are taking place — whichever are more stringent.

2. Strengthen national capacities to regulate, monitor, and enforce environmental laws regarding energy development and consumption.

3. Reduce the carbon contents of the energy supply by increasing renewable energy resources and the use of natural gas.

4. Improve measures for avoiding and/or controlling the negative environmental impacts along the energy chain for all energy sources.

5. Develop agreements between countries of the Americas that accelerate the adoption of more uniform environmental regulations. Some of the procedures used in the NAFTA agreement could be transferred to other Latin American countries.

F. Promote Energy-Efficient Transportation in the Americas

1. In urban and regional planning, "transit-led" development should be the guiding principle. Developing mass transit systems and discouraging automobile use then becomes the centerpiece of planning. Currently, the dominant dependence on road-based travel is leading to major congestion in cities, aggravating problems of economic productivity, air pollution, and growing energy consumption. Transit-led development is also an equitable economic development policy since it permits transportation for people who cannot otherwise afford it.

   Promote a cooperative effort among cities of the hemisphere to exchange information on maximizing energy-efficient urban planning and transportation development. Help build the capacity for this type of planning among cities in the South (another potential initiative for the Sustainable Development Program for the Americas).

2. The pledge by the United States and Canada to achieve the same level of overall greenhouse gas emissions of 1990 by the year 2000 is particularly commendable because the countries of LAC, which are not bound by the Climate Convention, could follow this strategy toward reducing their GHG emissions. The long list of actions being implemented by the U.S. administration to avoid climate change is valuable, but more significant actions are needed in the transportation sector. Overall, levels of CO_2 emissions are still increasing. Stronger actions in NA countries toward better performance standards and behavioral changes regarding transportation use could spread quickly to LAC countries.

Move toward setting hemispheric standards on fuel efficiency for automobiles.

G. Promote the Use of Renewable Energy Systems

1. A major effort should be undertaken to expand the use of renewable energy technologies (wind, solar, small hydro, biomass, etc.). This translates into a greater representation of such projects in the portfolios of multilateral development banks and agencies. Long-run energy investment planning should incorporate the environmental costs and benefits of different energy generation technologies.

2. Lower trade tariffs and barriers for renewable energy and energy conservation technologies.

3. The expansion of hydroelectricity in both NA and LAC countries should be promoted, taking care to minimize any negative environmental or social impacts. To reduce the need to flood large areas of land, special focus could be placed on developing small-scale hydro-power units.

4. Over the longer term, combine these efforts with the development of hydrogen as a clean substitute for fossil-derived fuels.

H. Modernize the Use of Biomass

1. Increasing the use of biomass could open new markets and lead to overall lower emissions of CO_2.

2. Biomass-gasification technology holds promise for rapid adoption by several LAC countries.

3. A Brazilian program to use ethanol from sugarcane has reduced CO_2 emissions of that country by 18 percent.

I. All Countries Should Commit to Implementing the Climate Convention

VII. FINANCING SUSTAINABLE HUMAN DEVELOPMENT IN THE AMERICAS

A. Overview

The current efforts to establish free trade throughout the Western Hemisphere are unprecedented in the histories of both regional integration and economic relations between rich and poor countries. Building on the NAFTA precedent, never have countries of such wide economic disparities and heterogeneous structures seriously contemplated such a new form of economic relations based on a mutual opening of each other's economies. While hemispheric integration can build on an already extensive linkage of trade, investments, and migration relations, it must also contend with huge asymmetries of power across countries and some of the widest income and regional inequalities within countries anywhere in the world. The move toward hemispheric free trade is occurring where disparities are two to three times wider than in the European Community's famed enlargement to include its poorer continental neighbors. The experiment of seeking rapid growth and development thorough mutual opening among neighbors is also alien to the export-led "Asian miracle." Setting a major global precedent, never before has such a broad attempt been made to integrate along North-South lines while simultaneously pursuing multilateral trade liberalization and South-South integration.

This bold experiment has captured the imagination of the hemisphere, which less than a decade ago was trapped in an acrimonious debt crisis with crippling stagnation. The rapid pace of this new integration, however, is also highlighting the challenge of huge disparities between the countries of the region as well as the income inequality and structural problems within countries. Increased integration can lead to faster growth for the more advanced sectors which will be further linked across countries, but it will also exacerbate already large inequalities within both rich and poor countries in the short term due to dislocations in the less competitive sectors, labor markets, and communities.

In the case of Europe, regional integration was accompanied by mechanisms for economic transfers from North to South. In Asia, massive capital flows for global export production are producing de facto adjustment mechanisms in already relatively egalitarian societies. What has been sorely lacking in the burst of enthusiasm for Western Hemispheric integration is an equally energetic focusing on the identification of investment mechanisms and domestic and international economic reforms that will be necessary if robust growth with equitable development is to be sustainable throughout the Americas. Such an effort will be necessary if hemispheric integration and cooperation is to serve as a foundation for sustainable human development.

Agenda 21 identifies priorities and elaborates strategies and programs to reverse environmental degradation and promote environmentally sound and sustainable development. Particular emphasis is placed on the need for a substantial flow of new and additional financial resources to developing countries for these purposes. Despite acceptance by many world leaders of the need for an "Earth Increment" during the UNCED held in Rio de Janeiro in June 1992, the response of the international community for new funds did not match or even come close to its ambitious pronouncements. Proposals put forth at the Summit must reflect this experience and be firmly grounded in the political reality of what is and what is not financially feasible. In practical terms, sustainable development must ultimately be self-financed, even though it may need a short-term injection of outside funds to solve a cash flow problem. To ensure that an initiative is financially self-sustaining, and politically feasible, we should first examine revenue-neutral reforms and mechanisms that do not require huge injections of new external resources.

Financing instruments for sustainable human development must always be in the form of incentive financing that mitigates a market failure; internalizes an externality; corrects an incentive structure; or plays a catalytic or leveraging role that raises additional resources or induces policy changes. Sustainable development is development that pays its full cost along the way. When it depletes resources, it charges itself a user cost; when it despoils the environment, it charges itself an environmental cost that fully covers the damage; it receives no subsidies except in proportion to the positive externalities that it generates. Outside financing can play only a catalytic, demonstration, or temporary role to alleviate cash flow problems in this process. Genuine development can only be sustained by internalizing the costs of environmental protection and the provision of social infrastructure into the very economic activities that place additional demands on these resources.

The following section will briefly review the experience of economic transfer mechanisms in the European Union and estimate what the size of those transfers would be if applied to the Western Hemisphere. Realistic options for the Americas are then reviewed and a proposal is made for a set of mechanisms to both address short-term dislocation and adjustment throughout the hemisphere as well as mobilizing long-term investment resources for a more efficient and equitable distribution of economic, social, and environmental infrastructure.

B. The European Union Experience

1. The European Union has made the elimination of regional disparities and the upward harmonization of standards an explicit goal since the signing of the Treaty of Rome in 1957. Currently, the European Union's structural adjustment and regional development programs include four separate components: three Structural Funds and the European Investment Bank (EIB). According to the Padoa-Schioppa Report of 1987, there was roughly a 1:5 differential in per capita income between the richest and the poorest regions, with unemployment ranging from 3 percent to 30 percent and basic infrastructure endow-

---

1. Canada, U.S., Mexico, Guatemala, (Belize), El Salvador, Nicaragua, Costa Rica, Panama, Honduras, Colombia, Venezuela, (Guyana), (Suriname), (French Guiana), Brazil, Paraguay, Uruguay, Argentina, Chile, Peru, Ecuador, Haiti, Bolivia, Dominican Republic, Jamaica, and Trinidad and Tobago.

ments 12 times higher in the wealthiest regions than in the least developed ones.

2. Structural Fund payments in 1991 totaled about 0.212 percent of total Community GDP. Total EIB lending was 0.279 percent of GDP. The total GDP of the Western Hemisphere[1] in 1991 was $7,193,935 million. Thus, a proportionally equivalent adjustment fund would spend $15,251 million per year, while an equivalent loan fund would lend $20,071 million per year.

3. However, it should be remembered that per capita income disparities are far greater in the case of the Americas than in Europe. Therefore, it is unreasonable to expect that the same level of funding will promote convergence, especially given the criticism that funding is not sufficient even in the European case. These figures make it clear that transfer payments, by themselves, will be insufficient to meet the challenge posed by hemispheric integration. Therefore, we must develop innovative strategies for financing education, poverty reduction, environmental protection, technology transfer, and the many other vital areas that must be addressed in the Americas.

C. Transition to Sustainable Development as a "Bankable" Project

1. The fundamental premise of Agenda 21 is that sustainable development is essentially a "bankable" project, that is, an investment that will reap much larger benefits in the long-run. The problem is that many developing countries are too poor and too indebted to secure long-term financing of their transition to sustainable development at commercial rates. Traditional development assistance is either inadequate or unavailable because of inadequate "conventional" returns or unaccounted global benefits. In such circumstances, a case can be made for longer-term loans with the incremental cost for the generation of global benefits funded by an outside grant.

2. However, in most cases the transition to sustainable development can be justified in conventional lending terms. In the long term, the project will more than pay for itself,

and therefore what we face is a cash-flow problem. To solve it, we need a loan, a collection mechanism (e.g., taxes or charges) and a favorable repayment schedule. To be sustainable, an activity must be ultimately self-financed.

D. Waste Reduction as a Financing Mechanism

Increasing emphasis on demand management and efficiencies in energy and water consumption will reduce the demand for major investments in new energy and water supply facilities. This would simultaneously benefit the environment and free up additional financial resources. The challenge for development agencies is to use their limited resources to leverage policy changes that will save a country millions while advancing sustainable development.

E. Increase Resource Rents

The rate of resource exploitation in most countries is excessive and possibly unsustainable. Little of the growing scarcity rent is captured by the government and reinvested in the protection and enhancement of the resource and the enlargement of the country's stocks of human and man-made capital as required by sustainable human development. For example, only 10 to 50 percent of the scarcity value or stumpage of tropical timber is being captured by governments, and a good part of whatever is captured is returned to logging companies through public construction of logging roads and timber processing subsidies which encourage increased logging. Similar situations exist in the mineral and fossil fuel extraction industries. Billions of dollars a year of additional foreign exchange earnings and government revenues can be obtained by a more efficient resource concession and taxation system.

F. Fiscal Reform

Conventional taxation systems throughout the world tax work, income, savings, and value-added, while leaving, consumption, resource depletion, and pollution untaxed (or even subsidized). The reduced incentives for work, savings, investment, and conservation and the increased incentives for consumption, resource depletion, and environmental degradation result in less growth and more environmental degradation. A reform of the fiscal system that would reduce conventional taxes and replace them with environmental taxes — leaving the total tax receipts unchanged — would bring the overall economy closer to sustainable development. Such revenue-neutral fiscal reform would not generate additional revenues in the short run, but it would save government expenditures on environmental regulation and pollution abatement while advancing the objectives of Agenda 21 of more economic growth with less environmental degradation. For example, income taxes could be reduced and the lost tax revenues replaced by taxes on gasoline, chemicals, and other polluting products. While an overnight shift from "taxes on value" to "taxes on vice" is unlikely and potentially disruptive, a gradual shift toward environmental taxes would be a move in the right direction. Care must be taken so that the overall tax burden is progressive rather than regressive.

G. The Removal of Subsidies as a Financing Mechanism

To put the economy on a sustainable development path, many changes needed may not involve any investments at all but simply a change in the incentive structure to induce less wasteful and more environmentally sound behavior. Removal of costly subsidies that distort the economy and subsidize waste and environmental degradation is the single most effective means of financing sustainable development. Examples include the removal of subsidies for fossil fuels, pesticides, logging, and land clering. This would realign the incentive structure in favor of environmentally sound practices; improve efficiency and raise economic growth by removing major economic distortions; improve income distribution since most subsidies disproportionately benefit the rich; and free up budgetary resources to spend on investments that advance sustainable development.

H. Brown Taxes and Green Subsidies

Economic activities such as logging and mining and products suchas pesticides and fossil fuels which generate negative externalities deserve to be taxed in proportion to the environmental costs they impose on society so that less of them will be produced. Activities and products such as reforestation, integrated pest management, and solar energy, which have positive externalities, deserve to be subsidized so that more of them will be produced. Such environmental investments can be financed from taxes on mining, soil erosion, and emissions without the need for higher

general taxation or increased foreign borrowing. Such cross-subsidization, if introduced gradually and designed to be revenue-neutral, is likely to have a positive impact on the structure of the economy without a negative impact on its growth rate.

I. Financing Through Privatization

Privatization of state enterprises is likely to save a substantial portion of the national budget for sustainable human development investments, as well as improve economic efficiency and reduce waste in the provision of public services and other products currently provided by state enterprises. Competitive bidding, with adequate safeguards for equity, anti-monopoly pricing, and environmental protection, can affect the private provision of many public services. Privatization of state enterprises would guarantee three direct sources of funding available for investments in sustainable development: additional government revenues from the sale of state enterprises, savings in government expenditures from no longer having to finance state enterprise deficits, and additional tax revenues from an expanded tax base.

J. Environmental Financing to the Private Sector

The state is often saddled with huge bills for cleaning up oil spills, hazardous waste, contaminated land, and reforestation. Many of these problems could have been paid for or prevented by the polluters or beneficiaries of the responsible activities. The government can reduce its share of the clean-up and restoration bill by instituting deposit-refund systems, environmental bonds, and bank guarantees for compliance with environmental rules. Induced self-regulation is more efficient and cost effective than direct government regulation because industries know best how to control their own waste, and the cost of policing and monitoring are significantly reduced and assumed directly by the source. Environmental bonds, for instance, ensure that:

   a. Resource extracting companies and potential polluters take adequate measures to minimize the environmental damage caused by their activities;

   b. These firms effect clean-up and restoration of residual damage in the most cost-efficient manner;

c. Adequate funds are available for clean-up and restoration of damaged environments by anyone who fails to comply. Environmental bonds need not be a constraint on economic activity as they can be invested in interest-bearing accounts or replaced by bank guarantees.

K. Economic Instruments and Environmental Regulations

Command and control regulations such as end-of-the-pipe effluent and emission standards and mandated pollution control technologies have been the standard approach to environmental protection in developed and developing countries alike. However, poor performance and high compliance and enforcement costs have encouraged many countries to explore the use of economic instruments instead. Environmental taxes, effluent charges, and tradable emission permits are more cost effective, and they could generate substantial revenues for environmental investments. Regulations, on the other hand, generate no revenues and require large budgets and bureaucracies to manage and enforce them. Thus, a move toward increased use of economic instruments for environmental management, either in support of or as a replacement for command and control regulations, should be regarded as an indirect mechanism for funding sustainable development. Unfortunately, the trend at present is for developing countries to copy the command and control regulations and rigid environmental standards of developed countries even as the latter are trying to escape from them.

L. Decentralize Government and Taxation

Most environmental problems are either local or global, and few, if any, are national. In many counties, local governments are no more than appointed local agents of the central government, accountable to the center rather than to their constituents. Therefore, they tend to be unresponsive to local needs and local problems and to advance top-down solutions. For example, only a small fraction of the tax revenues collected from many major tourist resort towns is actually retained in these towns to protect the natural environments that constitute the resource base of their major industry. While socially beneficial projects at the local and global level go unfunded, central governments are often busy taxing income and work to subsidize pollution, waste, and inefficiencies in the name of national development. A critical issue in financing sustainable development is how to decentralize government authority and revenue-generating power to the local level. Decentralizing taxation and public expenditure authority to local governments and municipalities is likely to both save tax revenues by trimming down a multilayer bureaucracy and to advance sustainable development. Clear rules for sharing authority and revenues from taxation and exploitation of natural resources among national and local governments is critical to the efficient financing of sustainable development.

M. New Mechanisms: The Multilateral Investment Fund and NADBANK

The Multilateral Investment Fund (MIF), first proposed in President George Bush's Enterprise for the Americas Initiative, was created on February 11, 1992, by twenty-one of the member countries of the Inter-American Development Bank (IDB).[2] A separate agreement was signed on the same date naming the IDB as the administrator of the Fund. Both agreements went into effect on January 7, 1993, and the first funding installments arrived shortly thereafter. The principal voters in the MIF are Japan, the U.S., and Spain. The $1.3 billion fund has two general goals:

a. To reduce the social costs of the transition to an open market economy, particularly by broadening participation in the enterprise economy among those people left out of the economic mainstream.

b. To boost private sector activity, streamline public sector institutions, and assist enterprises in entering the global marketplace.

2. MIF functions as part development institution and part venture capital fund, drawing on the resources of the IDB and the Inter-American Investment Corporation and providing assistance primarily in the form of grants. There are three facilities:

a. The Technical Cooperation Facility will provide assistance to governments and government agencies to study and imple-

---

2. Argentina, Brazil, Canada, Chile, Colombia, Costa Rica, France, Germany, Guatemala, Honduras, Italy, Japan, Mexico, Nicaragua, Peru, Portugal, El Salvador, Spain, the U.S., and Venezuela.

ment policy responses aimed at increasing investment.

b. The Human Resources Facility provides assistance to governments or other institutions to assist in developing the human resource base needed for increased investment and an expanded private sector.

c. The Small Enterprise Development Facility provides assistance to micro-enterprises, either directly or through intermediaries.

N. The North American Development Bank

1. Part of the NAFTA and its Side Agreements which came into effect as of January 1, 1994, is the establishment of a North American Development Bank (NADBANK). The NADBANK will serve as a regional lending institution designed to finance, coordinate, and implement border and nonborder environmental, infrastructure, and community development projects related to continuing North American integration. NADBANK will be organized to invest specifically in the environmental, physical, and social infrastructure that will be needed to bring about an improvement in environmental and social standards and practices between Mexico and the United States.

2. NADBANK's unique financing mandate covers both the United States and Mexico. A wide spectrum of border and non-border organizations, including local, state, and federal governments and agencies, community-based and other non-private organizations, and private business are able to submit project proposals. NADBANK would provide technical assistance to affected communities in developing project proposals. NADBANK projects would complement ongoing NAFTA-related worker retraining programs, seeking to open new viable employment options for less competitive regions. The goal of NADBANK funding is to enhance the quality of North American integration, not to supplant or subsidize the private sector. Its public interest purpose is to augment the following:

a. Leverage investment to develop socially beneficial environmental infrastructure;

b. Mitigate harmful effects of potential environmental hazards through user-fee based infrastructure financed on the "polluter pays" principle;

c. Participate in community economic development projects in targeted areas;

d. Assist in the development of small and emerging enterprises that benefit from NAFTA-generated opportunities and employ those displaced by industries threatened by NAFTA.

3. NADBANK represents a highly cost-effective way of using government funds to leverage private capital for needed investments. The U.S. and Mexican governments contribute a small amount of the total capitalization of the NADBANK in the form of "paid-in" capital or direct cash contributions. Paid-in capital would be $450 million or 15 percent of the total subscribed capital, with the U.S. and Mexico each contributing 50 percent ($225 million) paid in over five years. The United States and Mexico will also make available $2.55 billion in the form of guarantees know as "callable" capital.

4. The total NADBANK subscribed capital of $3 billion would then be used to issue bonds at a conservative gearing ratio to guarantee a AAA rating. These bonds will allow NADBANK to make available an estimated $3 billion for long-term financing at the lowest commercial rates possible. NADBANK's direct financing capacity will be used to leverage additional private and public funds in order to generate an estimated total of $20 to $40 billion in project finance for worthwhile projects that otherwise would not be financially feasible.

5. The evaluation for NADBANK support will be based on the NAFTA-related need for each project and the effectiveness of NADBANK funds to realize worthy projects that could not otherwise be supported solely through private capital markets and which provide an adequate rate of return to NADBANK. Projects supported by NADBANK must comply with domestic environmental and labor standards.

6. NADBANK governance is designed to be open, transparent, and highly participatory. While final decision-making authority rests with a Board of Executive Directors which represents the governments capitalizing the NADBANK, an Advisory Committee representing local government, community, environmental, labor, and business groups will also be appointed, and an Ombudsman Office will be created to assure public accountability and participation in the decisionmaking of the NADBANK.

O. Proposals for Cooperative Hemispheric Financing Mechanisms

1. Redeploy existing financial resources — development assistance agencies and environmental support groups must lead by example and redeploy their own resources to recast and restructure their existing projects and resources. The new criteria must be to elevate the capacities of developing countries for their transition to sustainable economies. The necessary changes call for more investments in people, analytical skills, institutional infrastructure, technical assistance, demonstration and pilot projects, and catalytic interventions.

2. There is a need for mechanisms that could accompany Western Hemisphere integration to address both short-term adjustment and long-term social development objectives. Other needs include direct investment in projects that can increase the capacity of less-developed regions to take advantage of new opportunities in increased hemispheric trade. Hemispheric mechanisms for sustainable human development that will help narrow disparities should be dedicated to two main goals:

   a. Funding investments necessary to accelerate growth with equity in the less-developed countries and regions with long-term investments in human capital, research and development, social and environmental harmonization, etc.

   b. Improving the basic infrastructure and removing structural impediments, thereby allowing those regions to reap the ben-

efits of increased integration and faster growth.

3. Retraining assistance is particularly needed to help alleviate unavoidable short-term dislocation problems in sectors, regions, and communities within both the developing and developed countries.

4. There are a broad range of possible means by which to finance and structure such a facility. Direct taxing of trade should be avoided due its negative effects on trade and employment. More innovative means that take into account the main beneficiaries of integration and the effects on current jobs and future environmental quality should be employed.

5. For large infrastructure projects, the most cost-effective way to leverage scarce public funds for needed investments is to capitalize financing through the direct support of regional governments and other governments that will invest and potentially gain from increased regional integration. AAA bonds could be issued and then provide low cost financing with long-term social returns. While this approach has been the standard funding mechanism used by the World Bank and Inter-American Development Bank, new institutions such as the European Bank for Reconstruction and Development, the MIF, and the NADBANK are expanding this mandate to lend not only to governments but also directly to the private sector and non-governmental organizations.

6. A proposal that could realistically gain acceptance by the Presidential Hemispheric Summit planned for December 1994 is the establishment of a series of adjustment and social development goals related to the goals of free trade and integration that could be financed through the coordination of existing government financing. Options include expanding the activities of:

   a. United Nations Development Programme;

   b. IDB/Multilateral Investment Fund;

   c. Organization of American States;

   d. North American Development Bank.

7. These same sources could make contributions to the new efforts undertaken by the

Sustainable Development Program for the Americas.

8. This approach would allow countries to commit and prioritize their own adjustment and social investment resources — particularly worker retraining and other targeted social, economic, and environmental funds —in order to meet each country's targets in a coordinated manner. In the U.S. and Canada, the NADBANK would serve as the financing vehicle, while the UNDP, OAS, and MIF/IDB would expand their activities to cover Latin American countries. As other countries join NAFTA or establish bilateral FTAs with NAFTA members or as other subregional groupings in Latin America (such as CACM or MERCOSUR) are deepened or expanded, the financing capacity and range of programs of these instruments would be expanded accordingly. Such an approach would provide incentives for social actors and countries in both the North and the South to accept the challenge of increased integration without feeling that the more vulnerable elements are being forced to absorb the costs of a broader social benefit. It would also establish explicit financing mechanisms in order to help developing countries realistically accept the move toward increasing standards for labor and the environment. In addition, it would commit the hemisphere to accepting the free trade and integration project as a means toward a set of social development goals.

ABOUT THE INTER-AMERICAN DEVELOPMENT BANK AND THE UNITED NATIONS DEVELOPMENT PROGRAMME

The Inter-American Development Bank (IDB), the oldest and largest regional multilateral development institution, was established in December of 1959 to help accelerate economic and social development in Latin America and the Caribbean. The Bank was created in response to a longstanding desire on the part of the Latin American nations for a development institution that would focus on the pressing problems of the region. A resolution calling for the creation of such a bank was adopted at the First International American Conference, held in Washington, D.C., in 1890. In 1958, President Juscelino Kubitschek of Brazil proposed that the countries of the hemisphere embark upon a bold cooperative effort to promote the economic and social development of the region. His proposal received support from throughout the hemisphere, and shortly thereafter a special committee of the Organization of American States drafted the Articles of Agreement Establishing the Inter-American Development Bank. The Bank's Charter states that its principal functions are to utilize its own capital, funds raised by it in financial markets, and other available resources for financing the development of the borrowing member countries; to supplement private investment when private capital is not available on reasonable terms and conditions; and to provide technical assistance for the preparation, financing, and implementation of development plans and projects.

The United Nations Development Programme (UNDP) is the world's largest multilateral source of grant funding for development cooperation. The United Nations General Assembly created UNDP in 1965 through the merger of two predecessor programmes for United Nations technical cooperation. Funding for UNDP comes from the voluntary contributions of member states. A 36-member Executive Board composed of representatives from both developed and developing countries approves major programmes and policy decisions. Through a network of 132 country offices worldwide, UNDP works with 174 governments with the aim of building developing countries' capacities for sustainable human development. The headquarters for UNDP's regional bureaus is located in New York and covers Africa, Asia and the Pacific, the Arab states, and Latin America and the Caribbean. There are also divisions for Europe and the former USSR and for Global and Interregional Programmes.

*Organization of
American States*

*Inter-American
Development Bank*

*United Nations
Economic Commission
for Latin America and
the Caribbean*

Toward Free Trade in the Western Hemisphere

EXECUTIVE SUMMARY

Since the 1980s the Latin America and Caribbean countries have been undergoing profound economic changes in order to renew growth and development and to participate more effectively in a competitive world economy. The changes have included an impressive unilateral trade liberalization process, far-reaching structural reforms, and a deepening and widening of a variety of subregional integration accords. Indeed, today's political and economic environment is such that the region is showing interest in the creation of a hemispheric free trade area. There is, however, the question of how to best achieve this objective.

In light of the upcoming Presidential Summit, and with a view to promoting consensus around a process that can effectively construct a hemispheric free trade area, this paper examines some potentially viable alternatives. The alternative paths presented, which are not necessarily mutually exclusive, fall into two broad categories: bilateralism and multilateralism. A discussion of the advantages and disadvantages of each alternative is prefaced by a list of the basic principles that should guide whatever mechanism is chosen to eventually form a hemispheric free trade area. These principles are a commitment to multilateral trading rules; explicit and flexible membership criteria; equal treatment for all members; transparency; complementarity of rules among agreements; effective institutions; and reliance on existing hemispheric institutions to give initial impulse to the construction of a hemispheric free trade area.

While it is possible to move toward free trade in the hemisphere through the realization of a series of bilateral accords that eventually converge, this type of option has several inherent limitations which make it less viable and attractive than a multilateral route. In contrast to bilateralism, multilateralism, while being potentially cumbersome at first, provides a more direct and explicit path toward the attainment of hemispheric free trade. Multilateralism involves an agreed-upon framework for collective consultation and negotiation of the terms of a broad-based trade liberalization process. Thus it can accommodate the different conditions among countries in a context of common principles that better facilitate a process of hemispheric free trade.

One possible route within the multilateral approach is the gradual extension of membership in one of the major existing subregional agreements until it incorporates all the countries of the hemisphere. Accession to NAFTA is potentially a strong option in this regard. NAFTA is a multilateral accord that includes the main economic partner and foreign investor for a large number of countries in Latin America and the Caribbean. The agreement's common set of rules already regulates three-quarters of intra-hemispheric exports. The agreement is consistent with GATT, and its accession clause is an expression of open regionalism. The

September 1994.

prospects of lowering investment risk through the locking-in of an agreement with a major industrialized economy also constitutes an additional motivation to accede to NAFTA.

Nevertheless, for further significant trade liberalization to occur in the hemisphere through an expansion of NAFTA membership, the procedures for accession and criteria for application to the agreement still need to be defined. In light of the heterogeneous levels of development in the region, an inclusive hemispheric process would likely demand flexible transitional arrangements and less uncertainty in areas that are sensitive to developing countries, such as labor and environmental standards. Hemispheric accession also would require committed political leadership, and, given the key role of the United States in this process, "fast track" authority should be granted to the Executive Branch.

While NAFTA accession is a major potential option for the goal of forming a hemispheric free trade area, the overall process can be strengthened and complemented through the progressive convergence and widening of all existing subregional agreements, such as NAFTA, MERCOSUR, CARICOM, CACM, and the Andean Pact, based on firm commitments to shared principles and to participation in a common negotiating framework. This paper outlines a way to develop a mechanism which could multilateralize free trade benefits among existing subregional accords within a mutually agreed-upon period of time, while at the same time generating a hemispheric consensus on common minimum standards for sensitive trade-related issues such as intellectual property, labor and the environment. Regular hemispheric ministerial level meetings could determine the precise form of the mechanism to multilateralize trade benefits as well as the interim measures that would ensure that the widening and deepening of existing subregional accords constitute effective building blocks for the larger hemispheric objective. The process could be facilitated by placing it in a hemispheric forum like the OAS Special Committee on Trade, with technical assistance provided by hemispheric organizations such as the IDB and ECLAC. In concluding, this paper points out that the mechanism to multilateralize free trade benefits among existing subregional accords is a new concept for hemispheric discussion, with its own set of complexities that will require the cooperation of all

countries. However, it has the advantages of building on existing progress in subregional integration and advancing the hemispheric free trade process on the basis of inclusion and consensus.

INTRODUCTION

Since the 1980s, the countries of Latin America and the Caribbean have been undergoing a profound economic transformation in order to face the competitive demands of a changing world economy and the challenges of renewing growth and development. At the same time, the United States and Canada have also been experiencing substantial economic restructuring, as they adapt to the increasing competitive pressures of a multipolar world economy. Meanwhile, in the political sphere, the end of the Cold War has introduced new opportunities and challenges for defining hemispheric relations.

These developments have contributed to a shift in hemispheric priorities within the realm of economic, social and political issues. Today, these changing priorities are reflected in the hemispheric agenda and include trade and investment liberalization, good governance, poverty reduction, and environmentally sustainable development.

One of the central aspects of the economic transformation in Latin America and the Caribbean has been impressive unilateral trade liberalization. This has been recently complemented by a surge of new subregional integration initiatives and growing hemispheric interdependence. Traditional subregional agreements have been revitalized, such as the Caribbean Community (CARICOM), the Andean Pact and the Central American Common Market (CACM). New initiatives also have emerged, including MERCOSUR, the North American Free Trade Agreement (NAFTA), the Group of Three (G-3) and numerous bilateral accords.

The combination of progressive unilateral liberalization and renewed subregional integration, all in the context of an outward-oriented development strategy, has led to a practice of "open regionalism." Within this context, there has been a growing interest around a new objective: development of a free trade area in the Western Hemisphere. Such an integration process can have many benefits, including increased scale of production; reduced transactions costs; fuller exploitation of geographic trading opportunities; absorption of technological progress; spurring of specialization within industries; the locking-in of economic policy reforms; and substantial institutional developments through cross-country cooperative programs.[1] The question that remains to be answered, however, is how best to achieve the objective of a hemispheric free trade area (WHFTA).

In an attempt to give more shape to the hemispheric discussion of this issue, particularly in anticipation of the Presidential Summit of the Americas, the present document will examine some basic principles and alternative paths to hemispheric integration. The first part enumerates a set of common principles that should guide any path towards hemispheric trade liberalization. Their purpose is to facilitate a common basis for achieving a more efficient and sustainable hemispheric integration process.

The second part of this paper explores two different paths for hemispheric trade liberalization. One is characterized by individual bilateral negotiations among countries, while the other relies on multilateral processes. Within the multilateral track, one route is the gradual extension of membership in one of the major existing subregional agreements until all the countries of the Americas are incorporated. In this regard, NAFTA is potentially a viable option. Hemispheric free trade could also be attained through the progressive convergence and widening of all existing subregional agreements based on commitments to shared principles and a common negotiating framework.

I. PRINCIPLES

While there is consensus that subregional agreements can serve as building blocks for freer trade in the region and indeed the world, the maintenance of open regionalism among the countries of the hemisphere is by no means assured or automatic. In order to promote trade initiatives that will complement rather than conflict with the objective of open regionalism and multilateral trade liberalization, the following principles can help guide subregional and hemispheric accords.

1. A Commitment to Multilateral Trading Rules

Integration efforts within the Western Hemisphere should advance global trade liberalization,

rather than the formation of restricted blocs. Authorities therefore should use GATT principles to guide the formation of regional trading arrangements. These principles include not raising protection above levels prevailing prior to the formation of a Free Trade Area (FTA) or Customs Union; eliminating trade barriers within a trading zone across substantially all sectors within an agreement rather than having sectoral or topic-by-topic coverage; and assuring that trade agreements have a precise interim plan and schedule for the staged introduction of benefits and disciplines.

2. Explicit Entry Procedures and Flexible Membership

Trade accords should contain explicit rules of entry, including clearly defined procedures and technical conditions for application and negotiation of accession. With this, countries can more effectively focus their attention on enhancing their "readiness to negotiate." The existence of clear and open rules of accession should moreover facilitate assistance and financing from regional multilateral agencies for this purpose. Open regionalism will be enhanced if agreements contain accession clauses and a commitment to initiate negotiations within a stated time frame for all nonmembers who formally apply for membership. Flexible terms of membership should also be promoted in order to broaden the participation of countries and to allow the new members to gradually adapt to all the parameters of an existing accord, after a mutually agreed transition period.

3. Equal Treatment

Trade liberalization in the Western Hemisphere should be based on reciprocity, whereby mutual benefits are attained through mutual obligations, without precluding flexible transition periods among the parties. Agreements that do not offer new membership on terms equal to those of existing members can introduce distortions and cause trade and investment diversion.

4. Transparent Rules

It is important that subregional accords adhere to basic standards of transparency regarding their key trading rules. This in turn will better support private sector investment initiatives within and across subregional accords and will also facilitate the procedures

---

[1] ECLAC (1994), *Open Regionalism in Latin America and the Caribbean*, LC/G.1801 (SES.25/4), Santiago, Chile.

of the new World Trade Organization. Some areas where transparent norms will be particularly important include rules of origin, rules for free trade zones, and staged phase-in periods for different member countries.

5. Complementarity

Countries must cooperate to promote accession clauses and trading rules which are compatible over time, thus establishing a basis for an eventual convergence of all subregional integration accords.[2] Without this cooperation, the hemisphere risks becoming encumbered by a bewildering maze of accession procedures, rules of origin, and tariff phase-outs that will actually increase transaction costs and protectionist practices.

6. Effective Institutions

Institutional mechanisms are essential to carry out operation and enforcement of trade accords. However, institutions should be kept simple in structure, tightly focused on essential functions, and properly staffed to adequately comply with given mandates. They should also be flexible enough to evolve with the changing requirements of the accord.

Among the most important institutional functions generally required are the resolution of disputes (set up to be flexible, speedy, and nonbureaucratic); the financing of adjustment, retraining and development (well focused on those sectors and regions that are bound to experience the most dislocation); and the monitoring of the execution of the agreed rights and obligations. The success of free trade accords will be further enhanced when institutional arrangements improve the efficient functioning of markets, including the enhanced flow of information and the harmonization of standards for quality and procurement.

To ensure transparency, all institutional mechanisms should be subject and accessible to public scrutiny.

7. Initial Reliance on Existing Hemispheric Institutions

The transition to a broader hemispheric free trade arrangement will require a great deal of preparation and coordination. The process should begin by relying on existing hemispheric institutional structures — for example, the OAS Special Committee on Trade and the OAS/IDB/ECLAC Tripartite Committee — to facilitate and enhance the "readiness to negotiate" of governments and the private sector. Existing institutional mechanisms will also be very useful for initial multilateral monitoring and dissemination of information, as well as for providing technical assistance for negotiators. The creation of more permanent institutional frameworks should be undertaken in due time so as to avoid the premature selection of structures which might not be the most appropriate in the long term.

II. ALTERNATIVE PATHS TO HEMISPHERIC INTEGRATION

There are several potential paths for reaching hemispheric trade liberalization. For example, individual countries could seek bilateral free trade agreements with the hope that these would ultimately spread into hemispheric free trade. Subregional groupings could conduct negotiations among themselves, potentially creating a free trade area that would eventually include all countries of the hemisphere. Individual countries or groups of countries in the hemisphere could also request negotiations for accession to an existing arrangement, which would ultimately evolve into a hemispheric agreement. In any event, if bilateral and subregional accords proliferate, at some stage an umbrella agreement will probably be required that pulls all arrangements together to optimize trade creation and to eliminate conflicting trade and investment arrangements.

Most of these scenarios are not necessarily mutually exclusive, since different countries or groupings may choose different options during the formative phases of integration. Indeed, to a certain extent, some of these options are already in progress.

In sum, hemispheric liberalization and convergence of existing schemes can be approached through a process of bilateral negotiations between individual countries. Alternatively, the process can follow a multilateral path toward hemispheric trade liberalization. These two paths are explored below.

II-A. BILATERALISM

Bilateralism has the potential to be rapid and simple vehicle by which countries can push forward national agendas for trade liberalization. The possibility of moving from bilateral agreements to hemi-

---

[2] Final Document of the Conclusions of the Fourth Ibero-American Summit of Chiefs of State and Government, Cartagena, Colombia, 14-15 June, 1994.

spheric liberalization, however, depends to a significant degree on the characteristics of the accords reached by the participants. Thus, a series of open bilateral agreements could conceivably be stepping stones towards broader subregional agreements and be compatible with eventual hemispheric liberalization, while exclusive bilateral agreements that raise barriers to third parties would clearly be a setback to the hemispheric process.

The emergence of hemispheric free trade thus depends on whether the agreements are easily converted into a multilateral framework. For instance, in addition to an open accession clause, it would also depend on whether the bilateral liberalization covers substantially all international trade and on whether commercial rules are broadly consistent with acceptable international practices.

Where bilateral agreements are open and compatible with the world trading system, and conducive to expansion of markets and investment, membership will be attractive to others. With time, a network of broadly compatible agreements could emerge. But in order to achieve hemispheric integration, at some point the process of hemispheric liberalization through the juxtaposition of diverse bilateral agreements would have to acquire a multilateral character.

While bilateralism could be a stepping stone toward a broader form of liberalization, it nevertheless has several inherent limitations. First, the benefits of trade liberalization tend to be concentrated in a few countries. In practice, these agreements tend to be discriminatory and some common characteristics of bilateral agreements make convergence difficult. They typically lack open accession clauses and establish differentiated rules of origin or preferential norms that are obstacles to convergence. In sum, the existence of a multitude of commercial rules exacerbates discrimination and potential trade diversion and raises uncertainties that dampen investment incentives.

With regards to institutional arrangements, bilateral agreements tend to establish *ad hoc* and opaque dispute settlement mechanisms. Once several bilateral mechanisms are operating, it can be even more difficult to harmonize trading rules across countries as precedents are set and vested interests are consolidated. Likewise, it is evident that countries encounter high costs when attempting to administer rules across many bilateral agreements. Once created, moreover, dismantling and replacing a complex network of

administrative rules may also prove costly and thus block the convergence of liberalization schemes.

In the realm of international relations, the proliferation of bilateral accords can provoke political and economic conflicts. The existence of different negotiating capacities across countries further complicates the situation, because smaller and weaker countries could tend to be excluded. In addition, bilateralism is prone to encourage sector-specific arrangements that favor interest groups which can obstruct the multilateralization of agreements in order to maintain their rents. Thus bilateralism tends to generate rigid conditions that are difficult to change later.

Bilateralism also tends to follow economic incentives which concentrate attention on the most attractive markets at the expense of others. This could easily lead to the creation of hub-and-spoke systems dominated by competing larger market countries, exacerbating the effects of trade and investment diversion. Firms within the hub country will have incentives to discourage multilateralization of free trade benefits in order to protect their own preferential position. Also, agreements between the hub and the various spokes may be inconsistent with one another, thus creating a trading maze that causes uncertainty and raises the costs of doing business, as well as slows down convergence in the hemisphere.

The hub-and-spoke system has a particularly perverse effect on investment. As long as there is no free trade and investment among the spokes, the hub country gains access to all spoke markets and each spoke is in a disadvantageous position to compete for direct investment, thus exacerbating trade and investment diversion.

In sum, the possibility of moving toward free trade in the hemisphere through the bilateral path could be complicated and very risky. To achieve the goal of hemispheric free trade, bilateral agreements would at the very least have to respect the common principles outlined above and ultimately be renegotiated and collectively administered in a way that clearly leads to multilateral convergence.

II-B. MULTILATERALISM

In contrast to bilateralism, a multilateral approach involves an agreed framework for collectively negotiating the terms of broad-based trade liberalization. Multilateralism can take the form of successive accessions to a major subregional agreement, such as

NAFTA, or the negotiated convergence of free trade among a number of countries or subregional accords. While multilateralism may appear more cumbersome than bilateralism in the initial stages, it has the advantage of more directly setting the stage for attaining a simplified common set of mutually agreed rules for hemispheric trade and investment.

Since countries and subregions find themselves at various levels of readiness to move forward on the free trade front, governments may have different preferences as to whether to pursue their objectives independently, as part of a group, or even to pursue both routes simultaneously. In general, any effective multilateral process towards hemispheric free trade must in some way accommodate the different national conditions regarding the disposition and capacity to negotiate, as well as preferred strategies, both at the subregional and hemispheric levels.

Whatever path is taken, hemispheric negotiations will likely test the cohesion of subregional integration schemes, particularly because both between and within subregional agreements countries are at very uneven stages of economic reform. In this context, deepening subregional integration arrangements could become an interim vehicle for achieving hemispheric trade liberalization, but on the condition that agreements remain open and share basic trading principles. At the same time widening subregional accords can begin to foster hemispheric links, with the largest market configurations like NAFTA and MERCOSUR possibly constituting the major attractions for other countries and subregional schemes. Convergence, moreover, might require some multilateral mechanism that promotes deepening and widening in a way that all subregional processes ultimately complement each other.

A hemispheric strategy thus should be inclusive, accommodating the widest possible objective differences among the countries. What needs to be avoided is exclusive hemispheric strategies, or potentially worse, the development of a vacuum in which there is no hemispheric strategy at all. Either situation raises the danger of a competitive race among bilateral and subregional trade pacts.

What follows below are two possible mechanisms for a multilateral path to hemispheric trade liberalization. One involves accession to NAFTA, an agreement which to date has attracted the broadest interest as a vehicle for hemispheric integration. The other is a framework for the negotiated linkage and convergence among a variety of countries and subregional accords, including NAFTA, MERCOSUR, CARICOM, CACM, ALADI, the Andean Pact, and incipient configurations such as the Association of Caribbean States (ACS) and the South American Free Trade Area (SAFTA).

II-B.1. NAFTA ACCESSION

Accession to NAFTA is potentially a straightforward option towards building a hemispheric free trade area. According to ECLAC, NAFTA "stands out as the most comprehensive free trade agreement in the hemisphere and the first to be negotiated between a developed and a developing country." It is also characterized as "a precedent...that could lead to progress in hemisphere-level integration, if other Latin American and the Caribbean countries eventually joined."[3]

For several reasons, accession to NAFTA could be a viable path to free trade in the hemisphere. NAFTA is a multilateral accord that includes the very large North American market, particularly the United States, which is the main economic trading partner and foreign investor for a very large number of countries in Latin America and the Caribbean. Moreover, exports among NAFTA partners represent three-quarters of intra-hemispheric exports and are now regulated by a common set of agreed rules and institutions. This makes NAFTA a powerful force in the drive towards hemispheric trade liberalization. Added to this are the prospects of reduced risk premiums and enhanced investment flows for those able to lock into a free trade agreement with a major industrialized economy. Indeed, consideration of these positive lock-in effects can be by itself a strong motive to explore entry into an accord with NAFTA or with the United States.

While the approval of NAFTA was a politically complex process, the continued existence of important constituencies in each member country that have demonstrated energetic and effective support of the agreement, coupled with the encouraging initial results of NAFTA trade, constitutes a potential basis for expecting future expansion of membership.

NAFTA rules are for the most part already operational, transparent, and consistent with GATT.

---

[3] ECLAC (1994), *Open Regionalism, op. cit.*, pp. 25, 28.

NAFTA is probably one of the most publicly account-able, coherent and fully implemented free trade agreements in the hemisphere. Uncertainty still prevails, however, in areas which are sensitive for many developing countries, particularly with respect to labor and environmental standards.

The accession clause, as it appears in NAFTA, is an expression of open regionalism, because accession is not geographically circumscribed to certain countries. This open accession clause helps protect NAFTA against the risk of becoming a closed trading bloc, thus reducing the inefficiencies generated by trade and investment diversion. It also allows nonmembers in principle to test the disposition of NAFTA members to practice open regionalism. However, while the accession clause is formally open, the procedures for application, acceptance and negotiation still have to be defined in order for NAFTA to become an effective vehicle for hemispheric integration.

There is agreement that few countries of the hemisphere are now in a condition to comply immediately with all existing disciplines of NAFTA. Given the heterogeneous levels of development in the region, a meaningful inclusive process of full hemispheric accession to NAFTA would demand flexible transitional arrangements. In practice, NAFTA already includes different calendars of execution adapted to particular cases and limited exceptions required by each negotiating partner. It also includes financing for trade adjustment and environmental infrastructure through the North American Development Bank (NADBANK).

In any case, multilateral trade liberalization through NAFTA accession will require committed political leadership, since the process promises to be lengthy and protracted. Leadership will require, inter alia, agreement among the NAFTA partners on the details of the open accession process. Moreover, given the importance of the United States, the executive branch of that country will need some form of "fast track" negotiating authorization from Congress.

II-B.2. FRAMEWORK FOR HEMISPHERIC TRADE NEGOTIATIONS

While accession to major subregional market accords will remain a major force in the drive for hemispheric free trade, the overall process can be strengthened and complemented by a mechanism which multilateralizes free trade benefits among existing subregional accords, such as NAFTA, MERCOSUR, CACM, the Andean Pact, CARICOM, and others. Indeed, a decision to establish such a mechanism could be one of the consensual initiatives at the December Summit meeting. This initiative could include the following components:

i) Summit participants would declare a collective commitment to construct a hemispheric free trade area.

ii) A target date could be set—for example the year 2000—to complete formal multilateral negotiations.

iii) Summit participants would agree that the widening and deepening of subregional accords could serve as effective building blocks for hemispheric free trade.

iv) It could also be agreed that a key minimum objective of hemispheric liberalization is multilateralization of basic free trade benefits and common minimum standards governing sensitive trade-related areas across all accords in the hemisphere. Some of these areas include intellectual property rights, development and adjustment assistance, financial services and regulation, labor and the environment. The trade benefits and standards would apply to all subregional and bilateral accords throughout the hemisphere within a period of transition to be established by subsequent negotiations.

v) To give credibility and momentum to the initiative, the summit would announce as an integral part of the overall agreement a commitment to establish annual trade ministerial meetings, with preparatory subministerial meetings, to discuss and eventually agree upon:

• Mutually acceptable and specific mechanisms, rules, procedures and principles to underline the negotiation of the multilateralization of free trade in the hemisphere;

• Additional common interim principles to guide future deepening and widening of all existing subregional and bilateral agreements, in order to ease or avoid obstacles to the construction of a common path of convergence to a WHFTA.

vi) The summit would identify an official and formally organized forum for the ministerial meetings which could be, for example, the OAS Special Committee on Trade, with technical support provided by other hemispheric multilateral agencies such as the IDB and ECLAC. In this way, the premature establishment of institutional structures, which may not be the most appropriate in the long term, could be avoided.

Existing and any new subregional secretariats and institutions would be encouraged to work with the hemispheric multilateral organizations to ensure that deepening of subregional accords and institutions would be compatible with hemispheric liberalization and open regionalism.

vii) The IDB and the NADBANK would be called upon to redouble their human and financial resource support for investments linked to integration and trade, with special attention to the sensitive areas of trade-related adjustment, environment, and infrastructure. As an incentive to a coordinated deepening and convergence of trade agreements, priority financing could be given to countries and subregional agreements which were in compliance with the interim guidelines that would eventually emerge out of the annual ministerial meetings mentioned above. The IDB funds would be allocated to all LAC countries while the United States, Canada, and Mexico would access NADBANK financing.

This mechanism has a number of potential advantages. First, it is centered on a principle on which all governments can probably agree: the desirability of an eventual free trade area in the hemisphere. Another consideration is that such an agreement would not be restricted by current trade commitments and political uncertainties, since the difficult details and principles regarding the "how" and "when" to achieve a WHFTA are backloaded to a period after the summit. This is an important consideration since many countries are not yet ready to decide on the exact course of hemispheric integration or the structure of negotiations, and indeed may even disagree on

important points. The initiative, however, is inclusive in the sense that all countries can actively participate (or be represented by a subregional group) and help shape their precise path of convergence into the agreed free trade area.

The backloaded free trade commitment is nevertheless not an empty one because it is given substance by the auxiliary commitment to accept the discipline of regular organized ministerial and subministerial meetings in an official forum such as the OAS. With the support of the IDB and ECLAC, the OAS could monitor, prod ahead, and technically support the process of achieving mutual extension of basic free trade benefits. Indeed, a summit agreement of this type would have the tangible result of moving forward the hemispheric trade agenda during a critical juncture.

Another consideration is that the interim as well as definitive processes and mechanisms for convergence will be defined multilaterally. This will facilitate the emergence of a fresh agenda that could phase in free trade and related disciplines in such areas as intellectual property rights, environment, and labor in a flexible way that could accommodate trade-offs and customized country-by-country schedules for sequencing and implementation. Such a multilateral process would moreover make all governments feel a larger sense of ownership regarding agreed standards in these sensitive areas and would also facilitate financing assistance from international institutions.

An agreement along these lines would also build on existing progress in subregional integration, which has been partly responsible for an impressive growth of exports and deepening "pro-market" liberalization of economies. The agreement would be politically realistic since it is consistent with countries pursuing their own immediate interests, whether by attempting to individually or subregionally accede to NAFTA, signing a bilateral or plurilateral reciprocal or nonreciprocal trade accord, or participating in a deepening of an existing subregional accord. The agreement only asks governments to commit to discussing a way to establish a set of common interim principles and rules to ensure that trade agreements evolve in a direction consistent with open regionalism, eventual hemispheric convergence and an open multilateral trading system.

A summit agreement of this type would allow leadership to be exercised in a multilateral forum where responsibilities and costs can be shared in a mutually agreed upon way, thereby enhancing the catalytic impact on hemispheric free trade with more predictable and enduring results. Indeed, this approach is consistent with the post Cold War trend to use multilateral forums for resolving issues of common concern.

Finally, since this mechanism is a relatively new concept for a hemispheric discussion that includes a large number of countries, it will require the cooperation of all. To the extent that free trade agreements promote hemispheric trade liberalization and take into account the different abilities and possible paths to achieve it, procrastination might be the exception rather than the rule. The free trade leadership and example of the NAFTA partners regarding open regionalism also represents a new potential catalyst to drive commitments forward.

PROPOSALS FROM NON-GOVERNMENTAL SECTORS

I. Preserving and Strengthening the Community of Democracies of the Americas

Americas: The Continent in Which We Want to Live

A Message from Amnesty International to the People of the Americas

Amnesty International is a worldwide movement of people acting on the conviction that governments must not deny individuals their basic human rights. The organization was awarded the 1977 Nobel Peace Prize for its efforts to promote global observance of the United Nations' Universal Declaration of Human Rights. Amnesty International works specifically for the release of prisoners of conscience — men, women, and children imprisoned for their beliefs, color, sex, ethnic origin, language, or religion, provided they have neither used nor advocated violence; fair and prompt trials for all political prisoners; and an end to torture, executions, political killings and "disappearances." Amnesty International's effectiveness depends on its impartial application of a single standard of human rights to every country in the world.

The organization is independent of all governments, political factions, ideologies, economic interests, and religious creeds. It accepts no financial contribution from any government and is funded entirely by donations from its supporters. To safeguard impartiality, groups do not work for prisoners of conscience held within their own countries. Since it was founded in 1961, Amnesty International has worked on behalf of more than 43,000 prisoner cases, of which 40,000 are now closed.

The future of democracy in the Americas will be high on the agenda when the region's presidents gather in Miami for talks in December. Significantly, human rights are not featured on that agenda.

During the years of military rule in the region, the human rights movement played a crucial role in opposing the military regimes and exposing their crimes. When formal democracy was restored in most Latin American countries in the 1980s, there were high hopes that newly elected governments would honor their pledges to uphold human rights. A decade later, at the threshold of the twenty-first century, there is still a gulf between governments' promises and reality. As the presidents of the Americas meet, the human rights movement is calling on them to fulfill their promises and ensure that human rights are respected.

There have been advances in the struggle for human rights. Most countries of the region have active and mature human rights organizations. Stronger civil societies mean that human rights victims are not at the mercy of the state as easily as in the past. There has been some progress in the inter-American system for the protection of human rights. Many of the region's countries are parties to the main regional and international treaties for the protection of human rights. The General Assembly of the Organization of American States (OAS) has just adopted the Inter-American Convention on the Forced Disappearance of Persons; twelve countries have signed this instrument to date. In many countries, the new freedom of the press has seen the growth of an independent media prepared to challenge the authorities.

Nevertheless, serious human rights violations persist in most countries of the Americas. The main reason for this is that those responsible for human rights violations operate with impunity. Extrajudicial executions and "disappearances" continue to be reported in Peru and Colombia, among other countries. In El Salvador, dozens of unresolved killings, some clearly political, have followed the 1992 peace accords, which ended 12 years of civil war. "Disappearances" and extrajudicial executions have also continued to be reported from Guatemala, even though its current President, Ramiro de León Carpio, previously served as the country's human rights procurator, while those responsible for the country's past human rights violations continue to enjoy impunity. In Haiti, hundreds of people "disappeared" or were extrajudicially executed by the army or their armed civilian auxiliaries, which until recently ruled the country.

In both Colombia and Peru, special courts and draconian anti-terrorist legislation have expedited trials of thousands of alleged "subversives," many of whom may be prisoners of conscience. In both countries, thousands of political prisoners, hundreds of whom are prisoners of conscience or possible prisoners of conscience, have been tried or are awaiting trial under judicial procedures which fall far short of international standards.[1]

In Cuba, where the Cuban Communist Party continues to be the only legal political party, some six hundred prisoners of conscience are serving prison sentences of up to fifteen years for offenses related to their attempts to peacefully exercise their rights to freedom of expression, association and assembly. Many are members of unofficial political, human rights, or trade union groups whose activities are severely hampered by the authorities. Trials in all political cases fall far short of international standards.

In the capitals of the region, particularly those of Brazil and Colombia, adolescents, street children, and young adults are killed or "disappeared" every year by the police or "death squads," which often include off-duty police officers. In Colombia other marginalized sectors of society — homosexuals, prostitutes, drug addicts — are also targeted for murder. In rural areas landowners continue to be above the law. They use their power and influence to intimidate indigenous leaders, peasants, rural union leaders, community activists, and anybody who dares to challenge their control over land, economic resources, and political privileges.

Although the death penalty has been abolished in law in most Latin American countries, it continues to be widely used in the United States (USA). There is now ample evidence demonstrating that the use of the death penalty in the USA is arbitrary, unfair and racially discriminatory, despite the existence of elaborate judicial safeguards. More than 2,870 men, women, and juvenile offenders are under sentence of death in the USA. More than 250 have been executed since 1977; 27 were executed between January and the end of October 1994. Nine juvenile offenders have been executed since 1985, in clear contravention of international human rights standards. In September 1993, President Clinton signed new legislation which authorizes the death penalty for some sixty offenses under federal civilian law. This is contrary to international human rights standards and treaties which encourage governments to restrict their use of the death penalty with a view to its ultimate abolition. The death penalty is also occasionally carried out in Cuba, where it is applicable for a wide range of offenses and is on the statute books of most English-speaking Caribbean countries and Chile. In Peru the scope of the death penalty was extended in contravention of the American Convention on Human Rights in December 1993, when the new Constitution came into force.

In response to the escalation of violent crime, the governments of the English-speaking Caribbean are turning to the death penalty and corporal punishment. In July 1994 the government of Trinidad and Tobago carried out its first execution since 1979. The execution was in violation of national and international law, as the case was still under judicial review. In August 1994, a judge ordered the first whipping in 25 years in Jamaica; further whipping sentences were imposed later in the year. The new government of Barbados, elected in September 1994, committed itself to the use of the death penalty and the reintroduction of corporal punishment, which was declared unconstitutional by the Court of Appeal in 1992. Despite numerous studies that have shown that such punishments do not deter violent crime more effectively than other penalties, other governments in the region are poised to adopt them.

Torture and ill-treatment continue to be widespread throughout the region. Beatings in police stations, near asphyxiation, electric shocks, and other forms of torture have been reported in Argentina, Colombia, Chile, Ecuador, Mexico, Paraguay, Peru, Venezuela, the USA, and others and were the norm in Haiti under the military government which only recently relinquished control of the country. Appalling prison conditions amounting to inhuman and degrading treatment and the torture of prisoners are common in many countries of the region, often leading to prison riots, which are violently suppressed. Prisoners have been massacred in Peru in 1986, Brazil in 1992, and in Venezuela in 1992 and 1994. Law enforcement officers have used excessive force, in violation of international standards, against criminal suspects and demonstrators in Bolivia, Brazil, Costa Rica, Paraguay, the USA, Uruguay, and Venezuela.

---

[1] Amnesty International regards prisoners of conscience as any person who is in prison, detention or subject to other physical restrictions by reason of his or her political, religious or other conscientiously held beliefs or by reason of his or her ethnic origin, sex, color or language, provided that he or she has not used or advocated violence.

Victims of Human Rights Violations

A disproportionate number of victims of human rights violations come from the poorest and most vulnerable sectors of society. Many were caught in the cross fire of political violence. The victims include human rights activists and those who struggle for the rights of their communities to a better and more secure life.

Political violence still features on the regional landscape, particularly in Peru and Colombia. "Disappearances," extrajudicial executions, arbitrary detention, and torture have characterized the security forces' counterinsurgency operations in these countries. Unarmed civilians in war zones, trade unionists, civic and popular activists, and human rights workers are among the victims.

In Colombia, more than 20,000 people have been killed for political reasons since 1986 — most by the armed forces and their paramilitary protégés. Paramilitary squads have overrun whole villages, taken control of the administration, and exacted "taxes" from the population. They have killed, terrorized, and driven out villagers and repopulated communities with their own supporters. Tens of thousands of people have fled from their villages to the shanty towns of Colombia's cities, where they face grinding poverty and further violence.

In neighboring Peru, a long and dirty war is being fought between the government and armed opposition groups. At least 27,000 people have lost their lives in the insurgency, approximately half of them killed by government troops. A significant proportion of the killings did not take place in armed combat; they were deliberate killings of defenseless people by either government troops or the armed opposition. Between 1983 and 1993, Amnesty International recorded details of more than 4,300 people who were detained by the security forces and then "disappeared"; the true figure is believed to be higher.

Amnesty International is aware of widespread human rights abuses by armed opposition groups in Colombia and Peru. The organization has repeatedly and unequivocally condemned the grave human rights abuses committed by these groups. These include the deliberate killing of civilians; the killing of members of the security forces who are *hors de combat*, or who have been incapacitated, have surrendered or been taken prisoner; the use of torture and the taking of hostages. In Nicaragua abuses, including summary executions and hostage-taking, have continued to be committed in the context of political violence by armed opposition groups made up of former *Contra* rebels and demobilized members of the army.

While open political violence has diminished in the region, poverty, unemployment, inequality, and discrimination breed potentially explosive unrest. Large sections of the region's population remain excluded from the benefits of economic development and without access to basic goods and services. Poverty and deprivation cannot be dissociated from current human rights problems throughout the region. The urban riots that shocked Venezuela in 1989, recent riots in Argentina's northern provinces, land conflicts in Brazil and Mexico, and widespread trade union and peasant protests in Bolivia, Ecuador, and Paraguay are the most visible manifestations of the social conflicts which affect almost every country of the region.

In the suburbs of Brazil's towns and cities, hundreds of youths and adults, most from the poorest sectors of the population, are killed or "disappeared" by the police or "death squads," which often include off-duty police officers. In Colombia's urban areas people regarded as "disposable" have also been killed by "death squads" in what amounts to a campaign of "social cleansing." Unlawful police violence against the poorest sectors of the population have been recorded in Venezuela and in the main cities of other countries in the region. Amnesty International is concerned by the high number of reports of police shootings, resulting in serious injuries and death in several U.S. cities, particularly Los Angeles and New York.

Among the urban poor children are the most vulnerable. Thousands of abandoned and orphaned children live a desperate existence on the streets of the Americas' main cities. They are attacked by "death squads," beaten and persecuted by the police, and threatened with starvation. Street educators who deal with the consequences of attacks on street children by the security forces are often singled out by the police. Even in countries which have advanced legislation for the protection of minors, the laws protecting them are often not applied and remain on paper. In the USA, death sentences are passed on juvenile offenders, although this is forbidden by international law and, in particular, by the International Covenant on Civil and Political Rights (ICCPR), the Inter-American Commission on Human Rights (IACHR), and the Convention on the Rights of the Child. At least thirty-four juvenile offenders are on U.S. death rows. Children have also been among the victims of past and present political violence in Argentina, Chile, Colombia, El Salvador, Guatemala, Haiti, Nicaragua, Peru, and Uruguay. Some of these children saw their parents killed, tortured, or taken away by the security forces never to be seen again. Other children "disappeared."

Women in the Americas suffer human rights abuse as well as discrimination. As human rights campaigners, political activists, and trade union leaders or as mothers, grandmothers, and wives, women have been subjected to human rights violations throughout the region. The mothers and grandmothers of the "disappeared" during the dirty war in Argentina, including over fifty children, are still trying to discover where their children and grandchildren are. So are the mothers and relatives of the "disappeared" in Chile and Guatemala as well as the mothers of the 11 adolescents and young adults from a shanty town in Rio de Janeiro who "disappeared" in July 1990.

In many cases, women suffered particularly vile forms of sexual assault and other forms of torture and ill-treatment. In Mexico, at least three women were raped by soldiers in June 1994 in the state of Chiapas, where early in the year there had been fighting between the Mexican army and the armed indigenous peasant movement, Ejército Zapatista de Liberación (Zapatista Liberation Army). In Haiti, women living in poor urban neighborhoods and rural villages, where support for President Aristide was strongest, were raped by members of the security forces of the recently deposed miliary-backed Haitian Government. In Peru, some women have been falsely accused of terrorism-related offenses on the basis of declarations forced from them under torture, including rape.

Indigenous people have been victimized by the security forces and by powerful local landowners and their allies for decades. Bitter land disputes have fuelled tensions, and the indigenous peoples have suffered the most. Discrimination against indigenous people means that they are more likely to have their rights trampled on in the first place and then be failed by the justice system. The circumstances in which indigenous peoples fall victim to human rights violations vary widely across the Americas. In Ecuador and Mexico, Indians involved in bitter struggles for land

have been arrested and tortured, and in Mexico, some have been extrajudicially executed. Tens of thousands died in Guatemala during the military counterinsurgency campaign of the late 1970s and the early 1980s. Native Americans are among those in the USA awaiting judicial execution in the horror of death row. Allegations of ill-treatment of Mohawk Indians during a land dispute in Canada in 1990 remain unsolved. The indigenous communities of Peru, caught in a decade of conflict between government forces and armed opposition groups, have suffered widespread abduction, torture and killings.

Despite important political changes in a number of countries during the 1980s, trade unionists in Latin America are still subject to illegal detention, torture and ill-treatment, "disappearance," and extrajudicial execution. Many trade unionists were among the thousands of people who "disappeared" in Argentina, Chile, Brazil, Uruguay, and Guatemala during the years of military rule. Amnesty laws passed in the first four countries mean that there is little prospect of those responsible for the "disappearance" being brought to justice, and there are indications that the same will happen in Guatemala. The whereabouts of the "disappeared" are still unknown.

Violent repression of trade unionists in Colombia has escalated since 1985. The country's largest trade union confederation reports that 500 trade union leaders have been killed since its creation five years ago. Union leaders and members have been subjected to extrajudicial executions, death threats, and harassment in Guatemala and El Salvador. In Costa Rica human rights workers reported that in May 1994, police attacked a demonstration by striking banana workers and opened fire on strikers.

Thousands of peasants, rural union leaders, and their advisers have been killed in Brazil since the country returned to democracy. Most were killed by hired gunmen, some of whom were off-duty or former police. Long delays in carrying out investigations and trials, disappearance of evidence and court records, failure to protect witnesses or those threatened with death, and police attacks on peasant settlers point to a pattern of official complicity with those who order the killing — the *mandantes*.

There is ample evidence that death sentences in the USA are imposed disproportionately on the poor, on minorities, on the mentally ill or retarded, and — crucially — on those without adequate legal counsel. More than 20 years after the U.S. Supreme Court held that the death penalty was unconstitutional in practice — largely because of racial discrimination — examination of the cases of prisoners now under sentence of death and of those executed since 1977 reveals pervasive evidence of continued racial discrimination. More than 49 percent of prisoners now on death rows across the USA are black, even though black people comprise only 12 percent of the U.S. population. The most marked disparities in death-sentencing, however, are seen on examining the race of the murder victim. Eighty-four percent of the prisoners executed since 1977 were convicted of murdering white victims, despite the fact that blacks and whites are the victims of homicide in roughly equal numbers.

The Governments' Reactions

In the 1990s, for the first time in history, most of the Americas' governments speak the language of democracy and human rights. But democracy can only be based on the rule of law and on equal respect for everybody's legally sanctioned rights. This equality of rights has not been respected in practice.

The new civilian governments have set up mechanisms for safeguarding civil and political rights. Official human rights agencies have been established in many countries of the region although the attributions, resources, and effectiveness of these agencies vary from country to country. New laws, constitutions, and constitutional amendments have been introduced, purportedly to reinforce the highest possible legal protection for human rights. International human rights organizations have regular access to governments.

Despite this, there is still a vast gulf between official statements and improvements in human rights in the Americas. Important as they are, constitutional provisions, institutional reforms, and free elections have not brought an end to gross human rights violations in the region. Many governments still operate under the pretence that passing a law amounts to enforcing the rule of law. However, the survival of special courts for the military and security forces, the inefficiency and lack of real independence of the judiciary, and the frequent violation of the principle of equality before the law are some of the means by which impunity is perpetuated. While institutionalization of agencies for the defence of human rights would be welcomed, these can never be a substitute for the governments' lack of political will to uphold

human rights under the rule of law enforced by an independent and efficient judiciary. If this political will is lacking, these government agencies become little more than lightning conductors to protect governments from taking direct responsibility for their human rights violations.

The impunity enjoyed by the perpetrators of gross human rights abuses during the years of military rule has eroded the legitimacy of the new democratic governments. Granting impunity to human rights abusers blatantly violates the principle of equality before the law which every democratic government is bound to uphold. The practice of impunity, however, is not limited to military regimes and civilian transition governments. It is rooted in the region's history of gross inequalities and authoritarianism; in the historically selective use of human rights standards as an instrument of cold war politics and national security; in the legacy of military rule and in the shortcomings of political and judicial reform since the return to democracy. In the Americas, the fact that human rights violators escape justice results from the persistence of structural factors, such as military jurisdiction and the lack of political will by the emerging civilian governments to carry out profound reforms of the administration of justice and the security forces.

The state has a duty to maintain social order. However, when impunity prevails, the rule of law breaks down in society at large. Popular anxiety about rising crime has provided the pretext for police to take the law into their own hands and for the state to execute convicted criminals. In these circumstances torture, judicial and extrajudicial executions, and "disappearances" become justified as a regrettable but unavoidable consequence of the growing threat to public order. In many cities shadowy forces have emerged to take the law into their own hands and impose their own forms of social regulation. These organizations blur the distinction between public and private power and between common crime and state repression. The "death squads" and their victims, from "common criminals" to street children, are the most visible actors of this parallel social order which regulates the lives of people who live on the fringe of society.

Social order cannot be preserved by unlawful killings by the police, by the expansion of the death penalty to more and more crimes, by torture or by "social cleansing" by "death squads." The politics of fear do not bring security. On the contrary, they degrade the societies which tolerate such crimes. Public security requires that states refrain from torturing or otherwise injuring their citizens, that they protect them from injury at the hands of others, and that they provide a system of justice to which all are equally accountable and have equal access. Only the rule of law can, in the long term, ensure social order. Justice requires that the guilty be held accountable for their actions. If those who have committed human rights violations do so with impunity, the ground is land for further abuses in the future.

A 10-Point Program for the Next Decade

The governments of the Americas are accountable both to the international community and to their own people in their obligation to ensure full respect for human rights. To this end, in a landmark judgment, the Inter-American Court of Human Rights ruled in July 1988 that states have the duty "to organize the governmental apparatus and, in general, all the structures through which the public power is exercised, so that they are capable of juridically ensuring the free and full enjoyment of human rights."

As the presidents of the American nations discuss the future of the region over the next decade, Amnesty International presents to the governments and peoples of the Americas a 10-point program for the free and full exercise of human rights in the region.

1. Abolish the death penalty.

Governments should abolish the death penalty and stop judicial executions. All death sentences should be commuted. In countries which retain the death penalty, minors, persons over 70 years of age, pregnant women, and new mothers should not be sentenced to death, in conformity with international standards. All people in these categories already under sentence of death should have their sentences immediately commuted.

2. Prevent torture, "disappearances," and extrajudicial executions by government agents and compensate the victims.

Ensure that torture, the commission of a "disappearance" or extrajudicial execution, or causing the death of a prisoner in custody is a criminal offence, punishable by sanctions commensurate with the gravity of the offense.

Inform families immediately of any arrest and keep them informed of the whereabouts of the detainee or prisoner at all times.

Make available judicial remedies (such as *habeas corpus* and *amparo*) to enable lawyers and relatives to locate prisoners and obtain the release of anyone who has been arbitrarily detained.

Prevent detention or imprisonment other than in official, known detention centres, a list of which should be widely publicized.

Order independent forensic investigations into reports of torture, killings, and deaths in custody, to be carried out promptly and thoroughly by qualified personnel.

3. Release all prisoners of conscience immediately and unconditionally.

Release all detainees and prisoners held because of their peaceful political beliefs or activities, ethnic origin, sexual orientation, language or religion.

4. Ensure prompt and fair trials for all political prisoners.

Governments should abolish all special courts and legislation for the trial of political prisoners, including military courts.

Ensure that all political prisoners charged with a criminal offense receive a prompt and fair trial by a competent, independent, and impartial tribunal.

Ensure that all political prisoners are treated in accordance with internationally recognized safeguards for fair legal proceedings.

5. End impunity.

Security forces personnel against whom there is evidence of involvement in extrajudicial executions, torture, "disappearances," or other human rights violations should be prosecuted. This principle should apply no matter how much time has elapsed since the commission of the crime. The perpetrators should not benefit from any legal measures exempting them from criminal prosecution or conviction.

The activities of "death squads" and all paramilitary organizations should be thoroughly investigated and members of such organizations responsible for human rights violations brought to justice.

Conduct prompt, thorough, and impartial investigations into all reports of "disappearances" and bring to justice those responsible.

Steps should be taken to strengthen national judiciaries and ensure that they are truly independent bodies able to carry out full and effective investigations into human rights violations. Military jurisdiction over human rights crimes committed by members of the security forces should be abolished.

It should be high priority of the governments to ensure that the civilian courts have the resources and legal means they need to administer justice. Procedures should be reviewed to reduce unacceptable long delays in investigations and in the gap between indictments and trials.

Governments should send a clear message to all law enforcement personnel that human rights violations such as torture, extrajudicial executions, and "disappearances" will not be tolerated under any circumstances and that those committing them will be punished in accordance with the law.

All incidents involving the use of lethal force by military and security forces should be thoroughly and independently investigated by an agency other than that to which those involved in the incident belong.

Investigations should establish chain of command responsibility for human rights violations and should investigate patterns of human rights violations as well as individual cases. Anyone found to have ordered, committed, or concealed human rights violations should be brought to justice.

6. Protect the victims and witnesses of human rights violations.

The rights of the victims and witnesses of human rights violations must be protected. Steps should be taken to ensure the protection of lawyers, prosecutors, officials, and witnesses, victims, or relatives of victims involved in cases of human rights violations.

All allegations of death threats should be promptly investigated and steps taken to ensure the safety of the recipient.

The appropriate authorities should review arrangements for the treatment and custody of all prisoners to ensure that they are treated humanely and in conformity with the UN Body of Principles for the Protection of All Persons Under Any Form of Detention or Imprisonment, the UN Standard Mini-

mum Rules for the Treatment of Prisoners, and Article 10 of the ICCPR, which states: "All persons deprived of their liberty shall be treated with humanity and with respect for the inherent dignity of the human person."

No one should be forcibly returned to a country where she or he can reasonably be expected to be imprisoned as a prisoner of conscience, tortured, "disappeared," or executed.

Every refugee or asylum-seeker must be given the opportunity of an individual hearing and be fully informed of his/her rights as a refugee or asylum-seeker under international law.

The state should provide appropriate reparation and compensation to the victims of human rights violations and their families.

7. Support the work of relevant intergovernmental, official, and non-governmental human rights organizations.

Governments should publicly state their commitment to collaborate with the work of international and regional bodies which monitor violations of human rights, including the United Nations High Commissioner for Human Rights, the UN Commission on Human Rights, and the Inter-American Commission on Human Rights, to accept their findings and recommendations.

Necessary resources, both human and material, must be provided to enable official human rights bodies to play their designated role in preventing and investigating human rights violations.

Governments should guarantee that human rights activists and members of non-governmental organizations working for the promotion and protection of human rights are properly consulted in the formulation and implementation of human rights policies.

The authorities should ensure that human rights defenders receive the full protection of the law so that they can carry out their vital work.

8. Promote human rights through official programs of education and training.

Governments should give high priority to education designed to promote human rights awareness, particularly among the most vulnerable sectors of the population, and to make society at large conscious of its duty to respect human rights and fundamental freedoms.

Governments should ensure that all law enforcement personnel and other government agents receive adequate training on the national and international standards which protect human rights and how to enforce them properly. Education in the human rights of women and children should be integrated into all education and training policies at both national and international level.

9. Ratify and implement all regional instruments for the protection of human rights without reservations.

Governments should ratify all regional legal instruments which provide for the protection of the human rights of all peoples of the Americas. These instruments include:

- The American Convention on Human Rights "Pact of San José, Costa Rica"
- Inter-American Convention to Prevent and Punish Torture
- Protocol to the American Convention on Human Rights to Abolish the Death Penalty
- Inter-American Convention on the Forced Disappearance of Persons
- Inter-American Convention on the Prevention, Punishment and Eradication of Violence Against Women — Convention of Belém do Pará.

Governments that have already ratified these instruments should reconsider any limiting reservations. In particular, governments should recognize the jurisdiction of the Inter-American Court of Human Rights.

10. Ratify and implement all international instruments for the protection of human rights.

Governments should also ratify without reservations and observe the provisions of all relevant international human rights treaties, including:

- The International Covenant on Civil and Political Rights (ICCPR) and its Optional Protocols
- The International Covenant on Economic, Social and Cultural Rights

- The Convention against Torture and Other Cruel, Inhuman or Degrading Treatment or Punishment
- The Convention on the Elimination of All Forms of Discrimination against Women
- The Convention on the Rights of the Child
- The Convention and Protocol relating to the Status of Refugees.

Governments should take due account of non-treaty instruments, including the Vienna Declaration and Programme of Action, the Declaration on the Elimination of Violence Against Women, the Basic Principles on the Independence of the Judiciary, the Code of Conduct for Law Enforcement Officials, the Basic Principles on the Use of Force and Firearms by Law Enforcement Officials, and the Safeguards Guaranteeing Protection of the Rights of those Facing the Death Penalty.

Governments should ensure that reports to treaty monitoring bodies are submitted in a timely manner and include detailed information on all rights protected by the reports.

Founded in Santiago, Chile, in 1957, the Facultad Latinoamericana de Ciencias Sociales (FLACSO) is an international organization dedicated to promoting teaching, research, and technical cooperation in the social sciences. With ten academic centers throughout Latin America and the Caribbean, it is the largest and most prominent post-graduate and research program in the region today. FLACSO-Chile conducts research programs in five issue areas: International and Military Relations; Political Structures and Processes; Education and Culture; Poverty, Social Policy, and Local Development; and Gender Studies. Among its linkages with institutions in the United States, FLACSO maintains permanent programs with the Wilson Center, Inter-American Dialogue, the University of Miami North-South Center, Florida International University, Ohio State University, and the University of California, San Diego.

Translated by Robert J. Barros for the University of Miami North-South Center.

Peace and Security in the Americas: Recommendations for Cooperative Hemispheric Security Policies

The creation of a post-Cold War system of hemispheric security should establish a new relationship among interests, deterrence mechanisms, and perceptions so as to protect peace effectively in the hemisphere.

Until these new linkages are established, gradual and consensual changes must be implemented to help maintain the intra-regional and hemispheric status quo while simultaneously working in diverse sectors.

We propose to develop a definition of Cooperative Security as a system of interstate interactions that, by coordinating government policies, anticipate and contain threats to national interests and prevent perceptions of threat from being transformed into tensions, crises, and open confrontations.

To put this concept into practice, we suggest that measures and operative mechanisms be adopted in ten areas: crisis prevention and status quo maintenance, modernization and regional balances, mutual confidence-building measures, arms control and limitation, disarmament, security regimes, bilateral responses, cooperative hemispheric security institutions, and constructive involvement of the United States and the United Nations in the development of a hemispheric security system.

The set of proposals that are described below may be appropriate elements for the creation of a cooperative security system in the hemisphere.

1. CRISIS PREVENTION AND MAINTAINING THE STATUS QUO

As long as a new relationship among interests, deterrence mechanisms, and perceptions is not established, it is essential to maintain the regional status quo and to implement gradual consensual changes that allow cooperative progress toward the creation of a post-Cold War hemispheric security order.

The project "Peace and Security in the Americas" (P&SA) is a joint academic activity of the Latin American Program of the Woodrow Wilson International Center for Scholars, the Area of International and Military Relations of the Facultad Latinoamericana de Ciencias Sociales (FLACSO)-Chile, and the Latin American Defense and Disarmament Center (Centro Latinamericano de Defensa y Desarme, CLADDE).

In order to maintain the current inter-regional and hemispheric status quo and to proceed to a new system, it is imperative to establish preventive mechanisms for peacefully handling and resolving crises and disputes.

Given the contemporary intra-regional political and economic transformations that are eroding the post-World War II status quo and the limits of existing hemispheric multilateral bodies, it is necessary to consider how to improve existing institutions while simultaneously creating new mechanisms for preventing, managing, and resolving crises.

2. MODERNIZATION AND REGIONAL BALANCES

We must ensure that the existing regional defensive deterrence mechanisms are sufficiently modern. Maintaining regional balances is not served by U.S. imposed limits on the transfer of military technology to Latin America. Such a policy, if implemented, would be ineffectual given the growing world supply of such materials and the inability of the United States or the United Nations to prevent such interchanges. On the other hand, the inclusion of the Latin American states in the principal arms control and limitation regimes would provide a global institutional framework for transferring military technology without the risk inherent to a process free of any controls whatsoever. In this way, arms limitation and control regimes could be transformed into mechanisms that facilitate a regulated military modernization. In such a framework, the necessary transparency of arms transfers as well as their equity would be more assured.

3. MUTUAL CONFIDENCE MEASURES

Despite the developments mentioned above, the realities and hypotheses of interstate conflict in Latin America have not varied substantially with the cessation of the Cold War. Insofar as the apparently common rhetoric of continental strategic unity has lost its force with the end of global military bipolarity, geo-strategic interests have reappeared. In this context, mutual confidence measures (MCM) take on new relevance and functionality for preventing the outbreak of unwanted conflicts and reducing the intensity of potential crises.

MCMs can include two broad types of measures: first, those actions that eliminate or lessen perceptions of danger in each specific geo-strategic situation, and, second, any other measures that increase trust among actors without necessarily referring to any particular concrete situation. The following issues lie within the range of MCMs: the exchange of military information and viewpoints; transparency regarding military expenditures and other sensitive matters such as arms transfers; prior notification of maneuvers; interchanges, visits, and the development of joint seminars, etc.; consultations; lowering levels of tension in specific geographic areas; and procedures for preventing and controlling crises.

Mutual confidence measures are one of the most developed aspects of interstate relations in the region. The exchange of information among neighboring countries has increased dramatically, and reciprocal military stances have moderated thanks to an increase in prior notifications, exchanges, and visits. There is greater transparency regarding military spending, and the countries of the region have begun to inform the United Nations of their defense allocations. There is a clear sense of the type and number of arms transfers. South American participation in joint seminars has increased, as have mutual consultations. All of this has led to a lessening of tensions in specific geographic areas. Nevertheless, much still remains to be done to develop procedures, training techniques, institutions, methodologies, and measures for preventing and controlling crises.

4. ARMS CONTROL AND LIMITATION

Given that military preparedness, in conjunction with other state instruments, is a fundamental aspect of national defense, regional arms control is a necessity for the Latin American states for three reasons. First of all, no economy in the region can withstand an unlimited expansion of military expenditures. It is sufficient to note the effects of unlimited military expenditures in the former Soviet Union and the United States. Second, the modernization of technology is a functional necessity in the area of defense. Third, regional military balances are dynamic, with each country having a natural ceiling for the development of its military capacity, which at the same time depends on that of other states. Given that the military industries of the region are relatively less developed than other international actors', this does not necessarily affect relative regional balances.

The maintenance of the status quo and regional balances, in conjunction with the modernizing of deterrence apparatuses, requires progress in controlling and limiting conventional weapons. Mutual confidence measures and disarmament agreements on weapons of mass destruction are not sufficient conditions for achieving a stable peace in the hemisphere.

Studies by the United Nations and academic researchers do not clearly conceptualize the difference between arms control and limitation. Throughout the Cold War, the notion of control was used as a euphemism for disarmament policies.

a. Arms Control

The meaning of the concept of "control" is structured around notions of verification, checking, inspection, supervision, and intervention. Theoretically, in contrast to MCMs, arms control implies some degree of abdication of sovereignty as a concession to understanding. For this reason, we will define as arms control those *previously agreed upon norms or regulations, whether self- or supra-imposed, to be observed in the process of acquiring and/or selling military materials*.

These norms or regulations concern, for example, self-limitations against selling arms to parties at war, the acceptance of norms prohibiting the resale of military goods without authorization from the original vendor, and agreements on norms regulating the acquisition of arms systems, including mechanisms of verification. These norms do not imply reductions or the elimination of specific types of arms; rather, they are measures that regulate the *quantity* and *type* of arms to have.

In this context, for example, a regional system of missile control or of entry into the Missile Technology Control Regime (MTCR) would favor the maintenance of strategic balances and prevent countries with greater missile development from continuing to advance their programs.

b. Arms Limitations

The term "limiting" implies "reducing, restricting, or fixing the upper range of one's jurisdiction, authority, rights, or faculties." In the case of arms limitations, there is a greater yielding of sovereignty than in that of arms control. Therefore, the concept of arms limitation refers to the *establishment of ceilings upon the number of arms systems and/or the freezing of acquisition and/or the production of specific types of armaments*. These ceilings or freezes are related to measures agreed upon or imposed regarding which arms *not to have*.

In these two areas, there have been few Latin American and hemispheric initiatives, and none of these have prospered. Numerous efforts were made after the "Ayacucho Declaration." These attempts did not bear fruit, however.

5. DISARMAMENT

A number of multilateral efforts have been implemented to *eradicate* ballistic missiles and other chemical, biological, and nuclear weapons of mass destruction. Thus, international support for the principal world disarmament and arms control treaties has increased considerably. According to the Stockholm International Peace Research Institute (SIPRI), over the past five years the number of parties to the Non-Proliferation Treaty has increased from 136 to 146, while adhesion to the Biological Weapons Convention has risen from 107 to 118 parties, and support for the Inhumane Weapons Convention has risen from 25 to 31 countries.

A similar trend can be seen in Latin America. The Mendoza Declaration establishes a complete prohibition on the production, development, stockholding, acquisition, or transfer of chemical or biological weaponry; the Declaration of Cartagena renounces any possession, production, development, use, testing, or transfer of all arms of mass destruction; and the additional protocols to the Treaty of Tlatelolco and the ratification of this treaty by states that had not signed (with the exception of Cuba) constitute the most important steps in securing peaceful cooperation in the region. As a result of a series of negotiations regarding pending border problems, agreements have been reached to resolve border conflicts, some of which have dragged on for decades.

6. SECURITY REGIMES

Other complementary steps toward developing a cooperative security system in the hemisphere involve establishing specific subregional security regimes circumscribed to groups of countries or organized around specific threats or dimensions. Such regimes might permit a combination of formulas which could, for example, increase joint action in inter-American operations in other parts of the world under the auspices of the United Nations; further advance the creation of a proposed naval force of the Americas to control jurisdictional waters, which could be combined with the initiative to maintain joint naval forces in the seas in which these navies have a presence; or limit the role of the Armed Forces to their professional tasks by excluding them from playing a central role in the fight against drug trafficking.

These subregional regimes ought to be supported by an inter-American system for the peaceful resolution of conflicts. This presupposes strengthening the inter-American juridical system as well as the Organization of American States (OAS), further mutual confidence-building measures among neighboring states, and the development of existing processes of subregional military cooperation.

These initiatives might allow the Latin American countries, along with the United States and Canada, to construct a hemispheric-wide strategic order that will correspond to the new political and economic trends of the twenty-first century.

7. BILATERAL RESPONSES

It is necessary to modernize *political-strategic relations* among neighboring countries in the Americas and to prepare to forge new relations.

This presupposes a frame of reference that makes it possible to articulate cooperative dimensions, incompatibilities and differences regarding economic issues, and military-political matters. This would mean working toward a unity that allows and respects the diversity of economic and foreign policy positions.

To achieve this end, it will be necessary to strengthen all present areas of convergence within international policy by broadening cooperative realms of security policy, while simultaneously developing mechanisms capable of preventing, managing, and eliminating divergences that arise as well as of reducing their impact.

In this regard, a number of different levels of action can be foreseen. On the one hand, there are the mutual confidence measures, which we will call low-intensity measures. They imply strengthening military

cooperation in response to catastrophes, environmental protection, and other contingencies. However, the establishment of a new political-strategic relationship among our countries requires heavy, harsh, *high intensity* measures. Progress in the development of high intensity measures is fundamental. Only in this manner will the Latin American countries be able to confront the present global and hemispheric challenges cooperatively and successfully, for these are challenges no country can overcome on its own.

For example, we can identify three areas of high-density bilateral relations that might be conducive to the new type of relationship we are suggesting.

The first would imply a radical alteration of those international policy divergences that are perceived as involving antagonistic national interests, which cannot be resolved through cooperative policies.

The second area concerns the make-up of each state's respective deterrence system. Progress could be made by clarifying mutual apprehensions concerning the quantity and type of forces and arms systems possessed by each party. Within this new framework, the difficult distinction between offensive and defensive systems should be reviewed. This transparency might lead to a reduction and limitation of certain arms systems.

The third area concerns the redeployment of forces. If this measure is successful, it might lead to holding joint exercises in certain regions. In this new context, early notification of individual maneuvers and exercises would lower the costs of stationing and maintaining forces.

This approach rests on the basic assumption that it is better to build constructively upon the set of existing initiatives than to set out with a grand design, which implies first having to reach difficult preliminary agreements on shared values and principles. In this manner, a system of hemispheric security could be built upon existing foundations by raising the current system to a higher level of coordination and coherence. The creation of instruments for preventing, managing, and reducing the impact of crises will make it possible to deepen and expand these areas of cooperation. The implementation of high-density measures may allow for the creation of a new political-strategic reality.

8. COOPERATIVE HEMISPHERIC SECURITY INSTITUTIONS

Existing hemispheric-level systems of military interaction should be reorganized along the lines of a relatively systematic proposal that arises from reflection on the future of inter-American cooperative security.

In order to advance the creation of this new system, it is necessary at the outset to recognize the multidimensional character of hemispheric security. This implies creating a system that will allow for a *coordinated* coexistence of new security regimes; existing global regimes; subregional, regional, and hemispheric arrangements; and agreements by area of interest in the ground, naval, and aerospace fields.

Such a change implies redefining the link between the Inter-American Defense Board (IADB) and the OAS. The IADB should be an advisory general staff without operational functions or forces under its command. Presently, a number of alternatives for the IADB are being debated, including the possibility of relocating the IADB in the OAS's Defense Advisory Committee or recycling it within an OAS Permanent Security Commission.

Regardless of which course is eventually taken, it is important to link the IADB, the Inter-American Defense College (IADC), and the inter-American armed forces conferences and initiatives in a coherent and systematic fashion within a new system of hemispheric security. This linkage should permit flexible coordination based on the principle of hemispheric cooperation regarding security, which should inspire these ties.

To summarize, existing mutual confidence measures, in conjunction with existing biological, chemical, and nuclear disarmament accords and eventual arms control agreements, constitute a framework which is capable of providing stability to the region without adversely affecting the deterrence capabilities of each state. Regional disarmament accords concerning weapons of mass destruction (Tlatelolco, the Non-Proliferation Treaty, and the biological and chemical weapons accord), a multitude of existing mutual confidence programs as well as a diversified network of hemispheric military interchanges — inter-American army, navy, and air force conferences — provide a sufficiently broad base made up of institutions and initiatives that are *open to coordination* within a more coherent framework. The growing coordination of policies at the regional, hemispheric, and global levels will make it possible to increase the levels of bilateral cooperation. As an integral element of this system, an eventual conference on hemispheric security and cooperation might be convoked.

9. CONSTRUCTIVE ROLE OF THE UNITED STATES

A first consideration in designing a policy conducive to the creation of a cooperative hemispheric security system consists of recognizing the existence of various elements that could be used in this task but are presently dispersed. In this sense, an undertaking of utmost importance is to identify a set of initiatives that could potentially be organized within a new perspective, beginning with a register of existing bilateral and multilateral endeavors.

Second, it is necessary to focus the agenda so as to avoid ambiguous objectives when developing a hemispheric security system. This implies that any set of policies in which the U.S. armed forces are principal actors should concentrate on limited but significant priorities, given that institutional resources and availability preclude covering a very broad array of issues and actions. This may imply a downsizing of the U.S. forces available for cooperative actions in the Latin American area.

Third, it is necessary to go beyond the traditional classification of Latin American countries into the three area groups of the Caribbean, Central America, and South America. Even when subregional approaches are useful for certain purposes, such as for naval programs, for example, it is necessary to design a future hemispheric security system capable of integrating a variety of functional, regional, institutional arrangements. Priority should be given to the type of country and the needs and nature of its military professionalism rather than to the region to which a country belongs.

The United States could make a positive contribution to the creation of a cooperative hemispheric security system through three types of policies: those supporting the upgrading of the level of professionalism of the Latin American armed forces, those supporting the regional status quo, and those supporting the creation of an effective multilateral system of hemispheric security.

a. Support for Professional Development

Support for the professional development of the Latin American armed forces presupposes the existence of shared security interests.

Assuming that there is a shared interest in protecting peace in the hemisphere, the United States, as a superpower, could cooperate so that the armed forces of the region become efficient counterparts in this collective endeavor.

Insofar as differences undoubtedly do exist in the level of professional development of the different Latin American armed forces, the specific content of these programs should be set by the interested parties of the region. However, assuming that ties with the United States have been shed of all ideological or political designs, it is possible to identify some areas in which there is broad space for the development of U.S.-Latin American security relations.

A first area of cooperation is the technological modernization of the Latin American armed forces. This modernization can be carried out through multiple channels and forms such as donations of equipment, sales, and associations in joint programs, whether with armies, navies, or air forces or in the form of joint ventures or co-production agreements.

A system of cooperative security cannot institutionalize the technological underdevelopment of one of its participants. On the contrary, military modernization is a necessary condition in order for the system of hemispheric security to be truly multilateral and cooperative and to allow the parties to act jointly. Otherwise, the huge asymmetries that exist will lead the Latin American armed forces to satisfy their needs of modernization in other parts of the globe. To assure that this permanent modernization does not imply an increase in the domestic social cost of the defense effort nor that it generate increasing regional insecurity, it is imperative that military modernization be accompanied by the measures previously discussed concerning regional balances and arms control.

Given the nature of this issue, such ties imply projecting cooperative security relations over the long run, without conditioning them to short-term demands.

A second area of potential cooperation is the modernization of military doctrines and joint land, air, and sea exercises. This type of cooperation might be best realized by gradually improving existing programs and by making them more multilateral or else by defining new activities that could grow out of existing bilateral initiatives and increasingly assume the form of multilateral actions.

Nevertheless, the identification of areas of cooperation should be an inductive process, whereby the Latin American armed forces formulate their demands and the United States responds by structuring its programs in accordance with the common terms that emerge from this exercise.

b. Support for the Hemispheric Strategic Status Quo

In a continent undergoing such an accelerated process of change, it is of fundamental importance to protect and care for the subregional and regional military balances. This is especially necessary if it is presumed that the process of technological modernization will proceed within a framework of cooperative security.

The United States' contribution to maintaining regional balances could be effected through a variety of existing initiatives and new programs to be developed.

The first is support for a policy of transparency in military exports and imports. A review of the first year of operation of the United Nations Conventional Weapons Register reveals that only twelve of the Latin American countries have complied with this agreement by reporting their international conventional weapons transactions. Of these, only three countries — Brazil, Chile, and Colombia — have fully complied by reporting all of the required information. The United States, especially through the Arms Control and Disarmament Agency (ACDA), could cooperate by distributing complementary information which would help generate greater transparency in these areas.

The second support task may be found at the level of the mutual confidence measures that are being developed in the region. As was recommended at the March 1994 Meeting of Experts on Measures for Fostering Confidence and Security Mechanisms in the Region, organized by the OAS and held in Buenos Aires, the member states should put into "practice, at the appropriate level and by the means that they regard to be adequate, diverse measures to foster confidence."

A third area involves mechanisms for the control and limitation of conventional weapons and the disarmament of weapons of mass destruction. Existing regimes should not be seen as instruments aimed at eliminating the armed institutions of the region. On the contrary, these regimes can provide vital support for modernization within specific areas. For example, the regime for controlling missile technology (MTCR) is an instrument which makes it possible to regulate the transfer of missile technology without risking developments that jeopardize regional security and stability. In this regard, information and cooperation from the United States could be important.

A fourth area of cooperation concerns the development of organizations for the *prevention and control of crises and conflicts*. To support this policy, it is necessary to develop subregional or hemispheric initiatives and/or institutions capable of preventing and controlling crises that might emerge in the future. This objective might take shape through broad-based conferences on cooperation and security in conjunction with specialized research centers and bodies that work on developing prescriptions for anticipating and controlling conflicts. The U.S. experience in these areas, particularly in Europe and other parts of the world, may be a source of valuable antecedents which the United States could make available to the Latin American governments and armed forces so as to make progress along these lines.

All of the previous initiatives could be incorporated into the U.S. military's agenda for action in the region, permitting interagency activities among the Department of Defense and other agencies, such as the Arms Control and Disarmament Agency (ACDA).

c. Increased Multilateral Action

A third set of policies conducive to the establishment of a cooperative hemispheric security system relate to the creation of an effective multilateral system. The creation of such a system implies developing concepts and policies for cooperative security. This type of revision demands that the United States go beyond its strategic self-absorption by creating coalitions, broadening the participation of the Latin American countries in decisionmaking on hemispheric security issues, and drastically limiting its unilateral action in the region. In concrete terms, this last point means an *explicit renunciation by the United States of any unilateral use of force in the hemisphere outside*

of existing multilateral mechanisms. This increasing use of multilateral institutions would imply an improvement and better coordination of existing institutional initiatives and organizations, such as the IADB, the IADC, the Inter-American Conference of Armies, Navies, and Air Forces, inter-service operations such as UNITAS and those of the air forces. The result would be a region integrated through common policies. The IADC should open itself up to training civilian and military personnel in new, cooperative hemispheric security policies.

Similarly, it is advisable that the United States fully participate in multilateral organizations, especially in those involved with peacekeeping efforts and the International Court of Justice. Regarding the former, though Presidents Bush and Clinton have assured support for equipment, training, logistical support, planning, crisis management, and intelligence, they have not accepted placing their peace forces under international control, thereby weakening the Military Staff Committee of the United Nations.

This reliance on multilateral action also implies an effective integration of new actors such as Canada into the hemispheric system. In this way, other European countries and countries that are supplying weapons to the region should be integrated as observers and cooperators in this system.

Along these lines, it will also be necessary to convert existing bilateral agreements with the United States into multilateral accords, particularly in those areas where there are shared interests. This would allow the creation of specific hemispheric security regimes, something we have proposed on a number of occasions. In this way, progress would be made by giving substance to new relations with the United States.

Nevertheless, regional stability and balance in the Western Hemisphere are not the exclusive domain of the United States. Given the existence of a broad and varied range of international military relations with other powers, it is essential that these ties be incorporated into the new system of hemispheric security so as to assure a healthy multilateralism.

In synthesis, the development of the set of previously mentioned policies could lead to the formation of a cooperative hemispheric security system that would in fact realize the *Cooperative Security*

Initiative for the Americas, which the twenty-first century so urgently demands.

10. THE UNITED NATIONS

The proposal *An Agenda for Peace* presents three types of risks that are not negligible.

First, the proposal involves a doctrinal revision of state sovereignty. The document asserts that "the time of absolute and exclusive sovereignty. . .has passed; its theory was never matched by reality. It is the task of leaders of states today to understand this and to find a balance between the needs of good internal governance and the requirements of an ever more interdependent world."

This may be even more problematic since a similar tendency has emerged within the hemisphere in recurrent proposals within the OAS to create multilateral intervention forces to protect democratic regimes.

Second, the notions of preventive deployment, even when such deployment is consensual or at the request of the states involved, and of the deployment of military forces on one side of a border to create demilitarized zones at the request of one of the parties entail the risk of producing regional imbalances, particularly if they are not mediated by institutional changes, because of the vying of a more powerful coalition against a weaker one in a specific region.

Third, unless the present composition of the organs of military command is modified, there is a risk that the actions of armed forces under international command may extend their authority beyond security matters to encompass other issues such as the control of international drug trafficking, as the United Kingdom unsuccessfully proposed in October 1989.

In regard to present trends within the United Nations, a broad regional consensus is needed to confront the emerging trend within this international organization to revise the notion of state sovereignty. Even though defenses of autarchy are rarely heard at present, any consideration of limits upon sovereignty must take into account that any such redefinition must generate equally powerful concepts that can be accepted as adequate principles for organizing hemispheric coexistence. Otherwise, the elimination of the principle of nonintervention in the internal affairs of other nations may prompt a period of great regional instability.

Likewise, it will be necessary to maintain and increase the Latin American contribution to peace-keeping operations and to confront the need to change the composition of the Security Council by enlarging it through the incorporation of Japan and the Federal Republic of Germany as well as by assuring a mandated, rotating representative position for the developing countries, which should have a veto capacity.

It will also be necessary to analyze the composition and modes of participation of the forces integrated into the Military Staff Committee's peace operations.

Insofar as peace operations are projected as part of the United Nations' new stage of development and to assure the adequate definition and implementation of policies in this area, it will be necessary to evaluate the Latin American experience in peace operations to date as well as the contributions made and results obtained by the countries of the region.

Francisco Rojas
FLACSO-Chile

Postscript:
The Miami Process
and Security Issues

The recent war in the Condor range, which still lacks a definitive resolution, has once again raised the issue of security to a prominent position on the Latin American and hemispheric agenda. During the recent Miami Summit, the heads of state reiterated that preserving and strengthening the democratic community of the Americas is one of the central objectives in the hemisphere. Democracy will reinforce peace within and among nations. However, this war and the tensions along the Colombian-Venezuelan border demonstrate that democracy in itself is not sufficient. A hemispheric security regime that can avoid conflicts and generate trust must be formed. Such a regime will be the foundation for stability in the area of security and will buttress the development of interdependence, trade, and economic integration. To attain the goal set in Miami of forming a *Free Trade Zone of the Americas by 2005 at the latest,* simultaneous progress is needed on an *Initiative for Security and Cooperation in the Americas.*

The Action Plan designed in Miami stated that the "objective consists of strengthening mutual confidence that contributes to the social and economic integration of our peoples." In this regard, the Summit supports actions aimed at assuring the success of the Conference on Promoting Confidence and Security, which will be held in Chile in November 1995.

The U.S. Secretary of Defense, likewise, has invited the ministers of defense of the Americas to a meeting to be held in July. Although the agenda for this meeting has not been fully established, the Secretary of Defense has signalled that the promotion of dialogue among civilian and military leaders regarding security and defense issues common to the hemisphere is in line with the objective of the Miami Summit to consolidate democracy in the hemisphere.

In this manner, a post-Summit process on defense issues has begun to take shape. The policy suggestions elaborated by the *Peace and Security in the Americas Program,* which are being carried out jointly by FLACSO-Chile and the Latin American Program of the Wilson Center, constitute a technical contribution to the agenda of discussion and analysis. These suggestions promote associational relations and multilateral action, and they establish alternatives for forming a cooperative security regime in the hemisphere.

INTEGRATION AND COOPERATION:
A VULNERABLE PROCESS

Initial perspectives in the early 1990s were marked by a strong dose of optimism: international cooperation could increase, and association, it was thought, would become the principal instrument of linkage among states. Nevertheless, the new reality revealed itself to be more complex; forgotten conditioning factors re-emerged. Ethnic and religious rivalries took on an intensity and importance unknown for over half a century. Nationalism appeared to be the most enduring force, and it erupted in a manner that shaped the international stage. The military conflict in the Persian Gulf demonstrated that conflicts could reach an enormous magnitude. The television, nevertheless, did not show the high costs that accompanied this technological war. The war in Bosnia, on the other hand, which is less technological and thus lacks the quality of a video game, reveals the horrors of war and the incapacity of the central actors who possess the greatest power to articulate policies and resolve ancestral tensions.

In Latin America, it was generally believed that the region was immune from these trends. Unfortunately, events have revealed the contrary. Two examples are sufficient: first, the emergence of the insurrection in the state of Chiapas, Mexico, and, subsequently, the conflict and confrontation between Ecuador and Peru. These events are combined with situations inherited from the colonial and Cold War periods. From the colonial period, we find the lack of complete and internationally recognized delimitation of the international borders of the states. Among the Cold War inheritances, we can mention the instability in the Caribbean and the continuation of conflict situations in the Central American region.

This set of situations reveals that a tendency toward confrontations also has a place in this region. Furthermore, social conditions can contribute to making tension and conflict a persistent factor in our region.

A reaffirmation of the region's commitment to resolving controversies peacefully is a fundamental requisite today. The creation of mechanisms designed to avoid conflicts and to increase mutual confidence has become an unavoidable stage given the new events in the region. The ties of association, integration, and interdependence can be consolidated only if the historical issues regarding the delimitation of borders are resolved.

HEMISPHERIC SECURITY: AN ELUSIVE ASPIRATION

Regarding security, no definite initiative exists comparable in scope to the efforts that have emerged on trade and economics. This points to a significant deficiency. The Condor War has made it clear that it is urgent to take up this issue.

Until the beginning of 1995, poverty appeared to be the principal internal defiance facing Latin American societies; whereas, international marginalization stood as the principal external challenge. This picture has changed. The situation today is more diffuse and complex. In addition to these two challenges, mistrust has been reinstalled to a prominent place on the agenda. In a short time, political-military tensions intersected with economic and financial crises. This has generated a strong perception of regional instability in key areas. Significant tendencies point to an increase in political-strategic distrust, perceptions of threat to territorial security, economic uncertainty, and the emergence of severe problems of governability in diverse subregions of Latin America.

Democracy is not a sufficient guarantee against violent confrontations among nations. Needed is an international security regime that possesses mechanisms for preventing conflicts and instruments for the verification and supervision of agreements. The open conflict between Peru and Ecuador has forcefully reestablished the need to build a cooperative security regime in the hemisphere for the post-Cold War scene.

In a matter of days, Latin America can lose one of its major assets: interstate peace. The escalation of the conflict that has arisen in the heart of South America generates uncertainty beyond the zone in dispute. Today, the conflict has been transformed into an international crisis with hemispheric implications. The very fact that the conflict involves countries such as Argentina, Brazil, Chile, and the United States as guarantors of the Rio de Janeiro Protocol imposes a level of diplomatic concern and attention that it concentrates the efforts of the most important countries in the hemisphere.

As a result of this situation, we can observe the lack of international instruments capable of preventing conflicts. These armed confrontations are placing old hemispheric institutions under a great deal of stress. These institutions have not managed to adjust themselves to this new era. Without an adequate international regime for preventing conflicts and for promoting cooperation, antagonisms will be expressed in crises that may have deplorable consequences not only for the states involved but also for the subregion or region as a whole because of their spillover effects in the area in which they occur.

NON-GOVERNMENTAL PROPOSALS

Concepts such as "cooperative security" may make it possible to generate new approaches toward cooperation in security matters. The coordination of government policies will arise from the formation of a common conceptual framework and the application of effective policies aimed at cooperation.

To place cooperative and associative policies at the center of choices implies reconstituting a basic trust. Confidence is sustained by an intangible asset which must constantly be reinforced. The great vulnerability of confidence lies in the simple fact that a single event is sufficient to transform a loss of confidence into a process of mistrust. In this sense, confidence entails a concept that is practically absolute. It increases in a gradual manner but is lost in a stroke. The reversal of the process is rapid. The logic in cases of reversal is to act before suffering greater losses or setbacks. The follow-up process to the Miami Summit should tackle this issue as a main point on the agenda. The shaping of a solid foundation of trust for designing a post-Cold War system of security institutions will only be possible by means of a cooperative security initiative.

The *Peace and Security in the Americas Program,* conducted by FLACSO-Chile and the Wilson Center in Washington, D.C., has proposed the implementation of ten security policies in the hemisphere as a step toward a *New Hemispheric Security System*: 1) prevention of crises and maintenance of the status quo; 2) modernization and regional balances; 3) mutual confidence measures; 4) arms control and limitation; 5) disarmament; 6) security regimes; 7) bilateral responses; 8) cooperative hemispheric security institutions; 9) constructive involvement of the United States in the development of a hemispheric security system (a. support for professional development, b. support for the hemispheric strategic status quo, and c. increasing multilateral organization); and 10) definitions in the United Nations.

Human Rights Watch/ Americas (formerly Americas Watch) was established in 1981 to monitor and promote internationally recognized human rights in Latin America and the Caribbean. Human Rights Watch/Americas is a division of Human Rights Watch, which also promotes human rights in Africa, Asia, the Middle East, and among the signatories of the Helsinki Accords. Human Rights Watch, founded in 1978 as Helsinki Watch, exposes and works to stop human rights abuses in over seventy countries worldwide. It is a nonpartisan, non-governmental organization funded by individual donors and private foundations.

The Center for Justice and International Law (CEJIL) was established in 1991 as a consortium of ten human rights organizations from North, Central, and South America and the Caribbean. CEJIL is the first human rights organization to offer an integrated program of international human rights protection, free legal advice, and monitoring of the Inter-American system. In coordination with domestic human rights organizations, CEJIL presents cases before the Inter-American Commission and litigates before the Inter-American Court of Human Rights, both of which are organs of the Organization of American States.

The Summit of the Americas Declaration on Human Rights

In an unprecedented joint effort, Human Rights Watch/Americas, the Center for Justice and International Law (CEJIL), and forty-three leading human rights organizations from the Americas [on December 1, 1994] presented the hemisphere's heads of state with the "Summit of the Americas Declaration on Human Rights." The groups, which drafted the declaration to reflect their shared human rights concerns, call on the governments attending the Summit to endorse publicly the Declaration as a demonstration of their commitment to basic human rights principles.

The following Declaration contains the most current human rights principles, taking into account the magnitude and seriousness of the structural and systematic violations that continue to occur in the Americas. The states attending the Summit should adopt the Declaration to reaffirm publicly their international human rights commitments, which they assumed voluntarily and in good faith with the goal of preventing violations and protecting the most vulnerable sectors of society.

The Presidents of the American States Present at the Summit of the Americas,

__Reaffirming__ our intention to consolidate in this hemisphere a system of personal liberties and social justice, within a framework of democratic institutions, based on the fundamental rights of the human person;

__Restating__ that, in accordance with the Universal Declaration of Human Rights, the highest aspiration of free men and women is the advent of a world in which all human beings, released from fear and misery, can fully exercise their economic, social, cultural, civil, and political rights;

__Recognizing__ that with the opening of markets and the growth of free trade among the states in the hemisphere, it is essential at the same time to guarantee full respect for the basic human rights of all people residing in the Americas;

__Recognizing__ that the full respect and guarantee of fundamental rights cannot be understood as an area reserved exclusively as the domain of the State, and that international supervision of these rights does not infringe on the principle of non-intervention;

__Recognizing__, in addition, that it is incumbent on the international community and, in particular, on the Inter-American system for the protection of human rights to demand that the States in the hemisphere guarantee the full and effective respect of the rights enshrined in both the American Declaration of the Rights and Duties of Man and the American Convention on Human Rights;

Have agreed on the following *Summit of the Americas Declaration on Human Rights:*

1. We reaffirm that every person has the right to have his or her life fully protected. With this objective, we commit ourselves to prevent crimes such as the forced disappearance of persons and extrajudicial executions and to investigate and punish those responsible for such atrocities. The death penalty will not be reestablished in the States in which it has been abolished, nor will its areas of application be expanded to include crimes not currently punished by said penalty.

2. We reaffirm the right to every person to have his or her physical, mental, and moral integrity respected and protected. In this regard, we commit ourselves to guaranteeing that no one be submitted to torture or to cruel, inhuman, or degrading treatment or punishment. We assume the commitment to protect persons, particularly women and children, who are victims of domestic violence and sexual assault, to strengthen the pertinent legislation, and to supervise its enforcement.

3. We agree to comply with the international humanitarian right that regulates the conduct of combatant parties during armed conflict in the hemisphere and, in particular, its application to conflicts which are not international in character. We commit ourselves to assure the humane treatment of combatants and non-combatants.

4. We reaffirm the right of every person to freedom of thought and expression — essential in all democratic societies that respect freedom of conscience — without discrimination for reasons of race, gender, sexual preference, religion, political opinion, nationality, or social origin. This right encompasses the freedom to look for, receive, and distribute information and ideas of any nature. We commit ourselves not to resort to penal measures such as contempt or defamation as a form of persecution against journalists, writers, or any person who publicly criticizes government officials.

5. We commit ourselves to support and promote the work of human rights defenders and to protect them from reprisals, harassment, violent attacks, and unjust accusations.

6. We commit ourselves to protect the right of the political refugee not to be expelled or returned to the State where his or her life or liberty may be endangered for reasons of race, religion, nationality, gender, membership in a particular social group, or political opinions. We agree, furthermore, that the facilities used to provide temporary haven to people escaping critical situations should have the adequate services and the appropriate conditions to satisfy the basic needs of this population. We commit ourselves to strengthen national and regional mechanisms for protecting and assisting internally displaced persons and others who are in refugee-like situations.

7. We reaffirm the right of every person to enter, exit, and move within his or her own country without restriction. We reaffirm the right of any foreign national, who is legally within a State's territory, to move freely and not to be expelled without full respect for the guarantees of legal due process.

8. We commit ourselves to carry out free and fair elections, under conditions which guarantee the equal access of all parties to the electorate and to the communications media.

9. We commit ourselves to renew our efforts — using the available resources — to achieve the progressive implementation of all of the rights recognized in the International Covenant on Economic, Social, and Cultural Rights. To this end, we commit ourselves to make greater efforts to eradicate poverty and discrimination from the continent and improve access to education and health services with special attention to those sectors of our society most discriminated against such as women, children, people with physical or mental disabilities, and ethnic minorities.

10. We reaffirm that the human rights of women and minors are an inalienable, integral and indivisible part of universal human rights. We reaffirm that gender-based violence and all forms of sexual harassment and exploitation are incompatible with the dignity and worth of the human person, and must be eliminated. We commit ourselves to guarantee the full and equal participation of women in the political, civil, economic, social and cultural life of our countries and to eradicate all forms of discrimination based on gender.

11. We agree to protect the rights of indigenous peoples of the hemisphere, in particular, the right to preserve their own cultures, customs and institutions, to practice their religion, and to use their own language.

12. We commit ourselves to guarantee the full respect of basic labor rights such as the freedom of association, the right to strike, the right to negotiate collectively, the right not to face discrimination in the labor market for reasons of race, gender, religion, political opinion, nationality, or social origin, and the right to work in conditions which do not endanger the health or safety of the worker.

13. We commit ourselves to promote the independent and impartial administration of justice which guarantees the right of due process recognized in international law. We commit ourselves not to participate nor to acquiesce to detentions or arrests in the territory of another state in violation of treaty-based

principles or customary international law on extradition, or those that violate the rights of the accused to due process.

14. We commit ourselves to ensuring that all abuses committed by State agents will be investigated, judged, and sanctioned according to existing penal and procedural standards. We further assume the commitment to review our domestic legislation with the purpose of restricting the jurisdiction of military tribunals to ensure that serious violations of human rights are punished. We commit ourselves, in addition, not to resort to the promulgation of amnesty laws or to grant pardons which benefit those responsible for serious violations defined as crimes against humanity.

15. We commit ourselves to assuring that police agents will conduct their operations with full respect for the rights of the accused during detentions, searches, control of demonstrations, or similar circumstances. The police should perform its duty to enforce the law while abiding by the same, without exercising excessive use of force, committing acts of discrimination, or denying procedural guarantees. We pledge to maintain police forces strictly under civilian authority.

16. We commit ourselves to guaranteeing that all people denied their liberty be treated with respect and with the dignity inherent to all human beings. We agree to adopt *The United Nations Standard Minimum Rules for the Treatment of Prisoners* as a legal model in reaching this objective and to incorporate its precepts into our domestic legislation. In addition, we commit ourselves to take effective measures to reduce the large number of individuals detained without sentences, who in many cases are detained in extremely precarious conditions for long periods of time.

17. We commit ourselves to promote the progressive development of the Inter-American System. Those States not currently belonging to the American Convention on Human Rights pledge to ratify it. Those States that have not recognized the compulsory jurisdiction of the Inter-American Court of Human Rights pledge to do so. We commit ourselves to implement the judgments of the Inter-American Court of Human Rights. We reaffirm our commitment to accept the resolutions and recommendations of the Inter-American Commission on Human Rights. We further pledge to sign the Inter-American Convention on the Prevention, Punishment, and Eradication of Violence Against Women, the Inter-American Convention to Prevent and Punish Torture, the Additional Protocol to the American Convention on Human Rights in the Area of Economic, Social, and Cultural Rights (Protocol of San Salvador), the Inter-American

Convention on Forced Disappearance of Persons, and the Additional Protocol to Abolish the Death Penalty.

The Presidents of the American States present at the Summit of the Americas in Miami on December 9, 1994, commit themselves to respect and, in a spirit of friendship, to cooperate to guarantee the rights and liberties recognized in this document.

The following human rights organizations join Human Rights Watch/Americas and the Center for Justice and International Law in submitting to you the attached Declaration:

Argentina: Fundación Servicio Paz y Justicia (SERPAJ), Centro de Estudios Legales y Sociales (CELS), Poder Ciudadano, Asamblea Permanente por los Derechos Humanos; **Brasil:** Núcleo de Estudos da Violencia, Instituto Brasileiro de Analises Sociais e Economicas (IBASE), Movimento Nacional de Meninos e Meninas de Rua, Movimento Nacional de Direitos Humanos (MNDH), Centro Luiz Freire/Gabinete de Assessoria Juridica as Organizações Populares; **Canada:** Inter-Church Committee on Human Rights in Latin America; **Colombia:** Corporación Colectivo de Abogados, Comisión Andina de Juristas-Seccional Colombiana, Comisión Intercongregacional de Justicia y Paz, Centro de Investigación y Educación Popular (CINEP); **Costa Rica:** Asociación Centroamericana de Familiares de Detenidos Desaparecidos (ACAFADE), Comisión para la Defensa de los Derechos Humanos en Centroamérica (CODEHUCA); **Cuba:** Comisión Nacional de Sindicatos Independientes, Human Rights in Cuba (Miami-based); **Ecuador:** Comisión Ecuménica de Derechos Humanos (CEDHU); **El Salvador:** Instituto de Derechos Humanos de Centro América (IDHUCA); **Guatemala:** Oficina de Derechos Humanos del Arzobispado de Guatemala, Consejo de Comunidades Etnicas Runujel Junam (CERJ), Centro de Investigación, Estudio y Promoción de los Derechos Humanos (CIEPRODH), Fundación Myrna Mack; **Guyana:** Guyana Human Rights Association; **Haiti:** Plate-forme des Organisations Haitiennes des Droits de l'Homme; **Honduras:** Consultorio Jurídico Popular; **Mexico:** Centro de Derechos Humanos Fray Bartolomé de las Casas, Comisión Mexicana de Defensa y Promoción de los Derechos Humanos; **Nicaragua:** Universidad Centroamericana (UCA); **Panamá:** Coordinadora Popular de Derechos Humanos de Panamá (COPODEHUPA), Comisión de Justicia y Paz; **Peru:** Coordinadora Nacional de Derechos Humanos (CNDDHH), Centro de Estudios y Acción para la Paz (CEAPAZ), Asociación Pro Derechos Humanos (APRODEH), Comisión Andina de Juristas, Comisión Episcopal de Acción Social (CEAS), Instituto de Defensa Legal (IDL); **Uruguay:** Servicio Paz y Justicia (SERPAJ-

URUGUAY), Instituto de Estudios Legales y Sociales del Uruguay (IELSUR); **Venezuela:** Programa Venezolano de Educación Acción y Derechos Humanos (PROVEA), Comisión Justicia y Paz de los Religiosos de Venezuela, La Red de Apoyo por la Justicia y la Paz, Comité de Familiares de las Víctimas de los Sucesos Febrero-Marzo (COFAVIC).

For more information, contact José Miguel Vivanco, HRW/A (202) 371-6592; Allyson Collins, HRW/A (202) 371-6592; or Susan Osnos, HRW/A (212) 972-8405.

Human Rights Watch/Americas, 1522 K Street NW, #910, Washington, D.C. 20005-1202; tel (202) 371-6592; fax (202) 371-0124; Email: hrwatchdc@igc.apc.org / cejil@igc.apc.org

Postscript: Summit Is a Major Disappointment on Human Rights

Human Rights Watch/Americas

The Summit's *Plan of Action*, approved today [December 11, 1994] sends a dangerous signal to human rights abusers in the region by making clear that violations will be tolerated as trade agreements are sought. José Miguel Vivanco, executive director of Human Rights Watch/Americas, states, "The Summit participants have sent precisely the wrong signal to human rights abusers in the region — that they can continue to get away with murder."

The Summit has become the latest example in an alarming trend in the Clinton administration's foreign policy to ignore human rights as it pursues trade, with administration officials claiming that free trade will bring respect for human rights. "This reliance on a 'trickle-down' human rights policy is deplorable," says Vivanco.

This policy was evident as International Human Rights Day passed on December 10, 1994, without even a mention of continuing human rights violations and impunity for those crimes. In fact, as Secretary of State Warren Christopher briefed reporters about the *Plan of Action*, the words "human rights" were not spoken, squandering an ideal opportunity to raise this important issue.

The *Plan of Action's* section regarding human rights is deficient on several fronts. Though the Plan acknowledges a gap between human rights concepts and norms and their effective implementation, it fails to mention the strongest contributing factor to that gap: the lack of political will to break the cycle of impunity for the most serious crimes and to make perpetrators accountable for their actions. The failure to issue a pledge against impunity is notable when compared to the Plan's section on corruption, where the leaders pledge to "make government operations transparent and accountable." Vivanco asks: "Why is it more important to investigate bribes than to end the secrecy that surrounds massacres, disappearances, and torture whose perpetrators go unpunished?"

Further, Vivanco asserts, "Human rights violations will continue in the region as long as the armed forces and police are not, in practice, subordinated to elected civilian governments. The *Plan of Action* fails to acknowledge that without civilian control of these forces, elections alone will not guarantee human rights."

While other sections of the *Plan of Action* include specific, concrete steps that will be taken by set dates, the human rights provisions are remarkably vague. And, of a dozen follow-up high-level meetings and conferences listed in the Plan's appendix, not one is devoted to human rights.

Finally, the *Plan of Action's* section on civil society is troublesome, as the governments pledge to "emphasize the management and oversight of resources as well as transparency and accountability to society of said [civil society] actors." According to Vivanco, this statement is ominous when pronounced by some hemispheric leaders who have frequently harassed and attacked organizations of civil society that attempt to fulfill their watchdog role on human rights. Further, a true civil society is formed by organizations that are independent not only in name but in practice, and such organizations are accountable only to their constituents — not to governments.

For further information, contact José Miguel Vivanco (202) 371-6592; Allyson Collins (202) 371-6592; or Susan Osnos (212) 972-8405.

*Lawyers Committee
for Human Rights*

*The Lawyers Committee for
Human Rights is an
independent, United States-
based non-governmental
organization. Since 1978,
the Committee has worked
to protect and promote
fundamental human rights
as established in the
International Bill of
Human Rights and other
relevant international
instruments. To this end,
the Committee conducts
fact-finding missions and
publishes reports which
serve as a starting point for
sustained follow-up
work in the international
community as well as in
the country concerned. The
Lawyers Committee employs
a total of thirty people in
New York and Washington.*

Statement on Human Rights and Civil Society and Recommendations for Action by Heads of State at the Summit of the Americas

Freedom of association and freedom of expression are universally recognized human rights; they are protected by the provisions of the Universal Declaration of Human Rights, the International Covenants on Human Rights, and the American Convention on Human Rights. When people exercise these rights and join in voluntary, nonprofit groups, the resulting organizations provide crucial and effective means for citizen participation in the affairs of the nation. This is the process by which civil society develops. Although the state has the primary responsibility to protect human rights, these non-governmental organizations also provide an effective, and necessary, voice for the protection of human rights and the articulation of rights-based norms and values which should govern individual as well as institutional behavior. Their role as advocates is crucial to the functioning of democracy, to the growth of civil society, and to the protection of human rights. They must be free to function without unnecessary governmental interference, even when their advocacy is in conflict with governmental policies.

Consequently, every state is subject to a fundamental imperative that freedom of association and of expression be clearly protected by the law of every state, as well as by administrative and judicial procedures, both formal and informal. This protection should be reflected in fair legal regulations covering, among other matters, taxation, incorporation, and corporate governance, which encourage the formation of nonprofit, non-governmental organizations and ensure their functioning free of unnecessary or politically motivated interference by the state. While NGOs are properly accountable to governmental bodies charged with oversight of nonprofit groups, this oversight must be exercised honestly and in accordance with established procedures for fair and impartial review; it may not be used as a tool to force an organization to conform its activities or advocacy to the wishes of the government or of politically powerful individuals.

A serious and growing problem which undermines democracy and civil society is bribery, and other form of corruption, in all types of international and local matters and transactions. It is imperative that all governments take the necessary steps to eliminate it. Permitting the continuation of preferential treatment for those who pay illicitly diminishes the freedom afforded to all other citizens who must rely on their elected representatives to manage the affairs of state faithfully.

Multilateral organizations have an increasingly significant impact in matters related to development and democracy in the hemisphere. It is important that these institutions promote practices of participatory democracy and good governance on the national level, and model such practices in their own decision-making.

NGOs must also act responsibly in society. As do all members of civil society, NGOs have a role to play in safeguarding and promoting democracy, civil society, and human rights. NGOs should, therefore, pledge:

To report annually on their activities and finances;

To ensure that their staffs and boards reap no financial benefits aside from reasonable compensation for services rendered and for expenses reasonably incurred;

To clearly state their organizational objectives in published documents and to ensure that these objectives include significant public interest dimensions;

To refrain from activities which are aimed at the destruction or limitation of democracy, civil society, or human rights.

In response to a pledge by NGOs to act as responsible members of civil society, the Heads of State participating in the Summit of the Americas should take the following actions:

First, to commit their government to ratify the American Convention on Human Rights, and to comply with its terms;

Second, in recognition of the crucial role which the Inter-American Court and the Inter-American Commission play in the protection of human rights and fundamental freedoms, to invite members of those bodies to play a prominent, public role at the Summit, and to pledge the support of their government for an adequate budget for those two bodies;

Third, to issue, on behalf of their government, as part of the final communiqué, the following statement:

We recognize that, for the purpose of promoting and protecting human rights, and to facilitate the growth of democracy and civil society, every member of society has the right to form and participate in non-governmental organizations. We also recognize that the state has the primary responsibility to promote and protect human rights and to insure the conditions which lead to the growth of democracy and civil society. Among those conditions is the elimination of corruption in all its forms.

To these ends, we pledge to undertake a review, in consultation with domestic NGOs, of governmental laws, policies and practices, both formal and informal. This review will examine, among other things, access to government information, the requirements for creation and operation of NGOs, tax exemptions and deductions, restrictions on fundraising and on relations between domestic NGOs and their foreign or international counterparts, and requirements for annual (and other public) reports. We will also examine all government laws and practices (including those relating to government regulation of, or relationships with, business, conflict of interest standards, and rules on political contributions) to identify those which foster corruption.

We pledge to remove the obstacles identified by this review and to adopt such legislative, administrative and other steps (including judicial and legal reform) as are necessary to create the social and political conditions and legal guarantees required to enable our citizens to associate, form non-governmental organizations, and pursue their objectives free of unnecessary or unduly burdensome restraints. We recognize that the only permissible limitations are those determined by law solely for the purpose of securing due recognition and respect for the rights and freedoms of others and of meeting the just requirements of public order and the general welfare in a democratic society and in accordance with applicable international obligations and commitments.

We recognize that NGOs have the following rights, among those others which are enumerated in the Universal Declaration of Human Rights, the International Covenants on Human Rights, and the American Convention on Human Rights:

To draw public attention to violations of human rights, to instances of corruption, and to inadequate compliance with the terms of this declaration; to complain about these policies and actions to competent national bodies; and to have those complaints promptly reviewed by independent, impartial and competent judicial (or other) authorities;

To have unhindered access to and communication with international bodies with competence to receive and consider communications on matters of human rights, corruption, and civil society in accordance with applicable international instruments and procedures.

Furthermore, we pledge to take all necessary steps to ensure the protection of everyone against violence or retaliation as a consequence of the legitimate exercise of these rights.

Finally, we recommend that hemispheric multilateral organizations, in consultation with civil society organizations, develop formal mechanisms for consultation with and participation by civil societies at hemispheric, regional, national, and local levels. In particular, we recommend that the Inter-American Development Bank work with civil society organizations to develop a mechanism that will provide for broad citizen participation in policy and program development, implementation, monitoring, and evaluation.

Policy Proposals on Democratic Governance

Pre-Summit of the Americas Workshop, Cartagena, October 9-11, 1994

THE DEMOCRATIC COMMUNITY OF THE AMERICAS: A COMMITMENT TO DEMOCRATIC INTEGRATION

The Summit of the Americas provides the democratically elected heads of government of thirty-four Western Hemisphere countries with an extraordinary opportunity to develop and begin to implement common strategies and policies aimed at achieving shared regional prosperity, based on solid economic growth, the strengthening of democratic governance, and sustainable development.

In an effort to contribute to the shaping of the Summit's agenda, the North-South Center at the University of Miami launched a hemisphere-wide effort to bring together leading experts from academia, bilateral and multilateral agencies, business and labor organizations, and non-governmental organizations in meetings to identify basic goals, analyze strategies for achieving those goals, and make concrete policy recommendations to the governments of the Americas concerning the issues on the Summit's agenda: Economic Integration, Democratic Governance, and Sustainable Development. Three Hemispheric Policy Working Group meetings, held in October 1994, in Buenos Aires, Cartagena de Indias, and Kingston, constituted the backbone of this effort.

The North-South Center's second Hemispheric Policy Working Group, co-sponsored by the Pontificia Universidad Javeriana, met in Cartagena de Indias, Colombia, on October 9-11, 1994. Charged with analyzing Democratic Governance, the participants were divided into three commissions, each of which examined a primary aspect of the subject: "The Viability of Political Institutions," "The Role of Civil Society," and "Threats to Democratic Governance." After a full day of deliberations, each commission presented its conclusions in a plenary session for discussion, modifications, and approval by all participants.

General Recommendation

The democratic nations of the Americas are in the process of implementing initiatives for economic integration within the framework of the accelerated globalization of the world economy. The North American Free Trade Agreement (NAFTA), the Southern Common Market (MERCOSUR), the Group of Three — Colombia, Mexico, and Venezuela — (G3), the Caribbean Community and Common Market (CARICOM), and the Andean Pact, among other bilateral subagreements, are regional processes that provide the foundation for effective economic integration in the Americas.

The process of economic integration poses a number of important institutional challenges. It is necessary to rethink the normative framework and the very nature of the hemispheric institutions related to the economic integration process and, in some cases, to create new trade agreements and other international mechanisms for economic integration.

At the same time, in response to the challenge of achieving economic integration within a democratic framework, it is necessary to strengthen the international norms and institutions responsible for overseeing democratic processes and human rights at the hemispheric level. In some cases, it will be necessary to create new international mechanisms to promote consensus building around common strategies and goals to reinforce democratic institutions in the Americas.

To move toward democratic integration, we recommend that the governments participating in the Summit of the Americas take the necessary steps to lay the foundation for a Democratic Community of the Americas (DCA).

To this end, we suggest the formation of governmental and non-governmental working groups 1) to evaluate the institutional and legal steps necessary for the creation of the DCA, 2) to determine the ability of the existing institutions and norms to contribute to the establishment of the DCA, 3) to propose the creation of new instruments and mechanisms necessary for the realization of this goal, and 4) to design a common strategy for the implementation of internal reform processes aimed at strengthening democratic norms and procedures in accord with the specific contexts of the diverse nations of the Americas.

COMMISSION NO. 1: THE VIABILITY OF POLITICAL INSTITUTIONS

Objective

The consolidation of democratic systems as a shared hemispheric goal. To achieve this objective, it is necessary to strengthen the democratic, participative, and accountable nature of political institutions. In addition, it is imperative to redefine the role of the state, enabling it to contend with the tensions arising from simultaneous consolidation of the democratic system and the deepening of market reforms.

GENERAL CONSIDERATIONS

1. The tension between the deepening of economic reforms and the consolidation of democratic regimes makes it difficult to reconcile the social cost of adjustment policies with the need to reaffirm the legitimacy of formal political institutions to the citizenry.

150

2. The notion of the state as responsible for a wide range of economic activities and social welfare functions is under varying degrees of scrutiny in the hemisphere. The common theme that arises from these discussions is that the state in the Americas must be redefined, not simply reduced in size. As a starting point, it is necessary to understand that the market itself does not provide sufficient mechanisms to respond to the problems of social well-being, especially those of the poorest sectors of the population. Nor has the state been able, in many cases, to generate appropriate initiatives or invest adequately in areas such as education and health necessary for the formation of the human resources to ensure that increased growth will produce new processes of economic development. For these reasons, it is necessary to:

a. Arrive at a new consensus with respect to the various areas in which government intervention is necessary and desirable for the consolidation of market economies.

b. Promote decentralization as a means of transferring and redistributing state power to various levels of government to make the state more efficient, as well as to facilitate the process of redistribution and promote the fight against poverty. Decentralization also broadens significantly the possibilities for citizen participation in public administration.

3. Political institutions in the Americas are experiencing varying levels of crisis in terms of the electoral system, the party system, and the system of government. Existing political systems, in some cases, contribute to polarization between the legislative and executive branches, resulting in governmental paralysis and even, at times, the instability of the democratic system. To overcome this situation, in addition to strengthening the balance of power, the role of the opposition must be recognized in all types of democratic governments. Similarly, opposition groups must assume a loyal and constructive role in the governing process.

4. The role played by political parties in contemporary society is under profound reevaluation. The relationship between government and civil society must be transformed in ways that permit political parties to transcend their simple electoral functions in order to participate in the governing process as vehicles for the expression of their constituents' interests.

5. Government administration and policy making must progressively foster new forms of access to

ensure popular participation in the public decision-making process. To this end, it is necessary to apply, wherever appropriate, procedures such as the impeachment of elected officials, popular legislative initiatives, and diverse forms of public consultation such as referendums and plebiscites.

Policy Recommendations

1. Strengthen democratic parties and the party system as fundamental intermediary mechanisms between the citizenry and the state. To achieve this goal, it is necessary to promote democratization within political parties and their decision-making processes. It is also important to provide traditionally marginalized sectors of the population access to party leadership positions.

2. Reform electoral systems to generate reliable voter registration lists, ensure the autonomy of institutions responsible for the supervision of electoral processes in order to contribute to their transparency and legitimacy, and strengthen mechanisms that promote a balance between popular representation and the creation of government majorities. Together with electoral reforms, it is important to encourage civic education campaigns toward the consolidation of a democratic culture.

3. Strengthen the balance of powers and the system of checks and balances, thereby fortifying legislative bodies in their law-making and supervisory capacities.

4. Strengthen judicial systems and assert their independence from other branches of government.

5. Call for a hemispheric consensus affirming the responsibility of governments to incorporate into stabilization and adjustment policies the measures needed to compensate for the negative social effects of these policies. Frame social policies within the broader goals of sustainable development and social and political stability. For these purposes, it is necessary to:

   a. Improve institutional performance in the implementation of social policies;

   b. Incorporate citizen and community participation in the social policy decision-making process.

6. Privatization initiatives must:

   a. Insure that activities transferred to the private sector result in a more equitable distribution of economic power;

   b. Promote a greater access to property rights for those individuals who traditionally have been alienated from these rights;

   c. Foster economic competition by developing and bolstering market regulatory mechanisms, such as anti-monopoly controls, free competition legislation, and systems designed to control natural monopolies.

7. Encourage decentralization of the state by:

   a. Strengthening regional, provincial, local, and municipal governments both economically and institutionally;

   b. Reforming fiscal systems and the allocation of public expenditures according to the needs of each level of government;

   c. Decentralizing the organizations that function as political intermediaries, such as political parties and associations, to ensure effective citizen participation and representation.

COMMISSION NO. 2: CIVIL SOCIETY

Objective

The strengthening of an integrated, vital, participative civil society in the Americas to assure the consolidation of democracy as well as sustainable economic progress and its equitable distribution.

General Considerations

1. Modern democracy requires the enhancement of citizens' civic capabilities as well as their increased political participation. This should be achieved through the strengthening of plural and competitive political institutions that consolidate and extend democratic achievements and norms throughout the diverse sectors of society. To this end, it is necessary to fortify the collective identity of intermediary groups and associations and to cultivate respect for the autonomy and the rights of indigenous populations, women, the poor, sexual minorities, and youth.

2. The viability of modern participative democracy requires:

   a. The formulation and implementation of viable, sustainable development strategies that enhance the possibilities created by the markets for addressing the deterioration of social conditions in the region;

   b. The reconciliation of the imbalances that exist among the state, the market, and civil society to the detriment of the latter;

c. The reversal of the fragmentation, exclusion, and increasing social inequalities that are present in the societies of the Americas;

d. The strengthening of governmental capacities to bolster mechanisms and implement policies which ensure that structural adjustment and trade liberalization do not infringe upon workers' rights or diminish their standard of living.

3. A modern, participative democracy requires citizens who are healthy, educated, informed, knowledgeable of their rights, and cognizant of their intellectual and material capabilities so that they can fully participate in public life. Without the assurance of a minimum standard of health and education, citizens are disempowered, and the very basis of democratic governance is undermined. In a global market characterized by an ever-increasing dependence on highly specialized labor, the continuing education of the workforce is essential to ensure the international competitiveness of the economies of the hemisphere.

4. Modern democracies demand an appropriate legal framework that ensures universal access to mass media in the context of full freedom of expression. This framework encourages the broadest possible participation in the formulation and reception of information and ideas and in the discussion of proposals. The communications media must be pluralistic in nature and must not be subject to any form of monopoly — be it legal, de facto, private, or governmental. Media pluralism is particularly essential in guaranteeing the voice of civil society during electoral processes.

5. Modern democracy demands the rebuilding of citizens' trust in the judicial system and in judicial processes, beyond the formal recognition of civil liberties, assuring all segments of the population — particularly the dispossessed — of effective, rapid access to the benefits of the legal system.

6. Solidification of modern democracy in the post-Cold War context, under new international circumstances allowing for the rechanneling of a significant portion of military expenditures, requires tax reforms. To generate the most resources possible without creating budgetary imbalances, these reforms must be promoted to ensure:

a. Access for all citizens to adequate health services, education, and the due process of law;

b. Financing of compensatory social programs aimed at ameliorating the social costs of structural adjustment;

c. Promotion of industrial restructuring required by the globalization of economic processes.

Policy Recommendations

1. Reinforce the political venues available to civil society by defining norms and institutions that permit increased participation of intermediary political parties and associations, such as labor unions, social movements, religious organizations, business associations, and all other groups that are part of the complex networks which distinguish the civil societies of modern democracies.

2. Create and/or perfect the necessary national and hemispheric regulatory framework to promote the efficient performance of markets. Generate modern, flexible regulatory systems that augment competition, minimize the possibility of monopolistic abuses, improve the quality of goods and services while lowering prices, and enable the citizens at large, as well as public agencies, to regulate the goods and services traded in the market.

3. Restructure educational systems to guarantee universal access to quality primary and secondary education, as well as strengthen public universities and fortify science and technology education to enhance the quality of human capital in our countries.

4. Ensure universal access to a balanced system in which the public and private sectors concur on the provision of health services for the population as a means of reversing the negative effects that the stabilization and structural adjustment programs may have had on the quality of health and social security programs.

5. Promote, via an adequate legal framework, civil society's access to mass communications media, especially television and radio, in order to maximize society's exercise of freedom of speech.

6. Assure the full independence and impartiality of judicial systems so that judicial processes go beyond the formal recognition of the civil rights of all citizens to guarantee their prompt, effective access to the benefits of the due process of law. To achieve this objective, it is essential to simplify legal systems and the various forms of administration of justice, making these more understandable and accessible, defining adequate mechanisms that provide access to those who are disempowered and marginalized. Provide the judicial branch the economic and legal support needed to ensure its effective performance.

7. Implement a progressive tax reform which would maximize the generation of public funds for the areas of education and health to compensate for the social costs of stabilization and economic adjustment and to stimulate the restructuring of industries. Also, it is necessary to establish mechanisms for the broader participation of civil society in the prioritization and use of public funds.

8. Highlight, according to the conclusions of the Commission on Economic Development within the Working Group on Shared Hemispheric Prosperity (Buenos Aires, 2-4 October, 1994), the need for governments of the Americas to:

a. Reaffirm their commitment to existing international rules and norms that appear in the regional and international statutes of the International Labor Organization (ILO).

b. Formulate specific policies and regulations to address the problems of migrant, undocumented or legal, workers and their families in order to eliminate all forms of discrimination and implement fair labor codes.

9. Formulate norms that create favorable conditions for the activities of non-governmental organizations, which have played a crucial role in the strengthening of associative networks in their function as nonpartisan monitors of electoral processes and human rights, as well as in promoting the self-organization of the most marginalized sectors of society for satisfaction of basic needs.

COMMISSION NO. 3: THREATS TO GOVERNANCE

Objective

To guarantee the consolidation of legitimate, participative, and efficient democratic governments by creating the conditions and generating the resources necessary to combat the national and international threats to democratic governance.

General Considerations

1. Governance is threatened by the diverse manifestations of organized international crime, especially drug trafficking and corrupt international financial exchange processes and relationships. The traditional concept of sovereignty prevents individual states from responding effectively to this situation, thus constituting a threat to the defense of the vital interests of nations and their democratic governance.

2. Democratic governance is threatened by the weakness of the mechanisms of supervision, control, and accountability to support the transparent exercise of power and create adequate conditions for the battle against corruption in the Americas. This weakness is fostered by the absence of adequate conditions and effective guarantees for the promotion and development of autonomous social actors, the insufficiency of institutional channels for the regulation of conflicts and the expression of social interests and demands, and the precarious nature of participatory culture. In many cases, there is a weakening and fragmentation of the political parties, ultimately reflected in the parliaments and decision-making entities. In other cases, the inequitable distribution of power undermines the legitimacy and representative character of the formal institutions of the state.

3. Democratic governance is threatened by the lack of full subordination of the armed forces to the legitimately constituted power.

4. Democratic governance is threatened by the crisis of the judicial system which weakens the autonomous and transparent administration of justice and, in many cases, stimulates the violation of fundamental human rights.

5. Democratic governance is threatened by the vastness of poverty in the countries of the Americas. The battle against poverty demands economic and social policies that effectively reach the most impoverished sectors of the society. These policies must be formulated and executed on the basis of mechanisms that ensure the participation of the affected population so that the attention to poverty ultimately contributes to a democratic citizenry.

Policy Recommendations

1. Promote the diversity of existing cooperative initiatives in the economic, social, and political realms by revising the procedures and functions of multilateral political or economic organizations. The impulse for this diversity of initiatives would constitute the basis of a new hemispheric institutionalization of a political and judicial order, in the context of globalization and in response to the threats to democratic governance associated with it.

2. Strengthen in the states of the Americas the guarantees of freedom of expression for political and social organizations and minorities. Secure competition, alternation, and the responsible exercise of opposition. In the same manner, promote innovative mecha-

nisms of popular participation such as referendums, popular initiatives, revocation of power, and so on.

3. Strengthen the process of internal modernization and democratization of political parties to fortify their programmatic, communicative, and mediating role between society and state. Define norms and mechanisms through which the state may ensure minimum conditions of independence and competition between the diverse parties and political organizations during electoral campaigns.

4. Fortify the representative character and institutional capacity of the parliaments in order to recover their credibility as forums for the democratic process. To this end, it is necessary to revise the mechanisms of representation and to upgrade the parliaments' legislative and oversight capacities, as part of an affirmation of an adequate division of power.

5. Strengthen the organisms of control, oversight, and accountability of public governance by fortifying the functions and capacities of the public entities responsible for combatting corruption.

6. Fortify the autonomy and technical efficacy of judicial power and the police forces in order to fight corruption and violence at the national and international levels. The governments of the Americas should:

a. Promote interstate cooperation agreements concerning judicial control of international economic processes and the sanction of transnational crimes;

b. Promote a continental strategy that seeks cooperation between security forces in order to confront threats of a transnational nature;

c. Fortify governmental and non-governmental, national and international institutions and mechanisms for the protection, promotion, and defense of human rights.

7. Fortify the civil administration of the armed forces. To accomplish this task, it is necessary to:

a. Mobilize and integrate the existing resources in the inter-American system to train civil leaders to conduct defense and security affairs successfully;

b. Differentiate between the tasks of internal security and those of national defense so that the mission of the armed forces is clearly defined in respect to both spheres;

c. Define mechanisms of cooperation, permitting governments to enhance their police forces' capacities to protect citizens through

adequate modernization of technological resources and growing professionalism of their members;

d. Open, wherever necessary, new channels of communication between military and the civilian police forces to contribute to the establishment of strong democracies.

WORKING GROUP ON DEMOCRATIC GOVERNANCE, OCTOBER 9-11, 1994

The Viability of Political Institutions

Chairperson, Ricardo Córdova, Fundación D. Guillermo Manuel Ungo (FUNDAUNGO), San Salvador, El Salvador

René Antonio Mayorga, Kellogg Institute, University of Notre Dame, Indiana, and Centro Boliviano de Estudios Multidisciplinarios (CEBEM), La Paz, Bolivia

Marcelo Cavarozzi, Georgetown University, Washington, D.C., and Facultad Latinoamericana de Ciencias Sociales (FLACSO), México

Efraín Gonzales de Olarte, Instituto de Estudios Peruanos (IEP), Lima, Perú

Milton Henríquez, Partido Demócrata Cristiano (PDC), Panamá

Adriana Delgado, Pontificia Universidad Javeriana, Bogotá, Colombia

David Roll, Pontificia Universidad Javeriana, Bogotá, Colombia

The Role of Civil Society

Chairperson, Sergio Zermeño, Universidad Nacional Autónoma de México (UNAM), México

Atilio Borón, Centro para Investigaciones Europeo-Latinoamericanas (EURAL), Buenos Aires, Argentina

Catherine Conaghan, Queen's University at Kingston, Canada

David Mercado, Universidad de Cartagena, Colombia

William C. Smith, University of Miami, Coral Gables, Florida

Steve Stein, North-South Center, University of Miami, Coral Gables, Florida

Threats to Democratic Governance

Chairperson, Fernando Cepeda Ulloa, Universidad de los Andes, Bogotá, Colombia

Felipe Agüero, North-South Center, University of Miami, Coral Gables, Florida

Pilar Gaitán, Secretaría de Derechos Humanos, Ministerio de Defensa, Bogotá, Colombia

Rodrigo Losada, Pontificia Universidad Javeriana, Bogotá, Colombia

Wilfredo Lozano, Facultad Latinoamericana de Ciencias Sociales (FLACSO), Santo Domingo, Dominican Republic

Anthony Maingot, Florida International University (FIU) and North-South Center, Coral Gables, Florida

Richard Millett, North-South Center, Washington, D.C.

Andrés Ramírez, Pontificia Universidad Javeriana, Bogotá, Colombia

Aldo Vacs, Skidmore College, Saratoga Springs, New York

PROPOSALS FROM NON-GOVERNMENTAL SECTORS

II. Promoting Prosperity Through Economic Integration and Free Trade

Text by Ambassador Julius L. Katz, President, Hills & Company and Robert C. Fisher, Managing Director, Hills & Company

Commissioned by the Council of the Americas, the Chamber of Commerce of the U.S.A., and the Association of American Chambers of Commerce in Latin America (AACCLA)

AACCLA is the most active and influential voice for American business operating in Latin America today. Founded in 1967, AACCLA is the umbrella group for 22 American Chambers of Commerce in 20 Latin American/ Caribbean nations. AACCLA advocates increasing trade and investment between the United States and the countries of the region through free trade, free markets, and free enterprise.

AACCLA represents over 16,500 companies and individuals managing the bulk of U.S. investment in the region.

Agenda for the Americas

INTRODUCTION

The Council of the Americas, Chamber of Commerce of the U.S.A., and the Association of American Chambers of Commerce in Latin America would like to take this opportunity to commend the Clinton administration for convening the Summit of the Americas. This unique event has the potential to be a truly historic catalyst, revitalizing relationships among the countries of the Western Hemisphere and building support for the trade-liberalizing commercial policies which have brought, and will continue to bring, prosperity to the Americas.

To support this important initiative, our organizations coordinated an effort to delineate the private sector's objectives for the Summit and communicate these objectives to the Summit participants. The following paper, entitled "Agenda for the Americas," represents the centerpiece of this effort. An earlier version of this paper was discussed in detail at the Pre-Summit Roundtable Conference, which we hosted at the Inter-American Development Bank in September 1994. This final text incorporates many of the comments and ideas expressed by the senior business executives from the United States and Latin America who participated in that conference and other meetings held with a wide variety of business representatives in the region.

The paper sets forth specific policy recommendations which lead to the creation of a Western Hemisphere Free Trade Agreement by the end of this century. These recommendations emanate from a set of general principles which have been broadly endorsed by business leaders in the hemisphere. In addition to circulation in the United States, the twenty-two American Chambers of Commerce in Latin America and the Consejo Empresario de América Latina discussed drafts of this paper with a variety of Latin American interests and provided valuable input for the final version.

We wish to express our appreciation to all the people who helped with the preparation of this paper, including the corporate members and staff of our and other business associations, such as The Business Roundtable, Consejo Empresario de América Latina, National Association of Manufacturers, National Foreign Trade Council, U.S. Council for International Business, and U.S.-Hispanic Chamber of Commerce.

Ambassador Julius L. Katz is President of Hills & Company, International Consultants. He served as Deputy U.S. Trade Representative from 1989 to 1993 and was U.S. Chief Negotiator for the NAFTA. He also had senior responsibility for bilateral and regional negotiations with Latin America and Europe and for the Uruguay Round of multilateral trade negotiations.

Robert C. Fisher is a Managing Director of Hills & Company, International Consultants. He served as Director, Mexican Affairs, at the Office of the U.S. Trade Representative from 1990 to 1993 and was lead market access negotiator for the United States in the NAFTA.

We are especially grateful to Ambassador Julius Katz and Robert Fisher of Hills & Company, who donated countless hours to the successful completion of the paper. Their wisdom guided our efforts and helped us incorporate, in a concise and cogent manner, a broad spectrum of the business community's goals for the Summit of the Americas.

We hope that the Summit leaders will find the principles and policy recommendations outlined in this paper to be useful and will join the private sector in the vigorous pursuit of hemisphere-wide economic integration, providing for free movements of goods, services, information, and capital throughout the Western Hemisphere.

Sincerely,

John E. Avery
Chairman
Council of the Americas

Richard L. Lesher
President
Chamber of Commerce
of the U.S.A.

Everett Ellis Briggs
President
Council of the Americas

David E. Ivy
President
Association of American
Chambers of Commerce
in Latin America

Summit of the Americas December 1994

The Summit of the Americas provides an historic opportunity for the Western Hemisphere's political leaders to inaugurate a new era of peace and prosperity in the region through the promotion of economic growth.

This hemisphere's commitment to freedom has strengthened dramatically in recent years. After decades of authoritarian governments and restrictive economic programs in most of the countries, there is now an enthusiasm for democracy and free markets. And with the freer exchange of ideas, goods, and services, there has arisen a new spirit of optimism and hope for the future.

The region's leaders must ensure that these favorable trends are strengthened, not merely by rhetorical support, but by policies and actions which will widen the opportunities for expanded trade and investment. This paper expresses the views of an important part of the hemisphere's private sector and sets forth the general principles that should underlie public sector policies within the region, with specific policy recommendations. At the heart of the recommendations is the call for negotiation of a Western Hemisphere Free Trade Agreement (WHFTA) by the turn of the century.

GENERAL PRINCIPLES

We believe that the rule of law and freedom of choice — whether in economics or in politics — are basic rights within the hemisphere.

Neither business nor society can thrive without clearly stated and consistently administered laws and rules. Independent and transparent legal systems that provide equal protection to all parties are necessary elements for sound market growth, for sustained capital development, and for strong, stable democracies.

Nor can societies grow without the ability to make choices. The ability to freely choose what business you conduct and with whom and when you do that business is central to competition. And without competition, economic growth stagnates and dies.

With freedom of choice, private sector economic activity is the principal instrument of economic growth for the region.

Nation after nation has learned a hard lesson — government should create an environment in which business operates and should not operate business itself. In almost every case, government involvement in business has led to excessive bureaucracy, waste, inefficiency, and, inevitably, economic stagnation. When government has divested itself of state enterprises, deregulated the economy, and allowed private sector entrepreneurship to flourish, productivity has improved, competitiveness has been strengthened, and the prospects for increased economic growth and incomes have brightened.

Without sustained economic growth in the region, no agenda for the Americas can succeed.

When economies stagnate or decline, workers, business, and consumers all suffer; investment is discouraged; social progress is retarded; and democracy comes under pressure. The surest way for governments to promote sustained economic growth is by creating a positive economic climate where individuals are free to compete in free markets. In so doing, they will advance economic prosperity, which is the precondition for job creation, rising consumer welfare, and the attainment of such social goals as improved worker rights, increased housing, greater access to education, and enhanced environmental protection.

In addition to assuring a proper economic climate, the nations of the region should work together to promote continued improvement in environmental protection, worker rights, education, housing, public health, and democratic institutions in the region.

Support within the United States and other countries for free trade, market economies, and democracy in the region will be strengthened if progress is made in addressing the broad range of issues our nations confront daily.

Free and open markets and sustainable development are not mutually exclusive, but mutually inclusive. Sustainable development should be pursued in the context of what is appropriate given each country's specific social and political goals, level of development, economic capacity, and environmental situation.

One of the best ways to encourage environmental awareness and to promote environmental protection and clean-up is through macroeconomic policies that promote strong, non-inflationary growth. Such growth will lead both to more resources for environmental protection and a growing demand among the citizens of the region that such protections be enacted. If the people of the Western Hemisphere earn rising incomes, they will be able to afford what they often now see as the "luxury" of environmental protection.

There is no single model for sustainable development. Neither the social nor economic interests of the region are advanced when countries are forced to adopt standards, procedures, or technologies that they cannot afford, maintain, or correctly implement. Therefore, market-conforming approaches that maximize transparency and returns to environmental investments and which accommodate differences in stages in development and circumstances should be adopted wherever possible.

Nor can we afford to ignore this hemisphere's most precious resource — its people. The public and private sectors must work to ensure that our children receive an adequate primary and secondary education and that our workers continue to be able to improve their knowledge and skills throughout their lifetime.

Rapid change today is a fact of life. If this hemisphere is to remain competitive in the global marketplace, our workers and our industries must be able to adjust to change swiftly and surely. They can only do so with a solid educational foundation and access to additional training as new technologies requiring new skills move into the market.

To promote the region's growth in trade and economic activity, our economic and labor policies and standards must meet the realities of a global economy characterized by fierce competition and rapid capital mobility.

At the same time, efforts to advance hemispheric cooperation on political, social, and environmental interests should be pursued in parallel with progress toward economic integration, and not as a matter of conditionality and linkage. Cooperative, voluntary exchanges of practices and experiences in these areas work and should be encouraged.

Unilateral trade conditions or sanctions are counterproductive to policies promoting sustainable development, labor rights, and other social issues. Rather than using the "stick" of unilateral trade sanctions, governments should work together cooperatively to promote improvements in and the protection of labor and the environment in the region.

SPECIFIC POLICY RECOMMENDATIONS

The Summit leaders should:

1. Commit themselves to the goal of negotiating a Western Hemisphere Free Trade Agreement (WHFTA) by the end of this century.

This is an ambitious goal. But the vision of a hemisphere without trade barriers, where goods, services, and investment flows can move freely must be expressed clearly and forcefully.

A strong commitment to a hemispheric FTA will reinforce and perpetuate the economic reform process already underway in the region, will enhance investor confidence, and will stimulate the region's economic growth.

2. Agree that the surest and swiftest path toward hemispheric free trade is the expansion of the North American Free Trade Agreement (NAFTA) and its principles.

Although specific agreements in areas such as investment, intellectual property rights, standards, and customs cooperation can serve as valuable stepping stones toward the WHFTA, these agreements should be seen as first steps toward the ultimate goal of a hemispheric FTA based upon the NAFTA.

Expansion of NAFTA should be based on NAFTA's core principles, while recognizing that transitional provisions will be necessary to smooth adjustments.

3. Pledge that regional trade liberalization will be pursued consistent with the multilateral trading system.

Subregional agreements such as MERCOSUR, the Andean Pact, CACM, CARICOM, and Mexico's agreements with Chile, Costa Rica, Colombia, and Venezuela can contribute to the overarching goal of hemispheric integration and could be expanded to include new members or merged with each other.

Hemispheric free trade should conform to the rules of the GATT. The level of protection against non-participants should not be increased beyond existing levels.

Particular care should be taken to avoid the trade-diverting effects that could result from overly restrictive rules of origin.

Free trade partners should pledge to support further multilateral trade liberalization so as to diminish any trade-diverting effects that result from regional trade arrangements.

4. Avoid further proliferation of new bilateral FTAs in the region.

New bilateral FTAs would almost certainly result in a competitive war in which trade would be diverted among the nations of the region rather than created within the region.

Each new agreement would result in different rules of origin, exceptions, and exclusions. Rather than simplifying trade rules, bilateral agreements would introduce new trade distortions. The potential for expansion of trade and investment would thus be diminished.

5. Dedicate their governments to adopt and maintain sound macroeconomic and microeconomic policies, which are the main prerequisites for hemispheric FTA negotiations.

Consistent macroeconomic policies to promote sustained, non-inflationary growth and microeconomic policies with minimal regulatory interference and red tape are critical to the success of a WHFTA. Without such policies, a future agreement will require overly long transition periods and may well self-destruct.

6. Commit that the NAFTA's core provisions establish a minimum for future obligations, whether in terms of potential "stepping stone" agreements or for a hemispheric FTA. These minimum obligations include:

Eliminating completely tariff and non-tariff barriers to trade in goods. Elimination of such barriers will enhance the competitiveness and prosperity of the entire region by allowing all our firms and consumers access to the best goods we have to offer at the lowest prices.

Liberalizing services trade to the maximum extent possible. Services now account for well over half of all economic activity in the Western Hemisphere. The elements of a thriving services sector — such as finance, telecommunications, tourism, and transportation — are essential both to economic development and to enhanced competitiveness.

Creating a free and open investment environment. New, sustained investment flows — both domestic and foreign — are essential to the long-term growth and competitiveness of the region. New investment will result in new jobs, increased technological development and transfer, enhanced workers skills, and improved competitiveness at home and abroad.

Enacting world-class intellectual property rights protection. Patents, copyrights, trademarks, and trade secrets embody one of this hemisphere's highest value-added commodities — knowledge. In an increasingly knowledge and information-dependent world economy, this hemisphere cannot prosper unless it adopts rules that provide sufficient rewards for those who develop new technologies and processes.

Establishing a mechanism for settling trade and investment disputes within the region. An effective dispute settlement mechanism is an essential component of a free trade agreement to provide confidence regarding the enforceability of obligations and to handle expeditiously disagreements which will inevitably arise as relationships expand.

7. The NAFTA contains exceptions in areas such as agriculture, energy, services, transportation, and government procurement. We urge governments to go beyond the NAFTA benchmark and thereby come closer to achieving the

region's full potential for expanded trade, investment and growth.

Governments also should consider provisions to harmonize MFN external tariffs at the lowest achievable levels wherever possible. Common external tariffs would eliminate the need for cumbersome and costly rules of origin that continue to impede trade flows throughout the region.

Canada, Mexico, and the United States could show leadership by beginning this process now in sectors such as electronics, auto parts, and chemicals. Such action would benefit trade within North America and between North America and the rest of the hemisphere.

8. Commit themselves to the goal of negotiating a Western Hemisphere Investment Code.

Investment is the engine of growth in the region. Timely development of necessary infrastructure — both physical and information — will depend on the ability to attract investment.

Negotiation and adoption of an investment code which lowers barriers to foreign investment (e.g., rights of establishment) and protects investments once they are made (e.g., protection against expropriation and dispute resolution mechanisms) will encourage investors to participate in Western Hemisphere markets.

9. Facilitate the flow of goods, services, information and investments within the region in advance of a hemispheric agreement. In particular, they should:

Standardize and simplify customs practices and procedures. The benefits of free trade can be maximized only when customs practices are consistent, predictable, and efficient. Governments should ensure that customs officials understand new FTA rules and work with the private sector to develop new, streamlined procedures.

Encourage the construction of the infrastructure needed to facilitate the trade and investment. Trade liberalization within the hemisphere has led to increased trade flows among the partners. As trade and investment grow, the hemisphere will require new and improved roads, railways, seaports, and airports; enhanced telecommunications capabilities and information infrastructure; and modernized ports of entry. **The governments of the hemisphere should work together to develop a cohesive trans-**portation and information infrastructure network. We urge them to look to the private sector to create this infrastructure whenever possible.

Harmonize standards' requirements and testing and certification procedures where feasible and work toward mutual recognition of national testing and certification procedures. Governments impose thousands of standards and testing and certification requirements to protect health and safety and ensure consumer welfare. Conflicting standards and testing procedures among governments impose needless costs on business and consumers and create significant obstacles to trade and competitiveness. **We encourage governments to work with the private sector to eliminate unnecessary standards and testing and certification requirements while maintaining a high degree of consumer protection.**

10. Require their trade and other concerned ministers to meet annually and report back to the Summit leaders on progress made toward the goals of regional integration and enhanced cooperation on environmental, labor and other policy interests.

Governments should develop cooperative workplans seeking coordination of policies in areas such as customs administration, investment, and the protection of intellectual property.

We also encourage technical exchanges among officials, as well as the use of technical assistance to promote the goal of regional cooperation.

In all of these efforts, governments should work in close consultation with the private sector, which most of these policies directly impact.

11. Ensure that appropriate legislative procedures are in place so that each country can act to approve the WHFTA as negotiated in a timely fashion. In particular, the United States should renew the "fast-track" authority to permit it to negotiate and implement trade agreements.

Such procedures must be sufficiently broad and unencumbered by conditionality to permit each country to negotiate effectively.

Without fast track, it will be difficult for the United States to persuade other governments in the region that it has the capability to negotiate in good faith and to deliver on what is negotiated.

• About AACCLA

• MEMBERSHIP

Twenty-two AmChams are located in twenty Latin nations:

- Argentina
- Nicaragua
- Ecuador-Quito
- Brazil-Rio de Janeiro
- Paraguay
- Guatemala
- Chile
- Trinidad & Tobago
- Jamaica
- Costa Rica
- Venezuela
- Ecuador-Guayaquil
- Bolivia
- Panama
- El Salvador
- Brazil-São Paulo
- Peru
- Honduras
- Colombia
- Uruguay
- Mexico
- Dominican Republic

• WHAT WE DO

The AACCLA Secretariat, located in Washington, D.C., works to alert business of the growing opportunities in Latin America through:

- Unique contacts in Latin America via the AmChams;
- Timely seminars on business opportunities in the region;
- AmCham publications available in the U.S. through the U.S. Chamber of Commerce;
- Publications, such as our *Latin American Country Profiles* (updated annually), which provide strategic analysis of the economic and political climate as well as trade and investment forecasts for the year ahead in 19 Latin nations.

• FOR MORE INFORMATION

If you would like more information on AACCLA and the AmChams in Latin America, please contact: AACCLA, International Division, U.S. Chamber of Commerce, 1615 H Street, N.W., Washington, D.C. 20062-2000. The phone number is (202) 463-5485; FAX (202) 463-3126.

Postscript:
The Summit of the Americas:
A Side by Side Analysis of Private Sector Recommendations and Summit Declarations

Association of American Chambers of Commerce in Latin America (AACCLA)

DECEMBER 15, 1994

White Paper Recommendations	Summit Declarations	Analysis
1. Commit themselves to the goal of negotiating a Western Hemisphere Free Trade Agreement (WHFTA) by the end of this century.	Leaders resolved immediately to begin work achieving a Free Trade Agreement of the Americas (FTAA), with negotiations to conclude in 2005. Also agreed to make concrete progress toward the attainment of this by the end of the century. After the Summit, the leaders of Canada, Mexico, and the United States agreed to begin NAFTA accession negotiations with Chile in May 1995.	*WIN:* Announcement of negotiations for Chile's accession to NAFTA has launched the process.
2. Agree that the surest and swiftest path toward hemispheric free trade is the expansion of the North American Free Trade Agreement and its principles.	Leaders "pledge to build on existing subregional and bilateral arrangements in order to broaden and deepen hemispheric economic cooperation."	*WIN/MIXED:* The U.S. has signaled that NAFTA accession is its preferred route. Work will begin immediately to add Chile to NAFTA. Since the Summit, Colombia, Trinidad & Tobago, and Jamaica have formally asked to join the trilateral pact. Work to decide what must be done to bring existing subregional arrangements to the point where they can accede to NAFTA will also begin.
3. Pledge that regional trade liberalization will be pursued consistent with the multilateral trading system.	The Summit Declaration and Program of Work reinforced the leaders' strong commitment to multilateral rules and disciplines of the GATT/WTO.	*WIN:* Consistent with White Paper.

White Paper Recommendations	Summit Declarations	Analysis
4. Avoid further proliferation of new bilateral FTAs in the region.	The Summiteers did not address this issue specifically.	*WIN/MIXED:* While the 34 leaders did not specifically address this issue, it was raised during the meeting by Chilean President Eduardo Frei. He emphasized that a proliferation of trade agreements with different standards and rules was a danger to the integration process and also warned that such agreements could raise, not lower, the cost of doing business in the hemisphere. The leaders agreed to make this issue a priority for the June 1995 Trade Minister Summit. This creates an opportunity for private sector organizations to continue to press this point forward in 1995 and further reinforce the message that while the rules of such pacts might be GATT/WTO consistent, they might unintentionally raise barriers for U.S. firms trying to access overseas markets.
5. Dedicate their governments to adopt and maintain sound macroeconomic and micro-economic policies, which are the main prerequisites for hemispheric FTA negotiations.	In the Summit Declaration of Principles, the leaders agreed that "our continued economic progress depends on sound economic policies."	*WIN:* Consistent with White Paper recommendation.
6. Commit that the NAFTA's core provisions establish a minimum for future obligations, whether in terms of potential "stepping stone" agreements or for a hemispheric FTA. These minimum obligations include: • Eliminating completely tariff and non-tariff barriers to trade in goods; • Liberalizing services trade to the maximum extent possible; • Creating a free and open investment environment; • Enacting world-class intellectual property rights protection; and	The 34 leaders agreed to "maximize market openness through high levels of discipline" and to "strive for balanced and comprehensive agreements." Among the issues to be addressed in Free Trade Area of the Americas are the following: • Tariff and non-tariff barriers affecting trade in goods and services; • Investment; • Intellectual property rights; • Dispute resolution; • Agriculture; • Subsidies; • Government procurement; • Technical barriers to trade;	*WIN:* The Summit Declaration not only meets but also surpasses the benchmark put forth in our White Paper. The topics set forth by the 34 leaders read like NAFTA's table of contents — all areas negotiated in trilateral pact, with the exception of customs procedures (which are covered in the Trade Ministers program of work), transportation standards (though in NAFTA they only relate to land transportation), agriculture standards, national treatment for both trade goods

White Paper Recommendations	Summit Declarations	Analysis
6. Continued		
• Establishing a mechanism for settling trade and investment disputes within the region.	• Safeguards; • Rules of origin; • Antidumping and countervailing duties; • Sanitary and phytosanitary standards and procedures; and • Competition policy.	and investment, energy, and telecommunications (covered by the Summit leaders in the infrastructure segment found below).
7. The NAFTA contains exceptions in areas such as agriculture, energy, services, transportation, and government procurement. We urge governments to go beyond the NAFTA benchmark and thereby come closer to achieving the region's full potential for expanded trade, investment, and growth.	NAFTA's exemptions were not addressed by the Summit leaders, though they did commit to "maximize market openness."	*WIN:* In spirit, the Summit Declaration and Plan of Work are consistent with the White Paper. The Western Hemisphere Task Force should monitor negotiations closely and be active in seeking opportunities to discuss negotiating strategies with the U.S. government.
8. Commit themselves to the goal of negotiating a Western Hemisphere Investment Code.	Leaders agreed to address investment as part of the FTAA and also agreed that "developing, liberalizing, and integrating financial markets domestically and internationally, increasing transparency, and establishing sound, comparable supervision and regulation of banking and securities markets will help to reduce the cost of capital by enhancing investor and depositor confidence." Also, leaders agreed to form a Committee on Hemispheric Financial Issues, designed to "promote the liberalization of capital movements and the progressive integration of capital markets, including...the negotiation of common guidelines on capital movements that would provide for their progressive liberalization."	*WIN:* The two positions agree conceptually. Precisely because the idea is so loosely defined, this topic is one in which the U.S. private sector can play a key role in shaping the investment code that emerges from this process. The Western Hemisphere Task Force should make this a priority item in its program for 1995.

White Paper Recommendations	Summit Declarations	Analysis
9. Facilitate the flow of goods, services, information, and investments within the region in advance of a hemispheric agreement. In particular, they should: • Standardize and simplify customs practices and procedures; • Encourage the construction of the infrastructure needed to facilitate trade and investment; and • Harmonize standards' requirements and testing and certification procedures, where feasible, and work toward mutual recognition of national testing and certification procedures.	The Summit leaders agreed that the 34 trade ministers should meet in order to "consider areas for immediate attention — such as customs facilitation — and produce testing and certification with a view to mutual recognition agreements." Infrastructure was also discussed; on this topic, the Summit leaders agreed that "development in this hemisphere depends on urgent infrastructure measures, including the priority allocation of financial resources, in accordance with national legislation and with the participation of both the public and private sectors."	*WIN:* Again, there appears to be a general convergence of positions. As a result, this provides an opportunity for the Task Force to provide input in 1995. Testing and certification language is wholly consistent with the White Paper. Infrastructure language is consistent with the spirit of our recommendations.
10. Require their trade and other concerned ministers to meet annually and report back to the Summit leaders on progress made toward the goals of regional integration and enhanced cooperation on environmental, labor, and other policy interests.	Summit leaders agreed that their trade ministers should meet in June 1995 and again in March 1996. At the latter meeting, they would set a timetable for further work.	*WIN:* Another area where the Task Force must work in 1995 to make sure its views are taken into account when the trade ministers begin their work. In sum, the ministers' agenda during the June 1995 meeting consists of the following items: • Prepare a preliminary report on status of work in existing trade and investment fora; • Receive and discuss the Organization of American States (OAS) Special Committee on Trade preliminary report; • Outline areas for immediate consideration. *In March 1996, the ministers will meet to:* • Receive the final report of the OAS Special Committee on Trade; • Report on their findings in the existing trade and investment fora; • Determine a timetable for further work. The Task Force might be particularly active in making known the priority issues for the business community.

White Paper Recommendations	Summit Declarations	Analysis
11. Ensure that appropriate legislative procedures are in place so that each country can act to approve the WHFTA as negotiated in a timely fashion. In particular, the U.S. should renew the "fast-track" authority to permit it to negotiate and implement trade agreements.	Leaders stated that they "recognize that decisions on trade agreements remain a sovereign right of each nation. In addition, recognizing the importance of effective enforcement of international commitments, each nation will take the necessary action, in accordance with its own legislation and procedures, to implement the agreements in the areas covered by the Plan of Action."	*MIXED:* A dialogue between the Congress and the administration on fast-track trade negotiating authority has begun. Speaker-to-be Newt Gingrich has reiterated his position that labor and environment standards should not be linked to trade. Action on fast-track is not expected until later in 1995.

MIAMI DECLARATION:
Hemispheric Entrepreneurial Leadership Summit

November 30, 1994
Miami, Florida

CAMACOL
hosted The Chambers of Commerce and Industry from the Latin American and Caribbean region prior to the 1994 Summit of the Americas, where this Declaration was generated.

Cámara de Comercio Latina de los Estados Unidos (CAMACOL), the Latin Chamber of Commerce of the United States, was created in 1965 by a small group of Hispanic business people and industrialists. They conceived the idea of building a non-profit organization that would join all Latin entrepreneurs for the common protection of their rights and for the promotion and development of commerce.

Today CAMACOL is a powerful Hispanic organization in the state of Florida and, with a membership of over 1,600, one of the largest chambers of commerce in the United States.

INTRODUCTION

The Chambers of Commerce and Industry from the Latin American and Caribbean region, as private sector representatives of our nations, hereby declare our responsible position, as defenders and promoters of the universal principles of political and economic liberty and representative democracy.

We demand for all of the citizens of the Hemisphere the right to property and to free economic initiative, as catalysts for the progress of our society.

We support the right of the consumers and producers to develop within a free and spontaneous market, without unnecessary state intervention that only ensures its protection, not its reduction.

We accept the need, within the judicial, moral and ethical framework, for the private and public sector to work within a climate of organized liberty to ensure social peace. Likewise, we recognize the supporting role of the modern state in its function and service to society within the concept of social cooperation.

We favor and work toward enabling our people to enjoy a high standard of living, both intellectually and materially, as well as social stability.

WHEREAS, the private sector of the Latin American region supports the principle of the expansion of trade globalization within the framework of the GATT and the World Trade Organization through the ratification of the agreements as a result of the Uruguay Round, and

that private activity, as it pertains to commerce and investment, is fundamental for the improvement of the quality of life of the citizens of the Hemisphere,

that this favors economic development, expansion and liberalization of regional trade and economic integration of the nations of the hemisphere, within a structure of "free regional trade," thereby not restricting nor excluding possible trade initiatives with a third nation outside our Hemisphere, or trade blocs,

that, in the forthcoming Summit of the Americas 1994, the participating heads of state are democratically elected, thus providing an unprecedented opportunity for the adoption of common policies and measures, earmarked toward shared prosperity, thereby strengthening the democratic system of government hence recognizing the important symbiotic relationship between economic integration and democracy.

The representative entrepreneurs attending this preparatory meeting of the XVI Hemispheric Congress of Latin Chambers of Commerce of the United States, CAMACOL,

DECLARE:

1. That we advocate the liberalization of Hemispheric trade as a continuation of the efforts in support of free regional trade, which for decades has been the desire and goal of our peoples. For this we support the timely establishment of a chronogram which will reflect the schedule for the establishment of a HEMISPHERIC FREE TRADE ZONE, also respecting the principal role of free regionalism.

2. That during the process of integration, the nations should move toward free access to market through:

- lifting of non-tariff barriers which continue to obstruct trade, as well as prompt elimination of all trade subsidies and all other impediments to commerce,
- harmonizing all norms of origin, technical standards, and sanitary norms,
- implementing effective measures concerning unfair trade practices,
- supporting harmonized policies which facilitate the integration of new frontiers, and which encourage the development of a transportation infrastructure which will physically integrate the nations and regions.

3. That the chambers of commerce and industry share the belief in the concept and are committed to sustainable development, as a means for economic growth, with access to the benefits arisen as a result of free trade for all of the members of society, and demanding the efficient and non-depleting use of natural resources, and the conservation of the environment, without using this as an unjust and disproportionate measure against free trade.

4. That we coincide in the support of policies of DEREGULATION which not only are earmarked toward the objective of obtaining open economies for international trade but also toward domestic issues, which contribute to the reduction of manufacturing costs and stimulate investment initiatives and projects which create new opportunities for employment which are vital for the sustainment of economic growth and development.

5. That, likewise, our institutions advocate for the just respect of labor conditions and for an understanding between workers and entrepreneurs in each of our nations.

6. That the key factor in the process of development of our region is education and that through it a higher standard of social well-being can be obtained.

7. That we urge for the establishment and implementation of effective measures against corruption in all of its forms. We focus on drug-trafficking, as well as corruption within both the public and private sectors which threatens the heart of the ethics and morals of our society.

8. That we express solidarity with the peoples of our Hemisphere who still cannot achieve human rights through the re-establishment of democracy, and we urge its prompt restoration.

9. That the entrepreneurs hereby united express our desires that the Summit of the Americas 1994 be commencement of a new era of understanding and cooperation between our nations, thereby facing the new XXI century with prosperity, growth, development, and freedom for our peoples and for humanity.

Participant Chambers in the Hemispheric Entrepreneurial Leadership Summit

HOST CHAMBER:

LATIN CHAMBER OF COMMERCE OF U.S.A.
(CAMACOL)
MIAMI, FLORIDA, U.S.A.

ARGENTINA

ARGENTINE CHAMBER OF COMMERCE
BUENOS AIRES, ARGENTINA

BOLIVIA

NATIONAL CHAMBER OF COMMERCE OF
BOLIVIA
LA PAZ, BOLIVIA

BRAZIL

FEDERATION OF COMMERCE OF
THE FEDERAL DISTRICT
BRASILIA, BRAZIL

CHILE

NATIONAL CHAMBER OF COMMERCE OF CHILE
SANTIAGO DE CHILE, CHILE

COLOMBIA

CONFEDERATION OF CHAMBERS OF COMMERCE
OF COLOMBIA
BOGOTA, COLOMBIA

COSTA RICA

COSTA RICAN CHAMBER OF COMMERCE
SAN JOSE, COSTA RICA

FEDERATION OF CHAMBERS OF COSTA RICA
SAN JOSE, COSTA RICA

DOMINICAN REPUBLIC

CHAMBER OF COMMERCE AND PRODUCTION
OF THE NATIONAL DISTRICT
SANTO DOMINGO, DOMINICAN REPUBLIC

DOMINICAN FEDERATION OF CHAMBERS OF
COMMERCE

(FEDOCAMARAS)
SANTO DOMINGO, DOMINICAN REPUBLIC

ECUADOR

CHAMBER OF COMMERCE OF GUAYAQUIL
GUAYAQUIL, ECUADOR

EL SALVADOR

CHAMBER OF COMMERCE AND INDUSTRY OF
EL SALVADOR
SAN SALVADOR, EL SALVADOR

GUATEMALA

CHAMBER OF COMMERCE OF GUATEMALA
GUATEMALA, GUATEMALA

HONDURAS

CHAMBER OF COMMERCE AND INDUSTRY OF
TEGUCIGALPA
TEGUCIGALPA, HONDURAS

FEDERATION OF CHAMBERS OF COMMERCE OF
THE CENTRAL AMERICA ISTHMUS
TEGUCIGALPA, HONDURAS

MEXICO

NATIONAL FEDERATION OF CHAMBERS OF
COMMERCE AND TOURISM
(CONCANO-SERVYTUR)
MEXICO, D.F.

NICARAGUA

CHAMBER OF COMMERCE OF NICARAGUA
MANAGUA, NICARAGUA

FEDERATION OF CHAMBERS OF COMMERCE OF
NICARAGUA
MANAGUA, NICARAGUA

PANAMA

CHAMBER OF COMMERCE, INDUSTRIES AND
AGRICULTURE OF PANAMA
PANAMA, PANAMA

FEDERATION OF CHAMBERS OF COMMERCE,
INDUSTRIES AND AGRICULTURE OF PANAMA
PANAMA, PANAMA

PARAGUAY

PARAGUAYAN-AMERICAN CHAMBER OF
COMMERCE
PARAGUAY, PARAGUAY

PERU

CHAMBER OF COMMERCE OF LIMA
LIMA, PERU

CONFEDERATION OF CHAMBERS OF COMMERCE
OF PERU
(CONFECAMARAS)

PUERTO RICO

CHAMBER OF COMMERCE OF PUERTO RICO
SAN JUAN, PUERTO RICO

URUGUAY

URUGUAYAN-U.S.A. CHAMBER OF COMMERCE
MONTEVIDEO, URUGUAY

VENEZUELA

NATIONAL COUNCIL OF COMMERCE AND
SERVICES (CONSECOMERCIO)
CARACAS, VENEZUELA

U.S.A. (States in alphabetical order)

CALIFORNIA

SAN DIEGO COUNTY HISPANIC CHAMBER OF
COMMERCE
SAN DIEGO, CALIFORNIA

FLORIDA

LATIN CHAMBER OF COMMERCE OF
THE TAMPA BAY AREA
TAMPA, FLORIDA

GEORGIA

ATLANTA HISPANIC CHAMBER OF COMMERCE
ATLANTA, GEORGIA

ILLINOIS

CUBAN AMERICAN CHAMBER OF COMMERCE OF
ILLINOIS
CHICAGO, ILLINOIS

LOUISIANA

GULF COAST INTERNATIONAL HISPANIC
CHAMBER OF COMMERCE
KENNER, LOUISIANA

NEVADA

NEVADA LATIN CHAMBER OF COMMERCE
LAS VEGAS, NEVADA

NEW JERSEY

STATEWIDE HISPANIC CHAMBER OF COMMERCE
OF NEW JERSEY
PATERSON, NEW JERSEY

NEW YORK

NEW YORK STATE FEDERATION OF HISPANIC
CHAMBERS OF COMMERCE
NEW YORK, N.Y.

TEXAS

SAN ANTONIO HISPANIC CHAMBER OF
COMMERCE
SAN ANTONIO, TEXAS

WASHINGTON, D.C.

UNITED STATES HISPANIC CHAMBER OF
COMMERCE
WASHINGTON, D.C.

GREATER WASHINGTON IBERO-AMERICAN
CHAMBER OF COMMERCE
WASHINGTON, D.C.

Text of the letter sent to the thirty-four heads of state attending the Summit of the Americas 1994

We join President Clinton and the members of the Summit of the Americas 1994 Host Committee in welcoming you to this important event, which we are certain will bring about a brighter future for all of the citizens of our Hemisphere.

Attached herewith is a copy of the Miami Document. This document reflects the concerns and recommendations of the private sector on the development of regional trade and the economic integration of the Hemisphere.

Accordingly, the document was generated during a Pre-Summit meeting of the members of the Permanent Secretariat of the Hemispheric Congress, comprised of the presidents of chambers of commerce who represent twenty-six nations throughout the Latin American and Caribbean region and their respective Minister of Commerce held on November 30, 1994.

The private sector is the backbone of a nation, and we affirm that united we can truly achieve the dream of true integration for the Americas in the century to come.

Sincerely,

Luis Sabines
President
CAMACOL

William Alexander
Chairman
Hemispheric Congress

The Columbus Group

This paper was prepared in response to an invitation extended to the Columbus Group by the Summit of the Americas 1994 to express its opinion on various aspects of the current situation in Latin America.

Latin America: Sustained Economic Growth

Grupo Columbus
Buenos Aires, November 14, 1994

Honorable Michael Skol
Principal Deputy Assistant Secretary
Latin America and the Caribbean
Department of State
2101 C Street N.W.
Washington, D.C.

Dear Mr. Ambassador:

We are pleased to write you in reference to the meeting that you, Ambassador Charles Gillespie, and Columbus Group members attended last June in New York regarding the Summit of the Americas.

At that time you kindly invited us to express a comprehensive opinion on the problems facing the hemisphere at the end of this century. The Columbus Group promised to write a paper for the Summit, which reflects its outlook on this important moment. The situation requires joint action on many of the matters our countries must face.

We are pleased to send you this paper which has been prepared with the collaboration of Chilean economist Hernán Buchi Buc.

Each member of the Columbus Group is also delivering a copy of this document to his respective government.

We trust we have made a positive contribution to this important Summit of the Americas meeting. We would also like to thank you for the fluid relationship, which we consider an honor, that our group has with the Bureau of Inter-American Affairs.

Sincerely,

Francisco Macri   *Carlos Ardilla Lulle*

c/c

Alexander Watson
Charles Gillespie

THE COLUMBUS GROUP

The Columbus Group was created in the mid-1980s. It is made up of Latin American and Latin European businessmen linked to Latin American economic, social, and cultural matters.

The members of the Columbus Group are committed to changing and revitalizing Latin America so that the region can respond efficiently to the profound changes affecting the world today.

The Columbus Group is a non-profit organization and is non-political.

Objectives

• To serve public and private activity in Latin America and to allow the region to benefit by its members' experience.

• To contribute to modernizing the region.

• To help identify the needs of each country.

• To promote industrialization and growth in Latin America.

• To assist in integrating capital and technology in Latin America's growth process.

• To increase inter-regional trade.

• To assist in the privatization of state-owned companies.

• To contribute to the creation of a serious and positive image of the region's current status, needs, and opportunities.

Principles

The Columbus Group is guided by the following principles:

• support for integration efforts.

• a belief that defining the region's future and independence is of crucial importance.

• the need to redefine the region's strategic priorities and foster development through the efforts and organizational ability of Latin Americans.

PRESIDENT
Carlos Ardila Lulle
Colombia

MEMBERS
Carlos Abedrop Davila
Mexico

Diego Arria
Venezuela

Gilberto Borja Navarrete
Mexico

Carlos Alberto Bulgheroni
Argentina

Angelo Calmon de Sa
Brazil

Oswaldo Cisneros Fajardo
Venezuela

Manuel Diez
Dominican Republic

Luiz Fernando Ferreira Levy
Brazil

Ignacio Fierro
Spain

Luis Garcia Miro
Peru

Carlos Hank Gonzalez (*)
Mexico

Francisco Macri
Argentina

Eduardo Martinez Lima
Dominican Republic

Manuel de Prado y Colon de Carbajal
Spain

Felipe Thorndike
Peru

Benito Zapata Cardenas
Venezuela

COORDINATOR
Victor Garcia Laredo
Argentina

(*) Currently on leave

Latin America: Sustained Economic Growth

Introduction

The number of problems facing Latin America today is enormous. To consolidate democracy, to overcome poverty, to conquer terrorism, to halt the effects of drug trafficking, to protect the environment, and to fight corruption at all levels — these are just a few of the most outstanding problems.

The list is so lengthy and urgent that one runs the risk of being ineffective if all the problems are attacked at once.

But true foresight, whether that of a statesman or a businessman, is knowing how to take advantage of real opportunities when they appear and, generating a great deal of energy around them, producing multiple wide-ranging effects.

We are convinced that Latin America has this opportunity right now. Practically the entire continent is enjoying a degree of freedom today that it has not had for some time. Economic reforms are being carried out almost in unison throughout the region. If they continue, we will make the same progress that allowed other nations to leap into the developed world in only one generation.

If this occurs, democracy will be reinforced, poverty will be effectively overcome, and there will be resources to protect the environment. Corruption and other scourges that affect many of our countries will be weakened or eliminated. But if we waste this opportunity to create an era of progress, no matter what efforts we make in other areas, we will probably be wasting our energy.

We would like for everyone to be aware of this great opportunity which unites us. We are just starting down the path of economic progress. Of course, enormous dangers and difficulties await us. While tremendous progress has been made in achieving stability and enormous changes have taken place, the goal of sustained growth has yet to be achieved. Impatience and real problems may make us stray from the path. It is important to recognize such situations and know how to overcome them.

Undoubtedly, some will legitimately try to skip stages and tackle future issues in the present, endangering the entire process. Consequently, we feel that, without questioning the values we all hold, such as freedom, honor, and solidarity, regional leaders have an historic responsibility to continue the process of economic changes until sustained growth is achieved. This should be the common point uniting us.

Every issue discussed in this report is based on the aforementioned thesis, with the intention of describing the current situation; detecting problems and difficulties present in our countries and proposing alternatives to counter them; pointing out emerging dangers; and lastly, defining the tasks and responsibilities to be assumed by the pertinent parties. Latin America urgently needs to take off. It needs to begin an extended period of sustained growth. It would be terribly cruel to the most poverty-stricken in our region if we do not continue the process we have begun.

1. Why Growth Is Important

1.1 The Summit of the Americas represents an historic opportunity for regional leaders to adhere to a new model for national organization and international cooperation, making the 20th Century an unequaled period of prosperity and peace.

1.2 Latin America is particularly hopeful. The Summit is taking place at a time when all the nations in the region — some more than others — have begun in-depth political, economic, and social reforms. They have abandoned authoritarianism and state-run economies and have moved on to building democratic societies and free market economies. This process has led to new optimism: now there are valid expectations for progress. But, at the same time, the process is tiring and causes impatience. The Summit of the Americas provides an opportunity for the continent officially to commit to democracy and free markets while agreeing on an agenda to make them a reality in long-suffering Latin America.

1.3 The Summit is taking place just a few years after Latin America began its "lost decade" caused by the foreign debt crisis. Between 1980 and 1990, the region's economic growth was only 0.9 percent, meaning a 1.2 percent drop in the per capita GDP. The debt crisis shook the entire region, affecting Mexico, Central America, and the Southern Cone at different times and with differing intensities. The decline in economic activity caused a notable increase in unemployment, a drop in real salaries, and many bankruptcies.

1.4 The economic turmoil at the beginning of the 1980s made many people think the Great Depression would make a comeback, that financial convulsions would lead the way to more political authoritarianism and stronger state intervention in economy. The end results were exactly the opposite. For a time it seemed the debt crisis and the crumbling capital markets would block the possibility of private initiative-based development and that ensuing social costs would indefinitely postpone democracy's arrival on the continent. These fears seemed especially valid in Argentina, Chile, and Uruguay, where the crisis hit after determined attempts at free market economies.

1.5 But history often takes strange courses. The "lost decade" was really a lesson: Latin America realized that the root of the problem lay in previous decades of bloated government; in the belief that legitimate expectations of well-being could be met by state intervention in the markets; in the consequent disdain for private initiative; in the frequent scorn for the basic macroeconomic balance, resulting from the demagogic desire to meet "social needs" with the fiscal budget without thinking about its costs. The crisis affected the conscience of political and business leaders and intellectuals and enabled the start of a profound cultural change. It clearly showed that progress is impossible without individual effort and that the government must establish conditions that make business efforts possible and worthwhile. This bitter lesson of crisis led to stability and structural reforms, which began in country after country throughout the 1980s and the early 1990s. These reforms have planted the seeds of progress and will prove that, in the long run, the decade of the 1980s, far from being lost, was enormously fruitful.

1.6 This planting has been arduous. Stability efforts are always arduous because they mean admitting the country has been living beyond its means, resulting in painful cuts in the fiscal budget, real salaries, and consumer habits. Efforts to change structures are difficult because they mean opening up economies, privatizing public companies and submitting markets to the rigors of competition. Powerful

bureaucratic, business, and union oligarchies are weakened in the process. This makes reform vulnerable. The process has advanced considerably, in various Latin American countries, but it hasn't been consolidated in any of them. The groups weakened by reforms have resisted during critical moments or have withdrawn to wait for more opportune moments. But they are there, ready to win back their previous prerogatives when the "social cost," erroneously attributed to the reforms, becomes politically intolerable.

1.7 The progress of these reforms has been greeted with understandable optimism in the Americas and in the world. If the reforms stay on course, in ten more years Latin America may be the next Southeast Asia. But the enthusiastic applause generally ignores the fact that it will be a while before the reforms bear fruit. Latin America continues to be burdened by the heavy crisis it inherited. Only in Chile and Colombia have the per capita income levels increased significantly over those of 1980. In spite of noticeable growth in recent years, Mexico and particularly Argentina and Brazil have income levels similar to or slightly lower than those of 1980.

The remaining economies, including Peru (in spite of its spectacular recovery in 1993-1994) and Venezuela, today have income levels considerably below those prior to the "lost decade." The same holds true for real salaries and purchasing power. The lack of sustained growth — not taking into account the cyclical recoveries already noted — explains why poverty has worsened. The events in Chiapas, Mexico, at the beginning of 1994 have placed Latin American poverty in all its dramatic dimensions at the center of the debate.

1.8 Unfortunately, it is common to associate current levels of poverty with stability and free market reforms. It is considered to be their "social cost." However, the truth shows it to be otherwise. Current poverty is the most visible and unfair manifestation of the social cost resulting from previous excesses — from the macroeconomic disorder and government-run systems that submerged the region in stagnation, inflation, and the debt crisis. The reforms are attempting to restart sustained growth, creating jobs and overcoming poverty. But in vast areas of the region, this growth has not yet arrived, or if it has arrived, it has not lasted long enough to reduce poverty. The Chiapas of the past and of the future show that the economic issue has yet to be solved, that we do not yet have growth, and that efforts must be increased.

1.9 Latin America has not yet been able to harvest the results of a prolonged period of strong growth, as it would expect to after undergoing reforms. Only Chile has shown such results: a real annual average growth of 7% during the past eight years. The benefits of this strong growth are noticeable in that country. Only strong and sustained growth is capable of fundamentally altering the economic, political, and social landscape of our countries. The "takeoff" by Japan, the southern European countries, and more recently Southeast Asia has proven this.

1.10 In effect, growth unleashes all sorts of virtuous cycles. When production capacity increases, a greater proportion of the population's legitimate consumer demands can be met without the threat of fanning the fires of inflation. The root of inflation lies in the imbalance between expectations and reality. Expectations become more desperate when growth is at a minimum and prospects are meager. Growth directly increases the income of the poor by improving the number and quality of jobs. While some people still see a conflict between accelerated growth and redistribution, the truth is that this does not exist. Only vigorous growth can give the government, which would otherwise have to raise taxes to an impossible level, the resources to complement poor people's income and support the acquisition of labor resources. Growth contributes to social peace by creating jobs, reducing poverty, and opening up the horizons to progress and by teaching the value of stability, which enables one's expectations to be met over time. An appreciation for stability makes democracy work better. Economic progress eliminates or undermines the more extreme political options, reduces political polarization, and makes election results less dramatic. The failure of many Latin American democracies has been associated with the perception that "everything was at stake" in each election. With stability and progress, there are more chances for consensus and justice. Contrary to what is often said, growth also favors environmental protection. Impoverished societies consider it a luxury to maintain the environment and don't hesitate to ruin it, if in the process they can satisfy their basic needs. An environmental conscience and the possibility of taking even minimum measures to protect the environment are directly related to the population's economic capabili-

ties, that is to say, their having had a sufficiently long period of strong economic growth.

2. Reform Program

2.1 Latin America has still not taken off economically. There are isolated cases of growth during a brief period or a mere cyclical recovery, but the region hasn't been able to come back totally from the "lost decade," much less position itself for a strong and sustained growth process. It urgently needs to do so, as poverty has reached desperate levels and the demands to see the fruits of the reforms are becoming increasingly stronger.

2.2 The lack of growth in Latin America is also due to the fact that reforms are far from over. In this respect, it is worth noting the stages of the reform process:

- In the first stage the emphasis is on stability: controlling inflation by means of appropriate changes to fiscal, monetary, and exchange policies. Efforts are made to reestablish access to foreign credit by balancing foreign accounts and restructuring or reducing foreign debts.

- The second stage includes structural reforms: opening up trade and finance; freeing prices, capital goods, and productivity factors; reducing government and public services.

- The third stage is one of sustained growth which demands a noticeable increase in investment, savings (both private and public), and careful management of macroeconomic policy to maintain positive growth conditions.

2.3 The different Latin American economies show varying degrees of progress on reforms. Some, like Brazil, Ecuador, Uruguay, and Venezuela, are still in the first stage. Their most immediate need is to obtain or consolidate a certain macroeconomic stability that will permit later growth. Some of these economies are advancing in the second stage, involving structural reforms. Argentina, Bolivia, Chile, Colombia, Mexico, Peru, and a good number of the Central American economies no longer experience big swings on a macroeconomic level. And some have made important progress in controlling inflation. Especially notable is the progress made on this front by Argentina, Bolivia, and Mexico, all of which had suffered previously from soaring inflation but today boast single digit rates. Chile, Colombia, and Peru are slowly advancing in the same direction. All these countries have simultaneously made great progress in the second stage, creating vigorous market economies. Chile was the region's pioneer in opening up and freeing its economy, as well as in privatization, but recently it has been surpassed in several areas by Argentina, Bolivia, Mexico, and Peru. However, Chile alone appears firmly rooted in the third stage of sustained growth. With estimated fixed investment rates and national savings at 27% and 25% of the GDP, respectively, in 1994, it is the only country in the region that seems to be enjoying a true economic takeoff. Argentina, Colombia, Mexico, and Peru appear to be the leading candidates to follow in Chile's footsteps.

2.4 Reform progress is complex, as it doesn't follow a strict sequence. It is clear that some degree of stability must precede the majority of structural reforms, that some should be made before others, and that only afterwards should savings and investment be expected to increase noticeably. But on the whole, progress on these three fronts should be simultaneous. Stability makes it easier to open up the economy, but an open economy also aids stability. Fiscal adjustments keep liberal financial policies from raising the cost of credit excessively, while at the same time, the expansion of capital markets allows the Treasury to finance itself without resorting to "inflation taxes." Opening economies without reducing taxes and deregulating and privatizing industry keeps exports from developing. Without labor flexibility, currencies may become overvalued, eventually causing a crisis in the balance of payment. Many of today's problems — unemployment, social impatience with the lack of progress, lagging exchange rates, and high interest rates — are a result of prior conditions but are also due to the difficulties in coordinating and synchronizing different reforms.

3. Important Objectives

3.1 Accelerating growth requires that reforms be accentuated and carried out in depth. In our opinion, the task ahead is still arduous, and as the crisis wanes, it is likely that the desire to carry out reforms will decline. Therefore, it is crucial to have a continental commitment and international cooperation for the agenda we propose. The agenda includes the following principal objectives: increasingly opening the economy through economic integration, continuing privatization, increasing competitiveness, achieving greater indices of human development, and overcoming new dangers arising from protectionism, desires for redistribution of wealth, and radical ecology.

a) Economic Integration

3.2 The opening of the economies' trade, finances, telecommunications, and technology is the key to Latin American growth. It is obvious that Latin America — whose GDP is only 9% of world GDP and whose exports are only 3% of total world exports — can only achieve sustained growth if it turns toward the large and vital North American, European, and Asian markets. World experience of "outward" growth strategies is so overwhelmingly superior to our traditional "inward" growth that it can't be debated. For this reason opening up the economy even further is essential.

3.3 Opening up the economy means more than simply eliminating non-tariff barriers to foreign trade or reducing the number and scope of customs duties. On both fronts, all the countries in the region have made notable progress, particularly Bolivia, Chile, and Peru, although they are not the only ones. Opening up the economy requires real international integration, including free trade as a medium-range objective. It also requires the elimination of subsidies for exports and tax benefits for domestic production, the unification of health and sanitation standards, the elimination of barriers on services, and an end to exchange controls and tax restrictions of any kind on transferring capital. It also means equal treatment for national and foreign investors, canceling double tax agreements, and reasonable immigration procedures. Opening up the economy also means fostering physical integration by eliminating excessive border controls, enabling joint use of road and port infrastructures, and encouraging connections between energy and information systems.

This subject may still awaken fears in groups or sectors who feel their survival is being threatened. The speed and way this process is carried out depends, of course, on each country. But the general direction should be clear. Hopefully, efforts will not be concentrated on finding permanent exceptions but rather on rapidly achieving various complimentary reforms. For example, in a more open economy, it is easier to have broad capital markets that offer better rates and terms, flexible labor markets and training programs for workers who have lost their jobs, with lower taxes and more efficient governments.

3.4 Every country in the region, in keeping with its particular characteristics, history, and current circumstances, has chosen its own path to opening the economy. Some have chosen a unilateral path, confident that the strength of their deeds and international pressure via the GATT will eventually tear down other countries' protective barriers. Others have opted for sub-regional trade agreements, some on a Latin American level (Mercosur, Andean Pact, Central American Common Market, and other specific pacts). Others chose free trade agreements with the United States and Canada, the most important being NAFTA. All these paths lead to free trade and should be considered initial steps toward a Pan American Free Trade Agreement (PAFTA).

3.5 Free trade treaties are positive because i) they strengthen and consolidate free market reforms without which the competitive ability of an integrated market would be severely hampered; ii) they are an efficient way to stimulate an intra-regional opening, combating protectionist pressures, and if like NAFTA they do not impede integration with the rest of the world, they will encourage worldwide free trade; and iii) make foreign investment easier because they reduce the perception of risk associated with investing in countries that may eventually change their minds about maintaining a market economy.

3.6 Free trade agreements do have risks. First of all, they may offer an excuse to close the borders to countries that are not members of the region. This could be a serious negative affect. To help Latin America, the leaders at the Summit should reiterate their support of the latest GATT agreements. Secondly, it is possible that exception clauses, schedules for partial tax reductions, complex rules of origin, complaints of unfair competition, and imposition of labor statutes could adversely affect the nature of these agreements. This could result in bureaucratic and protectionist free trade structures. Finally, there is the danger that treaty negotiations — especially entry into NAFTA — take too long, paralyzing the economic opening of the affected countries, as they wait to include these measures in the corresponding negotiations.

3.7 In spite of the above remarks, we feel that free trade agreements are the best possible way to further open the economy. Latin America's most important challenge is to establish compatibility in its efforts toward regional economic integration, including NAFTA, Mercosur, and Caricom, among others. These should slowly fuse to form the great Pan American agreement (PAFTA).

b) Continuing Privatization

3.8 Privatization in our economies is crucial because i) it assures that companies have the necessary incentives, management, and resources to take advantage of the new opportunities and increased efficiency that open markets make possible; ii) it gives private initiative the opportunity to participate in investment projects in mining, energy, telecommunications, infrastructure, and transportation, areas that are generally highly productive and prone to "bottlenecks" and which cannot be efficiently developed by the public sector due to the lack of adequate resources or incentives; iii) it allows the government to sell off unprofitable companies and money-making ones in order to concentrate its resources on developing human resources and fighting poverty, areas in which its efforts are essential; iv) it prompts greater property distribution with the accompanying economic, political, and commercial benefits. This is especially valid if the procedures lead to the creation of "new capitalists," as exemplified by either the Chilean case involving "popular capitalism" programs and the participation of privatized pension funds or the Bolivian plans regarding the "capitalization program for state companies;" and v) it is the most powerful weapon against the corruption often found in state-run companies and government contracts, which is a serious danger to young Latin American democracies.

3.9 Recently some Latin American countries have made significant progress in selling off public companies to the private sector: Argentina, especially, and to a lesser degree, Brazil, Chile, Mexico, and Peru. But real privatization of the economies goes even further. It also includes:

- Strengthening the legal system; property rights; protection against arbitrary state intervention and unfulfilled contracts. Latin America needs an in-depth modernization of its judicial system, a task still pending.

- Transferring to the private sector the responsibility for managing social services like social security, housing, education, and health.

All can be decentralized and privatized, with the government maintaining a regulatory and taxation function, together with additional support for the lowest income sectors so they can have access to such services.

- Reducing taxes and public spending in proportion to the size of the economy. Understandably, pressing fiscal needs have led many countries to increase taxes recently. Frequently this has meant placing a heavy tax burden on the (small) segment of economic activity that does not evade taxes, placing those companies at a disadvantage and causing large segments of the economy to work off the books. As the economy grows and public spending is controlled, it is possible to cut tax rates and even out tax pressures. Within the integrated economy we foresee, only those with low taxes and fair fiscal responsibilities will prosper.

- Suppression of regulations (laws, rules, norms) that unnecessarily hinder private initiative. Certain minimal regulations are necessary to protect property, maintain competition, rectify external situations, and control natural monopolies. But note should be taken of the dangerous practices of certain countries which substitute direct state intervention in business for indirect intervention through excessive regulation.

3.10 Privatization is a task for each individual government. The leaders attending the Summit should express their support for this process, pledging their technical assistance, either directly or through international entities, and encouraging the participation of their nation's businessmen in privatizations in other countries. This will facilitate American integration via the private sector.

c) Improving Competitiveness

3.11 Once the economic frontiers are open, competition promises to be fierce. Nothing sparks economic growth more than free competition. But this can hurt countries not prepared for it. The success of business and financial integration demands taking a long look at the obstacles which stand in the way of improving competitiveness and productivity in each country. Recent reforms in various Latin American countries have made considerable progress in this matter, but stumbling blocks still exist:

- protectionism in industrialized economies and also remnants of Latin American protectionism.

- high and uneven taxes, excessive regulation of key activities.

- insufficient fiscal belt-tightening and inadequate saving habits, which cause interest rates to rise while lowering the real rate of exchange; various Latin American economies are in danger of suffering from lagging exchange rates, which is not solved, as often thought, by a simple currency devaluation but rather an increase in public and private savings.

- high labor costs due to taxes, social security contributions, and demands by powerful union oligarchies. Labor reforms are seriously needed in Latin America. Their effect is obviously reflected in high unemployment rates and difficulties in triggering growth in Argentina, Brazil, and Mexico.

- lack of adequate highway and port infrastructure. Growth and business integration will demand improved infrastructure. If proper regulations are established, the private sector can take responsibility for investment and operation of these installations. However, governments remain ultimately responsible on a national level and should work jointly on transnational projects.

- increasing demands for environmental protection, which can become a source of regulations and impediments to increasing competitiveness.

3.12 Once again, the path chosen to encourage competitiveness is up to each individual country. The leaders attending this Summit should, nevertheless, pledge to fight protectionism, to give up the export subsidy race or competitive devaluations to stimulate market deregulations, especially labor, resisting new types of protectionism that attempt to put international codes on labor legislation, and to keep legitimate concern for the environment from turning into a source of inefficient regulations leading to loss of competitiveness.

d) Human Development

3.13 Latin America still has low human development indices. It is estimated that about 18% of the people live in poverty. Although this number can be used for political purposes, and is therefore difficult to reach agreement on, the fact is that the level of unfulfilled needs is enormous. Income distribution is notoriously unequal. The degree of infant mortality, poor nutrition, life expectancy, illiteracy, and education are quite unacceptable. In terms of infant mortality, only Uruguay, Chile, Costa Rica, and Cuba have acceptable rates. This task is overwhelming, especially because it is such a sensitive matter and lends itself so easily to demagoguery, that it should only be dealt with by professionals on a technical basis.

3.14 As mentioned above, the main danger is in interpreting the poverty figures as being caused by the reforms. The reforms are still too new to be held responsible for these problems. The figures reflect the dramatic inheritance from decades of slow or non-existent growth and disjointed social policies. The solution can be found in strengthening growth and improving social programs.

3.15 Under present circumstances, it is especially dangerous to talk about poverty in the context of the free trade agreements. It is a mistake to think that income distribution can be made fairer by labor legislation allowing workers to have part of the income that goes today to capital investment. This position is incorrect and a sure recipe for economic stagnation, unemployment, and poverty. It completely overlooks the fact that in many of the poorest countries, labor norms are extremely rigid and strict. But the idea enjoys political support because it appears simple and does not require governments to increase real wealth but rather simply to pass laws. Today it has supporters in North America: protectionist lobbies that charge that imported goods made by cheap labor are in effect "labor dumping." Their intention to subject free trade treaties to this concept could be fatal.

3.16 Eliminating poverty requires decentralizing and privatizing social security, government housing, education, and health. The government should limit itself to regulating and subsidizing the demand for these services for the poor sectors of society. The social security model used by Argentina, Chile, Colombia, and Peru is an example of this. The principles it is based on can easily be extended to other social areas. Basically, it singles out society's least favored sectors and directs defined programs to help them. These programs do not interfere with the markets or progress but rather are based upon them. They efficiently help increase labor resources and overcome serious problems. In practice, it has been shown that creating jobs plays an important role in these matters.

3.17 Every country should chose its own path according to its particular situation, but human development is a fertile area for international cooperation. Governmental agencies with international assistance and multilateral organizations, such as the World Bank and the Inter-American Development Bank, should be the first to be involved.

e) New Dangers

3.18 New issues and dangers arise from the flow of events and politics. Or rather, old problems take on new forms and can become powerful obstacles to growth.

3.19 The principal source of new dangers is veiled protectionism, disguised as labor rights or ecological protection. The danger is serious because it attacks the heart of our strategy: our ability to compete advantageously in an integrated world.

3.20 Labor protectionism maintains that anything produced at low labor costs is unfair competition because workers rights are supposedly abused. If such abuse exists, it should be brought to the attention of the respective national and international bodies that deal with this problem. But to suppose that free trade should be based on equal costs is to ignore the principle of comparative advantages. It is perfectly natural that labor costs are lower in poorer countries, just as their cost of capital is higher than in richer countries. As mentioned, job creation is one of the most effective mechanisms there is to fight poverty and labor protectionism is one of its principal enemies.

3.21 The situation is similar to "ecological dumping," or the principle of competitive products manufactured under lax environmental standards and exported to industrialized economies. Environmental standards are not similar in all countries, as each individual country must make its own decisions involving the proper balance between economic growth and the conservation of its own environment. The argument of ecological dumping only makes sense in those limited cases where the damage to the environment affects various countries or mankind, but in such a case it is mankind that should bear the corresponding blame. Unfortunately, in most cases it is just another attractive cover-up for protectionism.

3.22 Ecological concern is important. As we pointed out, in our countries, poverty, not growth, is the main enemy of the environment. However, it is a good idea to take advantage of the growing national and international awareness to concentrate on a limited number of priority environmental problems: water pollution; excessive exploitation of certain natural resources (whose ownership is not clearly defined); and disposal of industrial wastes, to name just a few. Analysis and cooperation, including financial assistance, to solve these problems would be valuable and very effective. Once again, specialized organizations should play an important role in this process.

4. Conclusions

4.1 Sustained growth is the determining and key element necessary to resolve the endemic problems of poverty in the region. Development is the best passport for personal advancement: jobs that allow men to progress thanks to their own efforts and not to the patronage of third parties.

4.2 As we already stated, Latin America urgently needs to take off. In the last few years, different Latin American economies have begun, one by one, to launch daring stability and restructuring programs. Several have been successful in halting inflation and reducing it to manageable levels, and several have made considerable progress in building open, competitive market economies. Some have begun to enjoy the fruits of these efforts. But for the majority of the countries and the majority of their people, growth in income levels is still insufficient or non-existent. During years of stagnation unfulfilled needs grew to dangerous levels. Therefore, efforts must be renewed to restructure the economies, open them further through hemispheric economic integration, intensify privatization, increase competitiveness, encourage the development of labor resources and face the new threats of labor and ecological protectionism.

4.3 We also know that sustained growth is indispensable if we want to consolidate the democratic process, halt corruption and begin protecting our environment.

4.4 The path the region has started down in recent years shows us that Latin America can develop. We have the necessary ability and energy. To achieve our goal, we only need to free our people's potential. They must be freed from the oppression of innumerable regulations and interventions that have restrained and continue to restrain the entrepreneurial spirit of our businessmen and our huge conglomerates. These are the impediments that keep them from realizing their full potential for growth.

4.5 We are living in crucial times. Until now, it was the pressures of crisis that inspired our societies to begin dismantling the bonds that had kept us from progressing. But the task is far from over. Now that the most critical moments are over, it is more difficult to continue advancing. Different interests and political pressures that created the restrictions in the first place, which explain our poverty, are returning to the scene. Only true statesmen can make the right decision to continue advancing.

4.6 We should not let a day go by without taking a step forward to make possible new endeavors or companies. We must be brave and break vicious prejudices. It has been proven over and over again that many rules which supposedly protect workers in reality only cause unemployment and stagnation. Nonetheless, a great deal of the region has yet to enact labor reform legislation. It is true that governments need a great deal of resources, but it is also true that they spend an enormous amount in useless tasks, unproductive bureaucracy, or sectors that are not the neediest. Many of the countries have made progress, but much remains to be done. The task will be complete only when it is possible to lighten the burdens paid by producers, whether small or large, so they can grow more every day. Giant steps forward have been taken with privatization, but there are still some areas where courage is needed to advance. Unfortunately, these areas are very important for development and progress. The courage with which some of the former Soviet Union or East European countries are progressing should serve as an example to us. The task can be completed only if we have the means to overcome poverty and create jobs that give our people dignity.

4.7 Historic responsibility rests on all of us, the private sector, governments, and international organizations for cooperation. We pledge to continue our efforts until the goal has been reached.

4.8 Private initiative has the starring role in this new model of Latin American development. Governments must support businessmen in their endeavors and trust in them. Businessmen are the ones who must believe in the possibilities this new model offers and place their bets on a Latin American takeoff. They are the ones who should create new initiatives, update their companies, invest in productive capital, infrastructure, and labor resources, encourage savings that will finance these investments, gain new markets in the region and abroad, increase employment and salaries, and pay taxes to finance governments. Business organizations should lobby for good economic policies and support free market reforms that are in the best interests of the companies and the country. This is essential because building a market economy is difficult and tends to provoke constant opposition from groups whose interests are affected. Businessmen need to undergo a cultural change: give up the traditional hunt for special favors and state protection, substituting it for efficiency and intelligent use of growth opportunities associated with a vigorous market economy. This action by the private sector should be supported and not be limited to the country but planned and coordinated on an international level. Internationalizing the continent's economies also offers a continental outlook on the problems, threats, and opportunities affecting them.

4.9 Governments should take the lead in modernization and growth by carrying out the agenda described above. This won't be easy. Reforms are still at the half-way point; much remains to be done and many difficulties must be faced. More than ever, the solution is to persevere down the road to reform. This requires a long-term outlook, overcoming short-term difficulties, placing general interests ahead of private ones, staying the course in spite of inherent political problems and remaining vigilant for opportunities to progress even though they may come in small steps.

4.10 The role of international cooperation is to support reforms that countries begin individually, creating an international framework for them to last and be successful. International cooperation should assist the countries in achieving economic integration. This means:

- backing GATT agreements that tend toward opening agriculture, services, and certain manufacturing sectors.

- fighting industrialized economies' protectionism, especially that of the United States, the EC, and Japan.

- setting up joint mechanisms to fight corruption in business transactions, both on national and international levels.

- facilitating the movement of capital, with equal treatment for international investment and credit funds.

- progress in hemispheric integration by expanding NAFTA.

- promoting physical integration as well as the integration of energy and information systems among the countries.

- facilitating mobility across borders.

- promoting the development of infrastructure with private sector participation and joint efforts by countries in the region.

- encouraging the protection of property rights in areas of common interest, for example, in oil exploration or air and water pollution.

- promoting labor reform that protects workers' basic rights, changes the region's economies, increases competitiveness, and assures more and better jobs. This is important in view of the recent resurgence of anti-market unionism encouraged by protectionism forces in the North.

- promoting highly trained government professionals so they can continue carrying out reforms.

- encouraging modernization and consolidation of democratic political institutions through decentralization and freedom of the press.

- promoting responsible ecology that recognizes the need to combine environmental protection with economic growth and the elimination of poverty. It should not be enacted by protectionist forces from developed countries.

- supporting understanding and peace among countries so as to gradually reduce multilateral armament spending; redirecting the Armed Forces toward pacific tasks, such as the colonization of uninhabited regions and fighting drug trafficking.

- redefining the goals of multilateral credit organizations, having the Inter-American Development Bank and the World Bank concentrate on programs to develop labor resources and overcoming poverty, and allowing them to finance the private sector. The International Monetary Fund should strengthen its stabilizing role, avoiding macroeconomic disturbances caused by industrialized economies that prolong greater macroeconomic difficulties in emerging economies.

4.11 The Summit of the Americas is an historic opportunity for American leaders to accept the agenda proposed in this document, pledging to apply it both nationally and internationally. The government of the United States has a fundamental role to play here. The government of the United States should make a public and unfailing commitment to do its best to obtain Congressional approval for the Uruguay Round of the GATT and employ the fast track method to expand NAFTA according to objective criteria.

It should be a real model of free trade and a champion of free trade in the world. It should aid the integration of the Americas in other areas mentioned in this document including energy, information, infrastructure, finance, and population. It should strengthen international organizations that give financial assistance. This will support the reform process and neutralize possible macroeconomic destabilizing pressures. The government of the United States should, above all, follow a stable and predictable course in its international policies concerning Latin America, as well as in its economic policies, which have always had deep repercussions on the entire continent and could affect the possibility of achieving several decades of sustained economic growth.

The Summit of the Americas is an historic opportunity not only to ratify the desire to achieve a better standard of living but also to work together to achieve this goal.

Statistical Appendix

LATIN AMERICA								
Country	**GDP Distribution (percent)**	**Evolution of GDP (Average Annual Rates) (percent)**				**Inflation (Avg. Annual Rates) (percent)**		
	1993	1970-80	1980-90	1991-92	1993	1985-90	1991-92	1993
Argentina	20.00	2.80	-0.90	8.80	6.00	564.20	47.00	7.40
Brazil	35.20	8.60	1.50	0.10	5.00	566.40	747.60	2489.00
Chile	3.50	2.10	2.90	8.60	6.30	21.00	15.70	12.20
Colombia	4.20	5.40	3.70	2.80	5.20	25.60	25.90	22.60
Ecuador	1.20	8.90	2.10	4.20	1.70	44.20	54.50	32.20
Mexico	27.90	6.70	0.50	3.20	0.40	65.60	15.30	8.00
Peru	3.20	3.90	-1.20	-0.10	7.00	746.20	93.60	39.50
Venezuela	4.80	1.80	0.40	8.20	-1.00	33.60	31.40	45.90
Total	**100**	**5.60**	**0.90**	**3.40**	**3.30**	**451.90**	**292.80**	**796.50**

LATIN AMERICA							
Country	**Exported Goods (FOB) (Annual Average in Billions of US Dollars)**			**Total Foreign Debt Exported Goods/Services (Annual Average Percentages)**			
	1985-89	1991-92	1993	1979-81	1982-86	1987-89	1990-93
Argentina	8.10	12.20	13.10	274	508	593	434
Brazil	28.50	33.00	38.60	330	406	351	337
Chile	5.70	9.10	9.20	227	399	227	153
Colombia	5.20	7.30	7.40	146	264	247	187
Ecuador	2.30	2.90	2.90	158	263	405	355
Mexico	30.30	42.80	51.10	267	360	336	279
Peru	2.70	3.30	3.50	234	343	433	496
Venezuela	11.30	15.50	14.00	153	226	285	214
Total	**94.10**	**123.30**	**132.90**	**236**	**354**	**350**	**296**

Period	LATIN AMERICA		
	Net Capital Revenue (Annual Average in Billions of US Dollars)	Net Capital Revenue Exported Goods/Services (Annual Average Percentages)	Net Transfer of Resources Exported Goods/Services (Annual Average Percentages)
1975-79	2100	36.50	21.00
1980-81	35.90	32.90	11.20
1982	20.10	19.50	-18.20
1983	2.90	2.80	-30.90
1984	10.40	9.20	-23.60
1985-89	8.60	7.50	-22.30
1990	20.70	13.70	-9.40
1991	39.30	26.00	5.50
1992	62.00	38.50	20.30
1993	54.60	32.30	15.20

Country	LATIN AMERICA									
	Real GDP Per Capita (12 Month Percentage Variation)									
	1985	1986	1987	1988	1989	1990	1991	1992	1993	1994*
Argentina	-6.4	3.8	1.3	-3.3	-7.4	.1.1	7.6	7.4	4.7	3.3
Bolivia	-3.4	-4.9	0.1	0.5	0.7	0.2	2.1	1.4	1.6	1.6
Brazil	5.7	5.5	1.6	-2.0	1.4	-6.1	-0.6	-2.5	3.3	1.6
Chile	0.7	3.8	4.8	5.5	8.1	1.6	5.5	9.1	4.5	2.3
Colombia	1.7	4.9	3.7	2.3	1.7	2.6	0.4	1.8	3.4	3.0
Ecuador	1.2	0.2	-7.0	6.2	-1.9	0.7	2.6	1.2	-0.5	0.2
Mexico	0.2	-5.9	-0.4	-1.0	1.1	2.3	1.4	0.6	-1.8	0.0
Peru	0.0	6.4	5.8	-10.3	-13.3	-6.3	0.7	-4.7	4.9	5.9
Venezuela	-2.5	4.0	1.3	3.4	-9.9	3.0	7.3	4.5	-3.1	-5.6

*Estimated

LATIN AMERICA										
Country	Inflation (12 Month Percentage Variation)									
	1985	1986	1987	1988	1989	1990	1991	1992	1993	1994*
Argentina	385	82	175	388	4924	1344	84	18	7	4
Bolivia	8171	66	11	22	17	18	15	10	9	7
Brazil	228	68	395	993	1864	1585	475	1149	2489	950
Chile	26	17	22	13	21	27	19	13	12	10
Colombia	22	21	24	28	26	32	27	25	23	23
Ecuador	24	27	33	86	54	50	49	60	31	23
Mexico	64	106	159	52	20	30	19	12	8	7
Peru	158	63	115	1722	2775	7650	139	57	40	18
Venezuela	7	13	40	36	81	37	31	32	46	75

*Estimated

ARGENTINA						
	1985-89	1990	1991	1992	1993	1994*
GDP	-0.8	0.1	8.9	8.7	6.0	4.5
Inflation	468.6	1343.9	84.0	17.5	7.4	3.4
Exports (in billions of US$)	8.1	12.4	12.0	12.2	13.1	15.0
Currency in Circulation (percent GDP)	-2.1	1.3	-1.5	-2.9	-2.9	-3.4

*Through August

BOLIVIA						
	1985-89	1990	1991	1992	1993	1994*
GDP	1.0	2.6	4.6	3.8	4.0	4.0
Inflation	273.0	18.0	14.6	10.4	9.3	7.0
Exports (in billions of US$)	0.6	0.8	0.8	0.6	0.6	0.7
Currency in Circulation (percent GDP)	-7.2	-4.8	-4.3	-8.2	-6.4	-6.2

*Through August

BRAZIL						
	1985-89	1990	1991	1992	1993	1994*
GDP	4.4	-4.4	1.1	-0.9	5.0	3.2
Inflation	453.5	1585.0	475.0	1149.0	2489.0	2362.0
Exports (in billions of US$)	28.5	31.4	31.6	35.9	38.6	41.0
Currency in Circulation (percent GDP)	-0.1	-0.8	-0.4	1.5	-0.2	-0.4

*Through September

CHILE						
	1985-89	1990	1991	1992	1993	1994*
GDP	6.3	3.3	7.3	11.0	6.3	4.0
Inflation	19.8	27.3	18.7	12.7	12.2	8.3
Exports (in billions of US$)	5.7	8.3	8.9	10.0	9.2	10.8
Currency in Circulation (percent GDP)	-4.5	-2.0	0.0	-1.7	-4.6	-1.5

*Through October

COLOMBIA						
	1985-89	1990	1991	1992	1993	1994*
GDP	4.7	4.3	2.1	3.5	5.2	4.8
Inflation	24.3	32.4	26.8	25.1	22.6	21.9
Exports (in billions of US$)	5.2	7.1	7.5	7.3	7.4	8.0
Currency in Circulation (percent GDP)	-1.1	1.4	5.4	1.9	-4.2	-4.6

*Through September

MEXICO						
	1985-89	1990	1991	1992	1993	1994*
GDP	1.0	4.5	3.6	2.8	0.4	2.2
Inflation	73.8	29.9	18.8	11.9	8.0	6.7
Exports (in billions of US$)	30.3	39.5	42.7	46.2	51.1	58.0
Currency in Circulation (percent GDP)	-0.6	-2.9	-4.8	-7.5	-6.5	-7.0

*Through September

PERU						
	1985-89	1990	1991	1992	1993	1994*
GDP	-0.4	-4.4	2.7	-2.8	7.0	8.0
Inflation	445.9	7649.6	139.2	56.7	39.5	18.0
Exports (in billions of US$)	2.7	3.2	3.3	3.5	3.5	3.7
Currency in Circulation (percent GDP)	-4.7	-3.7	-3.6	-4.6	-4.6	-5.8

*Through October

VENEZUELA						
	1985-89	1990	1991	1992	1993	1994*
GDP	1.6	5.3	9.7	6.8	-1.0	-3.5
Inflation	32.5	36.5	31.0	31.9	45.9	69.9
Exports (in billions of US$)	11.3	17.4	15.0	14.0	14.0	15.2
Currency in Circulation (percent GDP)	-1.1	17.2	3.3	-6.1	-3.6	4.6

*Through September

The Institute for International Economics is a private nonprofit research institution for the study and discussion of international economic policy. The Institute, directed by C. Fred Bergsten, provides analyses of key economic, monetary, trade, and investment issues and recommends practical approaches for strengthening public policy toward these topics. The Institute receives funding from a large number of private foundations and corporations. The Tinker Foundation, Inc., the Andrew Mellon Foundation, and the Inter-American Development Bank provided support for the research underlying this project, and the IDB sponsored seminars for the discussion of its preliminary results.

Western Hemisphere Free Trade Area Should Be Goal of Upcoming Inter-American Summit

INSTITUTE FOR INTERNATIONAL ECONOMICS

News Release
Embargo: July 6, 1994, 10:00 a.m., E.D.T.
News Conference: 10:00 a.m., 11 Dupont Circle, eighth floor

Washington, July 6, 1994 — Leaders of the Western Hemisphere nations should make a commitment at the Summit of the Americas, to be hosted by President Clinton in Miami on December 10, to achieve a Western Hemisphere Free Trade Area (WHFTA). They should do so by expanding the North American Free Trade Agreement (NAFTA) throughout the region. According to a new study from the Institute for International Economics, both the United States and the Latin American countries would benefit substantially from such an agreement.

In *Western Hemisphere Economic Integration*, Gary Clyde Hufbauer and Jeffrey J. Schott develop innovative "readiness criteria" to gauge the preparedness of each hemispheric country to undertake and sustain the free trade and investment obligations spelled out in the NAFTA. Their criteria assess both economic performance and democratic reforms over the past few years. Countries with higher scores are likely to be better prepared to meet the adjustment demands of integrating with the North American industrial powers, the United States, and Canada.

Comprehensive policy reforms in Latin America have moved several countries up the list that could soon be "ready" to enter into free trade talks. However, as summarized in Table 3, only a few countries now seem well-prepared:

— Chile tops the list of larger countries with a score of 4.4, out of a possible 5.0 (compared with 3.9 for Mexico just before it joined NAFTA);

— Trinidad and Tobago also scores 4.4;

— Barbados scores 4.1;

— Venezuela is next among the larger countries at 3.9, but recent events call into question the future pace of its market reforms;

— Colombia and Bolivia rate scores of 3.7;

— the region's largest country, Brazil, scores a dismal 2.3 and is clearly not ready at this time;

— Argentina rates only 2.6, but has made tremendous progress in arresting inflation, and its low scores on price stability and external debt will jump sharply if the reforms are maintained.

The authors strongly recommend that *the United States conduct enlargement talks through NAFTA rather than on a stand-alone basis with individual countries*. Politically, stand-alone talks would divide the hemisphere because existing NAFTA members would feel they were being played off against potential new U.S. partners. Economically, individual countries would be shortchanged in their trading relations with one another if the United States enters into separate arrangements with each. In addition, disparate rules on everything from investment barriers to product standards would create enormous confusion. For these reasons, U.S. talks with Chile and with the Caribbean Basin Initiative countries should be conducted within the NAFTA framework rather than through bilateral negotiations (or, for example, through a CBI parity bill that does not point to NAFTA accession).

Integration should proceed on a country-by-country basis, or through the accession to NAFTA of subregional groupings, *on a comprehensive basis. All* issues — manufactured goods, agriculture, textiles and apparel, services, investment, intellectual property rights, customs rules, and dispute settlement — should be addressed together. An "all-or-nothing" approach between North America and Latin America is now feasible because differences on labor, environmental, and human rights questions have become bridgeable with greater Latin American acceptance of internationally agreed social norms. In economic terms, such an all-or-nothing approach has two strong advantages over a sectoral approach:

— It creates the greatest scope for cross-sector concessions and thereby promotes a more rapid pace of liberalization.

— It creates the greatest amount of trade among the member countries relative to the trade diverted from outside suppliers.

Impact on the United States

The authors project that a WHFTA would substantially expand U.S. two-way trade with Latin America. U.S. exports to Latin America would be about $36 billion higher in the year 2002, a gain of 51 percent. U.S. imports would be about $28 billion higher in the same year, a gain of 43 percent. The U.S.

trade balance would improve, creating about 60,000 net U.S. jobs in 2002. Latin America could finance the corresponding decline in its trade balance because the WHFTA scenario would facilitate larger inward flows of capital into the region.

Even assuming that additional U.S. imports from Latin America would be heavily skewed toward labor-intensive goods, the authors calculate that net job creation due to a WHFTA is slightly biased toward higher-wage U.S. worker groups. However, even under extreme assumptions about the commodity composition of trade, the effect of trade changes on U.S. wage levels associated with each segment of the labor force will be small (see Table 4).

Gains to Latin America and the Caribbean

Latin America and the Caribbean would significantly benefit from closer trade and investment ties throughout the hemisphere. Assuming a WHFTA had started in 1990, the authors calculate that, by 2002, Latin America could have increased its exports by $87 billion and enlarged its imports by $104 billion — respectively, 42 percent and 51 percent higher than a baseline scenario of continuing reforms on a national basis by individual countries alone. The authors also project that $60 billion in cumulative additional inward direct investment flows could result from a hemispheric agreement by the year 2002. In conjunction with their more open economic systems and greater trade, Latin American GDP might be $273 billion (or 18 percent) higher in 2002 with a WHFTA than in the continuing individual-country reform scenario. This would represent a gain of about $525 per person throughout the region.

Latin American trade policy is not limited to increasing regional ties with North America. The authors conclude that beneficial subregional integration in Latin America should continue, driven by the logic of neighborhood trade links. After a certain point, however, economic considerations will prompt each of the Latin American subregions to seek closer ties with North America. The same considerations make a strong argument for the United States to expand its economic links to Latin America.

Trade and Investment Diversion

The potential diversion of trade and investment that could result from a WHFTA worries many observers. Nonetheless, the authors conclude that the scope of trade and investment diversion from Asia and Europe as a result of a WHFTA would be modest.

At most, a WHFTA would add manageable sums to the trade diversion already inherent in the NAFTA, MERCOSUR, Andean Group, and other subregional arrangements. By 2002, with a WHFTA in place, the loss of exports by affected third countries to the U.S. market would amount to those listed in Table 1.

Table 1.
Exports Diverted by WHFTA in 2002
(billions of dollars or percentage)

Exporting Region	Projected level of exports to U.S.	Exports diverted	
		Value	Percentage
South Asia	116.0	3.2	2.8
East Asia	281.2	7.4	2.6
Western Europe	163.3	5.7	3.5
All affected regions	560.5	16.2	2.9

The export diversion figures are stated in comparison with the baseline scenario of continuing individual-country reforms.

In addition, a WHFTA might increase foreign direct investment in Latin America by $60 billion by the year 2002, which in turn could divert some $30 billion of foreign direct investment from third countries (see Table 2).

Thus, the scope for trade and investment diversion within the hemisphere due to progressive implementation of a WHFTA is small.

WHFTA and the Global Trading System

It is critical, for both the United States and the rest of the hemisphere, that the creation of a WHFTA *not* be seen as undermining the global trading system. Such a perception could prompt emulation by other regions, notably East Asia, and substantially increase the costs of WHFTA's trade and investment diversion.

To the contrary, the WHFTA should be a building block for further global opening. Hufbauer and Schott thus recommend that the initiative proceed in parallel with two others: movement toward freer trade and investment relationships in the Asia Pacific region via the Asia Pacific Economic Cooperation (APEC) forum, which launched such a process at the Seattle

summit hosted by President Clinton in November 1993, and active pursuit of further multilateral liberalization and rule making in the new World Trade Organization, as already agreed with the European Union and the world's other major trading entities. The WHFTA should thus be part of a three-pronged initiative for future multilateral trade liberalization.

Table 2.
Foreign Direct Investment Diverted by
WHFTA in 2002
(billions of dollars or percentage)

	Projected level of FDI from all sources	FDI diverted	
		Value	Percentage
Developing Asia	192	6.2	3.1
Industrialized Asia	222	1.8	0.8
Western Europe	1,220	10.4	0.8
NAFTA and rest of world	1,089	11.5	1.0
All affected regions	2,942	30.0	1.0

The export diversion figures are stated in comparison with the baseline scenario of continuing individual-country reforms.

About the Authors

Gary Clyde Hufbauer is the Reginald Jones Senior Fellow at the Institute. He was formerly Marcus Wallenberg Professor of International Diplomacy at Georgetown University (1985-92); Deputy Director of the International Law Institute at Georgetown University (1979-81); Deputy Assistant Secretary for International Trade and Investment Policy of the U.S. Treasury (1977-79); and Director of the International Tax Staff at the Treasury (1974-76). He has written extensively on international trade, investment, and tax issues, including *Measuring the Costs of Protection in the United States* (1994); *NAFTA: An Assessment* (rev. 1993); *U.S. Taxation of International Income* (1992); *North American Free Trade: Issues and Recommendations* (1992); *Economic Sanctions Reconsidered* (second edition 1990); *Trade Policy for Troubled Industries* (1986); and *Subsidies in International Trade* (1984).

Jeffrey J. Schott, Senior Fellow, was a Senior Associate at the Carnegie Endowment for International Peace (1982-83) and an International Economist at the U.S. Treasury (1974-82). He is coauthor of *NAFTA: An Assessment* (rev. 1993); *North American Free Trade: Issues and Recommendations* (1992); *Completing the Uruguay Round* (1990); *Economic Sanctions Reconsidered* (second edition 1990); *Free Trade Areas and U.S. Trade Policy*(1989); *The Canada-United States Free Trade Agreement: The Global Impact* (1988); *Auction Quotas and U.S. Trade Policy* (1987); and *Trading for Growth: The Next Round of Trade Negotiations* (1985).

Table 3.
Performance Scores on Readiness Indicators[a]

Region/ Country	Price stability	Budget discipline	External debt	Currency stability	Market-oriented policies	Reliance on trade issues	Functioning democracy	Average
North America	4.3	3.7	4.0	5.0	5.0	4.3	4.3	4.4
U.S.	5.0	3.0	5.0	5.0	5.0	5.0	5.0	4.7
Canada	5.0	3.0	4.0	5.0	5.0	5.0	5.0	4.6
Mexico	3.0	5.0	3.0	5.0	5.0	3.0	3.0	3.9
Chile	3.0	5.0	5.0	5.0	5.0	4.0	4.0	4.4
Mercosur	1.3	3.8	2.8	4.0	3.5	2.8	3.5	3.1
Argentina	0	5.0	0	3.0	5.0	1.0	4.0	2.6
Brazil	0	0	2.0	3.0	3.0	5.0	3.0	2.3
Paraguay	3.0	5.0	5.0	5.0	3.0	2.0	3.0	3.7
Uruguay	2.0	5.0	4.0	5.0	3.0	3.0	4.0	3.7
Andean Group	2.4	4.8	1.8	5.0	3.0	3.0	3.2	3.4
Bolivia	4.0	5.0	0	5.0	4.0	4.0	4.0	3.7
Colombia	3.0	5.0	4.0	5.0	4.0	2.0	3.0	3.7
Ecuador	2.0	5.0	2.0	5.0	3.0	3.0	4.0	3.4
Peru	0	4.0	0	5.0	2.0	2.0	2.0	2.1
Venezuela	3.0	5.0	3.0	5.0	4.0	4.0	3.0	3.9
CACM	2.6	3.8	3.0	4.2	1.8	1.0	2.8	2.7
Costa Rica	3.0	4.0	4.0	5.0	3.0	0	4.0	3.3
El Salvador	4.0	5.0	5.0	5.0	2.0	2.0	3.0	3.7
Guatemala	3.0	5.0	4.0	3.0	1.0	0	2.0	2.6
Honduras	3.0	3.0	2.0	5.0	2.0	0	3.0	2.6
Nicaragua	0	2.0	0	3.0	1.0	3.0	2.0	1.6
CARICOM	3.6	3.6	3.8	5.0	2.8	2.4	4.4	3.7
Bahamas	4.0	4.0	5.0	5.0	3.0	0	4.0	3.6
Barbados	4.0	4.0	5.0	5.0	3.0	3.0	5.0	4.1
Guyana	3.0	0	0	5.0	2.0	3.0	4.0	2.4
Jamaica	3.0	5.0	4.0	5.0	3.0	2.0	4.0	3.7
Trinidad and Tobago	4.0	5.0	5.0	5.0	3.0	4.0	5.0	4.4

a. Scores for price stability are taken from table 5.2; scores for budget discipline are taken from table 5.4; scores for external debt are taken from table 5.6; scores for currency stability are taken from table 5.10; scores for market-oriented policies are based on the discussion in chapter 5; scores for international trade taxes are taken from table 5.11; and scores for functioning democracy are taken from the Freedom House rankings. (*Western Hemisphere Economic Integration.*)

Table 4.
Impact on Total U.S. Jobs and Median Weekly Wage Levels, Per Worker Group, under Two Scenarios, 2002

Job Impact	Base-year U.S. jobs, trading industries (thousands)[a]	Base-year U.S. jobs total (thousands)[a]	Continuing reform		WHFTA scenario	
			Net Impact on U.S. jobs (thousands)[b]	Percent change	Net Impact on U.S. Jobs (thousands)[b]	Percent change
$493-$451	3,693	63,519	165	0.26	326	0.51
$450-$422	5,480	9,922	178	1.79	342	3.45
$421-$396	4,863	29,727	-87	-0.29	-183	-0.62
$395-$271	4,698	6,679	-123	-1.84	-291	-4.36
Total	*18,734*	*109,847*	*133*	*0.12*	*193*	*0.18*

Wage Impact	Base-year U.S. wages for all industries[a]	Continuing reform		WHFTA scenario	
		U.S. wages for all industries	Percent change[c]	U.S. wages for all industries	Percent change[c]
$493-$451	472	474	0.52	477	1.03
$450-$422	435	450	3.59	465	6.89
$421-$396	404	402	-0.59	399	-1.23
$395-$271	328	316	-3.69	299	-8.71
Total	*441*	*442*	*0.24*	*443*	*0.35*

a. U.S. Department of Labor, Bureau of Labor Statistics figures.

b. From table B5.

c. Calculated by applying a demand elasticity of 0.5 to the percent change in total U.S. jobs associated with changing trade levels with Latin America. No allowance has been made for the normal real wage growth that would accompany the projected annual productivity gain of 2.4 percent per year.

Note: As explained in the text, these scenarios assume an extreme bias, in a labor-intensive direction, for additional Latin American exports to the U.S. market.

Western Hemisphere Economic Integration. Gary Clyde Hufbauer and Jeffrey J. Schott July 1994. Tables. Appendices. Index. 304 pp. 0-88132-159-1. $25.00 (U.S. and Canada); £19.99 (all other countries).

Customers outside the United States and Canada should order from Longman Group U.K., Ltd., P.O. Box 88, Harlow, Essex CM 19 5SR, U.K. Telephone: (0279) 623925, Fax: (0279) 453450.

Canadian customers can order from the Institute or from either: Renouf Bookstore, 1294 Algoma Road, Ottawa, Ontario K1B 3W8, Telephone: (613) 741-4333; Fax: (613) 741-5439; or La Liberté, 3020, chemin Sainte-Foy, Quebec G1X 3V6; Telephone: (418) 658-3763, Fax: (800) 567-5449.

A Project Sponsored by
- *North-South Center, University of Miami, Coral Gables, Florida*
- *Universidad de Belgrano and Fundación Integración, Buenos Aires, Argentina*

The mission of the North-South Center is to promote better relations and serve as a catalyst for change among the United States, Canada, and the nations of Latin America and the Caribbean by advancing knowledge and understanding of the major political, social, economic, and cultural issues affecting the nations and peoples of the Western Hemisphere.

Policy Proposals on Shared Prosperity in the Hemisphere: Trade, Investment, and Economic Development

Pre-Summit of the Americas Workshop, Buenos Aires, October 2-4, 1994

THE ECONOMIC COMMUNITY OF THE AMERICAS: A SHARED HEMISPHERIC GOAL

The Summit of the Americas provides the democratically elected heads of government of thirty-four Western Hemisphere countries with an extraordinary opportunity to develop and begin to implement common strategies and policies aimed at achieving regional shared prosperity, based on solid economic growth, the strengthening of democratic governance, and sustainable development.

In an effort to contribute to the shaping of the Summit's agenda, the North-South Center at the University of Miami launched a hemisphere-wide effort to bring together leading experts from academia, bilateral and multilateral agencies, business and labor organizations, and non-governmental organizations in meetings to identify basic goals, analyze strategies for achieving those goals, and make concrete policy recommendations to the governments of the Americas concerning the issues included in the Summit's agenda: economic integration, democratic governance, and sustainable development. Three Hemispheric Policy Working Group meetings, held in October 1994 in Buenos Aires, Cartagena de Indias, and Kingston, constituted the backbone of this effort.

The North-South Center's first Hemispheric Policy Working Group — co-sponsored by the Universidad de Belgrano and the Fundación Integración, in conjunction with the efforts of Ambassador Raúl Granillo Ocampo, Argentine ambassador in Washington, D.C. — met in Buenos Aires, Argentina, on October 2-4, 1994. Charged with analyzing Shared Prosperity in the Hemisphere: Trade, Investment, and Economic Development, the participants were divided into three commissions, each of which examined a primary aspect of the subject: "Trade," "Investment," or "Economic Development." After a full day of deliberations, each commission presented its conclusions in a plenary session for discussion, modifications, and approval by all participants.

General Recommendation

The participants in the Hemispheric Policy Working Group on Shared Prosperity: Trade, Investment, and Economic Development recommend that the governments participating in the Summit of the Americas, to take place in Miami on December 9-11, 1994, make a commitment to create an Economic Community of the Americas (ECA). An Economic Community of the Americas would express the common will of the hemispheric governments to foster trade liberalization and investment as part of a broader effort toward political, social, and environmentally sustainable development.

Toward this end, a process of negotiation should be launched at the Summit, leading to the signing of a formal agreement by the year 2000 to create an Economic Community of the Americas. The Community would establish a free trade zone compatible with the General Agreement on Tariffs and Trade (GATT) and would provide the structure for a progressive economic integration of the Americas to be completed by the year 2015, in accordance with existing international legislation and standards on labor, the environment, and democracy.

COMMISSION #1: TRADE

Objective

The expansion of trade flows should be the shared objective of all the countries of the Americas.

General Considerations

1. The major purpose of trade expansion should be to achieve a better quality of life for all people in the hemisphere, as well as to reinforce sustainable development.

2. The strengthening of multilateral rules constitutes the best vehicle for increasing trade flows in the hemisphere in order to promote shared prosperity. To this end, the governments of all the hemispheric countries should ratify the creation of the World Trade Organization (WTO).

3. The expansion of hemispheric trade should also be promoted by agreements that accelerate the process of liberalization and promote more profound integration among our countries. These arrangements should be developed within the framework of "open regionalism," compatible with the conditions established in Article 24 of GATT and subsequent agreements negotiated in the Uruguay Round as well as the terms of Article V of the General Agreement on Trade in Services (GATS).

4. In order to fit into a framework of "open regionalism," existing preferential trade agreements or those to be established in the hemisphere in the future should include clear and transparent rules of access for those hemispheric countries that have not yet subscribed to them. The pace and form of trade liberalization and economic integration in the hemisphere will vary according to particular national and subregional circumstances. Therefore, emphasis should be placed upon defining common rules designed to facilitate convergence.

Policy Recommendations

1. At the Summit of the Americas, begin negotiations for a free trade zone in the Americas with a formal agreement signed by the year 2000 and the creation of a Western Hemispheric free trade zone by the year 2015. This goal should be facilitated by the coordination and acceleration of ongoing processes of integration compatible with the rules of the multilateral system of trade.

2. Improve, in the interim, market access by means of:

   a. Harmonization of rules of origin applied by existing as well as future preferential trade agreements;

   b. Reduction of quotas, tariff escalation, and tariff peaks.

3. Avoid the erosion of existing market access conditions in the Americas in general as well as the suspension of existing preferential schemes such as those included in the General System of Preferences (GSP).

4. Ensure that the reduction of tariff barriers not be counteracted by higher non-tariff barriers and not be overcome by the growth of nonrestrictive tariff practices. In this context, the following measures should be promoted:

   a. Harmonization of technical standards and phytosanitary regulations;

   b. Effective implementation of multilateral regulations with regard to the application of anti-dumping regulations and countervailing duties;

c. The effective implementation of multilateral rules regarding safeguards.

5. Declare the Americas a zone free of export subsidies.

6. Establish a dispute settlement mechanism that will be rapid, transparent, and final and ensure a role for experts in the decision-making process. This vehicle should in no way preclude the use of existing GATT mechanisms or others to be implemented under the aegis of the WTO.

7. Address the potential conflicts that may arise out of the linkage of trade, environment, and labor issues by urging compliance with existing international agreements.

8. Emphasize the need to increase public awareness on these matters, especially with respect to the preservation of the environment. It must be made clear that the adoption of lax standards to attract investment as well as the insistence on harmonizing them at the strictest levels may provoke distortions in trade. These distortions could be avoided through cooperative efforts pointed at resolving differences in accord with existing multilateral agreements or those that may be established in the future.

9. Recognize the need, given different transition agreements and timetables that prevail in distinct countries and subregions of the hemisphere, for a diverse and multitrack approach to establish a free trade area in the Americas.

10. Establish a permanent forum or mechanism to:

a. Coordinate the negotiating process for the signing of a hemispheric free trade agreement by the year 2000;

b. Foster the development of a body of common trade regulations;

c. Identify the principal economic and/or institutional obstacles to the achievement of greater trade and economic integration in the Americas;

d. Promote the exchange of information on trade policy measures and on the evolution of preferential agreements, assessing their compatibility with multilateral rules.

Full consensus was not reached on the following point:

The ratification of the agreement that created the WTO was questioned with regard to deficiencies in the treatment of environmental concerns.

COMMISSION #2: INVESTMENT

Objective

The creation of the Economic Community of the Americas will generate confidence and establish an improved climate for the promotion of investment in the hemisphere.

General Considerations

1. The creation of an improved legal, economic, and social climate for investment in the region is essential to assure continuing economic growth. The building of a favorable climate for investment, including confidence among investors, is critical to the collective effort toward the creation of the Economic Community of the Americas. The principal strategies for achieving these goals are:

a. The development of efficient and transparent capital markets;

b. The establishment of mechanisms for broad access to market and investment related information;

c. The liberalization and harmonization of trade policies;

d. The provision by the public sector of the basic legal, physical, and human infrastructure and other public goods necessary to complement private investment.

2. The formation of parallel private working groups, consistent with the spirit and provisions of the Uruguay Round of the GATT and as a first step in a general process of harmonization, would serve as a catalyst to promote private sector dialogue as well as to advise intergovernmental working groups focused on the same areas. In addition, these working groups, intergovernmental and private, would create and nurture an environment of trust and understanding to achieve the goals of minimum standards and harmonization outlined above.

Policy Recommendations

1. The Summit should establish parallel private and intergovernmental working groups to institute minimum regulatory standards governing:

a. Flows of funds among countries;

b. Securities markets;

c. Commercial banking operations.

These and other proposed regional institutions and agreements are understood explicitly as complementary to subregional agreements such as NAFTA and MERCOSUR and larger multilateral groupings such as the Asia Pacific Economic Cooperation (APEC) and the WTO. One of the major tasks of the Summit will be to assure the compatibility of these efforts.

2. The establishment of regional framework agreements to encourage the utilization of existing mechanisms and the creation of new ones to increase investment in the region, including privatization, joint ventures, long-term private service contracts, debt swaps and similar initiatives.

3. The harmonization of legal instruments for the protection of private property, including real and intellectual property, as the necessary basis for deepening economic cooperation.

4. The establishment of clear guidelines for using the Multilateral Investment Fund (MIF) to support actively the aforementioned initiatives, urging the respective governments and other donor countries to become current in their subscriptions to the MIF.

5. The establishment of appropriate measures that would assist in the collection, harmonization, and dissemination of information on investment, trade, and technology by governments and intergovernmental organizations.

6. The establishment of a Regional Adjustment Fund to address macroeconomic and monetary problems created as a result of structural economic reform.

7. The establishment of a regional Private Investment Insurance facility as a regional option similar to the Overseas Private Investment Corporation (OPIC).

8. The establishment of a regional Export/Import Financing facility.

9. The creation of a regional mechanism for arbitration and dispute settlement, as an available forum for use within the Americas.

COMMISSION #3: ECONOMIC DEVELOPMENT

Objective

The elimination of poverty and the satisfaction of basic human needs should be, in conjunction with growth, the central goal of economic development in the Americas.

General Considerations

1. Economic adjustment, stabilization, and liberalization policies have been and continue to be necessary to assure favorable conditions for economic growth in the hemisphere.

2. Further steps toward a hemispheric free trade area as well as the definition of coherent policies to promote investment in the region are goals that this commission shares with commissions 1 and 2, as they contribute to hemispheric integration and economic growth. Such goals should be pursued in the context of the GATT agreement and with full respect for existing international legislation on labor and the environment.

3. The social and political viability of medium- and long-term economic growth depend upon the elimination of poverty, which currently affects 40 percent of the region's population. Along with growth, the improvement of the living conditions and the satisfaction of the basic needs of the largest possible number of the region's people should be established as shared goals by the region's governments as well as play a major role in both their national policies and those of the multilateral and bilateral agencies. These goals represent the consensus achieved by the member countries of the Inter-American Development Bank when they approved its Eighth Capital Replenishment and are consistent with the World Bank's Report on Development and the Draft Declaration of the Preparatory Committee of the UN's Summit on Social Development. Central concerns in the elimination of poverty include expanding access to:

a. Primary education aimed at the elimination of illiteracy;

b. Basic nutrition aimed at eliminating malnutrition;

c. Primary health care and voluntary family planning;

d. Clean water and sewage systems;

e. Minimum quality housing;

f. Information and knowledge.

Similarly, full employment should be a component of economic growth and development and a common goal shared by all sectors of society.

4. The current methods used to measure economic production and development should be redefined to include the qualitative factors of social development.

5. The medium- and long-term goals of a socially and politically sustainable strategy of development require the full participation of all sectors of civil society on the basis of the strengthening of mechanisms and institutions for democratic representation and participation.

Policy Recommendations

1. Education

Overcoming poverty and achieving economic growth and development are directly related to full access of the population to quality primary and secondary education and technical training. The governments of the hemisphere should launch a campaign aimed at:

a. Providing universal access to quality primary education;

b. Eliminating illiteracy;

c. Increasing facilities for technical training.

2. Debt

Debt has been a crucial problem in the recent Latin American experience and in the relations between North and South. Particularly with regard to the public debt, the governments of the hemisphere should:

a. Implement a mechanism for the permanent monitoring of the public debt in order to avoid the repetition of past crises;

b. Further explore and implement mechanisms of public debt cancellation in exchange for poverty alleviation and environmental protection programs.

3. Technology and Information

Economic growth and sustainable development demand the creation, promotion, and exchange of information and technologies. The governments of the hemisphere should:

a. Eliminate the restrictions that limit the access to and exchange of technologies and information;

b. Establish regional mechanisms and/or institutions for the promotion and exchange of technologies and information that contribute to economic development, fostering the role of the public sector in the creation and promotion of mechanisms for the exchange of technology and related information.

In order to assure that technological innovations are achieved without increased risk to people and the environment, the practice of disseminating products that have been banned in their countries of origin must be eliminated.

4. Employment

Aiming at full employment and recognizing the failures of past policies, governments in the hemisphere should:

a. Readdress the question of the relation between macroeconomic stabilization and employment creation goals;

b. Evaluate policies and legislation that facilitate micro and small enterprises, so that these enterprises and individuals have opportunities to achieve acceptable income levels;

c. As financing and educational strategies are established by governments and bilateral and multilateral agencies, assign priority to the development of 1) the agricultural sector; 2) micro, small, and medium-sized enterprises; and 3) programs that include youth and women.

5. Property

In order to distribute the benefits of growth to the broadest sectors of the population, the governments of the hemisphere should define strategies and policies to guarantee low income sectors and indigenous populations access to all forms of property and specifically secure these groups' access to vacant public lands.

6. Labor

Structural adjustment and free trade policies should not be built upon workers' losses of rights and real incomes. Therefore, the governments of the hemisphere should:

a. Reaffirm their commitment to the existing international norms and regulations as expressed in the regional and international statutes of the International Labor Organization (ILO);

b. Define specific policies to address the problems of migrant workers and their families, eliminating all forms of discrimination and enacting adequate labor legislation.

7. Social Expenditures and Social Compensation

Structural adjustment and stabilization policies have had acute social costs and in certain cases have caused significant reductions in public social expenditures. To overcome this negative impact, the governments of the hemisphere should:

a. Create and/or strengthen existing social compensation programs to minimize the negative effects of structural adjustments;

b. Direct the investment of social compensation expenditures toward productive activities.

8. State and Civil Society

Active participation by civil society is fundamental to the development process, which should comprise all social actors, including guilds, professional associations, and unions. Governments of the hemisphere should:

a. Establish channels of access to public authorities by creating an environment conducive to civil society's participation in the decision-making process. This would include the right to solicit civilian review of administrative decisions;

b. Promote the organization and representation of the informal sectors and establish forms of social dialogue for the purposes of problem solving and conflict resolution.

WORKING GROUP ON SHARED PROSPERITY: TRADE, INVESTMENT, AND ECONOMIC DEVELOPMENT BUENOS AIRES, ARGENTINA OCTOBER 2-4, 1994

TRADE

Chairperson, Roberto Bouzas, Facultad Latinoamericana de Ciencias Sociales (FLACSO) and Instituto del Servicio Exterior de la Nación (ISEN), Buenos Aires, Argentina

Carlos Alberto Primo Braga, World Bank, Washington, D.C.

Brennan Van Dyke, Center for Environmental Law, Washington, D.C.

Sergio Bustamante, Asociación Nacional de Industriales (ANDI), Medellín, Colombia

Javier Mujica, Centro de Asesoría Laboral del Perú, Lima

Luigi Manzetti, North-South Center, University of Miami, Coral Gables, Florida

Tim Plumptre, The Bank of Nova Scotia, Toronto, Canada

Renato Bauman, Comisión Económica para América Latina (CEPAL) Santiago, Chile

Roberto Alemann, Consultant, Buenos Aires, Argentina

Felipe de la Balze, Comité Ejecutivo del Consejo Argentino para Relaciones Internacionales (CARI), Buenos Aires, Argentina

INVESTMENT

Chairperson, Van Whiting, University of California, San Diego

Hugh Schwartz, Center for Behavioral Economic Analysis, McLean, Virginia

Janet Kelly, Instituto de Estudios Superiores de Administración (IESA), Caracas, Venezuela

Robert Grosse, American Graduate School of International Management, Phoenix, Arizona

John Avery, Americas Society, New York, New York

Norman A. Bailey, Consultant, Washington, D.C.

José Ma. Gonzales Eiras, MQM Argentina S.A., Buenos Aires, Argentina

Adalberto Rodríguez Giarvarini, Universidad de Belgrano, Buenos Aires, Argentina

Juan Yañes, Management Associates International, Inc. (MAI), Miami, Florida/Buenos Aires, Argentina

ECONOMIC DEVELOPMENT

Chairperson, Gonzalo Biggs, Universidad Diego Portales, Santiago, Chile

Patricia Wilson, University of Texas, Austin

Gabriel Misas, Universidad Nacional, Bogotá, Colombia

Roberto Lavagna, Universidad de Buenos Aires, Argentina

Victor Tokman, International Labor Organization, Lima, Peru

PROPOSALS FROM NON-GOVERNMENTAL SECTORS

III. Eradicating Poverty and Discrimination in Our Hemisphere

The Concerned Civil Society Organizations' Office on Development Policy in Washington, D.C., advocates public policies that address the root causes of injustice, poverty, and hunger worldwide. On behalf of Church World Service and Lutheran World Relief, the Office focuses its efforts on making U.S. government and international economic policy more responsive to the needs and aspirations of poor people in Asia, Africa, and Latin America.

The Office is regularly in dialogue with public officials, members of Congress and staff, and the media. It also seeks to arrange opportunities for overseas colleagues to share their perspectives directly with policymakers.

The Office's positions are influenced by the views of partner agencies worldwide. Policy efforts are carried out in cooperation with Bread for the World, Interfaith/ Impact, and InterAction. (Please refer to the last page of this chapter for a list of organizations that endorsed this document.)

Promises to Keep: The Unfinished Agenda for Human Rights and Economic Justice in the Americas

A STATEMENT AND RECOMMENDATIONS BY CONCERNED CIVIL SOCIETY ORGANIZATIONS TO THE SUMMIT OF THE AMERICAS

November 16, 1994

In this Summit of the Americas, our presidents will speak of democracy: making democracy work, making democracy prosperous, making democracy endure. While we welcome this theme and the strides toward elected governments in the Americas, we are concerned that vital elements of democracy — human rights and economic justice — are not on the table at this Summit and have not yet taken deep root in many parts of this hemisphere. Elected governments that do not guarantee their citizens full exercise of basic human rights and trade and development plans that are devised without participation and that do not guarantee that hungry people will be fed do not meet our standards for democratic life.

This document is the result of a wide-ranging consultation among hemispheric organizations that place particular value on human rights and the needs of the poor and excluded. Together, we call on our governments, north and south, to help a deeper democracy take root. We challenge our leaders to take actions that will make the full enjoyment of basic human rights a reality throughout the Americas. We hope that the Summit will be a call to action on the pressing issues of poverty and sustainable development, trade and economic integration for the benefit of all, and greater respect for human rights that face our hemisphere and demand our cooperation.

THE SUMMIT AGENDA

The vision and values within which governments act are generated and preserved by civil society. Thus, at a gathering such as this Summit, our role as civil society actors is to offer our vision and to ask whether the right issues are on the table and whether the initiatives under consideration reflect the experience and perspective of all of the hemisphere's peoples. We must also ask whether they incorporate those traditionally excluded from the political and economic life of the hemisphere. As we look around our hemisphere, we recognize progress in some areas, particularly in the growth of democratic traditions. At the same time, we are sobered by the gravity of the needs and challenges that confront us:

- We see economic growth and liberalization policies that do not redress the underlying causes of poverty and inequality and that in many cases further exacerbate poverty. We view with alarm disturbing evidence of continued concentration of wealth and increases in poverty that move the hemisphere farther away from fulfilling basic economic, social, and cultural rights protected under international law.

- We celebrate elected governments and the dynamic growth of civil society organizations, both vital elements of democracy. We note, however, that many nascent democracies face a variety of threats and challenges. Civil governments in many countries remain only weakly in control of their militaries. Respect for human rights continues to be an ideal, not a reality, in many nations. In Guatemala, Colombia, and Peru, for example, governments have attempted, through executive decrees and extraordinary legislation, to subvert the rule of law and distort Constitutional and legal processes. Freedom of association and of expression is still a dream in countries where human rights violations are routine. Human rights violations and other crimes too often go unpunished.

- We are concerned by the lack of recognition of the legitimacy of civil society, especially for its efforts to promote government accountability. In some countries civil society organizations operate under a cloud of fear; in others, they remain hampered by bureaucratic and legal constraints.

- We are concerned about the failure of governments to recognize either the economic contributions of women or their disproportionate poverty, their continuing underrepresentation in positions of power and policy decisionmaking and in the private sector, their lack of access to production resources, education and quality health care, and the high levels of societal and domestic violence.

- We are convinced that debate and decisionmaking on trade issues are too restricted. Trade agreements negotiated by a few are unlikely to benefit many. Mechanisms for strengthening labor rights and protecting the environment are weak or nonexistent, and immigration questions are largely excluded from the agenda.

Our concerns are directed equally to northern and southern governments, as we urge elected leaders to include in their deliberations the following questions:

How can countries throughout the hemisphere make strides towards guaranteeing fundamental economic, social, and cultural rights as well as civil and political rights?

How can poor and traditionally excluded people gain an integral role in economic development that addresses squarely the poverty and inequality that is crippling the hemisphere?

How can the region's citizens — particularly poor and low-income people — be ensured that trade and investment agreements will be negotiated in their interest?

We also wish to highlight our belief that one of the hallmarks of hemispheric cooperation should be **respect for the tremendous diversity and pluralism that characterize our corner of the globe.** It is essential that governments, peoples, and communities in this hemisphere find peaceful means of resolving differences that lead to conflict. **In this regard we are particularly troubled by the pointed exclusion from the Summit of a single country, Cuba.** We believe that the decades-long conflict between the United States and Cuba can and must be resolved urgently through peaceful means. **We call on all of the leaders of the hemisphere to commit themselves to actions that will facilitate a peaceful resolution of the conflict between Cuba and the United States.**

The Growing Role of Civil Society

The blossoming of civil society in this hemisphere is one of the most promising developments of recent years. Organizations of civil society, including those that are run by and represent the interests of women, have a growing capacity to carry out a wide range of programs in small business development, agriculture, self-help housing, health care, and organizational skills and training. Increasingly, too, through these organizations men and women engage in dialogue with governments to achieve consensus about needs and solutions and to collaborate in efforts to build societies that nurture human development.

We believe that a central element of inclusive, democratic, and economically competitive development is a new relationship between the state and civil society.

To this relationship our civil society organizations bring experiences and perspectives grounded in daily toil for human rights and economic justice. We also bring specific needs that must be met by government if we are to function effectively and to contribute to efforts to bring about a brighter future for all the people of the hemisphere.

Civil society organizations help to bring into the debate the voices of people who, although they are the majority, remain too often largely unrepresented in public life. Women's voices in particular are woefully underrepresented, despite the fact that they make up 50 percent of the population. Also underrepresented are indigenous peoples, small- and medium-sized agricultural producers, people of faith, laborers, trade unionists, neighborhood association members, children, and youth. We are gaining a clearer understanding of how the needs of each group differ from those of others. Together, these insights comprise a vision of just and sustainable development that protects human dignity and builds on and reinforces the values of caring and compassion.

For its part, as a contribution to a new state/civil society relationship, the government must agree to those actions that enable civil society organizations to function effectively. These include government respect for the human rights guarantees embodied in international and national law. They also include the creation of institutional mechanisms by which civil society can participate in the decision-making processes. In addition, government must operate in a transparent fashion, providing widespread access to information about government policies and programs. It must ensure the independent operation of an effective judicial system.

We acknowledge our own responsibilities to ensure a vibrant civil society. Toward that end, we pledge to:

- Report annually on our activities and finances;

- Ensure that our staffs and boards reap no financial benefits aside from reasonable compensation for services rendered and for expenses reasonably incurred;

- State clearly our organizational objectives in published documents and ensure that these objectives are in the public interest;

- Refrain from activities that are aimed at the destruction — or limitation — of democracy, civil society, or human rights.

We welcome this Summit of the Americas as a rare opportunity for our governments to make common cause in facing common problems. We ask that in the future our governments take the next essential step: opening up access in such meetings to representatives of civil society. The problems facing this hemisphere can not be solved by governments alone.

A Plan of Action

I. HUMAN RIGHTS

Human rights, including economic, social, and cultural rights, are the means by which society seeks to ensure human dignity and well-being for all its members. The human rights principles enshrined in international law are among the necessary conditions for progress toward such dignity and well-being. Those governments that enforce such principles through effective judicial institutions are more responsive and accountable to their citizenry. Where human rights are guaranteed, diverse groups can peacefully and nonviolently pursue their interests. In such settings, the role of military and security forces is highly limited. These are the human rights issues that should be addressed at the Summit:

A. INTERNATIONAL HUMAN RIGHTS SAFEGUARDS

Human rights include the full array of guarantees found in the International Bill of Rights: economic, social and cultural rights as well as civil and political rights. The Universal Declaration of Human Rights, the International Covenant on Human Rights, and — of particular significance to the Summit of the Americas — the American Convention on Human Rights provide important frameworks for ensuring the rights of all citizens. In addition, the Vienna Declaration of 1993, UN Resolution 48-104, and the OAS Convention of Belém do Pará recognize violence against women as a human rights abuse. The purpose of these instruments is to protect *all* citizens. The obligations undertaken by governments in ratifying these instruments are the standards against which they should be held accountable, both by their own citizenry and by actors in the international arena.

These guarantees should apply whenever a government acts against those who violate the law. Too often, counternarcotics operations, for example, have violated human rights. The threat posed by drug trafficking or by terrorism is sometimes used to justify counterinsurgency operations that result in gross violations of human rights. All too often, "extraordinary" legislation and courts instituted to prosecute accused violators lack the most basic due process guarantees.

Recommendations on International Human Rights Safeguards:

We call on the Heads of State of the Western Hemisphere to

1. Commit their government to ratify the American Convention on Human Rights and to comply with its terms or, if their government already has ratified the Convention, to pledge to comply with its terms;

2. Ratify and/or withdraw reservations to the UN Convention on the Elimination of All Forms of Discrimination Against Women and to commit resources necessary to comply with obligations under the UN Declaration on the Elimination of Violence Against Women;

3. Express their support for UN efforts to complete action on the draft Declaration on the Rights of Indigenous Peoples *and* on the draft Declaration on the Rights and Responsibility of Individuals, Groups, and Organs of Society to Promote and Protect Universally Recognized Human Rights and Fundamental Freedoms and pledge their efforts to secure speedy and deliberate consideration by national legislatures of these declarations, once completed;

4. Commit to ratify the basic human rights conventions of the International Labor Organization *and* the International Covenant on Economic, Social, and Cultural Rights;

5. Ensure that antinarcotic, antiterrorism and all other "extraordinary" legislation incorporates due process guarantees and respect for the rule of law as defined in international human rights law.

B. IMPUNITY

In many countries of the hemisphere, impunity is a serious problem. The willingness and ability of governments to carry out effective prosecution is an essential ingredient in fulfilling its obligation to ensure respect for human rights. Failure to ensure that those who violate the law are held accountable erodes the fundamental foundation of justice on which cohesive societies are built. It causes citizens to lose faith in the institutions of government, thereby undermining democracy and respect for the rule of law.

Recommendations on Steps Toward Ending Impunity:

We call on the Heads of State of the Western Hemisphere to redouble their efforts to

1. Remove obstacles to the investigation and prosecution of violations of the law;

2. Establish an independent judicial branch of government, where such does not exist, in accordance with their obligations under the American Convention and the International Covenant on Civil and Political Rights;

3. Take note of the personnel and resource needs of the judiciary and to pledge adequate budgets for its effective functioning;

4. Foreswear any improper interference with the judiciary, including in the resolution of individual cases;

5. Establish a judicial nominating commission to select judicial candidates based on merit, not political influence.

C. CREATING AN ENABLING ENVIRONMENT FOR CIVIL SOCIETY

Freedom of association and freedom of expression are universally recognized human rights protected by a variety of international conventions. When people exercise these rights and form voluntary associations and nonprofit groups, the resulting organizations provide crucial and effective means for citizens to participate in the affairs of the nation.

The state has the primary responsibility to ensure and protect human rights and to ensure the conditions that lead to the growth of democracy. However, the organizations of civil society — such as those we represent — also work to ensure the protection of human rights, to articulate rights-based norms and values that should govern both individual and institutional behavior, and to promote and implement development strategies that are equitable and sustainable. Our role as advocates is crucial to the functioning of democracy, the growth of civil society, the alleviation of poverty, and the protection of human rights. We insist on our right to function without unnecessary governmental interference, even when our advocacy conflicts with governmental policies.

Every state must ensure that freedoms of association and expression are clearly protected by law and by administrative and judicial procedures, both formal and informal. This protection should be reflected in fair legal regulations covering taxation, incorporation, and corporate governance, which encourage the formation of nonprofit, non-governmental organizations and ensure they can operate free of unnecessary or politically motivated interference by the state. While we recognize our legal accountability to governmental bodies that oversee nonprofit groups, this oversight must be exercised honestly and impartially. It may not be used as a tool to force an organization to conform its activities or advocacy to the wishes of the government or of politically powerful individuals.

Recommendations on Creating an Enabling Environment for Civil Society:

We call on the Heads of State of the Western Hemisphere to

1. Recognize formally that all members of society have the right to organize and to participate in voluntary associations, including trade unions, to protect and promote their interests;

2. Recognize formally that civil society organizations have the following rights, among those others enumerated in international law:

- To draw public attention to violations of human rights, to instances of corruption, and to inadequate compliance with the terms of this declaration; to complain about these violations to competent national bodies; and to have complaints promptly reviewed by independent, impartial, and competent judicial (or other) authorities;

- To have unhindered access to and communication with international bodies concerned with human rights, corruption, and civil society;

3. Pledge to ensure the protection of everyone against violence or retaliation as a consequence of the legitimate exercise of these rights;

4. Commit to undertake a review, in consultation with domestic civil society organizations, of governmental laws, policies and practices, both formal and informal. This review will examine access to government information, requirements for creation and operation of civil society organizations, tax exemptions and deductions, restrictions on fund-raising and relations between domestic organizations and their foreign or international counterparts, and requirements for annual (and other public) reports;

5. Pledge to remove the obstacles identified by this review and to adopt such legislative, administrative, and other steps (including judicial and legal reform) as are necessary to create the social and political conditions and legal guarantees required for citizens to associate, form non-governmental and other civil society organizations, and pursue their objectives free of unnecessary or unduly burdensome restraints. To recognize that the only permissible limitations are those determined by law solely for the purpose of securing respect for the rights and freedoms of others and of meeting the just requirements of public order and the general welfare in a democratic society;

6. Commit also to examine all government laws and practices (including those relating to government regulation of, or relationships with, business, conflict of interest standards, and rules on political contributions) to identify those that foster corruption.

D. CIVIL-MILITARY RELATIONS

An essential ingredient of democracy is civilian rule and respect for civilian institutions and constitutional guidelines. It is important to guard against the encroachment on civilian functions of government by the armed forces — both military and security forces. The armed forces must be subordinate to civilian institutions and subject to the same public scrutiny and accountability as the civilian government. In particular, military budgets and military involvement in the private sector should be subject to civilian control. External defense and internal security (police) functions should be separated. Scarce public resources should not be devoted to excessive military expenditures and military involvement in the private sector should be curtailed. Cases of alleged violation of the law by military personnel should be investigated promptly in accordance with recognized legal procedures.

Recommendations on Civil-Military Relations:

We call on the Heads of State of the Western Hemisphere to

1. Affirm the principle of civilian control of the Armed Forces and military budgets, including presidential review and control over personnel matters of the Armed Forces and of the accountability of the military to international human rights standards;

2. Pledge that civilians will be tried before civil, not military, courts;

3. Commit, on behalf of their governments, to full transparency in the consideration of military budgets and military involvement in the private sector;

4. Take steps to separate police forces from the armed forces.

II. ECONOMIC JUSTICE

Economic policies and practices that are fair and equitable and that enhance the quality of human life are the bedrock of economic justice. Increasingly, these policies and practices are defined not only at the national and local level, but at the global level, making the challenge of defining effective policies increasingly complex. Political will and greater citizen participation are needed to achieve economic justice.

A. MACROECONOMIC POLICY

The infamous "lost decade" of development in the hemisphere is testimony to the failure of an economic model that has focused more on macroeconomic variables than on the needs of the majority. This model, reinforced by economic structural adjustment programs, has placed greater priority on reducing the role of the state, lowering inflation, and opening Latin American and Caribbean economies to Northern businesses than on addressing the structural causes of poverty, the need to protect the environment, or the importance of reaching broad-based consensus on economic policies. Thus, while inflation rates have been reduced in many countries and a measure of growth has been restored in some,

the hemisphere simultaneously has experienced rising poverty, worsening income distribution, and increasing environmental degradation. Women have been especially hard hit by the effects of structural adjustment policies. Heavy debt loads remain a burden on many Latin American and Caribbean economies.

Those who have not benefitted from current economic policies have suggested alternate approaches to achieve economic stability and growth. The heavy emphasis on export promotion should be balanced with attention to developing domestic markets. Dramatic cuts in military spending and effective implementation of progressive taxation schemes can offset the need to slash funding for social services. The need to assure food security and increase domestic food production should be regarded as legitimate and valuable goals in national planning. A solution should be found to the region's debt problems. Social compensations funds, woefully inadequate as a means of addressing persistent poverty, should be linked to long-term development. The current accent on competition should be tempered by support for cooperation and social solidarity.

To date, governments and international financial institutions have not been responsive. Too often, far-reaching policies are decided with virtually no opportunity for public debate or influence. Genuine democracies should be judged in part by the degree to which economic policies are based on a consensus achieved through well-defined, accountable decision-making processes.

Recommendations on Macroeconomic Policy:

We call on the Heads of State of the Western Hemisphere to pledge to

1. Strengthen domestic markets as well as facilitate exports. While increasing exports is a goal shared by many countries, the critical need to expand local markets for goods and labor should not be neglected. Competitiveness should not be achieved at the expense of wages, employment, or worker rights; increasing domestic demand will distribute the benefits of expanded economic activity and create more stable markets;

2. Renegotiate bilateral debts using the Naples terms as the minimum provided to poor, highly indebted countries; encourage middle-income as well

as poor countries to use creative mechanisms, like debt swaps for social programs, to reduce debt burdens; separate structural adjustment conditionality from debt reduction; advocate multilateral debt reduction as recently proposed by the United Kingdom; and pledge to refrain from assuming unnecessary and expensive new debt obligations not in the public interest;

3. Implement accountable, participatory decision-making processes to achieve popular consensus on economic policies;

4. Increase funding for health, education, and social security in those countries where such spending is especially low, recognizing it as a public investment to increase productivity.

B. SUSTAINABLE DEVELOPMENT

The concept of *sustainable development* arose from the ashes of decades of "development" schemes that failed to achieve a lasting improved quality of life for those they sought to benefit and that too often contributed to environmental degradation. By contrast, sustainable development focuses on achieving improved quality of human life for all, while protecting the natural resource base. It concentrates on the specifics of what, beyond economic growth, is needed to ensure that all participate in and reap the benefits of development.

Sustainable development requires long-term strategic planning, the rational use of natural resources, investment that provides greater access to land and to credit, value-added enterprises, appropriate technology, research and innovation, and marketing assistance and human resource development — including basic health services and education — for those who traditionally operate on the margins of the economy, particularly women. In Latin America, appropriate agricultural policies to promote food security are indispensable elements of sustainable development.

Above all, sustainable development depends on active participation by those who seek to benefit from it. Such development is built on the insights, knowledge, and experience that reside within individuals, families, and communities. Civil society organizations often serve to articulate such knowledge and experience so that they can inform policy and program decisions.

Mechanisms for civil society participation in decisionmaking and program design, implementation, and evaluation should therefore be established at the global, regional, national, and local levels. Civil society experience in sustainable development confirms that participation at the local level is especially promising. It points to the importance of local government in helping to expand the scale of sustainable development efforts. Government authority and resources must be decentralized to increase the capacity of local governments to contribute to sustainable development.

It is particularly important that international financial institutions and intergovernmental organizations, which have an increasingly significant impact on democracy and development in the hemisphere, promote the practices of participatory democracy and good governance on the national level and model such practices in their own decisionmaking.

Recommendations on Sustainable Development:

We call on the Heads of State of the Western Hemisphere to pledge to

1. Improve the access of traditionally excluded sectors of society to productive resources including land, credit, and technical assistance, with priority given to the needs of women, indigenous peoples, and youth;

2. Identify or establish a mechanism that includes male and female representatives of organizations of civil society to monitor and report on national and hemispheric efforts to redress poverty. Economic policies should be evaluated not just on their success in improving macroeconomic indicators such as growth, inflation, and trade balances but also on their ability to lower poverty rates and improve income distribution;

3. Incorporate the traditionally excluded sectors of society, especially women, in development planning, including trade and economic integration, by involving their representatives in discussions and decisionmaking on policy and project formation, implementation, and evaluation;

4. Seek the establishment of consultative status at the Organization of American States for nongovernmental organizations and the establishment of permanent mechanisms within the Inter-American

213

Development Bank and other multilateral institutions that will provide for broad citizen participation in policy and program development, implementation, monitoring, and evaluation.

C. TRADE AND ECONOMIC INTEGRATION

The trade agreements currently underway or contemplated for the hemisphere are being crafted behind closed doors by governments with extensive input from transnational corporations. With such restricted decision-making processes, it is hardly surprising, therefore, that they are not designed to benefit our societies more broadly. We believe our countries can reduce trade barriers and remove some obstacles to investment as long as we embrace a new framework of initiatives for our hemisphere that steers trade and investment to promote fair-paying jobs, democratic and self-reliant communities, and a healthy environment.

We urge trade agreements that improve the quality of our lives. They should address the inequalities among nations with measures such as debt relief. They should improve environmental, social and labor standards, raising them, not lowering them. They should address not just the movement of goods, services, and capital, but the movement of people — immigration — proposing humane changes in immigration restrictions. Trade agreements should include codes of conduct for transnational corporations. Finally, they should include trade assistance adjustment programs to address the needs of those displaced by shifting trade and investment patterns.*

* These positions are adapted from a consensus document "A Just and Sustainable Trade and Development Initiative for the Western Hemisphere," created by organizations in Mexico, the United States, and Canada.

Recommendations on Trade and Economic Integration:

We call on the Heads of State of the Western Hemisphere to pledge to

1. Establish clear ways in which a broad range of organizations can have direct access to, and direct input into, trade agreements and integration plans. Draft trade agreements should be made public well in advance and should be open to debate in public fora;

2. Forge trade agreements that strengthen worker rights, that take specially into account the needs of small farmers, small business, indigenous communities, and women and that enhance environmental protection. Worker rights and environmental protection should not be discussed in side agreements but included as an integral part of any agreement, with clear mechanisms effectively to monitor and enforce compliance;

3. Forge trade agreements that do not preempt the power of individual countries to set higher standards than the minimum for labor, health, safety, and the environment. Trade agreements should raise, not lower, our quality of life;

4. Forge trade agreements that preserve the prerogative of governments to direct foreign investment to priority areas and/or to establish performance standards for foreign investment;

5. Include agreements over the movement of people — immigration — as well as the movement of goods and capital, that respect the dignity, health and human rights of migratory workers;

6. Adopt a Corporate Code of Conduct for the hemisphere that will call on all corporations to adhere to certain standards for worker safety, workers' freedom of association and collective bargaining rights, working conditions, liveable wages, and restriction of child labor. The Code should include environmental standards and require companies to disclose product hazards and ban exports of dangerous materials. The Code should be developed by unions, business, environmental organizations and other civil sector organizations throughout the hemisphere and should be ratified by governments.

CONCLUSION

The issues and recommendations outlined above reflect the priorities that have emerged from the experience of organizations and people laboring to build more just and equitable societies in the Americas. These "promises to keep" are presented with a sense of urgency and a spirit of collaboration. It is our hope that policymakers throughout the hemisphere will give serious consideration to these concerns and that a shared vision will lead to a brighter future for the peoples of the Americas.

The following organizations and
individuals endorse *Promises to Keep:
The Unfinished Agenda for Human
Rights and Economic Justice in the
Americas:*

(List in Formation, as of 12/2/94)

A Common Ministry in Latin America and the
Caribbean, DOM/UCBWM:

Christian Church (Disciples of Christ) in the United
States and Canada

United Church of Christ

Action Canada Network (Canada)

Agencia Latinoamericana de Información (Ecuador)

Asociación de Organizaciones Campesinas
Centroamericana para la Cooperación y el
Desarrollo (ASOCODE, Central America)

Canadian Environmental Law Association (Canada)

Center for International Policy (USA)

Central America Policy Alternatives — CAPA
(Canada)

Centro Para la Acción Legal en Derechos Humanos
(Guatemala)

Centro Félix Varela (Cuba)

Church World Service (USA)

CODEHUCA — Commission for the Defense of
Human Rights in Central America

CODEPU — Comité de Defensa de los Derechos
del Pueblo (Chile)

Comité de Servicio Chileno — Cuquero (Chile)

Common Frontiers (Canada)

Comunidad de Jóvenes Ambientalistas (JA!)
(Nicaragua)

Concertación Centroamericana de Organismos de
Desarrollo (Central America)

Debate Nacional por la Paz en El Salvador, CPDN
(El Salvador)

Development Group for Alternative Policies (USA)

The Ecumenical Program on Central America and
the Caribbean (USA)

Equipo Pueblo (Mexico)

Esquel Group Foundation (USA)

Foro Civil Nicaragüense para el Desarrollo
Sostenible (Nicaragua)

Forum Solidaridad (Peru)

Fundación Futuro Latinoamericana (Ecuador)

Guatemalan Human Rights Commission
(Guatemala, USA)

Guatemalan Partners (USA)

Lisa Haugaard, Central America Working Group*

Institute of Alternative Policies for the
Southern Cone of Latin America (PACS,
Argentina)

Instituto Interamericano de Servicios Legales
Alternativos (ILSA, Colombia)

Instituto de Desarrollo Urbano (CENCA, Peru)

International Center for Research on Women (USA)

International Council of Voluntary Agencies
(ICVA, Geneva)

International Labor Rights Education and Research
Fund (USA)

Jesuit Centre for Social Faith and Justice (Canada)

Lawyers' Committee for Human Rights (USA)

Lutheran Office for World Community, Evangelical
Lutheran Church in America (USA)

Lutheran Office for Governmental Affairs,
Evangelical Lutheran Church in America (USA)

Lutheran World Relief (USA)

Elsie Monge, Comisión Ecuménica de Derechos
Humanos (CEDHU, Ecuador)

Maryknoll Society Justice and Peace Office (USA)

Mennonite Central Committee (USA)

Neighbor to Neighbor (USA)

Network: A National Catholic Social Justice
Lobby (USA)

Network in Solidarity with Guatemala
(NISGUA, USA)

Nicaragua-United States Friendship Office (USA)

OXFAM America (USA)

OXFAM-Canada (Canada)

Peru Peace Network (USA)

Project on Demilitarization and Democracy (USA)

Quixote Center: Quest for Peace (USA)

Red Mexicana de Acción Frente al Libre Comercio
(REMALC, Mexico)

John Ruthrauff, Center for Democratic
Education (USA)

David Schott, Sister Parish Program (USA)

Share Foundation (USA)

Servicio, Paz y Justicia (SERPAJ) (Uruguay)

Servicio, Paz y Justicia (SERPAJ) (Argentina)

U.S./Guatemala Labor Education Project (USA)

Unitarian Universalist Service Committee (USA)

Washington Office on Latin America (USA)

Thom White Wolf Fassett, General Board of Church
and Society, United Methodist Church (USA)

Witness for Peace (USA)

Women Strike for Peace (USA)

* Organization listed for identification purposes only

*Cheryl Morden,
Associate Director for
Development Policy
Church World
Service/Lutheran
World Relief*

Postscript: The Measured and Unmade Promises of the Summit

The agreements reached at the Summit of the Americas fall short of the call to "action on pressing issues of poverty and sustainable development, trade and economic integration for the benefit of all, and greater respect for human rights" issued by organizations endorsing "Promises to Keep: The Unfinished Agenda for Human Rights and Economic Justice in the Americas." The Plan of Action's heavy emphasis on traditional approaches to trade and economic integration coupled with its weak provisions on human rights means that these organizations will continue to confront the same challenges that they faced prior to the Summit, although their efforts to promote more responsive and accountable government policies and programs may be bolstered by a number of provisions included in the Plan of Action. The Summit event did prompt collaboration among organizations that may strengthen their future efforts to ensure the needs of poor and excluded people.

The potential impact of provisions on trade and economic integration issues became more uncertain only days after the Summit as a result of the devaluation of the Mexican peso, which brought to a head the crisis that had been gathering there. This, coupled with the outbreak of fighting between Ecuador and Peru, gave new credence to earlier warnings by some civil society organizations that Summit results might be seriously flawed because of the tendency of planners to overstate significantly the degree of political and economic progress in the hemisphere and consequently to fail to address issues requiring urgent attention.

The Summit itself featured no surprises given the completion a week earlier by government ministers of the Plan of Action. Consultations leading up to the Summit produced a progressive dilution of actions initially contemplated on a range of issues. The governments rejected proposals to create new institutions and, instead, most actions are to be carried out by existing institutions, with international follow-up and accountability contemplated only on selected measures.

There were a few signs of rifts in the overall consensus among heads of state on key issues. Central American countries raised serious concerns about the implications of the recently passed anti-immigrant measure in California and about a spreading climate of xenophobia in the U.S. Caribbean countries, as they expressed reservations about the impact on their small economies of the trade and economic integration measures contemplated by the Plan of Action and raised concerns about the serious need for debt relief.

The willingness of officials in some governments, together with the determination of some civil society organizations to be heard, resulted in a measure of participation by civil society representatives in Summit planning and the inclusion of representatives of civil society in some Summit events. The extent to which this will contribute to acceptance and institutionalization of such participation within each country, within regional institutions, and at future gatherings of this sort remains to be seen.

Although the Plan of Action initiatives are not assigned priorities, it is clear that they do not carry equal weight. Implicit priorities can be deduced based on the degree to which follow-up is most ensured in the Plan. The likelihood of follow-up corresponds to the degree of concreteness of the action, whether timelines are indicated, and whether there is a mechanism that will facilitate international accountability with regard to fulfillment of obligations undertaken in the Plan of Action.

Not surprisingly, trade and economic integration emerge as the top priorities. Other initiatives that promise specific, concrete action and include follow-up mechanisms are those dealing with narcotics trafficking, democracy, capital markets, and corruption. Environmental initiatives fall in a second tier with less precision about entities responsible for national level follow-up and reliance on existing institutions and networks. Likewise, the measures on health and education lack precise definition of implementing mechanisms.

Human rights measures focus heavily on eliminating discrimination against minority groups, indigenous peoples, people with disabilities, women, and children but are otherwise weak. The leaders did not approve the creation of a Civil Society unit within the Inter-American Development Bank as had been proposed earlier but promised only to "consider the development" of such a program.

The Plan of Action does incorporate a handful of concrete measures, such as access of women to land and productive resources, that correspond to recommendations of "Promises to Keep." On the other hand, many of the recommendations, such as those concerning civil-military relations or the need for a hemispheric Corporate Code of Conduct, are not addressed by the Plan of Action. In between there are a variety of measures that correspond to "Promises to Keep" recommendations but are vague on action steps or coincide only partially with the recommendations.

The human rights commitments by the Heads of State are disappointing. Failure to agree to complete ratification of the American Convention is striking, as is the failure to address the issues of impunity and civil-military relations. The Heads of State agreed to review the regulatory framework for non-governmental actors in their countries, but the review contemplated in the Plan of Action is far more limited than that recommended in "Promises to Keep." Finally, the "Promises to Keep" recommendations concerning public participation in macroeconomic policy deliberations and the establishment of consultative status at the Organization of American States for civil society organizations go unaddressed by the Plan of Action.

The Summit of the Americas consolidates some of the trade and macroeconomic policies that "Promises to Keep" endorsers seek to change and at the same time provides some new opportunities and tools for their efforts to promote "a brighter future for the peoples of the Americas." The sense of urgency and spirit of collaboration with which the original recommendations were offered are both reinforced by the Summit's outcome.

By the Roundtable of Western Hemisphere Women Leaders

Sponsored by the Inter-American Dialogue and the International Center for Research on Women

Communiqué to the Presidents of the Americas

About the Inter-American Dialogue

*T*he Inter-American Dialogue is a forum for sustained exchange among opinion leaders of the Western Hemisphere and an independent, nonpartisan center for policy analysis on economic and political relations in the Americas. The Dialogue regularly convenes private and public leaders from diverse political perspectives to search for cooperative responses to hemispheric problems. It seeks to bring fresh, practical proposals for action to the attention of governments, international institutions, and non-governmental organizations. Founded in 1982, the Dialogue is currently led by co-chair Peter D. Bell and acting co-chair Alejandro Foxley. Peter Hakim is the Dialogue's president.

The Dialogue's 100 members — from the United States, Canada and 20 Latin American and Caribbean countries — include five former presidents, prominent political, business, labor, academic, media, military, and religious leaders. At periodic plenary sessions, members analyze key hemispheric issues and formulate recommendations for policy and action. The Dialogue presents its findings in comprehensive reports that are circulated throughout the hemisphere and widely regarded as balanced and authoritative. The Inter-American Dialogue's research and publications are designed to improve the quality of public debate and decision on key issues in Western Hemisphere affairs. The Dialogue emphasizes four broad themes — democratic governance, inter-American institutions, economic integration, and social equity.

The Inter-American Dialogue is funded by private foundations, international organizations, corporations, Latin American and European governments, individuals, and the sale of publications.

About the International Center for Research on Women

*T*he International Center for Research on Women (ICRW) is dedicated to promoting development with women's full participation. ICRW works in collaboration with policy-makers, researchers, and practitioners throughout Africa, Asia, and Latin America to address the economic, social, and health status of women in developing countries. ICRW is engaged in policy-oriented research, program support and analysis services, and an active communications program. ICRW's focus is on economic policies, such as the effects of structural adjustment on women's employment and their access to credit and other resources; on the formation and dynamics of family and household structures; on women's health and nutrition as these relate to their roles as economic producers, nurturers and health care providers for their families; and on the links between women and environmental degradation and protection.

Contents

ICRW is a private, nonprofit organization that is supported by grants, contracts, and contributions from international and national development agencies, foundations, corporations, and individuals. Established in 1976, ICRW has its offices at: 1717 Massachusetts Ave. N.W., Suite 302, Washington, D.C. 20036, (202) 797-0007; FAX (202) 797-0020; E-Mail: icrw@igc.apc.org

Foreword

Democratic progress in Latin America will require that women gain an increasingly significant role in shaping policy and managing power. Today, there are only a smattering of women occupying leadership positions in the region — whether in business, government or academia. But it is unlikely that large numbers of women will take on national leadership responsibilities until all women are guaranteed equal opportunities — for education, employment and access to productive resources — and until laws are revised so they do not discriminate against women and instead ensure their full civil and human rights. The bitter fact is, however, that these issues are not being adequately addressed, in part because there are so few women leaders to pursue them. This vicious cycle has to be broken by working on both problems: by promoting more women to positions of power and decision; and by pressing hard for improvements in the lives of all women. These are some of the ideas that inspired the Inter-American Dialogue and International Center for Research on Women to convene a group of distinguished women from throughout the Americas to review the economic and social issues that affect women, and discuss proposals for addressing them.

The Roundtable of Western Hemisphere Women Leaders brought together a politically and professionally diverse group of over 30 prominent women — none of whom occupy a national government position — from the United States, Canada and 11 countries of Latin America and the Caribbean. Participants included a former central bank president, foreign minister, and chair of the U.S. International Trade Commission; others were human rights activists, foundation officers, business executives, and leading academics. Although the group disagreed on many points, the participants sought and found a shared commitment to the fundamental values of democracy and equity, and agreed on common policy prescriptions for empowering women as key actors in development.

Participants in the Roundtable succeeded in accomplishing three key goals:

- They reviewed from the perspectives of concerned women the important economic, political, and social issues affecting the hemisphere, including democratic governance and the collective defense of democracy; hemispheric economic integration and extending the benefits of growth; and sustainable development and social investment.

- They agreed to pursue the idea of building a network of women leaders in the hemisphere that would seek the active participation of women in all aspects of inter-American affairs; promote policy changes required to expand opportunities for women; and monitor the actions of governments and international organizations toward women.

- They issued a *Communiqué* to the heads of state who will meet at the Summit of the Americas — scheduled for December 1994 in Miami — urging them to expand investments in women's education, health care and economic opportunities; to support the full range of human rights for women; and to promote national and regional policies to empower women.

With this publication, we are delighted to present the results of the Roundtable. They include the eloquent opening remarks of U.S. Assistant Secretary of State Alexander Watson, and of Sonia Picado, Ambassador of Costa Rica — both of whom called for giving greater visibility to women and women's issues — and the luncheon address of Nancy Birdsall,

Executive Vice President of the Inter-American Development Bank, who emphasized that hard-nosed investments in women are among the most effective means for addressing poverty and inequality. The participants' communique is also included: this is a group statement and not every participant agrees fully with every phrase in the text; different women would undoubtedly emphasize different points. But it does reflect a broad consensus among the participants, each of whom subscribes to its overall content and tone, and supports its recommendations.

The Inter-American Dialogue and ICRW would like to thank all who assisted in the preparation and conduct of the Roundtable. Joan Caivano and Jill Merrick played key roles in organizing the meeting. Donna Lee Van Cott drafted the Rapporteur's Report, and Carole Douglis prepared the background paper for participants. We are especially grateful to the Roundtable participants whose contributions were crucial to its success. We also wish to express our appreciation to the Ford Foundation and the Inter-American Development Bank for their support of this initiative.

Mayra Buvinic
President
ICRW

Peter Hakim
President
Inter-American Dialogue

Communiqué
To the Presidents of the Americas from the Roundtable of Western Hemisphere Women Leaders

We are committed to the objectives of making democracy work and advancing equitable development in the Americas. This means, first, recognizing the contributions women make to economic growth and family welfare, and second, promoting the full and equal participation of women in all aspects and at all levels of politics, the economy and society, without which no nation can be truly democratic or achieve its economic potential.

Because women's equality is essential for advancing the tightly interconnected goals of democracy, prosperity and justice, we urge the leaders of the hemisphere to:

Enhance the equal opportunity of all women to contribute to development by investing to ensure their full access to:

- Quality education, particularly in science and technology
- Health care throughout their lives
- Effective labor rights that will increase quality employment for women in all sectors
- Wage equity
- Financial resources, credit and services
- Affordable and reliable child care
- Anti-poverty policies and programs that enhance women's productivity and income

Ensure full human rights for women:

- Assure equal access to securing decision-making positions in government and the private sector
- Institute and enforce laws and programs to eliminate violence against women, including domestic violence
- Encourage men to share domestic and child-rearing responsibilities
- Ensure women's reproductive rights

- Promote the role of women's groups in strengthening civil society
- Promote responsible use by the media of programming that portrays violence against and negative stereotyping of women

Strengthen the capacity of government, multilateral and donor institutions to achieve the above goals:

- Set targets for recruiting and promoting women staff
- Fund research, programs and policies to benefit women
- Provide staff training on gender issues

Monitor progress on the above goals:

- Establish specific monitoring mechanisms in existing institutions
- Support the collection and publication of data disaggregated by gender to insure accountability.

*Roundtable of
Western Hemisphere
Women Leaders*

*Washington, D.C.
October 7, 1994*

Signatories of the Communiqué

Mariclaire Acosta
Mexico

- President of the Mexican Commission for the Defense and Promotion of Human Rights

Mariana Aylwin
Chile

- Christian Democratic Deputy to the Chilean National Assembly

Carmen Barroso
USA/Brazil

- Director of the Population Program at the MacArthur Foundation

Eva Blay
Brazil

- Senator from São Paulo to the Brazilian Federal Assembly

Mayra Buvinic
USA/Chile

- President, International Center for Research on Women (ICRW)

Joan Caivano
USA

- Associate, Inter-American Dialogue

Soraya Castro
Cuba

- Research Associate at the Center for the Study of the United States, University of Havana; Visiting Fellow at ICRW

Lynn Cutler
USA

- Senior Vice President of The Kamber Group

Joan Dassin
USA

- Director of Latin American Programs at the Ford Foundation

Carole Douglis
USA

- Writer

Ana Milena Gaviria
Colombia

- Economist

Margarita Guzmán
Colombia

- Founder and Advisor to Cali Affiliate of Women's World Banking

Peter Hakim
USA

- President, Inter-American Dialogue

Patricia D. Jacobs
USA

- President and CEO of Greenleaf Associates, Inc.

Ana Julia Jatar
Venezuela

- Senior Fellow at the Inter-American Dialogue

Elizabeth Jelin
Argentina

- Senior Researcher at the Institute for Social Research, University of Buenos Aires

Clara Jusidman
Mexico

- President of the National Accord for Democracy

Ana Raquel de Kessler
Argentina

- Deputy to the Argentine National Assembly

Ruth de Krivoy
Venezuela

- President of *Síntesis Financiera*

Barbara McDougall Canada	•	Director of E.L. Financial Corporation and Public Governor of the Toronto Stock Exchange
Amparo Menéndez-Carrión Ecuador	•	Director General of FLACSO-Ecuador
Jill Merrick USA	•	Director of Communications, International Center for Research on Women (ICRW)
Lourdes R. Miranda Puerto Rico/USA	•	President and CEO of Miranda Associates, Inc.
Isabel Nieves Guatemala	•	Coordinator, Applied Social Sciences, Interamerican Development Advisory Services (IDEAS), Ltd./DataPro
Laura Novoa Vásquez Chile	•	President of the Board of *Participa* and Corporate Legal Counselor
María Otero USA	•	Director of Acción Internacional and Chair of the Inter-American Foundation
Marta Oyhanarte Argentina	•	President of Citizen Power
María Eugenia Phenon de Cotter Costa Rica	•	Executive Director of the Arias Foundation for Peace and Human Progress
Susana Pinilla Cisneros Peru	•	President of the National Association of Institutes for the Development of the Informal Sector (IDESI)
Paula Stern USA	•	Senior Fellow at the Progressive Policy Institute and President of the Stern Group
María Elena Torano USA	•	Chair & CEO of META (Maria Elena Torano Associates, Inc.)

Participating Observers

Nancy Birdsall USA	•	Executive Vice President, Inter-American Development Bank
Inés Bustillo Mexico/Uruguay	•	Economics Affairs Officer, United Nations Economic Commission for Latin America and the Caribbean (UNECLAC)
Katy Button USA	•	Staff Assistant, Office of the First Lady, The White House
Monica Campano Argentina	•	Coordinator for Women, National Institute of Public Administration
Joelle Barbot Colderin Canada	•	Senior Women in Development (WID) Advisor, Americas Branch, Canadian International Development Agency
Pamela Hardigan USA	•	Program Coordinator for the Women's Health and Development Program, PAHO
Margaret Lycette USA	•	Director of the Office of Women in Development, U.S. Agency for International Development (USAID)

Armando Martínez USA	•	Program Associate, Ford Foundation
Cathryn Thorup USA	•	Senior Summit Liaison for Non-Governmental Actors, Directorate of Inter-American Affairs, National Security Council
Gabriela Vega USA	•	Acting Chief, Women in Development Unit, Inter-American Development Bank

What Happened at the Roundtable

Rapporteur's Report

What particular perspective do women bring to the broad range of policy issues facing the Western Hemisphere? Are any of these policy areas inherently *women's* issues? What meaningful contribution can women leaders in the region make to the debate on the agenda of the Summit of the Americas? This meeting was convened to address these issues. We found that while the assembled women approached policy issues — encompassing the expansion of free trade, consolidation of democracy, and sustainable development — from a variety of perspectives that reflect the diversity of their background, experiences and political views, all of the women share a commitment to equity, to empowerment of women as key actors in development, and the indivisibility of interconnected policy issues.

Conceptual Issues

Before making concrete recommendations to the leaders attending the Summit of the Americas, the group focused on defining several conceptual issues related to addressing "women's issues" in the region.

There was considerable agreement over the definition of the problem: it was universally acknowledged that women suffer discrimination and are under-represented in positions of power and policy decision making. Economically, women suffer disproportionately from poverty and are under-represented in the private sector and disadvantaged in terms of access to capital. In addition, women throughout the region have specific problems related to their gender: lack of access to safe and effective reproductive health care; high levels of societal and domestic violence; a demeaning portrayal in the media that reinforces and perpetuates dysfunctional societal attitudes toward women; and an unequal burden in the domestic sphere — bearing primary responsibility for childcare and domestic labor.

The first conceptual problem the group confronted was whether their purpose in meeting was to consider "women's issues," or rather to discuss the agenda of the Summit of the Americas from a "woman's perspective." If the latter, what is the "woman's perspective"? While this question was never resolved, the group decided to focus on issues of particular concern to women, but underlining the importance of these to all of society. For example, inequities that limit opportunities for women impair the attainment of development goals for society as a whole.

The group also agreed to place any policy prescriptions in the broader framework of a commitment to values. If the Clinton administration were to present its goals in terms of "Making Democracy Work; Making Democracy Prosper; and Making Democracy Endure," the group would ask: "Toward what end?" Trade and economic development should not be considered as ends in themselves but, rather, as processes to achieve larger social goals. By the end of the meeting, the group decided that the key values women bring to this discussion are democracy and equity. Democracy and equity should, thus, be the goals of the initiatives proposed at the Summit, and they became the pillars of the fundamental statement of principle that framed the group's *Communiqué*.

It was also agreed that women's public roles both as economic actors in the informal sector — the entrepreneurial, high-risk, "grey market" economy — and as prime movers in a vibrant civil society — comprised of organizations working on issues of participation and human rights — could be utilized for implementing whatever initiatives are agreed upon at the Summit, and for achieving, ultimately, society's goals of equity and well-being.

A further conceptual issue received unanimous support. Participants agreed that the three "baskets" of issues presented by the Clinton administration — roughly, economics, democracy, and sustainable development — cannot be addressed in isolation. The interconnectedness of these issue areas makes it impossible adequately to prescribe policy in one area without considering the impact on other policy areas. Thus, the group resisted speaking in isolation of "social" issues — education, health, and discrimination — without explicitly acknowledging their integral connection to trade, economic development and full democracy.

Finally, the women agreed that their group was not diverse enough to be representative of all women in the hemisphere. Their higher relative access to opportunities distinguished them from the majority of the region's women, who are more likely to suffer from poverty and discrimination based on gender or ethnicity. They recognized that this provided them the opportunity, however, to avoid focusing on women only as a constituency for social programs, as many women's forums tend to do. They saw the Roundtable as an opportunity to offer the perspectives of women as economic and political actors in a forum that might garner greater attention because of the prestige of the participants.

Policy Discussion

A key theme that ran through the discussion of policy issues was the fact that women lack the access to decision-making power necessary to influence policy on these issues. While many women urged the group to consider ways to create access for women's voices and perspectives in the policy process, no agreement was reached on how this could be done. Others argued that getting women into top positions was not necessarily the solution to the problems of women: women's problems are society's problems, and men should be equally concerned with resolving them. It was noted that only two women will be participating in the Summit of the Americas.

There was agreement that several policies are crucial to rectifying the mentioned inequities. First, participants agreed that a concentrated investment in educating girls and women is required. Many participants noted that educational opportunities for girls have proven to make a significant contribution to economic development. Participants also agreed that equal opportunity must include increasing women's access to finance so that they can utilize their proven entrepreneurial skills — witnessed by profitable microenterprise banking programs in the developing world — to empower themselves as economic actors. All participants further agreed that the issue of universal and affordable childcare must be addressed in order to free women to participate to their full potential as economic actors and otherwise.

On the issue of trade, the discussion reflected current debates within the hemisphere: Does sustainable economic development require more regulation or less? Should NAFTA be the starting point for regional trade integration? What role do *Mercosur* and other agreements play? Trade presented philosophical issues that remain unresolved. Some women questioned whether free trade is really beneficial to

the resolution of social problems. The majority acknowledged that while the region has embraced the neoliberal trade model, poverty and inequality have not decreased, and two distinct economies — formal and informal — coexist. It was noted that more women are involved in the informal economy. Is government regulation of free trade the way to address the inequities of the free trade model? Or should civil society take the lead in addressing worker and environmental rights issues? The question of labor rights as they relate to women was considered particularly crucial. Some participants argued that laws assigning specific benefits to women are positive, while others suggested they reduce women's employment opportunities. Women have benefited by expanded opportunities from trade, but some have also suffered decreasing wages due to international competition. No agreement was reached on the extent to which labor and environmental regulations should be introduced into international trade negotiations.

The majority concluded that equity means combining the market with values, such as a commitment to democracy and fairness. While some concluded that special regulations for women were necessary, others argued that treating women as handicapped would further marginalize them. Women should be offered equal opportunity but not be treated separately as a labor or investment issue. All participants did agree, however, that the question of equity is fundamental to the resolution of these contested points.

A challenge in addressing the economic issues noted above is presented by the process, underway in many economies of the region, of redefining the role of the state. Many responsibilities — the provision of social services, health care, education — are moving to the private sector. This requires solutions that are not solely oriented toward government; new models are needed to address the private sector and civil society as actors in resolving society's problems. The invigoration of civil society and the central role of women in non-governmental organizations present opportunities for women to take the lead in the creation of these new models.

Another policy issue currently on the Summit agenda that received considerable attention was the importance of women in microenterprise development. It was recommended that creating access to capital and technology would help equalize opportunities for women entrepreneurs. The Summit's focus on health and education was viewed as particularly critical for women, so an effort should be made to direct resources towards girls and women in these areas.

Policy issues not on the agenda included the role of the communications media. Some urged the group to recommend that governments use the media as a tool for the inculcation of more progressive values — much like television has been used to provide AIDS education. Others urged that the media be more responsible and restrict portrayals of women that are demeaning or that incorporate violence against women as entertainment. The roles of women in the domestic sphere — as caregivers and leaders of households — were also mentioned as areas absent from the Clinton administration's current agenda. Issues faced by women in this sphere — in particular, the need for affordable and accessible child care — were considered by the group to be issues of equal importance to government and the private sector. Finally, many in the group expressed the desire to see reproductive rights issues figure prominently in the agenda.

Recent and Upcoming International Conferences with Critical Debate on Women's Issues

UN Conference on Human Rights, Vienna, June 1993

IDB Board of Governors Meeting, Guadalajara, April 1994

International Conference on Population and Development, Cairo, September 1994

UN High-Level Regional Preparatory Meetings for the Fourth World Conference on Women, Djakarta, June 1994

    Mar del Plata, September 1994

    Vienna, October 1994

    Dakar, November 1994

    Amman, November 1994

Summit of the Americas, Miami, December 1994

UN Social Summit, Copenhagen, March 1995

UN Fourth World Conference on Women, Beijing, September 1995

Strategy

Having tackled conceptual and policy issues, the group approached the question of strategy. How should women's issues, problems, and perspectives be presented to the principally male audience that would attend the Miami Summit? After some discussion, the group decided that its statement should be framed in a positive light. Rather than list women's problems and demands, the group should offer ways the region's leaders can work together to maximize the significant contribution of women in the several spheres under consideration: government, the economy, and sustainable development. It was noted that women's contributions in these areas always have been significant but have gone unnoticed and unheralded. The Summit provides an opportunity to acknowledge the significant contribution of women to development and democracy and create opportunities to "formalize" and maximize that contribution.

However, the group acknowledged the danger of "objectifying" or "instrumentalizing" women as a tool for development. Women's contribution must be presented as her prerogative rather than as a tool to be used by policy makers for solving the region's problems. In addition, the participants should be sure not to portray women as victims, as this portrayal has marginalized women in the past.

Many women made reference to the fact that the Summit comes at the mid-point in a series of critical international forums for the discussion of women's issues. An April 1994 Inter-American Development Bank Board of Governors meeting focusing on women in development in Guadalajara; the United Nations Conference on Human Rights in Vienna; a regional meeting in Mar del Plata, Argentina, from September 26 to 30, in preparation for 1995's United Nations World Conference on Women in Beijing; and the recent United Nations Conference on Population and Development in Cairo were cited as crystallizing international awareness and consensus on the importance of empowering women in addressing economic growth and development. Women were treated as integral to the solution of population and development problems, rather than as instruments to achieve particular goals, as had been the case in the past. The resolve of Latin American and Caribbean governments to resist pressure from the Catholic Church at the Cairo meeting demonstrated the increasing political clout of women in the region. The Cairo meeting was equally important in defining a more integral role for women as key actors in international meetings for non-governmental organizations — which are more likely than governments to be led by women. On the horizon are a meeting for women in the region in Dade County, Florida; the United Nations Conference on Social Development, to be held in Copenhagen in the spring of 1995; and the UN World Conference on Women in Beijing, scheduled for June. The sequence of these events around the Summit of the Americas provides an opportunity for women in the region to focus the Western Hemisphere's leaders on women's issues and to generate momentum for next year. In particular, it was suggested that the group's *Communiqué* specifically urge the hemisphere's leaders to foster the compilation of data on the socioeconomic condition of women in the region in order that the information be available for the Copenhagen and Beijing meetings.

Given the Clinton administration's criteria for agenda items for the Summit — that initiatives be (1) presidential; (2) realizable; (3) that there be consensus on moving forward on the initiative; and (4) that the initiative provides an opportunity for partnerships among government, the private sector, and civil society — the majority of participants recommended limiting the group's recommendations to initiatives that meet these criteria. In particular, the group should take advantage of the Clinton administration's expressed desire to prepare initiatives in the area of civil society, in order to strengthen this sector in the region and to draw attention to women's crucial role in it.

Moreover, given the number of other sectors that will be competing for the attention of the Summit leaders, it will be important for this group to follow-up on its recommendations if they are to bear fruit. Specifically, women's organizations should lobby to be involved in the design and implementation of initiatives created at the Summit, and should participate in monitoring the results of such initiatives. Follow up will be particularly critical with respect to funding, and women should lobby elected officials, using the electoral clout of women to ensure that programs of interest to them are undertaken.

Finally, the group questioned what would be the appropriate audience for their *Communiqué* on the agenda of the Summit of the Americas. While governments in the region are their primary audience, the group agreed that the *Communiqué* should be disseminated more widely, through the media and through the personal activities of participants in today's meeting.

Follow-Up Plans

In addition to drafting a *Communiqué* on women's issues and perspectives for the Summit of the Americas, one of the tasks of the participants was to discuss ways to create a network of women leaders in the hemisphere. Various alternatives for doing this were discussed, particularly with respect to undertaking follow up on the implementation of the Summit initiatives. Several proposals suggested working within the framework of existing bodies within the Organization of American States. Specific reference was made to revitalizing the OAS' Commission on Women, or to creating a space in the Unit for Democracy for the analysis of women's rights. A recommendation in this area might fall under the rubric of "Making Democracy Work" on the Summit agenda, as it relates to the reform of the OAS.

Others recommended that a possible Commission on Women be developed. Such a commission could be (1) created within the OAS; (2) expanded to include representatives from the multilateral banks and non-governmental organizations; or (3) created around the participants in today's meeting, but incorporating women representing a greater diversity of the hemisphere's female population. Another suggestion entailed utilizing a multilateral, independent institution such as the Facultad Latinoamericana de Ciencias Sociales (FLACSO) to coordinate the collection and dissemination of data on the status of women in the hemisphere. It was also suggested that commissions were necessary at the national level to lobby for women's initiatives and monitor their progress in each country.

October 1994

Women as Full Partners in Development and Democracy

Keynote Address by
Alexander F. Watson
Assistant Secretary of State for
Inter-American Affairs

Thank you very much. It is indeed a pleasure to be here with you this evening, and an honor to be here with so many distinguished experts on issues of concern to women in the Western Hemisphere. Throughout the Americas, women have played central roles in historic events, such as the women soldiers or Adelitas in the Mexican revolution, women suffragists in the United States, and the Argentine mothers in the Plaza de Mayo. And, of course, women contribute more quietly and often at great sacrifice to the quotidian struggle for life and dignity throughout the hemisphere. Yet for reasons which have only been all too apparent, their contributions to society and the family are often overlooked, and they are very frequently the victims of discrimination. Perhaps the traditional pain and suffering of women in the Americas was best captured by the Argentine poetess, Alfonsina Storni, in her 1920 poem "La que comprende." In this poem, Storni portrays a pregnant woman in church, imploring: "Senor, el hijo mio que no nazca mujer" (Lord, let my child not be born a woman).

Despite progress in recent years, women in our hemisphere are disproportionately poor. Prior to and during the 1980s both the absolute numbers and the proportion of women among the poor increased. Many women in our hemisphere live in precarious conditions; one example is that maternal mortality rates are estimated at 270 per 100,000 live births. Women suffer more than men from anemia, stunted growth from lack of proteins and calories, and iodine deficiency. In nine countries of the region, female illiteracy is 15 percent or more, and in three of them more than half the women are illiterate.

Although many countries in the region have enjoyed steady economic growth for the last five years, we must really question the value of economic development if its fruits are not going to be enjoyed fully by half of the population.

In short, women are interested in and deeply affected by the central issues the United States and the other countries in this hemisphere are trying to address: issues of democracy, prosperity, and equity.

The Summit of the Americas at which the chiefs of state and heads of government of the Western Hemisphere will convene at President Clinton's invitation in Miami in a couple of months will focus explicitly on these issues through its three central themes of "Making Democracy Work: Reinventing Government," "Making Democracy Prosperous: Hemispheric Economic Integration," and "Making Democracy Endure: Sustainable Development."

We believe that specific initiatives generated by the Summit of the Americas will be tools to forge opportunities for both women and men, and to further the progress women have already achieved.

Making Democracy Work: Reinventing Government

Women cannot become full partners in the hemisphere's development until their right to live free from all forms of violence or discrimination in both public and private spheres is recognized and protected. Women's rights are human rights, and violence against women should be seen as a human rights violation and as a public rather than a private issue. Through an initiative under the rubric of "Making Democracy Work," the United States is proposing to our colleagues in the hemisphere actions to encourage development of private voluntary associations, many of which have been pioneers in protecting women's rights.

Although civil and family codes affecting women have been very restrictive in the past, many encouraging new laws have been passed to address these problems in our hemisphere. In the United States, some of the best examples have happened within our own lifetimes: legislation providing for widows otherwise facing destitution to gain access to the Social Security pensions of their husbands; legislation protecting women's rights to property and credit in their own names; and a judicial system and police force becoming more responsive and sensitive to women's needs for protection from domestic violence.

Important legislation has also been passed in other countries of the hemisphere, such as the new family codes in El Salvador and Trinidad and Tobago. For all of us, the continuing challenge is to see that such legislation is improved and — even more importantly — faithfully implemented.

In Brazil, another example, police stations staffed by women and for women have encouraged women to denounce attacks against them. These special police stations have been a model followed by other countries. I can remember when I was in Brazil as Deputy Chief of Mission of our Embassy these Delegacias were being established for the first time and I remember talking at great length with a leading Brazilian political figure and leader of this fight for women's rights in Brazil, Ruth Escobar, on exactly how these Delegacias were working.

But beyond legislation and government programs, the key to women's becoming full partners in our hemisphere lies in a generalized awareness that the future of society is dependent upon full partnership of citizens regardless of gender.

Women can only become full partners in the hemisphere's development, however, when they have an equal opportunity to influence and decide public policy at all levels. In Latin America and the Caribbean we have seen efforts to involve women in public policy through political affirmative action. For example, in Argentina a law requires political parties to present slates with a minimum of 30 percent of female candidates. The group assembled here tonight is a living example of what all women can achieve, if given the basic opportunities and resources.

The United States will propose an initiative at the Summit of the Americas, under the theme of "Making Democracy Work," which would commit governments of the region to take concrete actions to encourage the development throughout the hemisphere of civic-minded NGOs, and private voluntary organizations, such as Poder Ciudadano and Conciencia in Argentina, and Participa in Chile, which are major threads in the fabric of civil society.

Making Democracy Endure: Sustainable Development

Improving and implementing legislation to protect women is not enough by itself. Women make a significant contribution to economic development, and deserve recognition and encouragement in their endeavors in the informal economy and deserve an opportunity to participate in the formal economy. Women in urban areas are skillful entrepreneurs, starting up small businesses with next to no seed money. Estimates are that in the shantytowns or favelas surrounding large cities, a staggering percentage — up to 70-80 percent — of households are headed by women.

USAID and the Inter-American Development Bank have introduced microenterprise loans to encourage and nurture microenterprise as an employment alternative, with great success. At the Summit of the Americas, the United States will propose an initiative on Nurturing Microenterprise, an integrated set of projects that would further promote microenterprise and small business development. These projects could help non-governmental organizations provide financing on market terms, reduce legal obstacles that hurt microenterprises, lower transaction costs for small loans made by commercial banks to microenterprises, and encourage the development of business advisory services for small businesses — all of which should benefit women.

Another critically important area to improve women's standard of living throughout the hemisphere is health care. Women's health is a factor in the productive capacity of countries all over the world, and its importance was just recently recognized in the Cairo Conference on Population. The Summit of the Americas, through an initiative on equitable access to basic health services proposed by the United States, could call for each country's commitment to ensure equitable, universal access to basic health services so as to reduce child mortality rates in the region by one third and maternal mortality rates by half by the year 2000.

Although human rights, economic opportunities, political affirmative action, and health are all important, we must not forget education. In the very high-growth economies of East Asia, for example, resources were targeted in the 1950s and 1960s to give priority to universal primary education of girls and boys. I think that Nancy Birdsall has been a pioneer in analyzing this data. This front-loading of resources formed a solid base for girls and boys to continue successfully into secondary and university-level education.

In some countries there are still gender biases and stereotypes limiting women's occupational choices to dead-end, low-paying jobs. Let all of us in the hemisphere examine our educational programs with the objective of replacing gender-restrictive stereotypes with encouragement and opportunities for girls and boys throughout their lives. Careful and hard-hitting economic studies by the World Bank and others have shown that educating girls and women is an essential investment with a very high return in economic productivity, improved health, sustainable population growth, better natural resource management, and greater civic participation. All of these benefits will serve our hemisphere well in competing in the new world environment of free trade and economic integration.

Through an initiative of "Universal Access to Quality Primary Education," the United States proposes that the Summit of the Americas call for a hemispheric partnership to re-focus existing resources more effectively toward quality primary education through reforms in financing, decentralization, and a reordering of budget priorities so as to achieve 100 percent primary school completion rates and 75 percent secondary school enrollment by the year 2000.

There is still a long way to go before women are full partners in our hemisphere. But times are certainly changing. Today, from Rigoberta Menchu in Guatemala to dissident poet Maria Elena Cruz Varela in Cuba, women are speaking out with conviction, defending not only their rights but those of their fellow human beings. I believe that if she were here now, the woman in Alfonsina Storni's poem would be encouraged to see the changes forged by people like yourselves, and would share the hope which we all share for the future of women — and men — in our hemisphere. Thank you very much.

These remarks were given at the opening reception for the Roundtable of Western Hemisphere Women Leaders on October 6, 1994 at the Inter-American Development Bank in Washington, D.C.

Trade, Democracy, Rights Elude Latin American Women

Keynote Address by Sonia Picado Costa Rican Ambassador to the United States

Thank you so much for that very nice introduction. I always like to take opportunities like this: working with women and for women is working for human rights, and it is part of my life. I would definitely suggest that we send your words, Ambassador Watson, to all the people who are working on the Summit. In preparing this presentation I reviewed the summary of the first draft, that has been prepared for the Summit, and in that first draft women are quite invisible. I think complementing it with what you have said here would be extremely useful. Actually, many of the things that I am going to say you have already said, but I think it is always good to over-emphasize. Much of this will be, I am sure, the subject of a long and very rich discussion tomorrow.

I would like to start with something personal that shows how difficult it is to be a woman in any position that is classified as "masculine." I have felt very welcome in Washington, and I am very grateful for that. However, almost in every reception or meeting, people will come to me and say, "How is your husband, the Ambassador? Are we going to meet the Ambassador?" And when I say, "I am the Ambassador," people look at me embarrassed, not knowing what to say, or wondering, what is she doing here?

About two days ago a couple approached me and, of course, the question arose again, "Is your husband coming? Is the Ambassador coming?" I said, "I am the Ambassador." And so the man said, "And where is your husband?" I said, "I am divorced," and he looked at his wife and said, "Well, I guess that if she were an ambassador, I would be divorced from her too." And so I said, "That sounds very typical, but just think how unfair it is because had you been nominated ambassador, I am sure she would have been very supportive of you," and that is the reality of women.

The Summit of the Americas is going to be a meeting of powerful, political men with an amazingly small representation of women. For that reason I think it is important that dialogues such as this roundtable take place, because we have to be heard at the Summit.

I would like to take up the key issues that have been raised in the document regarding the Summit. Consolidating democracy, of course, is a key issue. The American Convention of Human Rights, Article 23, guarantees democracy and the right for every citizen to elect and to be elected. In this, the role of women is extremely important. Very recently, I visited the Electoral Tribunal in Mexico which was preparing for the election. They mentioned that one of the problems they encountered in implementing the new voter identity card was that men did not want their wives to be identified and to have a voting card. The men felt that they had the right to vote for the whole family, including sons, daughters and wives.

This gives me the opportunity to say that even though elections do not make democracy, as we all know, elections are a very important starting point. They are an important point to begin training women for participation, not only in political issues, but in civil, political life. Actually, there are many women that participate during political campaigns, but this does not translate into political positions, as we well know. I think it would be important in communities and municipalities to support women candidates because in Latin America men might "permit" their wives to serve in a municipality. Many would not, however, allow their wives to assume a cabinet post, and I can tell you that myself.

Not many women have the opportunity to participate after elections in a follow-up process of education in democratic values. International financial support and observer missions go to Latin America — as in the Haitian case or Nicaragua in 1989 — but afterwards, money for development or education is not forthcoming. I am very glad, Ambassador, that you emphasized education. I think it is the key issue if we want to have sustainable democracy.

We also need to change the very vertical mentality in Latin America. The vertical mentality starts at home, goes on in church, in school, and in the army. Our culture has been a culture of violence, a very discriminating culture, and you can only change culture through education.

I think it is also very important when we talk about consolidating democracy to talk about strengthening institutions. I feel worried about the lack of confidence that our people in Latin America have shown for political institutions, political parties, executive leaders and especially for the judiciary. If you consider the *autogolpes* of Fujimori or Serrano, they were issued in the name of a corrupt judiciary, corrupt Congress and corrupt politicians. For democracy to prevail it is necessary to trust the judiciary and to change the contents of the legal system. I would like to point out that women are now almost half of law faculties, and that we need to change the mentality of all lawyers — men and women. Let me tell you that as dean of a law school (I was former Dean of the University of Costa Rica's Law School), I tried very hard to change the legalistic approach that lawyers have in Latin America. Ambassador Watson, you mentioned the changes in family codes. Changing the law is always problematic, but it is indispensable if we want to reduce the gap between written law and reality. In the case of women, family codes are crucial in ensuring women access to the legal system. However, women do not know their rights and they do not dare use the law. In general, most women are afraid to go to a lawyer and to use the legal system.

In terms of the law, I would like to emphasize that in Latin America our legislation goes back to the Roman law, to the Napoleonic Code which compared women to the disabled and children. You may not be aware of the fact that in Argentina and Brazil, until a few years ago, there was no divorce, which meant that women had no legal rights over their children. For example, they could not take them out of the country. In Spain, until the death of Franco in 1975, women were not allowed to open a bank account or to own property. That is still true in some areas of Latin America.

Regarding land reform, we must emphasize that land has to go to the "family" in a very broad sense, because in our countries, due to the influence of religious tradition, you will find that "family" means mother, father and two, three or eight kids provided they are bound by legal and religious ties. In Costa Rica, 50 percent of the children in the two largest provinces are born without a father, so when you are talking about agrarian reform, unless you mention the extended family and specify that property should go to women, they will never be able to have access to it.

Following more or less the summary of the Summit document, we turn to strengthening the Organization of American States. I think the Organization of American States has tremendous potential and I am very hopeful that it will be able to play a key role in Latin America. However, I would emphasize that we must have gender awareness at the OAS. There are no women at the Inter-American Commission of Human Rights, and I was the only woman at the Inter-American Court of Human Rights. I can tell you that there is discrimination.

I feel also that everybody is talking about strengthening the different organizations of the system, but nobody has mentioned the Inter-American Commission of Women. I must say that in many ways the Commission has not worked up to expectations, but neither has the OAS. I wonder if the Summit should not propose that the Inter-American Commission of Women be strengthened and reformed. Instead of taking the conservative approach with which it works in many of our countries, it should be changed into an organization that will transform women, that will raise gender issues, the way this seminar wants them to be addressed. By the way, I think that before the Summit, you should distribute among the presidents of Latin America a definition of "gender" issues. Most of them don't know what we are talking about. I can tell you it's true.

In talking about economic integration, I think it is very important to decide how far we want to go. How far the United States is willing to go at the Summit to have Latin Americans as real partners in commerce, as real partners in NAFTA, in a more open Latin America. We are worried about the last events in Congress — Fast Track is postponed, and so is the Interim Trade Program. Let me say that the loss of the ITP — which was offered by Vice President Gore in Tegucigalpa and gave the benefits of NAFTA to textiles — marked a tremendous loss of jobs for women in Central America. Many women work in textiles and these factories are already going to Mexico. Unless we get something done very fast, a lot of women are going to be without a job.

I think it is important to understand that we emphasize trade because without trade we will not have democracy and we will not have sustainable development. Jose Figueres-Ferrer used to say "Don't give us aid, pay better prices for our products; don't give us aid, be partners in commerce," and this was 40 to 50 years ago. I think it still is a claim that is worth

listening to. In that respect I was very happy to hear you, Ambassador Watson, mention the fact that women are the poorest among the poor — *la pobreza tiene cara de mujer* — poverty has the face of a woman, and for them we need more trade, more jobs, more housing.

In that respect, let me say that we should not make the same mistakes of the 1960s. In the 1960s, development policies came to Latin America without any consideration of their impact on women, or on poor people for that matter. The aid came mainly to men — to high-class and middle-class men — to political men. A lot of the money went into Miami or Swiss banks and the gap between the rich and the poor was larger than ever. Women were excluded from the benefits of that development. They left their homes and land at the countryside which created even more poverty in our cities. Every time we talk about people we must emphasize that women are "people." Otherwise the technical assistance, the support will again be given to men, to politically connected men in Latin America.

It is important when we talk about an "alliance with nature" to realize that we need to fight poverty, which I consider the main violation of human rights on the continent. Every country lost income in what we call the "lost decade" in the 1980s and we must catch up. You cannot ask women to protect the environment if they need to cut wood to feed their family. Poverty is the most devastating aggressor of the environment; we can see this very clearly in Haiti.

In the Universal Declaration of Human Rights, it says that every person is entitled to equal rights. I think the Summit of the Americas will offer the possibility of achieving that equality. I am worried, however, that the wording of the agenda still talks about giving help to people — the poor, the indigenous population, and women — and by doing so women could again become invisible. Why? Because women's problems belong to all of America, while the problems of indigenous populations is not the same. It is very serious, but it has to be focused in a very different way than that of women. So when we say health, education, labor should go to cover minorities, we are making women more invisible. We are not minorities; we are in many cases a majority. Gender cannot be misunderstood in this respect.

The Summit is a wonderful opportunity for an agenda of the future, for hemispheric cooperation. I hope there is the political will to include among those goals the empowerment of women. I cannot find a word in Spanish that is equivalent to empowerment. I think it is a wonderful word that I cherish very much and it should be carried to the Summit.

Before I presented my credentials to President Clinton, a good friend said, "Sonia, I think you should use this as an opportunity to bring up one or two issues, instead of just making it a social event as many people do." Well, the main point I wanted to make was how much I admire the work that he and Mrs. Clinton have done for women. I said, "Mr. President, you have convened a Summit of the Americas. Latin America is a land of *machistas.* You have fought for women in the United States. Please help Latin American women by making them visible at the Summit."

We are here for that reason. I welcome the participants. Knowing many of them and knowing the wonderful work they have done, I am sure that they will help the President and all of you put women on the agenda of the Summit. Thank you.

These remarks were given at the opening reception for the Roundtable of Western Hemisphere Women Leaders on October 6, 1994 at the Inter-American Development Bank in Washington, D.C.

Economic Growth Follows Investing in Women: IDB

Keynote Address by Nancy Birdsall Executive Vice President of the Inter-American Development Bank

I want to start not by going directly to the issue of women, but by talking first about poverty and inequality in this hemisphere. I will go from there to some examples of what the IDB is doing to address poverty and inequality, in particular through programs for women. There is a message in this particular sequence — it is true that addressing the deep problems of poverty and inequality in the hemisphere means addressing the needs of women. But it is equally important, and I think an important point for the upcoming Summit, that hard-nosed investments in women are among the most effective and highest return investments for addressing poverty and inequality. And poverty and inequality must be addressed in Latin America, and I believe also in the United States, to ensure sustainable growth.

Here are a few facts about inequality in the Americas, in the northern part of the hemisphere as well as in the South. In the United States, as reported in the Washington Post, there are nearly 40 million people, 15 percent of the population now living in poverty — the highest since 1965, except for one year during the recession in the 1980s. This is despite healthy overall economic growth in the region in the last few years. Inequality in the United States has also risen with the top 5 percent of households increasing their income share to 20 percent and the share of the poorest 20 percent of households falling from over 4 percent several years ago to about 3.5 percent today. The situation in Latin America is even worse. Average incomes are lower, absolute poverty is higher, while inequality in the region is worsening. In Brazil, for example, the ratio of income of the richest 20 percent of households to the poorest 20 percent of households is 25 to 1. Of all the regions in the world, Latin America has had and continues to have the highest levels of inequality.

The setting for this, which is also the setting for the Summit of the Americas, is one which has also had tremendous success, particularly in the last five years, in macroeconomic stabilization, with inflation coming down, and in some fundamental structural reforms, especially trade liberalization; tax reform; and privatization, which has relieved the public sector of the budget strains of subsidizing inefficient state-owned enterprises. Investment and exports are increasing, private capital is flowing into the region and there has been a return to economic growth.

In some Latin American countries, these reforms and the resulting return to growth have helped the poor. They have also helped the rich — and much more. In other countries, particularly those in the early stages of these reforms, the poor have suffered — and the rich have suffered much less. Growth is necessary to relieve poverty and inequality and the economic reforms so successfully undertaken by so many countries in Latin America are critical to growth. But those reforms and this growth are far from sufficient in terms of addressing the deeply rooted problem of inequality in the region. A much more direct attack is needed.

This brings me to the issue of women. As Ambassador Picado said last night to those of you who were here, "la cara de la pobreza es la mujer" — "the face of poverty is a woman's face." This is true in Latin America as in other regions. Women, because they are poor, are least able to exploit the benefits of the economic reforms and of market-led growth. They have also been most vulnerable to the costs of these reforms. For the poor in general, and for women who are over-represented among the poor, the key in the future is equity-led growth. I believe that one path for this group is to ensure that the Summit, directly and indirectly, endorses those programs that constitute equity-led growth. A concerted attack on inequality is an attack on women's unequal status, and an attack on women's unequal status is an attack on inequality and on poverty.

Let me now go to some of the specific programs we are working on in the IDB that address the problems of inequality and poverty by addressing the needs of women. I will talk about three areas. The first of the three areas, social reform, is one in which the IDB and the other multilateral institutions have recently agreed to renew their efforts. There has been a lot of progress in Latin America in this area and women have benefitted from it. For example, the total fertility rate in Latin America has declined from 5.8 in

1965 to 3.2 two years ago, and contraceptive use has increased from 36 percent in the 1970s to just about 50 percent in the 1980s. (The issue of fertility and contraceptive use is a sensitive one in the region. The discussions in Cairo helped to provide a framework for addressing this issue in the region. I believe that further progress in these areas is absolutely key to unleashing women's potential and ensuring that women are fully empowered.) In addition, the literacy rate in Latin America for women as a percentage of the rate for men has increased in the last decade, while infant and maternal mortality have declined. All these are healthy signs.

The IDB has agreed through its shareholders to ensure that over the next four or five years at least 40 percent of the dollar volume of our new lending commitment and 50 percent of our operations address the social agenda, through support for programs in health and education, as well as civil society and the environment, that clearly help the poor and women. The approach to this agenda in the Bank is largely, though not entirely gender-neutral. The approach in the preliminary Summit document is gender-neutral. Because women are most vulnerable and because they are concentrated among the poor, it is women who will be beneficiaries of these programs, so that treating these programs as gender-neutral is reasonable. The greatest progress in health and education for women in the world in the last three decades has been in East Asia, and there was never any discussion in East Asia that was anything but gender-neutral. Women and girls benefitted because the emphasis was on universal education, universal health care, and universal access to family planning.

Let me go now to a second area of support, the private sector. In this area, it is critical to target programs for women. As a bank we have emphasized women's productive roles through projects in microenterprise finance, in technical and vocational training, and in support to women in the labor market. Let me give you a few details on each of these. In the microenterprise area, we estimate that credit programs we have financed have helped nearly 100,000 women to start, expand, or consolidate micro and small scale businesses. For example, the Centro Femenista de Acción e Información in Costa Rica is implementing an innovative self-help housing program, which I had the pleasure of visiting. This program provides credit, logistical support and technical assistance to women-owned businesses that construct low cost housing in and around San Jose. What is interesting about the program is that women are managing the construction of the houses — managing supplies, working with the carpenters and engineers, participating in the entire process both from the business and the engineering point of view.

Other programs that we support, such as a $24 million global credit program for microenterprises in El Salvador, do not single out women but support the informal sector. These programs for microenterprises exploit new technology developed by NGOs such as "Acción" and "Finca" that give women micro-entrepreneurs access to credit on fair market terms and at market interest rates, as well as provide advice on managing their businesses and marketing their products. Typically in these programs, no collateral is required and credit extends not only to manufacturing, but to services and commercial initiatives where women are concentrated. Financial institutions are finding that it is profitable to extend credit in these areas, despite the relatively small size of the loans. A credit program in Guatemala, for instance, has a default rate of 0 percent and a return of capital of 100 percent. What we have learned from these programs is increasingly well known: women make good investments.

Our unit on Women in Development is now undertaking a study on financial services for women microentrepreneurs. The objective of this study is to identify means not only to maintain these programs but to ensure that they expand, that they reach more and more women, and that they become sustainable. The critical approach here is to expand the programs to financial intermediaries outside the formal systems (such as credit unions and cooperative groups) and to gradually bring them in to the formal financial systems of bank supervision and prudential regulation.

In the area of vocational-technical training, there are two important loans that we have recently developed: a $40 million dollar loan for a labor force training program in Chile, and a similar $152 million loan in Argentina. These projects are open to men and women but have particular components focused on ensuring that women have access to and are encouraged to participate. To ensure that women have equal opportunities for technical and vocational training, there is funding for promotional campaigns that invite women to explore technical occupations and for demonstration programs in non-traditional, high demand occupations; funding to train counselors and

trainers in how to encourage women to take up new non-traditional occupations; and funding to ensure that there are subsidies or facilities for child care. Half (more than 50,000) of the beneficiaries of these programs are women, and many of them are receiving training in such non-traditional areas as welding and the installation of telephone equipment.

To support women in their efforts to enter into the labor market, we are currently developing pilot programs which make it easier for women to work — literally — by relieving them of the worry of child care. Centers in El Salvador and Nicaragua, for example, will be set up near employers and market areas, to provide not only child care but child health and nutrition services as well.

Finally, in this category of the private sector, I would like to mention briefly the glass ceiling issue. We don't see very many women in Latin America in the private sector — indeed, even among this group representing leadership of women in the region, the private sector is not very well represented. In the 1980s, only an estimated 16 percent of administrators and managers in the region were women. I am surprised that it is that high given that whenever I visit countries and have meetings with the private sector, including with the banking community (which has been more penetrated by women, at least in Europe and the United States), there has never once been a woman at those meetings. I think that as a group we need to think about what can be done to address the likelihood that there is a glass ceiling in the profit-making private sector in the region.

Now I would like to describe briefly a third critical area of IDB support for women: support for modernization of the state and for civil society. In terms of modernization of the state, the Bank is focusing on judicial and legislative reform. But we must go further. The economic reforms during the adjustment period of the 1980s focused on reducing the role of the state where it didn't belong. The reforms of the 1990s must build up the capacity of the state and of government institutions to do what they do need to do in areas where they need to be. An example is the area of security. Crime and violence is not just an issue for the middle class and the rich of clipped wallets and burglaries of condominiums. Crime and violence affect the poor, and especially affect poor women inside and outside the home. The threat of crime and violence in the streets as well as in the home affects women more than men. A recent

PAHO study estimates more than one quarter of women in the region have been physically abused or assaulted. This entire area of security is a critical one for women. Also important for women are property rights and improved enforcement of contracts.

The Bank is also taking major steps to improve our capacity to work with various institutions of civil society in the region — not only NGOs, but trade unions, community, church, and other groups that constitute a network of civil society. It is obvious that in Latin America women are the backbone of civil society. NGOs in the region that provide social services are, for the most part, led by women and include mostly women participants at the community level. The contribution of women via informal non-government groups came out very clearly in the Women's Forum that the Bank sponsored in April at the time of our Annual Meeting in Guadalajara. The energy and commitment of women to these groups shows the tremendous potential that can be unleashed in the region to work not only on the economic issues, which I have emphasized being an economist and a banker, but on social problems and on issues of democracy and human rights and of building institutions that make life civilized in the larger sense.

Let me end with a few conclusions. First, the IDB is a bank, and as a bank it sponsors these programs that address the needs of women because they are good investments, because they contribute to economic growth. They attack the problem of inequality which in turn can and will contribute to sustainable economic growth.

Second: What can this group do, different from what the IDB does, to advance this process in the context of the upcoming Summit? I have two suggestions. First, of all the recommendations which are in the draft communiqué for the Summit, I would focus on the need for a follow-up mechanism, to monitor how programs endorsed by the Summit affect women. Much of what the Summit is likely to endorse, as Assistant Secretary of State Watson said last night, will be potentially good for women. The issue is: will new or strengthened programs and new hemispheric policies reach women, ensure a level playing field for them, and ensure their full potential? While it is important to work toward the final Summit communiqué having an explicit reference to women, it is even more important to push for a mechanism of follow up.

This group has the potential to become a network to promote women into senior political administrative positions in the region. As leaders, you can focus on leadership. Such a focus would be different from the focus of the multilateral financial institutions on productive investments, and on poverty. Women's leadership would also clearly contribute to growth — and to the critical battle in the region against poverty and inequality. Thank you very much.

These keynote remarks were given at the luncheon session of the day-long Roundtable of Western Hemisphere Women Leaders on October 7, 1994 at the Inter-American Development Bank in Washington, D.C.

Investing in Women in Latin America and the Caribbean

A Contribution to the Summit of the Americas — Background Document

INTRODUCTION

During the 1980s, economic crises in the Latin American and Caribbean (LAC) countries virtually wiped out hard won gains in living standards made over the prior two decades. The gap between rich and poor widened in most countries, and the share of the population living in poverty rose sharply: from 26.5 percent of the population in 1980 to 31 percent in 1989, according to World Bank regional estimates, or from 41 to 44 percent in the same time period, according to the United Nations Economic Commission on Latin America and the Caribbean (ECLAC).[1,2]

Although the 1990s have seen renewed economic expansion — 1994 is expected to mark the fourth consecutive year of 3 percent growth — this growth has benefited primarily the wealthy. U.N. economists project that if current trends continue, poverty and inequity will continue to grow between now and the year 2000, carrying with them the threat of rising social unrest.[3] There is a consensus among governments, international donors and NGOs that top priority for public and private sector social reforms is investment in people and, more specifically, in raising the productivity and income of the poor.

Investing in girls and women is key to any social reform package seeking to reduce poverty and promote growth in the region. Two decades of research links investment in girls and women with improved performance in economic development projects, increased child well-being, and democratic participation.

It is now the stated policy of international financial institutions such as the Inter-American Development Bank (IDB) and the World Bank, and bilateral donors such as the U.S. Agency for International Development (USAID) and the Canadian International Development Agency (CIDA) to promote policies and projects that enhance women's capacity to earn income. However, there is far to go before such efforts realize their full potential. As recent reviews show, there remains a wide gap between policies that call for investing in women as economic agents and action toward those goals.

Therefore, we urge the leaders of the hemisphere to promote progress by endorsing a major commitment to invest in the region's women and women-based organizations as an initiative on the agenda of the Summit of the Americas. To a large extent, this is a commitment to reallocate international, bilateral, and national resources so that action will match stated policies. For rhetoric to become reality, the following is needed:

1. Reallocate national and international resources to invest in women and women-based NGOs throughout the region.

2. Reform policies and institutions to make concrete, measurable progress toward meeting women's needs. Strengthen women-based organizations throughout the region.

3. Establish mechanisms to assess and monitor progress toward enabling women to become full players in the economy and society at large.

Why Invest in Women?

- Investing in women is vital to economic development. Investing in women has led to long-term gains in health and reduction in fertility, which in turn helped Latin American and Caribbean women pour into the work force during the "lost decade" of the 1980s. Economic activity rates for women in Latin American countries grew by 13 percent on average during the 1980s — compared with virtually no growth in economic activity rates among men.[4] By increasing their work force participation and their contributions to household income, women helped poor families weather the economic crises of the 1980s.[5]

- Investing in women reduces poverty, since women are disproportionately poor. Despite their increased economic activity, estimates show that both the absolute numbers and the proportion of women in poverty grew during the 1980s in urban areas, and stayed at a high (56 percent) level in rural areas.[6] Women are poor because they have restricted access to land, capital, and modern technology. They are more likely than men to work in the informal sector, where pay is often below minimum wage and no social safety net exists. Even in the formal job market, women currently earn on average only 60-75 percent of what men earn.[7]

- Investing in women is investing in the future. A "virtuous circle" exists between increasing women's income and increasing children's health and education. This connection exists because women prefer to spend more of their income on their families, resulting in better outcomes for children. In Brazil, for instance, income in the hands of a mother translates into a positive effect on child health 20 percent greater than income controlled by a father. Similar benefits have been found in Guatemala and Chile.[8,9,10]

- Investing in expanding women's economic and social opportunities helps increase equity between urban and rural, privileged and poorer people. While progress has been made overall during the last 20 years, sharp differences exist among women in life expectancy at birth, total fertility rates, and primary school enrollment, both within and between countries. For instance, the life expectancy at birth varies by more than 20 years between countries. Similarly, the total fertility rate varies by up to five births per woman. The maternal mortality ratio varies from 5 mothers' deaths per 100,000 live births to nearly 500.[11,12,13]

- Investing in women contributes to free and stable democracies. Targeting women is an effective way to curb the poverty and hopelessness that is transmitted between generations of families and that can lead to social instability. Investing in women gives them the tools to increase their participation in civil society. No true democracy exists without the full participation of half the population.

What to Do Now:
Invest in Women as Wage Earners

The ability of women to increase their work productivity and wages translates into greater economic output and better nourished, healthier children with a brighter future. Yet although women now make up some 29 percent of the region's labor force — close to 50 percent in some Caribbean countries — they have far less access to useful technical and vocational training or financial capital than men, and tend to be shut out of higher paying work.[14]

Conventional vocational training for women is inadequate as it channels them into low-paying, traditionally female work.[15] Lack of training partly accounts for the fact that women work in industry in lower numbers than men — except in the assembly lines of export processing zones (EPZs). Employment in EPZs in a number of countries more than tripled between 1975 and 1986, with the majority of jobs going to women. Such jobs, however, tend to be low paid, repetitive, and dead-end.[16,17]

Recommendations:

- Promote labor-intensive economic growth policies.

- Legislate and enforce anti-discriminatory labor policies.

- Revamp technical and vocational training programs to help women gain non-stereotyped, higher-productivity, higher-paying positions.

- Provide tax and other incentives to the private sector to implement policies for the hiring and promotion of women.

- Design social investment funds and public works programs to ensure that women have equal access to funding offered and jobs created. Set target levels for women's participation in such funds and programs.

- Use intermediary institutions and social marketing techniques to inform women of their rights and new opportunities, and to challenge prejudices that keep women in low-paying, traditionally female occupations.

- Finance, from public and private sector sources, affordable and reliable child care options for working women.

Invest in Women in the Informal Sector and Self-Employment

Because of barriers to formal employment, women enter the informal sector in disproportionate numbers. There they operate the smallest marginal enterprises for payment that is often below minimum wage. In Bolivia, 61 percent of working women work on their own. In Mexico, women account for 52 to 62 percent of all informal sector workers.[18,19] While the informal sector grew throughout the region by about 20 percent during the 1980s, incomes in the sector dropped by 41 percent.[20]

It takes only modest funding to help women already in the informal economy to increase profits, generate more employment, and sometimes "graduate" into more stable positions in the formal sector. Increases in profits of women-operated enterprises range from 25 to 100 percent in some programs.[21] Payback rates approach 100 percent.[22]

Recommendations:

- Make the necessary changes in the financial system, legal structure, and overall economic environment to increase low income women's access to financial services, including savings.

- Promote and fund lending programs designed to bolster the economic performance of low income women entrepreneurs and producers.

- Promote and finance strong private sector financial intermediaries and business NGOs that lend to women.

- Set aside a quota of funds for women's enterprises that includes training and technical assistance to increase the productivity of these enterprises.
- Reform social security to include a safety net for women in the informal sector.

Help Women and Their Families Rise Above Poverty

Evidence suggests that poverty is becoming "feminized." Estimates show that during the 1980s both the absolute numbers and the proportion of women among the poor increased.[23] This feminization is tied to increasing numbers of women-headed households, male abandonment, and a rise in unpartnered teenage motherhood. Causes of poverty also include lower wages across the board for women, traditional discrimination in the job market, gender biases in the distribution of credit and ownership of land, and environmental degradation in rural areas that increases women's work.

Recommendations:

- Target poverty reduction programs to provide jobs to poor women — especially indigenous women and female-headed households.
- Promote and enforce laws to ensure that biological fathers help pay for their children's needs.
- Foster growth of intermediary agencies that increase poor women's understanding of their legal rights and access to state services and productive resources.
- Target sex education to teenage girls and provide access to reproductive health services, including safe contraception.

Invest in Women in Agriculture

Although they own little land, and are therefore not typically considered "farmers," nearly half of family income in the region's small farm sector is generated by women's work in agriculture.[24] And the proportion of women working in agriculture, both in subsistence and export crops, continues to rise. Yet, farm women are generally shut out of agricultural

extension programs as well as access to land, credit, and new technology.[25,26,27]

Recommendations:

- Balance policy reform in agriculture with sectoral strategies that raise women's productivity as farmers and wage laborers.
- Reform land tenure laws to eliminate gender bias in land acquisition and ownership and use.
- Make sure that agricultural research extends to food crops and processing done by women and includes women in farmer trials and studies.
- Increase women's access to agricultural extension services, credit, technology, and farmers' cooperatives.

Invest in Women's Health

Since women are key health providers and economic contributors to households, their illness or disability endangers the survival of the household. Investments in women's health pay off in terms of their economic productivity and their children's well-being.

Largely due to lack of access to safe and effective contraceptives, roughly four million clandestine abortions are performed in LAC countries each year, leading to high rates of infection, maternal mortality, and a burden on the health care system. In a number of LAC countries, including those where abortion is illegal, one out of three pregnancies ends in abortion.[28]

Out of wedlock adolescent fertility is on the rise as well in many countries. According to the World Bank, 16 percent of all births in 1992 in LAC countries were to teenage mothers.[29]

Recommendations:

- Reform health policies to increase access by the poor to quality basic preventive and curative services.
- Improve women's health throughout their lives, not only during the reproductive years.
- Improve the access to information and quality reproductive health services for all women including adolescents and unmarried women.

- Adhere to the principles agreed to in the 1994 International Conference on Population and Development regarding access to safe abortion and management of complications arising from abortion.

- Devise strategies to insure that men share responsibilities for sexual and reproductive health.

- Target a greater proportion of AIDS-related assistance on reducing the risk of HIV infection for women, whose rates of infection are rapidly rising.

- Promote joint medical and social science research on diseases and practices that affect women specifically — sexually transmitted diseases, reproductive tract infections, domestic violence, and unsafe abortions.

- Provide governments with public health and social statistics disaggregated by sex.

Invest in Girls' and Women's Education

The Universal Declaration of Human Rights confirms that education is a basic human right. In addition, education for girls and women is one of the most cost-effective social investments. It increases wages, reduces maternal mortality, and increases the use of family planning and child welfare.[30] While overall, girls now attend primary school in comparable numbers to boys, regional discrepancies persist. And adult females are disproportionately illiterate, with rates in some countries as high as 50 to 53 percent.[31]

Recommendations:

- Emphasize improving the quality of education for girls and women.

- Beyond the UN goal of universal primary education before 2015, help girls stay in school in secondary and higher education.

- Eliminate gender stereotypes from school curricula and materials.

- Encourage healthier school and community enabling environments for girls, including public awareness campaigns on the importance of schooling for girls.

Further Women's Participation in Democracy and Human Rights

Democracy depends on an educated, informed electorate, with free participation by all regardless of sex. And it depends on respect for human rights. Women are currently under-represented in government and political posts. And they suffer human rights abuses that endanger their health and keep them from fully contributing economically and politically.

The world community, in the Vienna Declaration of 1993, and again in UN Resolution 48-104, as well as the OAS Convention of Belém Do Para, recognized that violence against women is a human rights abuse. Yet it remains widespread in LAC as elsewhere. According to the World Bank, between one-fifth and one-half of women surveyed in many industrial and developing countries report that their partners have beaten them. In industrialized countries, rape and domestic violence account for nearly one out of every five healthy years of life lost to women of reproductive age. The burden on women in developing countries is similar per capita, although the percentage of healthy years of life lost to violence is smaller, due to greater health problems overall.[32]

Recommendations:

- Encourage governments to eliminate barriers to women's running for office and provide incentives to increase the participation of women in politics.

- Promote women in non-traditional roles in the public sector such as in the ministries of finance, agriculture, and industry.

- As the OAS broadens its mandate to promote and monitor democracy, ensure that the OAS includes at least 30 percent women in all its staff training and exchange programs for legislators.

- As the OAS helps strengthen educational and civic activities of NGOs, ensure that at least 30 percent of its support goes to women's NGOs.

- Help spread knowledge about laws promoting gender equality and human rights, through intermediary institutions, "barefoot lawyer" programs, social marketing techniques.

- Promote laws against domestic violence, enforce those that exist, and finance innovative institutions that can prevent and address violence.

Include Women as Full Partners in Development

While the educational level of many women in the region is high, women are rarely represented in high-level positions in the public sector, the international aid community, or lending institutions. This imbalance helps perpetuate a blindness to women's economic roles and needs. In traditional development projects, for instance, money for jobs training is channeled to men, while money for "welfare" — health, nutrition, and social benefits — is targeted to women.

General Recommendations:

- Ratify and implement the U.N. International Convention on the Elimination of All Forms of Discrimination against Women.

- Review national legal systems to remove barriers to women's full participation in society and the family.

- In public sector and international agencies, clarify commitment to women's issues in mission statements, policies, and programs, as well as in recruitment and promotion of staff, professional, and management positions.

- Substantially increase loan and concessional funding for projects that invest in women and women-based organizations, including funding to monitor progress and evaluate project impact.

- Develop and fund, jointly with national governments and international agencies, a broad-based, independent commission to monitor the implementation of the summit initiative on investing in women.

Recommendations for Selected Donor Institutions:

World Bank

The World Bank first addressed issues concerning women in development (WID) in 1973, but instructed regions to appoint WID personnel only in 1990. Not until 1994 did the Bank approve the first policy paper and operational guidance on gender issues. Projects with some stated gender-related ac-

tivities in Latin America and the Caribbean rose from 3 percent in 1985 to 33 percent in 1993. While this increase appears impressive, it is important to note that in most cases, gender-related activities form a very minor component of project objectives.

Recommendations:

- Gear up WID funding and staffing so that within five years, one-third of World Bank projects in LAC contain significant investment in women.

- To achieve this goal, the World Bank LAC regional vice-presidency needs to give priority to and provide strong endorsement for the implementation of WID policy in the region, assign sufficient financial and human resources to the task, and invest in evaluation research and monitoring of progress.

- Devote resources to assess the gender impact of macroeconomic reforms, and redesign these reforms so as not to penalize poor women.

Inter-American Development Bank

The IDB's operating policy on women in development was approved in 1987, and meaningful work on women's issues began after this date. Consideration of gender issues in project design increased from 6 percent in 1991 to 18 percent in 1992. During the Eighth Replenishment period, the IDB has made a significant commitment to civil society, the social sectors, and social reform.

Recommendations:

- Give priority to projects that address gender issues in the social sectors, so that at the end of five years, at least 50 percent of these projects invest in women.

- Similarly, by the end of the period, at least 30 percent of all concessional resources — including funds for special operations and technical cooperation — should flow to women and women-based non-governmental organizations.

United States Agency for International Development

USAID has incorporated policies on women since 1974; a major policy paper in 1982 reiterated the agency's commitment to women. However, implementation "has been slow," as stated in a recent Government Accounting Office (GAO) report to the U.S. Congress.[33]

Recommendations:

- Make investing in women and women-based NGOs explicit in LAC Bureau and Country Strategic Plans, in each of the five priority areas: population, health and nutrition, environment, democracy, economic growth, and humanitarian assistance.

- Allocate significant project and non-project assistance at the Mission level so that after five years, at least 30 percent of all Mission resources in LAC are devoted to women.

- To accomplish these goals, engage in broad consultation with women's groups in the countries, and take measures to research, monitor, and report progress.

Canadian International Development Agency (CIDA)

CIDA developed a WID policy in 1984 and a five-year action plan in 1986. CIDA has excelled in WID policy conceptualization and support to women-only projects and women-based agencies. Least effective has been implementation in productive sectors. Expenditures on WID rose between 86-89 and declined rapidly thereafter.[34]

Recommendations:

- Make the policy links between gender and poverty reduction, good governance and sustainability for LAC region and set WID priorities in country strategies and programs.

- Increase allocation of resources so that at least 1/3 of country resources flow to WID activities.

- Monitor progress and strengthen WID accountability.

Notes

1. George Psacharopoulos, Samuel Morley, Ariel Fiszbein, Haeduck Lee, and Bill Wood. 1993. *Poverty and Income Distribution in Latin America and the Caribbean: The Story of the 1980s.* LAC Technical Department Regional Studies Program, Report No. 27. Washington, DC: The World Bank.

2. ECLAC (Economic Commission for Latin America and the Caribbean). 1991. Panorama Social de America Latina. LC/G./688, October 31.

3. Nathaniel C. Nash. 1994. "Latin Economic Speedup Leaves Poor in the Dust." *New York Times.* September 7.

4. CELADE. 1992. "Demographic Bulletin, Latin America, Economically Active Population 1970-2000." Santiago, Chile.

5. Mayra Buvinic and Margaret A. Lycette. 1994. Women's Contributions to Economic Growth in Latin America and the Caribbean: Facts, Experience, and Options. Report prepared for the Inter-American Development Bank, Washington, DC.

6. Calculation for urban areas by ICRW. For rural areas, Jazairy, Idriss, Mohiuddin Alamgir, and Theresa Panuccio. 1992. *The State of World Rural Poverty: An Inquiry into its Causes and Consequences.* New York: New York University Press for the International Fund for Agricultural Development (IFAD).

7. George Psacharopoulos and Zafiris Tzannatos. 1992. *Women's Employment and Pay in Latin America: Overview and Methodology.* World Bank Regional and Sectoral Studies. Washington, DC: The World Bank.

8. Thomas Duncan. 1990. "Intra-Household Resource Allocation: An Inferential Approach." *The Journal of Human Resources* 25(4): 635-664.

9. Patrice Engle. 1993. "Influences of Mothers' and Fathers' Income on Children's Nutritional Status in Guatemala." *Social Science and Medicine* 37(11): 1303-1312.

10. Mayra Buvinic, Juan Pablo Valenzuela, Temístocles Molina, and Electra González. 1992. "The Fortunes of Adolescent Mothers and Their Children: The Transmission of Poverty in Santiago, Chile." *Population and Development Review* 18(2): 269-297.

11. World Bank. 1993. *World Development Report 1993: Investing in Health.* Washington, DC: The World Bank.

12. ECLAC (Economic Commission for Latin America and the Caribbean). 1993. *Población, Equidad y Transformación Productiva.* LC/G.1758/Rev.1-P, Series E, no. 37. Santiago, Chile: United Nations.

13. UN (United Nations). 1988. *Compendium of Statistics and Indicators on the Situation of Women 1986.* New York.

14. UN (United Nations). 1991. *The World's Women: Trends and Statistics 1970-1990.* New York: United Nations Publications.

15. CINTERFOR/ILO (Centro Interamericano de Investigación y Documentación sobre Formación Profesional). 1991. *Vocational Training on the Threshold of the 1990s: Volume I.* Montevideo, Uruguay.

16. Otto Kreye, Jurgen Heinrichs, and Folker Frobel. 1987. *Export Processing Zones in Developing Countries: Results of a New Survey.* Multinational Enterprise Programme Working Paper No. 43. Geneva, Switzerland: ILO.

17. Commonwealth Secretariat. 1990. *Engendering Adjustment for the 1990s.* Pall Mall, London.

18. Silvia Escobar de Pabon. 1993. Mujer y trabajo en unidades economicas de pequeña dimensión reflexiones sobre la situación actual y perspectivas. Presented at Seminario de Apoyo Técnico sobre Aspectos de Género y Desarrollo, ACDI-Contrapartes, Cochabamba, Bolivia.

19. Marguerite Berger and Mayra Buvinic, eds. 1989. *Women's Ventures: Assistance to the Informal Sector in Latin America.* West Hartford, CT: Kumarian Press.

20. PREALC (Programa Regional del Empleo para América Latina y el Caribe). 1988. *Sector Informal: Funcionamiento y Políticas.* Santiago, Chile.

21. Berger and Buvinic 1989.

22. Women's World Banking. 1994. *United Nations Expert Group on Women and Finance.* New York.

23. Calculation for urban areas by ICRW. For rural areas, Jazairy *et al.* 1992.

24. FAO (Food and Agriculture Organization). 1987. *Mujeres Campesinas en América Latina: Desarrollo Rural. Accesso a la Tierra, Migraciones y Legislación.* Santiago, Chile.

25. Agnes R. Quisumbing. 1993. Improving women's agricultural productivity as farmers and workers. (Draft). Washington, DC: The World Bank.

26. IDB (Inter-American Development Bank). 1990. *Economic and Social Progress in Latin America: 1990 Report.* Washington, DC.

27. Anne Ferguson and Marina Flores. 1987. *Resource Guide, Women in Agriculture: Guatemala.* East Lansing, MI: Michigan State University, Center for International Programs.

28. The Alan Guttmacher Institute. 1994. *Clandestine Abortion: A Latin American Reality.* New York.

29. World Bank. 1993. *World Development Report 1993: Investing in Health.* Washington, DC.

30. Lawrence H. Summers. 1992. "Investing in All the People." The World Bank Policy Research Working Paper 905 (May).

31. World Bank. 1993.

32. World Bank. 1993.

33. GAO (General Accounting Office). 1993. *Foreign Assistance: U.S. Has Made Slow Progress in Involving Women in Development.* Washington, DC.

34. CIDA (Canadian International Development Agency). 1993 (July). *Gender as a Cross-Cutting Theme in Development Assistance — An Evaluation of CIDA's WID Policy and Activities, 1984-1992.*

Biographical Information

Roundtable of Western Hemisphere Women Leaders

Mariclaire Acosta Urquidi

Mariclaire Acosta is president of the Mexican Commission for the Defense and Promotion of Human Rights, and is a founder of the Mexican Academy for Human Rights. She was previously president of Amnesty International in Mexico. Ms. Acosta is a member of the Inter-American Dialogue.

Carmen Barroso

Carmen Barroso is director of the Population Program at the John D. and Catherine T. MacArthur Foundation in Chicago. Dr. Barroso was a founding member of DAWN (Development Alternatives with Women for a New Era). She has been a visiting scholar at Cornell University's International Population Program, Hubert Humphrey Professor at Macalester College, and a sociology professor at the University of São Paolo.

Eva Blay

Eva Blay just completed Fernando Henrique Cardoso's term as Senator, and has now returned to teaching sociology at the University of São Paolo, where she chaired the department. She was the first president of the São Paulo State Council on the Condition of Women; founder and coordinator of the Nucleus for the Study of Women and Gender Social Relations at the University of São Paolo; and Inter-Regional Advisor of the U.N. Department for the Development of Women in Vienna.

Mayra Buvinic

Mayra Buvinic is founding member and president of the International Center for Research on Women, and past president of the Association for Women in Development. She is a member of the Board of Trustees of the International Child Health Foundation, has served on the Board of Trustees of the International Institute of Tropical Agriculture, and was a Scholar in Residence at the Bellagio Study and Conference Center and the Rockefeller Foundation.

Joan Caivano

Joan Caivano is an associate at the Inter-American Dialogue, where she serves as coordinator for the Dialogue's project on women leaders, as well as coordinator for its projects on Cuba, sovereignty, and on the Organization of American States. She recently left the private sector and received her master's degree in Latin American Studies from Georgetown University.

Soraya Castro Marino

Soraya Castro is a research associate at the Center for United States Studies at Havana University, where she directs research focusing on U.S. domestic and foreign policy. She holds a Ph.D. in law from Havana University and has pursued international law studies at the Institute of Foreign Relations of the University of U.S.S.R. in Moscow.

María Eugenia Phenon De Cotter

María Cotter is executive director of the Oscar Arias Foundation for Peace and Human Progress. She is founder of the Foundation's women's program; serves on the board of the National Center for the Development of Women and Family; and contributed to the 1990 Women's Equality Law.

Lynn Cutler

Lynn Cutler is senior vice president of the Kambler Group, a Washington communications firm, and a fellow at the John F. Kennedy Institute of Politics at Harvard University, where she teaches a course on Women Impacting Public Policy. She served three terms as vice chair of the Democratic National Committee, where she coordinated the Women's Division.

Joan Dassin

Joan Dassin is Regional Director for Latin America and the Caribbean for the Ford Foundation in New York City, for which she previously served as Representative in Rio de Janeiro, and Program Officer for Social Science and Human Rights.

Carole Douglis

Carole Douglis is a writer based in Washington, DC. She studied women in development issues at the Fletcher School of Law and Diplomacy from which she holds an M.A.L.D. She worked for the U.S. State Department in Niger helping design women's economic development projects.

Ana Milena Gaviria

Ana Milena Gaviria is an economist and professionally active former First Lady of Colombia and wife of the current Secretary General of the Organization of American States.

Margarita Guzmán

Margarita Guzmán, an economist, founded in 1980 the first affiliate of Women's World Banking in Cali, and currently serves as advisor in its transition to formal financial institutionalization. She worked for ten years with the Coffee Federation, most recently as General Manager of ten rural factories, working with poor women.

Peter Hakim

Peter Hakim is president of the Inter-American Dialogue. He was previously vice president for research and evaluation at the Inter-American Foundation and, from 1975 to 1980, he managed the international resource and environment program of the Ford Foundation. He is a member of the Council on Foreign Relations, and serves on the boards of the International Center for Research on Women and the Washington Office on Latin America.

Patricia D. Jacobs

Patricia Jacobs is president and chief executive officer of Greenleaf Associates, Inc., a development partner and project manager for 20 mid-size U.S. businesses. She is also president of the Cooperative Assistance Fund, Inc., an investment firm providing financial support for small businesses.

Ana Julia Jatar

Ana Julia Jatar, an economist, recently joined the Inter-American Dialogue as a senior fellow. She was formerly superintendent for the Promotion and Protection of Free Competition (the Venezuelan anti-trust agency); researcher and professor at the Institute for Advanced Administrative Studies (IESA).

Elizabeth Jelin

Elizabeth Jelin is professor of sociology at the University of Buenos Aires and senior researcher at the Institute for Social Research and the National Counsel of Scientific and Technical Research. She was formerly coordinator and researcher at the Center for the Study of Society and the State (CEDES).

Clara Jusidman de Bialostozky

Clara Jusidman is an economist for the National Autonomous University of Mexico. Former positions include researcher for the Bank of Mexico and College of Mexico, general director of Employment, and general director of the Center for Research on Rural Development. Currently she heads the National Accord for Democracy (ACUDE), which is preparing the national agenda for the IV International Women's Conference in Beijing in 1995.

Ana Raquel Sierchuk de Kessler

Ana Kessler is a National Deputy to the Argentine Congress. Ms. Kessler has held various public sector posts in the Ministry of Defense, the Ministry of Economics, the Ministry of Public Services, and others, as well as positions in the National Bank of Argentina, the Bank of the Province of Buenos Aires, and several regional banks.

Ruth De Krivoy

Ruth Krivoy, an economist, is currently head of *Sintesis Financiera*, a financial consulting firm. She recently served as president of the Central Bank of Venezuela, from 1992 to 1994. She was formerly President of the Presidential Commission for Industrial Competitiveness, and member of the Advisory Commission for Public Sector Debt Refinancing.

Barbara McDougall

Barbara McDougall is a director of E.L. Financial Corporation, public governor of the Toronto Stock Exchange, and director of the Canadian Institute of Strategic Studies. She was formerly Canada's Secretary of State for External Affairs, a member of Parliament, Minister of State, Minister of Finance, Minister of Privatization, Minister Responsible for the Status of Women, and Minister of Employment and Immigration.

Amparo Menéndez-Carrión

Amparo Menéndez-Carrión is director general of Facultad Latinoamericana de Ciencias Sociales (FLACSO) in Ecuador and professor of comparative politics and international relations. She formerly served as a Consultant for UNESCO, the International Labor Organization and the Ford Foundation.

Jill Merrick

Jill Merrick directs ICRW's Communications Program, and has 25 years experience in journalism, public affairs, media production, and marketing. As president of Merrick Communications for 15 years, she won national and international awards for her work associated with international social change and cultural agencies and Fortune 500 companies.

Lourdes R. Miranda

Lourdes Miranda is president and chief executive officer of Miranda Associates, Inc. She has served as President of the National Association for Women Business Owners and the National Conference of Puerto Rican Women, director of the National Foundation for Women Business Owners, and member of the Boards of the Center for Women Policy Studies, the Institute for Puerto Rican Affairs, and the Institute for Educational Leadership.

Isabel Nieves

Isabel Nieves, a social anthropologist, is coordinator of the Inter-American Development Advisory Services (IDEAS). She has been a consultant to the World Health Organization and the Pan American Health Organization, a social scientist for the International Center for Research on Women, and a researcher for the Institute of Nutrition, Central America.

Laura Novoa

Laura Novoa, an attorney, is counsel to the National Copper Corporation of Chile, and legal advisor to foreign and domestic investors in various fields. As President of the board of *PARTICIPA*, and as one of eight members appointed to the Commission for Truth and Reconciliation, she has been active in the democratic consolidation of Chile.

María Otero

María Otero is associate director for ACCION International, where she had been director of the Washington office since 1989. She is also chair of the board of both the Inter-American Foundation and of Bread for the World. She was previously a program officer for ACCION National in Honduras, and worked as an economist in the Women in Development office of the U.S. Agency for International Development. She was born and raised in La Paz, Bolivia.

Marta Oyhanarte

Marta Oyhanarte, an attorney, is president of and counsel for Citizen Power, a non-profit citizens group for democratic change in Argentina. Her legal practice has centered around investigating her husband's kidnapping and subsequent murder by the military and police in an effort to press the Argentine government to resolve the case.

Susana Pinilla Cisneros De Tantaleon

Susana Pinilla is founder and executive director of the National Association of Institutes for Development of the Informal Sector (IDESI Nacional), and the Institute for Development of the Informal Sector (IDESI). She was formerly general director for special projects for the National System for Popular Cooperation (COOPOP), and a consultant for UNICEF.

Paula Stern

Paula Stern is a Senior Fellow at the Progressive Policy Institute and president of The Stern Group, an economic advisory and trade analysis firm in Washington. She is former chairwoman of the U.S. International Trade Commission. Ms. Stern serves various boards and is a member of the Trilateral Commission, the Council on Foreign Relations, the Committee for Economic Development, and the Inter-American Dialogue.

María Elena Torano

María Elena Torano is chairman, founder, and chief executive officer of María Elena Torano Associates (META). Ms. Torano has been nominated by President Clinton to serve on the U.S. Advisory Commission on Public Diplomacy. She was formerly associate director for public affairs for the U.S. Community Services Administration under President Carter, and a member of the U.S. Commission on Minority Business Development.

*The Latino Alliance for the
Summit of the Americas
and The National Council
of La Raza*

*The National Council of La Raza
(NCLR) is a private, nonprofit,
nonpartisan, tax-exempt
organization established in
1968 to reduce poverty and
discrimination and improve life
opportunities for Hispanic
Americans. NCLR has chosen to
work toward this goal through
two primary, complementary
approaches:*

*• Capacity-building assistance
to support and strengthen
Hispanic community-based
organizations: providing
organizational assistance in
management, governance,
program operations, and
resource development to
Hispanic community-based
organizations in urban and
rural areas nationwide, especially those which serve low-
income and disadvantaged
Hispanics; and*

*• Applied research, policy
analysis, and advocacy: providing an Hispanic perspective on
issues such as education,
immigration, housing, health,
employment and training, and
civil rights enforcement to
increase policy-maker and
public understanding of Hispanic needs to encourage the
adoption of programs and
policies which equitably
serve Hispanics.*

*NCLR strengthens these efforts
with public information and
media activities and special and
international projects. These
include innovative projects,
catalytic efforts, formation of
and participation in coalitions,
and other special activities
which use the NCLR structure
and credibility to create other
entities or projects which are
important to the Hispanic
community and can
sometimes be "spun off" as
independent entities.*

U.S. Latino Communiqué to the Summit of the Americas

The following recommendations are necessary steps toward achieving our common purpose of democratization and higher standards of living for all peoples of the Americas:

RECOMMENDATIONS

Making Democracies Work

1. We urge the governments to protect the basic human political, civil, economic and labor rights of all men, women, and children through the unqualified ratification and enforcement of the American Convention on Human Rights, the U.N. Convention on Migrant Workers and their Families, the U.N. Declaration on the Elimination of Violence Against Women, the U.N. Protocol Relating to the Status of Refugees, the U.N. Genocide Treaty, and International Labor Organization worker rights conventions. We urge support for the U.N. draft declaration on the Rights of the Indigenous Peoples and call on the U.S. government to recognize the jurisdiction of the Inter-American Court of Human Rights.

2. We urge special attention be given to the rights and participation of disenfranchised groups, particularly women, indigenous peoples, refugees and migrants. International cooperation and assistance should be channeled to disadvantaged groups (women, minorities, and indigenous peoples) to promote their participation in and influence on political processes and government institutions, especially at the local level.

3. We support the principle of further civilian control of the armed forces, military budget priorities, and the scope and role of the military's involvement in the private sector.

4. We emphasize the need for free, transparent elections in the region with international observation and improved electoral administration, especially in the areas of voter mobilization and registration and voting procedures.

5. We call on the Heads of State to encourage the vigorous participation of non-governmental organizations in civil society through the elimination of the overt and subtle obstacles — political, legal, and economic — to their participation at the earliest possible opportunity.

Making Democracies Prosper

6. We support progress towards enhanced trade and economic integration in the hemisphere, accompanied by policies and institutions that address the costs of adjustment to dislocated urban and rural communities, workers and farmers, in both North America and Latin America, and provide investment resources that improve productivity and infrastructure to allow for harmonization of labor and environmental standards throughout the hemisphere.

PREAMBLE

By the year 2000, some 20 percent of the population of the United States will be of Latin American and Caribbean origin. This will make the United States the fifth largest Latin American country. The Latino community in the United States has abiding and profound economic, political, cultural, and social interests throughout Latin America and serves as an economic and cultural bridge between the Americas.

The undersigned members of the Alliance may have a diversity of views on the wide range of policy questions involving the United States and its neighbors in the hemisphere. However, we are united around the principle that, as a "bridge" community, U.S. Latinos have both an interest and an obligation to participate vigorously in the development and implementation of intra-hemisphere relations, which are inextricably linked to U.S. Latinos' interests with respect to immigration, trade, economic prosperity, and human and civil rights. We are further committed to achieving recognition of this principle within the policy-making arena. American Jews play an important role in shaping our policies regarding the Middle East; the African Americans play a similarly important role in shaping our policies toward Africa; in this tradition, it is entirely appropriate for U.S. Latinos to help shape our policies within this hemisphere.

STATEMENT

The Latino Alliance for the Summit of the Americas represents a broad coalition of Latino organizations united in recognition of the strong ties and mutual interests that bind the Latino community in the United States with the nations of Latin America. We strongly believe that the Latino community in the United States has an important role to play in the formulation and implementation of United States foreign policy and development assistance towards the Americas.

The Latino Alliance welcomes the historic meeting of the hemisphere's democratically elected Heads of State. The Alliance endorses the Summit's agenda and emphasizes the importance of commitments to achieve the following: 1) justice, human rights, and effective political participation for all individuals and respect for cultural identity, ethnic diversity, and immigrant status; 2) trade, investment, and migration flows which foster mutual economic benefits and improved labor and environmental standards throughout the hemisphere; and 3) the elimination of extreme poverty through sustainable, equitable development and improvements in education, basic health services and environmental infrastructure.

PROPOSALS FROM NON-GOVERNMENTAL SECTORS

IV. Guaranteeing Sustainable Development and Conserving Our Natural Environment for Future Generations

The Earth Council is a non-governmental organization founded in September 1992, as a direct result of the Earth Summit, held in Rio de Janeiro, Brazil, in June 1992. It consists of 21 members broadly representative of the principal regions of the world and the various sectors of the civil society, each appointed in his/her personal capacity.

Its creation was motivated by the need to empower civil society organizations; to monitor, review, and assess the implementation of the Earth Summit results; and to promote greater public awareness and support for the needed transition to more sustainable patterns of development worldwide.

A number of individuals and organizations constituted the Organizing Committee which outlined the basis for the establishment of the Earth Council. The Organizing Committee carried out extensive consultations with a variety of people and over 10,000 organizations from around the world, soliciting their views and proposals for the Earth Council.

Conclusions of the Inter-American Meeting of National Councils for Sustainable Development

José Maria Figueres Olsen
Presidente de la República

Open Letter

I had the honor to host and participate in the first meeting of National Councils for Sustainable Development held in my country on 10-11 October 1994. The inter-American meeting brought together for the first time on a regional level representatives from both official and non-governmental sectors. Twenty-five countries of the Americas sent representatives where these national coordinating mechanisms have been established or are under discussion.

It is important to note that this first gathering was organized by the Earth Council, an independent organization, whose global headquarters my country has the privilege of hosting. Its founder and chairperson is Maurice Strong, former Secretary General of the Earth Summit. The Earth Council task leader for the inter-American meeting was Jonathan Lash whose conclusions are summarized in this document and who is Co-Chair of the U.S President's Council for Sustainable Development.

The realization of the promise of the Earth Summit, as highlighted by Mr. Strong in his opening remarks, depends on the institutionalization at the national level of sustainable development coordinating and participatory mechanisms as recommended in Agenda 21. Supporting and facilitating the work of National Councils is thus an Earth Council priority. The focus is on their need to be participatory and multi-stakeholder as well as nationally and regionally integrative, stated Earth Council Executive Director, Alicia Barcena.

It is my pleasure to offer this summary report with the ideas and aspirations of participants representing the hemisphere's diverse cultural, political and environmental traditions, but who have in common the firm desire to initiate a new form of cooperation and dialogue between state and civil society within the Americas. The enthusiasm generated at this inter-American meeting has already encouraged other regions to carry out similar initiatives; its hopes and potential for change are an inspiration for our own Summit of the Americas.

José Maria Figueres
San Jose, 9 December 1994

"Sustainable development should become a lifestyle, permeating every aspect of national life."

—José Maria Figueres, President of Costa Rica

"The Councils represent a new species that has emerged from the turbulent conditions of a new world. Like all new species, they are both vulnerable and promising."

—Maurice Strong, Chairman of the Earth Council

"Until we realize that empowerment is not a threat, and that sharing power does not diminish us, we will not be able to realize our real potential to create different kinds of societies."

—Elizabeth Dowdeswell, Executive Director of UNEP

"Sustainable development cannot be an empty phrase or just a good intention; it must be a commitment of all."

—Carlos Aquino, Director General of the Inter-American Institute for Cooperation on Agriculture (IICA)

"Sustainable development does not fit the old ways of thinking about policy. We need changes in the way we produce and consume. Changes in values. Changes in politics."

—Johnathan Lash, Earth Council member and Co-Chair of the U.S. President's Council for Sustainable Development

Auspiciado por: Consejo de la Tierra, Programa de las Naciones Unidas para el Desarrollo (PNUD), Programa de las Naciones Unidas para el Medio Ambiente (PNUMA), Departamento para la Coordinación de Políticas y Desarrollo Sostenible (DCPDS) de la ONU, Instituto Interamericano de Cooperación para la Agricultura (IICA) y el Gobierno de Costa Rica.

Under the auspices of The Earth Council, the United Nations Development Programme (UNPD). the United Nations Environment Programme (UNEP), the United Nations Department of Policy Coordination and Sustainable Development (UNDPCSD), the Inter-American Institute for Cooperation on Agriculture (IICA). and the Government of Costa Rica.

Conclusions of the Inter-American Meeting of National Councils for Sustainable Development

San José, Costa Rica
October 10-11, 1994

Summary Conclusions

Participants examined the potential roles of National Councils: agents of change, a means to institutionalize citizens participation in Sustainable Development, guarantors of the post-Rio process, and as promoters of regional and international cooperation. The following is a synthesis of those conclusions and the main points raised in discussion.

a) Characteristics which may contribute to the success of the NCSD process include:

- Membership that is multi-stakeholder and multi-sectoral;

- Processes that are fair and inclusive and recognize the importance of creative conflict among different interest groups;

- Representation and democratic election of all development actors;

- Government commitment, especially from Heads of State or Government, without intentions to control;

- Policy issue-driven, non-bureaucratic, and non-hierarchical;

- Equal access to information;

- Engagement of society through a transparent process of exchange;

- Focus on sustainable development to break through sectoral barriers;

- Integration of long-term vision into current policies.

b) A number of problems and constraints were also examined:

- Difficulty in selecting participants who do not necessarily represent but who are representative of diverse constituents;

- Build commitment to constructive conflict resolution;

- Discover resource-balancing mechanisms between participants;

- Recognition of the urgency of alleviating poverty;

- The need for the active involvement of "non-environmental" ministries/departments, especially finance and trade;

- Credibility of NCSDs through meaningful citizen participation and policy results;

- The failure of industrialized countries to fulfil their Earth Summit commitments, especially those relating to financial and technological support;

- Lack of adequate consultation for the preparation of the Central American and hemispheric Summits, despite having democracy and sustainable development as key themes;

- The UN Commission on Sustainable Development must become a multi-sectoral forum reaching beyond environmental ministries.

c) Actions to be carried out:

- Establishment of networking facilities to promote NCSD processes, especially those underway;

- Strengthening of conflict management capacities;

- Integration of economic and environmental policy into NCSD processes;

- Building NCSDs capacity to evaluate international assistance priorities relating to sustainable development;

- Involvement of NCSDs in Agenda 21 reporting.

The meeting concluded with a strong sense of commitment and enthusiasm. The desire was expressed that the Earth Council continue its facilitating role, due to its capacity to bring various governmental, UN and non-governmental sectors together. The inter-American meeting helped set the stage for further regional NCSD meetings to be held in Manila (Asia) and Nairobi (Africa). Plans are also being made for a European meeting and a global forum in 1996.

It was clear that the National Councils, for all their different approaches and characteristics, had a well articulated goal and represented a significant follow-up to Rio. At their best, they embodied the principles and spirit of sustainable development and offered an opportunity to transcend longstanding differences between sectors of civil society.

List of Participants

Mr. Maurice Strong
Chairman of the Earth Council
700 University Avenue (H 1 9A27)
Toronto, Ontario, Canada
Fax: (416) 971-3691

Ms. Elizabeth Dowdeswell
Executive Director
United Nations Environment Programme
P.O. Box 30552
Nairobi, Kenya
Fax: (2542) 226-895

Ms. Joke Waller-Hunter
Director, Division for Sustainable Development
Dept. of Policy Coordination Sustainable Development
United Nations
New York, NY 10017
Fax: (212) 963-4260

Ms. Sarah L. Timpson
Acting Director
Bureau for Policy and Programme Support
United Nations Development Programme
One United Nations Plaza
New York, NY 10017
Fax: (212) 906-5313

Mr. Mohamed T. El-Ashry
Chairman, Global Environment Facility
GEF Secretariat, 1818 H Street, NW
Washington, DC 20433
Fax: (202) 522-3240/3245

Mr. Lars Hyttinen
Principal Officer
National Information Analysis Office
DPCSD, United Nations
One United Nations Plaza
New York, NY 10017
Fax: (212) 963-1267

Arsenio Rodriguez
Director Regional para América Latina y el Caribe
Programa de las Naciones Unidas para el Medio
  Ambiente y Desarrollo
Mexico, DF
Fax: (525) 202-0950

National Representatives

Mr. Eustace Hill *(Government)*
Chairman of the Historical Conservation
  and Environment Commission
c/o Ministry of Economy, Development, Industry
  & Tourism
Queen Elizabeth Highway
Antigua, West Indies
Tel: (809) 462-0092
Fax: (809) 462-2836

Mr. Hugo Ambrosio *(Government)*
Dirección Nacional de Relaciones Institucionales
Presidencia de la Nación
Secretaría de Recursos Naturales
  y Ambiente Humano
San Martin 459, 1 Piso
Buenos Aires, Argentina
Tel: (541) 394-6643 int. 8443
Fax: (541) 325-7677/79180

Dr. Victor Gonzalez *(Government)*
Permanent Secretary
Ministry of Tourism and Environment
Belmopán, Belice
Tel: (501) 823-393
Fax: (501) 823-815

Ms. Virginia Vasquez *(NGO)*
Executive Director
Belize Audubon Society
Ciudad Belice, Belice
Fax: (501) 234-985
Tel: (501) 234-987/235-004

Ms. Marianela Curi Chacón *(Government)*
Sub-Secretaria de Promoción
Ministerio de Desarrollo Sostenible
La Paz, Bolivia
Tel: (591) 315-983/354-522
Fax: (591) 329-304
Apdo Postal: #3116

Dr. Luis Alberto Rodrigo Gainza *(NGO)*
Director Ejecutivo de Lidema
Av. Ecuador 2131, Casilla 11237
La Paz, Bolivia
Tel: (591) 2-32-49-09/3-53-33-52
Fax: (591) 2-39-23-21
E/mail: lidema@unbol.bo

Ms. Nilde Lago Pinheiro *(Government)*
Presidente del IBAMA
SAIN, Via L4 - Norte
70 818900 Brasilia DF, Brazil
Tel: (5561) 316-1212
Fax: (5561) 224-5206

Mr. Rubens Harry Born *(NGO)*
Forum Brasilero de ONG's
Vitae Civilis
Instituto para Des., Meio Ambiente e Paz
R. MMDC, 172 Conj. 3 Butanta
São Paulo, SP 05510-001
Brazil
Tel/Fax: (5511) 815-8524
E-mail: rubinho@ax.apc.org

Mr. Antonio Carlos Alves de Oliveira *(NGO)*
Forum Brasilero de ONGs
Vitae Civilis
Instituto para Des., Meio Ambiente e Paz
R. MMDC, 172 Conj. 3 Butanta
São Paulo, SP 05510-001
Brazil
Tel/Fax: (5511) 815-8524
E-mail: tonhao@ax.apc.org

Mr. Ronald L. Doering *(Government)*
Executive Director
National Round Table on the
  Environment and the Economy
1 Nicholas St., Suite 1500
Ottawa KIN 7B7, Ontario
Canada
Tel: (613) 992-7189
Fax: (613) 992-7385

Ms.Susan Holtz *(NGO)*
Vice Chair
National Round Table on the Environment
  and the Economy
1 Nicholas St., Suite 1500
Ottawa KIN 7B7, Ontario
Canada
Fax: (613) 992-7385
For personal communication:
Fax: (902) 477-5464

Mr. José Goni *(Government)*
Director Ejecutivo
Comisión Nacional del Medio Ambiente
Ministerio Secretaría General de la Presidencia
Avenida Libertador Bemardo O'Higgins 949, P.13
Santiago, Chile
Tel: (562) 695-3080/699-2476
Fax: (562) 671-880

Mr. Bernardo Amigo (NGO)
Foro Chileno de ONGs de Medio Ambiente
  y Desarrollo
Casilla 197, Correo 13
San Jerónimo 5020, San Miguel
Santiago, Chile
Tel: (562) 522-52-35/522-51-96
Tel/Fax: (562) 522-26-07

Mr. Manuel Rodriguez *(Government)*
Ex-Ministro del Medio Ambiente
Departamento Nal. de Planeación
Ministerio del Medio Ambiente
Carrera 10 #86-89
Bogotá, Colombia
Tel: (57-1) 610-0136
Fax: (57-1) 610-8576

Ms. Consuelo Ordoffez de Rincón *(Government)*
Gerente General del INDERENA
Cra. 10a. #20-30, Piso 5
Bogota, Colombia
Tel: (571) 284-700
Fax: (571) 283-458

Ms. Juanita Castaño *(NGO)*
Centro de Investigaciones y
  Proyectos Especiales
Calle 12 No. 73 Este
Bogotá, Colombia
Tel: (571) 341-8715/282-6066 ext. 344
Fax: (571) 212-3463

Ministro René Castro *(Government)*
Ministerio de Recursos Naturales, Energía y Minas
San José, Costa Rica
Tel: (506) 233-4533/233-4025

Mr. José Luis Castillo Solano *(NGO)*
Mr. Tames Sin Arriola
Representantes de las ONGs
Costa Rica
Tel/Fax: (506) 758-2233 APDE/CONAO

Dr. Gisela Alonso Dominguez *(Government)*
Directora de Medio Ambiente
Ministerio de Ciencia, Tecnología y
  Medio Ambiente
La Habana, Cuba
Tel: (537) 61-02-61
Fax: (537) 33-86-54

Ing. Aracelli Mateo de Acosta Fernandez *(NGO)*
Secretaría Ejecutiva de Pronaturaleza
La Habana, Cuba
Tel: (537) 62-66-06
Fax: (537) 33-86-54

Dr. Roberto Troya *(Government)*
Asesor Permanente de la CAAM
Av. 10 de Agosto No. 3560 y Mariana de Jesus
Edif. Metrocar 4to. Piso
Quito, Ecuador
Tel: (593 2) 540-455/524-304
Fax: (593 2) 565-809

Lic. Vicente Pólit *(NGO)*
Presidente de CEDENMA
Italia 832 y Mariana de Jesus
Quito, Ecuador
Tel: (59 32) 230-746
Fax: (59 32) 434-449

Mr. Horacio Humberto Rios Orellana *(Government)*
Director Ejecutivo
Secretaria Ejecutiva del Medio Ambiente
Final de la 91 Av. Norte Entre 11 y 13 Calle
Poniente Colonia Escalon
San Salvador, El Salvador
Tel: (503) 79-3830/79-3970
Fax: (503) 223-9083/224-3886

Mr. Ernesto A. Freund *(NGO)*
Director de la Fundación Amigos de Ilopango
39 Calle Oriente, Pasaje Freund No.2
Colonia La Rabida
San Salvador, El Salvador
Tel: (503) 276-3333
Fax: (503) 276-3250

Mr. Bruno Busto Brol *(Government)*
Comisión Nacional del Medio Ambiente
Avenida Petapa 25 59 Zona 12
Guatemala City, Guatemala
Tel: (502) 276-1027/276-1029
Fax: (502) 276-1026

Mr. Raúl Velásquez *(NGO)*
Representante de ONGs
Comisión Nacional del Medio Ambiente
Avenida Petapa 25 59 Zona 12
Guatemala, Guatemala
Tel/Fax: (502) 276-1026/1027/1029

Mr. Carlos A. Medina *(Government)*
Ministro del Ambiente
Secretaría de Estado en el Despacho del
  Ambiente
Apartado 4710
Tegulcigalpa, Honduras
Tel: (504) 37-5667/38-5308/37-5664
Fax: (504) 37-5726

Licda. Rosalpina Mendoza *(NGO)*
Federación Ambientalista
Apto #3752
Tegucigalpa, Honduras
Tel: (504) 22-7107
Fax: (504) 37-5726

Mr. Franklin McDonald *(Government)*
Executive Director
The Natural Resources
  Conservation Authority
53 1/2 Molynes Road
Kingston, Jamaica
Tel: 1 (809) 923-5155/923-4241
Fax: 1 (809) 923-5070
E-mail: nrca@igc.apc.org

Lic. Enrique Provencio Durazo *(Government)*
Director General
Instituto Nacional de Ecología
Rio Elba #20, Colonia Cuautemoc
Mexico DF 06500, Mexico
Tel: (525) 553-9601/553-9969
Fax: (525) 286-6625

Ms. Julia Carabias *(Government)*
Instituto Nacional de Ecología
Rio Elba #20, Colonia Cuautemoc
Mexico DF, Mexico
Fax: (525) 286-6625

Mr. Luis Bustamante *(NGO)*
Coalisión de ONGs
Mexico DF, Mexico
Tel: (525) 202-7267
Fax: (525) 846-0280

Mr. José Leon Talavera *(Government)*
Presidente de la Comisión del
  Medio Ambiente
Parlamento de Nicaragua
Managua, Nicaragua
Tel: (505) 263-1271
Fax: (505) 263-1273

Ms. Rosario Saenz *(NGO)*
Fundación para el Desarrollo Sostenible
Managua Arbolito 2c. al sur
Managua, Nicaragua
Tel:(505) 668-172
Tel/Fax: (505) 223-254/799-122 (Habitación)

Ms. Silvia Ayon Ruiz *(NGO)*
Coordinadora Red de Desarrollo Sostenible
Managua, Nicaragua
Tel: (505) 2-28-13-12
Fax: (505) 2-66-69-09

Ms. Marla Esperanza Zelaya Ortega *(NGO)*
Directora Depto. de Ecología y RRNN de la
  Universidad Centroamericana
Managua, Nicaragua
Tel: (505) 2-621792
Fax: (505) 2-673638

Licda. Edilsa de Bellido *(Government)*
Departamento de Cooperación Internacional
Instituto Nacional de Recursos Naturales
  Renovables
Panama, Panama
Tel: (507) 32-6601/6643/6770
Fax: (507) 32-6612

Celeste Acevedo/ Jorge Pinazzo *(Government)*
Dirección de Parques Nacionales y Vida Silvestre
C.C. 303
Asunción, Paraguay
Hasta Dic. 1995: CATIE, Apartado 7170
Turrialba, Costa Rica
Tel: (506) 556-1533
Fax: (506) 556-6431

Biol. Ricardo Gutierrez Quiroz *(NGO)*
Supervisor de Areas Protegidas
INRENA
Calle 17 - 355
Urbanización El Palomar
San Isidro
Lima, Peru
Tel: (5114) 41-0425
Fax: (5114) 41-4606

Mr. Pedro Gelabert *(Government)*
Secretario, Departamento de Recursos Naturales
  y Ambientales
Apartado 5887
San Juan, Puerto Rico 00906
Tel: (1-809) 723-3090
Fax: (1-809) 723-4255/1464/2055

Ms. Carmen Reveron *(Government)*
Ayudante Especial, Técnico
Secretario de Recursos Naturales
  y Ambientales
Apartado 5887
San Juan, Puerto Rico
Tel: (1-809) 723-3090
Fax: (1-809) 723-4255

Ms. Clarissa Leon de Fernandez *(Government)*
Coordinadora de las Cumbres Mundiales
  de la Vicepresidencia de la República
Oficinas Gubernamentales
Edificio A ler Nivel
Santo Domingo, República Dominicana
Tel: (809) 221-6429/221-5140 ext: 206/208
Fax: (809) 685-8647

Mr. José Miguel Martínez Guridy *(NGO)*
Director Ejecutivo
Fondo Integrado Pro Naturaleza
Apartado 2956
Santo Domingo, República Dominicana
Tel: (809) 682-6343
Fax: (809) 685-8647

Mr. Victor Canton *(Government)*
Ministerio de la Vivienda, Ordenamiento Territorial
  y Medio Ambiente
Zabala 1427
Montevideo, Uruguay 11000
Tel:(598 2) 95-0211/96-1929
Fax:(598-2) 96-2914/96-5132

Mr. Leonardo Castagnola *(NGO)*
Representante de las ONGs de Montevideo
  en la Comisión Técnica Asesora
Santiago de Chile 1183 CP 11200
Montevideo, Uruguay
Tel: (598) 2-40-42-35/41-87-38
Fax: (598) 2-91-40-04/48-56-84
E-mail:ceuta.chasque.apc.org

Mr. Rafe Pomerance *(Government)*
Deputy Assistant Secretary for Environment
  and Development
Department of State
Washington, DC, USA
Tel: (202) 647-2232
Fax: (202) 647-0217

Molly Harris Olson *(Government)*
Executive Director
President's Council on Sustainable Development
730 Jackson Place NW
Washington, DC 20503, USA
Tel: (202) 408-5320
Fax: (202) 408-6839

Mr. Jonathan Lash *(NGO)*
President, World Resources Institute
Co-Presidente del Consejo Presidencial de los
  EEUU y Miembro del Consejo de la Tierra
1709 New York Avenue, NW
Washington, DC 20006, USA
Tel: (202) 662-2558
Fax: (202) 638-0036

Mr. Jared Blumenfeld
International Legal Consultant
National Resources Defense Council
1350 New York Ave., NW
Washington, DC, USA
Fax: (202) 708-5987

Mr. William Visser *(NCO)*
World Resources Institute
1709 New York Avenue NW
Washington DC, 20006, USA
Tel: (202) 662-3763
Fax: (202) 638-0036

Ms. Beatriz Pineda *(Government)*
Ministerio del Ambiente y de los Recursos
  Naturales
Oficina de Des. Prof. y Relaciones Internacionales
(ODEPRI)
Centro Simon Bolivar, Torre Sur, Piso 18
Caracas, Venezuela
Tel: (582) 483-4638
Fax: (582) 483-1148/483-2445

Ms. Alicia García Scarton *(NGO)*
Comité Ejecutivo
AMIGRANSA
Apartado 50460
Caracas 1050 A, Venezuela
Tel: (582) 623-484
Fax: (582) 921-884

Submitted by the Environmental and Energy Study Institute, March 24, 1994

The Environmental and Energy Study Institute (EESI) is a non-profit organization established by congressional leaders and dedicated to promoting environmentally sustainable societies. EESI believes meeting this goal requires transitions to social and economic patterns that sustain people, the environment, and the natural resources upon which present and future generations depend. EESI produces credible, timely information and innovative public policy initiatives that lead to these transitions. These products are developed and promoted through action-oriented briefings, workshops, analysis, publications, task forces, and working groups.

EESI's audience is Congress and other national policymakers — and the people who influence them. EESI enjoys a strategic position with national policymakers as the nation's only independent organization established by congressional environmental and energy leaders.

Declaration by Heads of State of Principles on Economic Integration and Sustainable Development: Proposal for the Summit of the Americas

Introduction: Economic integration is expected to figure prominently in discussions at the Summit of the Americas. Indeed, at this unique moment in the hemisphere's history, economic integration promises to provide a focal point for diplomacy and cooperation among all countries of the hemisphere for years to come. Summit of the Americas constitutes the best opportunity in a long time for leaders in the hemisphere to clarify and fortify the principles upon which economic integration among some or all of their nations will proceed.

Proposal: First, at the Summit, heads of state of each of the western hemisphere nations should issue a "Declaration of Principles for Promoting Sustainable Development through Economic Integration." Second, at the Summit, heads of state should call on their environment and trade ministers to establish regular and ongoing consultations for monitoring application of these principles. Specific principles should include:

1. Sustainable development as the main objective: All economic integration initiatives should explicitly state that their fundamental purpose is to promote sustainable development. Unlike trade and other forms of economic activity, sustainable development is an end in and of itself. Integration initiatives should be pursued which promote the ability of today's generation to satisfy its needs, without compromising the ability of all future generations to meet their needs.

2. Informed decision-making: In order to ensure that each economic integration initiative promotes, rather than hinders, sustainable development, it is necessary to identify and understand each initiative's potential positive and negative environmental effects. Among other things, this means that an environmental impact assessment should be undertaken of each initiative prior to agreement and implementation, and ongoing monitoring of the environmental effects arising from implementation of each initiative should be carried out.

3. Open decision-making: Because different parties are affected by and value environmental effects differently, all processes of negotiation, approval, implementation, and dispute-settlement relating to economic integration initiatives must be open and subject to influence by affected parties.

4. Precautionary principle: Because the environmental effects of integration initiatives may be uncertain and/or involve an unknown amount of risk, because some environmental impacts are irreversible within reasonable time frames, and because the needs of future generations are unknown, economic integration initiatives should incorporate the precautionary principle — "hedging on the safe side" — with respect to potential environmental impacts. That is, in the face of scientific uncertainty, policies should be adopted which allow an easing of environmental stress well before conclusive scientific evidence concerning environmental damage exists and which are adaptable as new scientific information becomes available.

5. Cost-internalization and polluter-pays: In order to promote efficiency of markets as well as environmental protection, economic integration initiatives should actively promote the internalization of environmental costs in prices of traded goods and full compliance with the polluter-pays principle.

6. Level of decision-making: Many environmental impacts, including deforestation, loss of biodiversity, and various forms of pollution, are of common concern to countries in the hemisphere. These problems should be dealt with through multilateral cooperation. At the same time, the right of communities at the national and all sub-national levels to set and maintain the highest environmental standards which they deem appropriate must be guaranteed.

For more information, contact:
Paul Speck
202-628-1400;
fax 628-1825

*This declaration was
prepared by the
Environmental and Energy
Study Institute
in Washington, D.C.*

Declaration by Non-Governmental Organizations to Heads of State Participating in the Summit of the Americas Regarding the Need for Public Participation

On December 9-11, 1994, the Summit of the Americas will gather Heads of State from the Western Hemisphere to discuss economic integration, democracy, and sustainable development. Decisions may be taken at this event that will affect the future of every citizen in the Americas.

Thus far, the interactive consultative process that has taken place between governments preparing for the Summit has not included much public participation. In the United Nations Conference on Environment and Development (UNCED), which took place in Rio de Janeiro in June 1992, and in other recent national and international fora, NGOs have played a central role in identifying sustainable development issues, crafting creative policy proposals, elevating these to high levels in public policy discussions, and offering reasonable amendments to international negotiating texts.

The undersigned non-governmental organizations respectfully request that the Heads of State participating in the Summit of the Americas ensure that a process of democratic participation, involving all segments of civil society, be adopted for the Summit. This process should be similar to that used for UNCED.

Specifically we ask that:

- NGOs have the right to attend all plenary meetings and formal working group meetings before and during the Summit. Special time should be set aside for NGOs to comment or intervene in those meetings by making formal statements.

- For these meetings, NGOs be encouraged to present statements representing consensus positions of a coalition of many NGOs.

- All working documents related to the Summit be made available and easily accessible to the public immediately upon their issuance.

- Individual governments actively include NGOs in their own preparatory processes for the Summit. For example, they should brief NGOs about their positions prior to meetings and share relevant documents. Also, they should include NGO leaders on their official delegations.

These important recommendations should be adopted in time to allow full NGO participation in all aspects of the preparatory process for the Summit of the Americas.

For more information about the Environmental & Energy Institute, including how to reach the other endorsing organizations, please contact Paul Speck at (tel) 202-628-1400 or (fax) 202-628-1825.

ENDORSING ORGANIZATIONS:

Argentina
Consejo de ONGs, Córdoba
Fundación Acción Ambientalista
Fundación Ambiente y Recursos Naturales
Fundación Bariloche
Fundación de Acción Ecológica, Córdoba
Fundación para la Defensa del Ambiente
Fundación Patagonia Natural
Fundación Proteger, Santa Fe

Brazil
Friends of the Earth International, Amazonia Program

Canada
Canada Parks & Wilderness Society
Canadian Environmental Law Association
Citizen's Clearinghouse on Waste Management
Ecology Action Centre
Environmental Resource Centre
Environmentalists Plan Transportation, Toronto
Great Lakes United
Guideposts For a Sustainable Future
McGill Faculty of Agricultural and Environmental Sciences, Québec
Nipissing Environmental Watch
Pembina Institute for Appropriate Development
Pollution Probe
Sierra Club

Chile
Casazúl
Casa de la Paz
Comité Nacional para la Defensa de la Fauna y la Flora
Conciencia 21
Consorcio Latinoamericano sobre Agroecología y Desarrollo
Defensores del Bosque
Participa
Red Chile de Acción para una Iniciativa de los Pueblos
Red Nacional de Acción Ecológica

Dominican Republic
Centro de Educación de la Realidad Campesina
Centro de Educación Popular
Club Amantes del Progreso
Club Cultural 16 de Agosto
Club Deportivo Cultural 27 de Febrero
Consejo de Unidad Popular
Fundación Educativa Pro-Democracia y Desarrollo
Fundación Los Hattises para el Desarrollo Sustentable
Instituto de Asistencia Jurídica Integral
Instituto para el Desarrollo de la Empresa Asociativa Campesina
Laboratorio de Investigación y Recuperación Ecológica
Solidarios

Ecuador
Fundación Futuro Latinoamericano
Fundación Natura

Mexico
Centro Mexicano de Derecho Ambiental
Grupo de los 100
Pacto de Grupos Ecologistas
Unión de Grupos Ambientalistas, I.A.P.

Nicaragua
Federación de ONGs de Nicaragua
Fundación Augusto C. Sandino

Declaration by Non-Governmental Organizations to Heads of State Participating in the Summit of the Americas Regarding the Need for Public Participation

NON-GOVERNMENTAL
PROPOSALS

Peru

Centro de Estudios para el Desarrollo
    y la Participación
Centro de Estudios y Promoción
    del Desarrollo
Centro de Investigación Social y
    Educación Popular

United States

Center for International Environmental Law
Community Nutrition Institute
Defenders of Wildlife
Environmental and Energy Study Institute
Environmental Defense Fund
Global Tomorrow Coalition
Institute for Agriculture and Trade Policy
Lawyers Committee for Human Rights,
    Washington Office
National Audubon Society
National Wildlife Federation
Natural Resources Defense Council
Sierra Club
Washington Office on Latin America

Uruguay

Centro Latinoamericano de Ecología Social
Fundación ECOS
Grupo Bosque
Instituto del Tercer Mundo

Submitted by the Environmental and Energy Study Institute in consultation with the International Institute for Sustainable Development

Postscript: A Western Hemisphere Agreement on Minimum Environmental Standards Governing Industry: Proposal for the Summit of the Americas

Introduction: Countries of the Western Hemisphere recognize the need to minimize pollution and other forms of environmental degradation associated with industry, including mining. However, the manner in which they undertake to minimize this degradation varies. Today some people are concerned that differing levels of environmental protection may adversely affect trade in the Western Hemisphere. The idea of using unilateral trade measures, including "environmental countervailing duties," to "level the playing field" has become very popular. Proponents argue that firms operating in countries with lower environmental standards are receiving a subsidy for their export and that they are engaging in "eco-dumping." Action must be taken to quell these concerns and to ensure that all countries promote sustainable development.

Proposal: At the Summit, heads of state should mutually call for the establishment of a "Western Hemisphere Agreement on Minimum Environmental Standards," with negotiations on this agreement to begin immediately. An outline of how the negotiations might be structured follows.

1. Negotiate a framework convention for international cooperation to reduce industrial pollution, similar to the framework conventions on ozone depletion, climate change, and biodiversity loss. In this convention, parties should agree to undertake national industrial pollution audits, based on a common model, and to share the data gathered from the audits with other parties through a conference secretariat.

Also in the framework convention, establish regional technical assistance centers and a conference fund for developing countries to obtain concessional loans to help firms comply with future minimum environmental standards. Authorize the use of technical panels of independent experts to receive and investigate complaints regarding individual firms' alleged failure to meet the future standards. And establish a mechanism to use trade remedies against countries in which firms are found to be out of compliance with the future standards.

2. Using data gathered from the environmental audits, negotiate a series of protocols on minimum environmental standards applicable to particular industry sectors. Each protocol should specify a period of time following the agreement's entry into force during which affected firms could take advantage of technical assistance provided by the agreement to adjust their operations before being held accountable to the agreed standards.

Rationale: Negotiating an international agreement on minimum standards for reducing industrial pollution, rather than imposing environmental countervailing duties, has several advantages for developing countries as well as developed countries in the hemisphere. First, a minimum standards agreement would *positively assist industries throughout the hemisphere to minimize environmental degradation,* whereas environmental countervailing duties would not. Second, a minimum environmental standards agreement would *help to avoid trade conflicts* over "environmental protectionism." Third, a minimum environmental standards agreement would *build on international cooperation that already is underway* on environmental control in industry.

It might be argued that domestic industrial pollution standards are not a legitimate subject for international negotiations, since industrial pollution does not always create global commons or transboundary environmental problems. However, precedents set by the United Nations Conference on Environment and Development and in negotiations on desertification, as well as the logic of global economic integration, suggest that international environmental conventions no longer have to be confined to issues with global commons or transboundary aspects. The international community has a general interest in minimizing industrial pollution within every country, just as it has an interest in preventing the further degradation of land within individual countries. Moreover, even if the argument that differential environmental standards distort trade is not always relevant, international environmental standards for industry will help to avoid trade controversy and restrictions in the future.

For more information, contact Gareth Porter or Paul Speck, 202-628-1400; fax: 628-1825.

The Canadian Foundation for the Americas (FOCAL) is an independent, non-profit organization that promotes business, academic, political, and cultural cooperation between Canada, Latin America, and the Caribbean.

Established in 1990, FOCAL acts as a national forum through which all sectors can collaborate in strengthening Canada's partnership role in the Americas. Its programs support four main objectives:

• Promoting the development of informed and effective policies enabling Canada to compete successfully in the Americas;

• Encouraging linkages between Canadian business, academe, and professional associations and their counterparts in Latin America and the Caribbean;

• Promoting dialogue on hemispheric affairs between policymakers and other sectors of Canadian society;

• Fostering mutual understanding between the peoples of Canada, Latin America, and the Caribbean.

To achieve these goals, FOCAL hosts workshops, conferences, and policy round-tables; administers an internship program for MBA students and media fellowships; and supports research on the impact of current trends and events. It also publishes papers and other documents on strategic issues.

Based in Ottawa, FOCAL has regional offices in Fredericton, New Brunswick; Québec City, Québec; and Calgary, Alberta.

Canadian Regional Consultations on the Miami Summit of the Americas Summary Reports from:

• Western Canada

• Toronto

• Atlantic Canada

• Québec

November 1994

This document provides summary reports from Canadian Regional Consultations on the Summit of the Americas. Meetings were made possible with the financial assistance of the Department of Foreign Affairs and International Trade Canada.

Collaborating Agencies

Department of Foreign Affairs and International Trade Canada

Inter-American Organization for Higher Education

The Canadian Council for the Americas

FOCAL-Atlantic

FOCAL-Québec

FOCAL-West

Table of Contents

INTRODUCTION

The following document compiles reports from a series of consultative sessions held across Canada between October 20 and November 2, 1994. These consultative meetings were developed in collaboration with the Department of Foreign Affairs and International Trade to provide a process through which the views of various sectors of Canadian civil society (NGOs, private sector, provincial governments, media, academia and other regional and national stakeholders) could be incorporated into the overall formation of the Canadian approach to the December 9-10 Summit of the Americas in Miami.

Four regional consultative sessions were organized across Canada, hosted by FOCAL-Atlantic (*Fredericton*); FOCAL-Québec and the Inter-American Organization for Higher Education (*Québec City*); The Canadian Council for the Americas (*Toronto*); and FOCAL-West (*Calgary*).

Each meeting brought together approximately 20 participants representing all sectors and addressed regional priorities, special initiatives, and proposed follow-up activities. Organized generally around the three "*baskets*" of issues identified in United States background documentation for the Summit — Making Democracy Prosperous, Making Democracy Work, Making Democracy Endure — each consultation focused on specific issues of importance to that region. The reports compiled in this document outline specific recommendations to the Canadian government position put forward during the consultations and highlight recommended priorities and initiatives.

This consultative process was made possible through the financial support of the Department of Foreign Affairs and International Trade. The views and recommendations contained in this document do not necessarily represent the views of all participants in the consultations nor of the coordinating agencies.

Special thanks are given to David Adam, Christon Archer, Chi Emeruwa, Lyne LaFlamme, Halina Ostrovski, Christiane Paponnet-Cantat, and Ruth Zeisler who took the lead to ensure the success of these meetings. Many others who cannot be mentioned here also made invaluable contributions to these consultations.

Western Canada Consultation for the Miami Summit of the Americas

Meeting Hosted by FOCAL-West
(The Canadian Foundation for the Americas-West, University of Calgary, Calgary, Alberta, T2N 1N4)
November 1, 1994.

A: Introduction

The following report summarizes the multi-sector consultation held in the International Centre at the University of Calgary on November 1, 1994, hosted by FOCAL-West. Participants from business, government, non-governmental organizations (NGOs), and the academic community of Western Canada reviewed a package of documentation distributed in advance that included "The United States Summary of Initiatives," "Towards Free Trade in the Hemisphere," "The Ad-Hoc U.S. NGO Working Group on the Summit," "Our Common Agenda for the Summit of the Americas," and a document presented at the meeting, "FOCAL: Toward a New World Strategy: Canadian Policy in the Americas into the Twenty-First Century." The Western Canada Consultation commenced with summary and overview reports from Ruth Zeisler (Deputy Director for Regional Coordination and the Summit, Department of Foreign Affairs and International Trade) **Canada's Perspective and Planning for the Miami Summit**; Stephen Randall, (Dean, Faculty of Social Sciences, University of Calgary), **the United States Initiatives**; Joel Prager, (Department of Finance, Government of Saskatchewan), **Review of the Organization of American States and IDB/UNDP Reports**; and Bradley Condon, (Simon Fraser University), **Perspectives on the Expansion of NAFTA**. In addition to the open discussions, all participants received two opportunities to make brief presentations and reactions, and student observers present were able to offer their views. Finally, the meeting broke out into small group discussion sections that reported major recommendations for inclusion in the Western Consultation Report.

B: The Thrust of Discussions at Calgary: the Perspectives of Western Canada

Delegates at Calgary expressed enthusiasm about the opportunity to advise the Department of Foreign Affairs on the Western Canada Perspective for the Miami Summit, but urged that in the future additional lead time should be made available so that participating individuals, governments, or organizations might have sufficient notice to consult more fully. Some participants requested the opportunity to prepare short briefs and position papers for circulation in advance at regional meetings. In the case of the Government of British Columbia, details about the Calgary Consultation did not reach officials in Victoria who otherwise would have sent representatives to Calgary. Participants from the business community advised that greater advance notice should be given so that calendars could be cleared and prior consultations within interest sectors and organizations arranged.

While some Calgary delegates expressed reservations, most shared a spirit of optimism for the 1994 Miami Summit, which grows in part from the restoration of democratic rule in the Americas, the end of the Cold War, and the ever-expanding networks and organizations for trade and exchanges of ideas. There was a suggestion that labour delegates should be present at a regional consultation, and several speakers commented about the silence from the United States regarding Cuban participation. Some speakers at Calgary expressed concerns that their particular views were interpreted by other members of the meeting as negative because they did not agree fully with the central emphasis upon trade and the economic agenda rather than aid, support for human rights, and environmental issues. The role of women, indigenous peoples, and minorities appeared to have been subsumed into the overarching objective to create stronger economic ties and organizations. Recognizing that the United States had initiated the Americas Summit, some delegates at Calgary suggested that Canada should play a stronger role in setting a date for a follow-up Americas summit conference in which other nations might have opportunities to set a different agenda. Indeed, one delegate recommended that Canada play a lead role in establishing a date for a follow-up summit and in extending an invitation to all other American nations.

In examining the United States background papers, it was noted that the emphasis in Miami would be trade rather than aid and that no one could expect a new Alliance for Progress. While Cold War themes were no longer present in many areas, Cuban participation would not take place. The major United States objectives under the present administration appeared to maintain rough continuity with the two previous administrations. In sum, the United States would continue policies reminiscent of the 1950s to channel assistance to private business. Many of the United States positions related to the internal domestic agenda concerning areas such as finding effective solutions to the drug trade. The United States appeals for collective action often echoed domestic concerns. On environmental cooperation, Calgary participants suggested that the United States wanted to direct other nations to "do it the U.S. way." Various participants at Calgary noted potential difficulties for the United States at Miami if fast track authority is not forthcoming. One participant noted that many of the United States initiatives were so general at present that it was difficult to anticipate exact policy directions. For example, Initiative No. 6 on Hemispheric Free Trade contained only six lines of text.

Moving to more general economic, political, and social issues, some speakers reflected upon the dangers of "magic wand economics" and of accepting hackneyed expressions that held the promise of panaceas. Despite the existence of many studies, the concept of sustainable development requires much better understanding, and some specialists have questioned whether economic development necessarily leads to enhanced democracy. Despite economic advances, unequal distribution of wealth in many Latin American states appears to be increasing with dangerous signs of political and social unrest that could interrupt the recent moves toward democracy and economic integration. Historians present pointed to previous periods of democratic activity in the 1950s, for example, and worried about continuing signs of unrest in Venezuela, Brazil, Chile, Bolivia, Argentina, and even Mexico. In Peru, where government successes against insurgency appeared to have taken hold, the sale of public corporations threatens new turbulence. Steps were proposed to promote inter-American cooperation to recover money pillaged by exiled dictators and better policies recommended to prevent the laundering of funds from the drug traffic.

273

Some delegates at Calgary criticized the United States and expressed disappointment at its Miami initiatives that appeared narrowly drawn surrounding trade, economic issues, and the domestic agenda. They argued that the United States had drawn an artificial line between human development and economic development. Delegates debated aspects of the United States initiatives, and some individuals pressed for the creation of a uniquely Canadian perspective. Many argued specifically against the creation of new organizations, meetings, and congresses, pointing out that the present framework of the Organization of American States (OAS), the Inter-American Development Bank (IDB), the Economic Commission for Latin America and the Caribbean (ECLAC), and other organizations provided suitable fora. Along these lines, a representative of the International Centre at the University of Calgary recommended that Canada seek to strengthen its presence in the OAS secretariat and bureaucracy commensurate with its financial contributions.

Responding to these positions, delegates representing government and business stressed that Canada must maintain a positive perspective and refrain from "blue-sky positions" or "grumbling negativism." After all, the United States had taken the initiative to call the Summit of the Americas and no other nation possessed sufficient clout to set the agenda. With regard to the Western Canadian petroleum industry, one participant stressed that Canadians had to identify their areas of expertise and excellence — and to see what this country can offer. It was proposed that Canada's delegation to Miami should seek ways to create micro-climates for small businesses that would link Canadian enterprises with those of other American nations. These ties would serve to foster local developing economies, give rise to local business leadership, and produce advantages for Canada and the other nations involved. Following along these lines, one participant argued that the Canadian delegation at Miami should emphasize assistance and exchanges in high technology, infrastructures, and interactions with regions and regional organizations such as Mercosur and CARICOM. Another participant joined this argument from the high technology perspective, underscoring that Canada must develop a unique role. Given its close proximity to its giant neighbour, this country has maintained its integrity and can bring a wealth of experience to other American nations that are looking for leadership.

Some delegates identified other high technology intermediary roles for Canada in communications, networking, and other systems for effective linkages. In some respects, Canada can use its lengthy experience to act as a broker or intermediary between other American nations and the United States.

Speaking for other constituencies, several delegates responded to the business agenda and proposed that in the communications area, Canada should also seek to foster hemispheric linkages between scholars, writers, artists, and poets. This would involve effective exchange programs for students of the Americas and open the way to exchanges between specialists in medical research, environmental areas, and in different fields of education. Delegates from NGOs supported Canadian initiatives to foster small business exchanges and loan projects, recommending that our Miami delegation seek to develop new and imaginative policies. They argued that Canada is uniquely qualified to handle leading roles in a number of these areas that over a longer term would enhance Canadian ties with the Americas.

In the next round of discussions, delegates stressed that Canada can play a dynamic role at Miami by virtue of its participation in NAFTA, its multicultural mosaic, and its traditional capacity to retain individuality despite proximity to the United States. However, the Canadian delegation should take concrete actions at Miami — announcing plans and initiatives. For example, programs could be announced for student exchanges, networking, small business initiatives, etc. Others suggested that Canada could develop positions on defining criteria for future admissions to NAFTA and to propose other approaches to share talent and pool resources within the Americas. Projects could be introduced to encourage economic ventures, business groups, and to stimulate a range of entrepreneurial activities. Notwithstanding these initiatives, several participants stressed the need for the Canadian delegation at Miami to base its policies on enlightened self-interest — that our nation must gain advantages from the advance of the nations of the Americas.

C: Proposals and Recommendations for the Canadian Delegation to the Miami Summit

1. Define a Canadian agenda that reflects our interests, unique strengths, and experiences that will enable Canada to exercise leadership without imposing our values. This would entail a) illustrating that we have maintained a close relationship with the United States without losing our distinct identity; and b) acting as a broker to seek solutions to hemispheric problems such as poverty and hunger.

2. Canada should press for the use of existing mechanisms and organizations. The tools are in place to oversee economic, cultural, and other exchanges. The creation of new agencies and organizations will cause further investment in bureaucracy.

3. Hemispheric security must be broadly defined to include all aspects of human existence and to combat deepening poverty, environmental degradation, and threats to order caused by corruption, drugs, and violence.

4. Canada should work with other American nations to bring Cuba to the table. The continued isolation of Cuba makes little sense in a post Cold War hemispheric system.

5. Ideas Exchanges: Canada should promote and facilitate the establishment of mechanisms for exchanges of business people, NGOs, teachers, university faculty, and above all of students. This would include electronic mail networks, exchange programs, and conferences.

6. Human Rights: The present United States initiative lacks any mention of human rights. Despite the restoration of democratic institutions, human rights abuses continue to occur. Canada should call for vigilance so as to prevent a return to the recent past.

7. Culture: The process of hemispheric integration must encompass non-economic endeavours. Canada should promote mechanisms for individual and group linkages in areas such as art, literature, and science. Stronger linkages in cultural areas will foster long-term understanding and education.

8. Youth, Education, Health Care: Canada should support NGOs and OAS initiatives, offering assistance based upon Canadian successes in these areas.

9. Canada should seek to define the criteria for any expansion of membership in NAFTA.

10. Canada should use its own specialized expertise to develop a Pan American electronic highway as a means of advancing technical, economic, cultural, and intellectual integration.

11. Canada should give special priority to small businesses that create jobs and take into consideration environmental issues. This would include exchange programs involving Canadian businesses as well as the fostering of small enterprises in Latin America.

12. Canada must promote a small number of attainable goals that will also advance Canadian self-interest.

13. Canada should support an end to corruption, money laundering, and drug trafficking as proposed in the United States Initiatives.

Conclusions

Following a full day of debate and discussions, the various sectors represented at Calgary achieved a remarkable level of agreement in outlining recommendations for the Canadian delegation to the Miami Summit. The participants stressed that Canada is uniquely situated to exercise leadership in fields embracing high technology, culture, diplomacy, and economic integration. Delegates stressed their agreement with aspects of the United States program relating to educational themes and social policy formulation. At the same time, members of the Calgary Consultation wanted to advise the Department of Foreign Affairs to develop an even stronger consultative planning process. They agreed that Canadians need to be better prepared and that additional advance time is required to develop Canadian positions. Although delegates were candid about Canadian problems, they felt that our national experience will permit us to play a major role at Miami and in the future of hemispheric integration. Finally, all members of the Calgary meeting praised the enthusiastic contributions and suggestions of students who participated in the discussions and demonstrated their commitment to a stronger hemispheric system.

Toronto Consultation for the Miami Summit of the Americas

Co-chaired by Gary German, Halina Ostrovski, and David Adam, the meeting was attended by twenty-three people. In attendance were two representatives from the federal government, two from the provincial government, two from universities, one from a college, two additional associations, eleven industry representatives and one graduate student (see complete list at the end of this document).

Meeting hosted by The Canadian Council for the Americas (CCA), Toronto, Ontario, October 20, 1994.

Meeting objective: to contribute views from the private sector to the agenda of the Canadian government for the Summit of the Americas.

The broad objectives of the Summit of the Americas were presented to the participants as:

- An important opportunity to move toward an economically open and integrated hemispheric community.
- A call for commitment by participating countries to market oriented and liberalized economies (including macroeconomics and structural policy reforms).
- A call for commitment by participating countries to take specific steps to bolster the move to free trade and investment flows.

Discussions at the meeting were conducted under the three main themes of the Summit and subdivided into eleven topics.

The themes were the following:

- Making democracy prosperous.
- Making democracy work.
- Making democracy endure: sustainable development.

The specific topics proposed for discussion:

1. Hemispheric free trade — WHFTA
2. WTO/GATT plus initiatives.
3. Infrastructure financing.
4. Transparency and accountability in the conduct of business.
5. Law enforcement — drug cartels.
6. Maximizing capital inflows.
7. Use of civic-minded NGOs and other regional institutions such as the OAS and BID to implement resolutions of the Summit.
8. Providing quality primary education to all.
9. Improving health care.
10. Integrating the poor into the formal economy.
11. Environment and conservation initiatives and enforcement.

Recommendations

- It was agreed that hemispheric economic and trade integration should be Canada's primary focus at the Summit.
- The following practical steps towards economic integration should be taken:
  - Look for assurances from all governments that existing barriers to trade will not be increased, and that, as of January 1995, no new barriers will be created.
  - Undertake a thorough examination and evaluation of obligations of all trade agreements in existence linking all the hemispheric partners (utilizing existing infrastructures such as the OAS or ECLAC).
  - Develop a code of principles for capital and investment flows between countries. This code ought to include provision for investment in equity and capital markets. (Discussion should centre around the financial benefits associated with investment. A "level playing field" where borders would be open on both sides is desirable.)
  - Establish clear explicit rules and obligations for international agricultural subsidies.
  - Define prerequisites for NAFTA accession and initiate the process of bringing Chile into NAFTA.
- It is time to resolve the Cuba problem. Cuba should be integrated into the hemispheric system.
- Canada should stand firm on its vision for the Summit.
- Canada should take a leadership role in the hemisphere.

Other Comments

NAFTA accession clause

President Bill Clinton issued a major statement last April regarding the accession clause. Many leaders throughout the Americas believe they are potentially eligible for entry into NAFTA. Still, the mechanics of accession have not been defined, and President Clinton has lost his fast-track authority for NAFTA. If additional partners are sought, NAFTA will have to incorporate international labour and environmental standards. All of the above will probably emerge as major issues at the Summit.

NAFTA accession and Chile

Although Chile was viewed favourably by meeting participants, some expressed caution feeling that Canada should not press for immediate Chilean accession to NAFTA. They felt that Canadians are not yet fully aware of all the implications of NAFTA and may want to consider alternative bilateral agreements (i.e., Canada-Chile bilateral) before admitting a new partner.

NAFTA accession and Brazil

Brazil presents an important exception to the exclusive use of NAFTA as a vehicle for expanding hemispheric trade liberalization. It was suggested that Canada should not be so committed to NAFTA accession and may wish to look at regional agreements such as the Mercosur as a building block. If Brazil rejects NAFTA accession, other Latin American countries may follow suit. Canada must then consider the danger of pitting NAFTA against other trade agreements.

Other economic integration concepts discussed

- Sector agreements such as the Canada-US Auto Pact may be desirable in some cases instead of bilateral or multilateral agreements.
- A South American Free Trade Agreement (SAFTA) may bring more benefits to investors than traders.
- An umbrella agreement between all hemispheric countries, with flexible rules, could prevent the proliferation of bilateral agreements potentially harmful to Canada.

Cuba

Participants expressed enthusiasm regarding evolving Canadian-Cuban relations. There was general consensus that Cuba should be integrated into the hemisphere and should have been invited to the Summit. It was agreed that it is time to resolve the Cuba problem.

Cuban integration into a future Western Hemisphere Free Trade Agreement (WHFTA) was discussed. Cuban policies in areas such as health standards, as well as the island's current lack of basic financial infrastructure (a central bank) would pose difficulties for its potential inclusion in such an agreement.

The effect of Cuba's development on the rest of Latin America was discussed. Some meeting participants felt that Canada should aim to be Cuba's primary trading partner; however, it was also stressed that caution must be exercised given that increased interaction with Cuba could create resentment in the United States.

It was pointed out that financial institutions are somewhat skeptical in their attitude towards Cuba. The country is still considered a "risky area," which would require considerable economic reform to assure the banks that Cuba is "investment worthy."

Additional theme discussion

All three themes were considered important. Economic growth was considered a necessary prerequisite for sustainable development and good governance. It can also be viewed the other way around: sustainable development and good governance are necessary prerequisites for economic growth.

It was agreed that Canada should "stick to what we know best" and focus efforts on economic integration. It was felt that the private sector should voice its desire for increased trade and economic relations at all times.

Concern was expressed regarding the issue of linking trade to human rights, aid to trade, and aid to investment. Concern was also expressed regarding CIDA's desire to tie trade to human rights and their ability to implement this principle.

There was concern expressed by some members of the group regarding the importance the Summit will give to the issue of sustainable development, and whether it could "capture the Summit" to the detriment of Canadian companies (in particular, mining companies). While sustainable development is important, it cannot be realized without investment and trade. It was suggested that, given Clinton's weakened political state, he may shy away from the issue of NAFTA accession and focus on sustainable development. It was generally agreed that while sustainable development could capture the attention

of the Summit, Clinton could not afford to ignore issues of economic integration. Clinton will probably push one sustainable development initiative instead, such as policies regarding climatic change and/or biodiversity.

It is in Canada's interest to support the concept of sustainable development in order to diffuse any negative impact.

Prior to the consultative meeting in Toronto, a questionnaire was distributed to participants. The responses of six of the participants are compiled in Annex 1.

Atlantic Canada Consultation for the Miami Summit of the Americas

Final Report

Meeting Hosted by FOCAL-Atlantic (The Canadian Foundation for the Americas — Atlantic), University of New Brunswick, Fredericton, N.B. November 2, 1994

The following is a summary of statements and recommendations that were expressed by participants at the Atlantic Canada Consultation for the Miami Summit of the Americas. These concerns are presented with both a sense of urgency and a spirit of collaboration. They should be given serious consideration and incorporated into the overall formation of the Canadian approach to the summit. Recommendations herein are in response to the three themes proposed by the organizers of the Summit of the Americas and the 14 Initiatives proposed by the U.S.

Theme 1 Good Governance

Workshop participants identified the following areas which needed to be strengthened in order to foster good governance:

- A need to build up a harmonious relationship between the state and civil society with a strong commitment to the development of a democratic culture;

- A need to make the Americas politically stable;

- A need to make institutions stronger and more open to public participation;

- A need for international organizations already in place (i.e., UN and OAS) to be actively involved in building up a democratic culture, in protecting the environment, and in combating drugs;

- A need to define democracy in a sense that would be devoid of any paternalistic or domineering attitudes.

The group agreed that Canada should endorse:

- The empowerment of judicial institutions,

- The strengthening of local courts,

- The decentralization of power,

- The reduction of violence,

- The strengthening of human rights, and

- The control of arms proliferation.

and that Canada should support:

- An orderly process of transition in Cuba. The exclusion of Cuba reflects "a cold war attitude," which is not appropriate;

- A position of "financial feasibility" as adapted to the political reality of each country;

- The promotion of education and literacy as these have an important socio-economic component and are crucial to the fostering of business opportunities.

The group also agreed that Canada should give priority to:

- Education which promotes not only schooling for children but also adult education,

- Population growth control and an improvement of the condition of women and children,

- Land reforms and the reduction of internal structural inequalities,

- Partnership between the state and NGOs, and

- Partnership between the OAS and NGOs.

and that Canada should be committed to:

- A type of sustainable development rooted in economic growth at the grass-roots level — economic growth requires community involvement;

- A harmonization between trade, the environment, and sustainable development — these three components must be mutually supportive;

- The development of mechanisms within the OAS that would deal with Latin America's national debt issues;

- The concept of cooperative security with the creation of a Permanent Committee on Hemispheric Security dealing with:

    - regional stabilization

    - peacekeeping and peace-making

    - drug enforcement

    - professionalization of military and police forces.

Recommendations

1. That all the nations of the world (including Canada and the United States) adopt an attitude of global partnership towards good governance and economic progress, which will take into account the special needs of the South which have often been ignored.

2. That grass-roots community organizations as well as existing international organizations promote good governance and sustainable development. People from all walks of life (including women) must become active participants in the development of a democratic culture.

Theme 2 Trade

The group agreed that there is a need for a clear trade policy vision and that Canada re-examine its model for sustainable development with global trade being its main engine.

Global trade must be re-examined with these considerations in mind:

- Partners are unequal.
- The existing trading system has built up inequalities that need to be addressed.
- Canada must endorse a concept of fair trade.

The group agreed that the following concerns be addressed by Atlantic Canada:

- How do we address the question of selection of trading partners?
- Atlantic export commodities are still based on natural resources.
- How do we address the question of transportation?
- Exporting partners for Atlantic Canada should be the Caribbean region including Cuba, Central America, Venezuela and Colombia rather than Chile.
- How do we address the question of economic integration without creating a competition problem? Assistance to Latin American economies will impact on our own industries.

The group agreed that in order to provide greater opportunities for Atlantic Canada it is necessary:

- To redefine the nature of investments in terms of partnership building;
- To take a long-term view so that trading is not detrimental to Atlantic Canada;
- To encourage small, medium and micro enterprises to link with the informal sector of Latin American economies;
- To promote cooperative and credit union organization;
- To put no limitation on information technology; and
- To protect culture and intellectual property rights.

Theme 3 Sustainable Development

The group agreed that the direction or path of the concept was the important thing and that the concept included:

- Sustainable local communities;
- Diversity (both economic and environmental);
- Per capita consumption and equity of distribution;
- The need to change attitudes (political/cultural changes);
- Low environmental standards are not sustainable in the long run from either an environmental or an economic point of view; and
- Sustainability does not necessarily imply or require equitable distribution of resources.

The group agreed:

- That sustainability in the hemisphere cannot be implemented as part of a Northern agenda. In fact, neither Canada (with its high debt) nor New Brunswick can be considered a model for sustainable development; and
- That existing institutions be strengthened.

The group disagreed on:

- Whether the OAS or UN agencies with a presence in the region would be effective and
- Whether promoting environmental protection and sustainable development in the hemisphere would affect business opportunities for Canada.

Initiative 9, Education

The group agreed with the importance of education, however:

- The time frame in the initiative is not realistic;
- Education, including adult education and improving literacy rates, is a key to sustainability and to the necessary change in attitudes;
- Community-based rather than institution-based programs are the most appropriate; and

- NGOs should be supported, especially local NGOs, as the most effective agent for delivery of aid.

Initiative 10, Health

The group agreed with the importance of universal access to heath care; however, it was pointed out that:

- The time frame in the initiative is not realistic;
- PAHO needs support, especially financial support;
- Increased participation of Canadians at the PAHO Secretariat is needed; and
- The role of women in the delivery of health care is important.

Initiative 11, Micro Enterprises (Small and Medium Sized Businesses)

The group pointed out that Atlantic Canada has considerable experience with small and medium sized businesses as well as with cooperatives and would be willing to assist the federal government in this area in the preparatory work for the Summit.

The group suggested that the following be incorporated in the Canadian position:

- Restructuring of debt is not strategic planning; these activities must be harmonized to integrate environmental objectives with other objectives;
- The NGO role, especially at the grass roots level, is important for effective implementation; and
- The Summit should avoid rhetoric; funding and political will are needed.

Initiative 12, Energy

The group agreed with the objectives of the initiative and suggested that pricing mechanisms could be used to meet these objectives. The most efficient electrical generating system that does not have a negative impact on the environment should be favoured. Further considerations include:

- Canada cannot be considered a model as Canada needs to change with regard to energy policy;
- Improved technology can help the problem; i.e., there is potential for reducing transportation costs by improving communication infrastructure;
- Small scale and private producers of energy should be considered; and
- Total cost accounting should be used to assess alternatives.

Initiative 13, Environmental Protection

The group advocated a strong support for Agenda 21 and the subsequent Biodiversity and Climate Change Conventions. Specific comments include:

- One central GEF should be set up, preferably not World Bank;
- Support should be given to existing institutions based in Latin America and the Caribbean;
- Project funding which requires matching dollars is not working; better to focus on fewer projects and provide full funding; and
- Biodiversity-ownership role and exploitation benefits should belong to country, not outside interests.

Initiative 14, Environmental Protection and Compliance Regimes

- Threat of nuclear pollution should be added to human health issues;
- Transboundary shipment of hazardous wastes and solid wastes should be limited (support for Basel Convention);
- Local communities should control the use of natural resources; and
- Harmonization of environmental regulations should be upward — regulations should provide a floor not a ceiling; individual countries should be allowed to enact more stringent regulations, and this should trigger a consideration of more stringent regulations in other countries.

Organisé par l'Organisation universitaire interaméricaine et FOCAL-Québec

Rapport de la réunion de consultation sur le Sommet des Amériques

Québec, le 31 octobre, 1994

Une vingtaine de personnes ont répondu à l'invitation de l'Organisation universitaire interaméricaine et ont consacré la journée du 31 octobre à émettre des avis quant à la participation du gouvernement canadien au Sommet des Amériques. Le groupe comprenait des universitaires, des fonctionnaires du gouvernement du Québec, des représentants d'organismes non-gouvernementaux et, malheureusement, un seul représentant du milieu des affaires.

Après avoir entendu le conférencier invité, Mme Chinyere Emeruwa, du ministère des Affaires étrangères et du Commerce international, les membres du groupe ont discuté du sujet sous quatre volets, un volet général et les trois thèmes proposés, soit la démocratie, l'intégration économique et le développement durable. Voici l'essentiel des avis qui ont été émis.

1. Principes et priorités

1.1 Bon nombre d'intervenants ont proposé que le Canada profite de l'occasion du Sommet pour se démarquer par rapport aux États-Unis. Il importe hautement, aux yeux de toutes les personnes qui se sont exprimées sur ce sujet, que le Canada ne soit pas perçu par les Latino-Américains comme une réplique des États-Unis, que notre position soit originale, mitoyenne entre la superpuissance voisine et les autres États américains. Au témoignage même d'un professeur latino-américain (invité à l'Université Laval et membre du groupe), le Canada est souvent perçu en Amérique latine comme une simple extension des États-Unis. De l'avis unanime des personnes réunies, il faut corriger cette perception. Il y aurait lieu, selon plusieurs, de nous rapprocher davantage de nos partenaires latino-américains et d'épouser à l'occasion, leurs points de vue.

Il est vrai, a-t-on souligné, que cela ne sera pas aisé au chapitre de l'intégration économique parce que le volume de nos échanges commerciaux avec les États-Unis ne nous laisse pas une grande marge de manoeuvre. Par contre, en ce qui a trait à la définition de la démocratie, au rôle de l'État et aux diverses questions relatives aux affaires sociales, culturelles et environnementales, nous aurions tout intérêt à insister pour que le modèle américain ne soit pas proposé comme le seul valable.

Plusieurs ont déploré le ton plutôt paternaliste, pour ne pas dire «néo-colonialiste», des initiatives proposées par Washington. L'impression qui semble se dégager du document états-unien, c'est qu'on demande à l'Amérique latine de modeler son comportement sur celui de l'Amérique du Nord. Le Canada devrait faire en sorte que cette impression soit corrigée.

1.2 En conséquence, le Canada devrait axer ses positions, comme il l'a fait si souvent dans le passé, sur une perspective multilatérale. Pour la plupart des intervenants, il importe à cet égard de renforcer la présence canadienne à l'Organisation des États Américains (OEA) et d'utiliser ce canal pour concrétiser les réformes proposées. Plusieurs ont mis en garde contre la stratégie américaine, dite du «hub and spoke» ou du moyeu et des rayons de la roue, qui consiste à tout réduire aux relations bilatérales entre les États-Unis et leurs divers partenaires. L'Accord de Libre-Échange Nord-Américain (ALENA) et d'autres organisations économiques, comme, par exemple, le MERCOSUR (pays du cône sud) devraient constituer d'autres cadres d'intervention.

1.3   Le Canada devrait encore profiter du Sommet des Amériques, selon plusieurs membres du groupe, pour manifester sa sensibilité particulière au respect des cultures. À cet égard, quelques intervenants se sont montrés déçus de ce que toute la documentation fournie soit en langue anglaise. On l'accepte volontiers venant des États-Unis, On l'accepte moins bien en provenance d'Ottawa ou de la Table ronde sur l'environnement et l'économie dont le rapport du 11 juillet 1994 est censé être disponible en français et en espagnol. Les membres du groupe souhaitent évidemment que l'image bilingue du Canada soit mise en relief auprès de nos partenaires des Amériques et qu'on exploite les affinités particulières des Québécois et des Latino-Américains.

1.4   On veut bien que le Canada privilégie l'intégration économique, mais on voudrait aussi qu'on porte attention au fait qu'une partie de la population latino-américaine (200 millions de pauvres) n'a pas encore fait ce choix historique en faveur de la démocratie et de l'économie de marché. On mentionne les fréquentes manifestations récentes et une certaine désillusion qui se fait jour à l'endroit d'une démocratie qui ne livre pas les fruits escomptés. L'intégration économique ne fonctionnera pas si on ne crée pas un marché de consommateurs.

1.5   À cet effet, l'éducation et la santé sont considérés par plusieurs intervenants comme les bases essentielles des réformes qu'il faut proposer. L'éducation surtout, car même la santé populaire repose sur une certaine forme d'éducation. On s'étonne de ce que les documents soumis fassent peu état de l'enseignement supérieur, en particulier. Car c'est l'université qui est la source des compétences, le réservoir des informations vitales, le lieu de la formation des maîtres du primaire et du secondaire. Pour participer à la démocratie et à l'économie, une population doit être formée, éduquée, instruite. On cite l'exemple de l'Union Européenne qui privilégie les capacités de recherche et de formation.

2. Démocratie

2.1   Les membres du groupe sont intervenus à plusieurs reprises pour souligner une tendance malheureuse à considérer que la simple tenue d'élections libres signifierait l'instauration de la démocratie. La démocratie constitue un processus beaucoup plus large et complexe. Les Américains eux-mêmes devraient bien le comprendre, car leurs Pères fondateurs ont insisté sur ce point et sur la nécessité d'une éducation à la démocratie. Thomas Jefferson, en particulier, considérait chaque citoyen comme un gouvernant en puissance et déclarait que la démocratie commence au lendemain des élections.

Il faut donc prendre conscience que la démocratie se développe dans un État de droits, dans la souveraineté populaire, dans la liberté de la presse et qu'elle suppose la santé physique et intellectuelle du peuple. À cet égard, on propose des entreprises communes aux Amériques (au delà des États particuliers) en matière de santé et d'éducation.

2.2   On signale aussi que le développement des valeurs démocratiques ne se poursuivra pas nécessairement selon le modèle américain. Bien au contraire, fait-on remarquer, la démocratie à l'américaine, à tort ou à raison, est souvent l'objet de suspicions chez les latino-américains. Le Canada serait bien placé pour faire valoir une conception de la démocratie qui laisse un rôle plus important à l'État et qui conviendrait davantage aux besoins de certains pays.

On fait valoir aussi que la démocratie politique ne saurait bien fonctionner ni être agréée des populations si elle n'est pas accompagnée par la démocratie économique, c'est-à-dire par une meilleure répartition des richesses.

On renvoie à cet égard aux pages 23 à 31 du document latino-américain «Our Common Agenda».

2.3   On propose encore une approche et des attitudes plus humbles de la part des citoyens de pays démocratiques comme le Canada qui sont appelés à faire état de leur expertise. On donne en exemple le rôle joué par la Direction générale des élections du Québec en Haïti. On a communiqué une expérience, on a fait des propositions, mais on a insisté pour que les Haïtiens organisent eux-mêmes leurs élections selon un mode qui leur est propre.

Il est important, fait-on valoir, que la démocratie se développe de l'intérieur et qu'on crée les institutions permanentes qui conviennent à chaque pays.

2.4. La plupart des intervenants se sont montrés sceptiques devant les propositions américaines relativement à des phénomènes comme la corruption, le trafic de la drogue et le blanchiment de l'argent. On signale d'abord que ces plaies sociales ont peu à voir avec l'absence de démocratie. Car elles se manifestent aussi bien aux États-Unis et au Canada qu'ailleurs. Nous serions très mal venus de nous montrer trop moralisateurs à ce sujet vis-à-vis de nos partenaires latino-américains qui auront tôt fait de nous ramener à nos responsabilités.

2.5 On signale que la seule protection des investissements n'est pas nécessairement liée à l'exercice de la démocratie.

2.6 Enfin, même si on a tendance, au sein du groupe, à valoriser le rôle de l'OEA, on met en garde contre des interventions trop directes de cet organisme, comme, par exemple, la création proposée de cellules de crise. (Le Canada verrait-il d'un bon oeil une intervention de l'OEA dans son problème constitutionnel?) L'OEA doit jouer un rôle de coordination mais les responsabilités immédiates de résolution de conflits doivent être plus décentralisées, croit-on.

3. Intégration Économique

3.1 En ce qui a trait à l'intégration économique, on a rappelé que le Québec y a toujours été très favorable. Mais, souligne-t-on, c'est avant tout pour contrer un certain protectionnisme américain que le Québec a appuyé l'accord de libre-échange avec les États-Unis. C'est encore pour diminuer quelque peu la contrainte américaine qu'on a appuyé l'ALENA et qu'on souhaite son élargissement à condition que cela ne se fasse pas selon le mode «hub and spoke».

3.2 On souhaite que l'intégration économique ne se poursuive pas selon un modèle ultralibéral d'économie de marché qui ne conviendrait pas aux économies du sud. Plusieurs font valoir qu'il devrait y avoir place dans une grande union économique régionale pour un certain rôle de l'État et d'organismes coopératifs. On signale que le Mouvement Desjardins du Québec a réalisé des expériences intéressantes au Mexique en suscitant la contribution du capital local à des entreprises coopératives.

On signale encore que tout n'est pas libéral aux États-Unis, qu'il y existe des règlements protectionnistes en matière de services financiers et quant à la libre circulation des biens et services. En d'autres termes, si le marché des Amériques doit s'ouvrir, celui des États-Unis doit s'ouvrir également aux exportations latino-américaines. On souhaite un équilibre des concessions.

3.3 Les membres du groupe sont unanimes pour souhaiter que l'intégration économique soit conçue dans un cadre respectueux des autonomies nationales et des cultures propres. Car c'est bien ainsi que les Québécois veulent se situer dans le processus de globalisation. Ils sont aussi soucieux de la protection de leur culture que de l'élargissement des marchés. On se fait fort de rappeler, à cet égard, l'esprit des accords de l'Uruguay Round (décembre 1993) qui ont laissé place à l'exception culturelle.

Dans un même ordre d'idées, on met en garde contre une extension des systèmes de télécommunications, en particulier du réseau Internet, qui ne serait pas respectueux de la diversité linguistique du continent. Le Canada bilingue devrait être aussi alerte en ce domaine que les pays hispanophones, lusophones ou autres.

On fait aussi remarquer que les infrastructures sociales sont tout aussi importantes que les infrastructures de communication.

4. Le Développement Durable

4.1 Au chapitre du développement durable, le groupe tombe facilement d'accord avec les propositions américaines. On craint cependant qu'elles demeurent des voeux pieux. On fait valoir aussi que les objectifs mentionnés sont plutôt utopiques, comme celui d'une fréquentation scolaire élevée à 100% au primaire et 75% au secondaire pour l'an 2 000.

4.2 On propose d'encourager les échanges d'étudiants et, en général, la rencontre des personnes entre le Canada et l'Amérique latine.

4.3 On attire l'attention sur l'importance de toujours tenir compte de la diversité des situations. À cet égard, des objectifs exprimés en pourcentages globaux n'ont guère de sens.

On propose la création d'États généraux de la santé et de l'éducation pour les Amériques.

4.4 Enfin, en matière d'environnement (une question que le groupe a très peu explorée), on souligne l'importance d'interdire l'importation des déchets, un phénomène qui pourrait s'accroître avec l'intégration économique.

Conclusion

Les membres du groupe demeurent bien conscients des liens particuliers qui nous unissent depuis longtemps aux États-Unis. Ils n'en sont pas moins conscients de l'urgente nécessité de nous ouvrir davantage et à notre façon à l'ensemble des Amériques. Car il leur apparaît que nous sommes de plus en plus voués à vivre la globalisation d'abord et avant tout sur le continent américain.

Annex 1

Prior to the consultative meeting in Toronto, a questionnaire was distributed to participants. The responses of six of the participants is compiled below.

1. NATURE OF THE BUSINESS OF RESPONDENT

Human biological / Assisting Ontario companies in securing international capital projects / Investment banking and brokerage / National trade association / Port corporation / Mineral exploration / Integrated mining and metal products.

2. COUNTRIES PRESENTLY INVOLVED

- Mexico, Argentina, Brazil, Venezuela, Peru.
- Entire region.
- Mexico, Argentina, Chile, Venezuela, Brazil, Panama, Uruguay, Guyana, Bahamas, Cayman, BVI, Netherlands Antilles, Barbados, Trinidad and Tobago, Bermuda, Dominican Republic and other Caribbean countries.
  - Mexico and entire region.
  - Central and South America.
  - Mexico, Panama, Peru, Chile, Argentina.

3. PLANNING TO EXPAND IN THE REGION?

- Yes (3).
- No.
- Yes, South America.
- Yes, in present countries.

4. COUNTRIES OF FUTURE INTEREST

- Mexico, Argentina, Chile, Brazil.
- Mexico, Argentina, Chile, Colombia, Brazil.
- Colombia, Costa Rica, Peru, Cuba, Ecuador, Paraguay.
- Argentina, Chile, Brazil, Mexico.
- Mexico, Central America and South America.
- Brazil.
- Mexico, Chile, Peru.

5. DIFFICULTIES IN DOING BUSINESS WITH THE REGION

- Legal, procedural and cultural difficulties in Mexico.
- Regulatory environment is not always conducive to private infrastructure investment; also, projects are difficult to finance given securities and rate of return available.
- Typically on underwriting US or European leads, dealers "crowd out" the Canadian after we have encouraged the issuer to offer the securities in Canada. In other words, the US or European lead "covers" Canada, and the Canadian dealers get nothing for the effort of selling the benefits of offering in Canada.
- N/A / No.
- Not international in nature - corruption in Mexico, Panama, crime in Peru. Hidden costs related to archaic bureaucratic legal system in Chile, petty bureaucracy, provincial system, semi-corruption in Argentina.
- None to state.

6. INDICATORS FOLLOWED IN DECISION TO DO BUSINESS IN A COUNTRY

- Access to, and potential size of, the market for our product, political and economical stability, legal aspect.
- Credit rating and future growth potential as well as interest of our client base.
- Credit rating, demand from investors, local capital markets, local investment laws.
- N/A (3).
- Personnel safety.
- Geological potential, geological climate, stable business climate.

7. INDICATORS WHICH POSTPONE OR ELIMINATE A COUNTRY IN BUSINESS OBJECTIVES

- Potential market size in volume and price.
- Political and economic instability and regulatory environment.

• Civil unrest, economic mismanagement, political instability, low reserves, default.

• N/A (2).

• Crime, political unrest, impossible investment laws, business climate.

8. HOW CAN CANADIANS DO MORE BUSINESS WITH THE REGION?

• Active government support services in the markets themselves. More direct flights from Toronto.

• Improved comfort to capital is key to increase the level of business activities.

• Centre for information, get on an airplane, speak Spanish or Portuguese, get away from the US middleman.

• More direct business contacts.

• Become more aggressive and focus on the long term prospects.

• Establish economically sound transportation systems to and from the countries and assist in the transport infrastructure of the countries.

• Solve difficulties referred to on question 7 of countries.

• Development of business infrastructure. Improved business to business links.

9. IS NAFTA WORKING?

• Greatest impact of NAFTA for us has been psychological.

• Yes, the level of interest in hemispheric trade has increased significantly.

• As an investment agreement, yes.

• Yes, at least in merchandise trade.

• Yes (2).

• Too soon to know.

10. WHAT ARE THE DIFFICULTIES IF ANY WITH MEXICO OR US AS RESULT OF NAFTA?

• N/A (3).

• More competitive but that is the objective.

• Rules of origin.

• None other time countervail, anti dump, rules of origin.

• No interpretive precedent in the uniform regulation.

11. WOULD YOU LIKE TO HAVE A WESTERN HEMISPHERIC FREE TRADE AGREEMENT "WHFTA"?

• Yes, most definitely.

• Yes, definitely.

• No, I would like to see AFTA (Americas Free Trade Agreement).

• Yes.

• Yes, very much.

• No. New time why not.

• If it is in Canada's best interest.

12. HOW WOULD YOU SEE WHFTA? (a) Countries would join NAFTA through accession clause. (b) A separate agreement should be examined?

• Add countries which meet certain criteria to existing NAFTA agreement.

• Accession clause.

• NAFTA should be used as the blueprint; however, the general agreement should be open to development. Countries should be able to apply to a central board based upon certain economic issues.

• (a) Yes. No separate agreement should be examined.

• A separate agreement should be examined.

• Accession clause. Joining through existing NAFTA not creating a whole new agreement.

13. HOW DO YOU PRESENTLY SEE GATT's ROLE IN GENERAL?

• Not clear to me.

• Their role would not change GATT. What would change is that WHFTA would take on an increased role in future.

• European community.

• Great idea, tough to implement.

• A world trade organization that sets the trading rules and a method to resolve disputes.

• GATT has a large role to play but the US administration must resolve their international difficulties first.

• N/A.

14. WOULD GATT's PRESENT ROLE CHANGE IN WHFTA?

- N/A (3).

- Let's work with NAFTA as the blue print and develop this document as time passes and different issues arise.

- GATT's role would not change.

- A WHFTA should stand on its own.

15. HOW DO YOU PRESENTLY SEE OAS' ROLE WITHIN WHFTA?

- Not clear to me.

- OAS is a political forum which complements WHFTA.

- Could be the board suggested above.

- No opinion (2).

16. WHAT WOULD YOU LIKE TO SEE INCLUDED IN THE CANADIAN AGENDA DURING THE MIAMI SUMMIT? PLEASE LIST PRIORITIES, IDEAS FOR INITIATIVES AND WAYS TO IMPLEMENT THESE PRIORITIES.

- Expansion of NAFTA to other countries in the Americas.

- Airline access rights from Canada.

- Harmonization of regulatory standards.

- Focus on regulatory environment for investment (infrastructure).

- Inclusion of services in many regional trade agreements.

- Financial services, brokerage, etc. We need "level playing field" and perhaps representation based upon region not number of companies.

- No loss to Canada of benefits achieved in the NAFTA.

- Accession of Latin American countries through NAFTA rather than a separate bilateral or other agreements.

- Explore the possibility of a hemispheric customs union. Improved dispute settlement mechanism for dumping and countervailing.

- Canada should focus on direct relationships with countries; i.e., not under the umbrella of US dominated policies.

- Investment/capital flow agreement.

- Foreign investment protection agreement.

- Coordination of crime, drugs, etc.

- Movement of personnel (technical) between countries.

- No opinion.

Participants in the Western Consultation

Christon I. Archer	University of Calgary, FOCAL-West, Chair
Sandra Block	University of Calgary
María Cashin	University of Calgary
Bradley Condon	Faculty of Business Administration, Centre for North American Business Studies, Simon Fraser University, Vancouver, B.C.
Louella Cronkhiten	World Citizen Centre, Lethbridge, Alberta
Mark Dickerson	University of Calgary
Wade Derkson	University of Calgary
Christopher Frazer	University of Calgary
Troy Fuller	University of Calgary
Joelle Gray	University of Calgary
Chris Hazeltine	Calgary Economc Development, Calgary, Alberta
Hannet Hefel	University of Calgary
Anette Hester	University of Calgary
Graham Knox	University of Calgary
Herman Konrad	University of Calgary
Daniel López	Student Participant, University of Calgary
Robert Lovsin	University of Calgary
Helmut Mach	Executive Director, International Economic Relations, Alberta Federal and

	Intergovernmental Affairs, Edmonton, Alberta
Dianna Massot	University of Calgary
Marianne Middelveen	University of Calgary
Ana María Peredo	FOCAL-West
Katherine Pérez	University of Calgary
Joel Prager	Director of Planning, Saskatchewan Finance, Regina, Saskatchewan
Stephen Randall	Dean of Social Sciences, University of Calgary
Thomas Routledge	FOCAL, Vancouver, British Columbia
Pat Shea	University of Calgary
Godfrey Tang	University of Calgary
Steven Walker	University of Calgary
Bill Warden	Director, International Centre, University of Calgary
David Wolf	President Stone Petroleum Ltd., Board Member SEAPAC, Calgary, Alberta
Ruth Zeisler	Deputy Director for Regional Coordination and the Miami Summit, Department of Foreign Affairs and International Trade
Hank Zyp	St Joseph's Save-the-Children, Edmonton, Alberta

Participants in the Toronto Consultation

Amb. David Adam	Department of Foreign Affairs and International Trade
Alan S. Alexandroff	Trade Policy Program Coordinator, Centre for International Studies, U of Toronto
Anthony L. Cooper	Vice President and Director, Scotia McLeod Inc.
Lisa Da Silva	International MBA Student
Alan Dean	Vice President, Brascan
Ruth Fothergill	Regional Vice President, Ontario, Export Development Corporation
Gary Gallon	President, Canadian Environment Industry Association
Gary German	CCA National Chairman and President and CEO of Bedford International Finance Corp.
Alan R. Hill	Executive Vice President, American Barrick Resources Corporation
W.L. Holt	Vice Chairman, Consoltex Group Inc.
Sen. James Kelleher	Partner, Gowling Strathy and Henderson
Mark Lievonen	Senior Vice President, Connaught Laboratories Ltd.
Michael Manjuris	Director, Officer of Int'l Business Relations, Ryerson Polytechnic University
Donald R. McArthur	President, Canadian Importers' Association
William Mercer	Manager, Latin America, Noranda Exploration

Christine Oldfield	Professor, School of Business, Centennial College	Chinyere Emeruwa	Foreign Affairs and International Trade, Ottawa, Ont.
Halina B. Ostrovski	National President, The Canadian Council for the Americas	Guy-Andre Gelinas	International Marketing & Entrepreneurship, UNB Saint John, N. B.
Maria Reda	Canadian Council for the Americas	Yola Georgiadou	Geodesy and Geomatics, UNB Saint John, N. B.
Brian Russell	Director, North American Polity Group, Dalhousie University	Dick Gorham	Former Roving Ambassador for Latin America, King's County, N. B.
Peter Sadlier-Brown	Assistant Deputy Minister, Ministry of Economic Development and Trade	Greg Gillis	Washburn and Gillis, Fredericton, N. B.
Wolfgang Schmitz	Director, Trade Development, Saint John Port Corporation	Sean Kelly	CUSO, Halifax, N. S.
		Karen Laine	Sustainable Communities Network of Nova Scotia, Halifax, N. S.
Denis Thibault	Director, Latin America and Caribbean Trade Division, DFAIT	Peter McKenna	Political Science, St. Mary's University, Halifax, N. S.
Glen Tugman	Assistant General Manager, The Bank of Nova Scotia	Christiane Paponnet-Cantat	Director, FOCAL-Atlantic, UNB Fredericton, N.B.
Adi Waksman	Canadian Council for the Americas	Mary Patterson	N. S. Centre for Environmentally Sustainable Economic Development, Halifax, N. S.
James Wessinger	Vice President, Ontario International Corporation	Neil Ridler	Economics, UNBSJ, Saint John, N. B.
		Carl Rufelds	Former Head of Missions in Latin America, Fredericton, N. B.

Participants in the Atlantic Consultation

		Frank Scheme	ADI Group Inc. Fredericton, N. B.
		Owen Washburn	Neil and Gunter Ltd., Fredericton, N. B.
Erick Anderson	Industry Canada, Moncton, N. B.	Frank Wilson	Vice-President (Research & Int. Cooperation), UNB Saint John, N. B.
Dave Besner	Environment, Fredericton, N. B.		
Jim Cromwell	Advanced Education and Labour, Fredericton, N. B.		
Jessie Davies	Sustainable Development, UNB Saint John, N. B.		
Richard Donald	Landmark Resource Consultants, Halifax, N. S.		

Participants à la reunion de Québec

Gérard Arguin	Directeur de la revue IGLU, Organisation universitaire interaméricaine
Louis Balthazar	Département de science politique, Université Laval
Michel Bellavance	Professeur, Sciences politiques, ENAP
Lincoln Bizzozero	Professeur invité, Programme de maîtrise en relations internationales, Université Laval
Maurice Boisvert	Directrice générale, Institut de développement Nord-Sud
Chiyere Emeruwa	Analyste de politiques, Division de la coordination régionale, Ministère des Affaires étrangères
Raymond Giroux	Adjoint au Directeur de l'éditorial, Le Soleil
Jean-Paul Gravel	Responsable des programmes, IRECUS, Université de Sherbrooke
Louis Fortier	Conseiller en politiques commerciales, Direction des relations commerciales, Ministère des Affaires internationales, Gouvernement du Québec
Jacques Jolicoeur	President de la Caisse Desjardins du Vieux Québec
Jean Jolin	Directeur général des élections, Gouvernement du Québec
Lyne Laflamme	Directrice de l'organisation et de l'information, Organisation universitaire interaméricaine
Gordon Mace	Département de science politique, Université Laval
Jean-François Motheron	Directeur, Directions des technologies, Ministère des Communications, Gouvernement du Québec
Léo Paré	Vice-president de l'Institut canadien des affaires internationales
Serge Paré	Conseiller au dossier industriel et à l'investissement, Ministère des Affaires internationales, Gouvernement du Québec
Denis Proulx	Professeur de management, École nationale d'administration publique (ENAP)
Alain Prujiner	Directeur de l'Institut québecois des hautes études internationales, Université Laval
Pierre Racicot	Directeur du Conseil régional de concertation et de développement de la région de Québec
Wayne Tessier	Conseiller-économiste, Centre mondial du commerce, Québec-Beauport Inc.
Christian La Tortue	Directeur adjoint, Institut de l'énergie, Gouvernement du Québec
Jacques Tousignant	Université du Québec
Robert Trudel	President de l'Institut canadien des affaires internationales, Direction des relations commerciales intercontinentales, Ministère des Affaires internationales, de l'Immigration et des Communautés culturelles, Gouvernement du Québec
Pierre Van Der Donckt	Secrétaire général exécutif, Organisation universitaire interaméricaine

These comments are excerpted from a special FOCAL report on the Summit of the Americas, prepared for the Canadian Foundation for the Americas by Ambassador John W. Graham, former Executive Coordinator of the Unit for the Promotion of Democracy of the OAS and currently consultant with the International Foundation for Electoral Systems, Washington, D.C.

Postscript:
Measuring the Summit's Success

In the years ahead, and well before the deadline of 2005, the Summit objectives will be judged on their implementation. The first test will be the extent of progress on FTAA, followed by democracy, governance, and sustainable development.

The Summit was essentially concerned with trade. But how securely can the Summit's promise rest on its commitment to free trade? On the last day, the Prime Minister of Canada, Jean Chrétien, and the President of the United States invited Chile to enter the process by which it would become the "Fourth Amigo." The route to full membership, however, must pass through the U.S. Congress. There was remarkably little discussion at Miami about whether a majority would be found in the new Congress to make hemispheric free trade viable. Chile, and everyone else who joins the procession, will require the "fast track" route through Congress for accession to the FTAA. But "fast track" is no longer available. A Republican Congress may not object to restoring it, but probably not on President Clinton's terms. Is there an alternative route?

The U.S. and Canada admitted Mexico to NAFTA with side agreements on labour and the environment. If these are attached, "fast track" is likely to be a non-starter for Congress. But Chile would hardly be allowed to enter FTAA on terms softer than those negotiated with Mexico. Clearly, opening the path to the FTAA will require political will and imaginative compromise.

What about those least developed countries, particularly in the Caribbean and Central America, that believe they could not survive on a level playing field? Apart from a very general recognition of the problem in the Declaration of Principles, nothing substantial has been offered to these nations. According to Mickey Kantor, concerns about the FTAA impact on microeconomies would be accommodated in the Interim Trade Agreement. However, not only is this agreement not mentioned in the Summit documents and still to be approved by Congress, but its terms offer little comfort to small, vulnerable economies because it provides lower U.S. duties only in some categories of garments and textiles. The mood of the new Republican Congress will likely not be amenable to special concessions or symmetrical arrangements. The Canadian government's attitude also appears increasingly less open to concessional trading terms. The Caribbean, particularly, faces difficult adjustments as the external economic environment changes. The Miami Summit was probably the last, best chance for several years for CARICOM heads of government collectively and rigorously to advance their concerns and their ideas for acceptable bridging arrangements.

Democracy, governance and sustainable development

Democracy, governance, and sustainable development raise other issues. A hemispheric commitment to preserve and strengthen democratic systems is listed in both the Declaration of Principles and the Plan of Action. In the latter, there is a non-binding undertaking by governments to ratify the Washington Amendment to the OAS charter. The closest that the final draft comes to the sensitive issue of region-wide support for conflict resolution is found in a request that the OAS engage in "fostering understanding, dialogue, and political reconciliation at the request of the affected state." This is a watering down of earlier and more supra-national concepts. More specifically, the OAS is expected to encourage exchanges of election-related technologies and assist national electoral organizations at the request of the interested state. This is a sensible, non-controversial proposal which will reaffirm an already active sector of OAS activities.

On the question of governance, the Summit added the administration of justice to the mandate of the OAS's Unit for the Promotion of Democracy (UPD). Reform in this area is, of course, critical, but should it be managed by the OAS? Probably not. The UPD is already seriously overstretched and its existing programs underfunded. USAID, the World Bank, and, to a lesser extent, the UNDP have projects in the administration of justice. The OAS should not expand its activities into an area where others are active and in which it has little expertise. The UPD does have expertise, however, in civic education and democratic development, a key area not mentioned in the Action Plan.

On the crucial issue of sustainable development and environmental conservation, the Action Plan draws up an ambitious, non-prioritized wish list. Given the breadth of issues, it is not surprising that deadlines are not attached. The IDB, World Bank, PAHO and the OAS, among others, are asked to finance, develop, and implement projects.

Long-term prospects

The Summit gave the OAS and the IDB a crucial role to play in following up these and other issues. To do so, OAS Secretary General César Gaviria undertook to reorganize the secretariat, but it is very unlikely that such changes will enable the OAS to assume its new responsibilities effectively without a significant fresh infusion of funds from member states. At the present time, there is virtually no prospect that either of the leading contributors, the U.S. and Canada, can increase contributions. And it is most improbable that other states would pitch in without a lead from the United States.

The Summit leaders have given Mr. Gaviria a splendid opportunity but little room to manoeuvre. There is hardly a substantive area of the OAS's present activities that has not been singled out for special action by the Summit. The IDB is much larger, more effective, and more amply funded. But despite its proven and far-sighted leadership — and recent restructuring — it suffers from turf battles and slow delivery.

It is unusual to ask international organizations "to do more with the same" and expect results. There is hope that the leadership of the OAS and IDB can rise to these extraordinary challenges. The Summit's success in the longer term will depend in part on their skill and energy. But to a far greater extent, it will depend on the U.S. Congress, the effectiveness of the Mexican financial rescue operation, and to what Mr. Clinton called the "spirit of Miami" in the majority of those other member states who have so much to gain.

This internal discussion document of the Global Forest Project (Friends of the Earth, Sierra Club, and National Wildlife Federation) was given to the University of Miami North-South Center with permission to reprint.

Forest Policy and the Summit: What Could the Summit of the Americas Accomplish on Forests and How?

By The Global Forest Project

A ROAD MAP FOR LAUNCHING A HEMISPHERIC PARTNERSHIP FOR THE CONSERVATION AND SUSTAINABLE MANAGEMENT OF FORESTS

For forests, the Summit of the Americas represents a significant opportunity to end the North-South acrimony of UNCED,* provide a stimulus to international policy accord, and bring the Western Hemisphere a step closer to sustainable forest management.

The Content

The forests of the Western Hemisphere are in trouble. Most of them are not managed sustainably. The multilateral forest policy debates of UNCED and since have made little progress and have produced sharp, North-South divisions. There are several promising initiatives which recently have been launched or proposed by Latin American governments for regional or hemispheric accord on forests. Building on those initiatives as a foundation, the people of the Western Hemisphere could make a leap forward regionally and set an example for the world. The Summit of the Americas is the ideal venue for beginning the process and for launching a new North-South forest partnership.

Primary Goal

Announce at the Summit the launching of a process to create a "Hemispheric Partnership for the Conservation and Sustainable Management of Forests," at which non-governmental organizations, indigenous peoples groups, the private sector, and others will be given a full seat at the table.

Supporting Actions and Goals

1. Praise the citizens of Central America and their governments for engaging in the process which led to the signing of the Central American Forest Convention (CAFC).

2. Give the CAFC a much higher profile, greater visibility, acknowledgement, congratulations, encouragement, promotion.

3. Encourage its early implementation.

---

*UNCED is the United Nations Conference on Environment and Development, also known as ECO-RIO '92.

4. Agree to support the CAFC's implementation with resources, technologies, training, etc.

5. Encourage other nations throughout the hemisphere to emulate the process the Central American nations used to craft their convention, and invite them either to craft similar instruments or to use the CAFC as a foundation to build on.

The National Audubon Society: Proposals Submitted to the Clinton Administration

The National Audubon Society is an international conservation organization with more than a half million members and over 500 chapters throughout the United States and Latin America. Audubon's principal mission is the protection of wildlife and habitat. Our international programs focus on the effects of population and trade on species and habitat and support international efforts to conserve biodiversity. Our interest in the environment of the Western Hemisphere is fueled, in part, by the decline of neotropical migratory bird species, a shared resource of all the Americas, and one indicator of the profound impact of trade on environmental resources.

This decline can be attributed to a number of factors, but chief among them is loss of habitat throughout their range, which runs from the far reaches of North America to the rain forests of South America. We recognized that the Summit of the Americas was an opportunity to influence environmental policy throughout the Americas and will continue to work for the preservation of biodiversity, and the minimization of the environmental impacts of trade, in the meetings which follow the Summit.

PROPOSAL FOR REVITALIZATION OF THE WESTERN HEMISPHERE CONVENTION

The environmental community has been asked to submit proposals to the Office of Environmental Policy for inclusion in the official agenda for the Summit of the Americas. Biodiversity and conservation issues are often marginalized in discussions and in actions taken under the sustainable development framework. However, these issues are important in their own right and should be a critical element of the Summit for the Americas. The Convention on Nature Protection and Wildlife Preservation in the Western Hemisphere,[1] commonly known as the Western Hemisphere Convention, provides an appropriate structure for conservation and protection of biodiversity on a regional level for the following reasons:

- first, the treaty has been signed by 22 states[2] — it is in full force and effect and does not require renegotiation, and its broad language allows for modern environmental perspectives to be included in treaty implementation;

- second, the Convention on Biological Diversity calls on signatories to the Convention to develop regional mechanisms to implement its terms — the Western Hemisphere Convention could be readily used to accomplish this goal;

- third, the Convention offers a comprehensive yet flexible legal framework for creating regional solutions to problems relating to the conservation of wildlife, migratory birds and their habitats;

- fourth, much of the international NGO community would enthusiastically support the revitalization of the treaty and would contribute considerably to these efforts; and

- fifth, an increasing number of signatories to the Convention have shown a serious commitment to revitalizing the Convention.

---

[1] 56 Stat. 1374; U.S.T.S. 981; 3 Bevans 630 (October 12, 1940).

[2] Argentina, Brazil, Chile, Costa Rica, Dominican Republic, Ecuador, El Salvador, Guatemala, Haiti, Mexico, Nicaragua, Panama, Paraguay, Peru, Suriname, Trinidad and Tobago, United States, Uruguay, Venezuela, Bolivia, Colombia, and Cuba have signed the Convention.

Thus, just as regional trade agreements provide the framework for an economic union extending from Patagonia to the Arctic, so too does the Western Hemisphere Convention provide a comprehensive framework for addressing conservation and biodiversity issues that are unique to our hemisphere, as well as the flexibility to deal with changing social priorities.

The United States should consider the following as means to address this issue at the Summit:

1. A joint announcement by the heads of state of a meeting of the environmental ministers of each country as a follow-up to the Summit. This meeting could take place in Latin America and its agenda could include a revitalization of the Convention and other biodiversity-related issues.

2. A joint declaration by the heads of state announcing a renewed commitment to implementation of the Western Hemisphere Convention.

3. An announcement by the United States of specific expanded commitments to implement the Western Hemisphere Convention, including funding for environmental education, training programs for park managers, improved management of protected areas, identification of important bird habitats, and capacity building of NGOs and relevant government institutions.

4. An announcement by the Organization of American States that it will undertake certain functions under the treaty, such as education and technology exchange.

5. An announcement by the Inter-American Development Bank (IDB) that it will accept funding proposals for implementation of the treaty. The IDB might also consider creation of a new biodiversity fund for the Western Hemisphere.

6. Announcements by heads of state regarding the creation of national parks and protected areas under the Western Hemisphere Convention.

7. *[For nonsignatory countries]* Announcements by heads of state that they will sign and ratify the Western Hemisphere Treaty.

- The National Audubon Society
- The Nature Conservancy
- The Environmental Law Institute
- International Council for Bird Preservation
- Natural Resources Defense Council
- Sierra Club
- Conservation International
- The Humane Society
- National Wildlife Federation
- Defenders of Wildlife
- Center for International Environmental Law
- Healing Forest Conservancy
- Interamerican Dialogue on Water Management

For more information please contact:

Kathleen Rogers
National Audubon Society
(202) 547-9009

Catherine Scott
The Nature Conservancy
(703) 841-7439

Susan Bass
Environmental Law Institute
(202) 939-3809

PROPOSAL FOR TRADE AND THE ENVIRONMENT

Increased economic integration and liberalized trade are at the top of the agenda for many governments in the Western Hemisphere. Trade and investment are certain to figure prominently at the Summit of the Americas. Environment and sustainable development should be first order priorities in any discussion of trade and investment initiatives for the Americas.

Including Environmental Safeguards in Future Trade and Investment Measures

Regional trade ties in the Western Hemisphere are likely to increase as other countries seek to join the North American Free Trade Agreement (NAFTA) or other trading partnerships. In addition, countries are actively pursuing investment agreements on a bilateral and multilateral basis, with little to no regard for the environmental impacts of those arrangements.

The NAFTA and its environmental side agreement represent significant progress in including environmental issues within the context of a trade agreement. In an effort to further those gains and ensure that the environmental safeguards included in the NAFTA provide the framework for any future agreements in the Western Hemisphere, the leaders of the Western Hemisphere should consider the following actions:

- Adoption of the relevant portions of the North American Agreement on Environmental Cooperation and all environmental provisions of the NAFTA including, but not limited to, Article 104 (which gives precedence to certain international environmental agreements) and Article 1114 (which prevents parties from weakening environmental laws in order to attract investment) when pursuing accession to the NAFTA, and the adoption of similar environmental safeguards when entering into other hemispheric trade and investment initiatives;

- Develop and strengthen an adequate legal framework for environmental protection, including avenues for public participation and transparency, enforcement and procedures for environmental impact statements;

- Provide full support for their environmental ministries in the development and enforcement of environmental laws as well as in the shaping of hemispheric trade and investment policy.

Proposed Trade, Investment and Environment Initiative

To ensure that environmental protection is a relevant aspect of strengthened trade and investment links in the Western Hemisphere, the United States should consider proposing a Hemispheric Trade, Investment and Environment Working Group. The Working Group will consist of representatives of the environmental ministries of the Western Hemisphere nations and will be charged with assisting governments in the upward harmonization of their environmental laws and regulations. Where such laws and regulations are missing, need strengthening or are not being enforced, the Working Group will develop

recommendations to improve their performance in these areas. In addition, the Working Group will be active in assessing the evolution of trade and investment linkages in the Western Hemisphere and their environmental impacts.

- Natural Resources Defense Council
- National Audubon Society
- National Wildlife Federation

For more information please contact:

Lynn Fischer
NRDC
202-624-9368
Fx 202-783-5917

Stewart Hudson
NWF
202-797-6603
Fx 202-797-5486

Kathleen Rogers
Audubon
202-547-9009
Fx 202-547-9022

PROPOSED STATEMENT OF TRADE AND ENVIRONMENT PRINCIPLES

Environmental principles must be reflected in all future bilateral and multilateral trade and investment agreements, including any bilateral or multilateral agreements to expand trade in the Western Hemisphere. The following principles will ensure that such agreements promote sustainable use of resources, conservation of species and ecosystems, and protection of public health, in addition to increased economic integration, equitable distribution of resources, and liberalized trade.

1. Countries participating in trade and investment agreements shall develop and strengthen an appropriate and comprehensive framework of environmental laws and regulations and should cooperate in and assist in the further development of multilateral agreements to address transboundary and global environmental problems.

2. Trade agreements must protect non-protectionist environmental and public health measures, including measures taken to enforce international environmental agreements, from challenge as trade barriers.

3. Participating countries shall demonstrate a commitment to strict enforcement of environmental laws and regulations by establishing as soon as possible a fully functioning and funded environmental enforcement agency, recognizing that lax enforcement of environmental laws distorts trade.

4. Countries entering into trade and investment agreements must allow public participation in judicial and administrative proceedings within a domestic environmental law framework and in the formation, negotiation, and implementation of trade and investment policies and agreements and must give appropriate access to environment related information on the community and national level. Trade agreements must permit public participation in dispute settlement mechanisms and other proceedings and public access to information relating to trade policy and trade agreement dispute settlement proceedings.

5. To encourage fully informed decision-making regarding trade and investment agreements, participating countries shall conduct environmental impact assessments prior to completion of an agreement and prior to its implementation, and trade agreements must include ongoing monitoring of the environmental impacts of increased trade and investment following implementation.

6. Trade agreements and participating countries must promote environmental cost internalization in traded goods, taking into account the principle that the polluter should bear the cost of pollution.

7. Recognizing the strains placed on the global environment by the disproportionate consumption of resources by industrialized countries, the nations of the Western Hemisphere should work together to reduce and eliminate unsustainable patterns of consumption and production in conjunction with efforts at economic integration.

8. Trade agreements should encourage a precautionary approach to the adoption of environmental policies which would allow countries to address serious threats of environmental harm in advance of conclusive scientific proof concerning that harm and which can be adapted as new scientific information becomes available.

9. Although environmental and health issues of common concern to countries in the Western Hemisphere should, where possible, be addressed through multilateral cooperation, communities at the national and sub-national level must be guaranteed the right to set and maintain higher environmental and public health standards as they deem appropriate.

10. Efforts at economic integration in the Western Hemisphere should promote conservation of biodiversity and ecosystems in the hemisphere and should ensure the adoption of policies for the sustainable use of resources, recognizing the need to ensure that increased trade does not jeopardize either the survival of the Western Hemisphere's diverse species and their habitats or the ability of future generations to meet their needs.

- National Audubon Society
- National Wildlife Federation
- Natural Resources Defense Council
- Environment and Energy Study Institute
- Community Nutrition Institute
- Defenders of Wildlife

For more information please contact:

Mary Minette or Kathleen Rogers
National Audubon Society
666 Pennsylvania Avenue, Suite 200
Washington, D.C. 20003
(202) 547-9009

Stewart Hudson
National Wildlife Federation
1400 16th Street, NW
Washington, D.C. 20036
(202) 797-6602

Lynn Fischer
National Resources Defense Council
1350 New York Avenue, NW
Washington, D.C. 20005
(202) 624-9368

Paul Speck
Environmental and Energy Study Institute
122 C Street, NW, Suite 700
Washington, D.C. 20001
(202) 628-1400

ENVIRONMENTAL REGULATORY FRAMEWORKS: ELEVATION AND ENFORCEMENT OF STANDARDS IN THE WESTERN HEMISPHERE

Recommendations for the Proposed Initiative to Raise Standards in the Western Hemisphere in Conjunction with the Summit of the Americas

We strongly support the initiative of the United States government to begin a cooperative effort to raise environmental standards throughout the Western Hemisphere at the Summit of the Americas. Weak standards and lax enforcement throughout the hemisphere have contributed to the overall degradation of the global environment. An initiative to develop strong environmental regulatory frameworks and to encourage strict enforcement of standards will promote sustainable development, conservation of species and ecosystems, and protection of public health throughout the countries of the Western Hemisphere.

To be effective, however, an initiative to raise and enforce environmental standards must reflect certain basic principles. Outlined below are our specific recommendations which would help to ensure that this initiative will be a success.

I. SECTOR-SPECIFIC INITIATIVES

We support the adoption at the Summit of a series of sector-specific initiatives to develop appropriate standards for substances which pose significant threats to the environment and human health. Such an approach would enable each country to develop and implement appropriate regulatory frameworks for the protection of their environments. Each of these initiatives requires a follow-up process and the identification of potential sources of funding.

Pesticides

Countries should develop and implement appropriate standards for pesticide use and should develop institutional and individual capacities for compliance with and enforcement of those standards.

Countries of the Western Hemisphere should pursue equivalence in data gathering and risk assessment methodology in order to ensure that policy decisions setting appropriate levels for pesticide use are based on the best available scientific information and are made with full knowledge of potential alternatives to that use. In addition, countries must develop mechanisms to ensure enforcement of and compliance with standards developed in this process.

As a first step, the countries of the Western Hemisphere should commit to a complete phase-out of the pesticide DDT by the year 2010.

Although banned in the United States and Canada, DDT is still widely used in Latin America, particularly in malaria eradication programs. New evidence suggests that this highly persistent chemical continues to cause contamination in countries where its use is outlawed, thus undermining the benefits of the ban. In addition, there is increasing evidence that DDT may have previously unknown human health effects, which include reproductive problems and higher incidence of breast cancer. The detrimental effects of DDT on wildlife are widely known. For example, DDT has been shown to result in a weakening of egg shells in eagles, condors, and a number of migratory species including peregrine falcons, pelicans, and ducks. Continued use of DDT in Southern Mexico, for example, places many North American migratory species at risk. There are safer alternatives to DDT in the control of malaria-carrying mosquitos, notably Malathion. However, alternatives are much more expensive than DDT, making a voluntary phase out unlikely, unless financing and other incentives are provided.

Nations should commit to studying the phase out of other pesticides which are banned for environmental or human health reasons by one or more Western Hemisphere nations.

The countries of the Western Hemisphere should consider phasing out the use of pesticides whose use has been banned by one or more countries in the region due to their environmental risks and the existence of acceptable alternatives. If one or more countries consider the risk of a pesticide significant enough to take the serious step of banning its use and have found or developed reasonable alternatives to its use, then other countries in the region should consider a similar ban on its use.

Countries should examine their exports of domestically prohibited pesticides to other nations in the Western Hemisphere and consider prohibiting those exports.

The practice of exporting products banned for domestic use not only places the citizens of importing countries at risk but also places the exporting country's citizens at risk when the banned substances return as pesticide residues in food or as long range transboundary pollution. Countries participating in the Summit should pledge to examine their exports of domestically prohibited pesticides and to report on their findings and plans regarding those substances at a follow-up meeting of environmental ministers.

Carrying out the Pesticide Initiatives

To carry out the initiative to raise pesticide standards throughout the hemisphere, to ban DDT, and to study the phase out of other banned pesticides, and the possible ban on exports of domestically prohibited substances, Western Hemisphere leaders must commit to:

- exchange information and technologies regarding risk assessment for the banned substances;

- transfer technologies supporting alternative approaches to pest and disease control;

- develop mechanisms for public participation in the policy-making process and in compliance with and enforcement of pesticide standards;

- develop educational and training capabilities regarding proper pesticide use;

- hold follow up meetings to discuss progress in implementing the initiatives, to address problems which may arise, and to develop new approaches to the issues.

Lead

The use of lead in gasoline should be phased out throughout the Western Hemisphere by the year 2010.

The negative human health effects of lead, particularly on children, are well documented. Exposures from leaded gasoline can result in impaired growth, mental retardation, and blood-related diseases. In addition, the possible transboundary effects of lead pollution are potentially serious. Lead in the air makes its way into the soil and then into produce which, if exported, can expose citizens of countries with limited use of leaded gasoline to serious health risks. A number of countries in the hemisphere have already taken steps to phase out their use of leaded gasoline; others are moving in that direction. In addition, relatively inexpensive and practicable alternatives to leaded gasoline exist and will ease the burden on countries participating in the phase out.

Countries should commit to further cooperation to eliminate additional sources of lead exposure, including ceramic and other manufacturing process, lead paint, and lead in drinking water.

While leaded gasoline presents the most immediate and widespread threat of lead poisoning, there are a number of other means of lead exposure that pose serious problems to specific populations. A number of ceramic glazing processes use lead, presenting a serious risk to employees and those living in close proximity to factories. In addition, improperly fired ceramics can allow lead to leach into food, placing consumers at risk. Lead paint is a serious threat to children throughout the hemisphere, including in the United States. Lead contamination of drinking water by lead pipes and solder also present problems in the United States and elsewhere.

Carrying out the Lead Initiative

To carry out a hemisphere wide phase-out of lead in gasoline, national leaders must commit to:

- exchange information and technologies for reducing and replacing lead in gasoline. The United States and Colombia are planning to host an international workshop in 1995 to discuss the transfer of technologies for replacing lead in gasoline;

- agree to widespread public health efforts to identify and reduce lead exposure risks throughout the hemisphere, including public education campaigns.

II. PRINCIPLES FOR RAISING AND ENFORCING STANDARDS

Heads of state gathered for the Summit could sign a declaration of principles relating to the development, implementation, and enforcement of environmental standards. Follow up to the declaration would include successful implementation of the sector-specific initiatives to raise standards and regular meetings of the Environmental Ministers of Western Hemisphere nations to report on progress in carrying out the initiatives and in implementing these principles, to exchange information and technology, and to develop cooperative approaches to other transboundary and regional standards issues.

Creating a Regulatory Framework for Environmental Management

National and sub-national governments should have the right to set standards higher than an agreed upon minimum.

In cases where higher standards are necessary to promote sustainable use of resources, conservation of species and ecosystems, or protection of public health, governments should be free to exceed international minimums without fear of commercial or other sanctions.

Any hemispheric initiative to raise environmental standards should include the precautionary principle.

Environmental effects are often uncertain, and irreversible impacts on public health and natural resources often occur before conclusive scientific evidence is available. Therefore, any agreement on environmental standards must preserve the right of countries to adopt standards which address serious threats of harm in advance of conclusive scientific proof concerning that harm and can be adapted as further scientific information becomes available.

Environmental laws and regulations should guarantee the right of the public to participate in environmental enforcement and decision-making processes.

Public participation is necessary both to the development of sound laws and policies and to the effective enforcement of those laws and policies. Maximum transparency and public participation in the development and implementation of environmental laws, regulations, and policies will ensure that these laws are both relevant and effective. The public must have the right to prior notice of proposed laws, regulations, and policies and to changes in existing laws, regulations and policies. In addition, the public must have the right to comment and be heard concerning proposed environmental standards and changes to existing standards and to request a response regarding those comments.

Individual citizens should have appropriate access to information concerning the state of the environment held by public authorities.

An informed citizenry is essential to effective enforcement of environmental laws and regulations. Governments should be required to make information on potential environmental and public health threats available to citizens, including information on hazardous materials and activities in their communities.

Environmental laws and regulations should reflect the principles of polluter pays and cost internalization.

In the interest of promoting market efficiency as well as environmental protection, any hemispheric initiative to increase environmental standards should encourage the development of laws and regulations that promote the internalization of environmental costs into the price of goods and services. Laws and regulations should also further the development of laws and regulations reflecting the principle that the polluter should bear the cost of preventing and cleaning up pollution.

Enforcement of Standards

Countries should demonstrate a commitment to enforcement of environmental standards by establishing or working towards fully functioning environmental enforcement agencies.

A strong commitment to enforce environmental standards must accompany an agreement to raise standards throughout the Western Hemisphere. Improvement of environmental conditions in the hemisphere will only occur if each government pledges adequate resources to enforcing standards through national enforcement agencies.

The public should have a right of access to judicial, quasi-judicial, and/or administrative remedies for violations of environmental standards.

Public participation in environmental monitoring and enforcement efforts is necessary to complement governmental efforts to enforce standards. Citizen involvement in enforcement proceedings extends the enforcement resources of national and sub-national governments.

Administrative, judicial, and quasi-judicial processes should be fair, open to the public, and allow all participants the right to confront their accusers.

Openness of enforcement proceedings enhances the effectiveness and accountability of the adjudicating forum and educates the public regarding its enforcement rights.

Technical assistance should be offered to affected persons and groups so that they may take a strong role in the enforcement of environmental standards.

The public can play a vital role in effective enforcement by augmenting governmental efforts to prosecute violations of environmental laws and regulations, and their participation in the enforcement process should be facilitated.

Monitoring and Building on the Regulatory Frameworks Initiative

The leaders gathered for the Summit should announce the beginning of a regular consultative process, with annual, or at least biannual, meetings of the environment ministers of the Western Hemisphere to continue consultations regarding the elevation and enforcement of environmental standards throughout the hemisphere.

The Summit of the Americas must be seen as the beginning of a cooperative process which will continue through the Bolivia 501 Summit of Western Hemisphere environmental ministers and beyond. If a sectoral approach is taken to developing regulatory frameworks, an ongoing consultative process will be vital to ensuring that the process continues and that other sectors of environmental enforcement are included in the process of raising standards. Finally, an ongoing consultative process will ensure that all countries are honoring their commitment to implement the above principles.

- National Audubon Society
- Natural Resources Defense Council
- Environmental and Energy Study Institute

Postscript:
The National Audubon Society:
Our Views on the Summit

Kathleen Rogers, Mary Minette, and Susan Murray

Although trade and investment in the Americas were prominently featured in the Summit Declaration and Plan of Action and received the lion's share of attention from the media, the Declaration also contained significant initiatives related to democracy and to sustainable development, which, if properly implemented, will have a profound impact on the future of our region. National Audubon worked hard to ensure that the Summit documents gave prominence to the protection and preservation of biodiversity and habitat throughout the region and to the development of strong environmental regulatory regimes in the Americas equivalent to that given to expansion of markets and investment opportunities.

Audubon drafted and, in conjunction with other groups, submitted proposals to the White House early in the Summit negotiations process regarding protection of biodiversity and the link between trade and environment. We strongly urged the inclusion of biodiversity and conservation issues in the Summit's agenda and urged that the leaders pledge to revitalize the Western Hemisphere Convention, a conservation treaty signed by many of the nations of the Americas but never fully implemented. The Summit Plan of Action gives prominence to these issues in the Partnership for Biodiversity initiative, which calls for governments to develop and strengthen management plans for parks and reserves, build capacity for conservation and sustainable use of biodiversity, and calls for the integration of biodiversity conservation and ecosystem protection into economic development activities. The Plan of Action additionally provides for a Sustainable Development Summit in 1996 in Bolivia and for annual ministerial meetings thereafter to discuss progress on biodiversity issues.

The failure of the Senate to ratify the Convention on Biological Diversity hampered our ability to achieve more concrete results on this issue. However, the biodiversity initiative is broadly drawn and could produce stronger results in the future.

Audubon's initial proposal on trade and environment called for the adoption of safeguards similar to those of the North American Free Trade Agreement and its environmental side agreement in future trade agreements in the hemisphere. It also called for the countries of the hemisphere to develop and strengthen environmental protection regimes and to commit resources to enforcement of environmental laws. We also proposed, with a number of other groups, that the leaders adopt a statement of trade and environment principles and make strong links between trade expansion in the hemisphere and environmental protection and conservation in the Summit Declaration.

The final Summit Declaration makes minimal links between trade expansion plans and environmental goals. The Declaration notes that "free trade and increased economic integration are key factors for raising standards of living, improving the working conditions of people in the Americas and better protecting the environment." The Declaration also commits the signatory countries to "advance [their] social well-being and economic prosperity in ways that are fully cognizant of [their] impact on the environment."

Nonetheless, the stature given to environmental issues in the Summit documents is an important first step towards a parallel and equivalent approach to both conservation and environmental protection, and trade and investment. However, we believe that the success of the Summit environmental initiatives, and the development of other regional approaches to environmental issues, must be linked to promises of open markets and greater investment opportunities. If this link is not made, a valuable incentive will have been wasted.

The Plan of Action contains a Partnership for Pollution Prevention initiative to strengthen national environmental protection laws and enforcement and to provide regional support for national initiatives. During the development of this initiative, Audubon and other groups submitted a short paper making recommendations for the implementation of aspects of the proposed initiative and setting forth principles which we believed should be reflected in the initiative. Several of these recommendations are incorporated in the final Plan of Action.

Finally, we recommended that the Summit be followed by annual ministerial meetings to ensure the full implementation of the Partnership for Pollution Prevention and the other sustainable development initiatives. This recommendation is reflected in the final declaration and will allow for further refinement of all of the initiatives. In addition, the Bolivia Summit will give prominence to sustainable development issues and will permit high level discussion of environmental issues outside the scope of the Summit documents.

In light of the successful integration of some members of the region's non-governmental community into the preparatory process for the Summit, we hope that all governments in the Americas will consider similar involvement for non-governmental organizations in the meetings which follow the Summit. The role played by NGOs in the preparations for the Summit was unprecedented for this type of presidential level meeting and conveyed a powerful message about the importance of citizen participation to government officials throughout the Americas. The open processes instituted by the Office of Environmental Policy and the National Security Council's Office of Latin American Affairs, including regular briefings, the solicitation of proposals, advice and expertise from the NGO community, and especially the inclusion of NGO representatives in the U.S. delegations which met with representatives of Latin American and Caribbean governments, allowed the U.S. NGO community an unparalleled opportunity to participate in the planning of the Summit. In response, the governments of Argentina and several Caribbean nations included NGO representatives on their negotiating teams.

Although we were disappointed by the continuing resistance of many governments to the participation of civil society in the preparations for this Summit and the universal resistance to NGO participation in the Summit meeting itself, we hope that future meetings of this magnitude, and the meetings planned to follow up on the work announced at this Summit, will include meaningful opportunities for the participation of civil society. We are asking the United States government to institutionalize the role played by NGOs in the Summit preparations for the follow up meetings and to permit NGO participation in the meetings themselves; we hope that other governments in the Americas will take similar steps. We must work to ensure that the governments and multilateral institutions charged with carrying out the work of this Summit develop effective mechanisms for harnessing the expertise of civil society.

Ensuring that the goals of the Summit are realized will require a significant amount of attention not only from government actors but also from industry and from NGOs throughout the hemisphere. The Summit documents mandate partnerships between governmental and non-governmental actors; however, NGOs must determine what role they wish to play in carrying out the agreements and must coordinate their efforts with other non-governmental actors in the hemisphere. NGOs can play a vital role in monitoring the progress of environmental protection and biodiversity conservation by governments throughout the region.

National Audubon sees the environmental initiatives of this Summit as a strong step towards protecting our region's common environmental heritage, and we hope to work with our government and with our colleagues throughout the hemisphere to ensure that the promise of these initiatives is fulfilled. Maintaining the Summit's spirit of cooperation is critical to solving shared environmental problems. We will look to the follow up meetings, including the 1996 Bolivia Summit, for real progress towards the goals set forth in the Summit documents.

John J. Kirton
Associate Professor
Department of
Political Science,
University of Toronto

and

Sarah Richardson
Foreign Policy Advisor
National Round Table
on the Environment
and the Economy

Advancing Sustainable Development at the Summit of the Americas

This paper has been adapted from the National Round Table on the Environment and the Economy's Task Force on Foreign Policy and Sustainability's background document used to guide the discussion at two international workshops held during 1994. The original paper is reproduced as Volume III of the NRTEE's Report Series on "Advancing Sustainable Development at the Summit of the Americas."

The National Round Table on the Environment and the Economy (NRTEE) was created in 1988 as Canada's principal institutional response to the challenge of sustainable development. In May 1994, the NRTEE entered a new phase of its existence, when the Prime Minister proclaimed the National Round Table Act, establishing it as an independent agency of the federal government.

Reporting directly to the Prime Minister and mandated by Parliament, the National Round Table's purpose is to play the role of catalyst in identifying, explaining, and promoting in all sectors of Canadian society and in all regions of Canada the principles and practices of sustainable development.

The National Round Table achieves its mandate by

- Providing advice to the Prime Minister and government on ways to progress toward sustainable development.

- Helping government address public policy questions as they relate to sustainable development.

- Providing a process and a neutral meeting ground for stakeholders to work together to tackle tough sustainability issues in areas such as forestry, pulp and paper, and fisheries.

- Providing a broad range of information and publications to encourage grassroots initiatives and to help decision makers address issues of sustainability.

Contents

Advancing Sustainable Development at the Summit of the Americas

INTRODUCTION

The Western Hemisphere should command a place at the centre of Canadian foreign policy in the 1990s, not only as a result of the economic power and potential of the region but, even more importantly, for its global ecological importance.

The countries of the Western Hemisphere, with only 13 percent of the world's population, together contain about 40 percent of the world's natural forest cover and renewable water, 36 percent of its coastlines, and account for almost 30 percent of its carbon dioxide (CO_2) emissions, energy production, and land area. More than any other single major region, the hemisphere is a global ecological treasure house. It thus has a critical role in implementing and extending the principles and practices of sustainable development articulated by the Brundtland Commission Report and adopted by the United Nations Conference on Environment and Development (UNCED) at Rio in 1992. Indeed, the Summit of the Americas presents a unique and timely opportunity to provide important follow-up to Agenda 21 and other Rio documents at a regional level.

Within the region itself, economic and environmental interdependencies are growing rapidly. Economically, the hemisphere, which provides over one-third of the world's gross national product (GNP, 1989), represents the first frontier for the prospective expansion of the *North American Free Trade Agreement* (NAFTA) regimes and institutions and offers a growing and modernizing market. This growth, with its accompanying natural resource demands, pollution, and impact on transportation networks throughout the region, threatens to cause significant ecological and, ultimately, economic damage unless pursued in sustainable ways.

Yet, in sharp contrast to other global regions, apart from the fledgling trilateral NAFTA community, the hemisphere, and particularly the Inter-American family of institutions, lags in the incorporation of fundamental aspects of sustainable development — the need to integrate economic and environmental concerns in a way that promotes equity, social accountability, and inclusive, multistakeholder decision making. Unlike the newer institutions governing the post cold-war world and serving as the primary instruments of Canadian foreign policy (the G-7, NAFTA, the Asia-Pacific Economic Cooperation forum (APEC), and even in part the Francophone, Commonwealth, and OECD) hemispheric institutions lack regular forums for ensuring collective direction by heads of government or by economic, natural resource, and environment ministers. It thus has been slow to recognize the regional interdependence and global importance of the hemisphere's ecology, the need to integrate economic and environmental considerations in its management, and to address this agenda according to, or as a follow-up to the 1992 Rio regime.

As demonstrated on a global scale at Rio, and at APEC from November 1993 onward, Canada has the capacity to lead. Among the countries of the hemisphere, it ranks first in coastlines and land area, and second in forest cover, freshwater, CO_2 emissions and energy production. It is thus in a position to pioneer bargains within the hemisphere that can address and forestall emerging regional problems and serve as a nucleus for building stronger global regimes. Canada has a strong interest, through a framework of multilateralism, in expanding its markets for trade as well as promoting international consensus for environmental protection and enhancement. In order to take advantage of its position and to advance sustainable development, Canada should pursue an action program based on the following recommendations at the forthcoming Summit of the Americas.

I. ECONOMIC AND TRADE ISSUES

The recent renewal of policy interest in the hemisphere as an integrated region and potential community flows primarily from dramatic developments in the economic sphere. Over the last decade, the trade and investment links in the Western Hemisphere have grown, as significant progress has been made in trade liberalization and concomitant measures of structural adjustment, privatization of state enterprises, and other market-oriented economic reforms in Latin America and the Caribbean. Tariffs have replaced licenses as the principal measure of import control and are undergoing scheduled reductions in many countries. All major Latin American countries are now members of and are subject to the disciplines of GATT. Many have signed and ratified the new World Trade Organization (WTO).[1]

At the outset of 1994, Canada, the United States, and Mexico successfully put NAFTA into force. The trade agreement was accompanied by two further, far-reaching agreements and institutions to address the related environmental and social challenges which might arise in North America as a result of the new regime of liberalized trade. In the past year, the three NAFTA governments have moved rapidly toward exploring the advantages of broadening the trilateral community into the full hemispheric domain and beyond, through intensified discussions about the accession to NAFTA of such partners as Chile.

In the last ten years, the economic recovery in Latin America has been encouraging. As a region, in 1992 Latin America and the Caribbean's economic expansion exceeded their population growth. Preliminary figures indicate the region's 1992 gross domestic product (GDP) increased by 2.4 percent, a slightly slower pace than the 3.5 percent registered in 1991. Although more and more countries in the region have progressed in consolidating their adjustment processes, 1992 was marked by widening variances in the performances of many of their economies. Apart from Brazil, regional output for the economies of Latin America and the Caribbean increased in 1992 by 4.3 percent (compared to 5 percent in 1991).

Inflation figures continued to drop. Only five countries experienced significant increases when compared to 1991. Only Brazil posted inflation over three digits. Fiscal austerity is being pursued as government budget surpluses are realized. Brazil remains the exception, but Argentina, which experienced inflation of some 50,000 percent in 1989, brought its rate down to 7.4 percent in 1993. Chile has also experienced rapid growth in the early 1990s. In 1992, its GDP expanded by 10.3 percent, and industrial production was up by 15 percent.

The countries of the hemisphere, with large populations and rapid economic growth, continue to present favorable opportunities for trade and investment. The process of trade and the economic activi-

ties associated with it are not only expanding; they are also becoming hemispheric. The unprecedented proliferation of sub-regional free trade agreements and the expansion of the trading relationships in the hemisphere, combined with changes to encourage reciprocal market access and the opening up of markets all over Central and South America, have led to tremendous increases in the volume of goods traded and economic activity. This should not be surprising as the hemisphere provides a market of 500 million people. Brazil alone contains over 150 million potential consumers and boasts a highly diversified economy, with a GDP of US$447 billion (compared to Canada's GNP of C$740 billion in 1994).

Adherents of sustainable development should welcome this increased activity, but be aware that it is having, and could continue to have, serious ecological and social implications. Environmental policies, laws, and regulations, particularly with respect to natural resource degradation, remain relatively weak in Latin America and the Caribbean, as do the resources and mechanisms for monitoring and enforcement. Intensifying economic growth presents a significant threat to the ecology of the hemisphere if pursued without concern for environmental and social protection. At the same time, increasing interdependence presents opportunities to undertake the increased economic activity in more sustainable ways.

In the process of expanding trade liberalization and NAFTA membership itself in the hemisphere, it is important, at a minimum, not to erode the environmental and social achievements of the existing NAFTA trilogy of institutions. Indeed, supporters of sustainable development should welcome the prospect of NAFTA expansion because it extends the highly developed NAFTA environmental and social regimes to the hemisphere, rather than having new entrants rely solely on the GATT or on existing regional agreements or agreements that they would otherwise have concluded without the same degree of environmental or social safeguards.

Expanding Trading Relationships in the Hemisphere

The trading relationships in the hemisphere are expanding on both bilateral and plurilateral bases. In North America, the Canada-U.S.-Mexico North American Free Trade Agreement of 1993 has linked the three countries of the continent and has superseded

---

[1] See Appendix A for a list of major international agreements, conventions, and organizations and the countries of the hemisphere that belong to them.

the pre-existing Canada-U.S. Free Trade Agreement. The NAFTA has created a market of 360 million people with a total purchasing power of US$6.2 trillion. Even as it is being implemented, other countries in the hemisphere, such as Chile and Colombia, have already shown signs of eagerness to join it.

In Central and South America, intraregional trade is growing. In 1986-90, intraregional exports represented 10 percent of global exports. In 1991, they were 14 percent; in 1993, 17 percent; and in 1993, they were as much as 20 percent of total exports. Four major subregional integration agreements have now been concluded: the Central American Common Market (CACM), the Cartagena Agreement, the Caribbean Community (CARICOM) and the Southern Common Market (MERCOSUR).

CARICOM is one of the older integration bodies within the broader region of Latin America and the Caribbean, tracing its origins as a trade body from 1968. It comprises 13 member countries which are among the smallest countries of Latin America and the Caribbean and often the most trade dependent countries.

MERCOSUR, expected to be established by January 1, 1995, will be the largest trading bloc in South America, uniting the countries of the Southern Cone — Brazil, Uruguay, Paraguay, and Argentina — in a common market. The agreement is intended to result in the substantial reduction in tariffs and non-tariff barriers to trade among its member countries. Even as MERCOSUR is being set up, other countries in South America are seeking to join. Intra-MERCOSUR trade, which was US$4.1 billion in 1990, was over US$10 billion in 1993. The environment is not considered a priority within MERCOSUR and is not an issue considered among the 11 working groups set up under the agreement.

A second major plurilateral agreement in South America is the Cartagena Agreement, also known as the Andean Group. Its members comprise Venezuela, Colombia, Ecuador, Bolivia and Peru. The Andean Group is now 25 years old and is in the process of defining for itself a new Andean agenda. This agenda will work toward a stronger free trade zone and customs union, a framework agreement for trade in services, and will tackle issues on the international economic agenda which could include sustainable development and human development. Intraregional trade in the Andean Group rose some 30 percent in

1993, climbing to a record US$2.9 billion from US$1.33 billion in 1990.

Finally, Mexico, Venezuela, and Colombia have recently finalized an agreement known as the Group of Three Agreement (G-3). This agreement is not confined to trade. It also includes other basic areas of the economy like services, investments, and industrial and intellectual property.

In the last ten years, over 20 bilateral agreements have also been signed — all with the aim of offering concessional treatment in the form of lower duties through preferential tariffs on targeted goods. Mexico has concluded a free trade agreement with Chile. Chile has concluded a bilateral agreement with Argentina. Venezuela has concluded a bilateral agreement with Colombia, which Ecuador would like to join.

Most recently, in April 1994, Mexico concluded a free trade agreement with Costa Rica, scheduled to take effect on January 1, 1995. This treaty is the most complete ever negotiated in Latin America and includes a set of rules that will lend transparency and security to the business sectors while fostering trade in goods and services.

Within the Latin American Integration Association (ALADI), which provides the overall framework for 11 countries in South America and Mexico to negotiate regional integration and regional trade, there are 120 existing trade agreements. Mexico is a party to 36 of these. The ALADI was established in 1980 by the Montevideo Treaty, which was one subject of a recent OAS Special Committee on Trade meeting. The Treaty might be in need of amendment and expansion to respond to structural and institutional, as well as economic realities and growth.

As the numbers of trading arrangements and free trade agreements increase, so too does the volume of trade among countries of the hemisphere. This increasing volume necessitates safeguards for the environment and other social imperatives more than ever. At present the newer trade agreements in the hemisphere, apart from NAFTA, do not contain adequate environmental or social safeguards.

If natural resources such as forests, land, water, and fisheries are traded freely without well-defined and secure property rights, trade liberalization might lead to expanded use or exports of natural resource-based commodities and agricultural and livestock products, at the expense of the resource base and long-term sustainability. For example, if there are no regulating mechanisms and economic instruments in place for internalization of environmental costs, increased exports of energy following trade liberalization could lead to increased air and water pollution, particularly if the product is subsidized.

From the perspective of prosperity, a recent report published by the Economic Commission for Latin America and the Caribbean (ECLAC), warns of the danger in the proliferation of bilateral agreements and other agreements with very limited geographical coverage, if these do not lead to broader, less discriminatory arrangements.[2] Bilateral relationships that are increasingly concentrated pose the risk that small countries will adjust their production structures to the conditions prevailing on the market of their main trading partner and thereby render themselves unable to adapt to more competitive conditions. The ECLAC report also warns of the increased concentration of investment in the regional "hubs" created by a number of bilateral relationships. The study suggests that Latin America and the Caribbean should advance, through a process of increasing economic interdependence among the countries of the region, toward an economic climate of "open regionalism."

Advancing Sustainable Development

Sustainable development can be promoted through increased economic integration to the extent that broadening existing trade liberalization agreements does not represent a de facto weakening of the achievements won for the environment and the social agenda in NAFTA. It is thus critical that the countries acceding to NAFTA be prepared to accept the environmental and social framework that was negotiated to accompany it, albeit with phase-in and assistance provisions reflecting their particular circumstances. The importance of the environmental and labor agreements for sustainable development notwithstanding, it is unlikely that the NAFTA partners will open up the agreements for renegotiation if countries from the hemisphere approach them one by one.

Some countries of the hemisphere may not aspire to accede to NAFTA. For others it might be a longer-term goal, especially for countries either unable or unwilling to enter into the commitments contained in the agreement. This could be particularly true if they are already members of one of the major free trade zones in South America and a member of the GATT. It thus becomes critical to examine closely the other plurilateral and bilateral agreements in the hemisphere to ascertain that they are concluded with an appropriate degree of attention to the environment and a concern for social equity.

Indeed, any future increase in economic activity generated by any free trade zones in the hemisphere should be carefully evaluated for potential negative or positive impacts on the environment and affected social groups. The task is even more pressing because the effort to formalize environmental protection within trade relations is not well advanced on a global level. Good environmental policies can help to improve gains from trade and avert trade conflicts. Moreover, trade liberalization can help to better environmental quality if conducted with adequate safeguards.

The recent study by ECLAC recommends broad trade liberalization. It suggests flexible, effective accession by countries to existing agreements, thereby facilitating a gradual extension of preferences and reducing intra-regional discrimination. Promoting effective accession has the two advantages of lessening the overlapping of areas caused by a multiplicity of bilateral integration agreements with different provisions and of spurring the formation of groups of countries that act as promoters of renewed processes of broader regional integration.

Sectoral integration is identified as a second option for advancing economic interdependence in the region. Flexible sectoral arrangements would help enterprises to reap the potential benefits of integration and could result in coordination that would promote and facilitate technological transfers and the creation of information networks and other channels.

Along with economic integration, social integration is crucial. The institutions in charge of implementing economic integration processes should encourage and facilitate greater participation by organizations representing various social interests, in accordance with the democratic spirit pervading the region. Social accountability remains a critical guarantor of responsible environmental stewardship.

The leaders at the Summit should commit to expanding trade in the hemisphere with the social and

---

[2] Economic Commission for Latin America and the Caribbean (ECLAC); *Open Regionalism in Latin America and the Caribbean - Economic Integration as a Contribution to Changing Production Patterns with Social Equity,* (Santiago, Chile: United Nations, ECLAC, 1994).

environmental protection afforded by the NAFTA trilogy of agreements and institutions. They should include a commitment to the socially and environmentally responsible accession to NAFTA. The leaders, however, should not assume that all countries in the hemisphere will accede to NAFTA, and they should agree to consider and conduct a review of the environmental and social implications of all trade agreements in the region. This could include research in the first instance which might be carried out by a joint Trade and Environment Committee at the OAS, or an ad hoc working party established by the leaders at Miami.

The "market integration" basket at the Summit of the Americas should consider issues of both trade and environment/sustainable development. Of primary importance is having a meeting of hemispheric trade ministers at which environmental questions are given full attention, to ensure that the integration of economic and environmental considerations can be better realized. Among the issues that could be discussed are the importance of building and maintaining capacity to ensure that countries are able to join other countries in free trade in ways which can promote sustainable development by ensuring that environmental and social standards are strengthened.

Trade ministers should consider the rapid phase-out of tariffs on environmental technologies and traditional technologies for pollution control in the hemisphere.

The leaders at Miami should agree to work toward the upward harmonization of environmental standards in the Americas, focusing on the strengthening of legal frameworks; the enhancement of environmental compliance and enforcement capacity; institution strengthening through technical cooperation, training and education; the possibilities for the development of eco-labelling and regional mutual recognition programs for eco-labelling; and the development of strategies for effective public participation in environmental policy making accession.

The OAS Special Trade Committee was created at the June 1993 Managua OAS General Assembly meeting. It held its first meeting May 16-18, 1994, in Washington, D.C. It replaces the previous OAS forum for trade (SECON, a body that some say focused its efforts on criticizing the United States). The new body, launched with American and Canadian support, was conceived as a forward-looking, effective organ, able to deal with the new trade liberalization issues in the hemisphere.

The new Trade Committee of the OAS should be invited to join with the recently established Environment Committee to initiate a joint work program. This program could begin with a comparative review of existing trade-environment regimes and provisions within the 25 hemispheric subregional trade agreements that now exist, and the applicability of the most advanced (including NAFTA) to a hemisphere-wide liberalization process or agreement.

Development of sustainability indicators should also be a subject for hemispheric cooperation, especially in light of prospects of economic integration. There is a pressing need to reform national accounting standards (GNP, GDP) to include information on social and environmental indicators, which can record the depletion or accumulation of natural, human, and man-made resources.

The leaders should support, in the context of the hemisphere, the future work of the North American Commission on Environmental Cooperation on sustainability indicators.

Building and Maintaining Capacity

A Hemispheric Standardization Forum

The approach of NAFTA led the private and non-profit consensus-oriented standards community in Canada, the United States, and Mexico to create, in 1990, the Trilateral Standardization Forum. In the spring of 1993, at Canadian initiative, an Environmental Standards Working Group was created within the Forum to exchange information about existing and anticipated environmental regulations and standards and standards-setting and conformity assessment processes within the three countries, to catalyze strengthened environmental standards and management systems and more effective compliance in the three countries, and to support the NAFTA institutions in their mandated standards activities. Such processes serve as a cost-effective supplement to, and substitute for, mandated government regulation and enforcement. By securing the support of industry and other operating institutions from the outset, they often generate greater environmental performance than even the most well-policed government enforcement regimes can ensure. With the expansion of NAFTA to other countries in the hemisphere now in prospect, it is timely to initiate, through the Standards Council of Canada and its partner bodies, a similar forum for information-sharing, cooperation, and environmental standards-setting and strengthening on a hemispheric basis (well beyond the limited accomplishments of the OAS' Environment and Juridical Committee's work on environmental legislation). Through such a forum, Canada could mobilize regional support for its leadership in the multilateral ISO TC 207 process on devising environmental management systems to accompany the ISO 9000 quality managements systems.

Following the North American Trilateral Standardization Forum's Environmental Standards Working Group among the United States, Canada and Mexico, a hemispheric forum should be created to exchange information about existing and anticipated environmental regulations and standards. Such a forum could also exchange information on the standards setting and conformity assessment processes within the countries of the hemisphere, and lead to strengthened environmental standards and managements systems and more effective compliance.

The leaders should support and take into account the work of the North American Commission on Environmental Cooperation on North American standards.

Environmental Technology Cooperation in Trade in Goods and Services

Resources from bilateral and multilateral institutions will be needed to enable local government to invest in environmental technologies. Local authorities in developing countries often lack the legislation to guarantee fair remuneration of patent rights as well as the necessary infrastructure to permit the transfer and absorption of technologies.

Serious consideration should be given to joint ventures between North-South partnerships, involving the private and the public sectors, as well as the reallocation of public funds.

The leaders should initiate a hemispheric program of environmental technology cooperation. From a trade perspective, this could take the form of enabling incentives, such as accelerated tariff reduction on goods and services that would curb environmental degradation, with current trading partners, and also from prospective partners who would commit to lower trade barriers on these goods and services. Items that should be targeted include technology necessary to

clean up existing industry, as well as new technology and services including environmental accounting, reporting, auditing and associated management systems.

Investment

A current estimate of Canadian investment in the other countries of the hemisphere is approximately $6 billion. Indeed, direct and portfolio investment flows to the five major Latin American markets of Argentina, Brazil, Chile, Mexico, and Venezuela more than doubled in 1991. Indeed, Brazil, at US$2.4 billion, is the third-largest recipient of Canadian investment abroad, after the United Kingdom and the United States. Similar increases are being experienced by other countries of the hemisphere. In Chile, for example, between 1992 and 1993, total foreign direct investment grew by 10 percent to $3.3 billion. Of this, U.S. investment accounts for $2.4 billion. New opportunities resulting from the privatization programs of the Salinas administration in Mexico, have resulted in the sale of over 1,000 state enterprises and are expected to attract increased capital to Mexico. For Canada, the most likely sectors of concentration will be mining, agro-industry, food, transportation, the environment, and tourism development.

The principle articulated in NAFTA's Article 1114, which prevents parties from weakening environmental laws in order to attract investment, should be endorsed by the leaders of the hemisphere, as applicable to their own countries.

II. ENVIRONMENTAL LINKAGES

As a result of increased interdependence on a hemispheric scale, we can anticipate some larger sustainable development challenges to emerge. We should seize this opportunity to enhance the environmental performance of the hemisphere as an organized community of interests and values, beyond those tentative moves that existing organizations such as the OAS have already taken.

The hemisphere can and should take a lead in those areas where it controls a strong plurality of the globe's environmental assets, where hemispheric performance lags behind that of other regions, and especially where the intensifying interdependence among hemispheric countries makes collective action urgent or present.[3] Three such ecological issues that have immediate hemispheric implications are climate change and energy, forests, and biodiversity. These issues are all interrelated. Forests are necessary to protect biodiversity — they provide the habitat for 10 to 80 million forms of life, ranging from species including the trees themselves as well as other plants, to mammals, birds, fish, insects, bacteria, fungi, algae, and other micro-organisms. Tropical forests contain by far the most examples of biological diversity. But even outside the tropics, forests are often extremely important habitat areas for the majority of species. In Canada, for example, 200,000 of the estimated 300,000 species of plants, animals, and micro-organisms reside in forests.

Thus, the loss of biological diversity on the planet and the fate of biological resources are closely tied to the fate of forests. Conservative estimates indicate that at current rates of global deforestation, at least 2 to 7 percent of all species will become extinct over the next 25 years.

Forests also help to protect the global climate against the effects of greenhouse warming. They filter the air and act as sinks for carbon dioxide, which, when released into the atmosphere, is the major greenhouse gas. In order to reduce CO_2 emissions to 1990 levels by the year 2000, it is critical to address issues in the energy sector, such as the inefficient use of fossil fuels, the reduction of emissions and sources of CO_2, and the preservation of sinks found in the forests of the hemisphere. While increases in CO_2 emissions are primarily (75 percent) due to the escalating combustion of fossil fuels, it is estimated that 25 percent are due to the destruction of global forests. Deforestation contributes to increasing concentrations of atmospheric CO_2, partly through the reduction in photosynthetic activity and partly through the release of the carbon stored in the forest biomass and soils.

Similarly, global warming, caused by current energy practices in the hemisphere, will have a negative effect on biodiversity both on land and in the oceans. Biological diversity will be affected by changes in climate. Projected temperature changes and sea level changes will have an impact on regional vitality, especially in low-lying islands and coastal areas. In some cases, a species' ability to survive will depend upon its ability to adapt to altered habitats and relationships with other species. Plants, which are directly affected by temperature and rainfall, cannot move if conditions become hostile.

Many analysts project an eventual sea level rise of 0.5 to 1 meter as a consequence of CO_2 doubling. Because Canada has the longest coastline of any country in the world, a 0.5 to 1 meter rise in sea level would be very costly for a number of Canadian communities, resulting in, for example, significant losses of coastal wetlands, which often provide a home for migratory birds. Similarly, the large number of small, low-lying islands in the hemisphere would be critically affected.

All of these issues are intricately linked to the economies of the countries of the hemisphere. These countries often rely upon their natural resource base or their climate for agriculture, or the biodiversity in their forests to sustain them. Given the environmental linkages among the countries of the hemisphere through the air, the sea, and over land, as well as the respective capabilities of the countries to address the issues in isolation (all countries in the Western Hemisphere except for Canada and the United States are classified by the OECD as developing countries), it is necessary to approach solutions as a hemisphere. Indeed, addressing these issues on a regional basis is called for in recent international Conventions and Principles. Both the Biodiversity Convention and the UN Authoritative Statement of Forest Principles recommend the strengthening of national, regional, and international capacities. Indeed, Chapter 38 of Agenda 21 calls for the promotion of regional and subregional cooperation in building and maintaining capacity and promoting the integration of environmental concerns in regional and subregional development policies. Regional cooperation is also needed to share experiences or alternative approaches toward establishing ownership security or responsible stewardship over natural resources.

Forests

Among them, the countries of the Western Hemisphere account for 42.9 percent of the world's natural closed forest cover (tropical and temperate). Indeed, Canada, the United States, and Brazil together

---

[3] Appendix B illustrates some environmental issues that are legitimately hemispheric, including fish, forests, biodiversity, climate change, and migratory species. Appendix C includes some indicators of the environmental performance of selected countries of the hemisphere on these issues, compared to each other and to other regions of the world. Appendix D illustrates, for comparisons' sake, population trends in different regions of the world.

account for 30.5 percent of the global total. The hemisphere contains over half (52.3 percent) of the world's tropical forest and 36.3 percent of the world's temperate forest.

Moreover, the Western Hemisphere is over-exploiting its forest reserves. The region leads the world in total tropical forest area lost each year. In general, between 1968 and 1990, the total forest cover of the hemisphere has dropped by 4 percent. This represents a rate of deforestation twice that of Africa and Asia which, as regions, both experienced rates of deforestation of 2 percent over the same period. In the Western Hemisphere, Mexico and Brazil stand out with rates of deforestation of 5 percent over the 22 year period. At the same time, the hemisphere experienced a 3 percent increase in area of pasture and a 2 percent increase in area of cropland.

Such rapid rates of deforestation contribute importantly to increased land degradation. The hemisphere, taken as a whole, includes 22 percent of the total percentage of the world's degraded land. While this degradation is not as extreme as in Africa, it is more extreme than that in Asia. The extent of degradation is worse in South America (14 percent of the total vegetated land) than it is in North and Central America (8 percent). Similarly, the causes of degradation are different in the North and the South. In South America, approximately half of the degradation is the result of rapid deforestation. In North and Central America, two thirds of the degradation is caused by agricultural mismanagement.

Of particular concern in the hemisphere are tropical forests, which originally covered 16 million square kilometers of the land surface. However, areas of this forest have been cleared for cultivation, agriculture, commercial timber, and fuel wood. By the mid-1970s, coverage had been reduced to about 10 million square kilometers of intact primary forest. Between 1981 and 1985, 4.4 million hectares per year of closed tropical forest were logged. Between 1981 and 1990, the hemisphere as a whole averaged a deforestation rate of its tropical forests of -0.7 percent, a rate identical to Africa. Some countries such as Mexico, at -1.2 percent, exceeded this rate. Tropical forests, due to their unique climatic and geographical conditions, are among the world's richest habitats and contain a large proportion of the world's biological diversity.

Acknowledging the importance of the environment in providing sources and sinks for greenhouse gases, the majority of countries in the hemisphere were concerned that any agreement at Rio recognize the needs of developing countries to benefit from their natural resources in an environmentally sustainable way. Some countries throughout the region have taken some steps to conserve forest biodiversity through, inter alia, the establishment of nationally protected areas. These actions can form a basis for international initiatives to learn from each others' domestic experiences and, possibly, promote the conclusion of a global or regional forestry convention.

One means of learning through others' experiences, pioneered by Canada, is the establishment of "model forests." A network of ten model forests now exists across Canada. In June 1992, Canada announced, and is now participating financially in the establishment of, an international network of model forests in Mexico, Malaysia, and Russia. There are two such forests in Mexico, a tropical one in the state of Campeche, and a temperate forest in Chihuahua. In the process of establishing a model forest, the various groups that have interests at stake in it form a partnership committee and reach agreement on a set of research projects by which aspects of sustainable development can be demonstrated and developed. These are then refined, approved, and jointly executed. It is believed that this interaction among stakeholders makes an important contribution toward reconciling forest objectives. Although still in its infancy, this program promises to provide a good track record and secure broad acceptance and success.

In the United States, President Bill Clinton announced a Forest Plan for a sustainable economy and a sustainable environment on July 1, 1993. Following the "Oregon Summit" of leading stakeholders early in 1994, the Plan was designed to provide guidelines for logging on public lands, to meet environmental requirements, to assist economic adjustment in the Pacific Northwest, and to clarify the roles of different federal agencies. The Plan used watersheds as the fundamental building block and designated reserve areas based on watersheds and old growth forests, within which only very limited activities would be permitted. Ten Adaptive Management areas were set aside to allow for "intensive ecological experimentation and social innovation to develop and demonstrate new ways to integrate ecological and economic objectives and to allow for local involvement in defining the future." The total timber output in board feet foreseen from the President's Plan, 1.2 billion, was about one-third the average output attained from 1980 to 1992. Cutting had been deadlocked by court actions under the *Endangered Species Act*, and the Plan was designed with the requirements of that Act in mind. Among aspects of the plan of possible wider interest are its gestation at a Conference of stakeholders and its orientation on watersheds.

Discussion of a possible global forest convention took place at Rio and elsewhere but encountered the main tropical forest countries' determined opposition to binding engagements. In view of this, the Intergovernmental Working Group on Global Forests, recently formed at the initiative of Canada and Malaysia, disclaims any intention of aiming at a convention. Nevertheless, the substance of its work has certain similarities to that which might go into a convention.

A document entitled "America's Forest Program" appeared in June 1994, the product of work by Ecuador and Argentina, and an Ecuadorean NGO, the Fundación NATURA. The Program called for the establishment of a continental convention to integrate forest ecosystems on a hemispheric basis by either converting the Rio Forest Principles into a convention or by amending the *1940 Convention for the Protection of the Flora, Fauna and Natural Landscapes of the Countries of the Americas* (the Western Hemisphere Convention). The initiative would involve designing and developing a Forest Evaluation System, strengthening forestry institutions, promoting training, encouraging demonstration regions, and favoring the creation of an America's Forest Fund to finance these activities. The program would be administered by a committee formed of government forest authority representatives and a representative of a designated NGO from each participating country.

Another alternative form of agreement is the *Central American Forestry Convention* signed by the Foreign Ministers of Costa Rica, El Salvador, Guatemala, Honduras, Nicaragua, and Panama in October 1993. This Convention reaffirmed the signatories' sovereign rights to develop their own forests as a function of their need for development, conservation and sustainable development, ensuring against environmental damage in other countries, and strength-

ened application of each state's Forestry Action Plan. It contains a commitment for a system of protected wildlands, integration of programs, and rehabilitation of degraded lands. The Central American Commission on Environment and Development is instructed to create a Central American Council on Forests to follow up the Convention and mandated to request support from friendly governments and international organizations. In substance, this convention is a form of general cooperation agreement.

Deforestation incentives and regulations should be reviewed to ensure that incentives for deforestation are phased out in the hemisphere. The leaders should explore incentives for maintaining and expanding existing forests. Existing work should be supported and further work encouraged on the criteria and indicators for sustainable development in the forestry sector.

The countries of the hemisphere should continue to explore methods for sustainable forest management. They should be encouraged to take up the issue of forests and to organize the region to move ahead of the Rio consensus (the Forestry Principles). This initiative might usefully be taken up by the OAS as a major agenda item in its new work plan.

It would be useful if the leaders at the Miami Summit recognized the sensitivities between the North and the South on forest issues in their deliberations. Should it happen that no model of a convention succeeds in attracting a consensus, there exist a range of other means for improving international forestry cooperation, building on the plans that already have the support of the developing countries in the hemisphere. Recognizing that this is a difficult issue and in light of Canada's abundant forest resources, the Canadian government should consider taking a lead on this issue.

Biodiversity

The Western Hemisphere is a treasure house of biological diversity. Brazil alone contained 1,573 of the world's known bird species in 1992. Indeed, Amazonia holds 20 percent of the world's bird species and thousands of species of butterflies and other insects.

From a global perspective, the 1988 list of the IUCN Red List of Threatened Animals contained 4,589 entries. The U.S. Global 2000 Report projected a loss of 15-20 percent of all species by the year 2000. A conservative estimate by IUCN's Threatened Plants Unit projects that, by the year 2050, up to 60,000 plant species will become extinct.

Within the hemisphere, of the OAS' [member countries'] known mammal and bird species, 6.9 percent of the mammals and 4.4 percent of the birds are threatened with extinction. More specifically, in 1992, Mexico contained 439 of the world's known mammal species, with 5.7 percent of those species threatened or in danger of extinction. In Brazil, the figure is almost double that at 10.2 percent of mammal species under threat. Moreover, 7.8 percent of the bird species in Brazil are threatened.

One reason for the extent of the diversity of species in the hemisphere is the presence, among those areas that contain exceptionally high biological diversity, of tropical forests. These forests, due to their unique climatic and/or geographical conditions, are among the world's richest habitats. They contain a large proportion of the world's biological diversity. The Western Hemisphere contains over half (52 percent) of the world's tropical forests. Thus, the loss of biodiversity is closely related to the rates of deforestation of tropical forests.

Tropical forests also have significant present and prospective economic and social value. One-half of all drugs and medicines dispensed have their immediate origins in wild plants and animals. Since tropical rain forests alone may contain 50-90 percent of all species, they are vast reservoirs of potential pharmaceuticals. As well, many industrial products such as oils, resins, gums, dyes, waxes, and tannins are derived from wild plants and animals.

The UN Biodiversity Convention and other Existing International Agreements

One means of protecting biological diversity is by acceding to and enforcing various international conventions on biodiversity and related matters. These include CITES, RAMSAR, the Biodiversity Convention, 1992, the Western Hemisphere Convention, 1940, and conventions that protect migratory species.

Not all the countries in the hemisphere are party to this range of conventions. If they are parties, many have not implemented them. For example, while all the countries in the hemisphere have signed the Biodiversity Convention, 1992 (The Convention on Biological Diversity entered into force on December 29, 1993), only five have fully ratified it. Even agreements such as CITES (Convention on International Trade in Endangered Species of Wild Flora and Fauna), which has been ratified by virtually 100 percent of the countries of the hemisphere, are sometimes not effectively implemented. For example, in 1990 the United States, Brazil, Chile, and Argentina were among a number of countries that consistently did not meet the CITES reporting requirements.

Under the Biodiversity Convention there is a provision requiring countries to produce national strategies. Canada has completed a first draft of this strategy. It is expected to be in final form by November 1994. Within Canada's national strategy there are a number of elements that support international action: international cooperation, the transfer of technology, the development of integrated programs, and the development of standards for products that are sensitive to biodiversity concerns.

Agreements which do not command all of the signatures of the hemispheric countries include the Convention on Wetlands of International Importance, especially as Waterfowl Habitats (RAMSAR); the Western Hemisphere Convention of 1940; and the Western Hemisphere Shorebird Reserve Network (WHSRN). The WHSRN was an initiative spearheaded by the Canadian Wildlife Service and has since been ratified by the governments of Canada, the United States, Mexico, Suriname, Argentina, Brazil, and Peru. Ratification by Panama and Chile is pending. WHSRN recognizes the importance of temperate and tropical wetlands for migratory shorebirds which breed primarily in arctic Canada and spend the boreal winter in South America. WHSRN is a program of Wetlands for the Americas, working with governments, multilateral banks, local and internationals NGOs, as well as research institutions throughout the Americas, in an effort to promote wetland conservation.

The leaders at Miami should consider whether the Convention on Biological Diversity has been well implemented in the hemisphere, whether it needs strengthening in ways the hemisphere could pioneer, and whether their countries have in place national biodiversity strategies.

The leaders of the hemisphere at Miami should commit themselves to join, ratify, and properly implement agreements such as CITES and RAMSAR, and the Western Hemisphere Convention of 1940.

The countries of the hemisphere should create a Hemispheric Biodiversity Inventory as part of an effort to monitor carefully the extent of and the loss of biodiversity in the hemisphere. This Inventory could be developed in conjunction with the United States, where a high priority has been given to creating a National Biodiversity Inventory. Alternatively, countries of the hemisphere should create their own national inventories which could feed into a hemispheric data base to assist in monitoring and in developing research agendas, conservation plans, and resource management schemes.

Migratory and Transboundary Species

In many cases, the species in the hemisphere are the joint responsibility of all the countries because the Western Hemisphere, as a region, provides the habitat for a number of species that migrate from one jurisdiction to another or where species' habitats are transboundary. In Canada, 24 percent of species migrate across international boundaries, while a full 81 percent of species span, or straddle, international boundaries.

There are 354 species of birds that migrate from Canada to the United States and Central and South America. About the same number of bird species migrate from the United States to Central and South America. As well, there are a number of species of birds that migrate within Central and South America. About half of the twenty species of bats in Canada are migratory, moving to the United States to avoid harsh winters.

A number of marine mammals migrate throughout the hemisphere as well. For example, two species of marine turtles migrate from Canadian waters to South American waters to feed and breed. Nine of the eleven species of great whales are found in Canadian waters. Of these, at least five species migrate to the equatorial waters of South America and the Caribbean to avoid ice and to breed. There are even a number of insects that migrate from North America to Central America and South America to avoid the harsh winters. For example, the monarch butterfly migrates from northeastern and northwestern North America to a few mountain valleys in Mexico and California, and the milkweed bug migrates from Canada to the southern United States.

Twelve percent of Canadian species are currently protected under international conventions or agreements such as CITES or the Migratory Birds Convention.

The Biodiversity Convention is explicit in its application to the national jurisdictions of its signatories. However, under Article 5, the Contracting Parties are encouraged to "cooperate with other Contracting Parties directly or, where appropriate, through competent international organizations, in respect of areas beyond national jurisdiction and on other matters of mutual interest, for the conservation and sustainable use of biological diversity." The Parties to the Convention are required to develop national strategies, plans, or programmes for the conservation and sustainable use of biological diversity (Article 6). Under the Biodiversity Convention, 1992, the signatory countries are encouraged to "[d]evelop or maintain necessary legislation and/or other regulatory provisions for the protection of threatened species and populations" (Article 8k).

In 1979 an international convention, *The Migratory Species Act*, 1979 (Bonn Convention), was signed in Bonn to protect migratory species that are endangered. Only five countries in the hemisphere have signed the Migratory Species Act, 1979. They are Chile, Jamaica, Panama, Suriname and Uruguay. Of these, Jamaica still has not ratified the agreement. Parties to the Convention are required to take steps to conserve endangered, migratory species and their habitats. The Bonn Convention is directly aimed at migratory species. Preserving their habitats could indirectly preserve the habitats of other non-migratory species. However, it leaves all plants, micro-organisms, and most invertebrates outside its application.

The Migratory Birds Convention Act between Canada and the United States (1917) is in the process of being extended to cover Mexico. Mexico is ratifying it, as it has been added to the list of environmental agreements that will take precedence over the provisions of the North American Free Trade Agreement.

The countries of the hemisphere should initiate joint research, data collection, monitoring, and protection of migratory species. International institutions should enable collaborative research and development.

The countries of the hemisphere should sign and implement the Bonn Convention to ensure, at a minimum, that threatened migratory species and their habitats are protected.

Building and Maintaining Capacity

Some countries lack the means to finance the protection of biodiversity, including resources for hiring personnel as well as equipment to monitor the state of biodiversity.

The leaders of the hemisphere should agree to examine government subsidies and tax policies with a view to identifying all those subsidies that contribute to environmental degradation or inhibit sustainable development in any way. They should also study the design and implementation of economic instruments for the conservation of biological diversity.

The leaders of the hemisphere could also begin the process of determining the value of ecological resources, including biodiversity, so that its value can be internalized in its calculations of national accounts.

Energy Production, Consumption, and Climate Change

The countries of the Western Hemisphere are major producers and consumers of energy. Taken together, in 1990 the countries of the Western Hemisphere produced 29.4 percent of global primary energy. This is more than any other single region in the world. It represented an increase of 11.5 percent from the energy production in the hemisphere over the ten years from 1980 to 1990.

The countries of the Western Hemisphere also rely heavily on energy produced by solid fuel (coal). This reliance has grown dramatically in the last 20 years. In 1991, the percentage of the hemisphere's energy produced by solid fuel (coal) was 24 percent. In North America, this figure is up 85 percent from 1971. In South America, the increase in the twenty years between 1971 and 1991, at 395 percent, is the highest of any region in the world.

Consumption of energy has also increased over the last decade, if not as rapidly as in other regions of the world. The countries of the hemisphere consumed 31.7 percent of the world's energy in 1990 — more than any other single region in the world. Although this was up 7.4 percent from 1980, the increase in consumption in the hemisphere is one-quarter that of any other region (except for Africa,

which experienced a decline of 13 percent in energy consumption in the same period).

Per capita, both North and South America experienced a decline in energy consumption between 1980 and 1990. Canada consumes only 2.6 percent of the world's energy, but the consumption of Canadians per capita is greater than any other country in the hemisphere, due in part to climate and distance.

Given the significant quantities of energy produced in the Western Hemisphere from solid fuels such as coal, the hemisphere is responsible for a considerable amount of the world's CO_2 emissions. Indeed, in 1991, the Western Hemisphere as a region was responsible for a full 28 percent of the world's CO_2 emissions. As a region, this is second only to Asia at 29.4 percent. Per capita, North Americans emit over six times the CO_2 of South Americans, and close to six times that of other regions (with the exception of the former Soviet Union, where per capita emissions are only slightly less than they are in North America).

However, since 1980 the emission figures in North America have been falling. In Canada there has been a 0.5 percent decrease in CO_2 emissions between 1980 and 1990. In the United States, the rise was only 4.1 percent. In South America, on the other hand, emissions have been rising rapidly since 1980. For example, Mexico's are up 25.9 percent, Brazil's 8.4 percent, and Chile's up 26.5 percent.

The UN Framework Convention on Climate Change

In 1992 at Rio, all of the countries of the hemisphere signed the *United Nations Framework Convention on Climate Change* (the Climate Change Convention). The Climate Change Convention entered into force on March 21, 1994, after the fiftieth instrument of ratification was deposited with the UN Secretary-General on December 21, 1993.

The Convention sets out general obligations for all Parties and additional obligations for "Annex 1 Parties," i.e., the member states of the OECD (not including Mexico, which was not an OECD state when the Convention was negotiated) and the states of Central and Eastern Europe with economies in transition. The most noteworthy obligation of Annex 1 Parties is to implement policies and measures to mitigate climate change by limiting anthropogenic emissions of greenhouse gases (GHG), and by protecting and enhancing sinks, such as forests. The Convention has, as one of its main goals, the return of levels of greenhouse gas emission to 1990 levels by the year 2000.

Developing countries are under the obligation to commit to a national plan for the reduction of greenhouse gases but are not bound by any specific targets. OECD countries must provide financial assistance to pay the full agreed incremental costs incurred by developing countries of implementing measures to meet their Convention obligations, as well as their full agreed costs in preparing national reports.

Among the signatory countries in the hemisphere, both Canada and the United States have ratified the Climate Change Convention. Indeed, in October 1993, U.S. President Bill Clinton announced a detailed global warming strategy, the Climate Change Action Plan, which is intended to meet the goals of the Convention to reduce greenhouse gas emission to 1990 levels. The plan also seeks to expand markets for U.S. technologies, create jobs, and reduce the deficit. The basis of the plan is a package of public-private partnerships with key industries to reduce all types of greenhouse gases without resort to regulation.

There is some concern that falling oil prices and increased economic activity will offset some of the gains that the Clinton plan relies on and that there is thus a shortfall of 70 million metric tons of carbon in the projected requirement — a major shortfall, given that the original Climate Plan was designed to reduce emissions by around 106 million metric tons.

The Canadian government has committed itself to reducing Canadian emissions of greenhouse gases by 20 percent from 1988 levels by 2005. It has not yet announced a strategy for achieving those targets. Its National Report (as required by the Convention) shows that unless additional measures are taken, Canadian GHG emissions in the year 2000 will be 10.6 percent higher than 1990 emissions. Through a Climate Change Task Group, the federal and provincial governments, along with environmental and business stakeholders, are developing a Climate Change National Action Program, which will set out options for achieving the stabilization goal and sustainable options for further reductions beyond the year 2000.

The leaders of the hemisphere should reaffirm their support for the Climate Change Convention and the science that underlies it.

The countries of the hemisphere should commit themselves to ratifying and implementing the Climate

Change Convention and rapidly producing the national plans it requires.

Joint Implementation (JI)

Article 4.2(a) of the UN Climate Change Convention introduced the concept of Joint Implementation, although it is not defined or elaborated.

Article 4.2(a): "The developed country Parties and other Parties included in Annex 1 commit themselves specifically as provided for in the following:

(a) Each of these Parties shall adopt policies and take corresponding measures on the mitigation of climate change, by limiting its anthropogenic emissions of greenhouse gases and protecting and enhancing its greenhouse gas sinks and reservoirs. These policies and measures will demonstrate that developed countries are taking the lead in modifying longer-term trends in anthropogenic emissions consistent with the objective of the Convention, recognizing that the return by the end of the present decade to earlier levels of anthropogenic emissions of carbon dioxide and other greenhouse gases not controlled by the Montreal Protocol would contribute to such modification, and taking into account the differences in these Parties' starting points and approaches, economic structures and resource bases, the need to maintain strong and sustainable economic growth, available technologies, and other individual circumstances, as well as the need for equitable and appropriate contributions by each of these Parties to the global effort regarding that objective. *These Parties may implement such policies and measures jointly with other Parties and may assist other Parties in contributing to the achievement of the objective of the Convention, and, in particular, that of this subparagraph;. . . ."* (emphasis added)

There are a number of problems that arise as a matter of interpretation of the joint implementation provision in the Climate Change Convention. Industry could see various scenarios under joint implementation which could include tradeable emissions, carbon sequestrations and offsets, technology transfer, and cooperation in the sharing of information and technology. Carbon sequestration could include planting trees in developing countries to earn credits that could be offset against emissions at home.

Many environmentalists, on the other hand, are opposed to carbon sequestration projects (at least for now) and interpret the commitments in the Climate

Change Convention as committing governments in the North to meet their own 20 percent targets before they can use credits earned in developing countries. As well, the task of quantifying and monitoring carbon sequestration projects is considered to be very difficult.

The developing countries in the hemisphere face difficulty with access to funds for training, research, technology, and information to assist in implementing the provisions of the Climate Change Convention. As well, there are political obstacles for joint implementation with the perception that the North will attempt to deal with its own commitments by engaging in offsets in the developing world, i.e., trying to solve our problems on the backs of the developing countries who will remain unable to help themselves.

The controversy over joint implementation raises the need to develop a framework to guide the conduct of pilot joint implementation projects. The legitimate concerns over the use of JI offsets need to be evaluated so that this issue can be dealt with in the most economic and environmentally sound way. The best option is to reduce emissions at the source through, inter alia, aggressive energy management programs. But, even with these efforts, it will not be feasible to eliminate emissions completely and it may be less costly in the interim to offset emissions through JI projects. Suggested criteria for JI projects have been developed by Canada, the United States, the INC Secretariat, and others. The framework for pilot JI projects should include criteria on:

- *host country acceptance;*
- *measuring, tracking, and verifying actual versus predicted net costs and benefits (emission reductions and sequestration);*
- *identification of other environmental, social, and economic benefits, including any associated non-greenhouse gas environmental impacts and/or benefits;*
- *eligibility of participants;*
- *project conformance with prevailing standards of environmental protection;*
- *permanence of and the offsets (long-term sustainability);*

- *potential for the project to induce changes in greenhouse gases elsewhere.*

Energy Efficiency and Renewable Energy Sources

Sustainable development requires the promotion of policies and the designing of instruments for the efficient use and sustainable development of energy resources. This includes the use of renewable and "cleaner" energy sources. The use of renewable energy sources and natural gas — thereby reducing the carbon content of the energy supply — will assist in reducing the emission of greenhouse gases and the environmental degradation associated with the development of conventional energy supplies.

Joint partnerships can promote interaction and partnerships between utility professionals to increase the capacity of utilities for technology transfer and information exchange to assist in implementing energy-efficient measures.

The leaders at Miami should consider whether it is advisable, and what steps can be taken domestically, to reduce the subsidies to fossil fuel industries in the hemisphere and determine how can those funds best be reallocated.

Building and Maintaining Capacity

There is a serious infrastructure deficit in Latin America and a continued failure to invest in infrastructure. In 1990, Latin American investment in construction was less than three-quarters of what it was in 1980. One of the biggest infrastructure deficits in the industrializing parts of Latin America is in the electricity sector.

Between 1989 and 1999, the energy needs of Latin America and the Caribbean countries are expected to grow by 60 percent. In many of these countries (including Brazil, Colombia, Guatemala, Argentina, Ecuador and many Central American countries) the percentage of the population presently without electricity exceeds 80 percent.[4]

These statistics confirm the fact that Latin America will soon require significant assistance in developing programs to supply and manage energy effectively.

---

[4] Figures taken from Gustavo Alanis Ortega, "A Latin American Perspective on the Summit of the Americas," a paper presented at a workshop on "Advancing Sustainable at the Summit of the Americas" hosted by the National Round Table on the Environment and the Economy, the National Audubon Society, and the National Wildlife Federation, July 11, 1994, Washington, D.C.

Assistance could include sharing of technology, information, and expertise. It could build on the 1993 Renewable Energy in the Americas Initiative which promotes present and future reliance on renewable energy sources.

The leaders at the Summit should suggest that the countries of the hemisphere establish a Continental Collaborative of Stakeholders to examine how to deal with the issues of climate change on a hemispheric basis. Among the issues that the Collaborative could look at are:

- *Alternative funding arrangements or mechanisms involving the traditional money-lending agencies, as well as different kinds of partnerships, public-private partnerships, energy efficiency technologies, more traditional pollution control technologies, training, and education at all levels. This could include an examination of how the countries of the hemisphere can encourage non-polluting, renewable, and energy-efficient forms of production.*

- *The use of market instruments in reaching climate change targets, including the possibility of emission trading.*

- *A serious investigation into the advisability of implementing CO_2 reduction strategies jointly throughout the hemisphere to reduce CO_2 emissions as a region. The Collaborative could address some of the difficult questions of interpretation in a North-South context and present its findings at the Conference of the Parties in Berlin in March 1995, at which point criteria for a Joint Implementation Pilot Phase are to be approved.*

- *How the countries of the hemisphere can best encourage non-polluting, renewable, and energy efficient forms of production.*

The leaders should also propose the creation of a pilot project for a public-private partnership in the electricity sector. It is an industry which is well-developed in both North America and South America, and it is an industry which is a major contributor, among the industrial sectors, to CO_2 emissions and to global warming. It is also an industry rife with inefficiencies in both the North and the South. The partnership could be designed to promote energy efficiency, building and maintaining capacity, technology transfer, information sharing, cooperation on research

agendas and other programs, including such items as demand management.

Toxics

The countries of the Americas use 26.7 percent of the world's pesticides. This is the highest level of any region in the world, although Europe is a very close second with 26.6 percent.

Transboundary Pollution

Human activities in the hemisphere and around the world emit millions of tons of polluting material into the atmosphere. Gases such as nitrogen oxides, carbon monoxide, and carbon dioxide — mostly from burning fossil fuels — account for a large part of this material. Dust and soot, as well as vapors and aerosols from chemical use, are other significant contributors to air pollution.

Not all toxic chemicals are a transboundary concern. Many highly toxic chemicals rapidly degrade or undergo chemical reactions to form other compounds under environmental conditions. The substances of concern from a transboundary or long-range transport perspective are generally grouped into three categories:

a) persistent organic pollutants (POPs), including industrial chemicals (e.g., PCBs), incineration by-products or contaminants (e.g., dioxins and furans), and pesticides (e.g., DDT);

b) man-made emissions of various forms of metals (e.g., lead, mercury, and cadmium); and

c) radionuclides (e.g., radon).

The transboundary movement of air pollutants results from the release of these substances in the form of gases, water droplets, and dust particles into the environment, where they may persist for long periods, meaning that a substance released in one area will almost inevitably be deposited somewhere else.

There is strong evidence to suggest that these persistent toxic substances can be carried long distances by air and water currents and have the ability to undergo may successive cycles, as warm southern winds lift these substances into the air and then redeposit them when these winds hit cool northern temperatures. This gradual cycling from warmer to cooler climates leads to their accumulation in regions far from their initiate release point, and eventually to the remote northern regions of Canada. Many of these substances have also demonstrated the ability to "biomagnify" in the food chain, i.e., to build up to many thousands of times higher concentrations going from lower organisms to fish, to the higher level species such as whales, polar bears, and humans. Indeed, the concentrations of these substances amongst the inhabitants of the Canadian Arctic, whose food intake comes primarily from fish and wildlife, are as high or higher than those found anywhere in the world.

As well as the atmospheric movement of toxics across national boundaries, the countries of the hemisphere can be linked in a transboundary sense through transport processes, such as rainwater and runoff, which can add to the toxic burden of waters throughout the hemisphere as the oceans and other large bodies of water are becoming a huge reservoir of these substances. Pesticides and chemicals that have been deposited on the ground are commonly washed into rivers and lakes. In addition, a substantial amount of toxic material can enter water bodies, especially those with large surface areas, directly from the air. More than 90 percent of the PCBs, DDT, and lead in Lake Superior, for example, is believed to come from atmospheric deposition.

Serious contamination can also occur as a result of toxic chemicals leaching into the water table from hazardous waste that has been buried in dumps and landfills. For example, an estimated 315 kilograms of toxic chemicals enters the Niagara River daily from several large U.S. sites located within 5 kilometers of the river.

The deposit of emissions raises a number of questions. Often, in the case of long-range transboundary pollution, it is not clear where a pollutant originated, or, once deposited, where it will travel and what its effects will be. One concrete effect of human emissions of sulphur and nitrogen dioxides has been to cause acid precipitation, which has had an adverse impact on hundreds of lakes and rivers in Europe and North America. However, long range transboundary air pollutants can also adversely affect human health, primarily respiratory systems, with sulphur dioxide, nitrogen dioxide, ozone, and particulate matter being the most common irritants. A number of persistent toxic substances have also been

shown to have adverse effects on human health, including cancer and reproducti[ve disorders], and recently many of these substances have been suspected of acting as synthetic versions of the hormone estrogen, upsetting the normal hormone balance. Plants, both domesticated and wild, show a variety of effects in polluted air, including a slower rate of photosynthesis, changes in enzyme activity, loss of foliage, and reductions in growth and seed production.

Toxics are an issue that must be dealt with jointly by the countries in the Americas. National and sometimes even regional bans on the use of specific chemicals cannot be completely effective in reducing contamination if the substances remain in use in other parts of the region.

The three NAFTA partners have already recognized their joint responsibility to deal with transboundary environmental issues. These could include atmospheric movement of toxics, notable assessment, notification, and mitigation.

The leaders at the Summit should advocate strongly the creation of a Hemisphere Toxic Release Inventory, building on the inventories that already exist in Canada and the United States, and supporting the work of the North American Commission on Environmental Cooperation.

There should be support for efforts for increased cooperation in research, data collection, and monitoring to identify where the toxics that are released into the atmosphere travel and the impact on regional populations and ecosystems. This information should be made widely available and accessible to the general public and other interested groups.

Movement of Hazardous Waste

The Lomé Convention bans all radioactive and hazardous waste shipments from the European Union (EU) to other signatories, and the signatories agree not to import any wastes from any other non-EU country. The Basel Convention sets global rules of procedure for the international waste trade. While many of the countries of the hemisphere are parties to the Basel Convention, only countries of the Caribbean have signed the Lomé Convention which, in effect, is a ban on waste exports from industrialized EU countries to less industrialized countries.

The countries of the hemisphere should be encouraged to sign and implement the Basel Convention to ensure that common procedures are in place to regulate the transboundary shipment of waste.

III. SOME ISSUES OF EQUITY AND SOCIAL JUSTICE

The third pillar of sustainable development along with economic prosperity and environmental enhancement is social justice and inter-generational equity. Poverty plays a critical role in shaping issues of social justice, equity, and quality of life. This is particularly true in some developing countries where the majority of the population lives in poverty and where there are inequities in the distribution of the wealth generated by increased economic activity. As noted above, in the hemisphere, with the exception of Canada and the United States, all of the countries are classified by the OECD as developing countries.

There has been considerable progress in the hemisphere toward the democratization of many governments. As one of the "baskets" for consideration by the leaders at the Miami Summit, democratic governance is critical in advancing issues of social justice. Indeed, social equity is contingent upon a broad, active, and democratic participation by the general population in a decentralized and participatory government, which has a basic respect for minority and individual human rights.

The issues involved in a consideration of social equity will influence importantly both the environment and the economy. A reduction of poverty, macroeconomic growth, and price stability, brought about by political stability, the adequate allocation of resources and land (including well-defined and secure property rights), and investment in people in the form of education, training, and employment will all promote economic stability and alleviate some of the environmental degradation brought about by poverty and inequities. This, in turn, will help to ensure the long-term and sustainable management of forests, land, biodiversity and water.

Sustainable development should be identified as the major focal point for the revitalization of the economies in the region and a basic theme around which to build new economic programs, as well as to address other social and environmental issues.

Poverty

Nearly one-half of the hemisphere's population lives in poverty. The number of Latin American households classified by the UN as "poor" rose 4 percent between 1980 and 1990 to a level that was only 1 percent lower than it had been in 1970. In 1990, 34 percent of Latin American urban households were classified as "poor," up 8 percent from 1970.[5]

Poverty has significant economic, political, environmental, and social costs. For many developing countries, poverty is linked to the lack of productive resources, overpopulation, environmental degradation, poor governance, and other development challenges.

From an economic perspective, natural resources provide a livelihood for billions of people in developing countries around the world. Natural resources also provide the raw materials for the economies of a number of countries in the hemisphere. The rapid loss of natural resources threatens to undermine the very structure and export capabilities on which many of these economies depend to sustain their economic growth, which is spurred on by increasing trade and investment throughout the hemisphere. A slow or negative economic growth rate will lead to low disposable incomes, low savings, and low investment rates.

From a political perspective, the recent progress toward democratic forms of government in many developing countries is put at risk by the persistence of widespread poverty. Democratic institutions will not be long sustained if large numbers of the population are marginalized due to poverty, disease, and lack of education. Poverty can lead to large-scale migration, social division, violent confrontation, and political instability. This, in turn, can affect levels of foreign investment and, thereby, injure the overall economic well-being of a country.

From an environmental perspective, about 80 percent of Latin America's poor live in environmentally degraded areas that threaten agricultural yields. They tend to live in ecologically fragile rural locations or on the peripheries of cities with low productive potential. They are becoming concentrated in resource-poor rural environments or on the margins of urban or peri-urban centers. The relationship between this lack of resilience and the demands made on natural resources by the poor is critical. The increasing pressure on marginal lands, causing defor-

---

5   Figures taken from Gustavo Alanis Ortega, *supra* note 4.

estation of tropical rain forests and land degradation, impacts on all the populations of the world through increases in greenhouse gases and loss of biological diversity. These areas are not resilient to stress or shocks, such as climactic variations, agricultural intensifications, or population pressures. Fuel wood is still the primary energy source for the majority of people in developing nations. This has an impact on rates of deforestation. And the burning of wood allows for its accumulated carbon to be released into the atmosphere in a relatively short time.

The poor are too busy satisfying the urgent needs of the present to plan for the future. They are thus unable to protect the resources they will be needing, and this failure leads to further environmental degradation.

From a social perspective, domestic policies regarding land tenure, titling, and ownership often act as a critical barrier to the rural poor's access to land. Institutional barriers prevent access to credit, training, land, water, or other inputs and work against fostering or promoting people's participation at the grassroots level. The environmental degradation brought about by poverty can have devastating effects on local communities.

Those sectors that are likely to remain excluded from the full benefits of development unless specific policy measures are taken are the poor, women, and Indigenous populations — and the UN Decade of the World's Indigenous People begins on December 10, 1994. Deforestation, in particular, threatens the well-being of Indigenous populations in the hemisphere. While forests directly support many subsistence cultures by providing a direct source of game and other food, the connection among the identity, culture, and rights of Indigenous peoples, often as forest dwellers, is well-known. Indeed, the human rights/environmental situation in Amazonia was among the earliest to come to international attention.

Building and Maintaining Capacity through Trade

In an effort to improve employment opportunities and the economic well-being of some of the poorer countries in the hemisphere, the Northern members could look at trade flows and their trade policies at home.

Countries in the North continue to keep in place subsidies to protect domestic production of crops, many of which would indeed be better grown elsewhere. For example, in the United States, domestic price supports, linked to a tariff-quota system, keep U.S. sugar prices two to three times the world level and have reduced imports, mainly from developing countries, by 75 percent since 1970. This has crippled the sugar industries in the Caribbean and other low-income countries and has resulted in the loss of some 400,000 jobs in Caribbean countries alone. The sugar protection program is a highly inefficient and uneconomic means of transferring income to large U.S. growers and processors from sugar producers in low-income countries and average U.S. consumers.

The effect on biodiversity is also staggering. For example, sugarcane is growing in the Everglades, where nearly one-third of the original Everglades has been drained and irrigated. This has changed the plant life in the Everglades, which adapts to new conditions, and the animal and insect life.

The countries of the hemisphere should identify protectionist measures in places which are causing environmental degradation, such as the destruction of biodiversity, and social inequities in the hemisphere.

Trade and Indigenous Peoples in Canada

A recent study completed for the United Nations Development Programme and Apikan Indigenous Network found that Indigenous Peoples in Central America unanimously supported sustainable development projects with a trade focus. Fifty-seven Indigenous organizations in Belize, Guatemala, Nicaragua, and Panama regard trade as essential to community economic, social, and cultural development. While development assistance is welcomed in Indigenous communities in the third world, these projects are often not fiscally sustainable. Traditional development assistance may help build badly needed schools, clinics, and other infrastructure, but assistance is often short term, leaving Indigenous communities without the resources to maintain these services. International trade offers opportunities for Indigenous communities to not only generate community wealth and employment, but also provide financial resources to sustain their own services.

Over the years, Aboriginal Peoples in Canada have developed expertise and knowledge in all areas of economic and social development. Currently there are over 10,000 Aboriginal non-government organizations (NGOs) in Canada. These NGOs have experience in economic development, including resource development, micro-enterprise development, agriculture, fisheries, forestry, communication, etc. Partnerships between Indigenous Peoples in Canada and Latin America and the Caribbean offer substantial opportunities for trade and development. For example, Unaaq, a successful Inuit fisheries corporation, is in the process of developing a joint venture with Miskito Indians in Nicaragua in their inshore fisheries.

Aboriginal Peoples also have successful social institutions in child care, health, education, social services, and urban institutions. Most Indigenous communities in the Americas do not have access to basic services such as health services and education. Social services also present substantial opportunities for Indigenous partnerships. Presently, the Winnipeg Indian and Metis Friendship Centre is building a school on the Miskito coast of Nicaragua.

Aboriginal Peoples in Canada believe that they have a competitive advantage in Indigenous trade and development. First, they are sensitive to the needs and culture of Indigenous Peoples, a barrier that still confounds international agencies and NGO's. Second, they know how to integrate cultural factors and values into project design and implementation. Third, they have had considerable success in building institutions which meet community and donor needs. Finally, they have the professional and technical expertise to manage complex projects.

There are numerous opportunities for Indigenous trade in the Western Hemisphere traditional products, community development, and Indigenous joint ventures and partnerships. Aboriginal Peoples' trade is appropriate for the transfer of knowledge, project delivery, and partnerships in trade and development.

One of the cornerstones of the Summit of the Americas is advancing equity. IPAFTA would incorporate all Summit "baskets": trade, sustainable development, and democratization. For Indigenous Peoples, trade fulfills national and international commitments of states, international agencies, and civil society to support the development of Indigenous Peoples.

In the general framework of liberalized trade in the Americas, special attention should be given to the development of opportunities for Indigenous Peoples' trade. One way might be to encourage the creation of an Indigenous Peoples' Americas Free Trade Agreement (IPAFTA) which would call for a phased-in process of Indigenous Peoples' trade liberalization in traditional products (based on a schedule that will be drawn up by the members of the IPAFTA).

A review of existing agreements, protocols, and policies could be undertaken to access the capacity for international, regional, and national support for Indigenous Peoples' trade and development.

An office of Indigenous Peoples' Trade and Development at the United Nations Development Programme and an Americas Ambassador on Indigenous Free Trade at the Organization of American States could be established.

Multilateral mechanisms to support Indigenous Peoples' trade and development could be established.

Public Participation, Social Accountability, and Security

The absence of participatory processes can lead to political turmoil and unrest. Indeed, equitable and participatory development is a prerequisite of social legitimacy that will allow the necessary policy reforms to encourage sustainable development. This is evident in Latin America where, despite successful economic reforms, the benefits of economic growth have not yet reached the poor or many in the middle class. The sustainability of improving economic and democratization prospects for the Americas is threatened by public policies that distribute growth benefits inequitably. The southern part of the Americas, which has the highest per capita income in the developing world (about US$2,000 per year), has the world's worst record of income distribution. Extreme poverty, when combined with inequitable distribution policies, has often led to political instability. It will hinder future investment and economic progress and contribute to the underlying causes of environmental degradation and poverty.

Redistribution of income, assets, land, or wealth is not sufficient. But it can play a catalytic role in poverty reduction and can promote equity when the root causes of poverty are associated with the misallocation of resources. This type of intervention can work to promote both access and control of assets, such as increasing the security of land tenure through land titling or equitable taxation schemes.

At a minimum, there is a need to empower individuals and groups at the local level in countries of the hemisphere to combat the most deadly forms of unsustainable development and to pursue their most basic environmental interests. Here, the sustainable development principles of open, multi-stakeholder, consensus-based decision making mean, at a minimum, the ability to receive and understand reliable and timely information about the health effects of environmentally altering economic, civilian government and military activity and the ability to organize at the local level to obtain such information and pursue shared ecological vocations and concerns. Reducing the burden which the maintenance of large national security establishments places on the process of poverty alleviation and addressing the environmental damage which closed military establishments have created is an important part of the move toward democratization in the hemisphere. On a more practical level, those national armed forces within the hemisphere that have done the most to reconfigure their capabilities from a focus on the old internal and international security concerns toward the next generation of ecological security threats (beginning with natural resource predation) should assist their hemispheric counterparts to move in this direction.

The leaders of the hemisphere should recognize the importance of access to information and of the broad participation of civil society in some of the institutions of government.

The leaders of the hemisphere should recognize that an important means for securing broad public participation and consensus is based on access to education, employment, and political representation.

The countries of the hemisphere should cooperate in establishing and monitoring poverty-reduction projects and their success in helping the poorest of the poor. Progress must be measurable (either qualitatively or quantitatively) for current and future planning.

IV. INSTITUTIONAL ARRANGEMENTS

There is a need for a plan of action to follow up on any declarations that are made at the Summit. Indeed, the hemisphere could well be used to pioneer global regimes to further the Rio Agenda and advance sustainable development. As an international institutional system that dates from the late nineteenth century, the existing Organization of American States,

as well as the array of other inter-American institutions have been slow to adapt to the new challenges of sustainable development in the hemisphere as the twenty-first century approaches.

The institutions of the hemisphere have lacked regular guidance from heads of state and government, whose purview uniquely embraces economic, environmental, and equity issues, in both their national and international dimensions, and who alone can inject political will and set new directions, priorities, and linkages. In sharp contrast to the OECD, APEC, or the G-7, where ministers other than those dealing with foreign affairs are regularly involved, hemispheric bodies have weakly institutionalized ministerial oversight, in either separated or integrated settings, from those responsible for economic, environmental or human development issues.

At the official level, bodies to deal with the environment have been of relatively recent origin and have had a narrow mandate reflecting the pollution, cleanup, and resources conservation approach of the Stockholm era rather than the sustainable development philosophy endorsed by UNCED. These institutions have also remained relatively isolated from the work of bodies in the economic and social development realms. Despite the impressive work of bodies such as the Economic Commission for Latin America and the Caribbean in some fields, the hemispheric system has had little capacity for analytical work on economy-environment interfaces (e.g., ecologically sensitive national accounts, ecological and resource capital and performance) or for coordinating or supporting relevant scientific research.

Finally, in contrast to bodies such as the OECD, and the North American Commission on Environmental Cooperation, the core hemispheric institutions have remained largely closed to participation from the business community, labor, and non-governmental organizations. Nor have they been quick to introduce other forms of accountability to stakeholders in their member countries and citizens in the hemisphere.

Thus, serious consideration, aimed at early action, should be given to the following proposals for institutional strengthening and reform:

Existing Institutions and Miami Follow-Up

It is noteworthy that the Miami Summit, in sharp contrast to the regular OAS General Assembly, has

NON-GOVERNMENTAL PROPOSALS

taken up sustainable development as a major component of its agenda. Moreover, the San José Summit of October 1989, and the recent call of the OAS General Assembly itself for a Hemispheric Heads of State and Government gathering underscore the value of periodic gatherings of the hemispheres leaders, in order to forge the new linkages and set the new directions that the hemisphere requires. The Ibero-American Summit, the annual G-7 Summit, and the annual APEC leaders meeting (in which Canada, the United States, Mexico, and prospectively Chile are involved) point in the same direction. Thus, it would be appropriate for the Miami Summit to authorize and to identify a date and location for a subsequent Summit, which would, inter alia, review progress and receive reports from any working groups that Miami established. While the European Council meets at least twice a year and the Commonwealth and Francophone every two years, the annual leaders' meeting of the G-7 and APEC could be an appropriate model. One possibility is to attach leaders' meetings to the annual OAS General Assembly, thus following its timing and location. In these subsequent gatherings of heads, the Miami agenda should be taken as a precedent, to ensure substantial, continuing attention to environmental and sustainable development issues.

All of the major, recently created plurilateral institutions to which Canada belongs also benefit from both regular collective direction from major portfolio ministers (as well as leaders) and from regular, high-level forums to deal with the environment and its relationship to economic concerns. At the G-7, environment issues have been a regular topic of discussion by leaders for almost a decade, and G-7 environment ministers have met several times since the spring of 1992 (most recently in Florence in March 1994). In the Asia-Pacific Economic Cooperation Forum, at their first meeting in November 1993, and at Canadian initiative, leaders called for an environment ministers meeting, which was held in Vancouver in March 1994. In NAFTA, the parallel environmental agreement and Commission is overseen by the environment ministers of the United States, Canada, and Mexico, who have begun meeting three times a year. Only in the western hemispheric system does the environment remain absent as a regular ministerial level concern.

In order to help ensure the implementation and elaboration of the Summit's sustainable development agenda, leaders at Miami could agree to meet on an *annual or biennial basis and/or ask their ministers responsible for trade, finance, the environment, natural resources, and other relevant portfolio ministers to meet annually.*

Of primary importance is a meeting of hemispheric trade ministers in which environmental questions are given full attention to ensure that the integration of economic and environmental considerations can be better realized.

Recognizing that some countries of the hemisphere do not have environmental ministries and that environment ministers often do not have responsibility for major ecological resources such as fisheries, forestry, land use or transportation, meetings should involve ministerial colleagues form these areas, appropriate to the particular agenda of the meeting. An environment ministers' forum could, inter alia, encourage countries of the hemisphere to set up domestic governmental bodies to deal with the environment within government, as well as give direction and focus to the work of the OAS and its recently created environment committee and trade committee.

The OAS Environment Committee

The OAS Environment Committee, one of several sectoral committees within the OAS, was established in 1991. Meeting once a week in Washington, it has provided the first, regular policy forum for regional discussion in a hemisphere where environmental issues are relatively new to many of the members. During its three years of operation, it has strengthened the attention given to environmental matters within the OAS. It has done so, in part, by liaising with other committees and engaging in joint projects such as Women and Environment (with the Women's Committee) and environmental legislation (with the Judicial Committee). The major items of interest to the Committee, thus far, have been fresh water, land degradation, and waste management. Environmentally committed countries have been able to use the Committee to good effect. For example, Canada was responsible for two resolutions on high seas overfishing, introduced into the Committee in 1992 and 1994, both timed before major conferences (Rio in 1992, the UN Conference on Straddling Stocks in 1994). These resolutions were passed by consensus and supported the broader multilateral effort to deal with these urgent issues of ecological, economic, and social devastation.

331

Yet, many other central issues of the Rio agenda, notably forests, biodiversity, and climate change, have remained absent from the Committee's agenda. Indeed, the Environment Committee is still operating under a 1991 Program of Action that predates Rio and thus does not reflect the perspective of, and new commitment of hemispheric governments to, sustainable development. Countries such as Canada have been active in trying to get the environment committee to focus its agenda, but progress to date has been slow. In 1994, some improvement was visible as the Committee dealt with hemispheric technical cooperation on environmental matters. But such major issues as trade and environment have been only touched on, rather than probed in depth, despite the members' considerable interest in the subject.

In the past year, there has been an emerging view that the OAS should conduct a re-evaluation of its activities in the light of Agenda 21. The Committee is setting its work plan for the next year in the coming months, providing an opportunity to move to the new Rio and post-Rio agenda. The Belém Declaration of June 6, 1994, began this process by noting the importance of environmental management, biodiversity, climatic changes, toxic waste, environmentally sound technology, additional sources of financing, and ecotourism. But issues such as forestry, energy, and fisheries remain absent.

The leaders should direct that the OAS Environment Committee take up the Rio agenda and define ways in which it can set priorities for and pioneer progress on the post-Rio agenda. They could direct that this work be done in ways that reinforce the multilateral work of the UN Commission on Sustainable Development. Promising possibilities for priority action are an expanded effort on environmentally sound technologies, environmental standards and indicators, forests, and energy.

The UN Economic Commission for Latin America and the Caribbean (ECLAC)

The UN's Economic Commission for Latin America and the Caribbean (ECLAC) is broader than the OAS. Its membership includes all countries with territorial possessions in the hemisphere, making Spain, the Netherlands, and France, as well as Canada and the United States, members. ECLAC meets every two years at the ministerial level, passing resolutions which its Secretariat, headquartered in Santiago, Chile, is asked to carry out. As ECLAC is a technical body, the

ministers who attend are those for finance, central banks, commerce, and planning. More recently, sectoral ministers, such as social affairs and education, have begun to attend when relevant matters are under discussion. In the interim periods, ECLAC is managed by a Committee of the Whole, for which representatives come from the embassies or member governments in Santiago. The Secretariat contains an Environment Division, which is co-financed by UNEP (as the Secretariat's agriculture division is co-financed by FAO).

In the lead-up to Rio, the Latin governments asked ECLAC to take on the task of preparing a common LAC position for UNCED. In January 1992, the ministers and representatives of the LAC members of ECLAC, at the Latin American and Caribbean Regional Preparatory Meeting for UNCED, adopted the "Tlatelolco Platform on Environment and Development" (LC/G.1712).

Most recently, ECLAC has sought to establish some guidelines whereby the UNCED agenda can be incorporated into ECLAC work programs. Flowing from the regional priorities identified in *Sustainable Development: Changing Production Patterns, Social Equity, and the Environment*, this effort has focused on trade, technology, decision making, environmental management, biodiversity, water, and hazardous waste. ECLAC has also released a report recently on *Open Regionalism in Latin America and the Caribbean — Economic Integration as a Contribution to Changing Production Patterns with Social Equity*, which advocates the gradual opening up of trade in the hemisphere among all countries, rather than the conclusion of bilateral treaties.

Building and Maintaining Capacity

The leaders at Miami should call for a systematic hemispheric examination of and approach to working with and strengthening the capacity of the most useful institutions and support those existing organizations best placed to support sustainable development.

In order to identify the ways in which increasing hemispheric interdependence in economic, ecological, and demographic matters raises problems of sustainable development and to provide a scientifically sound basis for the environmentally related disputes likely to arise, it is important to increase the scientific capacity for monitoring the hemispheric ecosystem as a whole. Such an enterprise could provide detailed assessments of members' ecological performance and a priority list of areas for intergovernmental action. Such a strengthened scientific capacity could come from improved networks of academic and research institutions, increased dialogue among governments, or by building the scientific capacity of intergovernmental hemispheric institutions. Canada's recent initiative, endorsed by the recent OAS General Assembly, to convene before March 1995, an experts' meeting focused on environmental technology, provides a practical example of what is required on a far more ambitious scale.

In advance of, or at Miami, the leaders should consider how and where this strengthened scientific capability should be developed. Items for consideration might usefully include research, data collection, and monitoring of toxics and biodiversity.

National and Hemispheric Multistakeholder Sustainable Development Dialogues

Despite the impressive recent moves to democratization in the hemisphere, and the establishment of such bodies as the Canadian Round Tables and the United States' Presidential Commission on Sustainable Development, forums for multistakeholder dialogue on sustainable development issues remain absent at the international level in the hemisphere.

The leaders at Miami should encourage the development of national, multistakeholder consensus-seeking bodies to promote sustainable development. The leaders should also announce the creation of a high-level, multistakeholder forum for the regular discussion of key, hemispheric ecological and linked economic issues and one linked to the work of the OAS itself in these areas. The Canadian initiative at the March 1994 Vancouver meeting of APEC environment ministers provides one model of how to proceed to build such a regional forum. This initiative could usefully be linked with existing institutions in the hemisphere such as the Earth Council, which might serve as a hemispheric focal point for the national bodies.

NGO Participation

On May 2, 1994, Canada presented a document to the OAS calling for a "Study of the Possible Granting of Status to Non-Governmental Organization (NGOs) at the OAS." The document was considered by the Permanent Council, which recommended it for fur-

ther study, thus ensuring it was not dealt with by Ministers at the General Assembly in 1994. It would be important for the Miami leaders to express their desire, at a minimum, for rapid attention to this matter, and, at a maximum, their willingness to develop appropriate mechanisms to achieve this result. Simultaneously, member states could act on ways to improve the ability of the NGO community and other interested stakeholders to participate more meaningfully in the operations of the OAS, the IDB, and their various committees with the North American Commission for Environmental Cooperation's Joint Public Advisory Committee serving as an important referent and possible model.

The strengthened capacity of NGOs and other stakeholders to participate in the preparations for Miami, subsequent summits, and other institutions should form part of this process. The model of the Rio conference provides some useful precedents regarding both the preparatory conference and follow-up phases.

The leaders might consider the creation of a separate, independent environmental agency to examine hemispheric environmental issues or, in the context of NAFTA accession, building on and expanding the North American Agreement on Environmental Cooperation (NAAEC). The hemisphere could also consider, given its particular interest, the optimum architecture of a prospective new global environmental organization as part of the major effort likely to take place in the coming years to reform international institutions. There is support for public participation, transparency, and access to information as an important part of any institutional reform in the hemisphere.

CONCLUSIONS — POST-MIAMI

The following advice was drafted by the NRTEE and sent to the Prime Minister on November 3, 1994.

Advice from the National Round Table on the Environment and the Economy on Advancing Sustainable Development at the Summit of the Americas

The NRTEE believes that Canada should continue to exercise its historic leadership role in promoting sustainable development by advancing the following initiatives at the Summit of the Americas.

1. Trade and Sustainable Development

The Prime Minister of Canada should encourage the leaders at the Summit to ensure that trade liberalization in the hemisphere is accompanied by appropriate environmental and social protection. The NAFTA and its parallel agreements and institutions could serve as a useful guideline for trade liberalization. The leaders should also be urged to consider the environmental and social implications of all trade agreements in the region, in order to ensure that other agreements are being negotiated with adequate protection afforded to the environment.

The Prime Minister of Canada should encourage the leaders at Miami to agree to work toward the upward harmonization of environmental standards in the Americas through systematic cooperation between and among governments, including the development of appropriate eco-labelling and their regional mutual recognition, with priority attention to pesticides.

The Prime Minister of Canada should also encourage the leaders to consider the various means of strengthening legal frameworks in the hemisphere. This should include:

a. enhancement, compliance, and enforcement capabilities in the environmental sector;

b. technical cooperation, training and education, as well as support for effective public participation, particularly in environmental impact assessment; and

c. ongoing support for existing institutions, in particular the newly created North American Commission on Environmental Cooperation.

The Prime Minister should invite the new Trade Committee of the OAS to join with the Environment Committee to initiate a joint work program to ensure the integration of environmental concerns into economic policy making in the Americas.

2. Biodiversity and Conservation

Considering Canada's historical commitment to biodiversity objectives, the Prime Minister of Canada should further advance Canadian leadership at the Summit of the Americas through the following:

a. *The Prime Minister of Canada should consider signing and ratifying a modernized 1940 Western Hemisphere Convention that embraces the living marine resources off the*

hemisphere's coasts, in ways that support Canada's multilateral objectives.

b. *The Prime Minister of Canada should confirm Canada's commitment to implementing the UN Biodiversity Convention and at the same time should encourage all the countries in the hemisphere, including the United States, to sign, ratify, and properly implement the Convention.*

c. *The Prime Minister of Canada should support the formation of an appropriate body in the OAS to implement activities in the hemisphere* and develop a hemispheric approach to the strengthening of biodiversity-related conventions and the capacities of countries to implement them.

3. Energy and Climate Change

The countries of the hemisphere should reaffirm their support for the UN Framework Convention on Climate Change and commit themselves to ratifying and implementing the Convention.

The Prime Minister of Canada should suggest that the countries of the hemisphere establish a Continental Collaborative of Stakeholders, which would be made up of representatives from, inter alia, the public sector, the private sector (including utilities), the financial institutions including the multilateral funding banks, and non-governmental organizations to encourage the emergence of a hemispheric approach to issues of climate change. The Collaborative could explore:

a. **The creation of pilot projects**, including public-private partnerships in the electricity sector designed to promote energy efficiency, building and maintaining capacity, technology transfer, renewable energy technology, information sharing, cooperation on research agendas, and other programs including demand management.

b. **The development of a framework and criteria on the evaluation and monitoring of pilot joint implementation projects** to ensure that such projects are carried out in an environmentally and economically sound manner.

c. Alternative funding arrangements or mechanisms involving the traditional money lending agencies, as well as new and different partnerships.

d. The use of market instruments in reaching climate change targets, including the possibility of emission trading.

4. Multistakeholder Forums

Considering the Government's recent proclamation, "An Act to Establish the National Round Table on the Environment and the Economy" (S.C. 40-41-42, C.31, 1993), Canada's extensive experience with multistakeholder forums, and building on the UNCED process, the Prime Minister of Canada should welcome initiatives in the hemisphere such as the new Central American Alliance for Sustainable Development, as well as support the development of national and regional multistakeholder consensus-seeking bodies to promote sustainable development, and the integration of environmental and social concerns into economic policy making and decision making.

5. Indigenous Issues

In the general framework of liberalized trade in the Americas, special attention should be given to the development of opportunities for Indigenous Peoples' trade. One way might be to encourage the creation of an Indigenous Peoples' Americas Free Trade Agreement (IPAFTA), which would call for a phased-in process of Indigenous Peoples' trade liberalization in traditional products (based on a schedule that will be drawn up by the members of the IPAFTA).

6. Follow-Up

In order to encourage the effective implementation and elaboration of the Summit's sustainable development agenda, the leaders at Miami should agree to meet again to review progress and to have their ministers responsible for trade, finance, the environment, natural resources, and other relevant portfolios meet on a regular basis.

Of primary importance is a meeting of hemispheric trade ministers in which environmental questions, as in the NAFTA regime, are given full attention to ensure that the integration of economic and environmental considerations can be better realized.

National Round Table on the
Environment and the Economy (NRTEE)
1 Nicholas Street, Suite 1500
Ottawa, Ontario
K1N 7B7
Tel. (613) 992-7189

Appendix A

SOME MAJOR INTERNATIONAL AGREEMENTS, CONVENTIONS, AND ORGANIZATIONS

	WTO[1]	Biodiversity 1992[2]	RAMSAR 1971	CITES 1973	Western Hemisphere	Bonn Convention	Climate Change 1992[3]	Montreal Protocol	Basel Convention	Lomé Convention
Antigua	S	CP	•	•	•	•	CP	CP	CP	CP
Argentina	S	S	CP	CP	CP	CP	CP	CP	CP	•
Bahamas	na	CP	•	CP	•	•	CP	•	CP	CP
Barbados	CP	CP	•	CP	•	•	CP	CP	•	CP
Belize	CP	CP	•	CP	•	•	S	•	•	•
Bolivia	S	S	CP	CP	CP	•	S	•	S	•
Brazil	CP	CP	•	CP	CP	•	CP	CP	CP	•
Canada	S	CP	CP	CP	•	•	CP	CP	CP	•
Chile	S	S	CP	CP	CP	CP	S	CP	S	•
Colombia	S	S	•	CP	CP	•	S	•	S	•
Costa Rica	S	S	CP	CP	CP	•	S	CP	•	CP
Dominica	•	CP	•	•	•	•	CP	CP	•	CP
Dominican Rep.	CP	S	•	CP	CP	•	S	CP	•	•
Ecuador	na	CP	CP	CP	CP	•	CP	CP	CP	•
El Salvador	S	S	•	CP	CP	•	S	CP	CP	•
Grenada	•	S	•	•	•	•	S	CP	•	CP
Guatemala	S	S	CP	CP	CP	•	S	CP	S	CP
Guyana	CP	S	•	CP	•	•	S	•	•	•
Honduras	S	S	•	CP	•	•	S	CP	•	•
Jamaica	S	S	•	•	•	S	S	CP	•	CP
Mexico	CP	CP	CP	CP	CP	•	CP	CP	CP	•
Nicaragua	CP	S	•	CP	CP	•	S	CP	•	•
Panama	na	S	CP	CP	CP	CP	S	CP	CP	•
Paraguay	S	CP	S	CP	CP	S	CP	CP	•	•
Peru	S	CP	CP	CP	CP	•	CP	CP	•	•
St.Kitts & Nevis	•	CP	•	•	•	•	CP	CP	•	CP
St. Lucia	S	CP	•	CP	•	•	CP	•	•	CP
St. Vincent	•	•	•	CP	•	•	•	•	•	CP
Suriname	CP	S	CP	CP	CP	CP	S	S	•	•
Trinidad & Tobago	S	S	CP	CP	CP	•	CP	CP	•	CP
USA	•	S	CP	CP	CP	•	CP	CP	S	•
Uruguay	S	CP	CP	CP	CP	CP	S	CP	CP	•
Venezuela	S	S	CP	CP	CP	•	S	CP	S	•

CP — Contracting Party
S — Signed but not ratified
na — Information not available
• — Treaty/Agreement not signed

[1] As of August 15, 1994
[2] As of April 15, 1994
[3] As of July 13, 1994

Appendix B
ENVIRONMENTAL POWER IN THE HEMISPHERE

	Western Hemisphere	Europe	Africa	Asia	Former USSR	Canada	USA	Mexico	Brazil	Chile	Argentina
Maritime											
EEZ as a % of world total	30.6%	15.5%	12.7%	21.4%	4.8%	3.1%	10.3%	3.0%	3.4%	2.4%	1.2%
Coastline as a % of world total	36.6%	11.9%	6.5%	27.9%	8.2%	15.5%	3.4%	1.6%	1.3%	1.1%	0.9%
Land											
Total Area 10^5 ha	38,906	4,727	29,642	26,790	22,273	9,221	9,166.6	1,908.7	8,456.5	748.8	2,736.7
% of total land area Cropland (1988-90)	19	29	6	17	10	5	21	13	7	6	10
Pasture (1988-90)	45	18	30	28	17	3	26	39	22	18	52
Forest (1988-90)	81	33	23	20	42	39	32	23	59	12	22
Fresh-water											
% of world's renewable fr.water	42.6%	5.7%	10.3%	25.8%	10.9%	7.1%	6.1%	0.9%	12.8%	1.2%	1.7%
Forests											
Total Area 10^3 ha	1,374,852	140,107	527,587	307,853	754,958	247,164	209,573	48,586	561,107	na	na
% of world's tropical forest, 1990	52.3%	na	30%	15.6%	na	na	na	2.8%	31.9%	na	na
% of world's temperate forest, 1990	36.3%	9.4%	na	8.6%	45.6%	22%	14.3%	na	na	na	na
Energy											
Primary energy production as a % of global (1990)	29.4%	12.1%	6.5%	28.2%	21.7%	3.4%	19.3%	2.4%	0.7%	0.1%	0.6%
% change in prod'n 1980-90	11.5%	4.3%	22.5%	26%	22.7%	na	na	na	na	na	na
Minerals											
Reserves of Base Metals (Cu, Pb, Sn, Zn) as % of global total '91	43.4%	10.8%	10.1%	13.2%	10.3%	7.4%	15.7%	4.2%	0.9%	15.5%	0.1%
Biodiversity											
No. of National Protected Areas 1993	2,419	2,177	704	2,181	218	411	937	60	214	65	100
and % of global total	28.1%	25.3%	8.2%	25.3%	2.5%	4.8%	10.9	0.7%	2.5%	0.8%	1.2%
No. of known mammal species 1992	na	na	na	na	276	139	346	439	394	91	258
No. of known bird species 1992	na	na	na	na	na	426	650	961	1,573	432	na

Appendix C
ENVIRONMENTAL PERFORMANCE IN THE HEMISPHERE

	Western Hemisphere	Europe	Africa	Asia	Former USSR	Canada	USA	Mexico	Brazil	Chile	Argentina
Maritime											
Fish % change in marine catch 1978-80 to 1988-90	+68%	+3%	+23%	+36%	+19%	+17%	+62%	+26%	no change	+129%	+5%
Land											
Total Area 10⁵ ha	38,906	4,727	29,642	26,790	22,273	9,221	9,166.6	1,908.7	8,456.5	748.8	2,736.7
% change Cropland 1968-70 to 1988-90	+2	-2	+1	+1	no change	no change	no change	+1	+3	+1	+1
Pasture 1968-70 to 1988-90	+3	-1	no change	+4	no change	+1	-1	no change	+4	+4	-1
Forest 1968-70 to 1988-90	-4	+1	-2	-2	+1	+4	-1	-5	-5	no change	no change
Pesticide use as a % of world total 1982-84	26.7%	26.6%	3.4%	15.7%	24.3%	2.5%	16.9%	1.3%	2.1%	0.1%	0.6%
% change in total fertilizer consumed 1968-70 to 1988-90	+58.2%	+27.8%	+146.8%	+411%	+167.1	+182.8%	+24.2%	+216%	+359.1%	+177.7%	+111.5%
Freshwater											
Annual water withdrawals as % of world 1980-91	26%	11%	4%	47%	11%	1%	14%	2%	1%	1%	1%
% change in fresh water fish catch 1978-80 to 1988-90	+112.6%	+43%	+41%	+120%	+26%	no change	+211%	+2,318%	+29%	+3,406%	+18%
Forests											
Tropical forest loss, % annual change 1981-90 (global change -0.8%)	-0.7%	na	-0.7%	-1.2%	na	na	na	-1.2%	-0.6%	na	na
Temperate loss as % of exploitable area 1981-90	Can. na US -1.6%	+1.4%	na	Japan -0.2%	+5.5%	na	-1.6%	na	na	na	na
Energy											
Consumption as % of world total in 1990, and % change from 1980	31.7% +7.4%	20.8% -13%	2.7% +44%	24.6% +61.6%	18.8% +28.1%	2.6% na	24.1% na	1.5% na	1.1% na	0.2% na	0.6% na
Consumption per capita in 1990 (10⁹ J) & % change from '80	NA 203 SA 29 NA -7.3% SA -3.3%	126 -4.5%	13 +8.3%	24 +33.3%	196 118.1%	301 na	292 na	51 na	22 na	37 na	53 na

Appendix C continued
ENVIRONMENTAL PERFORMANCE IN THE HEMISPHERE

	Western Hemisphere	Europe	Africa	Asia	Former USSR	Canada	USA	Mexico	Brazil	Chile	Argentina
Energy											
% Energy production by solid (coal) fuel, 1991	24%	34%	19%	34%	20%	14%	33%	3%	4%	30%	<1%
and % change between 1971 and 91	NA +85% SA +395%	-29%	+162%	+130%	-10%	+387%	+77%	+154%	+51%	+69%	-55%
Atmosphere and Air Pollution											
CO_2 emissions1991 % of global total	28%	18.1%	3.0%	29.4%	15.8%	1.8%	21.75%	1.5%	1.0%	0.1%	0.5%
1991 CO_2 emissions per capita (10^3 tons)	NA 13.59 SA 2.00	8.2	1.03	2.11	12.31	15.21	19.53	3.92	1.43	2.42	3.55
% change in CO_2 emissions 1980-1990	na	na	na	na	+17.9%	-0.5%	+4.1%	+25.9	+8.4%	+26.5%	+2.1%
Consumption of CFCs and halons per capita 1990(kg a^{-1})	na	na	na	na	0.05	0.58	0.88	0.17	0.06	0.07	0.20
% change in consumption of CFCs and halons 1986-1990	-55.3%	-39.9%	-66.4%	-18.5%	no change	-34%	-60%	+65.8%	-22.1%	+16.7%	na
Biodiversity											
CITES Reporting requirement met % 1990	na	na	na	na	75%	100%	88%	100%	41%	65%	82%
No. of threatened mammal species, and as a % of total national species	na	na	na	na	20 7.2%	5 3.6%	27 7.8%	25 5.7%	40 10.2%	9 9.9%	23 8.9%
No. of threatened bird species and as a % of total national species	na	na	na	na	38 na	6 1.4%	43 6.6%	35 3.6%	123 7.8%	18 4.2%	53 na

Appendix D
TRENDS IN WORLD POPULATION SIZE, 1960-2010
(million persons)

REGION	1960	1970	1980	1990	2000	2010
World	3,019	3,697	4,447	5,295	6,228	8,472
North America	182	226	252	277	306	330
Latin America	189	283	359	441	523	600
Caribbean	18	24	29	33	38	43
Central America	42	67	89	113	140	165
South America	128	191	240	294	344	391
Africa	248	363	479	642	856	1,116
Asia	1,513	2,101	2,583	3,118	3,691	4,213
Europe	414	466	492	509	523	536
Former USSR	190	235	258	281	297	317
Oceania	14	19	22	26	31	35

SOURCE: UN Department for Economic and Social Information and Policy Analysis
(Population Division) *1993 World Population Prospects: The 1992 Revision*, United Nations,
New York.

Policy Proposals on the Environment and Sustainable Development

Pre-Summit of the Americas Workshop, Kingston, October 23-25, 1994

A Project Sponsored by
• *North-South Center, University of Miami, Coral Gables, Florida*
• *University of the West Indies, Kingston, Jamaica*

• *Environmental Foundation of Jamaica, Kingston, Jamaica*

• *ICWI Group, Kingston, Jamaica*

The mission of the North-South Center is to promote better relations and serve as a catalyst for change among the United States, Canada, and the nations of Latin America and the Caribbean by advancing knowledge and understanding of the major political, social, economic, and cultural issues affecting the nations and peoples of the Western Hemisphere.

THE SUSTAINABLE DEVELOPMENT PROGRAM OF THE AMERICAS

The Summit of the Americas provides the democratically elected heads of government of thirty-four Western Hemisphere countries with an extraordinary opportunity to develop and begin to implement common strategies and policies aimed at achieving regional shared prosperity based on solid economic growth, the strengthening of democratic governance, and sustainable development.

In an effort to contribute to the shaping of the Summit's agenda, the North-South Center at the University of Miami launched a hemisphere-wide effort to bring together leading experts from academia, bilateral and multilateral agencies, business and labor organizations, and non-governmental organizations in meetings to identify basic goals, analyze strategies for achieving those goals, and make concrete policy recommendations to the governments of the Americas concerning the issues included in the Summit's agenda: Economic Integration, Democratic Governance, and Sustainable Development. Three Hemispheric Policy Working Group meetings, held in October 1994, in Buenos Aires, Cartagena, and Kingston, constituted the backbone of this effort.

The North-South Center's final Hemispheric Policy Working Group met in Kingston, Jamaica, on October 23-25, 1994. The meeting was co-sponsored by the University of the West Indies, the ICWI Group, and the Environmental Foundation of Jamaica. Charged with analyzing The Environment and Sustainable Development, the participants were divided into four commissions, each of which examined a primary aspect of the subject: "Regulatory Frameworks and Capacity Building," "Trade, Development, and the Environment," "Poverty, Fundamental Human Needs, and Sustainable Development," and "Biodiversity and Management of Ecosystems." After a full day of deliberations, each commission presented its conclusions in plenary session for discussion, modifications, and approval by all participants.

General Recommendation

The participants in the Hemispheric Policy Working Group on The Environment and Sustainable Development recommend that the governments participating in the Summit of the Americas make a commitment to promote and secure cooperation, coordination, and assistance among all countries in the Western Hemisphere to create and manage a Sustainable Development Program for the Americas. Through the strengthening of regulatory frameworks and capacity building, the eradication of poverty, and the reconciliation of economic growth with environmental protection, the Sustainable Development Program for the Americas would express the common will of the hemispheric governments to assure that increased trade liberalization and investment will occur in ways that promote the sustainable use of resources and the equitable distribution of economic benefits.

COMMISSION NO. 1: REGULATORY FRAMEWORKS AND CAPACITY BUILDING

Objective

Strengthen regulatory frameworks and promote capacity building for a Sustainable Development Program for the Americas.

General Considerations

1. Sustainable development policies must be based upon the recognition that human beings have the right to live in a balanced, ecologically diverse, and healthy environment.

2. Regulatory frameworks to date have not been entirely adequate for the implementation of sustainable development policies.

3. The creation and management of a Sustainable Development Program for the Americas depends upon the commitment of and cooperation among all countries in the Americas toward the goal of strengthening regulatory frameworks and promoting capacity building.

4. Capacity building for the ultimate goal of sustainable development requires caring for and nourishing the most valuable asset of the region: its people. At present, only 7 percent of government-to-government assistance is allocated for areas such as basic education, primary health care, nutrition, water supply, and family planning. Per capita spending on public education in the Latin American and the Caribbean region represents just one-tenth of educational spending in industrialized countries. Only half of the students in the region complete primary school.

5. Sustainable development policies must include the participation of all sectors of society, especially with regard to environmental policy making and implemen-

tation. Widespread participation is a key element for creating support among the citizenry, building compliance and enforcing regulatory frameworks.

6. National accounts are currently built upon procedures that measure only economic growth and disregard environmental and social indicators. New methodologies should be developed to take these indicators into account. The development of these new analytical tools could be an appropriate subject for hemispheric cooperation, especially in light of the growing multilateral contacts that will accompany increased economic integration.

Policy Recommendations

1. Operationalize a Sustainable Development Program for the Americas, through:

   a. The creation of a formal hemispheric network for information exchange on national and regional environmental policies, regulatory and institutional frameworks, science and technology issues, environmental inventories, project reviews, and financial options;

   b. A regularized program of intercountry delegation visits to build a body of knowledge on comparable experiences of sustainable development;

   c. The facilitation of joint partnerships among non-governmental organizations (NGOs), universities, the private sector, public agencies, community groups;

   d. The strengthening of sustainable development considerations in the policies, practices, and operations of multilateral, political, assistance, and financial organizations operating in the hemisphere, ensuring full enforcement of sustainable development principles.

2. Incorporate into environmental regulatory frameworks mechanisms for:

   a. Full access to information;

   b. Prior notice on environmental laws for community input and comment;

   c. Mandatory implementation of environmental impact assessment (EIA), which includes prior estimation of and consultation about environmental, socioeconomic, and human rights consequences;

d. Access to fair, open, and expeditious administrative and judicial proceedings to enforce and defend environmental rights.

3. Guarantee, at the constitutional level, the human right to live in a balanced, ecologically diverse and healthy environment. Individual states bear the responsibility of ensuring that these rights are respected and enforced. To this end, the governments of the Americas should:

a. Develop and incorporate these principles in the constitution and legal system of each country;

b. Establish, by law, restrictions on specific practices that directly result in the degradation of the environment, as well as incentives for activities conducive to sustainable development;

c. Build the organizational infrastructure necessary to oversee the preservation of the environment and the natural resources within the national territory.

4. Provide basic education to strengthen the quality of human resources required for sustainable development. To this end:

a. Strengthen educational programs to promote voluntary compliance with regulatory frameworks by educating all sectors of society on the corresponding legal issues; allow for the successful transfer and integration of new technologies within the hemisphere; develop ways and means to manage environmental problems at the local level;

b. Develop social and educational policies that address the specific obstacles faced by women and youth, particularly among the impoverished in rural and marginal areas.

5. Strengthen and implement social policies aimed at providing adequate primary health care, nutrition, water supply management, and family planning as key elements toward poverty eradication.

6. Reallocate resources from military spending toward the eradication of poverty and the promotion of sustainable development. To this end, the governments of the Americas should enter into negotiations to curtail the production, importation, and sales of conventional weapons in the hemisphere and create a Hemispheric Commission dedicated to halting arms proliferation.

7. Establish regulatory frameworks that incorporate the results of ecological and human health risk analyses that may arise from economic activities. These should be:

a. Consistent with prior assessments regarding the capacities for enforcement and compliance;

b. Devised to foresee progressive applicability and increasing tightening of standards;

c. Accompanied by a broad set of incentives to promote fast and full compliance.

8. Promote human and institutional capacity building in the Americas to protect the environment through:

a. Building public and private institutional capacities for financial resource allocation, land use planning, public participation, and administrative and judicial reforms for environmental protection;

b. Pursuit of joint commitments, where appropriate, for the use of economic instruments (such as taxes, user fees, permits, and bonds) as supplements to environmental regulations;

c. Establishment of mechanisms for internalizing environmental costs in regulatory frameworks.

d. Strengthening of the capacities of governments, NGOs, and private sector organizations to comply with existing environment-related conventions and agreements (such as the Convention on Nature Protection and Wildlife Preservation in the Western Hemisphere, commonly known as the Western Hemisphere Convention) in a manner compatible with the Rio Biodiversity Convention.

9. Define, harmonize, and implement a set of national and international instruments to regulate investments and trade in goods and services with undesirable environmental effects. To this end:

a. Identify priority areas for regulatory harmonization on a regional and sectoral basis;

b. Develop a work plan, with the participation of all affected and interested sectors of society, that contains short-, medium-, and long-term goals, as well as milestones for compliance;

c. Implement a mechanism to measure progress toward achievement of these goals;

d. Formulate international regulatory instruments for common resources management;

e. Ensure that exports are consistent, at a minimum, with existing standards in the country of origin;

f. Agree, in light of the prospect for hemispheric economic integration, to work toward common environmental standards for the Americas with different compliance schedules depending on each country's level of development and costs of adjustment.

10. Adjust national accounts and accounting methods to reflect environmental and social indicators.

COMMISSION NO. 2: TRADE, DEVELOPMENT, AND THE ENVIRONMENT

Objective

Ensure that increased trade and economic integration in the Americas contribute to the promotion of sustainable development.

General Considerations

1. In the past, in response to pressing human and social needs, economic growth has been given priority over sustainable development. At this time, there is the need for a fundamental departure from traditional notions of development toward the attainment of sustainable development. To this end, economic growth and environmental and social protection can be mutually supportive. For example, trade liberalization can facilitate technology transfer, innovation, and the development of environmentally sound products. Environmentally sound production methods can, in fact, be a source of competitive advantage and can increase trade opportunities. However, caution should be exercised so that environmental issues are not used to sanction unjustified barriers to international trade.

2. The recent trend to consider the Western Hemisphere as an integrated region flows largely from recent developments in both the political and economic spheres. Over the last decade, as the Cold War came to an end, economic growth has been fueled by an increase in the trade and investment links in the Americas, resulting from significant progress made in trade liberalization and other market-oriented economic reforms. This heightened level of economic activity brings with it increases in natural resources use and growing transportation infrastructure, which together threaten to cause severe ecological damage and social degradation, unless pursued in sustainable ways.

3. Building on the hard-won achievements of the United Nations Conference on Environment and Development and moving the Rio Agenda forward on a broadly hemispheric and cooperative basis, the transition to sustainable development will involve new partnerships for cooperation and the recognition of environment and social considerations as priorities of equal value to growth. Such a transition will also produce costs that must be offset by the development of appropriate financing strategies.

4. At the present time, the Americas lack the institutional capacity to put in place effective sustainable development oriented policies at the hemispheric level. There is a need to integrate economic and environmental concerns in ways that promote equity, social accountability, and inclusive multistakeholder decision making.

5. The lack of environmental standards or the lax enforcement of environmental laws can have distorting effects on both trade and investment flows. Failure to internalize environmental costs leads to environmental degradation and conflict in the trading system.

Policy Recommendations

1. Consider the importance of the environment and sustainable development for any truly successful process of economic integration, with a commitment to incorporate the fundamental concerns of sustainable development into trade and investment policies and practices and international agreements. This should be done taking into account fundamental principles of equity and special needs of particular countries and communities.

2. Establish domestic mechanisms to contend with the anticipated impact of further trade liberalization and growth by:

a. Expanding avenues for the participation of civil society in domestic policy decision making and implementation;

b. Strengthening national legal frameworks to promote environmental enhancement, compliance, and enforcement capabilities;

c. Working toward the harmonization of environmental standards based on genuinely sound scientific methods, which take into account domestic standard setting procedures;

d. Providing meaningful public environmental assessment on the impact of increased trade and infrastructure development and mechanisms for monitoring compliance with the recommendations produced by the assessment process;

e. Establishing effective mechanisms to promote appropriate environmental behavior and awareness among all sectors of the public administration and civil society, in particular the private sector.

3. Pursue innovative alternative funding arrangements and other mechanisms for building and maintaining a capacity to assist the governments and the enterprises of the hemisphere (including small and medium-sized businesses) in the transition to sustainable development. The following alternatives should be considered:

a. The creation of new partnerships and pilot projects with the private sector to increase technical capacity, facilitate technology transfer and innovation, improve training and education, and increase the exchange of information;

b. The removal and/or redirection of subsidies that distort international trade and encourage the unsustainable use of natural resources;

c. The generation of funds to underwrite the costs of the transition toward sustainable development, with the support of multilateral financial institutions, based on open and transparent practices;

d. The reexamination of the burden imposed by existing levels of private and public debt on the economies of some countries in the Americas. Resources liberated by debt rescheduling and/or renegotiation should be used to support the transition to sustainable development, including debt for nature swaps.

4. Sign, ratify, and properly implement international environmental agreements, in particular those that support the sustainable use of natural resources and regulate the trade of endangered species.

5. Support existing hemispheric institutions that are best suited to integrate effectively the issues of trade, sustainable development, and the participation of civil society. Special attention should be given to progress made on environmental standards, norms, and mechanisms within a number of trade agreements currently implemented on bilateral, regional, hemispheric, and international levels.

6. Agree not to weaken domestic environmental laws in order to attract investment. However, special efforts should be made to ensure that the environment does not become a tool for trade protectionism.

7. Establish a strategy designed to encourage and evaluate the progress made in the implementation of the Summit's sustainable development agenda, based on the scheduling of regular meetings of the ministers responsible for trade, finance, the environment, and natural resources and other relevant portfolios.

COMMISSION NO. 3: POVERTY, FUNDAMENTAL HUMAN NEEDS, AND SUSTAINABLE DEVELOPMENT

Objective

The governments and peoples of the Americas must immediately embark upon an accelerated process of poverty eradication through the design and implementation of new models for sustainable development.

General Considerations

1. The increasing percentage of those living in poverty in the Americas and the absence of environmentally safe and sound technologies pose serious obstacles for meeting the goals of environmental management and conservation essential to achieve sustainable development. The lack of economic opportunities — compounded by the proliferation of structural adjustment programs — lead the poor to perpetuate unsafe and unsound environmental practices.

2. Sustainable development requires a broadening of the definition of poverty. Rather than simply using economic criteria, poverty should be defined in terms of the degree to which fundamental human rights are satisfied. Providing for people's physical

(shelter and public health) and security (economic and physical) needs, as well as equal access to intellectual, spiritual, and cultural participation, should be the bases for a renewed commitment to the eradication of poverty.

3. Within both national and international domains, substantive political guidelines for new models of sustainable development already exist. Agenda 21 (guidelines for sustainable development agreed upon by the world's leaders at the UN-sponsored Rio de Janeiro Earth Summit of 1992) offers a comprehensive model. However, insufficient steps have been taken by governments toward its realization.

4. Environmental degradation in highly polluted and increasingly populated rural and marine areas and urban centers is aggravated by unmitigated migration to those areas.

5. Environmental crises (such as cholera, dengue, and chemical and oil spills) disproportionally affect the poorest populations, who are virtually helpless in mitigating them. Such crises often reach a scale beyond national borders and require regional or international responses.

6. Public efforts toward the eradication of illicit crops and prevention of drug trafficking and consumption drain important resources from development and social policies which otherwise could be targeted toward sustainable development.

7. Every nation is a composition of diverse micro-regions, each with its own ecosystems, patterns of production and consumption, ethnic mix, social organizations, and history. These micro-regions are often overlooked in national and international policies and planning.

8. Our current systems of education and welfare neither develop the leadership nor the specialized capabilities necessary for the design and implementation of comprehensive programs of sustainable development.

9. The generation and management of the funds needed to underwrite the costs of sustainable development demand new and creative approaches based on the concerted efforts of governments, the private sector, and multilateral financial institutions.

Policy Recommendations

1. Immediate action should be taken by all nations to:

a. Ratify and implement Agenda 21, the Global Forum Treaties and the biodiversity convention, endorse the creation of an Inter-American Water Resources Network, and support other protocols that reinforce progress for the eradication of poverty and promote sustainable development;

b. Integrate these instruments into regional and national policies and international aid programs, setting both specific objectives and timetables;

c. Establish criteria for the monitoring, evaluation, and assessment of each nation's progress toward achieving the goals outlined in endorsed international agreements, especially in the eradication of poverty;

d. Implement national judicial reforms and law enforcement in order to ensure accountability;

e. Ensure that each initiative is accompanied by adequate and earmarked sources of financing.

2. To foster sustainable development on the basis of micro-regions and small and medium-sized enterprises, governments and international organizations of the Americas should:

a. Recognize micro-regions as important units of sustainable development and give support for programs that work at the appropriate levels of human organization;

b. Focus planning efforts on micro-regions and increase funding for micro-regional projects, allowing for full participation by all social actors;

c. Encourage small- and medium-scale industries at micro-regional levels through technical assistance, financing, horizontal planning, and community participation and promote the competitiveness of these enterprises with the assurance that they be developed in a sustainable manner.

3. To ensure that impoverished populations do not continue to suffer from undue burdens of environmental crises, man-made or natural, leaders of the hemisphere should:

a. Fortify international agencies' and organizations' abilities to respond to environmental crises;

b. Ensure that response and recovery be done in consultation with affected communities, respecting issues of sovereignty;

c. Include local management and appropriate transfer of technical capacity in long-term recovery strategies to bolster local accountability and prevent environmental degradation.

4. Hemispheric countries should encourage and fund research programs focused on the sustainability of the environment and the eradication of poverty. To these ends, governments of the Americas should:

a. Provide adequate funding for research and development programs;

b. Stimulate sustainable development research efforts by the private sector;

c. Leverage funding through negotiated reduction of foreign debt to stimulate research and establish micro-enterprise lending for poor communities.

5. A key component of the sustainable development model is to maintain the local human and technical capacity and to ensure adequate participation, especially of the poor, in the decision-making process. To these ends, the governments of the Americas should:

a. Encourage community participation, voluntary or entrepreneurial, in environmental management programs to promote input in planning and ensure benefits for all local groups and sectors of society;

b. Encourage community participation in the review of environmental impact assessments and planning for new development projects;

c. Promote the commitment of all levels of national administration to sustainable development, supporting on each level business opportunities and employment for all citizens and immediate commitment to progress towards the eradication of poverty;

d. Encourage the private sector to increase labor opportunities and underwrite research and development of environmentally sound and safe technology, which reduces risks for the environment and society;

e. Strengthen the linkages among international, national, and local non-governmental organizations and private voluntary organizations with international non-governmental and development agencies to prioritize resources for building human capability and for the eradication of poverty;

f. Coordinate the implementation of a Hemispheric Human Resource Needs Assessment at all levels of society. This assessment would address the changes in the formal educational system that are necessary to develop training programs responsive to sustainable development and formulate new curricula for primary and secondary education, environmental literacy, and formal and non-formal educational methods to reach marginalized sectors of society.

6. To ensure environmentally sound and safe uses of energy resources the governments of the Americas should:

a. Work with the private sectors and local communities to develop and maintain programs for energy sufficiency and ensure universal access to this resource;

b. Provide funding to research and develop renewable as well as low-tech, low-cost energy sources.

7. Patterns of production and consumption must be transformed. To these ends, governments should:

a. Promote alternative sustainable patterns of production and consumption, concentrating on economically viable alternatives for the poor;

b. Promote alternative, environmentally sound production practices that are able to support successful small and medium-sized farms and industries.

c. Introduce tax policies and other incentives to stimulate investment for employment generation and production of environmentally advantageous technologies.

8. Creative generation and management of funds to respond to the diverse needs of sustainable development should include:

a. The participation of all sectors of society in the privatization of public services;

b. The allocation of new funds from the private sector and international financial institutions aimed at meeting fundamental human needs, education, and the strengthening of self-determination toward sustainable development of low income groups;

c. Debt swapping and restructuring plans and other financing mechanisms that target funds to locally managed initiatives for sustainable development.

9. Governments must institute a holistic approach to prevent further narcotics production, trafficking, and abuse. Programs should:

a. Focus greater attention, research, and funding to reducing illicit drug consumption on the basis of prevention and education in association with treatment and rehabilitation;

b. Renew efforts to identify alternative income generation in both urban and rural communities with high prevalence of illicit drug production and use;

c. Conduct research to identify eradication methods that do not result in irreparable damage to ecosystems;

d. Respect the traditional cultivation, distribution, and use of plants (otherwise illicit) for medical and cultural purposes within socially safe and environmentally sound standards.

COMMISSION 4: BIODIVERSITY AND MANAGEMENT OF ECOSYSTEMS

Objective

Conserve and protect biological and cultural diversity in the Americas as an essential component of sustainable development.

General Considerations

1. The Western Hemisphere, rich in biological and cultural diversity, contains over one-half of the world's biodiversity. The Americas' ecosystem is threatened by increasing levels of unsustainable economic growth and trade, resulting in destructive land use and the overharvesting of natural resources, which thereby shift the balance of ecosystems. The value of biodiversity to the region's economy is immense, as it provides germ plasm to the agricultural sector, contributes to adequate levels of food production and supply, and provides industrial and pharmaceutical feedstock.

2. Among the greatest challenges to sustainable development in the hemisphere are the simultaneous efforts to eradicate poverty, ensuring more equitable distribution of wealth, and to facilitate the adoption of effective conservation methods, curbing overconsumption and overpopulation.

3. A major cause of rural poverty is the inequitable distribution of land, which leads to encroachment on economically marginal and ecologically sensitive areas. Land redistribution and securing legal titles, therefore, are integral components of sustainable development, especially in so far as land ownership and access to appropriate technology encourage more judicious use of land.

4. Local communities and indigenous groups are often overlooked in the design, implementation, and evaluation of projects and conservation strategies. In many instances, disregarding these populations has contributed to the failure of projects.

5. Tourism is an important economic endeavor that both depends upon and affects the health of the region's ecosystems and biodiversity. Therefore, any plans to expand tourism, its infrastructure, and related services must consider the intrinsic value of forests, coastal, marine, and freshwater systems, and their products.

6. The non-sustainable harvesting of fuelwood in the context of rapidly increasing human populations and increasing demands for land for agricultural, commercial, and industrial purposes all negatively impact biodiversity. However, renewable sources of energy, including fuelwood, could be integral parts of sustainable development strategies.

7. Viable sustainable development programs and policies require a solid scientific foundation. However, current levels of research on the impact of ongoing developmental strategies on the environment and the value of natural resources and biodiversity for sustainable development are inadequate.

8. At the present time, a variety of sources exist that provide funding and adequate mechanisms for ecologically viable development.

Policy Recommendations

1. Sign and/or ratify the Rio Biodiversity Convention of 1992 and sign and/or ratify the Western Hemisphere Convention of 1940, while advancing proposals for the modification of the latter in accordance with contemporary prevailing views and agreements on sustainable development. Establish adequate mechanisms to implement activities under these conventions.

2. Promote and give priority to environmentally and socially sound production methods and products. To this end, governments should:

   a. Encourage, through incentives, availability of credit and appropriate technology for sustainable development projects;

   b. Give priority to production systems and products that are compatible with local and regional ecosystems;

   c. Require producing countries to disseminate information relative to banned products, through respected international and regional organizations, such as the World Health Organization (WHO), the Pan American Health Organization (PAHO), the United Nations Environment Programme (UNEP), the General Agreement on Tariffs and Trade (GATT), and the World Trade Organization (WTO);

   d. Devise mechanisms to compensate countries and communities financially for marketing traditional knowledge and products of biodiversity;

   e. Reinforce respect for the intellectual property rights of indigenous peoples.

3. Recognize the importance of the participation of local communities and indigenous groups often overlooked by development programs. To this end:

   a. Assure adequate access to land and corresponding titles and delink land titling from deforestation. Lands should not be cleared as a prerequisite for demonstrating occupation and obtaining titles;

   b. Involve local groups in the design, implementation, and evaluation of development projects, including technological and financial assistance aspects;

   c. Assign greater portions of development aid toward projects that prioritize the aspirations of local communities.

4. Incorporate mechanisms into national and regional tourism systems that support ecosystem conservation and development so that tourism is conducted in a way that makes sustainable activities economically attractive. To this end, tourism development should include:

   a. Participation of local communities as well as guidance by environmental impact assessments (EIAs). EIAs must determine environmental feasibility of tourism-related economic activities and be used as instruments in the design, development, and ongoing evaluation of the impact of tourism growth on sustainable development;

   b. Improvement of EIA methods by using scientific analysis, research, and biological inventories to assess the response of the ecosystem to change;

   c. Legislation that forces developers to comply with the recommendations of the EIAs;

   d. Government incentives that promote the effective and responsible management of ecosystems in tourism areas, thus furthering the goal of sustainable management of forests, marine, and freshwater resources;

   e. Government promotion of park and reserves management, including mechanisms that engage the participation of local communities and indigenous groups in decisions involving protection of and sustainable use of natural ecosystems.

5. Stimulate the appropriate uses of fuelwood as well as oil and gas and sustain further research on alternative sources of energy.

6. Current levels of research on the value and sustainable use of ecosystems and biodiversity should be increased and information disseminated to resources users and integrated into the decision-making process of these areas.

7. Continue efforts to reduce population growth and curb excessive consumption of resources.

8. Strengthen existing mechanisms and identify additional innovative ways to provide funding for sustainable development. Funds can be raised from a variety of sources by:

    a. Allotting a percentage of the budget of development projects toward local environmental mitigation;

    b. Using debt forgiveness and debt-for-nature swaps to establish trust funds, as successfully accomplished in Jamaica and the Dominican Republic;

    c. Increase multilateral development banks' financing of energy efficiency and nonconventional renewable energy projects to account for 25 percent of energy lending by the year 2000.

WORKING GROUP ON THE ENVIRONMENT AND SUSTAINABLE DEVELOPMENT, KINGSTON, JAMAICA OCTOBER 23-25, 1994

REGULATORY FRAMEWORKS AND CAPACITY BUILDING

Chairperson, Rodrigo Barahona Israel, Centro de Derecho Ambiente y de los Recursos Naturales (CEDARENA), San José, Costa Rica

Susan Bass, Environmental Law Institute, Washington, D.C.

James C. McGowan, UN Development Programme (UNDP), New York

Pedro Solano, Sociedad Peruana de Derecho Ambiental (SPDA), Lima, Peru

Valeria Merino, Corporación Latinoamericana para el Desarrollo, Quito, Ecuador

Gerald Lalor, University of the West Indies, Kingston, Jamaica

Manuel F. Olivera, Asociación Nacional de Industriales (ANDI), Bogotá, Colombia

TRADE, DEVELOPMENT, AND THE ENVIRONMENT

Chairperson, Sarah Richardson, National Round Table on Environment and Economy, Ottawa, Canada

Gustavo Alanis-Ortega, Centro Mexicano de Derecho Ambiental, Mexico City, Mexico

Rodrigo J. Prudencio, National Wildlife Federation, Washington, D.C.

Osvaldo Sunkel, Centro de Desarrollo Sustentable, Universidad de Chile, Santiago, Chile

Jeannine Horowitz, Programa Bolívar, Caracas, Venezuela

Patterson Thompson, Caribbean Association of Industry and Commerce Inc., Barbados

Robin Rosenberg, North-South Center, University of Miami, Coral Gables, Florida

Kathleen Rogers, National Audubon Society, Legal Department, Washington, D.C.

Mario G. Aguilar, Oficina de Medio Ambiente, Mexican Embassy, Washington, D.C.

Ambassador Don Mills, Ministry of the Environment, Government of Jamaica, Kingston, Jamaica

POVERTY, FUNDAMENTAL HUMAN NEEDS, AND SUSTAINABLE DEVELOPMENT

Chairperson, Stanley Heckadon-Moreno, Smithsonian Tropical Research Institute, Balboa, Panama

Eloy Anello, International Association for Development Learning, Universidad Nur, La Paz, Bolivia

Johanna W. Looye, College of Design, Architecture, Art & Planning, University of Cincinnati, Ohio

José Ochoa Iturbe, Jose Ochoa Iturbe & Associates, Caracas, Venezuela

Gonzalo Biggs, Figueroa and Valenzuela Law Firm, Santiago, Chile

Elizabeth Thomas-Hope, Centre for Sustainable Development, University of the West Indies, Mona, Jamaica

Mary Uebersax, North-South Center, University of Miami, Coral Gables, Florida

BIODIVERSITY AND MANAGEMENT OF ECOSYSTEMS

Chairperson, Terrence Thomas, Environmental Foundation of Jamaica, Kingston

Virgilio Viana, Escola Superior de Agricultura Luiz Queiroz, São Paulo, Brazil

José Martínez Guridy, Fondo Integrado Pronaturaleza (Pronatura), Santo Domingo, Dominican Republic

João Capobianco, Instituto Socioambiental, São Paulo, Brazil

Tia Nelson, Nature Conservancy, Washington, D.C.

Sponsors: Center for Latin
American Studies, Center
for Governmental
Responsibility, Office of
International Studies and
Programs, The University of
Florida; Latin American
and Caribbean Center,
Florida International
University; North-South
Center, University of
Miami; Florida State
University; Florida A&M
University; and Walter and
Betty Boardman
Professorship, University of
Central Florida

Prepared by participants in
"From Rio to Miami:
Sustainable Development
and the Summit of
the Americas,"
September 29-30, 1994,
Tallahassee, Florida

From Rio to Miami: Sustainable Development and the Summit of the Americas: Declaration of Principles for Sustainable Development in the Americas

PREAMBLE

Recognizing that "Making Democracy Endure: Sustainable Development" is one of three major themes of the Summit of the Americas, as identified by the United States, and

Recognizing that sustainable development is a dynamic, evolving process, not a static condition, and that it is equally a challenge for the developed as well as the developing nations of the Americas,

We commend the Presidents of each of the countries of the Hemisphere as they outline an agenda for our future at the Summit of the Americas and for identifying this vital issue as one of the three most important considerations for the Hemispheric Presidents, and

We challenge them to forge an effective hemispheric partnership to confront the challenges of sustainable development in the Americas.

Toward that end, as the Summit partners are seeking methods for establishing "Hemispheric Partnerships for Nature," as detailed in Initiative 13 of the Summit Initiatives Agenda, we commit to assist in the development and implementation of these partnerships, using the following principles:

TRADE AND FINANCE

Regional trade agreements should include provisions for promoting sustainable development because trade and sustainable development are irrevocably linked.

International financial institutions should be encouraged to support sustainable development in their loan policies and should refrain from implementing or supporting policies that jeopardize sustainable development.

EQUITY AND DEMOCRATIC PARTICIPATION

Equity and the reduction of poverty are integral elements of sustainable development.

Citizen participation, including that of the indigenous peoples of the Americas, is crucial to all phases of sustainable development policymaking.

Public education and public support are central to sustainable development.

RESEARCH AND TRAINING

Long-term multi-disciplinary research and training are essential to sustainable development.

Centers for Sustainable Development should be established at universities throughout the hemisphere in partnership with government, international financial institutions, non-governmental organizations, the public, and the media.

Appropriate technologies must be available and accessible to policymakers and local communities for environmental planning; and technological options for environmental purposes should be fostered.

NATURAL RESOURCES

Public policies should discourage overconsumption and waste and should encourage protection of resources for future generations.

A hemisphere-wide policy must be developed to protect water resources, which are our most vital and most threatened natural resource.

New approaches to managing ecosystems and natural resources across sub-national and national political boundaries must be developed. These approaches should include creative combinations of harmonized environmental standards, institutional development, enhanced enforcement mechanisms, and non-regulatory incentives.

In Conclusion,

We strongly recommend that the Presidents attending the Summit of the Americas develop a hemispheric agenda for sustainable development. We commit ourselves to respond with research, development, and technology to assist in developing and implementing those goals, as requested by Summit participants.

BACKGROUND

In preparation for President Clinton's Summit of the Americas, convened in December 1994, in Miami, several Florida universities sponsored an environmental summit, entitled "From Rio to Miami: Sustainable Development and the Summit of the Americas," in Tallahassee in late September. The conference was the only Summit-related event dedicated to environmental and sustainable development issues.

A "Declaration of Principles" for sustainable development for the hemisphere was prepared during the two-day conference, based on conference presentations from international, national, and state policymakers and researchers. The declaration included topics relating to trade and finance, equity and democratic participation, research and training, and natural resources. It recommended that Presidents of the countries attending the Summit develop a hemispheric agenda for sustainable development.

"Sustainable development was one of the major themes selected by the White House for discussion at the Summit. Florida's universities are conducting cutting-edge research in this field, and we developed the environmental summit to use our full resources in providing Summit officials with recommendations based on our experiences," said Jon Mills of the University of Florida's Center for Governmental Responsibility, one of the conference organizers.

Conference participants who developed the "Declaration of Principles" represented nine countries, eight universities or colleges, four state government agencies, two non-governmental organizations, and two private businesses.

The conference featured discussions on followup to the United Nations Conference on Environment and Development, trade and the environment, summit issues, World Bank projects, and the Chilean economic miracle. In addition, presentations were made on eight existing collaborations between Florida universities and academic institutions in the hemisphere. The "Declaration of Principles" was developed from these discussions and during an open debate at the conclusion of the conference.

FUTURE PLAN

Conference sponsors have been meeting since September to organize a network of academic institutions for continuing policy development and research in the field of sustainable development and trade. A post-Summit event, scheduled for Santa Cruz, Bolivia, in July 1995, will be convened to establish a network of universities and research institutes and develop a collaborative research agenda on sustainable development, leading up to the 1996 Summit Conference on Sustainable Development in Bolivia.

INSTITUTIONAL PROFILES

Center for Governmental Responsibility
University of Florida College of Law

The Center for Governmental Responsibility at the University of Florida College of Law is the State of Florida's senior law and public policy research center, with more than 20 years' experience in projects focusing on the environment, water law, growth management, land use, public policy, national health policy, elder law, guardianship, child health policy, juvenile justice, elder abuse, gender bias, race bias, victim advocacy, juvenile dependency, feminist jurisprudence, sexual harassment, and health and the law.

Internationally, the Center's staff conduct projects in Brazil, Poland, and Central America, specializing in international environmental and social policy development and in training of local government officials in emerging democracies.

Center for Latin American Studies
University of Florida

In 1963 the University of Florida (UF) established the Center for Latin American Studies (CLAS) to mobilize UF's considerable Latin American resources into an effective and coherent interdisciplinary program. CLAS is a free-standing, campus-wide program directly responsible to the university provost, with six tenure-accruing faculty lines. An original recipient of federal support for area studies, the Center and the Latin American and Caribbean Center at Florida International University currently share a U.S. Department of Education Natural Resource Center grant in Latin American Studies.

The core of Latin American studies at UF has traditionally been in the social sciences and humanities, but over the last decade it has developed strengths in such fields as agriculture, forestry, law, and journalism as well. Its program in Tropical

Conservation and Development integrates the social, natural, and agricultural sciences to address issues of resource conservation, development, and poverty alleviation in the humid neotropics.

Office of International
Studies and Programs
University of Florida

To ensure an educational response to the rapidly changing global environment, the University of Florida established the Office of International Studies and Programs (OISP) in September 1991 within the Office of the Vice President for Academic Affairs. OISP provides leadership for the university's rapidly evolving international work, promoting international education and research and training university-wide and mobilizing resources to support these activities.

Latin American and Caribbean Center
Florida International University

At Florida International University (FIU), the Latin American and Caribbean Center (LACC) is responsible for leadership in the field of Latin American and Caribbean Studies. As a federally supported National Resource Center for Language and Area Studies, LACC has a mandate to promote graduate and undergraduate education, faculty research, and public education on Latin American and Caribbean affairs.

Recognized as a national leader in research on Central America, the Caribbean, and Cuba, LACC has significant strengths in Mexico and Brazil as well. LACC's scholarly activities span the disciplines of economics, political science, sociology, anthropology, history, music, dance, educational administration, criminal justice, and business.

The North-South Center
University of Miami

The University of Miami North-South Center promotes better relations among the United States, Canada, and the nations of Latin America and the Caribbean through programs of education, cooperative study, training, public outreach, information, and research. Part of the University of Miami since 1984, the North-South Center conducts programs dealing with Latin American issues. A 1991 appropriation by the United States Congress enabled the Center to expand its programs and to draw upon wider intellectual resources throughout the hemisphere. The Center solicits proposals and provides funding for research grants by or in cooperation with other institutions.

Walter and Betty Boardman Endowed Professorship (in Environmental Policy) University of Central Florida

The Boardman Professorship — named for the late environmental advocate and his wife — targets research and educational programs in Volusia County and Central Florida. It is coordinated by the UCF Department of Public Administration and is housed at the UCF Daytona Beach Campus.

Walter Boardman was a patriarch of the conservation movement in Central Florida. He served as an educator in New York in the 1940s and 1950s. He then moved to Washington, D.C., to become executive director of The Nature Conservancy, one of the world's largest environmental organizations. In 1972, Boardman retired to Volusia County where he founded the Environmental Council, Volusia Land Trust.

Jon Mills, Director, Center for Governmental Responsibility, and Terry McCoy, Director, Center for Latin American Studies, University of Florida

Postscript:
Universities: A Key Partner in Sustainable Development

Hemispheric leaders who attended the 1994 Summit of the Americas identified sustainable development as one of their four overall goals. While sustainable development was listed in the Summit's "Plan of Action" as a separate goal, sustainable development touches directly each of the other Summit goals of sustained democracy, economic prosperity and free trade, and considerate and equitable treatment of people.

Sustainable development entails economic development, social development, and protection of natural resources. It is a future that balances every element of life in equal partnership. It is the vision of a healthy earth with a healthy economy and healthy people.

One key to achieving sustainable development is the partnership of government and universities. Governmental leaders in the hemisphere will set the goals and through laws and actions implement them, but universities must provide the information, analysis, and technology that spans the gap between goals and implementation.

As hemispheric leaders move forward into the next century with a renewed commitment to cooperation and a recognition of the necessity for removing barriers to collaboration, they must recognize the important, fundamental, long-standing partnership among institutions of higher learning throughout the hemisphere. Through those partnerships, universities in the hemisphere have addressed or are addressing many of the issues raised by the Summit. The institutions of higher learning can provide the best vehicle for implementing the recommendations from the Summit.

The Summit "Plan of Action" creates a foundation for the overall concept developed at "From Rio to Miami: Sustainable Development and the Summit of the Americas," a pre-Summit conference sponsored by Florida universities (September 29-30, 1994, Tallahassee, Florida). The conclusion of this conference was that sustainable development is one of the major issues facing the hemisphere and that universities are key components in creating a future of sustainable development. Why are universities the major building blocks?

1. Universities provide the largest body of expertise, research, and experimentation in the hemisphere at the least cost to government.

2. Universities throughout the hemisphere have hundreds of existing project linkages, extending into every component mentioned in the Summit documents.

3. Challenges of different languages and cultures do not exist within universities because of the diversity of the academic population and courses.

4. Universities are more stable and permanent than any government research agencies.

5. Universities are the investment of the future, training new generations of leaders and managers.

6. Universities can accurately interpret the policies of their individual governments because they frequently work under partial sponsorship of their individual governments.

7. Universities are an open marketplace of ideas.

8. Universities are a local, community delivery system.

9. Universities serve as a resource for government, business, local communities, the media, and the public.

While Summit documents make several references to the role of academic institutions in fulfilling the goals, realization of the complete resource offered by universities went virtually unnoticed. For example, each of the four overall goals articulated in the Summit's "Plan of Action" represents a concept that has been researched and refined at a university or a collaboration of universities in the hemisphere.

Participants in "From Rio to Miami" developed a new concept for partnerships in the hemisphere. They proposed a network of institutes for sustainable development, located at universities throughout the hemisphere, which will collaborate on priorities in sustainable development and serve as a resource for governments in developing policies to implement Summit recommendations.

The Summit's "Plan of Action" makes reference to the role of universities, noting that universities have a key role in the promotion of cultural rights (Section I.4) and in the production of scientific and technological knowledge (Section III.16).

However, universities can fulfill a major linkage in the "Decade of Discovery" (Section IV.22), envisioned as a way of promoting "hemispheric technical and scientific cooperation and to facilitate the exchange of information relevant to the conservation and sustainable use of biological diversity." Universities can also play a major role in training and education needs of the hemisphere (Section IV.22) and offer economic and policy analysis regarding free trade issues (Section II).

"From Rio to Miami" featured discussions of sustainable development issues facing the hemisphere, using existing research and collaboration as

problem-solving models for the future. Ongoing programs exist between Florida universities and Brazil on analysis of environmental laws and practices; between Florida and Central America on non-governmental organizations; between Florida and Bolivia on conservation and indigenous people; between Florida and Brazil on agroforestry in the Amazon; between Florida and Mexico on water management; between Florida and Central America on ecosystem management; and between Florida and Brazil on strategies for sensitive areas.

Each of these multi-year projects developed policy recommendations based on two-way input and comparative analysis between the hemispheric partners. Most continue to contribute to policy development and information exchange that is replicable throughout the hemisphere. These projects are only a few of the collaborative efforts between Florida universities and colleges and academic institutions throughout the hemisphere.

In opening "From Rio to Miami," Florida State University System Chancellor Charlie Reed said, "This is a great place to come and talk about sustainable development. Florida began sustainable development policy. In this state, we focus on partnerships — among and between public and private universities, community colleges, state agencies, environment and economic agencies, and between state and federal agencies. It's not always easy, especially in environmental and economic areas."

The role of universities was recognized at the United Nations Conference on Environment and Development (UNCED) in 1992. Universities were cited as partners with government in capacity building in the hemisphere. UNCED leaders acknowledged that "skills, knowledge and technical know-how at the individual and institutional levels are necessary for institution-building, policy analysis, and development management, including the assessment of alternative courses of action with a view of enhancing access to and transfer of technology and promoting economic development" (37.2).

UNCED participants identified university roles to include "long-term cooperative arrangements between municipalities, non-governmental organizations, universities, training and research centers and business, public, and private institutions with counterparts in other countries or within countries or regions" (37.7); research to assist in policy decisions

(8.9); training and post-graduate programs (8.20); curriculum development in sustainable development (8.38); and public awareness (36.3).

With the institutionalization of institutes for sustainable development at universities throughout the hemisphere, a blueprint can be developed for implementing the policies of the Summit of the Americas. That plan can be presented at the 1996 Summit for Sustainable Development in Bolivia.

PROPOSALS FROM NON-GOVERNMENTAL SECTORS

V. General Proposals

*Submitted by the American
Federation of Labor and
Congress of Industrial
Organizations and the
Inter-American Regional
Organization of Workers/
International Confedera-
tion of Free Trade Unions*

Declaration of Concern of the Inter-American Regional Organization of Workers

STRUCTURE OF THE AFL-CIO

Membership

The American Federation of Labor and Congress of Industrial Organizations (AFL-CIO) is made up of 83 national and international unions which in turn have more than 45,000 local unions. It is not a union, but a federation of unions. The combined membership of all the unions affiliated with the AFL-CIO is approximately 13.3 million.

Affiliated Organizations

Unions may also affiliate with a variety of trade and industrial departments. Those departments are separate organizations within the AFL-CIO which promote the interests of specific groups of workers with strong common interests.

Many of the national and international unions are affiliated with one or more of the nine departments: Building and Construction Trades, Food and Allied Service Trades, Industrial Union, Maritime Trades, Metal Trades, Professional Employees, Public Employee and Transportation Trades. The ninth, the Union Label and Service Trades Department, seeks to promote consumer interest in union-made products and union services.

The AFL-CIO is organized nationally into state and local AFL-CIOs in each of the 50 states and Puerto Rico. The local unions in the particular states form the state AFL-CIOs. The federations advance the statewide interests of labor, particularly in state legislative matters. Similarly, in each of 610 communities, the local unions of different national and international unions band together in local AFL-CIOs.

American Federation of Labor and Congress of Industrial Organizations

October 27, 1994

The President
The White House
Washington, D.C. 20500

Dear Mr. President:

This month, the Executive Council of the Inter-American Regional Organization of Workers, (ORIT/ICFTU) representing 25 national trade union centers in 21 countries throughout the hemisphere, adopted the enclosed Declaration of Concern on the upcoming Summit of the Americas.

The AFL-CIO, together with the ORIT, believes that if the Summit is to make progress in promoting democracy, shared prosperity, and sustainable development, the interests and concerns of workers and their unions must have a significant place on the Summit agenda and be addressed directly by the Summit participants. This is particularly important in the context of increasing economic integration and potential trade negotiations.

It is my understanding that proposals for the Summit agenda do not, at this point, include any mention of trade unions or the importance of labor policy or worker rights. This is a serious omission with far reaching consequences.

The AFL-CIO stands ready to work with your administration to ensure that the Summit reflects the interests and aspirations of workers throughout the hemisphere as the surest path toward the realization of our common goals.

Sincerely,

Lane Kirkland
President

Enclosure

DECLARATION OF CONCERN OF THE INTER-AMERICAN REGIONAL ORGANIZATION OF WORKERS

International Confederation of Free Trade Unions and the National Confederations of Workers to the Representatives of the Heads of State attending the Summit of the Americas

December 9-10, 1994, Miami, Florida, USA

The American Federation of Labor and Congress of Industrial Organizations and the Inter-American Regional Organization/International Confederation of Free Trade Unions sincerely applaud the convening of the Summit of the Americas, which will bring together the Presidents of the countries of this Hemisphere for the purpose of arriving at a consensus for solving the major problems we face. With equal sincerity, however, we believe that the inclusion of organized labor in the deliberations would assure the success of the meeting. More importantly, the future of hemispheric political and economic development depends on workers' participation and support for constructive change.

The AFL-CIO and the ORIT/ICFTU have repeatedly gone on record in favor of those institutional and economic changes which will allow our society to break the vicious cycle of poverty and replace it with a virtuous cycle of sustainable development. We believe that this can only occur in the presence of democracy, which requires the active involvement of workers and the sharing by those workers in the prosperity promised by integration. Without such participation, in fact, the promise will be hard to fulfill.

We subscribe to the three stated themes of the Summit of the Americas: the encouragement of democracy, the sharing of prosperity, and the promotion of sustainable development.

To these ends:

1. The inclusion of worker rights in trade agreements is essential if the process of hemispheric integration is to proceed. The sharing of prosperity and narrowing the gap between rich and poor in our society will be enhanced if the rights of workers are considered in trade agreements to be of equal importance with the protection of property rights.

2. Democracy is threatened if workers lack internationally recognized rights to form unions, to negotiate the terms and conditions of their employment, and to withhold their labor, if necessary, in pursuit of their common interests.

3. Workers, far more than other groups or interests in our society, are aware of the tremendous and growing need for jobs. We are concerned that unscrupulous investors may see opportunity for additional profit in the development of industries and industrial processes which are destructive of the environment, including our workplace environment. Such industries must not be allowed to pollute in the name of competitiveness or threaten to relocate if environmental standards are enforced.

The AFL-CIO and the ORIT/ICFTU is concerned that the Summit of the Americas might not include labor as an integral part of these deliberations or related development issues including:

— the need to create jobs which are *not* based on low wages but rather on more socially acceptable comparative advantages such as proximity to markets, availability of natural resources, and favorable business climates.

— the need to better educate and train the current work force and the work force of the future.

— the need to encourage labor participation in the search for "flexibility," a term often used as an excuse to destroy hard won labor benefits through disingenuous and ill-conceived labor reforms.

— the need to provide safety nets for workers who may be negatively affected by economic restructuring such as privatization.

If the goal of the Summit of the Americas is to arrive at a consensus on economic policy, it cannot be achieved without the cooperation of organized labor. In this sense, we stand ready to assist with this potentially important and historic meeting.

THE INTER-AMERICAN REGIONAL ORGANIZATION OF WORKERS

ORIT

The Inter-American Regional Organization of Workers (ORIT) represents the interests of democratic workers throughout the Western Hemisphere. ORIT is one of several regional affiliates of the International Confederation of Free Trade Unions (ICFTU) and is composed of 25 national labor confederations operating in 21 countries.

The following is a list of ORIT's affiliates by country:

Argentina	General Confederation of Workers
Barbados	Barbados Workers Union
Brazil	General Central of Workers Union Force Workers' Central Union
Canada	Canadian Labor Congress
Chile	Unitarian Workers Central
Colombia	Confederation of Workers of Colombia United Front of Democratic Workers
Costa Rica	Confederation of Workers Rerum Novarum
Dominican Republic	National Confederation of Dominican Workers
Ecuador	Ecuadorean Confederation of Free Trade Unions
El Salvador	Confederation of Democratic Workers Salvadoran National Federation of Workers
Guatemala	Confederation of Trade Union Unity of Guatemala
Guyana	Guyana Trades Union Congress
Honduras	Confederation of Workers of Honduras
Jamaica	Jamaica Confederation of Trade Unions
Mexico	Confederation of Workers of Mexico
Nicaragua	Confederation of Trade Union Unity
Panama	Confederation of Workers of the Republic of Panama
Peru	Confederation of Workers of Peru
Trinidad & Tobago	Trinidad and Tobago Labor Congress
USA	American Federation of Labor — Congress of Industrial Organizations
Venezuela	Confederation of Workers of Venezuela

AFL-CIO: Press Release, Description of Structure, and Declaration of Concern of the Inter-American Regional Organization of Workers

PRESS RELEASE OF DECEMBER 8, 1994

AFL-CIO Calls Summit "Squandered Opportunity"

In response to requests for comment on the upcoming Summit meeting, Thomas R. Donahue, secretary-treasurer of the AFL-CIO, issued this statement:

In the Summit of the Americas, the United States and nations of the western hemisphere had an opportunity to address the real concerns of working families throughout the Americas. Unfortunately, we are squandering that opportunity.

The Summit draft declaration barely pays lip-service to the needs and interests of working people — worker rights, adjustment policies for those hit hard by trade, a just share in economic expansion. Our efforts — and those of workers throughout the hemisphere — to raise these concerns to at least the level of protection automatically awarded corporations and investors have been rebuffed.

Freedom of association and the right to organize and bargain collectively as well as minimal workplace standards in such areas as safety and health and child labor are ignored; intellectual property rights, investments and other items on the corporate "wish list" are extensively protected.

The administration's design to extend the North American Free Trade Agreement into Latin America, beginning with Chilean accession to that agreement, offers nothing to the hemisphere's workers. We have argued for months for a bilateral agreement with Chile which could set new standards for decency in trade matters.

We support the position of House Democratic leader Richard Gephardt, who expressed his opposition to the negotiation of traditional accession agreements in a December 7, 1994 letter to President Clinton. "I do not want the NAFTA to become the high water mark in our trade relations," Gephardt wrote. Rather, he added, "We must not accept the NAFTA agreements in these important areas (labor and environmental issues) as the ceiling on our efforts."

We also stand with ORIT, the Inter-American Regional Organization of Workers and our sister federation, which represents some 45 million workers throughout Latin America. In a November 4, 1994 letter to President Clinton, ORIT stated that unless worker rights and standards are placed at the center of hemispheric integration, these trade arrangements will result in "a race to the bottom: the further weakening of laws that protect worker and trade union rights, health and safety and the environment, while increasing the freedom of businesses to exploit men, women and child workers in the struggle for competitive advantage."

A so-called free trade area which is designed to encourage U.S. investment in other countries and which ignores the social conditions of workers in those countries leaves those workers depending on "international trickle-down economics" and opens the hemisphere to allow U.S.-based corporations to transfer production from the United States more easily.

Contact:

Candice Johnson	(202) 637-5010
Mark Anderson	(202) 637-5166

A Hemispheric Commitment for Sustainable Development

Proposals from Latin American Civil Society to the Americas Summit

The attached document is the outcome of a consultation process undertaken between July and October 1994 among the civil society organizations of fourteen countries of the Region and the Business Council for Sustainable Development Latin America (see annexed list). This participatory process included, inter alia, business and labor sectors, non-governmental organizations, academia, and indigenous peoples. The proposals attached reflect the regional consensus among participants. Additional outcomes of this endeavor are documents with recommendations at the national level, which were sent to the authorities responsible for Summit preparations in each country.

Fundación Futuro Latinoamericano fosters the attainment of sustainable development in Latin America through a participatory decision-making process.

It is a private not-for-profit organization, created on November 1, 1993, and, although regional in scope, is incorporated under Ecuadorean laws. Its headquarters are located in Quito, and it intends to open offices or establish representations in other countries of the region.

Fundación Futuro Latinoamericano gratefully acknowledges the positive reception given by the hundreds of entities and organizations that participated in this endeavor and the Latin American governments that received the initiative constructively, and likewise, thanks the United Nations Development Program (UNDP) and the J. Altman Foundation for their financial support.

The Proposed Agenda

1. In reference to the proposed agenda for the Americas Summit, we must note that trade expansion and promotion of technological and financial cooperation and of investment are necessary means for the attainment of sustainable development, but they are not sufficient. Strengthening of democracy and the promotion of good governance are essential conditions towards this end.

Principles of Hemispheric Action

2. The main objective of Hemispheric cooperation and integration shall be the attainment of sustainable development.

3. The Hemispheric debate on sustainable development, trade and integration shall be undertaken with exclusion of no country in the Hemisphere.

4. Joint efforts for political, economic, social and physical development in the Hemisphere shall be aimed at the enhancement of the Continent's quality of life, including poverty eradication and treatment of the environmental component, through the expansion of opportunities in a framework of inter-generational and inter-regional equity.

5. In Hemispheric relations, States shall act with due respect to development priorities democratically defined inside each country and in full consideration of each country's ethnic and cultural endowment.

6. The definition of these priorities shall result from democratic and participatory processes of consultation and decision-making, incorporating governments, business and labor sectors, NGOs, research centers, academia, and any civil society grouping with a legitimate interest.

7. The States of the Hemisphere shall pledge full compliance of binding commitments undertaken at Rio's United Nations Conference on Environment and Development in 1992; Agenda 21; the Convention on Biological Diversity and the Framework Convention on Climate Change.

8. Hemispheric cooperation for development shall ameliorate conditions for governance and support the strengthening of democracy in our countries. For this purpose, cooperation resources shall be directed towards the reinforcement of capacity and efficiency of local and regional governments as well as towards new and ongoing processes of modernization, decentralization and enhancement of public participation. All of these shall help eradicate poverty.

9. These principles of sustainable development shall constitute the reference framework for Governments in the Hemisphere and the multilateral institutions to evaluate, deepen and/or reformulate the current processes of physical and trade integration, implementation of structural adjustment policies, reinvigoration of social policies, the broadening of capital and services markets, the facilitation of transboundary movement of personnel and of productive investment, and the establishment of conduct codes and regulation aimed at the elimination of corruption practices in the performance of commercial endeavors, all of the above, through strategies that guarantee the duration of the processes through several generations.

10. In the framework of the sustainable development objective, securement of Hemispheric bonds (agreements, conventions, treaties, etc.) related to environmental policies, shall be sought with full respect of both basic principles of sovereignty and responsibility of States and of international commitments.

11. The treatment of the relationship between trade and environment in the Hemisphere shall strictly observe the multilateral trade principles and commitments. In no case, would there be recourse to unilateral actions.

12. As a concrete expression of cooperation and as a result of this Summit meeting, a Hemispheric partnership for sustainable development should be advanced based on principles of equity and reciprocity, taking into account the relative advantages of each country in the region with respect to its natural, financial and technological resources. This partnership shall power relative dynamic advantages in each of the countries involved.

13. In a Hemispheric context, the solution to external debt problems as well as technical and financial cooperation from bilateral and multilateral sources shall be directed towards sustainable development goals, giving priority to the regions and sectors with the most urgent needs.

14. Special attention shall be given to investment in human capital and in environmentally sound technology as instrumental tools for sustainable development.

15. Strengthening of civil society in the Hemisphere requires the subjection of military and security bodies to civil authorities and the re-orientation of the

sector's expenditure to the benefit of sustainable development objectives.

Proposals for Hemispheric Action

16. Establish a democratic intra-hemispheric—multilateral and multisectoral—process of negotiations, open to participation of representatives of the civil society, to deal with economic and trade issues. The process shall have as a forum and secretariat one of the existing entities (ALADI, SELA, or other).

17. Establish a democratic intra-hemispheric—multilateral and multisectoral—process of negotiations, open to participation of representatives of the civil society, for the treatment of environmental issues, including the assessment and eventual revision of existing environmental agreements and the establishment of processes of definition of environmental standards. To this end, consideration shall be given to the feasibility of adapting one of the existing fora or bodies or, if necessary, the creation of a new specialized body. (Issues to be treated include, *inter alia*: revitalization of The Western Hemisphere Convention; a proposed Hemispheric Convention on Forests; the establishment of viable schemes for reinvestment of external financial flows in environmental programs; agreed guidelines on development, standardization or mutual recognition of national environmental legislation and standards; an eventual agreement on trade in prohibited or severely restricted goods in their country of origin.)

18. Establish a participatory process of reformulation and re-engineering of plurilateral continental, regional and subregional organizations (OAS, IDB, and other) so that their mission and functions be re-oriented and/or broadened, positioning them as genuine institutional support for integration, cooperation and sustainable development among the countries of the Hemisphere.

19. Establish a participatory process at the Hemispheric level for the definition and further elaboration of indexes of performance, measurement and assessment of the policies and commitments towards sustainable development of the Western Hemisphere.

20. Establish, immediately, the necessary ways and means for strengthening and intensification of policies, measures and actions for the struggle against drug-trafficking, particularly by means of combatting

drug consumption and dollar-laundering through financial and commercial activities, all of which shall be carried out with the same intensity currently applied to actions against production and traffic. Repression of drug-trafficking shall not affect traditional production and use of the coca leaf and, instead, work shall be undertaken towards the research and development of viable alternatives of licit use.

21. Establish a commitment among all participating States of the Hemisphere to make operational the jurisdiction of the Inter-American Court of Human Rights in each country.

Bogotá, October 1994

The English version was provided by Fundación Futuro Latinamericano; the original was written in Spanish.

List of the National Coordinators for the Summit of the Americas Project

- Argentina, FARN, Pedro Tarak
- Chile, PARTICIPA, Laura Novoa
- Uruguay, ECOS, Miguel Reynal
- Paraguay, Fundación Moisés Bertoni, Raül Gauto
- Bolivia, Fundación Milenio, Horst Grene
- Ecuador, Fundación Natura, Teodoro Bustamante
- Peru, PROTERRA/DESCO, Raúl Guerrero
- Colombia, Centro de Investigación y Proyectos Especiales, Juanita Castaño
- Venezuela, FUDENA, Glenda Medina
- El Salvador, SALVANATURA, Carlos A. Linares
- Honduras, CODDEFFAGOLF, Jorge Varela Marquez
- Guatemala, Defensores de la Naturaleza/Mario Dary, Oscar Iván Maldonado
- Dominican Republic, Instituto para el Desarrollo de la Empresa Asociativa Campesina (IDEAC), Pedro Franco
- Brazil, IDEAC, Miguel Darcy de Oliveira

FUNDACIÓN FUTURO LATINOAMERICANO

Fundación Futuro Latinoamericano fosters the attainment of *sustainable development* in Latin America through a participatory decision-making process.

Institutional structure: Fundación Futuro Latinoamericano is a private not-for-profit organization, created on November 1, 1993, and, although regional in scope, incorporated under Ecuadorean laws. Its headquarters are located in Quito, and it intends to open offices or establish representations in other countries of the region if necessary.

The Board of Directors comprises a group of representatives of nine Latin American non-governmental organizations, independent research centers and other entities (development, environment, etc.), and six individuals with regional recognition for their individual talent.

An academic advisory board, formed by Latin American experts, provides guidance to Fundación Futuro Latinoamericano's activities.

Fields of interest: For the achievement of its objectives, Fundación Futuro Latinoamericano makes use of the best available Latin American, subregional, national, and local fields. It has begun work on the organization and promotion of dialogues of broad participation. The aim is to bridge the institutional gaps which limit the perspectives of sustainable development in the region.

Similarly, it seeks actively to contribute to remedy current communication a and information voids which obstruct the implementation of public or private actions oriented toward sustainable development. In the context of Latin America confronting global challenges, Fundación Futuro Latinoamericano serves as a catalytic agent for the identification and ripening of Latin American interests vis-à-vis third regions, with an emphasis on strengthening the economic, social, political, and physical integration of the Hemisphere.

Ricardo Meléndez O.
Director General,
Fundación Futuro
Latinoamericano

Postscript:
The Summit Agreements and Their Immediate Future: Collective Processes on Hemispheric Ends

The Miami Summit jump-started a refreshing and promising wave of processes on hemisphere-wide agreed objectives. Democratic change and dynamics of economic, trade, and physical integration in the region had been exercising enormous pressure in that direction over the last few years. To celebrate the Americas' issuing a Declaration of Principles and agreeing on a Plan of Action constitutes, in itself, a notable accomplishment. But only the materialization of the hopes inscribed in Miami will make of it a success, a real triumph. That shall not be assessed but way down the road. Thus, the community of the Americas, its civil society and governments, will most probably stand as overseer of the agreements signed last December.

Enhancement of democracy by promotion of regional, economic, and social prosperity and sound environmental management, as praised by the Central American Alliance for Sustainable Development, should be the path to be followed by inter-American relations. That has been the message conveyed to Miami by hundreds of civil society voices. The aspiration is that the forthcoming hemispheric summit in Santa Cruz in 1996 will materialize this view.

Democracy has always been the focus of the inter-American system. The Organization of American States, as its preeminent forum, has embraced from the outset the struggle for and enhancement of democratic mechanisms in the Americas as its foremost goal. The Summit's outcome is to be commended as it provides a new opportunity to turn the OAS forum into an effective instrument, a tool for radiating improvement of economic conditions and betterment of the quality of life of the peoples of the hemisphere as pillars for viable democracy.

Only under conditions of peace can societies and economies prosper. Military tensions among bordering states bring about not only death and chaos in the conflictive area but also the alteration of people's lives and of countries' financial markets and trade flows. Domestic democracy and democratic ways should serve as a catalyst for long-standing disputes. Recent eruption of such an instance along the Ecuadorean-Peruvian border shall serve as an alert on the priority that definite resolution of these queries should receive. A community of neighbors will advance on the same path and prosper only as long as there is no animosity among the respective governments and peoples.

The Summit agreements propose *economic integration and free trade* in the Americas as means to higher states of development. These means shall evolve under conditions of equity in all spheres: social, economic, political, and environmental. Strengthening and creation of competitive factors shall underpin this purpose as well as higher levels of productivity, primarily based on better training and education of the work force. Production methods and technologies, management and marketing techniques, and investment capital shall freely move across borders to push productive machineries all over the hemisphere into a level playing field. Rule-making in the context of trade integration schemes shall see that this purpose is accomplished. Integration shall evolve at a viable pace in a manner which systematically approaches subregions for mutual benefit.

Improved social policies, with special emphasis on the eradication of poverty, are a priority for the attainment of sustainable development. The programs agreed upon in the Summit reflect a good start, which shall be consolidated in time. A major role should be given to health organizations and social-development private groups with field experience. Once again, participatory decisionmaking should be encouraged in order to reach real stake-holders.

On natural environment (the prevention and control of pollution, protection of ecosystems and use of biological resources, and promotion of clean, efficient, and sustainable energy production and use), the outcome of the Summit falls short. Natural resource management can only be viable if it is part of a strategy toward sustainable development. Old approaches have proved to be partial solutions at best, and lack of coherence with strategies for improvement of political ways, betterment of social programs, and economic models render them inadequate. Much more should be proposed and done in terms of hemispheric coordination in this respect, keeping sustainability as an umbrella objective. Civil society groups, including business and industry as well as indigenous communities, have expressed on more than one occasion their desire to participate in the construction of such coordination. They need to be taken into account and their proposals must materialize if we care for the hemisphere of our children and the quality of life of future generations.

As a main by-product, the Summit has been able to generate processes of collective thought and participatory mechanisms from its preparatory phase onwards. That momentum should not be left to weaken. The moment should be appraised. The hopes raised should serve as inspiration, and we all should keep working, gathering more and more people, on the ideals of inter-American progress and the challenge to attain sustainable development for the peoples of the New Continent.

Summary of
Recommendations from
the Inter-American
Dialogue

The Inter-American
Dialogue is a forum for
sustained exchange
among opinion leaders of
the Western Hemisphere
and an independent,
nonpartisan center for
policy analysis on
economic and political
relations in the
hemisphere.

The Americas in 1994:
A Time for Leadership

Summit Priorities

• The priority goals of the summit should be (a) to set the foundation for a hemisphere linked by free trade and economic partnership and (b) to strengthen the capacity of the Organization of American States (OAS) and other regional institutions to help safeguard democracy and human rights. These are issues that must be dealt with multilaterally. Progress requires international agreement, joint initiatives, and the cooperation of many countries.

• The assembled leaders should commit their governments to confront actively the challenges of fortifying democracy, protecting human rights, and reducing poverty and inequity. The solution to these problems, which face every country of the Americas, mainly falls to each nation's government and citizens.

The Multilateral Issues

I. Joining our Economic Futures

• The nations of the Americas should agree on a blueprint for building hemisphere-wide free trade arrangements. These should eliminate nearly all restraints to the free flow of goods and capital; include mechanisms for resolving disputes; and offer a strategy for dealing with countries unable or unwilling to join in regional free trade. They must also be consistent with the global GATT agreements. In addition, the governments should establish a timetable for achieving the new trading arrangements and develop a regional mechanism to coordinate progress.

• The United States should make clear in advance of the summit its vision of a hemispheric free trade system. Approval of "fast-track" authority would do most to reaffirm the U.S. commitment to free hemispheric trade.

II. Strengthening Inter-American Institutions

• When the credibility of an election is at stake, the Permanent Council of the OAS should authorize the Secretary-General to organize a monitoring mission and issue a judgment on the integrity of the election. Where the constitutional order is endangered in other ways, the Secretary-General should be empowered to (a) undertake anticipatory diplomatic action to help avert impending threats and (b) manage OAS responses to outright violations of democratic process.

• The OAS's Unit for the Promotion of Democracy should work with governments and NGOs on a longer-term basis to help strengthen

September 1994.

key institutions of democracy: electoral machinery, judicial and legislative systems, and networks of nongovernmental groups.

• The Inter-American Commission and Court of Human Rights should redirect their work to investigating and adjudicating individual human rights violations, and to establishing a body of case law for national and international courts. Every country of the Americas should agree to ratify the American Convention on Human Rights and accept the jurisdiction of the Court.

• Governments should review all regional security arrangements and consider recasting or dismantling them in view of the changing regional context. The Inter-American Defense Board and College must be clearly subordinated to the civilian authority of the Secretary-General of the OAS. Governments should halt military-to-military programs that exclude civilian participation.

Recurring National Issues

I. The Consolidation of Effective Democracies

• All governments should rededicate themselves to forging vigorous democracies by consistently supporting democratic politics, denouncing violations, and defending regional norms. Every government should pledge to critically evaluate its own democratic practices and institutions, including executive-legislative relations, the administration of justice, civil and human rights protections, civilian control over security forces, and the accountability of political institutions. The effectiveness of public institutions must be enhanced, including efforts to eliminate corruption and expand access to all groups.

II. The Challenge of Poverty and Inequality

• The presidents and prime ministers should affirm their commitment to reducing social and economic inequities. Governments must sustain sound macroeconomic policies to encourage investment and growth; increase the collection of taxes to finance social spending; improve the delivery of services to their poorest citizens (who are disproportionately women, minorities, and indigenous peoples), and invest more in them.

• Every leader should commit to undertaking programs to improve the quality of schooling for all groups and agree to establish realistic goals, monitor student achievement, and evaluate school performance.

A Time for Leadership

• The nations of the hemisphere have an important opportunity to achieve real progress toward more enduring and productive ties, if the assembled leaders are prepared to meet three challenges: to face up to the failings of democratic practice and commit their nations to active programs of political renewal and social advance; to agree on a blueprint for building an economically integrated hemisphere joining countries through free flows of trade and investment; and to map out a plan for strengthening the OAS and other key regional institutions.

*A Report of the
Inter-American Dialogue
to The Summit of Presidents
and Prime Ministers of
the Americas*

The Americas in 1994:
A Time for Leadership

In December 1994, the presidents and prime ministers of the Americas will meet in Miami — at a time of broad inter-American convergence on three powerful ideas: democratic politics, free markets, and regional community.

Political democracy is now widely accepted as the only legitimate form of government in the Americas. Market-oriented economic policies — emphasizing macroeconomic stability, exports and foreign investment, and private sector initiative — have been adopted in most countries of Latin America and the Caribbean. Closer political and economic cooperation among the nations of the hemisphere is seen as crucial for defending and consolidating democracy, promoting human rights, achieving sustained economic progress, combatting poverty and inequality, and protecting the environment.

Rapid and dramatic changes throughout the hemisphere are responsible for this remarkable convergence on basic principles:

- Twenty years ago, most Latin American and Caribbean countries pursued inward-oriented development strategies behind high tariff walls. Today, virtually every country of the region has sharply reduced barriers to international trade and investment.

- Fifteen years ago, dictatorships ruled in all but a handful of Latin American countries, and human and political rights were brutally repressed in many places. Today, elected, constitutional regimes govern nearly all nations of the region, and human rights violations have been sharply curtailed in most.

- Even ten years ago, most Latin American governments would have had difficulty contemplating close economic cooperation with the United States. Today, the United States and Mexico are joined in a free trade agreement, and most other countries in the region say they want free trade with the United States as well as with each other.

- Just five years ago, Latin America and the Caribbean, after enduring nearly a decade of debt crisis, were still mired in economic depression. Today, the crisis has substantially receded, and growth has resumed in most countries. Throughout the 1980s, capital fled from Latin America; now more than $50 billion a year is flowing in.

- Five years ago, concern was widespread in Latin America that — with the end of the Cold War and other global changes — the United States and other industrialized nations would turn their political attention and economic interest to other parts of the world. Today, the countries of Latin America and the Caribbean are more fully engaged in the global community than ever before. International business has a growing stake in their

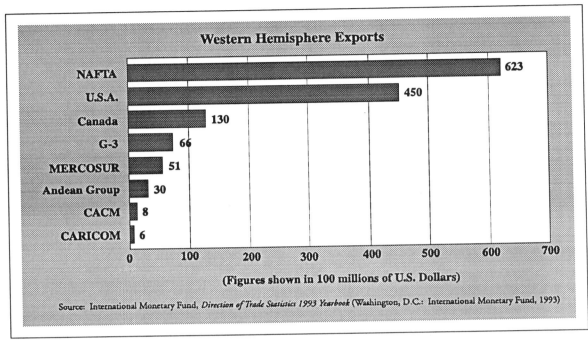

Figure 1. Western Hemisphere Exports

economies. Latin Americans serve worldwide in U.N. peacekeeping missions. Within the hemisphere, the two key international institutions — the Inter-American Development Bank (IDB) and the Organization of American States (OAS) — are more vigorous than ever and are poised to play expanding roles.

Latin America and the Caribbean still face formidable problems, however. Cuba remains a dictatorship, and its leaders so far have rejected democratic reform. After only seven months in office, Haiti's first freely chosen president was overthrown in 1991, and a cruel military regime holds power there. In Peru, the elected president suspended democratic rule and closed down parliament in 1992; formal constitutional rule has been restored, but power remains centralized in the presidency. President Balaguer retained office in the Dominican Republic through a tainted election in May 1994. And Venezuela's government is ruling under emergency powers that include the suspension of constitutional guarantees. Other elected governments — in Guatemala, Panama, and Trinidad and Tobago — have been threatened by coups d'ètat in the past few years. Human rights abuses are common in some countries, and security forces escape the control of elected authorities in many.

With few exceptions, economic policy reforms in Latin America and the Caribbean are still fragile. Economic growth remains sluggish in most countries, and export performance lags expectations. Decaying infrastructure stands as an obstacle to sustained growth. Overvalued exchange rates pose a risk to financial stability in several countries. And Brazil, the region's largest and most economically important country, has only recently shown progress in bringing inflation under control. By 1994, fewer than a third of the countries of Latin America and the Caribbean had regained the level of income per capita they had in 1980.

Most disturbing is the persistence and pervasiveness of poverty, inequality, and social injustice throughout Latin America and the Caribbean. Economic growth rates in the region are insufficient to reduce the number of persons living in poverty; these are disproportionately women, racial minorities, and indigenous peoples. Income inequality is the worst of any major region in the world, and there are no significant signs of improvement. (See Figure 2.) The failure of most Latin American and Caribbean countries to address effectively the problems of poverty, illiteracy, and malnutrition has placed the credibility of democratic institutions at risk and endangers macroeconomic progress.

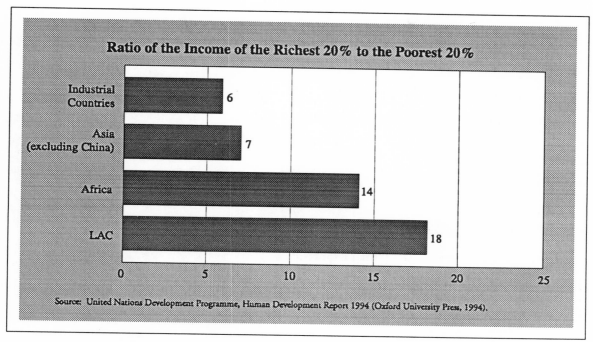

Figure 2. Comparative Indicators of Inequality by Region

Finally, although U.S.-Latin American relations today are mostly free of conflict, U.S. policies toward Haiti and Cuba, as well as U.S. antidrug programs, are controversial and opposed by many in the region. They could lead to increased confrontation in hemispheric affairs.

The upcoming Summit of the Americas — bringing together the elected presidents and prime ministers of the hemisphere — will be a time to celebrate the important gains of the past years, reaffirm shared principles and goals, and seek ways to take effective advantage of new opportunities for economic and political cooperation. Just as important, it will be a time to take stock of our common problems and concerns and to chart a future course of action that deals honestly and effectively with them.

In fixing the agenda for the summit and developing a mutually agreed program of action, the first emphasis should be on those issues that can only be dealt with multilaterally — on which progress requires international agreement, joint initiatives, and the cooperation of many countries. The main priorities should be (a) setting the foundations for a hemisphere linked by free trade and economic partnership and (b) strengthening the capacity of key

regional institutions and other mechanisms for inter-American cooperation.

The summit will also be an opportunity to focus attention on a second group of issues: those that recur in many countries of the Americas, but whose solutions must be sought mainly within each nation by that nation's government and citizens. The key issues here are fortifying democratic practice, enhancing protection of human rights, and reducing poverty and inequity through sustainable development. The assembled leaders should be prepared to commit their governments to confront these problems actively, to establish basic norms for progress, to share information and experiences, and to set in place mechanisms for monitoring and evaluation.

THE MULTILATERAL ISSUES

I. Joining our Economic Futures

Regional free trade is an idea that has taken hold among Western Hemisphere governments. Nearly every country of the Americas now participates in some form of free trade arrangement with its neighbors. NAFTA — which joins the United States, Canada, and Mexico — is only the most recent of six

MERCOSUR		
	US$100M	Total Exports
To:		
MERCOSUR	7	14%
United States	9	17%
Latin America & Caribbean	13	26%

NAFTA		
	US$100M	Total Exports
To:		
Latin America & Caribbean	80	13%
NAFTA	270	43%

Andean Pact		
	US$100M	Total Exports
To:		
Andean Pact	2	6%
Latin America & Caribbean	7	24%
United States	13	42%

United States		
	US$100M	Total Exports
To:		
Mexico	41	9%
Latin America & Caribbean	76	17%
NAFTA	131	29%

Latin America & Caribbean		
	US$100M	Total Exports
To:		
Latin America & Caribbean	28	18%
United States	62	42%

Source: International Monetary Fund, *Direction of Trade Statistics 1993 Yearbook* (Washington, DC: International Monetary Fund, 1993)

Box 1. Intra-Regional Trade

subregional trade pacts to go into force. Indeed, the proliferation of subregional and bilateral trade agreements, albeit a constructive and encouraging development, poses a challenge of coordination.

These trade initiatives, coupled with the broader restructuring and revitalization of Latin American and Caribbean economies, have led to an upsurge in intraregional trade — among the countries of Latin America and the Caribbean and between them and the United States and Canada. Particularly significant increases have occurred between countries joined in free trade pacts — like Argentina and Brazil in MERCOSUR; Venezuela and Colombia in the Group of Three and the Andean Pact; the members of the Central American Common Market; and the United States, Canada, and Mexico in NAFTA. (See Box 1.)

The lesson is that reduced import barriers and agreements to promote freer trade can, and do, lead to substantial trade expansion. Most countries of the hemisphere are counting on that expansion to help propel growth in the coming years. They are also looking to free trade arrangements to achieve other benefits — more stable and predictable access to major markets; a secure anchor for trade-liberalizing measures and other economic reforms; greater flows of overseas investment; and enhanced coordination

on a widening array of economic and financial matters.

The summit is the right setting for the nations of the Americas to agree on a blueprint for achieving a hemisphere-wide free trade system. This should be the priority objective of the meeting. Such an agreement would make a major contribution to sustained economic advance and, in addition, would facilitate cooperation on the range of other critical issues affecting the Americas. It should aim at achieving six basic goals:

- *A regional free trade and investment regime that eventually includes every nation of the Americas.* There should be no "second class" economic citizens in the hemisphere, and regional agreements should not discriminate against countries outside the hemisphere. The objective is more open and productive commercial relationships with all nations.

- *The elimination of restraints to the free flow of goods and capital.* The more barriers that are removed, the greater the economic gains over time. The end of most protection should be the objective of all countries within a reasonable phase-in period.

- *The development of effective regional mechanisms for resolving trade disputes.* Because such disputes are inevitable, the establishment of sound, mutually agreed procedures to resolve them may be the single most important benefit to be derived from regional integration.

- *A practical strategy for managing relations with those hemispheric countries that are either unable or unwilling to meet the requirements of a regional free trade pact.* It is important that no country be isolated economically or suffer unduly from trade and investment diversion during the transition period to an economically integrated hemisphere.

- *A specific timetable for achieving free hemispheric trading arrangements.* Although symbolically attractive, the year 2000 might well be too ambitious a target. The year 2005, hardly more than a decade from now, would be a more realistic time frame.

- *The development of a regional mechanism, consistent with the rules of the General Agreement on Tariffs and Trade (GATT), to guide progress toward a Western Hemisphere free trade area.* No existing regional organization currently has the mandate and expertise to exercise leadership on trade issues or to serve as a continuing source of data, analysis, policy review, and technical assistance. The first task of the new mechanism would be to coordinate the implementation of trade-related agreements reached at the summit.

Besides agreeing on these central goals for a hemispheric free trade system, participants in the summit should map out the next key steps that must be taken to proceed.

The countries of the hemisphere must first agree on how to go about building a free trade system. There are two main alternatives. NAFTA, given its economic importance within the hemisphere, could become the core of an expanding free trade area that incorporates other countries (or groups of countries) as they qualify and demonstrate an interest in joining. The advantage of this NAFTA-centered model is that it appears more straightforward than any other procedure and would lead directly to a unified set of trade and investment rules for all countries, producing the benefits of a single integrated market. Proceeding in this way, however, might well disrupt the important progress toward open trade that has already been achieved by other subregional groupings.

The second approach would emphasize the deepening and consolidation of economic integration within each subregion. That deepening and consolidation would be followed by negotiations between, and the eventual merging of, the different groups. This approach has the advantage of building on existing arrangements and strengthening partnerships that are already in place. It could, however, lead to a patchwork of separate trade groups with distinct rules, thereby frustrating the eventual formation of a single, hemisphere-wide free trade area.

In either case, the countries of each subregional group need to make explicit the conditions they expect other nations to meet in order to join or merge with their group. Ideally, the conditions required of new participants should not be significantly different from those demanded of current members. The NAFTA partners, for example, might agree to incorporate any country that is willing and able substantially to comply with the accord's current provisions, including its side agreements on labor rights and the environment.

At the summit, the nations of the Americas will have, for the first time ever, both the opportunity and responsibility to set in motion the building of a regional economic community that would over time enable every nation to become more productive and compete more effectively in the global economy. The foundation can be laid for enduring economic and social advance and for sustained political cooperation as well. The summit has no more important goal. To make it achievable, all countries will have to engage in intensive consultations prior to the hemispheric meeting and be prepared to reach agreement on some difficult issues.

Given the size of its economy — six times larger than all the economies of Latin America and the Caribbean combined — the United States must demonstrate leadership. If the summit is to succeed in reaching accord on free trade, the United States must make clear in advance its vision of hemispheric trade arrangements and how it proposes to pursue that vision. Approval of "fast-track" negotiating authority prior to the summit would, more than anything, reaffirm the United States' commitment to hemispheric free trade.

Inter-American Institutions*

The Organization of American States

The world's oldest regional organization, the OAS dates back to the First International Conference of American States, held in 1890. Its charter entered into force in 1951. The OAS currently has 35 member states and has granted permanent observer status to 25 states in Europe, Africa, Asia, the Holy See, and the European Economic Community. The purposes of the OAS are: to strengthen the security and peace of the continent; to promote and consolidate representative democracy; to prevent possible causes of and ensure pacific settlement of disputes that may arise among member states; to provide for common action on the part of member states in the event of aggression; to seek solution of judicial, political, and economic problems and to promote, by cooperative action, their social, economic, and cultural development; and to achieve an effective limitation of conventional weapons in order to devote the largest amount of resources to the social and economic development of the member states. Among the most important organs of the OAS are:

The Inter-American Economic and Social Council promotes cooperation among the nations of the Americas to achieve economic and social development.**

The *Inter-American Council on Education, Culture and Science* promotes hemispheric cooperation in these fields.**

The *Inter-American Juridical Committee* advises the OAS on juridical matters and promotes the development and codification of international law.

The Inter-American Commission on Human Rights was established in 1959 to promote the observance and protection of human rights and to advise the OAS in this area.

The Inter-American Court of Human Rights, established in July 1978, is an autonomous judicial institution whose purpose is to apply and interpret the American Convention on Human Rights. Seven judges from member countries sit on the bench of the Court.

The Unit for the Promotion of Democracy was established in 1990 to provide advisory services (research, training, and information exchange) and direct assistance (technical assistance, election monitoring, and other aid requested by member states). Priorities for its agenda are technical support to electoral organizations, legislative training, and civic education.

Inter-American Development Bank

The largest and oldest regional multilateral development institution, the IDB was founded in December 1959 to promote social and economic development in Latin America and the Caribbean. Its principal functions are to finance the development of the borrowing member countries, to supplement private investment, and to provide technical assistance for development plans and projects. The Bank emphasizes industry and agriculture, transportation and energy, and health, education, and urban development. Bank membership includes 46 nations.

The Pan American Health Organization

PAHO was established in 1902 to promote and coordinate the efforts of the nations of the Americas to combat disease, prolong life, and improve the mental and physical health of their peoples.

United Nations Economic Commission for Latin America and the Caribbean

ECLAC provides a variety of statistical, analytical, advisory, and training services to Latin American and Caribbean countries.

*See also Box 4 - Regional Military Institutions

**These two councils are to be merged into the Inter-American Council for Integral Development under a pending reform of the OAS Charter.

Box 2. Inter-American Institutions

II. Strengthening Inter-American Institutions

In 1928, Franklin Roosevelt wrote, "It is possible that, in the days to come, one of our sister nations may fall upon evil days; disorder and bad government may require a helping hand be given her citizens as a matter of temporary necessity to bring back order and stability. In that event it is not the right or the duty of the United States to intervene alone. It is rather the duty of the United States to associate itself with other American Republics, to give intelligent joint study to the problem and, if the conditions warrant, to offer the helping hand or hands in the name of the Americas. Single-handed intervention by us in the internal affairs of other nations must end; with the cooperation of others we shall have more order in this hemisphere and less dislike."

Roosevelt's advice explains the need for strong inter-American institutions to make cooperation work among the nations of the Americas. Such institutions are required to give the governments of the hemisphere the capacity to act collectively to secure peace, assist countries in distress, defend democracy and human rights, and advance social justice. The summit will allow the presidents and prime ministers an opportunity jointly to review the institutions of inter-American cooperation, assess their mandates and performance, and decide how to reshape the hemisphere's institutional framework to manage hemispheric affairs better. (See Box 2.)

The two most important regional institutions — the Inter-American Development Bank (IDB) and the Organization of American States (OAS) — have made important progress in the past several years, gaining in stature and competence and expanding their roles.

The nations of the hemisphere, as well as the other participating countries, affirmed their confidence in the IDB earlier this year at the Bank's annual meeting in Guadalajara, Mexico. The capital available to the IDB was nearly doubled to about $100 billion, allowing for a lending program of some $7.5 billion a year for the countries of Latin America and the Caribbean. (See Figure 3.) In the past few years, the Bank has redefined its priorities so that they are fundamentally consistent with those that should be emphasized at the summit, including the fight against poverty and inequality; initiatives to strengthen public institutions in such areas as education, health, social security, and the administration of justice; new efforts to promote environmental protection and sustainable development; and expanded investment in infrastructure to overcome years of dissaving and facilitate export-led growth. The IDB is poised effectively to advance each of these priorities.

Defending Democracy

The OAS is also a more active and important institution today than it was several years ago. Since 1990, it has taken on an important role in safeguarding democracy — particularly in monitoring elections where there is potential for fraud or conflict and responding to violations of constitutional order. (See Box 3.) The pathbreaking decision was the OAS General Assembly's June 1991 approval of Resolution 1080, which mandated that the governments of the hemisphere act collectively against challenges to democracy in the hemisphere and seek to restore democratic rule when it is ruptured. By allowing the OAS to suspend the membership of governments that come to power illegally, the Washington Protocol, approved in 1992, reinforced the idea that the OAS is a "community of democracies."

OAS actions to restore constitutional government in Haiti, Peru, and Guatemala — the three cases in which it was forcibly interrupted since the approval of Resolution 1080 — have produced mixed results. An attempted coup in Guatemala in June 1993 was aborted and the constitutional order reinstated. Although the formal trappings of democracy have been restored in Peru, power remains concentrated in the presidency and the army, which operate with few effective constraints. In Haiti, the OAS failed to return elected President Jean-Bertrand Aristide to power, and the effort has largely been taken over by the U.S. government and the United Nations.

With a new secretary-general of the OAS now in office, the summit is the right opportunity for leaders of the hemisphere to agree upon a program of action to bolster the capacity of the OAS — to turn it into a more effective mechanism for strengthening the basic institutions of democracy, for safeguarding democratic rule when it is threatened, and for helping to repair breakdowns in the constitutional order. The presidents and prime ministers should endorse two initiatives to accomplish these goals.

First, the secretary-general of the OAS should be granted the authority, and necessary financial and

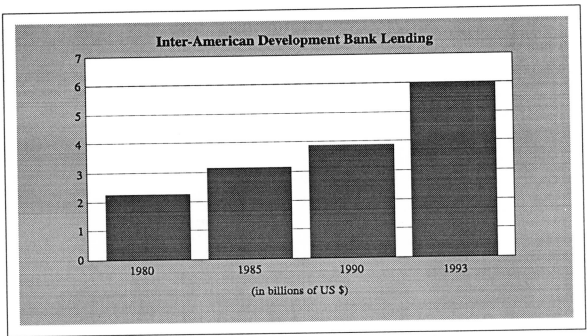

Figure 3. Inter-American Development Bank Lending

staff resources, to exert leadership in cases where democratic rule is endangered. Whenever the honesty and credibility of an election is at stake, the Permanent Council should authorize the secretary-general to organize an electoral monitoring mission, issue a judgment on the integrity of the election, and recommend OAS action in response to irregularities. Where the constitutional order is threatened in other ways, the secretary-general should be empowered by the Council (or, when appropriate, by a special meeting of the foreign ministers) to (a) undertake anticipatory diplomatic action to help avert the impending threats and (b) manage OAS responses to outright violations of democratic process. To carry out these responsibilities, the Secretary-General will require a significant professional staff with capacity to gather and analyze information in difficult situations, devise alternative strategies of response, and organize reconciliation and mediation efforts.

Second, the OAS's Unit for the Promotion of Democracy should be assigned a professional, long-term role. It should not engage in crisis management, but work with governments and NGOs to help build and strengthen key institutions of democracy: electoral machinery, judicial and legislative systems, and networks of nongovernmental groups. To do this, the Unit will require increased financing and better-

trained staff and will need to develop close working relations with many public and private institutions, including think tanks, human rights and democracy advocacy groups, and local community organizations. The Secretary-General, in turn, should be able to count on the assistance of the Unit's staff and

---

**Organization of American States
ELECTION MONITORING MISSIONS**

1990: Nicaragua, Haiti
1991: El Salvador, Suriname, Paraguay
1992: Peru, Paraguay
1993: Peru, Honduras, Venezuela
1994: Panama, Dominican Republic

*Box 3. Organization of American States:
Election Monitoring Missions*

expertise in election monitoring missions and other efforts to defend democratic practice.

Advancing Human Rights

The OAS agencies established to protect human rights — the Inter-American Commission and the Inter-American Court — should be reshaped to fit the evolving political circumstances of Latin America and effectively meet the new challenges to individual and civil rights. During the 1970s and 1980s, when dictators dominated Latin American politics, the Commission played a critical role in defending the rights of opposition groups; it responded to gross and systematic rights violations in many countries, and it exposed the governments and individuals responsible. With the return of constitutional rule to nearly all of Latin America, both the Commission and Court appear to have lost their clarity of purpose. Their vitality has ebbed, and they seem to be losing support in some countries. Their efforts to protect and advance human rights must continue. They should be redirected, however, now that violations result mainly from the inability or unwillingness of weak elected governments to control their security forces, rather than from the deliberate abuses of repressive regimes.

The work of the Commission and the Court should be refocused on the investigation and adjudication of individual cases of human rights violations — although country reports should still be prepared where patterns of persistent or gross violations appear. The idea is to depoliticize the handling of human rights claims, allow for their quick disposition, and establish a body of case law that could be drawn upon by both national and international courts. The emphasis of the Court and Commission, in short, should be on resolving individual cases and developing legal precedents. The leaders assembled at the summit should pledge to (a) substantially expand the staff and financial resources available to both institutions; (b) support the election of judges and commissioners who meet the highest standards of competence and integrity; and (c) respect fully the autonomy of the institutions.

Finally, it is fundamental that every country of the Americas ratify the American Convention on Human Rights and accept the jurisdiction of the Court. Nothing would do more to reinforce the inter-American system of human rights. (To date, 25 of 35 member countries are parties to the Convention; only 16 have accepted the Court's jurisdiction.)

Military Institutions

With the end of the Cold War, the military institutions established for the common defense of the Americas no longer serve their initial purposes. The presidents and prime ministers should be prepared to review all regional security arrangements and consider recasting or dismantling them. (See Box 4.)

Founded in 1942, prior to the OAS, the Inter-American Defense Board is the region's oldest military institution. The Board is an independent agency

---

Regional Military Institutions

The Inter-American Defense Board was established in 1942 to study and recommend measures for the defense of the hemisphere during World War II. An independent agency whose members are active-duty military officers, the IADB's principal functions are to plan the hemisphere's collective defense and to help strengthen military cooperation among the countries of the Americas.

The Inter-American Defense College provides one or two years of special military training to U.S. and Latin American military officers.

The Conference of American Armies annually assembles the commanding officers of the U.S. and Latin American armies in an atmosphere of professional exchange and consultation. *The Conference of Air Force Chiefs* is a similar, although less institutionalized, exchange for that branch of the service.

Operation UNITAS is a joint naval exercise involving many countries of the hemisphere.

Box 4. Regional Military Institutions

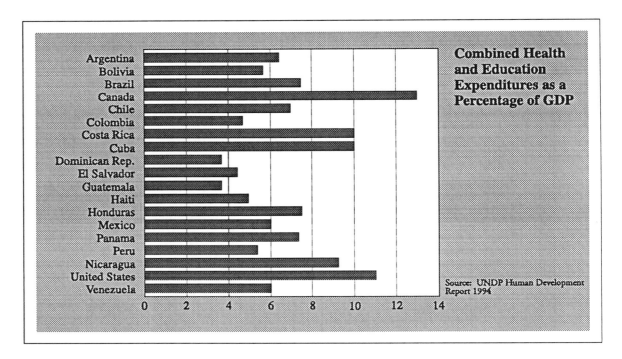

Figure 4. Health and Education Spending in Latin America

whose members are active-duty military officers; it was originally intended as a coordinating mechanism for regional defense initiatives and policies, but today no longer serves that purpose except as a point of exchange for military leaders. One course would be for the governments of the hemisphere to reformulate its structure, mandate, and mission and make it an integral part of the OAS system. An alternative would be to abolish the Board.

The governments should also review the Inter-American Defense College, which provides training to U.S. and Latin American military officers, and decide whether it serves an important need. The College should, at a minimum, also be placed firmly under the authority of the OAS and instructed to incorporate far more civilians and assign more attention to issues related to civil-military relations and the defense of democracy.

The leaders assembled at the summit should initiate a reassessment of the many military-to-military programs that exclude civilian participation and oversight. The Conference of American Armies, for example, regularly assembles the commanding officers of U.S. and Latin American armies for strategy and policy discussions. The Conference of Air Force Chiefs has a similar purpose. Operation UNITAS is a

joint naval exercise involving many countries of the hemisphere. It is time to reconsider these exclusively military activities. The governments of the hemisphere should call for a meeting of their ministers of defense — who more clearly respond to civilian authority — to rethink what kinds of exchanges among the region's armed forces would be appropriate and useful and to assure they are subordinated to civilian control.

RECURRING NATIONAL ISSUES

I. The Consolidation of Effective Democracies

The presidents and prime ministers participating in the summit should celebrate Latin America's turn toward democracy in recent years — but they must also confront the hard fact that the region's democratic trend has yet to produce robust and vigorous democracies. In many countries, citizens are increasingly disaffected. Presidential power is inadequate in some countries and excessive in others. Parliaments, legislatures, courts, and political parties are often inept, powerless, and unaccountable. Corruption is widespread in the Americas, and common crime has

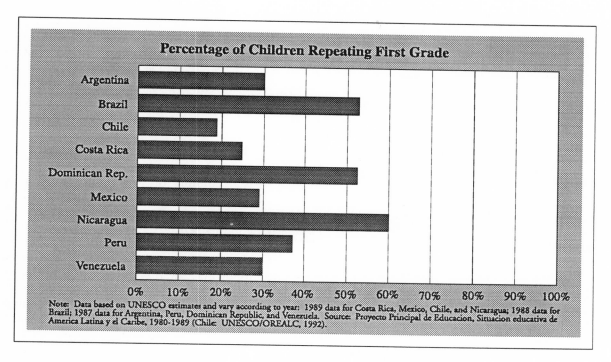

Figure 5. Percentage of Children Repeating First Grade

become pandemic. The dismal performance of democratic institutions has left them vulnerable — threatened by armies in a few countries and by the growing alienation of common citizens in many.

In nearly every country, a dramatic and welcome shift occurred in the quality and openness of political life following the transition from authoritarian rule to elected, civilian government. Yet sustained progress toward effective democratic practice has not occurred in most places. There has not been a satisfactory deepening and widening of democratic norms, procedures, or institutions in the region. Few countries have made steady advances toward the building of judicial systems and legislatures that are competent, honest, and accessible — or parties that are responsible and representative. Human rights abuses declined sharply with the end of military rule but are still common in many places. In only a handful of nations have the armed forces withdrawn from politics and been brought under civilian authority.

At the summit, the nations of the hemisphere together must come to grips with the political failures that have left democratic rule ineffective and increasingly vulnerable in many countries. All governments should rededicate themselves to the task of forging vigorous democratic systems. Collective international

efforts can be helpful in important ways — by consistently supporting democratic politics, by disclosing and denouncing violations, and by setting and defending regional norms. The primary challenge of protecting and deepening democracy falls to the governments and citizens of each country, however.

There is no ready diagnosis or easy remedy for the multiple shortcomings to democracy in the hemisphere. Every government at the summit should pledge to undertake a critical self-evaluation of its own democratic practices and institutions — making sure to include attention to such key areas as executive-legislative relations, the administration of justice, civil and human rights protections, civilian control over armies and police forces, and the broad accountability of political institutions. Such an evaluation — if done right, with the participation of many groups inside and outside of government — can become the basis for a broad national debate on democracy and for a systematic program of action. Each country is likely to take this initiative seriously to the extent that others do.

For most Latin American nations, securing and consolidating stable democracy will require even more than sustained political and legal reform. Efforts must be made to enhance the effectiveness of public institutions — including the elimination of widespread governmental corruption and the expansion of access to all groups. The credibility of democratic governments, and ultimately democracy itself, depends on the performance of public institutions — on whether they are viewed as honest, effective, and serving all citizens.

II. The Challenge of Poverty and Inequality

The presidents and prime ministers gathered for the summit should affirm as well their commitment to reducing social and economic inequities in their own societies. This is an immense challenge that few Latin American nations have confronted successfully during this century. There are no new or easy solutions to poverty or inequality. What governments must do is sustain sound and disciplined macroeconomic policies that will encourage investment and growth; increase the collection of taxes to finance greater social spending; and improve the delivery of services to and expand investments in their poorest citizens. (See Figure 4.) International and bilateral financing agencies can assist in critical ways, but facing up to the social challenge — like democracy building — is mainly a task for each nation.

Improvements in education are especially crucial to raising the productivity of low-income groups and narrowing income disparities — as, indeed, they are to bolstering international competitiveness and to promoting democracy. Yet, most countries of the hemisphere have allowed the quality of their educational systems to deteriorate in recent years. (See Figure 5.) The summit is the right time for a collective commitment to reverse this trend.

Every leader should commit his government to undertake substantial programs to enhance the quality of schooling for all groups — but particularly for the most disadvantaged and vulnerable. Each country should agree to establish realistic goals, monitor student achievement through national testing, and create mechanisms for evaluating school performance. Although each nation will require its own reform program, key elements will inevitably include a combination of decentralized management; better-trained and more professional teachers; and increased involvement of parents, employers, and other social groups in devising and implementing programs. Educational policy should link secondary education to labor markets and foster partnerships between schools and businesses. Ideally, the presidents and prime ministers should agree to develop a few concrete programs that could be applied hemisphere-wide—as a guide and a prod to educational reform in all countries.

A TIME FOR LEADERSHIP

The Summit of the Americas is a special event. Some 35 heads of state will assemble to discuss the shared interests and concerns of their countries. It will be disappointing if the summit turns out to be mainly a symbolic affair. Participants should not be content simply to celebrate the democratic gains of the past 15 years or to applaud existing economic and political cooperation. At the summit, the nations of the hemisphere will have an important opportunity to achieve real progress toward more enduring and productive ties—if the assembled leaders are prepared to meet three challenges:

- To face up to the failings of democratic practice in country after country and truly commit their nations to active programs of political renewal and social advance.

- To agree on a blueprint for building an economically integrated hemisphere joining all countries through free flows of trade and investment.

- To go beyond reaffirming commitments to cooperative ties—and to map out a plan for jointly attacking the hemisphere's common problems and for strengthening the OAS and other key regional institutions.

It will require courage and imagination from the leaders assembled at the summit to take on the substantive decisions needed to build genuine partnerships in the Americas. The summit will be a test of their leadership and their commitment to hemispheric community.

Supplemental Comments

From Members of the Dialogue

Raúl Alfonsín

I wish to express a reservation about free trade. Trade liberalization must be accomplished through a careful process that does not harm national industry. Also, I believe we should urge that the U.S. embargo against Cuba be lifted, as recently proposed by the Rio Group of Latin American countries.

Peggy Antrobus

While recognizing the "persistence of poverty, inequality, and social injustice throughout Latin America and the Caribbean," the report ignores the contradiction between macroeconomic policies favoring corporate interests and the welfare of ordinary people. Instead of free trade, the report should emphasis that fair trade is required between unequal partners. Given the concerns of labor and environmental groups, it is too soon to consider NAFTA as a framework for the entire region.

Economic globalization presents the island states of the Caribbean with special problems. Because they are so small and vulnerable, government policies are needed to protect disadvantaged groups and fragile ecological systems. Under market-oriented policies, the gap between rich and poor likely will widen with poverty, unemployment, and social disintegration increasing. The leaders at the Summit of the Americas should seek to place macroeconomic policies at the service of people rather than powerful interest groups. It is time for more reflective leadership.

Lee Cullum

As a journalist who might write about this report, I must stand on the disclaimer in the introduction: the views expressed in the document are not necessarily my own. Especially, I would add my reservations at this point about the U.S. accepting jurisdiction of the Inter-American Court. This seems to me premature. The report overall, however, strikes the right tone and holds much promise for the hemisphere.

Karen DeYoung

As a practicing journalist involved in coverage of United States government policy, I make no endorsement of the policy recommendations on trade and U.S. involvement in multilateral organizations contained in this report.

Maurice Ferré

As a firm supporter of the Cuban Democracy Act, I would oppose any recommendation in the economic section that does not require full adherence to this legislation.

Richard W. Fisher

I wish to disassociate myself with any recommendation for greater taxation in the Americas. What is needed is more efficient tax collection in Latin America and sound macroeconomic policies to bring central government spending under control. Also, the report fails to note that the United States has a significant debt problem. The U.S. government should be urged further and sharply to reduce its budget deficits.

Douglas A. Fraser

I want to disassociate myself from the report's references to NAFTA.

Andrew Goodpaster

The section on military institutions has an excessively negative slant. With the rise of democracy and the demise of communism, the Americas, like most of the rest of the world, have come to a new era of security and confidence and a time of redefining the role of military force. Military institutions and associations that were developed and proved their value in the past can play a highly constructive role. The reduction and restructuring of military forces, the building of civilian-military relationships appropriate to democratic governments, the shared understanding of the new strategic environment, and the relation of multinational military institutions to the OAS, offer a challenging avenue for both civilian and military participation, to which the military institutions cited in the report can contribute in important ways. This is a time, and that is a way, to "accentuate the positive."

Xabier Gorostiaga, S.J.

I wish to offer three comments. First, I am concerned about a growing crisis of leadership and credibility, perhaps even legitimacy, in many countries of the region. Market economies must be democratized in order to create stable, deeply rooted, and enduring democracies. Second, I believe that NAFTA should not be emphasized as a path to hemispheric integration since it corresponds more to a U.S. strategy than to real partnerships among all countries. Third, Haiti and Cuba are being excluded from regional initiatives; in both cases, U.S. unilateralism is part of the problem, not of the solution.

Carla A. Hills

I am concerned that seeking hemispheric free trade through the "deepening and consolidation" of multiple agreements would inevitably lead to undesirable complexity. One trade model, such as the core obligations of the North American Free Trade Agreement, should be the operative premise for achieving free trade in the hemisphere.

John T. Joyce

I fundamentally agree with the Dialogue's report, although I believe that its emphasis is misplaced in several key areas. Free trade, for example, is a worthwhile objective—but it should not take precedence over efforts to strengthen democratic institutions, eliminate poverty, or promote equality and social justice. Indeed, these objectives must be addressed together in policy and in practice. Free trade agreements should be designed to achieve economic and social advance among all groups; they should be conditioned on respect for democracy and human rights; and they should include provisions for cushioning the inevitable economic dislocations they cause individuals and communities. These are the kinds of free trade arrangements that we should all be working toward.

Elsa Kelly

I disagree with the idea of making NAFTA the core of an expanding free trade club. The MERCOSUR was established to increase the size of markets and raise productivity through specialization and sectoral cooperation. But it also has the purpose of strengthening our capacity to negotiate with the United States and other industrialized countries. The idea is to transform the MERCOSUR countries into actors in the global economy—which could not be achieved under NAFTA's "umbrella."

Celso Lafer

I welcome this report as a positive contribution to the debate on the key issues of Western Hemisphere relations. I am not, however, comfortable in endorsing it in its entirety since many points, I believe, require further analysis and qualification. For example, I am not sure, considering the complexity of negotiations on "rules of origin," that a NAFTA-centered model is the most straightforward for a hemisphere free trade system. Also, even though I agree that regional security arrangements must be reexamined and recast, more extensive analysis is needed before proposing that the existing arrangements be dismantled.

Fernando Léniz

The document fails to emphasize sufficiently the main cause of poverty and political instability in Latin America: the crisis confronting education throughout the region. Educational reform is our most urgent need. The resources devoted to education should be increased threefold. We must prepare our people to understand the rapidly changing world and give them the knowledge and skills to be productive and creative. Unless this is done, efforts to strengthen national and international institutions cannot be effective.

Manuel Moreno Fraginals

I agree in general with the report but have three observations. First, the dictatorial and oppressive regimes of Cuba and Haiti should not be paired with the *provisional* suspension of constitutional guarantees in Venezuela, which confronted an unprecedented and inherited economic crisis, in accord with the country's laws. Second, the section on democracy avoids discussion of Cuba and Haiti, which should be fundamental topics at the summit. The Latin American presidents are likely to raise the issue of the U.S. embargo as they did at their recent meeting in Rio. Should not the Dialogue demand effective steps toward democracy in Cuba in exchange for an end to the embargo? Third, I think the report should include a paragraph about freedom of information as an elemental human right.

Celina Vargas do Amaral Peixoto

It is important to improve regional communication not only among states but also among citizens and their groups. Ordinary citizens and nongovernmental organizations should be represented at the OAS and allowed to express their ideas and concerns.

Charles Pilliod

I have reservations about the use of economic trade sanctions on behalf of human rights. Over time, this works out to our economic detriment, as we lose markets that are hard to regain later.

Alberto Quirós Corradi

I am concerned about the weaknesses of hemispheric leaders and institutions, which prevent them from agreeing on serious solutions to the crucial issues discussed in the report and to such others as Cuba and Haiti. I fear that the summit will wind up avoiding the most important problems. Although I support the report's analysis and recommendations, I disagree with its implicit endorsement of the summit.

Shridath Ramphal

The statement "Cuba remains an oppressive dictatorship" oversimplifies a complex reality. I would prefer to say, "Despite the rigors of a U.S. economic embargo, Cuba remains obstinately authoritarian." NAFTA's side agreements retain a substantial *sui generis* character. The notion of "signing on" without negotiation is not, I believe, an ideal way forward for the Hemisphere.

Augusto Ramírez Ocampo

The summit should adopt a new paradigm for the hemisphere: sustainable human development. A common agenda should be developed in the next ten years and joint mechanisms established to deal with the potentially most controversial issues, including environmental protection, antidrug initiatives, and regulation of migration.

Brent Scowcroft

I disagree with the tone of the recommendations regarding inter-American military institutions and exchanges. The U.S. military should be working closely with Latin American militaries, giving particular emphasis to the development of a greater commitment to democratic practices in the region's armed forces.

Paula Stern

I want to emphasize that hemispheric free trade agreements should be models of "open regionalism," specifically allowing for the accession of countries outside the hemisphere that are willing and able to meet the agreed-upon conditions. It should be recalled that four countries of the Americas—Canada, Chile, Mexico, and the United States—are participants in APEC, the Asia and Pacific trade group.

Mario Vargas Llosa

I do not share the optimistic appraisal of the Organization of American States, an organization which I think has failed — particularly in the cases of Peru, Haiti, and Cuba — in its obligation to promote and defend democracy in the Americas.

Members of the Inter-American Dialogue

FROM LATIN AMERICA, THE CARIBBEAN, AND CANADA

Mariclaire Acosta Urquidi

Mariclaire Acosta is president of the Mexican Commission for the Defense and Promotion of Human Rights, and a founder of the Mexican Academy for Human Rights.

Raúl Alfonsín

Raúl Alfonsín was president of Argentina from 1983 until 1989. He is president of the Radical Party and was cofounder of the Permanent Assembly for Human Rights.

Peggy Antrobus

Peggy Antrobus, of Barbados, is tutor and coordinator of the Women and Development Unit at the University of the West Indies.

Oscar Arias

Oscar Arias was president of Costa Rica. He is president of the Oscar Arias Foundation and earned the Nobel Prize for Peace.

Nicolás Ardito Barletta

Nicolás Ardito Barletta is president and general director of the International Center for Economic Growth. He was formerly president of Panama and vice president of the World Bank for Latin America and the Caribbean.

Sergio Bitar

Sergio Bitar is a national senator from the northern region of Tarapaca in Chile.

José Octavio Bordón

José Octavio Bordón is a national senator and former governor of the province of Mendoza, Argentina.

Rodrigo Botero

Rodrigo Botero served as minister of finance of Colombia and is the founder of the Foundation for Higher Education and Development in Bogotá.

Margaret Catley-Carlson

Margaret Catley-Carlson is president of the Population Council. She was deputy minister for health and welfare in Canada and president of the Canadian International Development Agency.

Roberto Civita

Roberto Civita is chairman and CEO of Abril, S.A., Brazil's largest publishing and pay TV company.

Oliver F. Clarke

Oliver F. Clarke is chairman of the board and managing director of The Gleaner Company, Jamaica's largest newspaper publisher.

Gisèle Côté-Harper

Gisèle Côté-Harper, Q.C., is a barrister who teaches law at Lavalle University in Quebec. She is chair of the International Center for Human Rights and Democratic Development.

José María Dagnino Pastore

José María Dagnino Pastore is professor of economics at the Catholic University of Argentina. He served as minister of finance, minister of economy and labor, and ambassador-at-large in Europe.

Enrique Dreyfus

Enrique Dreyfus was foreign minister of Nicaragua. He has served as president of Nicaragua's principal business federation.

Oscar Espinosa

Oscar Espinosa is managing director of Enrique Ferreyros, S.A. in Peru. He was the chairman and president of Peru's National Development Corporation.

Carlos Filizzola, M.D.

Carlos Filizzola is the first democratically elected mayor of Asunción. He served as deputy secretary-general of Paraguay's largest labor association.

Alejandro J. Foxley (acting co-chair)

Alejandro Foxley is president of the Christian Democratic Party in Chile. He was Chile's finance minister.

Xabier Gorostiaga, S.J.

Xabier Gorostiaga is the rector of the Universidad Centroamericana in Nicaragua and president of the Regional Center for Economic and Social Research (CRIES). He was director of national planning for Nicaragua.

Ivan L. Head

Ivan Head is a professor at the University of British Columbia. He was president of the International Development Research Centre of Canada and special assistant to the prime minister for foreign policy issues.

Osvaldo Hurtado Larrea

Osvaldo Hurtado was president of Ecuador. He is president of CORDES, a research center in Ecuador.

Elsa Kelly

Elsa Kelly is a congressional deputy to the Argentine National Congress. She has served as deputy minister of foreign affairs, ambassador to UNESCO, and as a member of the OAS Commission on Human Rights.

Pedro-Pablo Kuczynski

Pedro-Pablo Kuczynski is president and chief executive officer of Westfield Capital and vice chairman of CAP, S.A., of Chile. He was previously minister of energy and mines in Peru.

Celso Lafer

Celso Lafer is professor of public international law and jurisprudence at the University of São Paulo and the chairman of the board of Metal Leve. He served as Brazil's minister of foreign relations.

Augustín Legorreta

Augustín Legorreta is chairman and chief executive officer of Grupo Financiero Inverlat. He has been president of the Mexican Bankers Association and president of the Business Coordinating Council.

Jorge Paulo Lemann

Jorge Paulo Lemann is founder and senior partner of Banco de Investimentos Garantia S.A., of Brazil. He serves on the board of the Catholic University of Rio de Janeiro, Ação Comunitária, and Fundação Estudar, a scholarship program for university students.

Fernando Léniz

Fernando Léniz is chairman of the board of several major companies and foundations in Chile. He served as finance minister of Chile.

Marcos McGrath

Monsignor Marcos McGrath, C.S.C. is retired archbishop of Panama. He served as vice president of the Council of Latin American Bishops.

Barbara McDougall

Barbara McDougall was foreign minister of Canada. She is an international business strategist.

Beatriz Merino

Beatriz Merino is representative for corporate affairs at Procter & Gamble Latin America. She was a national senator in Peru.

Manuel Moreno Fraginals

Manuel Moreno Fraginals is a leading Cuban historian and has participated in collaborative international projects on the history of the Americas.

Roberto H. Murray Meza

Roberto Murray Meza is president of La Constancia, S.A., El Salvador's largest brewery. He has served as president of the Social Investment Fund and as an advisor to the minister of culture.

Sylvia Ostry

Sylvia Ostry is chancellor of the University of Waterloo, chair of the Centre for International Studies, chair of the Canadian Institute of International Affairs, and a member of the G-30 in Washington.

Celina Vargas do Amaral Peixoto

Celina Vargas do Amaral Peixoto is general director of the Getulio Vargas Foundation. She was director of Brazil's National Archives and president of the Latin American Association of Archives.

José Francisco Peña Gómez

José Francisco Peña Gómez was a candidate for president of the Dominican Republic this year. The election has been rescheduled because of irregularities. He earlier served as mayor of Santo Domingo.

Jacqueline Pitanguy

Jacqueline Pitanguy is the founding president of CEPIA, a private research organization on women's issues in Brazil.

Alberto Quirós Corradi

Alberto Quirós Corradi is president of Seguros Panamerican in Caracas. He was president of Shell of Venezuela and director of *El Nacional*.

Augusto Ramírez Ocampo

Augusto Ramírez Ocampo served as foreign minister of Colombia and led the U.N. mission in El Salvador.

Shridath Ramphal

Sir Shridath Ramphal was the secretary-general of the Commonwealth and later chairman of the West Indian Commission. He is now cochairman of the Commission on Global Governance and a member of the Latin American and Caribbean Commission on Development and Environment.

Julio María Sanguinetti

Julio María Sanguinetti was president of Uruguay. He is president of the PAX Institute.

Juan Manuel Santos

Juan Manuel Santos was vice president and minister of trade in Colombia. He is now deputy-publisher and editor-in-chief of *El Tiempo* of Bogotá.

Javier Silva Ruete

Javier Silva Ruete has served as a senator, as minister of economy and finance, and minister of labor of Peru.

Maurice Strong

Maurice Strong is the chairman of Ontario Hydro and chairman of the Earth Council. He was the first president of the Canadian International Development Agency, executive director of the United Nations' Environment Program, and secretary-general of the 1992 United Nations Conference on Environment and Development.

Gabriel Valdés

Gabriel Valdés is president of the Chilean senate. He served as Chile's minister of foreign relations and as president of the Christian Democratic Party.

Mario Vargas Llosa

Mario Vargas Llosa is a distinguished novelist. His latest book is *Lituma in Los Andes*.

FROM THE UNITED STATES

Michael D. Barnes

Michael Barnes is a partner at Hogan & Hartson. He was a member of Congress from Maryland and chaired the Subcommittee on Western Hemisphere Affairs.

Peter D. Bell (co-chair)

Peter D. Bell is president of the Edna McConnell Clark Foundation. He is chairman of CARE and of Americas Watch.

Kathleen Brown

Kathleen Brown is the treasurer of the state of California and a candidate for governor.

McGeorge Bundy

McGeorge Bundy is a scholar-in-residence at the Carnegie Corporation of New York. He was president of the Ford Foundation and national security advisor to presidents Kennedy and Johnson.

Terence C. Canavan

Terence Canavan was executive vice president of Chemical Bank. He is the chairman of Acción.

Jimmy Carter

Jimmy Carter was president of the United States. He is chairman of the Carter Center of Emory University in Atlanta and of the Council of Freely Elected Heads of Government.

A.W. Clausen

A.W. Clausen served as president of the World Bank and chairman and chief executive officer of BankAmerica Corporation and Bank of America NT&SA. He is now an honorary director of the Board of Directors of the Corporation and the Bank.

Lee Cullum

Lee Cullum is a columnist for *The Dallas Morning News* and a featured commentator on the "MacNeil/Lehrer NewsHour."

Ralph P. Davidson

Ralph Davidson was chairman of Time, Inc. and president of the John F. Kennedy Center for the Performing Arts.

Karen DeYoung

Karen DeYoung is assistant managing editor for national news at *The Washington Post*.

Jorge I. Domínguez

Jorge Domínguez is the Frank G. Thomson professor of government at Harvard University.

Lawrence Eagleburger

Lawrence Eagleburger was U.S. secretary of state. He is senior foreign policy advisor at the law firm of Baker, Worthington, Crossley & Stansberry.

Dianne Feinstein

Dianne Feinstein is a U.S. senator from California and a former mayor of San Francisco.

Antonio Luis Ferré

Antonio Luis Ferré is president of *El Nuevo Día*, Puerto Rico's major newspaper, and vice president of the Economic Development Committee of Puerto Rico. He is vice chairman of the board of Banco Popular and of Puerto Rican Cement.

Maurice A. Ferré

Maurice Ferré served twelve years as mayor of Miami and is the vice chairman of the Metropolitan Dade County Commission.

Richard W. Fisher

Richard Fisher is candidate for U.S. senator from Texas. He is managing partner of Fisher Capital Management of Dallas and chairman of the Dallas Committee on Foreign Relations.

Albert Fishlow

Albert Fishlow is professor of economics at the University of California at Berkeley, where he earlier served as director of international and area studies.

Douglas A. Fraser

Douglas Fraser is professor of labor studies at Wayne State University and co-chair of the Michigan Governor's Commission on Jobs and Economic Development. He was president of the United Auto Workers.

Andrew J. Goodpaster

General Andrew Goodpaster, U.S. Army (Ret.), is co-chairman of the Atlantic Council of the United States. He was staff secretary to President Eisenhower, superintendent of the U.S. Military Academy at West Point, and supreme commander of the Allied Forces in Europe.

David Hamburg

David Hamburg, M.D., is president of the Carnegie Corporation of New York. He was president and chairman of the board of the American Association for the Advancement of Science and president of the Institute of Medicine of the National Academy of Sciences.

Antonia Hernández

Antonia Hernández is president and general counsel of the Mexican-American Legal Defense Fund.

Theodore M. Hesburgh

Theodore M. Hesburgh, C.S.C., is president emeritus of the University of Notre Dame. He serves as president of the Board of Overseers at Harvard University and as a director of the United States Institute of Peace.

Carla A. Hills

Carla A. Hills was U.S. Trade Representative. She is chairman and CEO of Hills & Company, an international consulting firm that advises clients on trade and investment matters abroad.

Hanna Holborn Gray

Hanna Holborn Gray was president of the University of Chicago. She also served as provost and acting president of Yale University.

John T. Joyce

John Joyce is president of the International Union of Bricklayers and Allied Craftsmen of the AFL-CIO.

Juanita M. Kreps

Juanita Kreps served as secretary of commerce. She is vice president emeritus of Duke University.

Sol M. Linowitz

Sol Linowitz was the founding co-chairman of the Inter-American Dialogue. He is honorary chairman of the Academy of Educational Development. He served as President Carter's representative for the Middle East peace negotiations, co-negotiator for the Panama Canal treaties, and Ambassador to the Organization of American States.

Abraham F. Lowenthal

Abraham Lowenthal directs the Center for International Studies at the University of Southern California. He was the founding director of the Inter-American Dialogue and the Latin American program of the Woodrow Wilson International Center.

Mónica Lozano

Mónica Lozano is associate publisher and editor of *La Opinión*, the largest Spanish-language daily newspaper in the United States.

Jessica T. Mathews

Jessica Mathews is a senior fellow at the Council on Foreign Relations and a columnist at *The Washington Post*. She was deputy to the undersecretary of state for global affairs and directed the Office of Global Issues on the staff of the U.S. National Security Council.

Charles McC. Mathias, Jr.

Charles Mathias is a partner at the law firm of Jones, Day, Reavis & Pogue. He was a senator and member of Congress from Maryland.

David T. McLaughlin

David McLaughlin is chairman of the Board of Trustees and CEO of The Aspen Institute. He was chairman and CEO of the Toro Company and president of Dartmouth College.

Robert S. McNamara

Robert S. McNamara served as president of the World Bank and as secretary of defense. He was previously president of the Ford Motor Company.

William G. Milliken

William Milliken was governor of Michigan. He has chaired the National Governors Association and the Republican Governors' Conference.

Ambler H. Moss, Jr.

Ambler Moss is director of the University of Miami's North-South Center. He served as U.S. ambassador to Panama.

Edmund S. Muskie

Edmund Muskie is a senior partner at the international law firm of Chadbourne and Parke. He served as U.S. secretary of state and was senator and governor from Maine.

Luis Nogales

Luis Nogales is president of Nogales Partners, a media acquisition firm. He was president of UNIVISION and chairman and CEO of United Press International.

John R. Petty

John Petty is chairman of the Czech and Slovak American Enterprise Fund. He was chair and CEO of Marine Midland Bank and assistant secretary of the treasury for international affairs.

Charles J. Pilliod

Charles Pilliod is chairman and CEO of ABF Investors, Inc. He served as ambassador to Mexico.

Robert D. Ray

Robert Ray is president and chief executive officer of Blue Cross/Blue Shield of Iowa and chairman of the Indo-Chinese Refugee Panel. He served as governor of Iowa.

Elliot L. Richardson

Elliot Richardson was U.S. attorney general, secretary of defense, secretary of commerce, and deputy secretary of state. He is a senior partner at Millbank, Tweed, Hadley, & McCloy.

Rozanne L. Ridgway

Rozanne Ridgway is co-chair of the Atlantic Council and vice chair of the American Academy of Diplomacy. She is a retired career diplomat.

Brent Scowcroft

Brent Scowcroft is president of the Forum for International Policy. He served as national security adviser to President Bush.

Anthony Solomon

Anthony Solomon served as president and CEO of the Federal Reserve Bank of New York and was undersecretary of the U.S. Treasury, as well as assistant secretary of state for economic affairs. Currently, he is chairman of the Economics Program at the Institute for East-West Studies.

Paula Stern

Paula Stern is a senior fellow at the Progressive Policy Institute and president of the Stern Group. She was chairwoman of the U.S. International Trade Commission.

Viron P. Vaky

Viron Vaky was assistant secretary of state for inter-American affairs and served as ambassador to Costa Rica, Colombia, and Venezuela. He is a senior fellow at the Inter-American Dialogue and teaches at the Georgetown University School of Foreign Service.

Cyrus R. Vance

Cyrus Vance served as secretary of state, chairman of the Federal Reserve Bank of New York, secretary of the Army, and the Defense Department's general counsel.

Fred F. Woerner

Fred Woerner is professor of international relations at Boston University. He was commander-in-chief of the U.S. Southern Command.

*A Statement of the
Inter-American Dialogue
April 10, 1994*

The Hemispheric Summit: An Opportunity for the Americas

The members of the Inter-American Dialogue — from the United States, Canada, Latin America, and the Caribbean — applaud President Clinton for calling the first summit of Western Hemisphere leaders in a generation. It is now up to all governments of the Americas to make the summit succeed in its promise of advancing the hemisphere's common goals. Their challenge is to assure the summit is not a single event, but the foundation for continued regional cooperation and broad hemispheric progress. Many issues deserve attention, but three — expanding trade, strengthening democratic institutions, and fostering social progress — belong at the top of the summit agenda for action.

First and foremost, the summit is an opportunity for hemispheric governments to agree on the basic architecture and the next important steps toward building a comprehensive free trade system that can incorporate every country of the Americas. To make that possible, we urge that all summit participants be prepared to offer and discuss concrete proposals for developing a Western Hemisphere free trade area within a decade. As by far the largest economy and market in the region, the United States, in particular, should bring to the summit its strategy and specific conditions for proceeding toward hemisphere-wide free trading arrangements.

The people and governments of each individual nation are primarily responsible for building democracy and making it work. But the governments of the hemisphere should together take action to enhance their collective capacity to safeguard democratic practice. They should agree on measures to reinforce the Organization of American States' capacity for dealing with violations of human rights and democratic processes, and set out clearly the responsibilities that the OAS must undertake whenever democracy is threatened in the hemisphere. The nations of the Americas should also commit themselves to the immediate suspension from the OAS and from other inter-American institutions of any country in which democratic rule is interrupted.

Democratic politics and economic cooperation in the hemisphere are jeopardized by persistent poverty and profound inequalities of income and wealth. We urge all governments of the Americas to pledge themselves to opening new social opportunities for their citizens, recognizing these as crucial to democratic stability and sustainable economic progress. We make a special call for a new commitment to education — especially for girls, indigenous groups, ethnic minorities — in every country of the hemisphere. Each government should start by committing itself to establish goals and standards for educational advancement, and to develop adequate systems of measuring and monitoring progress toward these goals.

Peter Hakim,
Inter-American Dialogue

Postscript:
The Summit and Beyond

When Vice President Gore traveled to Mexico in early December 1993 to celebrate NAFTA's passage, he announced U.S. plans to host a summit meeting of Western Hemisphere leaders, the first in more than a quarter-century. Latin America and Caribbean governments welcomed the announcement because they assumed that the administration was setting the stage for extending free trade arrangements throughout the Americas.

The path to the Summit was hardly smooth, however. For much of 1994, the problems seemed to overwhelm the opportunities in Latin America, and U.S. policy seemed inadequate to the task of either dealing with the problems or effectively pursuing the opportunities. Within the region, expectations for the Miami meeting seemed steadily to diminish as attention was diverted from the hemispheric trade agenda — by other international trade priorities and by troubling developments in several Latin American countries.

It was only in September that the administration finally announced that trade would, indeed, be the centerpiece of the Summit — not merely one of many issues on the agenda. U.S. trade officials then also began consulting, although still tentatively, with Latin American and Caribbean governments on how to address the trade questions. This all coincided with the appointment of Thomas McLarty, the former White House chief of staff, to oversee the Summit preparations. With less than three months to go, the administration began to give the Summit priority attention. It also started to take seriously the concerns, now widely heard in Latin America, that continued U.S. silence on trade matters could condemn the meeting to irrelevance.

Still, the administration found it extremely difficult to gain agreement on what should be discussed and decided at the Summit. There were important unresolved differences within the administration, for example, over how forthcoming the United States should be on hemispheric free trade. Disagreements persisted between the United States and the countries of Latin America on several key issues — for instance, on whether specific procedures and a timetable should be proposed for free trade negotiations, whether labor and environmental matters should be included in trade talks, and how significant a role the OAS ought to have in defending democracy and human rights. And, of course, the Latin American and Caribbean governments did not always agree among themselves on these and other issues.

Agreement was ultimately reached — in the final two weeks before the Summit — when an intensive series of consultations yielded significant concessions and compromises on all sides, demonstrating the good will that virtually every government would bring to Miami. (There were critics of the process, however, who argued that, while strengthening the sections on trade, the concessions and compromises ended up diluting further already weak statements regarding the protection of human rights, democratic practice, and labor standards.) Brazil and the United States — which, of all countries, had been most at odds — managed to find common ground on the important issues, and both the Brazilian president and president-elect participated in the meeting, as Washington had hoped. One of the most significant outcomes of the Summit — and the consultations preceding it — may have been improved communication between Washington and Brasilia and a greater appreciation by U.S. officials of Brazil's central role in Latin America.

The three-day Summit — from December 9 to 11 — was a success. The meeting itself and the final declaration of the hemisphere's leaders reaffirmed the impressive convergence of interests and values that exists between the United States and the nations of Latin America and the Caribbean. It also produced a constructive plan of action that should influence the agenda of Western Hemisphere affairs for the next several years.

The most significant agreements reached at the Summit were about hemispheric free trade; for most countries, this is what made the meeting worthwhile. The 34 participating governments agreed to forge a free trade area incorporating every country of the Americas by 2005 — and to seek to achieve significant progress toward that goal by the turn of the century. Although somewhat vague about precisely who does what, a 15-month consultative process — extending to March 1996 — was designed to lay the groundwork for subsequent negotiations on free trade arrangements. And one very concrete step was taken at the Summit toward building hemispheric free trade: the three NAFTA partners — Canada, Mexico, and the United States — finally announced plans to negotiate Chile's accession to their pact.

Although less dramatic than the trade accords, the Summit also produced agreements on a range of other goals, such as preserving and strengthening democracy, defending human rights, eradicating poverty, combatting corruption and illegal drugs, greatly expanding access to education and health services, and protecting natural environments. In many cases, the goals are too ambitious and unlikely to be achieved, but they do express a striking consensus in the hemisphere on a range of fundamental principles. Moreover, most of the proposed program initiatives would produce useful results, even if they fall short of

their declared objectives. And the expanded responsibilities assigned to the OAS and IDB should encourage greater regional cooperation.

The Summit, in short, turned out to be an event of some significance, which has already contributed constructively to U.S.-Latin American relations. Whether it has any lasting importance depends on what happens now, whether the governments actually put into practice and remain committed to the agreements reached in Miami. According to Ambassador Sol Linowitz, who organized the 1967 Summit in Punta del Este, Uruguay, the final communiqué of that earlier meeting "included a 23-page action program, which did not produce a great deal of action." Expectations are higher today.

U.S. leadership will be crucial in the coming months. The first task is for Washington to move quickly to prepare the way for free trade talks — both to get Chile into NAFTA and, jointly with the other nations of Latin America and the Caribbean, to begin plotting a course that will open the way to negotiations on broader hemisphere-wide trade arrangements. The crucial discussions will be those between the United States and its NAFTA partners, on the one hand, and the four countries of the Mercosur, led by Brazil, on the other. These two trading groups together account for the great bulk of the hemisphere's economic activity; an agreement between them on how to proceed is the key to building a regional free trade area.

To make the negotiations meaningful, most observers believe President Clinton will need to secure fast track authority from the new Republican Congress. This will almost certainly require the administration — in the face of intense opposition from organized labor and other key Democratic constituencies — to accept Republican demands to exclude labor and environmental matters from trade negotiations. It is unclear at this point whether a compromise solution can be shaped or whether the president will have to make a very hard choice.

The countries of the hemisphere want to move forward on trade and will try to make the Summit agreements in this area work. There is not much, however, to propel the implementation of the non-trade initiatives. For one thing, most of them depend on the actions of individual governments rather than on a collective effort by many countries. They may end up being mostly treated as statements of principle, not as guides to policy action, unless the governments are prepared to establish more specific goals, agree on practical means for getting to them, and develop clear benchmarks and review procedures to measure progress.

The Summit agreements, particularly on trade, should set the course for U.S. policy toward Latin America in 1995. They express the collective interests of the hemisphere's governments and offer important new opportunities for regional cooperation on many issues. But they do not reduce the other difficult policy challenges that Washington faces, for example, in Mexico, Haiti, and Cuba. Indeed, the implementation of the Summit agreements will be made far more difficult by the recent economic setbacks in Mexico, which for many confirm that NAFTA was a bad idea and that it would be unwise to pursue other trade agreements in Latin America.

In the next two years, however, the administration's policy toward Latin America and the Caribbean importantly will be judged by whether it sticks to the commitments it made at the Summit — particularly whether it effectively pursues negotiations toward hemispheric free trade and sets the stage for eliminating trade and investment barriers in the Americas. Success will depend on how well the United States manages its relations with Brazil and Mexico and how productively the administration works with the Republican-controlled Congress.

SUMMIT CORRESPONDENCE

Indian Law Resource Center

October 7, 1994

Ms. Cathryn L. Thorup
Associate Director & Senior
Summit Liaison for Non-Governmental Actors
National Security Council/Inter-American Affairs
Room 361, OEOB
Washington, D.C. 20506

Dear Ms. Thorup:

We appreciated our meeting of October 3 with you and Richard Feinberg, but we remain troubled by the marginal treatment of indigenous peoples' concerns in the agenda for the Summit of the Americas. Throughout the consultative process in preparation for the Summit, we have urged that the administration take a leadership role on indigenous rights issues. This should include U.S. support for the draft UN Declaration on Indigenous Rights and for initiatives that specifically address the issues of indigenous self-determination, land demarcation, and the legalization of land rights, resource rights, and cultural rights. Unfortunately, these critical matters have been virtually eliminated from the administration's draft agenda.

I am enclosing these materials about indigenous rights for your office's consideration:

1. President Clinton's address at the recent White House meeting of U.S. tribal leaders.

2. The Clinton/Gore statement on this administration's Indian rights policy. Note that under the heading "Guarantee Rights" there is a commitment to "support sovereignty and self-determination of Native American tribal governments."

3. The draft UN Declaration on the Rights of Indigenous Peoples. This draft Declaration has been in preparation for over a decade. It has widespread support among indigenous peoples, many of whom have been active participants in its development. (The effort of the OAS Inter-American Commission on Human Rights to develop a similar new juridical instrument on indigenous rights began much later and has not yet produced a document.)

4. The statement of U.S. Representative John Crook in support of the draft UN Declaration on the Rights of Indigenous Peoples. The draft Declaration was approved by the Subcommission on Prevention of Discrimination and Protection of Minorities. It will be reviewed by the UN Human Rights Commission in February.

5. Statements by the National Congress of American Indians a) in support of the draft Declaration and b) to the President at the recent White House meeting of tribal leaders.

6. Statements by our Center a) in support of the draft Declaration, b) on the issue of self-determination, and c) introducing the statement of Erica-Irene Daes, chairperson of the UN Working Group on Indigenous Populations, the author of the draft Declaration.

7. Letter of September 15, 1994, from Raymond Apodaca of the National Congress of American Indians to the White House, expressing concern about the marginalization of indigenous peoples' concerns in the Summit agenda.

8. Letter of October 6, 1994, from the President of the Indigenous Parliament of America to President Clinton, requesting inclusion of the issue of indigenous peoples and sustainable development on the Summit agenda.

We respectfully urge reconsideration of indigenous rights in the Summit preparatory process. The agenda should be reformed to feature indigenous concerns under each of the Summit baskets of trade, democracy, and sustainable development. We encourage Mr. Feinberg to draw on the enclosed materials in his drafting of a declaration for the Summit.

Thank you for your consideration. Please do not hesitate to ask for additional information. We would be pleased, of course, to meet with you again at your convenience.

Sincerely,

Steven M. Tullberg
Senior Attorney
Indian Law Resource Center

Letter from non-governmental organization leaders to the leaders of the Western Hemisphere

November 4, 1994

To the Leaders of the Western Hemisphere:

We are writing to emphasize the need for transparency and public participation in carrying out the initiatives that will be announced at the upcoming Summit of the Americas. The involvement of non-governmental organizations (NGOs) and the public could be instrumental in ensuring that the programs initiated at the Summit successfully address critical hemispheric issues. Strong partnerships between governments and civil society are essential to the development and enforcement of sound laws and policies and will be vital to ensuring that the initiatives related to democracy, economics, and sustainable development meet their ambitious objectives.

In light of the above, we are concerned about the significant role proposed for the Organization of American States (OAS) in many of the Summit initiatives. It has been suggested that the OAS take a leadership role in advancing both human rights and environmental protection in the hemisphere, that many Summit initiatives will be "mandated" to the OAS, and that the Summit will enhance the authority of that organization. We are concerned about this proposal because, with the exception of its relatively autonomous Inter-American Commission on Human Rights, the OAS currently has no formal mechanisms for participation by NGOs and the public. Recently, the Canadian ambassador to the OAS proposed that the organization merely *study* granting observer status to NGOs. This proposal was vigorously opposed by some OAS members and was ultimately tabled.

The significant role envisioned for the OAS in carrying out the work of the Summit is especially troubling because of the prominent role assigned to democracy issues in the agenda for the meeting. Giving OAS the "mandate" for these important and ground-breaking initiatives will, given current OAS procedures, prevent the full participation of civil society in their implementation and may inhibit their ultimate success.

Solutions to the complex problems facing the hemisphere call for creative and visionary collaborations between governments and civil society. Such innovative partnerships are not currently possible at the OAS. While we realize that international institutions will be needed to carry out the Summit initiatives, it is essential that such institutions be more open and transparent. If the OAS is to be involved in carrying out these initiatives, it should be required to consult with civil society. An oversight mechanism must be established to ensure that such consultations occur, and reform of the OAS should be a topic for discussion at the Summit.

We hope that you will direct your respective OAS representatives to consult with NGOs regarding reform of the OAS and regarding the work of the institution. In addition, each of the undersigned groups will be contacting their respective governments to set up meetings to discuss this issue.

Sincerely,

Eugenia Bec
Abogada
Fundación Ambiente y Recursos
Naturales
Buenos Aires, Argentina

Silvar Excobar de Pabón
Carlos Villegas Quiroga
Centro Estudios para el
Desarrollo Laboral y Agrario
La Paz, Bolivia

Miguel Castro
Director
Centro de Estudios Regionales
para el Desarrollo de Tarija
Tarija, Bolivia

Leonor Arauco
Directora
Unión Nacional de Instituciones
para el Trabajo de Acción Social
La Paz, Bolivia

Brig. Luis Antonio
Friends of the Earth International-Amazonia Program
São Paulo, Brazil

Janine Ferretti
Executive Director
Pollution Probe
Toronto, Ontario, Canada

Elizabeth May
Executive Director
Sierra Club, Canada
Ottawa, Ontario, Canada

Martin Garate
Director
Comité de Servicio Chileno-Cuaquero
Santiago, Chile

Brenda Hannu
Directora
Asociación para la Conservación
y Manejo de Bosques Tropicales
San Pedro, Costa Rica

Roxana Salazar
Directora Ejecutiva
Fundación Ambio
San José, Costa Rica

Chris Wille
Co-Director
Rainforest Alliance, Central
American Office
San José, Costa Rica

Yolanda Kakabadse
Presidente Ejecutiva
Ricardo Meléndez
Director General
Fundación Futuro
Latinoamericano
Quito, Ecuador

Lic. Mario Vásquez
Director Ejecutivo en Funciones
Asociación Audubon de
El Salvador
San Salvador, El Salvador

Barbara McKinnon de Montes
President
Amigos de Sian Ka'an, A.C.
Cancún, México

Susan Porter-Smith
Audubon de San Miguel de
Allende
San Miguel de Allende, México

Gustavo Alanis-Ortega
President
Centro Mexicano de Derecho
Ambiental
Mexico City, México

Dr. David Barkin
Professor of Economics
Universidad Autónoma
Metropolitana
Xochimilco, México

Wilson Campos
Coordinador General
Asociación de Organizaciones
Campesinas Centroamericanas
para la Cooperación y el
Desarrollo
Managua, Nicaragua

Pedro Félix Obregon
Foro Civil para el Desarrollo
Sostenible de Nicaragua
Managua, Nicaragua

Raul Gauto
Director Ejecutivo
Fundación Moisés Bertoni
Asunción, Paraguay

Lider Sucre
Vice President
Sociedad Audubon de Panamá
Balboa, Panamá

Roco Valdeavellano Roca Rey
Directora
Instituto de Desarrollo Urbano
Lima, Perú

James Matlack
Director
American Friends Service
Committee, Washington Office
Washington, D.C., United States

Preston Hardison
Projects Director
Center for Indigenous Development and Environment
Seattle, WA, United States

Robert Housman
Staff Attorney
Center for International Environmental Law
Washington, D.C., United States

R. Lawrence Turnipseed
Executive Director
Church World Services
New York, NY, United States

Paul Speck
International Program Associate
Environmental and Energy Study
Institute
Washington, D.C., United States

Arthur Domike
President
Esquel Group Foundation
Bethesda, MD, United States

Stephen Hellinger
Executive Director
The Development Group for
Alternative Policies
Washington, D.C., United States

Steven M. Tullberg
Senior Attorney
Indian Law Resource Center
Washington, D.C., United States

George Shillinger
International Council for Bird
Preservation
Washington, D.C., United States

Pharis J. Harvey
Executive Director
International Labor Rights
Education and Research Fund
Washington, D.C., United States

Kathryn Wolford
Executive Director
Lutheran World Relief
New York, NY, United States

Kathleen Rogers
Wildlife Counsel
National Audubon Society
Washington, D.C., United States

Barbara J. Bramble
Director of International
Programs
National Wildlife Federation
Washington, D.C., United States

Alice Walters
Mark Sauchier
National Coordinators
Peru Peace Network
Jefferson City, MO, United States

Cara Siano
Research Fellow
Project on Demilitarization and
Democracy
Washington, D.C., United States

Daniel A. Seligman
Senior Trade Fellow
Sierra Club
Washington, D.C., United States

George Vickers
Director
Washington Office on Latin
America
Washington, D.C., United States

Clemencia Rodner
Sociedad Conservacionista
Audubon de Venezuela
Caracas, Venezuela

Indigenous Parliament of America

Office of the Permanent Secretary

"International Decade of the Indigenous Peoples"

October 6, 1994

His Excellency
The Honorable William J. Clinton
President of the United States of America

Your Excellency Mr. President:

By means of this letter, I am pleased to send you my cordial greetings on behalf of the Indigenous Peoples of Nicaragua and as leader of the Indigenous Parliament of America, taking advantage of the opportunity to refer to the very important "Summit of the Americas" which will be held this coming December in Miami.

Considering that this Summit must not leave out the theme of "The Indigenous Peoples and the Sustainable Development of America," permit me to present this theme as our initiative so that it will be debated within the Summit agenda, for highest priority consideration and as a substantial component of the development of the countries of the Continent.

The United Nations Resolution which initiates the Decade of the Indigenous Peoples on December 10 provides that indigenous peoples must be treated with care in regard to the sustainable development of the countries of the Continent because the majority of these countries have a large indigenous component—indigenous peoples who speak in their own language, conserve their ancestral culture, and constitute an important factor in each one of the National States.

The Indigenous Peoples of America are profoundly tied to the land and to nature and therefore to ecology, with their obligation of continuing that which they have been doing with their work and by necessity for centuries—the protection and conservation of the natural environment. This commitment obligates the governments to take into account the participation of the indigenous peoples in the conservation and protection of the forests and biodiversity.

Moreover, taking note of the principles of democracy and equal protection, the indigenous peoples not only should participate in the benefits provided by the countries' sustainable development but also should support with their indigenous institutions the consolidation of democracy in order to strengthen the rule of law, as one of the most important national goals.

Confident that these considerations will move Your Excellency definitively to include the theme "The Indigenous Peoples and the Sustainable Development of America" in the agenda for the "Summit of the Americas," I gratefully solicit your favorable attention to my request.

Unofficial Translation

With my highest consideration and esteem,

Sincerely,

Alfonso Smith Warman

Member of the Nicaraguan National Assembly

President, Indigenous Parliament of America

President, Commission on Indigenous and Ethnic Affairs
of the Latin America Parliament (Parlatino)

cc: Her Excellency

The Honorable Violeta Barrios V. de Chamorro
President of the Republic of Nicaragua

His Excellency
The Honorable Al Gore
Vice President of the United States of America

National Audubon Society

October 19, 1994

The Honorable Katie McGinty
Office of Environmental Policy
The White House
Washington, D.C.

Dear Katie:

With the Summit of the Americas less than two months away, I am writing to express my concern regarding two issues which are not being adequately addressed in the planning for this historic meeting. First, the proposed "economics" agenda, which will be the centerpiece of the Summit, fails to make any link between trade expansion and environmental issues. Given the profound impact of economic development on the global environment and the interest of the United States and other Western Hemisphere nations in entering into new trade relationships, the agenda for the Summit must clearly link trade expansion in the hemisphere with environmental protection and conservation of resources.

The link between trade and environmental issues was successfully made in the North American Free Trade Agreement and its environmental side agreement. Countries in the hemisphere hoping to join the NAFTA expect to hear that their entry into the agreement will be conditioned on progress toward a comprehensive system of environmental regulations. This belief has been reinforced by our experiences as a member of the team consulting on the agenda for the Summit with Latin American and Caribbean nations.

Next, I am deeply concerned by the apparent failure of the Summit coordinators to provide a suitable role for non-governmental organizations during the Summit itself. We were advised that the administration would prefer that NGOs refrain from holding parallel events that might distract attention from the accomplishments of the Summit. We now understand that the business community, with the blessing of the Host Committee and the U.S. Departments of Commerce and Treasury, will be holding various functions in Miami during the Summit. This places the environmental community in a difficult position. Having agreed to forego holding our own meetings and unable to participate in the official events of the Summit, we are left with no forum for expressing our views regarding and support for the Summit initiatives. This situation is particularly disturbing in light of the prominent role assigned to democracy and public participation issues in the Summit agenda and in light of the forceful and effective leadership which the administration provided on these issues at the UN Conference in Cairo last month.

I would like to have the opportunity to speak with you regarding my concerns at your earliest convenience. Thank you for your efforts to include NGOs in the preparatory meeting for the Summit. I believe that we can work together to resolve the issues outlined above.

Sincerely,

Peter A.A. Berle
President & CEO
National Audubon Society

410

Inter-American College of Physicians & Surgeons

October 4, 1994

The President
The White House
1600 Pennsylvania Ave., N.W.
Washington, D.C. 20500

Dear Mr. President:

Shortly after you announced the Summit of the Americas to be held in Miami in December 1994, the Inter-American College of Physicians convened a meeting of its Board to discuss our shared interests in the health sector and propose recommendations that could help outline the health agenda of the Summit.

The Summit of the Americas will be a unique opportunity to improve life and enhance the quality of health care in the Continent; to make a difference in the way we fight disease, provide opportunities and training for our physicians, and better health conditions and health education for our people. We believe that a health agenda focused in identifying critical health issues and promoting equitable policy developments through leadership and collaboration will expand access to health care and set the necessary basis for economic development and partnerships in the health area.

Therefore, responding to your call to help define the Summit agenda, we have taken the initiative of outlining the following recommendations for the development of strong links between the United States and the Latin American health sector.

The Summit must develop a health agenda that advances common interests between our medical societies and health care providers and promotes professional and scientific collaboration as well as economic growth.

The health agenda should, in our view, consider two main issues: first, the empowerment of non-governmental health care provider associations and the health care private sector in Latin America to participate in health care policy-making; and second, the integration of economies in the health sector to facilitate scientific and professional exchanges and improve health care delivery services.

The arguments for the empowerment of medical societies and the health care private sector are based on the need of a grassroots-informed planning and the need to expand and improve medical care in an affordable, efficient manner. The political climate is now supportive of this empowerment, which will give health care providers a voice in the process.

Please find enclosed a concept paper of an initiative for the Americas, "The Health Professional Leadership Initiative to Latin American Medical Organizations," developed by the Inter-American College of Physicians and Surgeons, which is planned to start in March 1995 following the Presidential Summit. This paper describes a collaborative action to provide leadership and to strengthen links between medical societies in the continent as a starting point for future endeavors.

We will be very pleased to assist you in this initiative, and we look forward to collaborating with you.

Sincerely yours,

Rene F. Rodriguez, MD
President
Interamerican College of
Physicians & Surgeons

National
Audubon Society

Environmental
Law Institute

Partners of the
Americas, Inc.

The Humane Society
of the United States

International
Institute for Energy
Conservation

Center for
International
Environmental Law

Healing Forest
Conservancy

Indian Law
Resource Center

National
Wildlife Federation

World Wildlife Fund

Sierra Club

Natural Resources
Defense Council

February 21, 1995

The Honorable Albert Gore, Jr.
Vice President of the United States
The White House
1600 Pennsylvania Avenue, N.W.
Washington, D.C. 20500

Dear Mr. Vice President:

We are writing to thank you and the Clinton administration for the access given to non-governmental organizations (NGOs) in the preparation and negotiation of the sustainable development agenda for the Summit of the Americas. The role played by NGOs in the preparations for the Summit was unprecedented for this type of presidential-level meeting and conveyed a powerful message about the importance of citizen participation to government officials throughout the Americas.

The open processes instituted by the Office of Environmental Policy and the National Security Council's Office of Latin American Affairs—including regular briefings, the solicitation of proposals, advice and expertise from the NGO community, and especially the inclusion of NGO representatives in the U.S. delegations which met with representatives of Latin American and Caribbean governments—allowed the U.S. NGO community an unparalleled opportunity to participate in the planning of the Summit. In addition, the example set by U.S. inclusion of NGOs in the negotiations encouraged a number of Latin American and Caribbean governments to include representatives of their own NGO communities in the process.

In light of the successful integration of the non-governmental community into the preparatory process for the Summit, we hope that you will consider a continued and broadened role for non-governmental organizations in the meetings which follow the Summit. This would include not only the planned sustainable development ministerial meetings but also the 1996 sustainable development Summit in Bolivia, and the ministerial meetings which will monitor and direct the Summit's democracy and economic initiatives, such as the trade ministerial meeting planned for March 1995.

The initiatives announced at the Summit promise useful changes for the future of the Americas; however, the problems facing our region cannot be solved by governments working in isolation or by governments working only with commercial interests whose focus is on expanding hemispheric markets. The success of the Summit showed that a broad spectrum of civil society can bring unique and important opinions and information to the preparatory process. The talents and expertise of the civil society of the Americas must be put to use if real change is to occur.

We look forward to working with you and with your staff to implement these ideas. Thank you for your consideration of these important issues.

Very Truly Yours,

Peter A. A. Berle
President and CEO
National Audubon Society

William S. Reese
President
Partners of the Americas, Inc.

Deborah L. Bleviss
President
International Institute for Energy
Conservation

Katy Moran
Executive Director
Healing Forest Conservancy

Lynn Greenwalt
Vice President, International Affairs
National Wildlife Federation

Larry Williams
Director, International Program
Sierra Club

William J. Futrell
President
Environmental Law Institute

Paul G. Irwin
President
The Humane Society of the United States

Durwood Zaelke
President
Center for International Environmental
Law

Robert T. Coulter
Executive Director
Indian Law Resource Center

Diane Walton Wood
Vice President, Latin American and
Caribbean Program
World Wildlife Fund

Jacob Scherr
Director, International Program
National Resources Defense Council

Participating Organizations

AACCLA (Association of American Chambers
of Commerce in Latin America)
1615 H Street, NW
Washington, DC 20062-2000
Tel: 202-463-5485
Fax: 202-463-3126

AFL-CIO
815 16th Street, NW
Washington, DC 20006
Tel: 202-637-5166
Fax: 202-508-6767

Amnesty International
304 Pennsylvania Ave., SE
Washington, DC 20003
Tel: 202-544-0200
Fax: 202-546-7142

CAMACOL (Cámara de Comercio Latino)
1417 W. Flagler St.
P.O. Box 350824
Miami, FL 33135
Tel: 305-642-3870
Fax: 305-642-0653

Center for Latin American Studies
University of Florida
319 Grinter Hall, P.O. Box 115530
Gainesville, FL 32611-5530
Tel: 904-392-0375
Fax: 904-392-7682

Church World Service
475 Riverside Drive
New York, NY 10115
Tel: 212-870-3300

Columbus Group
c/o Victor García Laredo
Avenida Eduardo Madero 940
Fl. 14 Capital Federal
Buenos Aires, Argentina
Tel: 541-313-7105

Council of the Americas
680 Park Avenue
New York, NY 10021
Tel: 212-628-3200
Fax: 212-517-6247

Earth Council
Apdo. 2323-1002
San José, Costa Rica
Tel: 506-256-1611
Fax: 506-233-1822

ECLAC (United Nations Economic Commission
for Latin America and the Caribbean)
1825 K Street, NW Suite 1120
Washington, DC 20006
Tel: 202-955-5613
Fax: 202-296-0826

Environmental and Energy Study Institute
122 C Street, NW, Suite 700
Washington, DC 20001-2109
Tel: 202-628-1400
Fax: 202-628-1825

FLACSO (Facultad Latinoamericana
de Ciencias Sociales) - Chile
Leopoldo Urrutia 1950
Santiago, Chile
Casilla 3213 Central de Casillas
Tel: 562-225-6955/9938
Fax: 562-460-4333

FOCAL (Canadian Foundation for the Americas)
55 Murray Street, Suite 230
Ottawa, Canada
K1N5M3
Tel: 613-562-0005
Fax: 613-562-2525

Fundación Futuro Latinoamericano
Casilla 17-17-558
Quito, Ecuador
Tel: 5932-435-521/491
Fax: 5932-462-204

Indian Law Resource Center
601 E Street, SE
Washington, DC 20003
Tel: 202-547-2800
Fax: 202-547-2803

Institute for International Economics
11 Dupont Circle, NW - 6th Flr.
Washington, DC 20036-1207
Tel: 202-328-9000
Fax: 202-328-5432

Interamerican College of Physicians & Surgeons
915 Broadway, Suite 1105
New York, NY 10010-7108
Tel: 212-777-3642
Fax: 212-505-7984

Inter-American Development Bank
1300 New York Ave., NW
Washington, DC 20577
Tel: 202-623-1200
Fax: 202-623-3615

Inter-American Dialogue
1211 Connecticut Ave., NW, #510
Washington, DC 20036
Tel: 202-822-9002
Fax: 202-822-9553

Latin America and the Caribbean
United Nations Development Programme
1 UN Plaza, Room 2218
New York, NY 10017
Tel: 212-906-5400

Latino Alliance for the Summit of the Americas
National Council of La Raza
1111 19th Street, NW, Suite 1000
Washington, DC 20036
Tel: 202-785-1670
Fax: 202-785-0851

Lawyers Committee for Human Rights
100 Maryland Avenue, NE, Suite 502
Washington, DC 20002
Tel: 202-547-5692
Fax: 202-543-5999

Lutheran World Relief
110 Maryland Ave., NE
P.O. Box 45
Washington, DC 20002
Tel: 202-543-6366/6336
Fax: 202-546-6232

National Audubon Society
700 Broadway
New York, NY 10003
Tel: 212-979-3000

National Security Council
Office of Inter-American Affairs
Old Executive Office Building
17th & Pennsylvania Avenue, NW - Room 361
Washington, DC 20506
Tel: 202-456-9131
Fax: 202-456-9130

North-South Center
1500 Monza Avenue
Coral Gables, FL 33146-3027
Tel: 305-284-6868
Fax: 305-284-6370

NRTEE (National Round Table on the
   Environment and the Economy)
1 Nicolas Street, Suite 1500
Ottawa, Ontario K1N 7B7
Canada
Tel: 613-992-7189
Fax: 613-992-7385

Organization of American States
17th and Constitution Ave., NW
Washington, DC 20006
Tel: 202-458-3000
Fax: 202-458-3967

Summit Coordinating Office
Room 3250
Department of State
Washington, DC 20520
Tel: 202-736-7533
Fax: 202-736-7618

Wilson Center
1000 Jefferson Drive, SW
Washington, DC 20560
Tel: 202-357-2429
Fax: 202-357-4439